FABIAN FREEWAY

HIGH ROAD TO SOCIALISM IN THE U.S.A.

FABIAN FREEWAY

HIGH ROAD TO SOCIALISM IN THE U.S.A.
1884–1966

by Rose L. Martin

with foreword by Loyd Wright

"No man can serve two masters. For either he will hate the one, and love the other, or he will sustain the one, and despise the other."

Matthew 6:24

HERITAGE FOUNDATION
—CHICAGO—

To the memory of
the late Senator Pat McCarran

First Printing

Contents

28265

CONTENTS

Appendices

Foreword

THE American people have been and are complacently unfamiliar with Communism's helpmate, Fabian Socialism. For over fifty years but especially since the middle nineteen-thirties there have been insinuated into high places in our government at Washington men whose collaboration in this socialistic movement has been greatly responsible for breaking down our constitutional form of government and substituting therefor the Socialist idea of centralized government.

Every loyal American should read this book. It is well documented, and proves beyond doubt that those who have wielded such vast influence upon successive Presidents, especially since Franklin Roosevelt, do not have a desire to retain the freedom of the individual and the free enterprise system, but rather seek to establish the very coercion from which our forefathers fled.

The reader will be shocked when he comprehends that there are those in high places in government who are dedicated to this Socialist movement. The ultimate objective of the Fabian Socialist movement is *no different* than the ultimate objective of the Communist movement. The gangsters in the Kremlin tell us they will bury us. George Bernard Shaw, one of the originators of the Fabian movement, puts it another way. He states in effect, "When we come to power, you will do what we tell you or we will shoot you."

To those who have an inquiring mind, and to those who wish to understand the tragedy of abandoning our form of government under which we prospered and under which our people have freedoms never enjoyed before in the history of the world, this book is a "must." It will enlighten the American people, and it is hoped that a reaction will set in demanding that the Walter Lippmanns, the Schlesingers, the Rostows and a vast number of others disclosed in the book as Fabians, be exposed for what they are so that their influence on government will terminate.

The author has rendered a great public service. Whether you agree or disagree with the conclusions or the philosophies enunciated herein, you cannot close your eyes to the documentation of the progress of this evil movement.

Loyd Wright

Everything Has A Beginning...

EVERYTHING has a beginning. This book tells how the Fabian Socialist movement, which exists under many names in many places, began and grew in Britain; and how, under the guise of an innocent-looking reform movement, it became a ruling force in the United States as well.

Started by a small group of middle class revolutionaries in nineteenth century England, its respectable influence now pervades the English-speaking world which is still largely unaware such a movement exists.

In Britain its present-day leaders control the Parliament and the Ministries, in the name of the Labour Party.

In the United States, where its identity has been even more carefully concealed and where its practitioners are usually known as liberals rather than Socialists, it has very nearly succeeded in reversing that movement of national independence which began in 1776.

Originally advancing with the slow but steady gait of a tortoise on a country road, Fabian Socialism has now adapted itself comfortably to a high speed age and attempts to lead the Free World with unprecedented velocity towards a financial, military and moral breakdown, of which World Communism is the only logical beneficiary.

Still carefully restricted in size and as shy of inspection as the keepers of the Soviet missile sites, the parent Fabian Society of London is today what it has always been: a revolutionary secret society, behind a beguiling false front of benevolence and learning. One of the traits of a secret society is that a handful of its officers and publicists may be known, while the majority of its followers remain as hidden as its operations.

Let no one tell you the Fabian Society has faded or is only a pale relic of a bygone day. Let no one tell you it is mild, gentle or harmless. Here is the evidence that it has neither declined nor passed away, even if it sometimes chooses to play dead.

It is not that the Fabian Society is dead, but that our own world is threatened with death. Nearly all the conditions necessary for such demise have been set up, including the barefaced announcement that God is "dead."

In spite of outward semblances of prosperity and freedom, the America we have known and think we still possess lies gasping—its constitutional separation of powers blurred; its wealth expended in the vain hope of nourishing a largely hostile world; its military security endangered by invisible civilian planners and irresponsible brokers of disarmament; its union, which was its strength, crumbled into a powder of racial minorities and special interest groups.

Altogether this no longer spells creeping Socialism but *onrushing* Socialism, of which Communism is merely the final stage. Incredible? Not to those who have kept their eyes open and their senses alert, instead of being anesthetized by slogans or lulled by promises of perpetual affluence.

If the tortoise was once an appropriate symbol, a speedier and deadlier device would be suitable for today's faster moving Fabian Socialism, effective leader of the Socialist International. And if the turtle's obscure trail once seemed the proper path, the multi-lane highway or freeway is the avenue today.

Indeed, executive-type socialist errand-boys, diplomats and hatchet men in a hurry, range modern America's freeways, impatiently carrying out the schemes of unseen Fabian master planners, redeveloping American cities, reorganizing local governments along regional lines, keeping the farmer relatively happy despite the trend towards a collectivized agriculture. So instead of the tortoise and its tortuous trail, we have the fast car and the freeway.

How did all this come about? To understand, we must go back to New York's Turtle Bay of the nineteen-twenties and then back a greater number of years to a certain modest parlor in one of London's less fashionable streets, where a few brash young people met on a certain evening to plan a New Life—and then we must follow through from there!

Rose L. Martin
Los Angeles, 1966

1

Make Haste Slowly!

Introduction

AS A very young college graduate, searching for literary employment in the New York City of the middle nineteen-twenties, the author of this book happened to discover a colony called Turtle Bay. It included about a dozen remodeled town houses on East Forty-eighth and Forty-ninth Streets, arranged for gracious living before the phrase was current. One of the first modern restorations in the Forties and Fifties near the East River, it bloomed unexpectedly in a neighborhood of tenements and abandoned breweries. Evidently its builders were versed in the colonial history of Manhattan Island, when the entire region consisting of a few large farms had been known as Turtle Bay. For its twentieth century revivalists, the name had a double meaning.

The colony was planned by Mrs. John W. Martin (the former Prestonia Mann), wife of a British Fabian Socialist who had transferred his activities to the United States before the turn of the century.† Founded as a quiet haven for a little group of serious thinkers, the Turtle Bay restoration listed among its early settlers the Pulitzer prize winning novelist, Ernest Poole, and several editors of the *New Republic*.

There was Philip Littell, whose family once owned the *Living Age* in Boston; Francis Hackett, popular Anglo-Irish biographer and book critic; and a perennial summer and fall tenant on leave from the University of Chicago English Department, Robert Morss Lovett. Some had permanent summer cottages and others were recurrent weekend guests at Cornish, New Hampshire, in the White Mountains,

---

† The colony real estate was owned by Mrs. Walton Martin, nee Charlotte Honeywell, also of Boston, not a relative of Prestonia, but also thought to be a founder.

1

where they fraternized annually with Harvard alumni Edward Bur-
ling, Sr. and George M. Rublee, members of the same prosperous
Washington law firm to which a future Secretary of State, Dean
Acheson, belonged.

All were charming, witty, well-bred, industrious, solvent: clearly
superior persons and all aware of the fact. The Harvard men among
them typified in one way or another the revolt against New England
Puritanism and utilized the Bible as a prime source of wit and humor.
(Philip Littell named his canary Onan, because it scattered its seed.)
These were the American cousins of a species commonly cultivated
in England by the Fabian Society, because such individuals made
Socialism appear attractive as well as respectable. Being socially
beyond reproach, it would be difficult to attack them, however dubious
the doctrines they favored.

Turtle Bay colonists of the twenties personally knew and admired
a good many of the English Fabians, a fact frequently reflected in
their writings. Ernest Poole had retired in 1918 from a six-year term
as vice president of the Intercollegiate Socialist Society, which changed
its name in 1921 to the League for Industrial Democracy and was
hailed at its 40th Anniversary dinner as "America's Fabian Society." [1] The chief activist among Turtle Bay residents was Robert Morss
Lovett, whom the others affected to regard as an *enfant terrible*
because of his pacifist stand during World War I.

Besides serving as literary editor of the *New Republic* six months
of the year, Lovett was an official of the American Civil Liberties
Union and the League for Industrial Democracy, the latter occasionally listed in British Fabian Society literature among its overseas
branches. He was also a trustee of the American Fund for Public
Service, known as the Garland Fund, which financed a swarm of
so-called liberal organizations hospitable both to Socialists and covert
Communists, as well as to old-fashioned social reformers. In those
days, the terms "front organization," and "fellow traveler," were still
unknown.

A central feature of Turtle Bay was its pleasant Italian-style garden,
shared by all the residents and wonderfully green in spring. Set in
the flagstone walk was a small figure of a turtle in mosaic with the
inscription, Festina lente ("Make haste slowly"). To casual visitors,
the turtle merely added a picturesque touch. Few recognized this

[1] *Forty Years of Education*, (New York, League for Industrial Democracy, 1945),
p. 56.

unobtrusive little beast as an emblem of Britain's Fabian Society, which, since its formation in 1884, has preached and practiced a philosophy of achieving Socialism by gradual means.

Over the years to the present, the Fabian turtle has won a series of gradual victories that could hardly have been predicted in 1920, when the possibility of Socialist control in England and the United States seemed remote to its own leaders. Even now the results are hardly credible to the great majority of people in this country.

In England the Fabian Society, numbering at most five thousand listed members, has succeeded in penetrating and permeating organizations, social movements, political parties, until today its influence pervades the whole fabric of daily life. At one time, with a Labour Government in power, 10 Cabinet Ministers, including the Prime Minister, 35 Under Secretaries and other officers of State, and 229 of 394 Labour Party Members of Parliament held membership in the Fabian Society.[2] After World War II Fabians presided, as England's Winston Churchill declined to do, over the liquidation of Britain's colonial empire, and today, through their control of opinion-forming groups at the highest levels, they play a powerful role in formulating foreign policy on both sides of the Atlantic.

In the United States the progress of the Fabian pilgrims, though more difficult to trace, has been impressive. On the whole, United States Fabians in public office have been more cautious than their British models about admitting that Socialism is their goal. The gradualist and freewheeling character of the movement, plus the generally unsuspicious nature of the American people where gift horses are concerned, has allowed our native Fabian Socialists to pursue their goals step by step without disclosing their direction. Their once slow and cautious pace has been gradually accelerated to a breakneck speed.

In the past, Fabians were more successful in capturing administrative than legislative posts in the United States. They have left their mark on three decades of legislation largely through a combination of Executive pressure and the allure of free spending. The interpretive role of the Judiciary and the power of Executive decree have assumed new importance for Fabian-inspired officials unable to legislate Socialism by more direct methods.

With the multiplication of Federal agencies and employees (2,515,-

---

[2] *The General Election and After,* Fabian Research Series, No. 102, (London, The Fabian Society, 1946).

870 Federal civilian employees in November, 1962, as compared to 605,496 in June, 1932 [3]), the progress of Fabianism through government channels was further veiled. Not only the general public but many public officials as well were confused, and still remain so. The Romans had a word for it—*obscurantism*—which means the purposeful concealment of one's ultimate purpose.

By September, 1961, at least thirty-six high officials of the New Frontier Administration were found to be past or present members of an Anglo-Fabian-inspired organization calling itself Americans for Democratic Action. The tally included two Cabinet members, three White House aides, Under Secretaries and Assistant Secretaries in various departments of government, and holders of other policy-making posts ranging from ambassadors to the director of the Export-Import Bank.[4]

Americans sometimes wonder why so many members of a leftist elite occupy posts of great influence in Washington today. Others ask why United States spokesmen at home and abroad seem so often to be following policies counter to our traditional interests as a nation, and why in Cold War operations we so frequently lose by default to our declared mortal enemy, international Communism.

We will try to discover the honest answers to such puzzling questions. First, we will trace the movement represented by Americans for Democratic Action and related groups from its historic origin in British Fabianism to the present day. Second, we will make plain, beyond the shadow of any future doubt, the tactical service rendered by the Socialist International, with which the Fabian Society is allied, in advancing the ultimate goals of the Communist International.

A curious thing about our American Fabians—so reticent as public officials about admitting their Socialist motivation—is that in private life they tend to express themselves rather freely in signed articles for publications reaching a limited circle of readers. With research, it becomes possible to demonstrate their Socialist views in their own words. However, any attempts to confront them with the evidence or to interpret their programs in the light of their own confessed philosophy are promptly and vigorously denounced as "unfair," if not downright wicked.

---

[3] Figures obtained from Legislative Reference Division, Library of Congress. (The payroll for Federal civilian employees for the month of November, 1962, was $1,295,088,000, an annual rate of 15.5 billion dollars. This annual payroll exceeds the total national budget for 1932.)

[4] From a list compiled by Robert T. Hartmann, Washington Bureau of the Los Angeles *Times*, September, 1961.

In the past thirty years a whole series of loaded epithets has been invented for that purpose, beginning with "reactionary" in the early nineteen-thirties and proceeding through "Fascist" and "McCarthyite" to "Birchite." At present, "Right Wing extremist" is the automatic catchword applied to any person who seeks to expose or oppose the Socialist advance, and even to persons expressing the mildest sort of patriotic sentiments.

Still, men must be judged by what they advocate. Arthur M. Schlesinger, Jr., Pulitzer prize winner and Harvard history professor, writing on "The Future of Socialism" for the *Partisan Review* in 1947, said: "There seems to be no inherent obstacle to the gradual advance of Socialism in the United States through a series of 'New Deals.'" Elsewhere he describes the New Deal as "a process of backing into Socialism."

In 1949 Schlesinger was advocating "liberal Socialism" and calling on a powerful state "to expend its main strength in determining the broad levels and conditions of economic activity." Three years later he insisted that those who called him a Socialist were seeking to smear him; but he still asserted that he was a "New Dealer."[5] In 1954 he contributed what the *Fabian News* described as "an important article on foreign policy" to the *Fabian International Review*.

From 1961 to 1964 Arthur Schlesinger, Jr. was Administrative Assistant to the President of the United States. Since his case is by no means an isolated one, and since we have the example of England to show us what a well-placed group of dedicated Socialists can accomplish in transforming the economic and political life of a nation, it would seem reasonable to inquire where all this is leading us.

Where, indeed? In a rare moment of candor Gus Hall, General Secretary of the Communist Party of the United States, told us just where. Addressing a capacity audience of University of California students at the off-campus YMCA in January, 1962, Hall announced that the trend in the United States is towards Socialism, "not like in other countries but based on America's background, and still Socialism." And he predicted that "the United States will move gradually from Socialism to the higher state of Communism."

Though he was then under criminal indictment for refusing to register as a foreign agent, pursuant to provisions of the McCarran Act, Hall seemed to consider this no more than a passing annoyance.

[5] Peter Minot, "Inside Schlesinger . . . Slingshot of the New Frontier," Washington *World*, (January 17, 1962).

With Socialists of established respectability sitting in high places today in many countries, the Communists evidently feel they can afford to parry with a smile attacks on their own visible party organs. The Kremlin agents are unconcerned as long as an untouchable Socialist elite continues with increasing speed to prepare this nation and others for what Communists believe will be their own final victory.

Military men will recognize the procedure as an elementary tactic in warfare. An infantry commander only orders his front line troops into action after the territory to be occupied has been properly softened up by artillery and airpower based behind the lines. In the world-wide theater where Marxists wage class war, the Communists can be regarded as front line troops; while the Socialists serve as the big guns in the rear, firing over the heads of the men in forward positions and enabling them at a well-chosen moment to seize their objective rapidly.

It is a simple pattern, which any GI can recognize. Politically, it was the pattern of events in Czechoslovakia, in the Hungary of Bela Kun, even in Russia itself, where Socialist governments prepared the ground for a Communist seizure of power. Seen in this light, the value of the Socialist International to the Communist International becomes plain.

Popular confusion on the subject has given rise to a dangerous myth; namely, that a basic and irreconcilable enmity exists between Socialists and Communists. This is by no means true. Though superficially different and sometimes at odds about methods or timing, both are admittedly followers of the doctrines of Karl Marx or "Social Democracy" and they go together like a horse and carriage. In every country not yet under Communist control, the Socialists remain Communism's most potent and necessary allies. In fact, if they did not exist, the Communists would have had to invent them.

When Khrushchev insulted British Fabians, his insult was in all likelihood a calculated one. His gesture only heightened their respectability and enhanced their ability to promote Marxist programs piecemeal. A survey of the Fabian record will disclose how often Fabian policies have had the effect of serving Communist objectives. It will show not only that Fabian tolerance for what was once called "the Soviet experiment" insured its survival and expansion, but also that avowed Communists have been personally tolerated in Fabian circles. Finally, it will reveal how often founders and leaders of the

Fabian Society have, in their later years, openly traveled the road to Moscow.

This survey of Fabian Socialism is offered for people who feel they need to know where this country is heading and why. Since the movement is one about which many Americans are confused, and since an understanding and a healthy distrust of its activities seems vital to our survival as a nation, clarity is the prime objective.

As to why this writer feels called upon to undertake a task so apt to invite abuse and reprisals from persons who may feel themselves touched by it, the laconic last words of a New York newspaper editor at the turn of the century can be cited. He had killed his wife, and, asked why he did it, replied: "Somebody had to do it!"

I

GREAT BRITAIN

2

Sowing The Wind

ONE chilly October evening in 1883—the same year a Prussian-born war correspondent, free-lance economist and lifelong conspirator named Karl Marx died obscurely in London lodgings—sixteen young Britishers met for a parlor discussion of the higher things of life. They were guests of a twenty-six year old junior stockbroker, Edward R. Pease, who was bored with his job and with typical Victorian rectitude sought grounds for condemning it as immoral.

All were young, earnest, ambitious, of middle class origins and decent if by no means glamorous ancestry. All were groping for some sort of secular faith to replace the old God-given certainties as a basis for living and shaping their future careers. Like many restless young people of our own day, they hoped to find it in an atmosphere of mingled culture and social change. About half were personal friends of Pease and the rest were members of a budding cultural group called the Nuova Vita.

They had come to hear Thomas Davidson, a Scottish-born American and itinerant schoolmaster then visiting England, give a talk on "The New Life." Known as the Wandering Scholar, Davidson was a man of considerable learning and personal magnetism. He had toyed with the philosophy of Rosmini, an Italian priest who tried to fuse the systems of St. Thomas Aquinas and Hegel. At the moment, he was also flirting with a species of Utopian Socialism in the manner of Robert Owen, who favored setting up ideal communities of choice and noble souls.[1] (With Owen, an Englishman who visited America, the term "Socialist" first came into general use in 1835.)

[1] In a letter written some years afterwards to Morris R. Cohen, eventually to occupy a chair of Philosophy at City College of New York, Davidson said: "That

11

When Davidson returned to the New World to preside at various impromptu summer schools and to found the Educational Alliance on New York City's lower East Side, he had left behind him in London a lasting monument to his visit. From that casual gathering on October 24, at 17 Osnaburgh Street, the Fabian Society of London was born. Its character, however, was not immediately apparent. After a few meetings, at which the possibility of forming a religious-type community without benefit of religion was discussed, the group voted to remain in the world.

Within a few years the more bohemian elements from the Nuova Vita drifted away. Among them were Edward Carpenter, the future poet laureate of British Socialism, and Havelock Ellis, harbinger of free love and forthright sexual discussion, whose impact on the morals of young intellectuals in his own time would prove similar to that of Freud after World War I. Leaders of the Fabian Society at a later date viewed Ellis uneasily as a threat to that image of respectability which was to prove their most highly prized asset. An examination of the early minutes book of the Fabian Society suggests that the name of Havelock Ellis has been carefully removed from the list of original signers of its credo. Scandals provoked by the unconventional love-life of certain early Socialist leaders evidently convinced the Fabian high command that an appearance of prudery was preferable.

From the outset, the nine young men and women who remained to found the Fabian Society had grandiose plans. Quite simply, they wanted to change the world through a species of propaganda termed "education," which would lead to political action. To a rather astonishing degree they have been successful. For over three generations, members and friends of the Fabian Society have dedicated themselves to promoting an anglicized version of Marxism. Started as a discussion club, the Society has become the most important and long-lived Socialist organization in England. Without advertising the fact, it has also assumed leadership of a world-wide Socialist movement and is today the dominant influence in the Socialist International. Its originality lies in the techniques it has developed for permeating established institutions and penetrating political parties in order to win

---

you are attached to Socialism neither surprises nor disappoints me. I once came near being a Socialist myself and in that frame of mind founded what afterwards became the Fabian Society. But I soon found out the limitations of Socialism. . . . I have not found any deep social insight or any high moral ideals among the many Socialists I know." *Memorials of Thomas Davidson*, William Knight, ed., (Boston and London, Ginn and Company, 1907), p. 142.

command of the machinery of power. Historically speaking, perhaps its most remarkable feat has been to endow social revolution with an aura of lofty respectability.

The hole-and-corner beginnings of the Fabian Society offered no clue to its destiny. In the tranquil and prosperous British Empire of the early eighteen-eighties, the future of Socialism appeared dim. The working classes were docile and churchgoing, the landed aristocracy was firmly entrenched. Only the middle class seemed apt for the Socialist bait, particularly the younger intellectuals and professionals. Lacking any profound group loyalties, their religious convictions shaken by popularized versions of Darwinism and scientific materialism, many yearned for some new creed to make life worth living. All over London discussion clubs, debating clubs, study clubs sprang up and bloomed ephemerally. Movements like Psychical Research, Vegetarianism, Spiritism and Theosophy flourished for a decade or two and declined.

Edward Pease, who in due time became the perennial general secretary and chronicler of the Fabian Society, had dabbled in such diversions and found them disappointing. During a Psychical Research expedition to a haunted house in Hampstead, where he tried and failed to locate a ghost, he struck up a friendship with Frank Podmore, the man who subsequently provided the Fabian Society with a name and a motto. The name was symbolic and, like that of the conservative John Birch Society[2] today, had no reference to the actual founders. But it lent a touch of classical elegance to a tiny left wing organization, few of whose original members had attended England's better public schools and universities.

The Fabian Society was named for Quintus Fabius Maximus, a Roman general and dictator who lived in the third century B.C. In his lifetime Fabius was nicknamed "Cunctator"—the Delayer—because of his delaying tactics against Hannibal in the second Punic War. By avoiding pitched battles at a time when Rome was weak, he won time for the Republic to build up its military strength. Though Fabius eventually met and defeated Hannibal at the Battle of Tarantum, he was not, in spite of what is often said today, "the patient vanquisher of Hannibal." In fact, he died before Hannibal was decisively van-

[2] The John Birch Society, is an American membership group of dedicated anti-Communists/anti-Socialists who call themselves Americanists. It is described in a book by Robert Welch, *The Bluebook of the John Birch Society*, (Belmont, The John Birch Society, 1966), fifth edition.

quished and Carthage destroyed. The final blow was dealt by a more aggressive and ruthless Roman, Scipio Africanus, a detail omitted from references to Fabius in the Society's literature. In this respect, also, Fabius' strategic role resembles that of the Society which has borrowed his name. (One cannot help wondering how the Roman patriot would have responded to the far from patriotic question posed by a well-known early Fabian, Graham Wallas: "When a man dies for his country, what does he die for?")

The motto of the Fabian Society, published on page 1 of *Fabian Tract No. 1*, stressed the value of delayed action. It stated: "For the right moment you must wait, as Fabius did most patiently when warring against Hannibal, though many censured his delays; but when the time comes, you must strike hard, as Fabius did, or your waiting will be in vain and fruitless." Time and repetition have given this motto a spurious patina of antiquity, but no one has ever been able to cite a Latin text as its source. On the cover of many a Fabian publication it was shortened to read, "I wait long, but when I strike, I strike hard." Usually it accompanied a sketch of an angry tortoise by the Fabian artist, Walter Crane, which first appeared on a Fabian Christmas card and has since been reproduced on literally millions of Fabian tracts and pamphlets distributed throughout the English-speaking world. So the tortoise became the heraldic device of the Society—emblem of persistence, longevity, slow and guarded progress towards a (revolutionary) goal. Not until the nineteen-sixties, for reasons best known to the Fabians themselves, did this tell-tale emblem abruptly cease to appear on the covers of most official Fabian publications.

Both name and motto were adopted on January 4, 1884, which may be presumed to be the actual founding date of the Society. It was half a dozen years before the program and leadership assumed definitive shape. Meanwhile, the deliberate tempo and very British complexion of the new Society distinguished it from the numerous small groups of foreign revolutionaries who took refuge in London throughout the nineteenth century and which invited surveillance by the police of several countries. Clever young Englishmen with a world to win obviously could not afford to be identified with foreign radicals, not if they hoped to attract any substantial following in Britain.

And yet, contrary to general belief, the gradualist policy of the Fabians did not conflict essentially with the doctrines of the lately deceased leader of world Socialism, Karl Marx. Had not Marx himself told German Communists in 1850 that it would take years "of civil strife and foreign wars not only to change existing conditions, but to change yourselves and make yourselves worthy of world power"? At an open meeting in Amsterdam reported by the Leipzig *Volkstaat* of October 2, 1872, Marx also said, "We know that we must take into consideration the institutions, the habits and the customs of different regions, and we do not deny that there are countries like America, England and—if I knew your institutions better I would perhaps add Holland—where the workers can attain their objectives by peaceful means. But such is not the case in all other countries."

At least one original leader of the Fabian movement had been definitely exposed to Marxist doctrines before joining the Society. In May, 1884, when the organization was still in its infancy, there appeared at its meetings an impertinent young Irishman with flamed-red hair and beard, of whom nobody had yet heard. The name of this apparition was George Bernard Shaw, and he claimed to be looking for a debate. In September of the same year he was admitted to membership and the following January was elected to the Fabian Executive.

Shaw was then twenty-eight years old, a free-lance journalist living on an occasional stipend. For nine years he had drifted from one leftist group and radical colony in London to another. In later life he was fond of telling how he was suddenly converted to Socialism in 1882 as the result of hearing a London lecture by Henry George, the American single-taxer and foe of "landlords." Obviously, Shaw's experiences as a penniless youth in the metropolis had not disposed him to love landlords, but he was stretching the truth when he dated his interest in Socialism from that lecture.

As early as 1879 he had joined the Zetetical Society, an offshoot of the Dialectical Society formed to explore the dialectical materialism of Karl Marx, though its alleged purpose was to discuss the works of John Stuart Mill. Before coming to the Fabians, Shaw had also belonged to a Marxist reading circle, politely called the Hampstead Historical Club, and had been at least a candidate member of the militantly Marxist Social Democratic Federation whose leader, Henry Mayers Hyndman, trailing clouds of costly cigar smoke, often visited Karl Marx at home.

Thereafter Shaw proceeded to school himself and others by making speeches on all the current issues about which he wished to be informed. For twelve years after joining the Society, he spoke as often as three times a week to audiences small and large, ranging from soapbox speeches on street corners to public debates in crowded halls, from formal papers before the nascent British Economic Association to four-hour addresses at large open-air meetings. As his mentors, he preferred to cite Henry George, or John Stuart Mill, the British Utilitarian; Professor W. S. Jevons, or David Ricardo, the early nineteenth century English economist from whom Marx derived his theory of surplus value.

Whether Shaw was ever personally acquainted with Karl Marx is not recorded. He could hardly have failed to see the ponderous Prussian in the reading room of the British Museum, where Marx was a fixture for nearly thirty years. Before and after joining the Fabians, Shaw, too, frequented the British Museum almost daily. There he read the first volume of *Das Kapital* in French and was vastly impressed by it; and there he became friendly with Marx's daughter Eleanor, a dark, rather striking young Socialist, working as a copyist in the reading room for eighteen pence a day. It is hard to see how he could have avoided meeting her father—the more so because, throughout his long career, Shaw never displayed the least reticence about introducing himself to anyone he wished to know.

Failure to mention meeting or even seeing a man whose work had impressed him so profoundly is a significant omission, especially on the part of a notorious name-dropper like Shaw. He refers casually to having once met Frederick Engels, Marx's alter ego who remained in London to edit the posthumous portions of *Das Kapital* until his own death in 1892.

The possibility has been raised—and remains an interesting subject for speculation—that George Bernard Shaw, the self-styled mountebank with his Mephistophelian eyebrows and carefully cultivated air of diabolism, who in his later writings equated Jesus and Lenin, as spiritual leaders,[3] was commissioned by the fathers of Marxian Socialists to help found a select company for the propagation and defense of their Socialist views. Early in the game, Shaw confided to the German Socialist, Eduard Bernstein, that he wanted the Fabians to be "the Jesuits of Socialism." [4]

Any serious consideration of Fabian Socialism must allow for the

[3] George Bernard Shaw, "Preface on Bosses," *Complete Plays. With Prefaces,* (New York, Dodd, Mead and Company, 1962), Vol. VI, p. 202. (Dated August 28, 1935.)

[4] Eduard Bernstein, *My Years of Exile,* (New York, Harcourt & Co., 1921), p. 226.

very real possibility that Communists early saw their opportunity to introduce Communism into America *through the Anglo-Saxon* tradition: enter at stage Left, the Fabian Society!

In any event, Shaw came into the Fabian Society as if *propelled;* promptly pushed himself into a position of leadership where he remained for decades; and to the end of his days retained a paternal and financial interest in its affairs. This was true even after his meteoric success as a playwright and propagandist prevented him from participating in its day-to-day activities. The average American of today, who knows Shaw chiefly as the author of *Pygmalion,* on which the libretto of *My Fair Lady* is based, may be surprised to learn that Socialism was the consuming passion of his rather anemic, vegetarian life.

Acidly outspoken on some matters, frankly blasphemous on others, the one subject on which he ever waxed sentimental was the Fabian Society. As a speaker, playwright and essayist, Shaw did more than any other human being to establish the fiction that the polite conspiracy called Fabian Socialism is a "peaceful, constitutional, moral and economical movement," needing nothing for its "bloodless and benevolent realization except that the English people should understand and approve of it." [5]

In January, 1885, Shaw introduced a friend into the Society whose contribution was to be as fateful as his own. This was Sidney Webb, a squat, dark, determined young clerk in the Colonial Office, with a photographic memory, a gift for assembling statistical data and a taste for political manipulation. Because his father, a bookkeeper from Westminster, had once served as a committeeman for John Stuart Mill, Webb claimed to have unique knowledge that Mill had died a Socialist.

As a boy Sidney Webb attended schools in Germany and Switzerland and presumably read German as fluently as English; yet he always took pains to disclaim any knowledge of or interest in the works of Karl Marx—although Shaw noted in his diary that in August, 1885, he and Webb together read the second volume of *Das Kapital,* just published in German. Webb's disclaimer can therefore be doubted, especially in view of his monumental, if masked, contribution to the practical advancement of Marxist programs in England during his lifetime and the fact that his final work (written jointly with Mrs.

[5] George Bernard Shaw, "The Revolutionist's Handbook," *Seven Plays. With Prefaces and Notes,* (New York, Dodd, Mead and Company, 1951), p. 710.

Webb and the Soviet Foreign Office[6]) was a paean to the "new civilization" of the Soviet Union. Even his loving wife in her *Diaries* has charged Sidney with possessing a most "robust conscience."

Shaw and Webb had met in 1879 at the Zetetical Society, when both were exploring the uses of Marxian dialectic as a weapon in debate. As Fabians, they formed a two-man team pacing each other like a pair of well-gaited carriage horses. They collaborated smoothly in the production of pamphlets, essays, and reports, drafted plans for political activity, and formulated internal and external policies of the Society in advance of executive meetings. Sidney Webb supplied the direction, George Bernard Shaw, the literary style.

Soon they were joined by a third friend, Sydney Olivier (afterwards Lord Olivier), also a clerk in the Colonial Office, who, many years later, was to become the Fabian-inspired Secretary of State for India. Like Sidney Webb, Olivier proved to be a fertile source of confidential information gleaned from official contacts in government service.[7] With the advent the next year of Graham Wallas, M.A.—future missionary-in-chief of Fabian-type Socialism in the United States—the first Fabian high command was complete.

The facility with which that oddly assorted quartet captured and retained the Society's top leadership bears some resemblance to the methods of Marxist-Leninist factions in front organizations of the nineteen-thirties. It suggests that the Fabian Society may, in fact, have been the first Marxist innocent front in history. True, members of the Fabian Executive did not hesitate to damn the ghost of Karl Marx as they saw fit. With equal impunity they "damned each other's eyes twelve months of the year," yet remained loyal to the Society and its secrets.[8] Differences of opinion and verbal battles between individual Fabians were routine, yet did not preclude the factor of Fabian discipline. The half-humorous insults they tossed back and forth so lightly only served to veil the deadly seriousness of their common objectives.

These objectives were broadly outlined in the *Basis,* a credo to which every member from 1887 on was obliged to subscribe. With a single change it survived until 1938, when it was recast to become the constitution of the Society. All three versions began by announcing,

[6] *Hearings of the Subcommittee on Internal Security of the United States Senate Committee on the Judiciary.* Testimony of Col. I. M. Bogolepov, April 7, 1952.
[7] Cf. S. G. Hobson, *Pilgrim to the Left,* (London, Longmans, Green & Co., Ltd., 1938). (See Chap. VIII.)
[8] *Ibid.*

"The Fabian Society consists of Socialists." The original *Basis* went on to say:

It [the Fabian Society] therefore *aims at the reorganisation of society by the emancipation of land and Industrial Capital from individual and class ownership,* and the vesting of them in the community for the general benefit. . . . *The Society accordingly works for the extinction of private property in land.* . . . *The Society further works for the transfer to the Community of such Industrial Capital as can conveniently be handled socially.* For the attainment of these ends the Fabian Society looks to the spread of Socialist opinions, and the social and political changes consequent thereon. . . . It seeks to achieve these ends by the general dissemination of knowledge as to the relation between the individual and Society in its economic, ethical and political aspects.[9]

Like other movements small in their beginnings but destined to cast a long shadow, the Fabian Socialist movement, which was called a Society, has never strayed from its original objectives. What the *Basis* proposed was nothing less than social revolution, to be achieved by devious means over a period of time rather than by direct action. Violence as an ultimate measure was not renounced—it simply was not mentioned. Religion was not attacked—it was merely ignored.

Cautiously phrased to disarm the unwary and to reassure any who might consider the term "social revolution" indiscreet, the *Basis* was probably the most genteel war cry ever uttered—but it was a war cry for all that! Propaganda and political action were the twin weapons by which Great Britain's unwritten constitution was to be subverted and the traditional liberties of Englishmen exchanged for a system of State Socialism. More precise instructions for putting into effect the Fabian scheme for nationalization-by-installments were issued many years later in a volume by Sidney and Beatrice Webb boldly entitled *A Constitution for the Socialist Commonwealth of Great Britain.*

For so ambitious a plan to be launched by so small a group must have seemed slightly absurd at the start. Certainly it caused no alarm in 1887 among authorized spokesmen of an Empire on which the sun never set. How could a few conceited young people hope to overturn the basis of England's mercantile power and, in fact, of civilization itself? And yet, less than twenty years before, an equally obscure group of assorted radicals had contrived to set up the Commune and ended by delivering Paris into the hands of the invading

[9] (Italics added.)

Prussian armies. That happened in France, however, a notoriously excitable country. Englishmen did things in a quite different fashion.

From the start, Fabian leaders were fully aware of the stamina of the system they hoped to abolish. They did not imagine, any more than Karl Marx or Lenin did, that Socialism could be achieved at one bound in a nation as strong as nineteenth century England. They did believe, however, that with some help, the people of Great Britain, and eventually the world, could be persuaded psychologically to accept Socialism as inevitable. It might take a long while, a full fifty years or more, but Fabians were willing to work and wait. Their time to strike, and strike hard, would come later.

In their first years the Fabians displayed as much irritation as the bearded Prussian, Karl Marx, had displayed towards some of his more impatient followers. They were furious at Henry Mayers Hyndman and his openly Marxist Social Democratic Federation for predicting so positively that the world-wide social revolution would take place on July 14th, 1889, the hundredth anniversary of the fall of the Bastille.

Failure of this widely advertised event to occur proved indirectly helpful to the early Fabian Society by bringing a number of embarrassed radicals and nervous liberals into the gradualist camp. Just before Christmas, the first edition of *Fabian Essays,* edited by Shaw and written by members of the Fabian inner circle, was published. On the strength of favorable book reviews by Fabian journalists[10] in such respected publications as the London *Star,* the *Chronicle* and the Edinburgh *Review,* the *Essays* attracted readers and stimulated some interest in Socialism. By 1890 the Fabian Society was definitely on its way, *and it has never stopped since.*

[10] Hubert Bland, H. W. Massingham, and Harold Cox, M.P.

3

The Dangerous Fabians

THAT year, in the flush of his first faint triumph, Sidney Webb began courting Beatrice Potter, a statuesque and well-heeled bluestocking. The contrast between them, both in station and stature, was acute. Beatrice was one of eight daughters of a Canadian-railway magnate; while the mother of her pint-sized suitor had been a London hairdresser. Beatrice once dreamed of a quite different future, but an earlier romance with Joseph Chamberlain, the great reformist Mayor of Birmingham, proved ill-starred. Sidney would channel her pent-up intellectual energies and resentments into a lifelong attack against the social class which had wounded her pride.

In 1892 this formidable couple—"very clever, very conceited," as an acquaintance remarked—agreed to merge their differences. The marriage was something of a milestone in Fabian history. It was not only because Beatrice, by a fortunate coincidence, had inherited an income of one thousand pounds a year in Canadian railway stocks, which relieved Sidney of the necessity of earning a living and enabled him to concentrate with quiet intensity on undermining the system that sustained him. Their union was also the prototype of a ménage soon to become characteristic of the Fabian set—the husband-and-wife "partnership" that applied itself with peculiar devotion to shattering the existing scheme of things and remolding it nearer to the (Fabian) heart's desire. It permitted a pattern of radical feminism combined with domesticity, and it proved appealing to ladies of strong views. The Fabian movement always emphasized the importance of female support, both personal and financial—though it alienated some by

21

its insistence that all but the most prominent women should do their own housework.

With the publication of their *History of Trades Unionism* (which Lenin translated into Russian for his followers) the names of Sidney and Beatrice Webb began to appear jointly on a series of ponderous volumes intended to conduct the English-speaking world along the road to Socialism. Their intellectual progeny were numerous, and the effect on their own and succeeding generations was considerable. In addition, Beatrice Webb was closely identified with the development of a product known as Fabian Research. Organized fact-finding designed to lend weight to predetermined opinions was to provide the basis for Fabian propaganda, educational and political.

Fabian "research" as practiced by Beatrice Webb and her school combined the turgid German type of scholarship, noted for massive detail and much admired by nineteenth century intellectuals, with a kind of airy legerdemain. It specialized in reaching conclusions on social and economic topics which were quite unrelated to the facts themselves. These dangerous *non sequiturs* escaped challenge because the preliminary facts were often obtained from unimpeachable official sources and because they were so voluminous.

The Fabian way was to bury an opponent, when possible, under mountains of exhaustive detail. Fabian research supplied the content for the "educational" material distributed by the Society, a good deal of it in the form of tracts and pamphlets presenting the Fabian stand on successive issues of the day. At a later date Beatrice Webb was made formally responsible for setting up the Fabian Research Department, which in due time became infiltrated by Communists and in the end was abandoned to them.

The decade of the eighteen-nineties has been poetically referred to as the period of the Society's "first blooming." The phrase is apt if one recognizes the movement to be a species of deadly nightshade rather than a wholesome growth. It is true that provincial affiliates of the Society sprang up all over England and Scotland, and general membership soon exceeded two hundred—not a very impressive figure. In 1891, the Society began publishing the *Fabian News*, "for members only," which is still published today.

A scattering of Fabians sat on town councils where, as "gas and water Socialists," they agitated for municipal control of public utilities. They got themselves named to local school boards, where they did their bit towards steering the education of the common-school masses into Socialist channels. In London, Sidney Webb became a member of the County Council and Graham Wallas headed the School Management Committee of the School Board.

In those years Fabian lecturers roamed the hinterland. Book boxes and tracts were shipped in bulk from the newly-opened headquarters at Clement's Inn. All that bleak superficial bustle helped to create an impression, still carefully fostered in the general press, that the Fabian Society was no more than a small, rather harmless, busybody organization chiefly involved in fraternal squabbles. Nothing could be further from the truth.

In reality, the Society took only a passing interest in the new members who had drifted rather aimlessly into its ranks, and soon released many of them to other radical organizations of lesser status.[1] While it was concerned at all times with creating a favorable climate for Socialist opinion, the particular mission of the Fabian Society was to develop a Socialist elite—in short, to discover and mold the leaders of an evolving Socialist world.

It is on this point, rather than on their gradualist procedure, that the Fabians appear to differ most obviously from classic Marxists, though the difference may be more apparent than real. Fabians have insisted from the start that in advanced capitalist countries like England and the United States, Socialism must *begin at the top* and meet the industrial masses half way.

Hence, the Fabians' emphasis on leadership, and their solicitude for higher education through which the leaders of the future were to be formed. The Fabian Society, which ceased publishing membership lists in 1945 to "assure privacy" to its many notables, has always contained the elite of left wing society, open and covert. It was no coincidence that when the Labour Party finally came to power in England, figures like Ramsay MacDonald and Clement Attlee, Sir Stafford Cripps, Herbert Morrison and a host of equal and lesser luminaries were found to have been Fabian-trained.

There was jubilation at Fabian headquarters when the first— though by no means the last—student group at Oxford was formed

---

[1] By 1893, in addition to the mother society in London, there were about 1,500 members organised in over seventy societies. But on its formation the Independent Labour Party absorbed most of these and by 1897 only eleven local groups remained. *Fabian News,* (September, 1959).

back in 1895. This one small chick caused more rejoicing than the whole brood of new provincial societies, since England's great universities were traditionally the hatcheries for Members of Parliament and the Civil Service. By 1900 there were three more university groups, and as one academic generation followed another, quite a number of England's future rulers submitted to brainwashing by Socialist tutors. In 1912, university students accounted for more than one-fifth of the Society's membership,[2] with the Cambridge group led by such obviously coming young men as Hugh Dalton, a future chairman of the Labour Party, and Clifford Allen, later chairman of the Independent Labour Party. The priority which the Fabian Society gave to this proselytizing is evident from the fact that such leading members as R. H. Tawney, G. D. H. Cole, afterwards president of the Society, former Foreign Secretary Patrick Gordon Walker and Prime Minister Harold Wilson taught for years at Oxford, shaping the young mind to the Socialist idea.

Another pilot operation begun in the nineties and steadily expanded to the present day is the London School of Economics. The circumstances of its founding are worth examining because they furnish so clear an example of Fabian duplicity at work.

A benefactor of the Fabian Society, Henry Hutchinson, M.P., had committed suicide in the summer of 1894, leaving a hastily drawn will in which he bequeathed a trust of nine thousand pounds to further the "propaganda and other purposes of the Society." As chairman of the Society, Sidney Webb was to be chairman of the Trust, but the will did not specifically authorize him to administer outlays. Without informing his colleagues of the precise terms of the will, Sidney proceeded to use the bulk of the money to establish the London School of Economics and Political Science. Nominally, the school was not established under the auspices of the Society, which, however, retained indirect control.

Before taking this step, Sidney privately consulted the well-known legal authority R. B. Haldane, Q.C. Haldane asked Webb pointblank if he was still a Socialist, and if the new school would really advance the cause of Socialism. On getting an affirmative answer to both questions, Haldane advised going ahead.

Nevertheless, the first Director of the School, who had been selected by Webb, solemnly assured the London Chamber of Commerce that "the School would not deal with political matters and *nothing of a*

[2] One-third of the present-day membership is composed of university students.

THE DANGEROUS FABIANS

socialistic tendency would be introduced."[3] That this pledge was honored chiefly in the breach is evident from an entry in Beatrice Webb's *Diary* of March, 1898. "The London School of Economics,"[4] she confided, "is growing silently but surely into a center of collectivist-tempered research and establishing itself as *the* English school of economic and political science."[5]

Since the Webbs themselves taught at the London School, it can be assumed that Beatrice knew the facts. Many other prominent Fabians have since served on its staff, including such leading lights of Socialism as Harold Laski, chairman of the Fabian Society from 1946 to 1948. Among Professor Laski's students at the London School were two sons of a United States Ambassador to the Court of St. James: Joseph P. Kennedy, Jr. in 1933-34 and John F. Kennedy in 1935-36.

Like the Catholic Society of Jesus—which the Fabian Society, being secular and materialistic in its approach, does not otherwise resemble —the basis for future action was so firmly defined in its first years that its subsequent growth was assured. A contemporary once said of Ignatius of Loyola, "When Ignatius drives a nail, no one can pull it out!"

Without attributing supernatural motives to the freethinking authors of the Fabian Society, it can be noted that the essential elements of purpose, organization and method on which the development of the Fabian movement depended were defined in its first decades, primarily by those two profane zealots, Sidney Webb and George Bernard Shaw. Despite the increased tempo and range of its present-day activities, the Fabian Society has not deviated in any essential way from the patterns initially devised for it. It remains today, as it was at its inception, a dangerously subtle conspiracy beneath a cloak of social reform.

Organizationally, the movement operated in ever-widening circles, like ripples in a pond. The Fabian Society of London was the mother society, source of programs, directives and propaganda which were handed down to the more variable local societies. The Executive Committee of the London Society constituted an inner circle with which the general membership enjoyed only fleeting contacts, at lectures, meetings, Easter, New Year's, and Summer Schools or weekend semi-

[3] Minutes of the Chamber's Commercial Education Committee: Janet, Lady Beveridge, *An Epic of Clare Market*, (London, Bell Publishers, 1960), p. 27. (Italics added.)
[4] Shortened form, in popular usage for London School of Economics and Political Science.
[5] Beatrice Webb, *Our Partnership*, (New York, Longmans, Green & Co., Ltd., 1948), p. 145.

nars. Then came the handpicked membership. And finally, there was a very much larger and continually expanding ring of sympathizers, who supported immediate or long-range programs of the Society, in whole or in part.

The influence of the Fabian movement, which has always been more real than apparent, cannot be measured by the Society's limited membership, but must be gauged by other factors. Such factors, for instance, as the practical influence each member was able to exert in his chosen profession or field of action. Even during the days when membership lists were published, the Society already operated to a large extent as an invisible and toxic force. As the Machiavellian Webb so often said, with an air of candid innocence, "the work of the Fabian Society is the sum of its members' activities."

At the heart of those concentric circles, ringed around and shielded from scrutiny, was the small, hard core of the Fabian leadership, which acknowledged no responsibility for the sometimes contradictory acts of individual members—even after stimulating such action. For almost fifty years Sidney Webb remained the guiding force of the Society, discreetly controlling its rather loose organizational reins and seldom letting his right hand know what the left was doing. Edward R. Pease, who replaced Sydney Olivier as general secretary from 1890 to 1924, remained Webb's faithful watchdog, enforcing the authority and masking the often devious maneuvers of his small master.

The Society's function from its earliest years coincided perfectly with the formula of Wilhelm Liebknecht, nineteenth century German Marxist: "to forecast a practical program for the intermediate period; to formulate and justify measures that shall be applicable at once and that will serve as aids to the new Socialist birth." Grafting itself on the century-old British reform movement, the Fabian Society combined sociology with politics in an effort to propel its members into positions of national influence.

Unlike their European Socialist comrades, the Fabians established themselves as a private Society of limited membership rather than a political party. The Society was neither doctrinaire nor given to philosophical hairsplitting. All it exacted was a broad pledge of allegiance to Socialist goals, leaving each member free to justify them by any logic or philosophy he preferred. He was also free to join any political party he chose, provided he utilized every possible opportunity to further the Fabian cause. In fact, he was encouraged to do so, for political activity was only second to *education* on the Fabian agenda.

The practice of joining a political party for the sake of advancing Fabian programs, and of placing Fabians in elective and appointive posts, became known as "penetration." Since the first loyalty of Fabians was to the Society, rather than to any party, their motives were sometimes suspect. Thus, Edward R. Pease was almost ejected from the Bradford Conference of 1893, when the Independent Labour Party was formed. He managed to remain and some years later was able to report that two-thirds of the Fabian Society belonged to the Independent Labour Party.[6]

After 1919 Fabians transferred their allegiance en bloc to the British Labour Party, at whose foundation other Fabians had assisted—and for all practical purposes the Independent Labour Party was no more. It remained a mere wandering voice on the far Left, calling for militant action when more "peaceful" Fabian programs seemed in danger of bogging down and, in effect, winning liberal support for the Fabian way as being "less dangerous."

Fabian penetration of the Liberal Party of Great Britain, though less extensive, proved no less lethal. From 1903 Sir L. G. Chiozza-Money, a member of the Fabian Executive, went to Parliament as a Liberal. When Liberals came to power in the elections of 1906, twenty-nine seats in Parliament were held by Fabians. By 1911, forty-two Fabian Socialists sat on the Liberal-Labour benches. Eventually their intimate knowledge of Liberal constituencies enabled Fabians to divert a number of election districts to the upcoming Labour Party, and to aid the Labour Party in detaching trade union support from the Liberals. Penetration created new political alignments more profitable to the cause of Socialism.

What George Dangerfield called *the strange death of liberal England* [7] was hastened by the fact that the Fabian Society—on the strength of "tips" from its members in the Liberal Party, as well as gossip leaked from government offices—was able to release a steady barrage of printed matter politically damaging to Liberalism and its leaders. The intention and the effect was to build up the Fabian-dominated Labour Party that emerged full-blown after World War I.

A twin to "penetration" was the time-honored Fabian practice called "permeation." Much favored by the ladies—Beatrice Webb actually believed she had invented it!—Fabian permeation dates from

---

[6] Edward R. Pease, *The History of the Fabian Society,* (London, A. C. Fifield, 1916), p. 208.
[7] Also the title of his book.

an era before women could vote. Permeation meant getting the ear of important or key persons and inducing them to push through some action desired by Fabians. It was not considered necessary that such persons be Fabians. Often it was preferable that they should be outsiders. The important thing was that they should act on the advice and instructions of Fabians. The rather startling appointment of Beatrice Webb to the Royal Commission on the Poor Law from 1905 to 1909 was an example of something achieved at second hand by permeation; for the unhappy official who named her to that post was neither aware of the lady's Socialist bias nor her forceful nature. Permeation failed at this time to get her recommendations written into law, but the unauthorized printing of her Minority Report was a propaganda coup for the Society. Interestingly enough, the copy that went to the printer was in Sidney's handwriting.[8]

One advantage of permeation, developed to a fine art by the Fabians, was that it could be practiced almost anywhere—at teas, dinners and weekend house parties, as well as in committee and board meetings. Doubtless the same black art was known under other names to the Medes and Persians, and was old in Cleopatra's day. It has even been seen to rear its head along the social circuit in modern Washington. The Fabian Society, however, appears to have been the first organization ever to advocate this technique openly as an instrument of political policy.

A final pattern for the future, established by those two long-lived patriarchs of the Fabian Society, Sidney Webb and George Bernard Shaw, solved the problem of where Socialism is going. When all is said and done, where *could* it go? With many of the preliminary steps accomplished and the end plainly in sight, only one road would be open to the Socialists and it would lead inexorably to the *Left*. After the Directory, the Terror. After July, October. That is the historic pattern, and to date it has never varied.

Shaw and Webb, both hardened professionals, pointed out the way to their followers. It was no accident of old age that led them separately in 1931-32 to the Union of Soviet Socialist Republics and to full-throated capitulation. After some earlier expressions of distaste for Communist violence and the iron hand of Communist Party discipline, they could no longer restrain themselves from making public professions of their allegiance.

Perhaps they had always known what the journey's end must be.

[8] Pease, *op. cit.*, p. 213.

Perhaps in their secret hearts they had been there all the time. At the turn of the century, Joseph Fels, a soap magnate from Philadelphia and an early member of the Fabian Society,[9] had, in 1907, loaned money to Russian revolutionaries at the time when Lenin quarreled with the majority of Russia's Social Democrats and formed the "Bolshevik" wing of the party. In those struggling early days there had seemed to the Fabians to be no enemies on the left, and perhaps it has remained so.

Weighted with years and honors, the Webbs and George Bernard Shaw traveled royally to Moscow to announce their full support for the Soviet system of rationalized barbarism. Shaw, by then the dean of English letters, told Stalin that the words "the inevitability of gradualness" should be engraved on Lenin's tomb. Webb, now Baron Passfield, exchanged ideas on colonial policy with Stalin, who had launched his own public career with a study of subject nationalities. In 1929-30 Webb had served as Britain's Secretary of State for the Dominions and Colonies, and in 1930-31 as Secretary of State for the Colonies.

Among the poisoned fruits of the Webbs' sojourn in the Socialist Fatherland was a two-volume work entitled *Soviet Socialism—A New Civilisation?* (The question mark was dropped in later editions.) Even before publication, portions of the manuscript placed in the right hands helped to spark a movement leading to United States recognition of the Soviet Union in 1933. The Webbs had known Maxim Litvinoff, the Soviet Foreign Minister, and his British-born wife, the former Ivy Low, during that couple's years of "exile" in London.

Like the character in Stendhal's historical novel who rode through the Battle of Waterloo without being aware of it, the Webbs were present at a wholesale slaughter and did not see or choose to see it. Their visit to the Union of Soviet Socialist Republics in 1932 coincided with the huge man-made famine that swept the Ukraine and Crimea, where a minimum of two to three million persons was deliberately starved to death in order to hasten the Soviet program of farm confiscations. Such horrors were handily omitted from the Webbs' encyclopedic volumes, whose publication was withheld until after the 1935 British elections. Their index refers to "famine, alleged."

The actual sources of this book were revealed some years later, in testimony given to the Internal Security Subcommittee of the United States Senate Committee on the Judiciary. Appearing before that

[9] Listed as a Fabian in *Fabian News,* (March, 1905).

body on April 7, 1952, Colonel I. M. Bogolepov, a former Soviet Army officer who had been attached from 1930 to 1936 to the Soviet Foreign Office, recalled his dealings with the Webbs. He stated bluntly that *the entire text of the Webbs' book had been prepared in the Soviet Foreign Office.* Material for the chapter on Soviet prison camps, stressing the "humane" methods employed in those factories of death and minimizing the vast scale of their operations, was specially compiled by the Secret Police and also delivered through the Foreign Office to the learned couple. The Colonel happened to know these things because, as he explained with some amusement, he had done most of the ghostwriting himself in the line of duty.

Colonel Bogolepov added that after fleeing to the West he read the Webbs' book with much interest and found they had used his prepared material almost verbatim. "Just a few changes for the English text, just a little bit criticizing!" he remarked ironically. Which is almost, but not quite, the last word on Fabian Research!

For some reason, their gyrations did not estrange the Webbs from the Fabian Society, or vice versa. When Sidney died in 1947, a few years after Beatrice, he left their joint estate of thirty thousand pounds to the Fabian Society and the London School of Economics. For services rendered, a grateful Labour Government interred the ashes of Sidney and Beatrice Webb, who had been practicing atheists most of their lives, in the hallowed precincts of Westminster Abbey. Concerning the final disposition of Beatrice, who once wrote that "the character of Jesus has never appealed to me," Shaw commented on a postcard to her niece, Barbara Drake: "B. must be sizzling to hear the name Jesus spoken over her!" Shaw,[10] carrying his defiance of everything holy into the hereafter, ordered his ashes to be scattered in the garden of his home at Ayot St. Lawrence "to make the soil of England more fertile for the growth of Socialism."

At the Beatrice Webb House in Surrey, used today for Fabian Summer Schools and weekend conferences, there is a rather grotesque stained glass window ordered by Shaw in 1910. It depicts himself and Webb smashing the world with workingmen's hammers. Among the Fabians kneeling below in attitudes of mock adoration is the novelist H. G. Wells, thumbing his nose irreverently but still close to the old

[10] In a letter dated January 14, 1948, and written just a few years before his death to Miss Fanny Holtzmann, a New York attorney, Shaw stated: "My dear Fanny: I am not a Cobdenite Liberal, but the very opposite, a Communist, though not a member of the so-called Communist Party." Washington *Post*, (February 3, 1948).

gang. On a streamer overhead is the legend, "REMOULD IT NEARER TO THE HEARTS DESIRE." That much-quoted line comes, of course, from a quatrain in Edward Fitzgerald's translation of Omar Khayyam:

> Dear Love, couldst thou and I with fate conspire
> To grasp this sorry scheme of things entire,
> Would we not shatter it to bits, and then
> Remould it nearer to the heart's desire!

To an outsider those verses might seem no more than a quaintly Victorian literary relic, but to the Fabians they are still a literal statement of destructive intent.

4

A Chosen Instrument

THE demonic spirits of the Fabian Society, Shaw and Webb, lived long enough to see a number of their destructive hopes fulfilled. Progress of their brainchild in the twentieth century far outstripped its *fin de siècle* promise. Still guarded in its movements and as nearly invisible as possible, the Society became the directing force of Socialism not only in Britain but throughout the Empire it schemed to dissolve. Leading Fabians had been making world tours since 1898, and since that time colonial units of the Society had multiplied and prospered. When the colonial administrators departed, native Fabians, educated at the London School of Economics, were ready and all too willing to take a hand in shaping Socialist-oriented Commonwealth governments.

In Britain the influence of the Society had grown steadily, if imperceptibly, until it dominated a major political party—a far cry from its small beginnings. Even in its fledgling years, however, the Society had been able to obtain cooperation whenever required from all domestic Socialist factions, because individual Fabians were active in each of these splinter groups. At one time or another, Fabian projects and candidates had received support from the Radical Clubs, the Progressives, the Cooperative Union, the National Reform League, the Social Democratic Federation, the Independent Labour Party, and other left wing bodies. By refusing to identify itself with any of them, the Fabian Society survived them all and went on to larger things.

An exception to this rule was eventually made in the case of the Labour Party, founded and directed throughout its history by top-echelon Fabians. (Today, members of the Fabian Society must be

32

eligible for membership in the Labour Party, though the reverse is not the case.) As Fabians gradually moved into positions of power with the support of British Labour, they have utilized that power for the advancement of Socialism abroad as well as at home.

It is not surprising that their first decisive action in foreign affairs was undertaken for the benefit of their brothers-under-the-skin in Moscow. The sweeping threat by British trade unions to "down tools" in 1920 was instigated by an arch-Fabian, Arthur Henderson. This threat effectively ended British military intervention in Russia and enabled the Bolsheviks to capture large stores of British-made munitions—a decisive factor in the survival of Bolshevik armed rule, as Joseph Stalin suggested in an interview with George Bernard Shaw and the Liberal Party leader, Lord Lothian,[1] later Ambassador to Washington.

Throughout the nineteen-twenties, Fabian-instructed Labour groups and Fabian Members of Parliament pressed for renewal of trade relations by Great Britain and other nations with Soviet Russia. Their pretext was that such trade would provide more employment for British workers and more votes for the Labour Party—though it is hard to see how revived commerce between the Soviet Union and Weimar Germany could have aided the British working man. What the Fabians aimed at was a three-cornered interchange between themselves, their Social Democrat confrères in Germany and the Soviet Socialist Republics, all leading, as Shaw remarked, "to Socialist control of trade at the consular level."

Arthur Henderson, long a member of the Fabian Executive, was the Foreign Minister, who in 1929 engineered British diplomatic recognition of Bolshevik Russia and paved the way for similar recognition by the United States, in a period when the Soviets' internal economy and external prestige were perilously low. Little was said or even hinted as to just how far such "cooperation" advanced the various Communist five-year plans and permitted the Soviet Union, with its technique of bloodbaths, intrigue, sedition, and guerilla warfare, to acquire the imperial status abandoned after World War II by England. It is noteworthy that Fabian publicists today no longer refer to Great Britain, but simply to Britain.

The once-imperial island, which no foreign force for a thousand years could violate, finally succumbed to Fabian guile. What Phillip's

[1] Hesketh Pearson, *Bernard Shaw*, (London, Methuen & Co., Ltd., 1961), p. 358.

Spain, Napoleon's France, the Kaiser's and Hitler's Germany had all failed to achieve, a small band of home-grown Socialists peacefully accomplished. How Fabians performed this feat in approximately three-quarters of a century is a mystery that the Society would now prefer to dismiss as fiction. A glance at the record, however, confirms the facts and provides a neat object-lesson for other nations where allegedly "gentle" and "humane" Socialists aspire to power.

From the beginning, the destructive nature of Fabian Socialism was never made sufficiently clear to the British public. The good manners of the Fabians tended to veil their revolutionary purpose and render it improbable to all but the initiate. To gain popular sympathy, the Society concealed its will-to-power behind a series of apparently benign social welfare programs and preached the brotherhood of man for the attainment of purely material ends. Whenever possible, its members attached themselves to existing reform movements which in the long run gained prominence and preferment for Fabian leaders. In every decade of the twentieth century, Fabians have claimed the credit for every Liberal reform.

Thus, gradual and penetrating Socialism came to be accepted as mere reformism, and its practitioners escaped the censure directed at Socialists of the catastrophic school. As George Bernard Shaw announced in 1948, the Fabian Society was "still alive and doing its work, which is to rescue Socialism and Communism from the barricades." One no longer even needed to read Marx and Engels in order to advance their programs. Cunningly, Fabian Socialism represented itself as "a constitutional movement in which the most respected citizens and families may enlist, without forfeiting the least scrap of their social or spiritual (sic) standing." [2] To emphasize the Society's regard for family ties, a single membership sufficed for both husband and wife. Their children, instructed in Fabian nurseries for adolescents, grew up into revolution without ever realizing there was any other way.

In the course of nearly four generations, some highly respected names in modern British letters and learning have been connected with the Fabian Society, either as dues-paying members or willing collaborators.[3] In the field of history, there were such gifted individ-

[2] George Bernard Shaw, "Sixty Years of Fabianism," *Fabian Essays,* Jubilee Edition, (London, The Fabian Society and Allen and Unwin, 1945), p. 287.
[3] All the names which follow are listed by official Fabian historians, Edward R. Pease and Margaret Cole, or recur frequently in the pages of the official Fabian publications, *Fabian News* and the *Fabian Annual Reports.*

uals as G. M. Trevelyan, Philip Guedalla, Arnold Toynbee. Philosopher-statesman Lord Haldane also belonged to the Society, according to a *Fabian News* obituary. There was R. H. Tawney, economist, social historian and long time member of the Fabian Executive, known for his personal piety, devotion to the Virgin Mary and bitter anti-capitalist bias. A whole series of Fabians held membership in the Royal Economic Society, which George Bernard Shaw and a few fellow Social Democrats had helped to launch many years before, and contributed regularly to its *Journal* edited for a time by John Maynard Keynes.

In science, the Society claimed Sir Julian Huxley as well as a number of Nobel prize winners, more noted for their scientific attainments than their political acumen. University tutors and professors were legion—among them such venerated figures as A. D. Lindsay, the Master of Balliol, and Sidney Ball, don of St. John's, Oxford, until his death in 1918, and founder of the Oxford Social Club that sponsored Fabian lecturers. Military opinion was represented by the late Brigadier General C. B. Thomson, and Captain B. H. Liddell Hart, military correspondent for the *Times* and proponent of the theory of defensive warfare, who, in recent years, has addressed official Fabian Society gatherings.

Fabian poets included Maurice Hewlett and Rupert Brooke, the Cambridge undergraduate who died in military service during World War I. Among editors holding membership in the Society were Harold Cox, M.P., of the Edinburgh *Review*, A. J. Orage of the *New Age*, and S. K. Ratcliffe of the *New Statesman*, who also served as London representative of the *New Republic*. The publishing fraternity was represented by Raymond Unwin, of the firm of Allen and Unwin, whose books were reprinted in America by Macmillan; Leonard Woolf, husband of the well-known writer Virginia Woolf, and himself the author of a Fabian document, *International Government*, which was an early blueprint for the League of Nations; and Victor Gollancz of Left Book Club notoriety, who also published the *Fabian News*.

So many successful writers and publicists have been aligned with the Fabian Society that an innocent observer might easily have mistaken it for a kind of logrolling literary society. Among them were Arnold Bennett, H. G. Wells, Rebecca West, John Galsworthy, Granville Barker, Harold Nicolson, St. John Ervine, Constance Garnett,[4] Francis Hackett, Jerome K. Jerome, Robert Dell, E. M. Forster, Aldous

[4] Constance Garnett was a translator of Tolstoi and other pre-revolutionary Russian novelists.

Huxley, J. B. Priestley, J. C. Squire, Desmond McCarthy, Naomi Mitchison, and a host of others. They have ranged from the frankly Marxist John Strachey to the neo-Catholic Barbara Ward, propagandist for African nationalism. Even Monsignor Ronald Knox confessed to having joined the Oxford Fabian Society and G. K. Chesterton was once a Fabian, but both withdrew from the movement prior to their conversion to the Catholic faith.

As an authority on the subject has remarked, "Fabians appeared in so many desirable liberal (and cultural) connections that they could scarcely be believed to be subversive of private property or of liberty." [5] The London School of Economics, aided by grants from the Rockefeller Foundation, was growing to world renown as "the Empire on which the concrete never sets." Scant attention was paid to the fact that its lecturers in economics and the so-called political and social "sciences" were almost invariably Fabian Socialists or their bedfellows. Many persons who disagreed with its politics relished the good style and literary flair of the *New Statesman*—a weekly "journal of opinion" founded by the Webbs in 1913, financed, edited and written largely by Fabians though nominally independent of the Society.

In their mannerly, welfare-bent, cultivated and studious fashion, Fabian Socialists were progressively undermining the foundations of the British Empire and the age-old liberties of Englishmen as a more stridently revolutionary movement could hardly have succeeded in doing. "As much freedom as possible consistent with public control of the means of production" became their slogan: a formula that denies liberty itself as a basic human right, and begs the question as to how much of it is possible under State control of private initiative. Only Shaw, in his old age, warned that a great deal more regulation than most people anticipated, including stern restriction of trade union activity, would be inevitable in the elite-ruled Socialist state; but his realistic view of the promised land was dismissed as just another tired, Shavian paradox.

While the Fabian Society consists chiefly of middle class intellectuals, it has never been intolerant of affluence or noble birth if they furthered the Fabian cause. Peers like Lord Parmoor and Lord Henry Bentinck, offshoot of a famous Liberal family, graced the membership lists of the Society even before a Labour Party Government created

---

[5] M. P. McCarran, *Fabianism in the Political Life of Britain, 1919-1931*, (Chicago, Heritage Foundation, 1954), p. 439.

its own non-hereditary peerage. One of the earliest aristocratic converts to Socialism had been the Countess of Warwick, young, beautiful and a friend of King Edward VII. The Countess was so much impressed by what her new-found friends were doing to "help the poor" that she donated her country house, Easton Lodge, to the Fabians for a perpetual weekend haven and conference center.

Earlier still, Charlotte Payne-Townshend, an Anglo-Irish convert to Socialism known as "the millionairess," had been induced by Beatrice Webb to contribute a thousand pounds to the London School of Economics. As a reward, Beatrice Webb introduced her to the indigent Fabian, George Bernard Shaw, whose poverty was soon abolished by marriage to Charlotte Payne-Townshend. Before wedding her in a civil ceremony, Shaw insisted on extracting a marriage settlement from his Charlotte—a somewhat cold-blooded procedure, but a clear indication of how highly prized by Fabians was personal solvency. Shaw later earned substantial sums from his propagandizing plays and essays; but fortunately for him and many another Fabian, royalties and dowries were never a form of wealth marked for nationalization by the Society.

It was the wily Shaw who also perceived the possibility of utilizing the poor to finance the political advancement of Socialists. As early as 1893 he had been the first to propose using trade union funds to elect Socialists to Parliament—a scheme whose vast potential was not fully apparent in an era when only a small segment of British labor was organized. As the trade unions grew in numbers and wealth under Fabian-tutored leaders, the method suggested by Shaw would propel Fabian Socialists into positions of national control. Much slow, painstaking political and educational work by Fabians, culminating in a brand-new alignment of political parties in Great Britain, was necessary to bring those hopes to fruition.

When *Fabian Essays* was published in 1889, only a little over 10 per cent of Great Britain's industrial workers belonged to trade unions. It was understandable—though not quite pardonable—that the *Essays* should have failed to include any mention whatever of the subject. This omission was hastily repaired with the publication in 1894 of a *History of Trades Unionism* by the Webbs, who saw the light in ample time to take advantage of it. As a practical step towards political power, the Labour Representation Committee was formed at Sidney Webb's suggestion in 1899.

Despite its resounding title, that committee was at first no more than a representative collection of Socialist splinter groups, convoked to find ways and means of obtaining parliamentary seats for Socialists in the name of Labour. Discreetly, the Fabian Society sent only one delegate, the mole-like Edward R. Pease. A well-disciplined committeeman, Pease avoided controversy and in a shadowy way exerted much influence on organization through the years. The Society, as such, remained in the background.

One reason why the Fabian Society preferred to avoid the limelight was in order to avert any direct challenge to its leadership role in the Socialist movement. Another was the harsh fact that some Labour men, then as now, regarded the Society as being almost too high-toned for comfort. For a good many years its sole working-class member was a London house painter, W. L. Phillips, author of *Fabian Tract No. 1, Why Are the Many Poor?* As late as 1923 there was not one "proletarian" on the Fabian Executive; and even today there are still Divisional Labour Party leaders and agents in Great Britain to whom the term Fabian merely implies "that snob Society."

Anonymity in the Labour Representation Committee involved no real sacrifice for the Society, because individual Fabians wearing other hats were on hand to defend its interests. Keir Hardie was there as head of the Independent Labour Party, at that early date the leading Socialist political party in Great Britain. Hardie was a member of the Fabian Society, though some called him undisciplined. Similarly, Ramsay MacDonald, who was chairman of the Committee and also headed the new Labour Party, belonged for some years to the Society. Arthur Henderson, a former Wesleyan minister and an admitted Fabian from 1912, was permanent treasurer of the Committee as well as MacDonald's chief personal aide. Originally the British Labour Party, which grew out of this committee, was just another Socialist splinter group.

It was a strange masquerade, which deceived no one except the public, but in the end it served its purpose—namely, to decoy organized labor into the Fabian Socialist trap. Results were not immediately apparent, and patience was recommended. Though trade unions were urged to affiliate with the Committee, and the Independent Labour Party worked to infiltrate the trade unions, the first acceptance did not come until 1903, from the Gasworkers' Union. Fabian historians complain that the initial fee for union affiliation was fixed much too low, provoking some difficulties when the Committee found itself obliged to raise the tariff. Socialists were finding that it cost more money to win elections than they had supposed.

The rather modest success of this committee in gaining seats for Socialists in the parliamentary elections of 1906 and 1911 justified its existence. During those years the Labour group in Parliament operated chiefly as a pressure bloc within the Liberal Party, and due to its relative weakness it was neither disliked nor feared. As yet, no one except its Fabian mentors could be sure whether the little Labour Party was an advance guard of Socialism or a mere appendage of Liberalism. It was the outbreak of war in 1914 that offered Fabian Socialism its big opportunity to organize a mass Labour Party on the home front, while the flower of old England was dying on the first traditional, thin, red battle lines.

Many years before, Karl Marx had predicted that a general European war would give Socialists an opening to capture power. That proved to be the case in Russia, and to a more limited extent in other parts of Europe. In England, the country where the capitalism of our era was born and originally demonstrated its dynamic force, the advance of Socialism was more deliberate. Not one, but two World Wars were needed to reduce that island fortress. Nevertheless, the Fabian tortoise, as if guided by Marxian precepts, moved during World War I to strike its first major blow. The men most responsible for inciting it were Sidney Webb and Arthur Henderson, who combined their treacherous efforts in a period of political truce to form a new-style Labour Party quite unlike the old semi-pressure group.

On August 6, 1914, the War Emergency Workers' Committee was born and proved to be the most influential single event in the creation of the revised Labour Party. The Emergency Committee's chairman, until he joined the Government, was Arthur Henderson; and its secretary was J. S. Middleton, Assistant Secretary of the Labour Party. Both were members and tools of the Fabian Society. While Sidney Webb held no official position on the War Emergency Workers' Committee, his skill in drafting statements and bringing unlikely groups together under one roof assured him a leading role.

Looking more than ever like a tintype of Napoleon III, the aging but agile Sidney was cast for the role which suited him best—that of a mastermind behind the scenes, exerting influence without responsibility, the Gray Eminence of a Socialist mass party to be manipulated in Labour's name. Within a week after the wartime Committee

was set up, Webb had prepared and issued *Fabian Tract No. 176,
The War and the Workers,* for distribution throughout the country.
This tract urged branches of all participating groups to set up local
Emergency Committees, presumably to defend the wartime and post-
war living standards of labor and to help keep the working force on
the production lines. It is noteworthy that a series of conferences on
"Restoring Trade Union Conditions after the War" was held in Fabian
Hall, and the audiences heard Beatrice Webb and other Fabian So-
cialists reject the Whitley Council System of capital-labor-government
cooperation.

The War Emergency Workers' Committee, in effect, delivered organized British labor into Socialist hands. It embraced The Trades
Union Congress and the General Federation of Trades Unions; the
powerful Miners', Railwaymen and Transport Workers' Unions; the
Cooperative Movement and Wholesale Society; the Women's Labour
League and Cooperative Guild; the London Trade Council; the National Union of Teachers—in addition to the Labour Party and the
Socialist Societies. Joint local committees of all these organizations
would provide the base for a new national party to include "workers
of hand and brain."

Not even the urgencies of wartime can explain why the Cabinet of
Lloyd George was so incautious as to present the Labour Party and
the Fabian Society with virtually unlimited access to future working-
class votes. Obviously, both groups were considered innocuous, a
public impression the Party and the Society had taken pains to foster.
As far as the War Government was concerned, the Emergency Committee proved quite useful in the summer of 1915 when the penalty
clause of the Munitions of War Act was found inapplicable to a
large-scale work stoppage. Since Lloyd George could not jail 200,000
striking Welsh coal miners whose output was badly needed, he welcomed the Committee's diplomatic intervention.

In December, 1915, Sidney Webb was named the Fabian Society's
official representative on the Labour Party Executive and his collaboration with Arthur Henderson became still closer. By war's end the
Labour Party had a skeleton network of local units reaching from
the Shetlands to Land's End. It also boasted a new constitution and
an overall program, both the work of Fabians.

The circumstances that produced the Labour Party's constitution
should be remembered because they illustrate so plainly the emotional effect of the Russian Revolution on British Fabians. The 1917

Revolution was hailed as a victory by Socialists of every stripe throughout the world—even though it cost Allied lives by releasing a number of German Army Divisions for service on the Western Front! In his enthusiasm, Arthur Henderson asked permission for British Labour representatives to visit Sweden along with other Allied Socialists and confer with the Russian revolutionaries. When the War Cabinet bluntly refused such facilities, Henderson was so outraged that he sat down and, with Sidney Webb's help, wrote the new constitution for the British Labour Party.

Promptly adopted in February, 1918, it established the Labour Party as a federation of affiliated bodies to include the trade unions, the Royal Arsenal Cooperative Society, the Socialist Societies and local Labour Party units. Only delegates of these constituent groups were entitled to sit on the Party Executive or vote at its congresses—a provision that forever excluded the mere Labour Party sympathizer and independent voter from any voice or influence in Party affairs. At the same time, its Fabian architects cleverly managed to identify the Labour Party with labor as such; so that anyone opposed to its Socialist program appeared by inference to be a foe of the working man.

It is interesting to note that a similar trick of language was exploited at a later date by the authors of Franklin D. Roosevelt's New Deal, who contrived to equate the Democratic Party in the United States with the idea of democracy, thereby implying that all opponents of Roosevelt's policies were enemies of democracy itself—a prime example of false logic purveyed through mass suggestion.

The new Labour Party constitution accomplished the long-hoped-for Fabian fusion of trade unionists, who furnished the votes and the money, and Socialists who dictated policy. It was an unnatural creation resembling the two-faced pagan god Janus, with, in this case, one face looking to labor for power and the other looking to Socialism for heaven on earth. To bind labor more effectively to Socialism, Sidney Webb had organized his first "tutorial class" in 1916 at the London School of Economics. There he lectured on Fabian economics and "doctrineless" Socialism to Britain's future trade union leaders—as G. D. H. Cole and Harold Laski did after him.

This so-called adult education movement, designed to bring the Socialist-oriented university professor and the labor movement together, had been initiated at Oxford in 1906 under the sponsorship of the Workers' Educational Association. Sometimes described as the fruit of Edwardian liberalism, it was supported from the start by such eminent Fabian Socialist dons as A. D. Lindsay, R. H. Tawney and Sidney Ball.[6] Fabian Society locals at Oxford and Cambridge sent their most promising young men and women to teach at Workers' Educational Association evening courses in nearby working class centers. It was while teaching at such a school that Lord Pakenham, the Catholic Fabian, met his future bride, a niece of Lord Curzon.

Through the Adult School and the "Labour Church," Socialist intellectuals were able in a single generation to shape the minds and politics of those who were to bring the trade unions into the Labour Party. Such men as Ernest Bevin, who headed the Transport and General Workers' Union representing 4,000,000 electoral votes, and Emanuel Shinwell, who succeeded Ramsay MacDonald as the idol of the radical Clydesiders, had known only four or five years of grammar school education.[7]

While Shinwell claimed to have educated himself through reading at public libraries, Bevin supplemented his formal schooling, or the lack of it, by attending the Fabian-backed Adult School classes of the Bristol Town Council.[8] In after years, as Britain's Foreign Minister, Bevin paid tribute to the Adult School movement and especially to his teacher, H. B. Lees-Smith, a Fabian Socialist labor theoretician who later served in the MacDonald government of 1929 and for a time during World War II was Acting Leader of the Parliamentary Labour Party. A good many Labour M.P.'s of 1945 owed their "university education" to the Workers' Educational Association and its off-shoots.[9]

Fabians estimated that only 5 per cent of the working class was worthy of being groomed for leadership; but every member of their own handpicked Society was regarded as a potential leader in his chosen field. After 1918, Fabians wishing to enter politics would do so through the Labour Party. At the same time, the Society continued to disclaim responsibility for the political views or activities of its

[6] J. F. C. Harrison, *Learning and Living*, A Study in the History of the English Adult Education Movement, (London, Routledge and Kegan Paul, Ltd., 1961), p. 264.
[7] Emanuel Shinwell, *Conflict Without Malice*, An Autobiography. (London, Odhams Press, Ltd., 1955), pp. 18-19.
[8] Francis Williams, *Ernest Bevin*, Introduction by the Rt. Hon. Clement Attlee, O.M., C.H., M.P. (London, Hutchinson & Co., Ltd., 1952), pp. 15-22.
[9] Margaret Cole, *The Story of Fabian Socialism*, (London, Heinemann Educational Books, Ltd., 1961), p. 208 (footnote).

members—just as it also disclaimed responsibility for the tracts published under its imprint—asserting that the world movement towards Socialism was above and beyond mere individual or Party bias. This delicate distinction puzzled and sometimes irritated the more forthright trade union men.

The revolutionary program of the reborn Labour Party, which in essence has not changed to this day, was primarily the work of one Fabian, the durable Sidney Webb. In 1916 Sidney had published a series of "studies" on *How to Pay for the War.* There he proposed nationalizing mines and mineral production, railways and canals. He advocated a State Insurance Department, and a revolution in income taxes and inheritance taxes (in England called "death duties"). It was the first public announcement of what Fabian Socialism had in store for postwar Britain—and nearly all of its proposals have since been put into practice.

Less than two years later a special committee of the Labour Party Executive issued a report entitled "Labour and the New Social Order." While embodying the suggestions previously made by Webb, it went a great deal further. Everyone familiar with Sidney's cast of mind and style of writing recognized it as a product of his peculiar genius —even to the characteristic parade of capital letters. A subsequent president of the Fabian Society, the widow of G. D. H. Cole, has described this egregious document as being "purest milk of the Fabian word."

It began by announcing cheerfully that, as a result of World War I, "the individualist system of capitalist production has received a deathblow." And it continued:

We of the Labour Party . . . must insure that what is to be built up is a *new social order*—based not on fighting but on fraternity—*not on the competitive struggle* for a means of bare life, but on a *deliberately planned cooperation in production and distribution* for the benefit of all who participate by hand and brain . . . *not on an enforced domination over subject nations, subject races, subject colonies, subject classes or a subject sex* . . . .

The Four Pillars of the House that we propose to erect, resting upon the common foundation of the Democratic *control of Society in all its activities,* may be termed respectively:

(a) The Universal Enforcement of the National Minimum
(b) The Democratic Control of Industry
(c) The Revolution in National Finance
(d) The Surplus Wealth for the Common Good.[10]

   [10] (Italics added.)

Under those four discreetly phrased headings (Pillars), the intention of Fabian Socialists to destroy the competitive system of production, strip the Empire of its overseas possessions and vest control of all domestic activities in the State was spelled out with precision. The first Pillar covered most of the proposals for State-financed social "welfare" that Fabians had supported from time to time. The second Pillar advocated women's suffrage, whose vote-getting potential the Fabians had been somewhat slow to recognize; abolition of the House of Lords; nationalization of land ownership, electric power, maritime and railway transport, and the mining and metals industries; and "elimination of private profit" from insurance and from the liquor trade.

The third Pillar supported confiscatory increases in taxation (including the capital levy) which in time would abolish private savings as well as private investment. The fourth Pillar foreshadowed the transformation of the British Empire into the British Commonwealth; limitation of armaments and abolition of profit in the munitions industry; an international court; international economic controls; international legislation on social matters—and finally, a supranational or "one world" authority. Many of the objectives listed under the fourth or final heading had appeared in a Fabian-prepared Labour Party pamphlet published in 1917 under the title *Labour's War Aims*, which antedated and supplied the basis for Woodrow Wilson's Fourteen Points.[11]

Labour and the New Social Order was a sweeping Fabian prospectus for the gradual and orderly achievement of Socialism in the Empire and the world—so thoroughly revolutionary in what it proposed to do that more sober Englishmen, if they knew of it at all, must have dismissed it as mere campaign verbiage. It is a document that deserves to rank with *Mein Kampf* or the *Communist Manifesto* as one of the most plain-spoken announcements of destructive intent ever framed. In June, 1918, it was adopted as the official program of the British Labour Party, and except in details, such as the temporary inclusion of a birth control plank in 1927, it has never been really changed.

Strangely enough, when the program was concocted, there were labor groups in Britain who favored an even speedier rate of nationalization. To please them, Arthur Henderson in September, 1919,

[11] To be treated in a later chapter.

asked Sidney Webb to submit a plan for nationalizing the whole of British industry. Arthur explained that it "would be better for electioneering," but Sidney declined to oblige. Already Webb perceived, as some others did not, that by nationalizing certain key industries and at the same time securing State control of both finance and social welfare, total nationalization could be achieved in fact, if not in name.

The irony of it is that a majority of British labor today, after some unhappy experiences with State-administered industry and some snubbing at the hands of State-appointed managers, no longer demands speedy nationalization but, on the contrary, mistrusts and fears it. As a result, the late Leader of the Parliamentary Labour Party and veteran member of the Fabian Executive, Hugh Gaitskell, M.P., was forced to take the alternate route conveniently left open by Webb and to stress the more oblique methods of attaining State capitalism, as foreseen in general, if not always in detail, by the Fabian master planner.[12] For this, Gaitskell was unfairly criticized as being a lukewarm Socialist by more impetuous elements among his own followers. The question of how to satisfy both Right and Left wings of the Labour Party, while presenting a bland non-Socialist face to the Liberals and Independent voters, is a dilemma he has bequeathed to his successor, Harold Wilson.

In origin, policy and leadership, the British Labour Party was definitely a creature and a creation of the Fabian Society, and remains so today. Guided by Fabian Socialist politicians, whose ties with the Society were seldom noted outside of official Fabian publications, that Party became the Society's chosen instrument for wrecking the national economic structure and dismantling the overseas Empire.

[12] Hugh Gaitskell, M.P., "Socialism and Nationalisation," *Fabian Tract No. 300*, (London, The Fabian Society, 1956).

5

Sedition Between Two Wars

IN 1918 a revitalized Labour Party marched to the polls in the "khaki election" and was spankingly defeated in a first test of strength. Confidently it plugged organizational loopholes and intensified its propaganda in labor and Liberal as well as university circles, where Fabian groups were transformed into "Labour Clubs." Following the initial defeat, Sidney Webb in 1919 openly took charge of affairs as head of the Labour Party Executive, which sent him to Parliament in 1920 and 1922.

One of the industrious minor characters who went to the House of Commons with Webb was Harry Snell, offspring of agricultural laborers. Long a member of both the Fabian and Labour Party Executives, he had represented the Society many years before on the board of the London School of Economics. Besides being a dyed-in-the-wool Socialist, Snell was also a prime mover in American as well as British Ethical Culture Societies of the day, having long since abandoned the Protestant faith of his boyhood. His biography in *Who's Who* contains the grim notation: "Recreations: None."

Suddenly in January, 1924, to the surprise of almost everyone, the Labour Party was called to power as the better half of a Labour-Liberal coalition. The circumstances were peculiar and have never been satisfactorily explained. As against 258 Conservatives sent to Parliament, there were 191 Labourites and 158 Liberals. Over the protests of Lloyd George, the old war-horse, the Liberal Party chose to throw its votes to Labour instead of to the Conservatives. Some interpreted this move as an expedient on the part of the Liberals to

46

rid themselves of Lloyd George. Others like Lord Grey, the former Foreign Minister who had seen the lamps go out in 1914, described it as a well-calculated risk.

Years of Fabian penetration and permeation of Liberal circles, including the long, close friendship of George Bernard Shaw with the Liberal Party leader, Lord Asquith, may also help to explain this curious domestic application of the balance-of-power theory, that is, throwing one's weight behind the second strongest power. The volatile Lady Asquith, as well as Lord Lothian, accompanied Shaw in 1931 on his triumphal trek to Moscow; and in Shaw's final years as a nonagenarian, the ever-loyal Margot Asquith was among the few surviving intimates who visited and cared for him.

The decision to back the Labour Party in 1924 proved suicidal for British Liberals of the day, recalling those gifted patricians of Imperial Rome who at the most unexpected moments chose to open their veins and watch their lifeblood ebb away. From its self-inflicted death-blow the Liberal Party has not yet recovered, growing more and more feeble until by 1945 it could muster only twelve seats in Parliament and no more than six in 1959.[1] Following World War I the Labour Party under Socialist tutelage usurped the Liberals' reformist role, and thereafter every social reform introduced by the Fabian-steered Labour Party was carefully contrived to weaken one sector or another of the national economy.

Ramsay MacDonald, an ex-Fabian surrounded by Fabian advisers, became the first "Labour" Prime Minister in England's history. His twenty-five man Cabinet contained at least five "old" Fabians of the London Society, and there were many more in lesser posts. Sir Sydney Olivier became Secretary of State for India. Sidney Webb—who with Beatrice had recently published a long essay entitled, *The Decay of Capitalist Civilisation*, in which they declared that Karl Marx and John Maynard Keynes had "called the moral bluff of Capitalism" [2]—became, of all things, President of the Board of Trade!

Climax to years of Socialist effort and scheming, the new administration proved premature and short-lived. MacDonald's first go-round at 10 Downing Street lasted less than a year, owing largely to an indiscretion on the part of his supposed Soviet friends. By October

---

[1] "Election Guide," *Socialist Commentary*, (October, 1964), p. 20.
[2] Sidney and Beatrice Webb, *The Decay of Capitalist Civilisation*, (London, The Fabian Society and Allen and Unwin, 1923), p. 177.

his government had crashed spectacularly, in an atmosphere of popular excitement and fear, stirred by publication of the Zinoviev "Red Letter."

So many shock waves have assailed the world's nerves since then that people have almost forgotten the impact of the notorious Red Letter found in a Secret Service raid on the offices of Arcos, the Soviet Trade Bureau in London. Apparently the Zinoviev Letter was a directive from the Third International in Moscow, advising British Communists how to seize power from the "weak" government of MacDonald. Their coup was to be effected by disarmament and corrupting the allegiance of British military forces, as well as by arming the workingmen in key areas. Action was to be taken when the MacDonald-sponsored trade treaties with Russia were signed, possibly because Soviet merchant vessels could then more readily transport munitions for an insurrection.

Promptly denounced as a forgery by Communists, the Red Letter was considered genuine by the British public and by MacDonald himself, whose Foreign Office penned a protest to Rakovsky, the unofficial Soviet representative in London. Few Englishmen believed the time-honored British Secret Service to be guilty either of committing or abetting a public forgery. Although the contents of the Letter appeared fantastic, only the year before Germany had narrowly escaped a Moscow-planned Communist revolution—called off at the eleventh hour everywhere but in Hamburg, where the stop order arrived too late! Events of 1923 in Germany supplied a pretext for the emergence of Adolf Hitler, who staged his first National Socialist demonstration that year in Munich. In Great Britain, publication of the ill-fated Zinoviev Letter merely insured the electoral defeat of Ramsay MacDonald, whose subsequent attitude towards the Union of Soviet Socialist Republics appeared to be no less compounded of "love and pity" than before.

The consensus of sober opinion is that publication of the Red Letter just three days before the election was purposefully timed by Opposition elements in the Civil Service; but that the document itself was authentic. The Fabian historian, C. Delisle Burns, asserted it was and said the Secret Service furnished a copy.[3] The former Fabian solicitor, Henry Slesser, confirmed this view.[4] George Bernard Shaw himself

[3] C. Delisle Burns, A Short History of the World, 1918-1928, (New York, Payson and Clark, 1928), pp. 186-188.

[4] Henry Slesser, Judgment Reserved, (London, Hutchinson & Co., Ltd., 1941), pp. 96-98.

accepted the missive at face value, for in December, 1924, he published an open letter simultaneously in the Labourite *Daily Herald* of London and *Izvestia* of Moscow, informing the Russian comrades that British Socialists were quite capable of handling their own show and would appreciate not being embarrassed in future.

Shaw asked the Soviet Government "to tell Mr. Zinoviev plainly that he must choose definitely between serious statesmanship and cinematographic schoolboy nonsense if the Soviet Government is to be responsible for his proceedings, which will otherwise make Mr. Rakovsky's position here almost impossible." And he added, "From the point of view of English Socialists, the members of the Third International do not know even the beginnings of their business as Socialists." Plain language from an old revolutionary to his fellows, and the fact that it was printed verbatim in the official newspaper *Izvestia* suggests that Shaw was already *persona grata* in the very highest circles in Moscow. Zinoviev at a later date paid with his life for this and other miscalculations.

The same puzzling ambivalence—a combination of love and occasional hatred which psychologists assert is characteristic of all true affairs of the heart—marked the attitude of Fabian Socialists towards Moscow throughout the nineteen-twenties and thirties, and exists today. Following the Russian Revolution, a wing of British industrial labor pressed increasingly for "Socialism Now," threatening to upset the somewhat more gradual program envisioned by Webb.

Soviet agents were active and hospitably received in Labour as well as Fabian circles. One of the more conspicuous was Rajani Palme Dutt, a half-caste of mixed East Indian and Scandinavian parentage, who after perfecting his dialectic in Moscow worked from 1923 to 1926 with Fabians G. D. H. and Margaret Cole in the Labour Research Bureau, formerly the Fabian Research Department. The Bureau printed a monthly circular, a kind of leftist *Ministry of Labour Gazette,* intended to furnish factual ammunition for Socialists in their day-to-day political battles. Eventually Dutt ousted his Fabian hosts at which point Communists brazenly took over the Labour Research Bureau. Rajani Palme Dutt became editor of the Communist *Labour Monthly* and was listed in 1962 as vice president of the Communist Party of Britain; yet former Fabian colleagues refer to him without rancor as "that cuckoo in the Fabian nest."

The General Strike of 1926 was touched off at Communist instigation by direct actionists in the Trades Union Council.[5] Once more

[5] Margaret Cole, *Beatrice Webb,* (New York, Harcourt, Brace, 1946), p. 157.

Fabians yielded easily to pressure from the catastrophic Left. This revolutionary strike, which Fabians had not provoked but found it necessary to support, placed them in the same situation as a citizen of the French Revolution who was once seen racing down a Paris street in the wake of a milling crowd. When asked where he was going, he replied breathlessly, "I am their leader—I must follow them!"

During the strike emergency the Fabian-edited *Daily Herald,* then being run by one William Mellor (an erstwhile noncomformist preacher), published the official strike newspaper, the *Workers' Gazette.* Other Fabian publicists tried painfully to justify the very doubtful legality of a revolutionary general strike. When Cardinal Bourne, the Roman Catholic primate of England, expressed the view that the General Strike was unconstitutional and violated the Trade Union Act of 1906, he was publicly rebuked by Socialist Members of Parliament led by the nominally Catholic Fabian, John Scurr.

With the collapse of the strike movement, the emphasis shifted once more to politics, and there Fabians were in their element. Working-class groups, discouraged by the failure of direct action, and middle-class liberals, alarmed at what had seemed to be the first hot breath of revolution, turned to the Labour Party for salvation. Forgetting the debacle of 1924, the electorate was even prepared to approve the Labour Party's Soviet-oriented foreign policy that still promised to provide full employment at home. In a few short years the Fabian Socialist tail was again in position to wag the trade-union dog.

By the summer of 1929 the Labour Party returned to power with the largest number of seats in the House of Commons, though still something less than a majority. Forty-seven seats were won by Fabians, of the forty-nine Fabians who ran.[6] Among them were such clever and ambitious younger men as Hugh Dalton, Herbert Morrison and Sir Stafford Cripps, a nephew of Beatrice Webb, who was to serve as president of the Fabian Society from 1950 to 1952.

The *Fabian News* for July, 1929, reported eight Fabians in the Cabinet and eleven Fabian Under Secretaries in the Government. Eleven out of seventeen new Labour peers, created to block possible veto of Labour Party measures in the Upper House, were veteran members of the London Fabian Society. They included the solemn Lord Henry Snell who was assistant to a delighted Sidney Webb, by then Lord Passfield, at the Colonial Office. That year also saw the publication of *Fabian*

[6] *Fabian News,* (July 1929).

Tract No. 230, entitled *Imperial Trusteeship.* Signed by Lord Sydney Olivier, who had served in the West Indies and India, it advocated release of the colonies to independent native governments under Socialist tutelage and looked forward to eventual Socialist world control of raw materials. Owing to a relatively brief term in office, however, the Labour Party was compelled to postpone dismemberment of the Empire until a later date.

A feature of the 1929 elections was the part played for the first time by British women. Some seven hundred thousand new women voters joined the Labour Party, lured by the promise of jobs for their men and by various social benefits to be bestowed free of charge—except, of course, for the eventual tax bill which was not mentioned. The Labour Party had been late in announcing support for women's suffrage, even though a number of early suffragists like Inez Milholland and Annie Besant had been Fabians; yet it managed somehow to reap the benefits of the Liberal Party's record in that field, as it did on the freedom-for-Ireland issue.

Among the first three Labour women to be elected to Parliament was the redoubtable A. Susan Lawrence, who had just written a novel, *Clash,* purporting to tell the inside story of the General Strike. Like her friend Ellen Wilkinson, later head of Preparatory Commission for UNESCO, "our Susan" was typical of those Fabian lady politicos with iron in their souls and a bright red bee in their bonnets, to whom secular Marxism was a substitute for religious profession. For thirty-three years of her life she sat on the Executive of the London Fabian Society. Long a member of the Labour Party Executive and active in garnering the women's vote, she served as its chairman in 1930, gazing absently through her lorgnette at unruly males as in her youth she had disconcerted her professors at Newnham College. To a colleague Susan remarked significantly, "I don't preach the Class War, I live it." [7]

The common philosophical basis of Socialism and Communism was more evident to observers in 1929 and succeeding years than it had been before. All that distinguished many a Fabian Socialist from the local Communist gentry was the lack of a Communist party card and a preference for indirect over direct action. If a few like Ellen Wilkinson in 1929 [8] or Ivor Montague in 1941 [9] admitted to carrying the

[7] *Fabian Quarterly,* (Summer, 1948), p. 23.

[8] M. P. McCarran, *Fabianism in the Political Life of Britain,* (Chicago, Heritage Foundation, 1954), p. 439.

[9] Margaret Cole, *The Story of Fabian Socialism,* (London, Heinemann Educational Books, Ltd., 1961), p. 277.

Communist party card as well, this was held to be their privilege, and an understanding Fabian Executive did not reprimand them.

Arthur Henderson, the Fabian politician, stage-managed the Labour Party's return engagement of 1929. In the process he angled for Communist votes and placated the British Communist Party leader Harry Pollitt, who demanded "Socialism in every sentence" of the program. Henderson came to the Foreign Office pledged to European disarmament and recognition of Soviet Russia, as outlined in the Geneva protocol written by Fabian Socialist R. H. Tawney. Sharply reduced appropriations for the British armed services (shades of the Zinoviev Letter!) were advocated in 1928-29 as a means of paying for State-financed social welfare benefits, and a strange new type of internationalism that demanded "the sacrifice of national self-interest" was propounded.

For many months prior to becoming Foreign Minister the sonorous voiced Henderson, with other traveling Fabians, had been active in rebuilding the Socialist International—which, despite Ramsay MacDonald's verbal sparring matches with the "giants of the Communist International, Radek and Bukharin," displayed unwavering loyalty towards the Soviet Union in practical matters of trade and diplomacy. Even the Soviet Union's wholesale dumping of commodities was defended by Sidney Webb, who described it as being "no more than the competition of cheaper commodities."

Britain's second Labour Government, like the first, was undone by its own contradictions. Caught in the grip of a world-wide depression, its Socialist leaders moved to cut the dole and raise taxes on the poor as well as the rich. Ramsay MacDonald resigned in 1931 only to join over his Party's protest, a new disaster coalition composed of unfrocked Labourites, Conservatives and Liberals.

The Monarch who at Conservative Leader Stanley Baldwin's request formally invited MacDonald to return to the Government—although his former party had just been definitely whipped at the polls—was denounced by the Left Wing for "interference." For the first but by no means the last time, Fabian Socialists like Professor Harold Laski attacked the throne as an institution, calling it a "dignified hieroglyphic" and warning that future interference would be grounds for revolution. During the next few years Fabian faith in constitutional action waned visibly, as symbolized by the visits of the Webbs and Shaw to Moscow.

Organizationally, the Fabian Society could not help but suffer from the crushing defeat of the Labour Party with which it had allied itself so closely; yet like the Party it preserved the spark of life. Though its financial resources appeared to shrivel and provincial Fabian Societies in Britain—most of which had been turned into Labour Clubs—declined from 120 in the middle twenties to a mere six in the late thirties, the London Society and its Executive brain trust were far from extinct.

Like the tortoise, the Fabian Society had withdrawn temporarily into its shell, to emerge at a more favorable moment. The *Fabian News* still published notices of meetings, lectures, municipal and overseas Socialist activities; A. Emil Davies of the Fabian Executive continued to rally the morale and retain the support of hard-core Fabians; the individual members devoted themselves as assiduously as ever to world travel and a variety of left wing causes chiefly identified with the Popular Front activities of the thirties.

There was always a Fabian in the person of W. Stephen Sanders or Philip Noel-Baker at the International Labour Office in Geneva, and Fabian voices were prominent at the annual International Socialist congresses. A Fabian idol who had penetrated the Liberal Party years before and never resigned from it, the economist John Maynard Keynes, acquired immense prestige as a financial oracle. By turns he terrorized financiers with predictions of doom and induced his own and foreign governments to adopt policies of deficit spending calculated to assure the long-range destruction of the capitalist system he pretended to "save." Fabian mischief makers of Marxist inspiration were by no means lacking during the Society's apparent quiescence.

In the field of popular education, sometimes termed propaganda, individual members of the Society were never more dangerously active than during the years leading up to World War II. The Left Book Club—an enterprise similar to book clubs in the United States, in that it furnished pre-selected popular reading at cut-rate prices—proved a most profitable venture, both financially and propagandawise. Its political bias was plain from the fact that its first literary offering was a volume by Maurice Thorez, secretary of the Communist Party of France. So faithfully did its output follow the Stalinist line that in the *Daily Worker* of London for May 9, 1936, Harry Pollitt, secretary of the British Section of the Communist Party, praised the Left Book Club as a project "worthy of support."

In a few years its membership exceeded fifty thousand and its annual income neared $400,000—proof of a substantial following in

Britain. Actually the circle reached by the Club was much wider, since subscribers were urged through the *Left News* to organize Left Book Groups in their neighborhoods for purposes of reading and discussion. In March, 1938, the *Left News* announced that 831 such groups had been formed under the wing of the Left Book Club. Whether Communist- or Socialist-led, their trend was frankly Marxist and clearly catastrophic. The fine lines of demarcation between one brand of Marxism and another were blurred in those days of the Popular Front.

What is interesting for purposes of this study is that the Selection Committee of the Left Book Club was controlled by three well-known members of the Fabian Executive. They were Victor Gollancz, publisher of Left Books who also published *Left News* and the *Fabian News*; Professor Harold Laski of the London School of Economics, who from 1946 to 1948 was chairman of the Fabian Society and in 1945 served as chairman of the Labour Party; and John Strachey, a frequent Labour Member of Parliament who became Minister of Food and Supply in the post-World War II Labour Government.

Concerning Strachey, the admiring *Left News* for March, 1938, wrote, "In American newspaper jargon John Strachey would be described as 'Marxist No. 1' and the title would be deserved." His claim to that title might well have been challenged by Professor Harold Laski, whose revolutionary influence on the youth of many nations has proved so decisive a factor in our times. Laski is quoted by his personal friend and biographer, Fabian and late *New Statesman* editor Kingsley Martin, as saying to a questioner at one of his lectures: "My friend, we are both Marxists—you in your way and I in Marx's!"

Both the late John Strachey and Professor Laski had occasion to deny under oath that they ever held membership in the Communist Party, and it may be inferred they spoke the truth. Such a technicality as a party card would merely have restricted the broad range of their privileged activities. When asked by a reporter for *The New York Times* [10] whether he preferred Socialism or Communism, Fabian John Strachey replied, "Like all Socialists, I believe that the Socialist Society evolves in time into the Communist society." With this statement —which was echoed in 1962 by the American Communist, Gus Hall— most Fabians would feel compelled to agree.

Closely linked with the Left Book Club was a still more impudent contrivance known as the Christian Book Club, whose sole publisher

[10] *The New York Times*, (October 11, 1938).

was Fabian Victor Gollancz. Its general editor was the Dean of Canterbury, Dr. Hewlett Johnson, often referred to as the "Red Dean." The first book this Club recommended for Christian readers was *Soviet Socialism, A New Civilisation,* by Sidney and Beatrice Webb—the same work which had been prepared with the aid of the Soviet Secret Police and which announced the Soviets' fabled policy of tolerance towards religion. Members of the so-called Christian Book Club were also privileged to purchase virtually the whole list of the Left Book Club selections at the reduced prices.

The inference seemed to be that, since Christians were not overly bright, they could easily be led down the garden path to Socialism by a false appeal to ideals of brotherhood and social justice. In the Fabian Socialist movement, as in Soviet Marxism, there was always a strong element of political messianism, diametrically opposed to the religious messianism of One who proclaimed: "My Kingdom is not of this world." Both Socialist and Communist literature stressed the supposedly communal character of early Christianity, undetectable to anyone familiar with the Epistles of St. Paul. Revolutionary Marxism, open or disguised, was presented as being the "Christianity of today." Voluntary charity and renunciation of one's own goods were confused with the forcible confiscation of other people's property, as illustrated in the phrase of John Maynard Keynes, "the euthanasia of the rentier," that is, the mercy-killing or painless extinction of those who live on income from invested capital.

From the beginning, the personal coolness of many Fabian leaders towards religion—ranging from polite agnosticism to the frank atheism of Shaw and Laski and the amorality of a Bertrand Russell—had been balanced by their far from indifferent attitude towards the religious-minded electorate. To churchgoers among the voting population, Sidney Webb had reasoned shrewdly, Socialist goals must be presented cautiously—in terms that did not appear to conflict with their religious beliefs.[11] Thus, *Fabian News* recorded that from 1891 to 1903 one Bruce Wallace, an honorary Minister of a Congregational Church, held a conference every Sunday afternoon, and after a fifteen-minute prayer service a Fabian lecturer spoke at considerably greater length.

[11] Bernard Shaw, "Report on Fabian Policy," *Fabian Tract No. 70,* 1896. "The Fabian Society endeavors to pursue its Socialist and Democratic objects with complete singleness of aim. For example: it has no distinctive opinions on the Marriage Question, Religion, Art, Abstract Economics, Historic Evolution, Currency or any other subject than its own special business of practical Democracy and Socialism."

From that day to this, a good many nonconformist ministers of the Gospel have deserted their pulpits to pursue political careers under the auspices of the Fabian Society, one of the most notable being Arthur Henderson who negotiated Britain's recognition of Soviet Russia.

It was not accidental that the endless series of pamphlets launched by the Fabian Society were piously called "tracts," like the earlier publications of the "Christian Socialists" in England. With the formation of the Labour Party, even Catholic workingmen could vote for Socialist programs without subscribing directly to a Socialist philosophy. Catholic Members of Parliament on the Labour benches were permitted to "vote their conscience" on such matters as birth control and aid to Catholic schools, which to most Fabians seemed of minor importance. Though the Fabian Graham Wallas differed with Webb on the school issue and found an early audience for his views in the United States, Sidney Webb and his successors were understandably reluctant to provoke any controversy that might block their route to power by popular consent.

In this connection, however, it must be emphasized that Karl Marx is the natural father of all modern Social Democracy, not excluding those groups which for reasons of propriety choose to deny or dissemble the relationship. As the writings of Marx disclose, that herald of "the new social order" hated all religions with impartial fervor. Marx visualized the Class War—since his time a basic concept in both Socialist and Communist philosophy—as being essentially an inverted crusade against the Deity whose existence he denied. *Non serviam* ("I will not serve"), the phrase of Lucifer before the Fall, is innate in the dogmas of Marx.

The blasphemous slogan, "Religion is the opium of the people," was emblazoned for years on a billboard overlooking Red Square. A fellow Georgian and boon companion of Stalin, Orjonokidze, headed the official Soviet Society of the Godless and fomented militant action against religion at home and abroad. Until his death he was a member of the Politburo, superior organ of Soviet policies which Christian Book Club readers in Britain were invited to approve.

Napoleon Bonaparte, product of an earlier revolution, reached somewhat different conclusions on the subject of religious faith. "Without religion, France would be a nation of highwaymen," remarked Napoleon, who had retained few illusions about the perfectibility of human nature by government decree. Not yet arrived at that pinnacle of power, the Fabian Society viewed religion less from the angle of the Public Prosecutor and more from the standpoint of the aspiring politician and social propagandist. For the most part its spokesmen prudently avoided outraging the beliefs of religious-minded persons, while soliciting their support for Socialist candidates and projects. The Christian Book Club was a unique but significant venture for which the Society, as usual, disclaimed any official responsibility.

The vogue of the Left Book and Christian Book Clubs in Great Britain declined with the announcement of the Nazi-Soviet Pact, which plunged the world into war and ended the diversions of the Popular Front. More exacting tasks lay ahead for the Fabians, who organized, planned and plotted unceasingly during the whole of World War II to put a Labour Party Government into office at war's end with Fabian Socialists at the helm. Harold Laski's death a few years after the war was ascribed by his biographer, Kingsley Martin, to the fatigue induced by his intensive noncombat activities in a wartime era of political truce.

6

Dirge For An Empire

1.

SHORTLY after the atom bomb burst upon a war-weary world, the Labour Party swept to power in Britain by an overwhelming majority. Both events illustrated vividly the destructive possibilities of long-range research, a type of activity commonly regarded as harmless and benign. Conducted in relays by anonymous teams and applied with explosive effect at a psychological moment, modern Fabian Research more than any other factor assured the comeback of the Labour Party—which had been the third, then the second and was suddenly the first political party in England.

For a number of years prior to that disruptive climax, "research" had been the prime point of Fabian concentration. It flowed from the New Fabian Research Bureau[1] where the rejuvenated leadership and direction of the movement were centered. This source not only supplied a Socialist elite and its allies with tactical guidance on the climb to power, but also produced a series of strategic plans and programs that became the basis for public policy. Thus Fabian Socialists heading the victorious Labour Party in 1945 became the first government leaders in British history to *employ privately controlled research as an official weapon* for wrecking the economy of the nation and dissolving its far-flung system of Empire.

The process leading to such tragic results began unobtrusively in the summer of 1930. At that time a group of hard-core Socialists, rep-

---

[1] "Our research department has not yet discovered (though success is hourly expected) how to produce *any* virtue." C. S. Lewis, *The Screwtape Letters*, (New York, The Macmillan Co., 1960), 1960 ed., p. 146, Letter XXIX.

58

resenting many fields of Fabian endeavor, met in rustic privacy as guests of the Socialist Countess of Warwick at Easton Lodge in Essex, the idyllic setting for many a Fabian policy meeting until the spacious old building was finally torn down in 1948. There the cry of peacocks on well-tended lawns mingled with the insistent call of a neighboring cuckoo. Easton Lodge was just next door to East Glebe, country estate of the novelist and errant Fabian, H. G. Wells, where representatives of the Soviet Government were frequently entertained over the years[2] and where Maxim Gorki's agent and common-law wife, Baroness Boudberg, a mysterious character who wore three wedding rings, was a regular visitor.

Before the house party at Easton Lodge ended, its busy guests had formed a Society for Socialist Inquiry and Propaganda with Ernest Bevin as chairman. The Society was known to its familiars as ZIP— a quality it tried unsuccessfully to instill into the flagging and badly split Labour Party Government of the moment. When that government fell in 1931, ZIP was transformed into the New Fabian Research Bureau which would plot the future course of Fabian fortunes at home and abroad.

Both organizations were initiated by G. D. H. and Margaret Cole, an energetic husband-and-wife team aspiring to the mantle of the superannuated Webbs. Like so many Fabians of the new generation, G. D. H. Cole did not scruple to call himself a Marxist and an atheist. He proclaimed that the main effort of a Socialist government should be "to destroy confidence . . . in the prospect of sustained profits" by removing "the very foundations on which the opportunities for capitalist profit-making rest." As a tutor at Oxford and the London School of Economics, Cole recruited a number of promising young disciples—one of whom, Hugh Gaitskell, M.P., became Leader of the Parliamentary Labour Party as well as a top figure in the Socialist International.

An academic charmer, handsome, petulant and adored by Fabian women who gladly expended themselves in volunteer political work at his request, the alphabetical Cole was less ponderous but also less patient than Sidney Webb. Prolific in print, Cole was credited with having written ninety-one published books before his death in 1959. Some Socialist leaders, including Beatrice Webb, privately regarded his pert wife Margaret as the more able and tenacious member of the

---

[2] Kingsley Martin, *Harold Laski: A Biographical Memoir*, (New York, The Viking Press, Inc., 1953), pp. 52-53.

family team, and not wholly on the theory that the female of the Fabian species is deadlier than the male. The Cole household could have served as a model for the three-child family, which Fabian social theorists seek to popularize today—and which Professor Richard M. Titmuss, of the University of London faculty, recommends be encouraged by special family allowances in the far-off and primeval island of Mauritius.[3]

According to G. D. H. Cole, the collective leadership of the New Fabian Research Bureau included the most outstanding figures in the Fabian Socialist movement, some already well-known, others marked for future prominence.[4] Its first chairman was Clement Attlee, a member of the Fabian Society since 1909, who succeeded Ramsay MacDonald as Parliamentary Leader of the Labour Party and became Prime Minister of Britain. The vice chairman was C. M. Lloyd of the *New Statesman,* for the benefit of whose knowledgeable contributors the Bureau often collected material and even ghosted entire articles. G. D. H. Cole was honorary secretary, and his active assistant was young Hugh Gaitskell, whose labor of love for the Bureau was only briefly interrupted when he went to Austria in 1933-34 on a Rockefeller Foundation scholarship. Professor Harold Laski and Leonard Woolf, who headed its international committee, joined the Bureau's Executive the following year.[5]

The New Fabian Research Bureau proved to be another of those mysterious hybrids so dear to Fabian organizers and so difficult for outsiders to fathom. For eight years it led a nominally independent life as an affiliate but not a unit of the Fabian Society. Founded to perpetuate the tradition of Fabian "research" after the old Labour Research Bureau had been conveniently captured by Communists, it was the true repository of Fabian leadership during a period of transition and political reverses in Britain. Its modest offices staffed by pretty young volunteers sheltered a top-level Socialist brain trust seeking immunity from Labour Party discipline.

This arrangement offered continuity and privacy for the general staff of the Fabian Socialist movement, self-designated apostle to the gentiles of the English-speaking world. Subservient neither to the

[3] Richard M. Titmuss and Brian Abel-Smith assisted by Tony Lynes, *Social Policies and Population Growth in Mauritius.* A report to the Governor of Mauritius. (London, Methuen & Co., Ltd., no date).
[4] G. D. H. Cole, "Remembering the New Fabian Research Bureau," *Fabian Journal,* No. 19, (July, 1956), pp. 2-5, (Newsletter).
[5] *Ibid.*

Labour Party nor the Fabian Society itself, the Research Bureau operated as a remote-control unit and planning body for both. Control was maintained through a system of interlocking memberships on the Executives of all three organizations, a system still faithfully copied by Fabian-inspired groups in the United States. Top authority, however, resided in the Research Bureau which issued its Executive-approved directives in the form of personal briefings, as well as custom tailored material for speeches, reports, resolutions, articles and books. For publicists and politicians too busy to do their homework or lacking literary skills, it was a most opportune arrangement. Few were aware how closely the functions of the Research Bureau's Executive resembled those of a master-control unit like the Soviet Politburo, with which one leading Fabian or another usually maintained cordial relations.

With the blessing of the Webbs, Shaw, Henderson and the rest of the Fabian old guard, the New Fabian Research Bureau was formally launched at a House of Commons dinner on March 2, 1931. Sentimentalists noted that the founders' group numbered about one hundred persons, approximately the size of the Fabian Society in 1889 when the first *Fabian Essays* had been published. Without a qualm, the new Bureau pledged itself not to engage in direct propaganda, nor to take part in political or electoral activities. Subsequently it published pamphlets on such "nonpolitical" and "nonpropagandist" topics as *How to Win a Labour Majority*, *Labour Propaganda* and *Class Favoritism in the Armed Services*.

Displaying the usual eagerness of Fabians to forgive past Communist aggression, the first field project sponsored by the new Research Bureau was a study of Soviet Russia, the land of full employment and forced labor by forgotten men. A select investigating team trailed the Webb cortège to Moscow in the summer of 1932. After being led around for six weeks by official guides, the team returned to write *Twelve Studies in Soviet Russia*. Like the Webbs' book it included a lyric account of "Soviet justice," evidently derived from similar official sources. As for the famine in the Ukraine, the team's agricultural "expert," John Morgan, perceived that dietary conditions on collective farms in the South left something to be desired; but he did *not* ascribe them to bad weather.[6]

[6] As late as 1946, Margaret Cole stated cold-bloodedly: "It was not until after the experiences of the winter of 1932-33 that the Soviet collective farming really got on its feet." Margaret Cole, *Beatrice Webb*, (New York, Harcourt Brace, 1946), p. 195.

One and all were uplifted at discovering among the Soviets "that sense of collective purpose and planning so notably lacking in England and the United States in 1932." [7] A less publicized effect of the trip was to establish channels of communication between the Socialist Fatherland and the new Fabian leadership. Informed circles in Britain also aver that in the course of this visit arrangements were made for the return of the old Fabian-Labour Research Bureau files, purloined by the Soviet agent Rajani Palme Dutt and containing names, records and statistical data of special value to Socialists.

By 1934 the Fabian Society had turned over all its research activities and most of its propaganda work to the New Fabian Research Bureau. With the "nonpolitical" help of the Bureau, a number of Fabian intellectuals won parliamentary seats in the 1935 elections. That year the Labour Party formally renounced the slogan, "No Arms for a Tory Government," but as a matter of practical politics the Party's spokesmen and allies still contrived to delay every effort by patriotic Britons to rearm their country swiftly in the face of Hitler's mounting military might. How much the Labour Party politicking and Fabian-fabricated propaganda in educational, trade union and social circles weakened the position of British diplomats and speeded the drift to war is a chapter Fabian historians prefer to pass over lightly. Those pacifist intrigues were calculated to transcend party lines and to enlist confused individuals at all levels of society.

Most people today have forgotten that Sir Oswald Mosley and his wife, the former Cynthia Curzon, were ardent Fabian Socialists in the nineteen-twenties and early nineteen-thirties. A wing of the Society shared their misplaced admiration for Hitler, who also called himself a Socialist. Even George Bernard Shaw—more intimately informed than some on Soviet trends, and possibly anticipating the Nazi-Soviet Pact—uttered warm words in favor of the former Austrian house painter. In the years leading up to World War II the Mosley faction, due in part to Sir Oswald's elegant antecedents, succeeded in permeating certain upper-class circles and inducing them to oppose arms appropriations by Parliament.

As leader of a neo-Fascist Party in Britain today—a noise-making fringe organization which gives no evidence of mass support—Sir Oswald still appears to serve Fabian ends by indirection. His frequent rowdy weekend demonstrations tend to alarm moderate ele-

[7] Margaret Cole, The Story of Fabian Socialism, (London, Heinemann Educational Books, Ltd., 1961), pp. 228-229.

ments among British voters and give Socialists an opportunity to picture themselves as the desirable happy medium between a largely fictitious right-extremism and a very real left-extremism that Fabians at no time have seriously opposed.

With the announcement of the Munich Pact, dictated as much by Britain's military weakness as by the visible strength of the Nazi war machine, it became obvious to almost everyone that a general European war was imminent. Though Fabians have invariably depicted themselves as the world's greatest peace lovers, their political philosophy obliged them to welcome the coming cataclysm as a priceless opportunity for Socialist expansion. Here was the long-awaited conflict which (as Karl Marx had foretold, and as every Socialist devoutly hoped) would at last destroy the capitalist system and lead straight to social revolution in even the most persistently capitalist countries! In a mood of preparedness which they had notably failed to display in their country's defense, Britain's Fabian Socialists closed ranks and regrouped their forces in expectation of a postwar takeover.

After some preliminary palaver, the New Fabian Research Bureau and the Fabian Society agreed in 1938 to amalgamate, thus making a long-standing liaison official. The fifty-five year old *Basis* was scrapped in favor of a new constitution with more modern phrasing but identical aims, which remains the present constitution of the Society. After announcing as usual that "The Fabian Society consists of Socialists," the revised document stated:

It therefore aims at the establishment of a society in which . . . the economic power of individuals and classes (shall be) abolished through *the collective ownership and democratic control of the economic resources of the community*. It seeks to secure these ends by the methods of political democracy.[8]

The new constitution also specified:

The [Fabian] Society shall be affiliated to the Labour Party. Its activities shall be the furtherance of Socialism and the education of the public along socialist lines by the holding of meetings, lectures, discussion groups, conferences and summer schools; the promotion of research into political, economic and social problems, national and *international;* the publication of books, pamphlets and periodicals; and *by any other* appropriate means.[9]

---

[8] (Italics added.)

[9] As a condition for full membership, the Fabian Society required that applicants be eligible for membership in the Labour Party. Associate memberships in the Society were provided for "members of other radical parties," including the Communist Party. (Italics added.)

In self-defense, the rules of the modernized Society included the same "self-denying ordinance" adopted by the Research Bureau. No resolution of a political nature, taking a stand or calling for action, was to be issued *in the name* of the Society. Delegates to the Labour Party and other conferences were to be nominally uninstructed. Thus the Fabian Society retained freedom from Labour Party discipline, while its informally coached members could exert their influence separately or in concert within the Labour Party and other outside organizations.

The Research Bureau still remained supreme, being authorized to name nine members to the joint Executive "by co-option," that is, *without the formality of election* by the Society's general membership—a strange example of political democracy at work. It continued, as before, to transmit Executive-approved material to allegedly "independent" persons and organizations that might or might not be known as Socialist: a classic subterfuge reminiscent of that old master of the political black arts, Sidney Webb.

Though the total listed membership of the Fabian Society then numbered fewer than two thousand, every one was a hard-core Socialist, frequently boasting a personal following and a well-established reputation in the political, labor, education or communication fields. As a symbol of the Society's longevity, the elderly Beatrice Webb was invited to serve as first president of the reconstituted body. Despite the rigged Moscow treason trials and blood-purges, the Nazi-Soviet Pact that triggered World War II, the rape of Finland, the seizure of Poland and the Baltic States, the old lady's devotion to the Soviet Fatherland never wavered.

Other Fabians, who sometimes found such vagaries hard to explain, were almost indecently prompt in condoning them when the Nazis invaded Russia in June, 1941, and the Soviet Union became a wartime Ally of Britain. While Winston Churchill remarked wryly, "If the devil declared war on Hitler, I should feel obliged to mention him favorably in the House of Commons," members of the Fabian Society took a more cordial view. Communist treachery and brutalities were forgotten in their delight at feeling together again.[10] Hastily the Research Bureau assembled a volume of essays entitled *Our Soviet Ally* and issued a best-seller pamphlet. Fabian lecturers, following the example of Victor Gollancz, stirred intellectual and trade union audiences by telling them that as allies of the "noble Socialist State" it

[10] Cole, *op. cit.*, p. 270.

now became their duty to achieve Socialism in Britain as rapidly as possible!

"Leave the conduct of the war to the Tory politicians, and prepare yourselves to take over at war's end," Fabian insiders were coolly instructed. Obviously, the advice was not meant to deter Fabian stalwarts from securing the best available civilian openings for themselves in the wartime Ministries and Civil Service; it rather urged them to utilize such positions for advancing postwar aims, as formulated by the Society's War Aims Research Committee.

With the fall of the Chamberlain government in 1940, four veteran Fabians had already been named to the War Cabinet—Clement Attlee, Hugh Dalton, Arthur Greenwood [11] and Herbert Morrison. Four junior Ministers were Fabians, and more than a dozen others served as parliamentary private secretaries. As wartime Ambassador to Moscow, Beatrice Webb's favorite nephew, Sir Stafford Cripps, labored to ensure the survival of the Socialist Fatherland. Cold-shouldered in public by the Russians, he continued to treat them with loving kindness.

While the war lasted, Fabians of Cabinet rank were obliged to render lip service to the War Government, which they did in a bland and superficially correct manner. At the same time, they were able to open many official doors to Fabians of secondary rank, who pursued their Socialist objectives freely. Various members of the Society, including Hugh Gaitskell and E. F. M. Durbin, climbed happily in the wartime Civil Service; while other Fabian Socialist nominees were planted in key spots on special commissions and investigative bodies. Sir William Beveridge, a protégé of the Webbs for over thirty years, bluntly asked Ernest Bevin, Minister of Labour, to put him in charge of a manpower survey for the United Kingdom, including colonial manpower. When his request was granted in 1940, the liberal Sir William quickly enlisted the services of G. D. H. Cole and a whole crew of Fabian researchers, who familiarized themselves at first hand with a wealth of current data relating to the working-class electorate.

In 1940, while the rest of the country was mourning the disaster at Dunkirk, the fertile planners of the Fabian War Aims Research Committee spawned a sinister offshoot—their own private Colonial Bureau! It was set up to deal directly with the colonial territories, then

---

[11] Arthur Greenwood's son, Anthony Greenwood, M.P., became the Fabian Socialist Secretary of State for Colonies in the Labour Party Government of October, 1964.

becoming increasingly involved in the war. Under cover of war's confusion and Great Britain's desperate need for support, this conspiratorial Bureau devoted itself to fostering nationalist movements in colonial areas—chiefly, but not exclusively, British. The Fabian Colonial Bureau (since renamed the Fabian Commonwealth Bureau) was established in October, 1940, as a separate section of the Society, with the globe-trotting Arthur Creech-Jones as chairman and Rita Hinden, Ph.D., as permanent secretary.

Although questions relating to India and Palestine were still routed to the Fabian Society's Executive, the rest of the colonial world was the Bureau's oyster and Africa its particular pearl. The first research pamphlet published by the Fabian Colonial Bureau, *Labour and the Colonies*, gave a Socialist twist to material obtained from the manpower survey. Its first book-length offering was Rita Hinden's *Plan for Africa;* and it printed at least one pamphlet, *America's Colonial Record*, by John Collier who headed the United States Government's (American) Indian Bureau under Harold Ickes!

Flagrantly anti-imperialist, the Fabian Colonial Bureau fanned the sparks of discontent by publicizing every controversial aspect of British colonial rule—through parliamentary questions, briefing of M.P.'s for debate, letters to the press and a monthly journal, *Empire*.[12] During the war and after, it maintained personal contacts with a network of chosen native politicians, many already versed in Socialist doctrines derived from Fabian professors at English universities—including Kwame Nkrumah of Ghana, Tom Mboya, Secretary of Kenya's KANU Party and Jomo Kenyatta,[13] leader of postwar Mau Mau atrocities in Kenya. While Great Britain battled for survival against the most efficient war machine in history, this strictly unauthorized, private Bureau had the hardihood to draft postwar plans for separating the colonies from the mother country, according to a gradualist Fabian timetable.

When a Labour Party Government was acclaimed in 1945, the chairman of the Fabian Colonial Bureau, Arthur Creech-Jones, was promptly posted to the Government's Colonial Bureau—first as Assistant Secretary for the Colonies, then as Secretary. There he was at liberty to translate Socialist programs, privately concocted by Fabian researchers, into official action by the British Government. In a remarkably short time one jewel after another was plucked from the Imperial

[12] "The Fabian Commonwealth Bureau," *Fabian News*, (April, 1958).
[13] Nkrumah and Kenyatta also studied in Moscow.

Crown, sometimes to the accompaniment of native turmoil and blood-shed—India first, then a succession of territories step by step. What the various colonial demands for independence, presented by a handful of highly articulate native leaders skilled at arousing the primitive masses, owed to Fabian tutelage and prodding is a question that still merits research. Certainly Great Britain's postwar decision to divest herself progressively of her colonies (as the *Fabian News* proudly proclaimed) "owes more than can yet be properly assessed to pains-taking Fabian work which permeated, in true Fabian tradition, the thinking, not only of the Labour Movement, but gradually of wider circles as well." [14]

With the creation of the Fabian International Bureau in December, 1941, the structure of the mid-century Fabian Society was complete. Nominally, the International Bureau was organized as a secretariat and clearing house for Socialists in exile, who had found asylum in wartime London and dreamed of heading postwar governments in their homelands after liberation. Actually, it became the directing force of the Socialist International in which German Social Democrats had once played the leading role. Due to its interest in the political aspects of the various liberation movements and its connections with underground groups in the occupied countries, the Fabian International Bureau operated from the start under rules of extreme secrecy. No membership lists or details of its activities were ever published, although the names of its officers and Advisory Committee were always public property.

The first chairman of the International Bureau, which like the Colonial Bureau operated as a separate section of the Society with its own membership lists and affiliates, was Philip Noel-Baker, M.P.—a future Nobel peace prize winner like Dr. Martin Luther King and a Minister in the 1945-51 Labour Governments. This particular Bureau combined underground work with research in international matters; ran a lecture bureau that scheduled propaganda tours for selected publicists; and drafted plans for Britain's postwar foreign policy, which it proposed to dovetail with an international Socialist policy in foreign affairs. Failing to take into account factors of power-politics, the Fabian International Bureau looked forward starry-eyed to an era of mutual trust and reciprocity between the Soviet Union and Britain after the war. For the United States, the Bureau advocated the scheme of Federal Union with Britain as a prelude to Socialist World

[14] "The Fabian Commonwealth Bureau," *Fabian News*, (April, 1958).

Government—a Fabian doctrine promoted even before America entered the war by R. W. G. Mackay, member of the International Bureau's first Advisory Committee, together with the well-known Anglo-American publicist, Clarence K. Streit.

2.

The Labour Party's return to power at war's end was virtually assured three years earlier, as the result of a shrewdly planned and carefully stage-managed propaganda coup that bypassed the political truce which all parties in Britain had pledged themselves to respect during the war. On December 9, 1941, just two days after Pearl Harbor, the very social-minded Sir William Beveridge celebrated the ending of his War Manpower Committee with a cocktail party—"the high point," as he remarked frivolously, "of a day which included a thirty-five minute personal interview with H. M. the King."[15] On December 11, he submitted a basic memorandum to the Government regarding the cause and cure of poverty. Within a month, at the instigation of two Fabian Cabinet Ministers, Arthur Greenwood and Ernest Bevin, Sir William was appointed a one-man committee to report on the possibilities of ending poverty through a system of State-financed social insurance.

Since his youth, Fabian patronage had molded the career of Sir William (later Lord) Beveridge. Back in 1909, when Fabians were busily penetrating the Liberal Party, Sidney and Beatrice Webb had recommended "the boy Beveridge" to Winston Churchill, himself an active Liberal at the time. Ten years later Beveridge was the Webbs' chosen candidate for director of their beloved London School of Economics. Before assuming that position, which he held from 1919 to 1937, Sir William recalls that Sidney Webb was the only trustee with whom he conferred. In 1923 Beveridge received a postcard from Graham Wallas—one of the original Big Four of the Fabian Society—informing him that Beardsley Ruml, a director of the Laura Spelman Rockefeller Fund, was en route to England and would make a special trip to Liverpool to confer with him. As a result of that meeting and the contacts ensuing from it, Sir William eventually extracted some millions of dollars from private foundations in the United States to

[15] Lord Beveridge, *Power and Influence*, (New York, The Beechhurst Press, Inc., 1955), pp. 306 ff.

endow chairs in the social sciences, as well as to erect the new buildings in Bloomsbury now occupied by the leftist school.

Sir William was something of a social lion in his later years. His Olympian dignity, conversational gifts and talent for moving in high society made him a priceless tool of Fabian permeation on both sides of the Atlantic. Always one of Beatrice Webb's "obedient young men," his reputation for profundity was assured by a succession of Fabian researchers and ghostwriters—who at one time included Harold Wilson, M.P.[16] Through the agency of this synthetic but imposing personage, the Fabian turtle struck—and struck hard enough to assure the political defeat three years later of the noblest Briton of them all, Sir Winston Churchill!

Early in the war, a subcommittee of the Fabian Society had prepared a volume of essays on *Social Security*, edited by W. A. Robson of New Fabian Research but not published until 1943. All the material contained in those essays was presented to Beveridge in the form of "collective evidence" when the authors "testified" before Sir William and a group of interdepartmental employees called in for appearance's sake to "assist" him. Such testimony formed the basis for a report signed and submitted by Sir William alone—"one man disguised as a Committee," he noted gleefully, a situation without precedent in British Government circles.[17] Published in December, 1942, the widely-touted Beveridge Report had repercussions which in the opinion of Sir William and his friends quite eclipsed the painful war news of the day from North Africa.

In his effort to muster the virtually unarmed British people for the battles and sacrifices ahead, all that Winston Churchill had honestly been able to promise was blood, toil, tears and sweat. Unless and until the war was won, there was no security on earth; and in December, 1942, the outcome of the war was still problematical. Yet here was Sir William Beveridge offering everyone paradise unlimited, as if victory were already assured. He announced that poverty could and should be abolished through a species of State-administered insurance extending from the womb to the tomb. To a bomb-shattered, blitz-shocked nation and to the anxious troops overseas, his message was enticing. That was precisely what the Fabians, with their cynical grasp of mass psychology, had planned.

[16] Beveridge, *op. cit.*, p. 260.
[17] *Ibid.*, pp. 317-318.

If the Beveridge Report had been shelved until after the war, as at first seemed likely, it might have caused little commotion. Fabian Socialists had no intention, however, of allowing their master stroke to be quietly deflected. Somehow, word of the Report's "exciting" contents was leaked in advance to news correspondents, not by Sir William in person, but by a "friendly Embassy" to which he had submitted a preliminary draft. It was the friendly *American* Embassy, headed by John G. Winant—whose appointment as an "ideal Ambassador" to the Court of St. James had been suggested to President Roosevelt by the arch-Fabian, Harold Laski.[18] For several weeks following the news leak, Sir William was in disgrace and ignored by his government.

All at once, Beveridge was summoned to a press conference at which the Minister of Information, Brendan Bracken, presided. The same evening he was invited to discuss his report over a world-wide British Broadcasting Company hook up that reached the fighting troops abroad. Brendan Bracken, who had served as Winston Churchill's private secretary, did not act in this instance without authorization. Pressure had been exerted by highly placed "friends" in America to insure the widest possible publicity for the Beveridge Report—pressure which Prime Minister Churchill, as a suppliant for United States war aid, was in no position to resist and to which he yielded without comment.

As Sir William himself confided, in a memoir modestly entitled *Power and Influence:* "My friend Mrs. Eugene Meyer of the Washington *Post*, when at last I did manage to get a copy to her *by the Embassy bag*, cabled to me on December 9 that the effect over there was electrifying. Professor A. D. Lindsay, just returned from a visit to America, wrote me on December 24 that he had found universal interest in the report all over the United States, and that President Roosevelt had talked of getting it made into a congressional document and having a million copies distributed. Though this did not happen, the British Government [sic] arranged with Macmillan's in New York for an American edition to be printed at top speed and netted $5,000 for the [British] Treasury." [19]

In Britain, the public boom of the report was fantastic—partly due to skillful briefing of the press, partly because the report itself played

[18] Letter from Harold Laski to Felix Frankfurter, quoted by Kingsley Martin, *op. cit.*, p. 139.
[19] Beveridge, *op. cit.*, p. 320. (Italics added.)

so shamelessly on the deep-rooted hopes and fears of ordinary Englishmen. Lord Pakenham, the Fabian peer and absentee Irish landlord who served as Sir William's aide, admits to having been "extremely active" in his contacts with the newspaper world. Describing the effect of those news stories on the British housewife, His Lordship tells how, early in the morning after the Beveridge Report was made public, he stopped at a newspaper shop to see the headlines he had helped to plant.[20]

"Papers?" said the old lady in charge. "You don't think I've got any left. It's that Sir William Beveridge!"

"What's he done now?" asked Lord Pakenham, pretending innocence as usual.

"It's what he's going to do!" answered the poor old lady. "HE'S GOING TO ABOLISH WANT!"

In retrospect the whole performance seems a cruel farce, perpetrated for the shabbiest reasons of political advantage on a hungry and hopeful nation at war. Within a few weeks Sir William was the best-known character in England, more conspicuous for the moment than Sir Winston Churchill himself. A Gallup Poll showed that nineteen of every twenty adults in Britain had heard of his report, and the average Briton was dazzled by that picture of a bright, new world. Such results were not casually achieved. Lord Pakenham confesses that he alone made 250 speeches to help sell the Beveridge Report to the public; and other Fabian propagandists swung simultaneously into action throughout the land.

Shortly after its publication, the National Council of Labour (representing all trade unions), the Cooperative Union and the Labour Party unanimously approved the report, and called on the Government to introduce the necessary legislation for an overall program of cradle-to-grave "security"—literally, an impossibility in time of war or peace! Generously, the Fabian Society loaned its research secretary, Joan Clarke, to the Labour Party to aid in organizing a nationwide Social Security League and in keeping the issue alive among the voters. Whenever the agitation seemed in danger of subsiding, Fabian Members of Parliament on the Labour benches revived it by needling the War Government for an official statement of postwar intentions, and by demanding proof that government leaders could be "trusted" in that regard. Socialism was never mentioned—only social benefits.

[20] Lord Pakenham, *Born to Believe, An Autobiography*, (London, Jonathan Cape, 1953), pp. 125 ff.

Most Englishmen were unaware that the blessings so freely promised must be paid for in time, not merely out of earnings but at the price of total dependence on a bureaucratic State.

On February 3, 1945, Arthur Creech-Jones, M.P., member of the Executive of the British Labour Party and chairman of the Fabian Colonial Bureau, addressed the 40th Anniversary dinner event of the League for Industrial Democracy at the Hotel Astor in New York City. There he announced brazenly: *"We anticipate before long that our movement will be in power . . . .* We believe that the time will not be very far after making of peace in Europe . . . . The movement is preparing for this great opportunity."* [21]

Before the year ended, his prediction had become a reality. To the astonishment of most of the world, the British people renounced their wartime leader, Winston Churchill. Instead, they voted into office a Labour Party government dominated by a secret society of Fabian Socialist intellectuals who were pledged to dissolve the Empire and the economic structure sustaining it. Only the Fabians and their friends showed no surprise. That little band of prophets knew in advance what the election returns would be. Through a combination of long-term "research," a coldly calculated appeal to mass psychology and a deep-dyed duplicity, Socialism had achieved full power in Britain by "constitutional" means. While congratulating themselves on exploiting the methods of political democracy, Englishmen overlooked the fact that only a few years earlier the late Adolf Hitler's party had been elected no less legally and democratically—and with equally firm intentions of subverting the constitution that made possible its rise to power.

So Britannia won the war and abandoned her symbol of victory. In doing so, she moved to release colonies which promptly developed into pensioners instead of assets—and of which many have since signed separate trade and "technical aid" treaties with Soviet Russia or its satellites. At the same time, Britons voted themselves quite cheerfully into Socialist bondage at home, transposing the major strains of "Rule Britannia" into a plaintive minor key. What had once been a stirring victory march became, for the time being, a dirge. So Britons never, never, never shall be slaves? *Never?* Well, hardly ever!

[21] *Forty Years of Education.* (New York, League for Industrial Democracy, 1945), p. 31.

7

Trial By Ordeal

1.

"A THOUSAND years of English history went out the window" between 1945 and 1951—to borrow a phrase from Harold Wilson, M.P., chairman of the Labour Party in 1962. Wilson was subsequently Fabian leader of the Labour Party in Parliament in 1963, and Prime Minister from 1964. That headlong dissipation of national glories and personal liberties was effected *by strictly lawful means*. Indeed, this was accomplished by a whole series of parliamentary acts drafted well ahead of time by the ebullient pioneers of the New Fabian Research Bureau.

Over a decade before, in 1934, the Bureau had published a study on what it termed *Parliamentary Reform*, over the signature of Sir Ivor Jennings. Little noticed at the time, it later proved to be quite significant; for it prescribed certain changes in established parliamentary procedure, by means of which a Socialist government could work its will "democratically" on a trusting people. In 1945, most of those suggested changes were hastily adopted by the newly elected Labour Party majority in the House of Commons, over two-thirds of whom belonged to the Fabian Society. No legal or moral barriers remained to block the rush of the prefabricated Socialist legislation that followed. Within a few short years a Labour Party government, manned at every key point by Fabian Socialists, had, for all practical and impractical purposes, socialized the economy of Britain. This was done by nationalizing about one-quarter of the island's economic processes outright and socializing the rest indirectly through an overall system of government planning that controlled both production and credit.

Basic industries and services commandeered by the State included: the Bank of England (finance and credit); utilities (gas and electricity, which furnished the power for industry); coal mines (which supplied the basis for electrical power); internal transport (railways, bus, truck and inland waterways); civil aviation (both domestic and overseas); cables, wireless and broadcasting (which afforded control of propaganda channels as well as communications). In 1949, the Fabian-packed House of Commons finally voted to nationalize the iron and steel industry.

The inconvenience resulting from these State-run enterprises was only exceeded by their inefficiency. Former stockholders, who were paid off in bonds, proved to be the sole beneficiaries,[1] since the bonds drew interest when dividends were unwarranted. Could the Fabians have failed to foresee that unless nationalized industry was operated at a profit, either the British taxpayer or Uncle Sam would be called upon to make up the losses? The railroads ran at a deficit. Each ticket sold on British Overseas Airways cost the government, on the average, $250 more than was taken in. While production and export figures in most sectors of industry showed a monetary paper increase, the rise was in terms of inflated postwar values but obscured a decline in the real amount of goods and services.

Under political management, British coal production in 1947 fell seven million tons below the output of privately owned mines ten years earlier, even though several hundred million dollars had been spent to modernize the mines and increase their output! That year Emanuel Shinwell, Fabian-trained Minister of Fuel and Power, was obliged by the coal shortage to cut off industrial electricity in the London and Midlands areas for a three-week period. The effect was to close down 75 per cent of British industry, put two million working-class families on the dole, and lose Britain over three-quarters of a billion dollars in much needed export orders.

Moreover, it appeared that national planning involved other arbitrary features for which the public was unprepared. Planned production, while failing visibly to produce abundance, had certain other unavoidable corollaries. It demanded wage controls, price controls, rationing at home; currency control and export control in foreign

---

[1] Permission was secured from the U. S. Commission to use some 80 million dollars in United States funds advanced to Britain, to pay interest on these bonds.

trade. Though such measures might be accepted as necessary during a war, in time of peace they proved as oppressive as they were economically unsound.

At a moment when other victorious nations were moving as quickly as possible to lift war-imposed restrictions, Britain's Fabian Socialist Government acted to prolong them. In addition to being continued, their effects were multiplied, almost beyond the capacity of the people to endure, by a swarm of subsidiary regulations. Daily the press announced new decrees affecting not only the management of business and industry but the lives of every householder and small shopkeeper as well. The earthly paradise Labour Party spokesmen had promised the common man still glimmered beyond the horizon, more distant than ever. But even the glimmer was imaginary.

Far from ending wage slavery, the Fabian Socialist leaders of Britain gave literal meaning to what had formerly been a figure of speech. Ignoring trade union protests, they actually decreed a job freeze in 1946. Their Control of Engagements Order enabled the Ministry of Labour to compel workingmen and women to take and hold specific jobs at a fixed wage. Rules, permits and excessive paper work not only killed personal initiative but poisoned the daily life of the average citizen. In cases of dispute, which were frequent, some indifferent bureaucrat in London always enjoyed the final word.

In February, 1947, as Fabian Prime Minister Attlee admitted in the Commons, seventeen Government Ministries were free to enter private homes without search warrants. Ten thousand officials had authority to invade the Englishman's traditional castle for purposes of inspection. Due process was abandoned as farmers and workingmen became subject to arrest or eviction by official order. In a single year, over thirty thousand prosecutions for violating routine regulations were recorded—an impossible burden on the law courts as well as the tax-paying public.

For all the boasts of Labour Party propagandists about new housing provided for the masses, progress in that department was slow and extremely dear. The Government constructed 134,000 fewer houses per year at a much higher per unit cost than were built in either of the two years preceding the war. The Government was consciously building Socialism into the community structure of its dreary New Towns. As late as 1949, in one Midlands industrial city alone, nearly fifty thousand families were still on the waiting list for unfinished public housing.

While wages were frozen at wartime levels, prices soared as stocks of food declined—a fact hardly improved by the government's donation of $2.50 per week to each householder's grocery bill. Premiums for social insurance were a further drain on the income of employed persons and pensioners. Failure to make these payments was punishable by fine and/or jail. Yet the cost to the Government of such social services far exceeded the sums collected annually for the purpose.

Although the widely touted Beveridge Plan was in effect, it had by no means succeeded in abolishing want. As one left wing American commentator noted,[2] the plan merely furnished a thin cushion against total disaster for the most impoverished third of the population. True, every citizen (whether or not he needed it) was entitled to prenatal care, a birth subsidy, hospitalization and medical care of sorts, unemployment insurance, an old-age pension, funeral costs, and an allowance for his widow and dependent orphans. The subsidies and allowances were tiny, and, with mounting inflation, barely sufficed for the poorest—sixteen dollars at birth and eighty dollars for a pauper burial. Medical services were spread so thin that even at the price of nationalizing the existing medical profession, it was impossible to guarantee first-rate care. With food rations hovering near the starvation level, sickness became more frequent and national production fell still lower.

So poverty was not eliminated but increased to plague proportions, and life was a nightmare for everyone but the most dedicated bureaucrats. A man might have "social security," yet he could not go out and buy a dozen eggs. After four years of Socialist government, he was only entitled to an egg and a half per week, as decreed by Marxist No. 1, John Strachey, Fabian Minister of Food and Supply.

A vacation in Ireland where food was plentiful became the dream of every famished Briton. In those years an Irish-American writer for the *New Yorker* magazine described his stay at a seaside resort in Ireland, once known as a land of famine. He marveled at the huge breakfasts being consumed by an English family sitting near him in the hotel dining room, and was touched by the concern of the Irish waiter who remarked: "I'll just run and get some more eggs for the children. They still look a little hungry to me!"

Inadequate as the British social services were, their overall costs, added to deficits in nationalized industries and to swollen administra-

[2] John W. Vandercook, "Good News Out of England," *Harper's Magazine*, (March, 1947).

tive payrolls, created a condition verging on national bankruptcy. This would have been evident much sooner, except for the fact that a free-handed administration in Washington had been paying most of the bills for Britain's Fabian Socialist experiments at home and in the dwindling colonies. In 1947 alone, the Labour Party used over two and three-quarter billion dollars from funds voted by the United States Congress. During the same year British planners drew an impromptu one-quarter billion dollars from the International Monetary Fund, of which the late Harry Dexter White was chief architect[3] and first Executive Director from the United States.

As Under Secretary of the United States Treasury from 1934 to 1946, wielding powers far beyond public knowledge and beyond his nominal title,[4] White had personally engineered arrangements for the multi-billion dollar American loans to Britain's postwar Socialist Government. Negotiations for the first of these so-called loans—all handled independently of the Marshall Plan—began even before the Labour Party assumed office, but at a time when informed British Fabians like Arthur Creech-Jones and Harold Laski already felt assured of the election results. Without the active connivance of Harry Dexter White, it would have been impossible for Britain's spendthrift planners to carry on as long as they did. A crony of Lord Keynes, who fathered the theory of deficit spending, White was also a warm admirer of Professor Harold Laski, whose Marxist views he once extolled in an hour-long interview with a United States Treasury Department publicist, Jonathan Mitchell.[5]

Shortly after Harry Dexter White's mysterious death, documentary evidence in White's own handwriting was introduced on the floor of the United States House of Representatives. This document, made public January 26, 1950, proved conclusively that, in addition to his

[3] *Post War Foreign Policy Preparation.* U.S. Department of State, (Washington, U.S. Government Printing Office, 1949), p. 142.

[4] United States Treasury Department Order No. 43, dated December 15, 1941, and signed by the Secretary of the Treasury, gave Harry Dexter White "full responsibility for all matters with which the Treasury had to deal having a bearing on foreign relations." Pursuant to a further Order of February 25, 1943, White became the official Treasury representative on all interdepartmental and international bodies. Cited in the *Report of the Subcommittee on Internal Security to the Committee on the Judiciary,* U.S. Senate, 83rd Congress, First Session, (Washington, U.S. Government Printing Office, July 30, 1953), pp. 29-30.

[5] *Hearings of the Subcommittee on Internal Security of the Committee on the Judiciary,* U.S. Senate, 83rd Congress, *Interlocking Subversion in Government Departments,* (Washington, U.S. Government Printing Office, March 25 and April 6, 1954), Part 19, pp. 1933 ff.

other key functions, the late Under Secretary of the Treasury had also acted as a Soviet agent and informer.[6] So for several years the Labour Party Government owed its survival as much to undercover Soviet favor as to American largesse! Were British support of Soviet policy in Asia and recognition of Red China the favors exacted in return?

When the United States Congress finally served notice that it would no longer finance the Socialist fiasco in London, there was consternation in the Fabian Executive now meeting for convenience's sake at the House of Commons, because so many members of that Executive held seats in Parliament.[7] As a final expedient, Fabian Chancellor of the Exchequer, Sir Stafford Cripps, was reduced to telling the British people the truth: that future costs of Socialism in Britain must come from the taxes, production and privations of the British workingman. Attempting to prolong the agony a little further, he submitted his notorious budget of "taxation and tears."

Socialism in practice, unlike its glowing predictions, was turning out to be a dreary treadmill for the great majority of the British people. Confiscatory taxes on land, inheritance and income, coupled with the restrictions on productive investment, had driven into flight whatever capital was left, or forced it to remain idle. By 1949, according to statistics cited by a sympathetic reporter, there were just forty-five individuals in Britain with incomes of $24,000 a year or more after taxes, and only thirty-five thousand with incomes from $8,000 to $16,000. Yet the disappearance of affluence for the few did not insure it for the many. Future government payrolls, even under a pattern of deficit financing, could only be met by imposing still heavier taxes on the common man, by limiting food imports still more rigidly and increasing per man production for export.

Though the best brains of the Fabian Society were engaged in the futile effort to make Socialism work, it was becoming obvious that the new system of improvisation and promises simply could not deliver the goods. Socialist theory in action was wrecking the economy of Britain, which for several centuries had prospered from the profitable sale and brokerage of goods and services around the world. If persisted in, the new policy would end by reducing the once tight little

[6] *Report of the Subcommittee on Internal Security of the Committee on the Judiciary*, U.S. Senate, 83rd Congress, (Washington, U.S. Government Printing Office, July 30, 1953, p. 32.

[7] Margaret Cole, *The Story of Fabian Socialism*, (London, Heinemann Educational Books, Ltd., p. 309. Of the twenty-five members of the Fabian Executive, at least ten held seats in the Commons, 1945-1951.

island to a status no more impressive than some Caribbean isle like Cuba. Several Socialist Members of Parliament and Labour Peers[8] openly announced their disillusionment in 1949 and resigned from the Labour Party. The bright slogan, "Fair Shares for Everyone," on which that Party rode to victory four years earlier, turned out to mean ever smaller shares in a contracting and top-heavy economy.

To the mounting chorus of popular complaints, the Labour Party Conference at Blackpool retorted by approving an expanded program of nationalization and public spending. Defiantly, it proposed to take over cement manufacture, sugar refining, cold storage and meat packing, much of the chemical industry, and, most controversial of all, industrial and marine insurance. Fortunately for British consumers and their commercial creditors overseas, more pressing problems intervened before this plan could be put into effect. Faced by labor unrest, vanished gold reserves and the threat of total fiscal collapse, Britain's Labour Party Government was booted out of office a year later by a popular vote of no confidence.

Repudiated in the General Elections, the Party was forced to postpone new nationalization schemes for a future day. It retired in confusion, leaving behind it a truncated Empire, a bankrupt economy, and as many Socialist officials as it had been able to blanket with permanent Civil Service. No wonder that the Fabian Society declined responsibility and chose to minimize its controlling interest in the discredited Labour Party Government of 1945-51. More than ever the Society's "self-denying ordinance" proved to be a self-serving device.

The Society's preference for the shadows was dictated by instincts of preservation rather than modesty. While incoming Conservatives were left to repair as far as possible the damage caused by their predecessors, Fabians (starting with Lord Attlee) who had served in the defeated Administration sat down comfortably and dictated their memoirs. In that avalanche of ghostwritten prose, it is noteworthy

---

[8] John T. Flynn, *The Road Ahead*, (New York, The Devin-Adair Company, 1949), p. 58. In July, 1949, Lord Milverton, Labour Whip in the Lords, who had been created a peer by the Labour Party in 1947, renounced his party affiliation during the debate on steel. In a speech on the floor, quoted in the *Times* of London, he declared that "he had certain aims and ideals, and he had thought the Labor Party could 'deliver the goods'." Previously, Albert Edwards, M.P. had stated in the Commons, "I have spent years discoursing on the defects of the capitalist system. I do not withdraw those criticisms. But we have seen the two systems side by side. And the man who would still argue for socialism as the means of ridding our country of the defects of capitalism is blind indeed. Socialism just does not work."

that even veteran and dedicated Fabians mention the Society in the briefest, most fugitive manner, if at all! Confirmation of such long-standing ties can be more readily obtained from the files of the *Fabian News* and *Fabian Journal,* from the information sheets of the Socialist International, and from official histories of the Society all destined for more or less limited circulation.

Though the enthusiasm with which rank-and-file labor had spurned them was a slight shock to Fabian Socialist chiefs of the Labour Party, outwardly they accepted it calmly as no more than a battle lost in the long-range struggle for power. In a sense, they could hardly help but count it a blessing in disguise. Defeat saved them, after all, from having to cope with the consequences of their own folly and provided a timely exit from the house of cards they had erected. They did not foresee that it would be a full thirteen years before they returned to power in Britain.

2.

As they had done after previous political reverses at home, British Fabians promptly consoled themselves with adventures abroad. Among other projects, they moved to reorganize the old Labor and Socialist International, where they occupied the lordly position once held by the German Social Democrats. The Fabian Society's hand-writing was plain in the International's 1951 Frankfurt manifesto which declared "democratic planning" to be the basic condition for achieving Socialism.[9] Statism and the welfare state, as demonstrated by the British Socialists during their spell of majority Labour Party Government, were being packaged deceptively for export around the world.

Gilded with the prestige of the high offices they had recently held and the patents of nobility conferred on them, top Fabians now applied themselves discreetly to promoting the same system in other lands that had just failed so dismally in Britain. Their plans provided for leveling the wealth of nations as well as individuals—with the United States the prime target and natural victim. The barbarian

---

[9] C. A. R. Crosland, "The Transition from Capitalism," *New Fabian Essays,* edited by R. H. S. Crossman, (London, Turnstile Press, 1952), pp. 59-60. Crosland, a long time member of the Fabian Executive, became Economic Secretary to the Treasury with rank of Minister in the Fabian-dominated Labour Party Government of October, 1964.

practice of stripping the more developed nations to satisfy the primitive hordes of Asia and Africa had been advocated centuries before in less polite accents by the Tartars, Huns and Moors. It was urged again in September, 1962, by Fabian Socialist Hugh Gaitskell, M.P., writing in *Socialist International Information* on "The British Labour Party's Foreign Policy." Calling for a "mobilisation of our Western resources for the crusade against world poverty," that none-too-Christian soldier concluded:

The British Labour movement dedicated to equality and the ending of the divisions between the haves and have-nots in these islands, recognises that a Socialism which stops at our own shores is a hypocrisy; *that the coexistence of the privileged with the under-privileged is as indefensible between nations as it is within nations.*[10]

Coexistence with the Soviet Union and its satellites, however, was defensible, and remained a basic point of Fabian foreign policy. It was echoed by the Socialist International, whose forty-two member and "observer" parties claim to speak for 11.8 million persons and to control 64.5 million votes around the world;[11] it was echoed by a succession of Fabian Socialist Ministers in the Commonwealth countries, typified by Prime Minister Walter Nash of New Zealand.[12] In August, 1954, Morgan Phillips of the Fabian International Bureau, a former chairman of both the British Labour Party and the Committee of the International Socialist Conference (COMISCO), had led a British Labour delegation that included Lord Attlee on a junket to Moscow and Red China. En route, the group also visited Stockholm, Helsinki, Singapore, Beirut and Tokyo; met representatives from Malaya and Burma; and "exchanged views with many Socialist Parties at these places." As a result, the Asian Socialist Conference met for the first time in a joint congress with the Socialist International in July, 1955.

Before departing on that global tour, Morgan Phillips had a warm and animated meeting in Geneva with Chou En-lai, Red China's Foreign Minister. The Chinese Communist leader, "wearing his simple blue-gray uniform," came in hurriedly and announced through an interpreter that he had just seen Charlie Chaplin, so much admired and touted by Fabians in other years. After a further exchange of civilities, Phillips "reflected that a great new age was now dawning for Asia, an age that the Labour Government in Britain had helped

---

[10] (Italics added.)
[11] *Socialist International Information*, Vol. XIII, No. 34-35, (August 24, 1963).
[12] *Fabian News*, (March, 1958).

to usher in when it granted independence to India, Pakistan and Burma." And he reflected, too, "that Chou En-lai must inevitably play one of the leading roles in guiding the newly-awakened Asia." [13]

Fabian lenience towards Communist movements and leaders was held to be justified not only by their joint Socialist heritage, but by their common purpose of achieving Socialism throughout the world. In the lead essay of the *New Fabian Essays,* published in 1952 as a "restatement" in modern terms of unchanging Fabian objectives, R. H. S. Crossman[14] of the Fabian Executive noted that Communist movements are often the most effective way of introducing Socialism into backward countries which lack parliamentary experience.

By inference, "Democratic Socialism" as preached by Fabians is designed primarily to captivate advanced industrial nations, where the more direct Communist methods of attack do not appeal and cannot so easily penetrate. Plainly the two movements supplement each other, even if their vocabulary is different and their tasks are divided. Thus Crossman urged coexistence with the Communists; though he protested almost too emphatically that coexistence did not mean cooperation.

Evidently Fabian Socialists still preferred to retain their separate identity and their perennial "right to criticize," which is the Fabian definition of freedom. A critical attitude towards friend and foe alike has characterized the movement from its earliest days, and confirmed in its practitioners a satisfying sense of being superior persons. At times, that habit makes it difficult for an outsider to distinguish the Fabians' friends from their foes. Anyone reading the critical "tributes" to G. D. H. Cole in the *Fabian Journal,* following his death in 1959, finds it hard to believe they were penned by some of his warmest friends and admirers. Similarly, Fabian Socialist criticism of Communist behavior cannot be interpreted as pure hostility.

Outspoken cooperation with the Communists, Crossman implied, must be reserved for a future day when every country on earth should be either Communist- or Socialist-ruled; and the two kindred movements could finally merge their differences on the basis of some higher dialectic not yet apparent. Meanwhile, Fabian contacts with Communist leaders were cultivated at the uppermost level; and the vice

[13] *Socialist International Information,* (August 21, 1954).
[14] Named Minister of Housing and Local Government with Cabinet rank in the British Labour Party Government after the October, 1964 elections.

president of the British Communist Party, Rajani Palme Dutt, was invited to speak at the Fabian Society's Autumn Lectures in 1956.

The Fabian-steered Socialist International continued, through its socially acceptable friends and individually respected leaders, to put pressure on its various home governments in support of Soviet foreign policy goals in Asia, Africa and Latin America. Thus the Socialist International, which takes precedence historically over the Communist International, presented itself as a kind of Third Force, maintaining and manipulating the balance between the two major world powers, the United States and the Soviet Union, but somehow always leaning towards the latter.

Among the North Atlantic Treaty nations already joined in a military defense pact, British Socialists promoted the cause of Atlantic Union and continue to do so today. This high-flown scheme was merely an enlargement of Federal Union, the scale model engineered at the outbreak of World War II by a key member of the Fabian International Bureau, R. W. G. Mackay, aided by the Fabian-approved Rhodes Scholars, Clarence K. Streit and Herbert Agar.[15] Federal Union calls among other things for the Government of the United States to reunite with Britain, while Atlantic Union marshals European support for the same plan. Both in its original and expanded forms, Federal Union has appropriated the secret dream of nineteenth century Empire builder Cecil Rhodes and remolded it along lines more adapted to the schemes of the Socialist International. Such eminent personages of the International as Foreign Minister Paul-Henri Spaak of Belgium have lent the luster of their names to Atlantic Union.

What it proposes is that the world's most advanced Christian nations should revise their idea of national sovereignty and pool their economic as well as their military resources. Its Fabian framers attempt to justify the plan by quoting copiously from the writings of early American Federalists, although the new type of union projected is very far from anything James Madison or Alexander Hamilton had in mind. Atlantic Union, or Atlantica, would embrace a group of fifteen highly industrialized welfare states on both sides of the North Atlantic and culminate in one World Government. The Socialist character of that eventual World State is not emphasized in the smoothly written propaganda and even smoother social functions

---

[15] Both have been cited favorably in *Fabian News*.

designed to attract industrialists, financiers, educators, statesmen and military figures of the several NATO nations. Many no doubt believe they are merely helping to further the cause of mutual defense.

Seeking to permeate the upper crust of the North Atlantic community, Atlantic Union has made membership on its 538-man international council a status symbol, and, in some instances, a springboard to higher business and professional opportunity. By indirection its authors also aim to weaken resistance among the socially elite to the adoption of Socialist-sponsored programs in their homelands and in the world. Significantly, a number of British peers who achieved nobility by the grace of the Labour Party have been active in Federal Union and related enterprises. Prominent among them was that well-known international bleeding heart, Sir William (later Lord) Beveridge, the much-publicized "father" of the Welfare State.

After the collapse of Britain's Socialist Government of 1945-1951 (which in 1949 named him chairman of the British Broadcasting Corporation), Lord Beveridge says he "returned to Federal Union across national boundaries, as a necessary step towards World Government and substitution of world justice for war." [16] Previously, he had been a charter member of the Inter-Parliamentary Committee for World Government. Indeed, he headed a coterie of economists who actually undertook to draft a "practical" plan for Atlantic Union merger[17] and to apportion the wealth of nations on an "equitable" basis. Reports prepared by his committee on the economic aspects of federation, though perhaps a trifle dated, would no doubt prove edifying to members of the United States Congress today.

While striving to render patriotism outmoded and to discredit the concept of national sovereignty in the more literate countries, British Fabians at the same time speeded up their efforts to promote nationalist movements in so-called backward areas of the globe. At first glance, this might seem a contradiction. Closer scrutiny reveals that Fabian aid to national independence movements in colonial and semi-colonial lands stems from theories advanced as long ago as 1902 by the early Fabian, John Atkinson Hobson, in his book *Imperialism,* which antedated and influenced Lenin's writings on the subject.

Among latter-day Fabians such aid has assumed two principal

[16] Beveridge, *Power and Influence,* (New York, The Beechhurst Press, Ltd., 1955), p. 356.
[17] George Catlin, *The Atlantic Community,* (London, Coram, Ltd., 1959), p. 82.

forms. First, education of native leaders under Fabian tutelage. In 1951 the Labour Party Government had four thousand colonial students in England,[18] most of them being carefully schooled in the "social sciences" by Socialist professors. And second, the promotion of trade unions in colonial territories, not simply to raise standards of living for native labor, but as organs of mass pressure for independence. It is planned that ex-colonial nations shall eventually form regional federations under Socialist leadership.

In 1949 Sir Stafford Cripps, then a Minister of the Crown, made the remarkable announcement that "The liquidation of the British Empire is essential to Socialism." This statement appeared in the March, 1949, issue of *Venture*, published by the Fabian Colonial Bureau (renamed the Fabian Commonwealth Bureau in 1958). During the same year the International Confederation of Free Trade Unions (ICFTU) was formed, as an adjunct of the Fabian-led Socialist International, to speed colonial liquidation not only in British territories but in other regions as well—excluding, of course, the Soviet Empire! Making certain that the coolies of Asia and the tribesmen of Africa would not suspect it of being pro-Christian, the Confederation refused to accept the Christian Trade Unions of Europe as affiliates.

After the fall of the Labour Party Administration, Fabian spokesmen continued to urge Empire liquidation from the Opposition benches. Since their ranks in the Commons were thinner, they were obliged to lean more heavily than ever on outside sources of support and agitation in order to complete this unfinished business. In 1953 the mild-mannered Sir Stafford—who had just completed a term as president of the Fabian Society—urged the need for exerting all possible pressure on Britain's Conservative Government to carry out the Fabian-planned schedule of Empire dissolution.

By that time, the ICFTU boasted one hundred affiliated organizations in seventy-five countries, including Poland and Yugoslavia. It claimed the support of fifty-four million trade unionists throughout the world, many of whom had certainly never heard of that body as such.[19] As a "labor-minded" international pressure group oriented towards Socialism, the Confederation maintained close and cordial

---

[18] *Socialist International Information*, (October 16, 1954).

[19] Ten years later, in a press release of May 20, 1963, from its world headquarters at 37-47 Rue Montagne aux Herbes Potageres, Brussels, the ICFTU claimed over fifty-seven million members in 108 countries.

relations with the "political-minded" Socialist International. It also worked closely with the Fabian Colonial Bureau, much of whose own globe-girdling activity was financed by donations from the large British trade unions.[20]

The ramifications of Fabian Socialism in Africa, Asia, Latin America and the West Indies, during the nineteen-fifties and after, can be traced in the pages of *Venture*. Here Fabian ties with international unionism are plainly revealed, as well as the drive to use the trade unions as mere stepping stones to Socialism.

The methods and aims of those fantastically widespread operations were summarized with perfect clarity by Fabian Socialist Arthur Skeffington[21] in a speech delivered before the Commonwealth Section at Transport House, headquarters of the British Labour Party. His speech was reprinted in *Socialist International Information* for October 16, 1954, under the title, "From Crown Colony to Commonwealth," and it is by way of being a historic document.

First of all, Skeffington noted "the fine practical cooperation of the British Trades Union movement in sending out colonial trade union officers, assisting the budding trade unions in the colonies, bringing their officials over here for training and advice, and now agreeing to a levy of 2d. per member on their whole [British] membership to increase their colonial activities." In the next breath he praised the initiative of the defunct Labour Party Government in promoting colonial independence, saying, "We introduced no less than forty new colonial constitutions—bringing Nigeria and the Gold Coast to the doorstep of self-government, besides giving independence to 400 million people in Asia."

While admitting that the same Administration had freed India with no assurance or evidence of "democratic" government except the Socialism of Nehru, on the whole Skeffington opposed self-government in colonial countries unless it was sure to be "democratic"— that is, socialistic. "We must be certain," he continued blandly, "that all the people have the machinery and the ability to express their own will before self-government is accorded." Then, in a burst of frankness, he concluded: "We must take the opportunity, indeed, we must create the opportunities to associate them with our movement, for, as Socialists, we surely believe that the only future healthy

[20] Cole, *op. cit.*, p. 318.
[21] Named Parliamentary Secretary to the Ministry of Land and National Resources in the Labour Party Government of October, 1964.

development [sic] in the colonial territories must be based on the principles of Socialism."

This speech, which gives every indication of having been prepared in the New Fabian Research Bureau, unquestionably reflects the policy of the Fabian Society which named Skeffington its chairman three years later. Trade unions around the world were to be inoculated with Socialism and to press for the political independence of colonial regions. Such pressure was employed to spur the further dismemberment of the British Empire. It strengthened the hand of the enfeebled Labour Party Opposition in the Commons, and eventually helped to win acceptance for such Communist-trained and Fabian-approved native leaders as Jomo Kenyatta in Kenya. (As Crossman remarked in the *New Fabian Essays,* the success of Communist methods in backward countries must be recognized!)

More feverishly than ever before in the history of the Society, overseas contacts and affiliations were cultivated under the personal supervision of leading British Fabians. New front organizations and their offspring in the political, educational and cultural fields sprang up all over the map, usually based on plans originating in the fertile New Fabian Research Bureau. There seemed to be Fabians everywhere, Rita Hinden of the Colonial Bureau reported in 1957.[22] In Tokyo she and Arthur Lewis were feted, together with Fabians from India and Yugoslavia, by the Fabian Institute of Japan—a body "quite independent of the British Society, but performing a similar function."

Delegations from Poland, Germany, Scandinavia and all the Commonwealth countries visited London, to be entertained graciously at Lord Faringdon's town house in Brompton Square and to confer with representatives of the Fabian International and Commonwealth Bureaus on matters of peculiar interest to Socialists. Members of Americans for Democratic Action from the United States were welcomed regularly at Fabian Summer Schools.[23]

In recent years top British Fabians, taking advantage of jet-age facilities and, at times, of their own privileged positions as Members of Parliament, have become world commuters on a grand scale. Typical of the breed was Kenneth Younger, Minister of State at the Foreign

[22] "Fabians in a Japanese Tea House," *Fabian News,* (July, 1957).

[23] "Invitation," *Fabian News,* (July, 1957). This item states: "The Society has often welcomed to summer schools members of Americans for Democratic Action . . . . Now A.D.A. is offering places at its summer school at half-rates to visitors from Britain . . . . Lecturers will include Mrs. Eleanor Roosevelt, and the school is to be held in Dutchess County overlooking the Hudson River . . . ."

Office in 1950-51, whose schedule of arrivals and departures would have exhausted a diplomatic courier—though his colleague on the International Bureau's Advisory Committee, Denis Healey, seemed to be a close runner-up for the title of Most Traveled Fabian. In the space of a week or two, Younger might be reported flitting in and out of half a dozen countries, and he slipped through the Iron Curtain as if by osmosis.

On his travels Kenneth Younger wore a variety of hats. He was billed as a Member of Parliament; as a representative of the Fabian Executive; as the chairman of the British-Asian and Overseas Fellowship, an organization set up to establish residential centers in Britain for "overseas comrades"; or as director general of the august Royal Institute of International Affairs (British counterpart of the American Council on Foreign Relations), with headquarters at Chatham House, 10 St. James Square, London. Whatever title he might have used at a given moment, there is little doubt that he ranked for many years as Fabian Socialism's foremost flying salesman.

In the summer of 1962, just a fortnight after it had been announced that Kenneth Younger was in Saudi Arabia, the world press carried a pronouncement in favor of Socialism by a younger member of that oil-rich country's royal family. Prince Talal, challenging the rule of his brother, King Ibn Saud, in the age-old Middle Eastern tradition, had discovered a new approach. "I am a Fabian Socialist," he told reporters.[24]

Combining infiltration and propaganda with ceremonial duties, the globe-trotting routine merely confirmed the leadership role of British Fabians in world Socialist affairs. Almost any issue of *Fabian News*, selected at random, contained items like these:

Arthur Skeffington, the Society's Chairman, is spending a very busy Parliamentary recess. He returned from a visit to East Germany to direct the Summer School at Oxford, and then left on a Parliamentary delegation to Tanganyika. He will return for the Labour Party Conference at the end of September.

Another Fabian with a tight schedule is T. E. M. McKitterick, who is at present commuting between France, Turkey, British Guiana and New York.

Colin Jackson is again visiting the Middle East, and James MacColl is visiting Virginia for Tercentenary Celebrations.[25]

²⁴ *Fabian News*, (November, 1962).
²⁵ "Busy Chairman," *Fabian News*, (September, 1957).

Or this:

Travellers.
There were probably some eminent Fabians still left in the UK [United Kingdom] during the summer [of 1963] but not very many. Robert Heild has been in India studying India's economic problems under the auspices of the M.I.T. Center for International Studies; Thomas Balogh has been in Algeria on behalf of a U.N. agency; Anthony Crosland was lecturing in Australia, and Brian Abel-Smith was last heard of in the Congo; John Parker and Tom Ponsonby are leading lots of other Fabians around Russia.[26]

Returning to England, eager voyagers regaled the more earthbound and anonymous majority of the Society's members with eyewitness accounts of "conditions" in other lands. Their reports were featured events at Fabian Summer Schools and weekend conferences, giving audiences the vicarious and cost-free pleasure of foreign travel as well as the feeling of being directly involved in exciting events abroad. All of which stimulated the rank-and-file in the local societies to carry on the more pedestrian work of home research, propaganda and organization needed to prepare for a Labour Party comeback in Britain.

In July, 1952, a weekend school headed by Kenneth Younger and sponsored by the Fabian International Bureau was announced in *Fabian News*. Lectures were devoted to various aspects of Anglo-American relations. Among others attending it were a French Senator belonging to the left-of-left NRP; a representative of the Yugoslav Embassy in London; and an unnamed United States Embassy attaché. Although Younger, in answer to an inquiry from a non-Fabian, conceded that other Americans were present as well, he firmly declined to identify them.

Occasionally, there were "reports" from other foreign friends of the Society which suggested a deeper degree of involvement in foreign intrigue than the Fabian Society officially admits. During a 1962 Easter Weekend School held at Beatrice Webb House, Dorking, the young unofficial Algerian envoy to London, Cherif Guellal, foretold with uncanny accuracy the role an independent Algeria would play in international affairs. He not only predicted that his country would range itself after "liberation" with the "non-aligned"—neutralist and pro-Soviet—nations; but made it clear that on the domestic front *Algeria would pursue a So-*

---

[26] "Travellers," *Fabian News*, (September, 1963).

cialist policy.[27] This prophetic declaration was made several months before the rest of the world had heard of Ahmed Ben Bella or could guess he was plotting a left wing coup to seize power in Algeria.

While accelerating its movements and expanding its influence outside the British Isles, the Fabian Society is never idle at home. True, its listed membership (which rose to an all-time peak after 1945, when many people regarded the Society as a means of entry into politics and government) was cut back to the usual serviceable hardcore following the defeat of 1951. Much of that trusted membership has proved to be hereditary. It includes children and grandchildren, nephews and nieces of bygone Fabians—an ironic touch, since the Society objects so vigorously to the hereditary principle in other areas, especially in the House of Lords. Its present (unpublished) list of dues-paying members, which the Society estimates at about five thousand,[28] gives no inkling of the uncounted thousands who quietly follow the Fabian line in Britain. Long before Communists adopted the practice, the Fabian Society found it convenient, in the main, to abolish card-carrying memberships.

[27] "Easter School," *Fabian News*, (June, 1962).

[28] According to the *Fabian Society Annual Report*, national membership figures were listed at 2,692 full members and 91 associate members as of June 30, 1963. These figures are somewhat misleading, since the national membership figures include subscribing bodies and organizations which are listed as individual members. As of June 30, 1963, subscribing bodies numbered 137 Labor Parties, Cooperatives and Trades Unions, and 92 libraries. On the same date the Commonwealth Bureau claimed 167 members and the International Bureau 57; but these apparently modest figures also included subscribing bodies. Since that time the Commonwealth and International Bureaus have merged to form a single bureau. Membership of local societies as of March 31, 1963, was listed at 1,848, organized into 76 societies. Total: 4,855.

8

Tomorrow, The World?

1.

TODAY, as ever, the Fabian Society of London together with its affiliated provincial societies consists of several hundred well-known publicists and politicians whose connections with the Society can readily be confirmed, although the general public seldom identifies them as Fabians; plus a larger number of unknown and unsung adherents, engaged in a wide variety of more or less obscure tasks. Frequently, their long and faithful services are recorded only by a brief death notice in *Fabian News* or the *Fabian Society Annual Report*. On the whole, it is a case of "join for five years, join for fifty, and Fabians are notoriously long-lived." [1]

As always, the Society is composed mainly of middle class professionals, many engaged in writing, teaching and various types of "research." Leading symbol of Fabian Research in 1963 was a lean, hollow-eyed pundit from the London School of Economics, with a name reminiscent of the Mad Hatter's tea party: Professor Richard Titmuss. More and more, the Society seeks to enlist engineers, technicians and managerial personnel; and a special effort has been made to penetrate the modern communications industries—radio, television

---

[1] "Fabians Old and New," *Fabian News*, (May, 1958). As an example of that longevity, *Fabian News*, (May, 1960) reported that Percival Chubb, who attended the first meeting of the Fabian Society at 17 Osnaburgh Street, Regent's Park, on January 4, 1884, died on February 10, 1960 in St. Louis, Missouri at the age of 99.

and motion pictures[2]—with an eye to their "educational," that is, propagandist value for Socialism.

There is a firm nucleus of Fabian civil servants in every government department, and Fabian Socialists have been regularly appointed as Opposition members on government Advisory Boards, notably Labor, Commonwealth Affairs and Immigration—as well as to key posts in the United Nations. A. D. K. Owen, better known as David Owen, who served as personal assistant to Sir Stafford Cripps in 1941-43, has been a fixture at the United Nations since its inception.[3] As director of the Office of Technological Services in the UN Secretariat, he has been for years in a position to dispense patronage to Fabian Socialists on a world-wide basis.

Though the terminology has changed with the times, the Fabian Society remains a secret society of Socialists, dedicated to transforming the existing world order by methods necessarily devious and not always short of sedition. Despite its nominal emphasis on "democratic" practices and parliamentary means to accomplish its ends; despite its respectable front of good manners, charm and learning; despite the fact that its Summer Schools stress such sources of innocent merriment as croquet, table tennis and country dancing—in essence, the goals of the Fabian Society parallel those of the Communists and at some point short of infinity find a common meeting place.

Rosa Luxemburg, the Left Wing Polish Social Democrat who was "executed" under mysterious circumstances in Germany following the abortive Spartacus revolt of 1919, long ago noted a disturbing likeness between the British Fabian Society and Lenin's Bolshevik Party. Each, she pointed out, was a secret society of intellectuals grasping for power through control of the working-class—and she feared and distrusted them both.[4]

It is true that methods of discipline governing the two organizations vary—the Bolshevik parties being operated along quasi-military lines, while the Fabian Society appears to impose little or no control

[2] *Fabian News,* (May, 1958). "The Chairman and Vice Chairman [of the Society] share a serious interest in the Cinema: Roy Jenkins as a Governor of the British Film Institute, and Eirene White as a member of the Cinematograph Film Council."

[3] An alumnus of Leeds University, David Owen flew from New York to attend the memorial service honoring the late Hugh Gaitskell, M.P., at Westminster Abbey on January 31, 1963. The *Times* of London, (February 1, 1963).

[4] Robert Hunter, *Revolution,* Committee for Constitutional Government, (New York, Harper & Brothers, 1940), p. 350.

over its members. Inquiry reveals, however, that major policy decisions of the Fabian Executive are binding; and that virtually all important speeches or publications by Fabians are prepared and/or cleared by the New Fabian Research Bureau, even when they appear for tactical reasons to be mutually contradictory. The Society's bylaws provide that members or associates may be dropped for "want of confidence," and in some cases, individuals condemned to that silent treatment have been known to drop completely from political sight. Except in the strictly superficial give-and-take of conversation and debate, the boasted Fabian tolerance is a myth, and Fabians are by no means the "gentle people" they claim to be.

During a prolonged period of political Opposition in Britain, Fabian Socialists nursed their strength at the municipal level, while gradually increasing the number of their seats in Parliament. For instance, on the London County Council, Sidney Webb's old stronghold from which he moved into national politics, Fabians still retain a majority (including the chairmanship) that assures them control of local educational institutions. In September, 1956, *Fabian News* announced that "the new leader of the Labour Group (majority) on the Leeds County Council, Frank O'Donnell, is a member of the Leeds Fabian Society" and that "all four sitting M.P.'s" (including Hugh Gaitskell, M.P. and Denis Healey, M.P.) are "members of the Leeds Society."

This item was interesting in the light of an Associated Press dispatch of November 12, 1962, announcing that Owen Lattimore, the former Johns Hopkins University professor, had just been appointed to a teaching post at Leeds University, a public institution. Many Americans will recall that Owen Lattimore, author of books on Communist Asia and alleged secret agent of the Soviet Foreign Office, was indicted for perjury for his testimony before a United States Senate Subcommittee investigating the notorious Institute of Pacific Relations case. Fabian writers and publicists in England rallied volubly to his defense at the time—though the same circles later professed to be shocked by reports that Soviet spies and informers had succeeded in filching some British Government secrets.

From 1956 to his sudden death in January, 1963, Hugh Gaitskell of the Leeds Fabian Society was Parliamentary Leader of the British Labour Party. As a member of the Leeds County Council, he could scarcely have failed to be aware of Lattimore's appointment to Leeds University. Yet Gaitskell was the man slated to become Britain's next Prime Minister, in the event of a Labour Government's return to power! While publicly mourned, his demise may have proved providential for British Socialism. At least the Labour Party was able to present a new, youthful and relatively noncontroversial face to the world, at a time when aggressive new tactics were urgently needed.

Gaitskell's successor, Harold Wilson, M.P., was named on St. Valentine's Day, 1963. A Fabian victory in the mock contest for the post was a foregone conclusion, following an "election" in which all three candidates for the Opposition leadership turned out to be long-standing members of the Fabian Society. Harold Wilson, a former chairman of the Society who more recently headed its Local Societies section, had been an active Fabian Socialist since his undergraduate days at Oxford. Somehow, that pertinent fact was not featured in general press and television accounts, which heralded his "election" as Opposition Leader as respectfully as if he were already the effective Prime Minister.

Like his "rivals," George Brown, M.P., and James Callaghan, M.P., Wilson belonged to the Opposition's Shadow Cabinet chosen to man a future Labour Government. His place as "Shadow" Foreign Minister was promptly filled by Denis Healey, M.P., member of the Advisory Council of the Fabian International Bureau as well as a stalwart of the Leeds Fabian Society. Of the twelve Labourites named to the Gaitskell Shadow Cabinet in 1959, nine belonged to the Fabian Society.[5] If and when they became Cabinet Ministers in substance, it was certain beyond the shadow of a doubt that plans and programs prepared in advance by New Fabian Research would once more become the official policies of the British Government.

In February, 1957, the official *Fabian News* reported: "Fabians are playing a major part in the preparation of Labour policy documents. The Party's National Executive has recently set up working parties to report to the Party Conferences in 1957 and 1958 on the Ownership of Industry, Control of Industry, Public Industries, Agriculture and Education. The first working party is composed entirely of Fabians, and there are several Fabians on each of the others."

Whatever the Fabian Society had in mind for Britain, the privations, indignities and follies from 1945 to 1951 were merely a foretaste of things to come. Enlarged schemes, glimpsed in publications of the

---

[5] "Shadow Fabians," *Fabian News*, (November-December, 1959). Cited as Fabians in the Shadow Cabinet were: Harold Wilson, James Callaghan, Anthony Greenwood, Tom Fraser, George Brown, Patrick Gordon Walker, G. R. Mitchison, Fred Willey and Denis Healey. Two peers on the Parliamentary Committee, Lord Faringdon and Lord Lucan, were also described as Fabians.

Socialist International, seemed to include a coolly calculated timetable for synchronizing "peaceful social revolution" in England with simultaneous developments in the other nations of Atlantica. Even emigration would no longer afford an escape for the regimented Britons of the future.

Domestic plans for a Socialist Britain were outlined in the flood of publications which the Society continued to issue on virtually every subject under the sun. Over the signature of John Hughes, a basic plan to renationalize the steel industry was distributed to all members of the Society in 1962 as Document No. 198 of the *Fabian Research Series*. Other happy suggestions, guaranteed to finish off the free enterprise system by more indirect methods, have been announced since 1956. They propose to control existing industrial and business corporations via government purchase of shares (stocks); to set up new plants with government funds, plants that will work towards the gradual extinction of competitive private industry; to "decentralize" the management of nationalized industries[6] and to require government-owned enterprises to show a profit (along lines remarkably similar to those proposed in Soviet Russia as of November, 1962).

There were political plans for "reforming" the House of Lords and for downgrading and humiliating the Monarchy, approved by Eirene White, M.P., a chairman of the Fabian Society.[7] In fact, more outspokenly radical elements of the Society—typified by Hugh Gaitskell's teacher, the late G. D. H. Cole, and until recently by Harold Wilson himself—had long urged complete abolition of the Monarchy and the watchdog House of Lords. A favorite pupil of the departed G. D. H. Cole tells how the latter, after freely describing the various revolutionary changes he hoped to see the next Labour Party Government make, suddenly realized he had failed to mention a particular reform dear to his heart. As the students to whom Cole had imparted his plans were leaving, he exclaimed: "Why, I forgot to include the abolition of God!"[8]

Since the day when that graceless quip was uttered more in earnest than in jest, G. D. H. Cole has gone to his reward. He died in 1959 as president of the Fabian Society, a post awarded to his widow in

[6] Hugh Gaitskell, M.P., "Socialism and Nationalisation," *Fabian Tract No. 300*, (London, The Fabian Society, 1956).
[7] Eirene White, "Noble Lords and Others," *Fabian News*, (May, 1958). Eirene White, M.P., was named Parliamentary Under Secretary of State for Colonies in the Labour Party Government of October, 1964.
[8] "Tribute to G. D. H. Cole," *Fabian Journal*, (April, 1959).

1962; but his destructive ideas still survive among his numerous disciples in Britain and the Commonwealth countries. G. D. H. Cole's influence on the current crop of Fabian Socialist leaders has been profound, however obliquely it was sometimes expressed in statements from the Opposition benches. When Hugh Gaitskell and Harold Wilson opposed Britain's entry into the Common Market in 1962, even Socialists seemed puzzled by the unaccustomed strain of patriotism in their arguments. Yet, on closer inspection, their stand was neither surprising nor prompted by abnormal respect for tradition.

For any Cole-tutored Marxist, the obvious if unspoken complaint against the Common Market was quite simply that it did not "destroy confidence in the prospect of sustained profits," but on the contrary seemed to produce general prosperity by a capitalist formula. If Socialist administrations held office simultaneously in France, Holland, Italy, West Germany, Belgium and England, as they have long been striving to do, opposition to the Common Market by British Fabians might be expected to subside. Gaitskell and Wilson left the door open against that eventuality; but General de Gaulle,[9] for reasons best known to himself, slammed it shut.

The imminence of a Labour Party victory in England was somberly underscored by the tribute paid to the departed Fabian Socialist, Hugh Gaitskell. On January 31, 1963, memorial services for him were held in Westminster Abbey, an honor usually reserved for a Prime Minister. The Queen, so often derided from the Labour benches, was courteously represented in the Abbey by the Earl of Eldon; the Duke of Edinburgh by Rear Admiral D. C. Bonham-Carter; and Sir Winston Churchill by Lady Churchill.

Prime Minister Harold Macmillan and his colleagues in the Government shared the choir stalls with the Shadow Cabinet of the Opposition. In the procession to the sanctuary, the Archbishop of Canterbury was accompanied by the Moderator of the Free Church Council. At the close of the service, spectators seated in the nave and standing in the cloisters joined with mixed emotions in singing William Blake's hymn which envisages the building of Jerusalem in England's green and pleasant land.[10]

[9] Margaret Cole states that in the early years of World War II the Fabian International Bureau, after "receiving de Gaulle at first with caution, then backed him strongly . . . . returning after the Liberation to more strongly expressed doubts of his political intentions . . . ." Margaret Cole, *The Story of Fabian Socialism,* (London, Heinemann Educational Books, Ltd., 1961), p. 288.

[10] The *Times* of London, (February 1, 1963).

In that overflow congregation of diplomats, nobles, civil servants, parliamentarians and trade unionists, the Socialist International was well represented. The Prime Minister of Denmark, J. O. Krag, head of the Danish Social Democratic Party; Willy Brandt, Socialist Mayor of West Berlin; and D. Segall, of the Social Democratic Party of West Germany, flew to London for the occasion. Other representatives of foreign Socialist groups who were present remained discreetly nameless, including a delegation from the United States. Gaitskell's stepson, Raymond Frost, who came from Washington for the funeral, could not attend the Abbey tribute because he had to leave England on a World Bank mission to Colombia.[11]

The obsequies over, Britain's Fabian Socialists applied themselves hastily to transmuting Gaitskell's cold-eyed successor into what they fondly hoped would be the irresistible image of a future Prime Minister. In this alchemy they were assisted by the British version of a Madison Avenue advertising agency, which distributed photographs of Harold Wilson in several unlikely attitudes. One showed the forty-seven year old Opposition Leader with eyes downcast, hands prayerfully raised as in the Duerer etching—and a pipe clamped between his teeth! Another was a photomontage of Harold Wilson at the age of eight, posed outside the door of 10 Downing Street.

Such primitive publicity stills made older and more sophisticated Fabians shudder, and were frowned upon by trade unionists who paid the bills. Soon it was announced that a new group of assorted image-makers, resembling the Advertising Council in the United States, had volunteered to promote Harold Wilson's campaign gratis. They would use billboards, buttons, stickers and other visual aids to which the frugal British electorate was still unaccustomed. Names of advertising men involved and the amounts of money to be spent were not revealed. Labour Party spokesmen at Transport House, however, were quoted as saying their early-bird campaign would be styled along the lines of the 1960 campaign that put John F. Kennedy into the White House, with Theodore H. White's book, *The Making of the President, 1960,* serving as a text.[12]

It was a neat compliment to those "democratic" Americans who, after having been initially trained and cued by British Fabians (as we shall subsequently see), were now in a position to furnish aid and comfort to their tutors. Returning from a visit to Washington in April,

[11] *Ibid.*
[12] United Press International dispatch from London, (May 19, 1963).

1963, Harold Wilson wrote ecstatically: ". . . for sheer quality, the United States Government from President Kennedy downward, is without equal in any administration in any country." [13] The harsh treatment accorded Prime Minister Macmillan in the Skybolt affair, followed by the exquisite kindness shown to visiting Opposition Leader Harold Wilson in upper echelons of the New Frontier, helped to convey the notion that Conservative Party leaders could not "deal effectively" with Washington.

In England the shopworn promises of "a new dynamism" to "get the country moving again," heard during the 1960 Kennedy-Johnson campaign in America, were dusted off by Fabian orators and presented as fresh merchandise to the British electorate. Wilson was billed as the only leader capable of "mobilizing the energies of Britain in the sixties." One advantage of such rousing generalities was that they sounded vigorous and bold, without obliging the speaker to commit himself to any particular philosophy of action. They tended to reassure moderates, and to head off discussion of specific methods by which Harold Wilson and his associates planned to impose full-scale Socialism in Britain and the Commonwealth, once they succeeded in recapturing power.

If any doubted this to be Wilson's intention, his answer to Sir Gerald Nabarro's query on the floor of the Commons was plain enough to dispel uncertainty. Brusquely, the newly chosen Opposition Leader *reaffirmed his Party's Socialist pledge to work without qualification for public control of the means of production, distribution and exchange.* Wilson has long been identified with the irreconcilable or Jacobin wing of the British Labour Party, which views taxation more as a means of "ensuring social justice" than of raising revenue. His Party's program of "tax reform" disclosed on February 26, 1963—extracts from which were proudly published in *Socialist International Information*[14]—included a scaled increase in Social Security contributions obtained via payroll deductions; a steep rise in corporation taxes; and an annual capital levy on all wealth exceeding twenty thousand pounds. Personally, Wilson has favored retributive

[13] From an article signed by Harold Wilson and distributed by North American Newspaper Alliance. It appeared on April 14, 1963, in the San Francisco *Chronicle* under the headline, "Future British Premier."

[14] *Socialist International Information,* (March 9, 1963), Vol. XII, No. 10. "British Labor Party Proposals for Tax Reform", by James Callaghan, M.P., British Labor Party Spokesman for Economic and Financial Affairs.

taxes ever since he decided, as a precociously embittered schoolboy in Huddersfield, to become Chancellor of the Exchequer someday and to tax phonograph records because his family did not own a phonograph! This bit of prophetic nonsense was related in campaign biographies of Wilson, and may or may not be true. Eventually, of course, he would decide to serve as First Lord of the Treasury rather than Chancellor of the Exchequer, the better to negotiate funds for his government in the course of discreet periodic visits to Washington.

Another Fabian Socialist spokesman for the Labour Party, James Callaghan, M.P., explained mildly that the proposed capital levy would not affect more than one voter out of a hundred.[15] He failed to mention, however, that confiscatory taxation, by sharply reducing the area of private investment, could affect the employment of millions, and within a relatively short time make them wholly dependent on government bounty. To cope with unemployment—or "redundancy," as it is quaintly called by present-day Fabian economists—Harold Wilson proposed that new factories be built, equipped, financed and run by the State. "We have to have State factories," said Wilson brightly, "to provide some of the goods the Commonwealth is going to want." [16]

The plump, prematurely silver-haired Oxonian, whose formal speeches and occasional witticisms are handily supplied by Fabian Research, was described by news correspondents as a Socialist in a gray flannel suit. He might just as well have been called a wolf in sheep's clothing—the Aesopian symbol, which George Bernard Shaw long ago suggested was more appropriate than the tortoise as a heraldic device for the Fabian Society—and which appears in the Shavian stained-glass window at Beatrice Webb House in Dorking. It is not the outer apparel, but the inner nature of the Fabian Society that has made Harold Wilson what he is today.

As a scholarship student at Oxford during the middle nineteen-thirties, he attached himself to the Society in an era when Marxist doctrines were openly professed by its leaders, and when Socialist and Communist undergraduates merged in the activities of the Popular Front. The pacificism of the Oxford movement was perpetuated in Wilson's prolonged association with the extreme left wing Fabian,

---

[15] *Ibid.*

[16] Harold Wilson, M.P., "The Labour Party's Plan for Britain's Future," *Socialist International Information*, (February 23, 1963), Vol. XIII, No. 8.

Aneurin Bevan.[17] It persists today in Harold Wilson's frank opposition to nuclear deterrents for Britain,[18] and his advocacy of conventional military forces for Western Europe to confront the Soviet hordes. He is committed to abandoning Formosa and to procuring a seat for Red China in the United Nations.[19] Though no trace of traditional Marxian phraseology appears today in the cautiously stated Aesopian programs of Harold Wilson and his Fabian associates, to paraphrase Napoleon: Scratch a Fabian, and find a Marxist.

Wilson succeeded to the political leadership of Britain's Labour Party at a moment when International Socialism appeared more confident of being able to move into a position of world-wide control, than at any time since the Russian Revolution. With left wing Social Democratic administrations in office or on the verge of it in a majority of countries throughout the so-called Free World, few Socialists doubt that they can readily establish a *modus vivendi* with the economically embarrassed Socialist Fatherland and its satellites. As in the nineteen-twenties—though on a far more imposing scale—world trade once more becomes the medium by which Socialist governments plan to aid each other to retain power at home, as well as to strengthen the strained Communist economies. Production surpluses are to be siphoned off without counting the cost, to build or bolster Socialism in other lands.

Having served at the age of thirty-one as president of the Board of Trade in Britain's former Labour Party Government—he was the youngest member of any British Cabinet since William Pitt!—Harold Wilson was the logical candidate to promote Socialist world hegemony via foreign-trade channels. He envisaged Socialist control, not only of raw materials but of manufactured goods as well, through price-fixing commodity agreements and foreign-exchange control. The ever generous United States would be expected to supply the "monetary lubrication."

"Now, for the first time," exulted Harold Wilson on February 11, 1963, "we have an American government in active sympathy!" What

[17] Bevan's widow, Jennie Lee, M.P., a frequent guest speaker over the years before Socialist and left wing labor bodies in the United States, was appointed Parliamentary Secretary to the Minister of Public Buildings and Works in the Wilson Cabinet of October, 1964.
[18] Article written by Harold Wilson for the North American Newspaper Alliance, (April, 1963).
[19] *Ibid.*

Wilson meant was that the United States now had a program of international commodity agreements. He went on to say:

Commodity agreements for temperate foodstuffs must provide the machinery for channelling the overspill of our advanced countries into the hungry countries. But why food only? There is a surplus of steel in many advanced countries, and in this country the steel mills are working at 60 per cent capacity. We all want to help India and a score of other developing countries. *Why not send them a million tons of ingot steel? We might go further* . . .[20]

We might, indeed, go further! The world giveaway program projected by Harold Wilson and his colleagues of the Socialist International has endless possibilities, limited only by the resources of the donor countries. Launched by an international cartel of Socialist rulers and administered by a supranational authority,[21] it might well go on and on—until the advanced nations of the earth are drained, exhausted and reduced to a common level of weakness and confusion. At that point, the sole military power still permitted to retain its independence, the Union of Soviet Socialist Republics, can move to take over, with hardly a struggle, its progressively enfeebled benefactors.

Initially, the Fabians propose to maneuver within the "mixed economy," part nationalized and part seemingly free, but in fact wholly controlled by government fiat, punitive taxation, and negotiated price-fixing arrangements inside and outside the British Commonwealth. By such means they hope to disarm preliminary opposition and to accomplish their ends more adroitly than by outright confiscation. The more extreme dangers and discomforts of a manipulated world economy, based on international agreements between all-powerful Socialist planners, still remain to be experienced. As with other attempts to subject living creatures to a totally controlled environment, unpredictable malignancies and painful side effects can be expected to result.

Still, as Harold Wilson points out, "the sacrifices, if sacrifices there must be, will at least be fairly shared"[22]—that is, by the captive industrialists and the helpless, security-drugged population. Only the

[20] Harold Wilson, M.P., "The Labour Party's Plan for Britain's Future," *Socialist International Information*, (February 23, 1963), Vol. XIII, No. 8.
[21] Harold Wilson, North American Newspaper Alliance, (April, 1963).
[22] Harold Wilson, M.P., "The Labour Party's Plan for Britain's Future," *Socialist International Information*, (February 23, 1963), Vol. XIII, No. 8.

salaried bureaucrats of the Fabian-approved inner circle can hope to better themselves individually. For the rest, we are led to believe, there will at least be freedom of discussion, if not of decision. In the New Britain, the Go-Ahead Britain, as planned by the fertile brain trusters of Fabian Research, men will learn to bear with docility the yoke of public happiness!

2.

A new generation of voters had grown to manhood and womanhood since a previous Labour Party Government ruled the United Kingdom. Children of a Fabian-permeated educational system, they were exposed from infancy to a barrage of direct and indirect Fabian Socialist propaganda, not only in the schools and universities, but also through the popular news and entertainment media. Those young people never knew that virtually every key post in the Government between 1945 and 1951 was filled for some time at least by a Fabian.[23] As for their elders, the painful memories of postwar scarcity had dimmed, and many were prepared to gamble that Labour would do better next time.

Among nearly thirty-six million Britons who went to the polls in October, 1964, few realized that Fabian Socialists invariably framed the policies and supplied the top personnel for the so-called Labour Party. In 1964 (as in the 1959 General Election) over one-third of all Labour Party candidates belonged to the Fabian Society;[23] but they refrained from mentioning that interesting fact in their campaign speeches and literature. Of 220 Fabians seeking election to Parliament, 120 were successful.[24] Blandly the *Fabian News* assured its own limited circle of readers that the proportion of Fabians in the Executive branch of the new government would be very much higher.

So, for the fourth time in precisely forty years, the Fabian-controlled Labour Party came to power in England. It received only a plurality of the total vote, winning by a frail majority of six parliamentary seats. Immigrants of color moving to Britain from Commonwealth countries reputedly furnished the margin of victory— even though popular feeling against the newcomers in some localities led to the defeat of several old Fabians. Prominent among the casualties was Patrick Gordon Walker, who lost the Smethwick seat he had held since 1945.

[23] *Fabian News. General Election Supplement.* (December, 1959).
[24] *Fabian News.* (November-December, 1964).

As a student and teacher at Christ Church College, Oxford, Gordon Walker was a contemporary of Dean Rusk, Walt Whitman Rostow and other liberally disposed Rhodes Scholars who attained high office in Washington under the Kennedy-Johnson Administration. After World War II he served as parliamentary private secretary for a year to Harold Laski's great friend and ally, Herbert Morrison. Appointed Under Secretary of State for Commonwealth Relations in 1947, Gordon Walker was properly helpful in "solving the Palestine question." As Commonwealth Secretary in 1950-51, he speeded the dissolution of the British Empire: a process initiated by his former chief, the late Arthur Creech-Jones, an early chairman of the Fabian Colonial Bureau.[25]

Following an American visit in 1947, Gordon Walker had played host in London to moving spirits of Americans for Democratic Action,[26] a group whose outlook on world affairs closely resembled his own. Members and friends of that organization were frequently in a position to exert decisive influence in Washington. Like them, Gordon Walker was an enthusiastic advocate of the Socialist International's plan for aid to underdeveloped countries:[27] a plan whereby, among other things the United States was induced to assume the major burden of financial support for Britain's orphaned ex-colonies.

When a debate on foreign affairs was held in the British Parliament on June 16-17, 1964, it was Gordon Walker who spoke for the Labour Party, expressing views shortly to become the official policy of Her Majesty's Government. It happened to be the occasion of Winston Churchill's final appearance in the House of Commons. For that old warrior the debate must have stirred painful memories of the arms limitation arguments of the nineteen-thirties, which encouraged Adolf Hitler to plunge the world into war.

Like a voice from the tragic past, tinged again with overtones of disaster, Patrick Gordon Walker declared: *"The supreme objective of foreign affairs must be the achievement of disarmament . . . . The*

---

[25] R. W. Sorenson, "Obituary: Arthur Creech-Jones," *Venture*, (London, The Fabian Society, Vol. XIV, No. 12, December, 1964), p. 5.

[26] *Fabian Society 67th Annual Report.* (July, 1949-June, 1950).

[27] "Socialist Policy for the Underdeveloped Territories. A Declaration of Principles Adopted by the Second Congress of the Socialist International," Milan 17-21 October, 1951. *Yearbook of the International Socialist Labour Movement 1956-1957.* Edited by Julius Braunthal, Secretary of the Socialist International. Under the Auspices of the Socialist International and the Asian Socialist Conference, (London, Lincolns-Prager, 1957), pp. 47-52.

most important hope of advance lies, I think, in the idea of a *minimum deterrent.*" Naively, he continued, "The Soviet Union seems genuinely interested in this." And well it might be, since a minimum deterrent is as good as none at all! Persons seated near Churchill saw his eyes flash as in the past, and heard the old patriot growl quietly under his breath. The speaker concluded by saying hopefully that "when the British and United States elections are over there may be a real chance of a breakthrough in disarmament." [28]

Considering Gordon Walker's failure at the polls in October, 1964, Prime Minister Wilson must have had strong personal reasons for appointing him to the post of Foreign Secretary. In the normal course of events, that place would have gone to Denis Healey, M.P., an equally devout Fabian Socialist and a past chairman, like Gordon Walker, of the Fabian International Bureau. As a consolation prize Healey was named Secretary of Defense in a government pledged to the gradual erosion of Britain's military defenses.

Such assurance was given by Prime Minister Wilson himself, who told the House of Commons on November 23: "*A Defense policy which does not contain within itself the seeds of further progress towards disarmament is one which in the present state of the world we can no longer regard as appropriate.*" [29] He did not deign to explain how it is possible to arm and disarm at the same time. Apparently Healey knew the answer without being told.

Nevertheless, it was evident to Fabian insiders that with Gaitskell's death Denis Healey lost his best friend at court. He, too, knew a number of important people in America, and in 1962 had been a featured speaker before a Council of World Affairs seminar at Asilomar in California. But what John Freeman of the *New Statesman* charitably described as Healey's "offbeat sense of humor" almost proved his undoing. In 1958, for instance, a political journalist from West Germany interviewed various prominent Britons on the technical question of the Bonn Government's reluctance to accept the Oder-Neisse boundary for a united Germany. They were asked: "Would the British nation, in a similar situation . . . ever accept the loss of one-quarter of the United Kingdom, including the complete denationalization of those territories by the mass expulsion of their

[28] Patrick Gordon Walker, "Foreign Policy in a Changing World," *Socialist International Information,* (July 4, 1964), Vol. XIV, No. 14.

[29] Official text supplied by British Information Services, References and Library Division, T 48, New York, (November 24, 1964).

inhabitants?" With one exception they replied, "No, of course not." The exception was Denis Healey, M.P., who said, "Certainly, we would agree." [30]

There is some question as to whether Healey's famous sense of humor might not again betray him and his associates. His answer in 1964 to the question, "Why are we still fighting overseas?" contained statements that could prove lethal to multitudes, if taken seriously in high quarters. "The idea that international Communism is the problem which we face in Africa and Asia is a nonsense from the start," declared Healey, "because Communism is no longer as it once was, a single monolithic bloc." [31] Did he, with typical Fabian conceit, regard himself as more than a match for the wily Russians and wilier Chinese?

Like his colleagues of the Socialist International at home and abroad, Denis Healey accepted at face value the Communist world's amoeba-like application of the ancient adage, Divide and Conquer. In a fine-spun argument that undoubtedly caused some mirth in Moscow and Peking, Healey pointed out that it was Britain's duty to seek agreements with other world powers, and above all with the Soviet Union, for achieving stability in Asia and Africa. Ever mindful of the "necessity" for being fair to the Red Chinese, he explained:

. . . in those parts of Asia where Communism is clearly at work subverting institutions of the non-Communist world, it would be a mistake to assume without evidence that Communism is centrally directed from Moscow or even from China. There is much evidence to suggest that even the Vietnamese Communist Party, although it holds heavy responsibility for Laos and South Vietnam, is not acting as a satellite of Peking.[32]

The names of Denis Healey and Patrick Gordon Walker appeared on an unusually long list of official appointments marking the advent of the Labour Party Government in Britain. A number of brand new departments had been created, sometimes with functions that overlapped the old. More than ever veteran Fabians predominated. According to the *Fabian News* of November-December, 1964, which printed a list of government appointments and conveniently marked with a cross the names of members of the Society, they filled nearly

[30] Bolko von Richthofen, "All Out of Step But Healey." *Sudeten Bulletin.* A Central European Review. (Munich, December, 1958), Vol. VI, No. 12, p. 266.

[31] Denis Healey, "Why Are We Still Fighting Overseas?" *Socialist International Information,* (July 4, 1964), Vol. XIV, No. 14.

[32] *Ibid.*

two-thirds of all ranking government posts.[33] The cross mark was inadvertently omitted from some well-known old Fabian names, such as Lord Gardiner, a former member of the Fabian Executive, Jennie Lee, Alice Bacon and others, who may have allowed their formal memberships to lapse. So the actual count was probably higher. Far from being a composite picture of youthful vigor, the Cabinet represented the unchangeable old guard of the Society. Practically all had served in one capacity or another in the Labour Government from 1945 to 1951, and their average age was fifty-seven years.

On the authority of *Fabian News,* nineteen of twenty-three Cabinet Members could be counted as belonging to the "National Fabian Society"—a term not hitherto used.[34] The others (such as Sir Frank Soskice, the new Home Secretary, or Frank Cousins of the Transport Workers Union, appointed to head the new Ministry of Technology and Science) were almost equally well-known and trusted in Fabian circles. Yet no whisper of that open secret reached the air waves or percolated into the general press.

So strictly was Fabian security maintained, that the informed *New Statesman* felt free to indulge in a little discreet private fun on the subject. "Most of the reformist movements," remarked a columnist on that Fabian-controlled weekly, "seem to have lost to the Government either a chairman or a valued committee member. Flourishing limbs have thus been lopped off the National Campaign for the Abolition of Capital Punishment, the Howard League, the Albany Trust, the New Bridge, the Josephine Butler Society and the Prison Reform Council, to name only a few. Letters of congratulatory regret have been flowing into ministers' offices." [35]

Unmentioned, of course, was the fact that names of five past chairmen of the Fabian Society turned up on the revised roster of Her Majesty's Government,[36] released by British Information Services in November, 1964. Or that nine Cabinet Members and at least five Ministers outside the Cabinet had seen service on the Fabian Execu-

---

[33] "The General Election," "The Labor Government," *Fabian News,* (November-December, 1964). See Appendix I, pp. xxxix-xli.

[34] *Ibid.* See Appendix I, p. xxxix.

[35] Quoted in the *National Review Bulletin,* (January 5, 1965), p. 7.

[36] Cf. *Fabian Society Annual Reports,* 1954-55 through 1961-62. (The five former chairmen were: Prime Minister Harold Wilson, chairman of the Society, 1954-55; Arthur Skeffington, Parliamentary Secretary to the Ministry of Land and National Resources, chairman of the Society, 1956-57; Roy Jenkins, Minister of Aviation, chairman of the Society, 1957-58; Eirene White, Under Secretary of State at the Colonial Office, chairman of the Society, 1958-59; C. A. R. Crosland, Economic Secretary to the Treasury, chairman of the Society, 1961-62.

tive.[37] These statistics were already known to delighted members and friends of the Fabian Society (sometimes referred to by Communists as a "reformist movement"), which had also relinquished most of its current officers and committee heads to the Government.

Chief Secretary of the Treasury with rank of Minister was John Diamond, a longtime honorary treasurer of the Society. Postmaster General Anthony Wedgwood Benn was the Fabian Society's current vice chairman, as well as the chairman of its combined International and Commonwealth Bureau. William Rodgers, general secretary of the Fabian Society, went to the Ministry of Economic Affairs as a parliamentary Under Secretary. Few, indeed, of that suddenly exalted company saw fit to record in *Who's Who* their lifelong organizational ties with Britain's oldest and boldest Socialist Society, bellwether of the world-wide Socialist International.

Dedicated for years to the idea of social revolution and the gradual but total extinction of private enterprise, they now preferred for publicity purposes to be described as "moderate" Socialists. In reality, there is no such breed. There are only patient and impatient Socialists—just as Dorothy Day, a left wing Catholic newspaper editor in New York, suggested long ago that there are patient and impatient virgins.[38]

So the same dreary old programs that had proved incapable once before of producing a brave new world were freshened up and given a new look by Fabian Research. Like rabbits pulled from a magician's hat, they were presented with an air of proud discovery and some variations in the patter designed to divert attention from the timeworn routine. The new Minister of Economic Affairs, George Brown, M.P., might talk ever so brightly about "the development and implementation of a national incomes policy covering all forms of income and related to productivity." But in the end, it still meant wage controls, price controls, export-import controls, and a capital levy.

Management and unions were invited to collaborate in the "plan," with government holding the whiphand and deciding just "where the

[37] *Ibid.*, p. 2. Cabinet members formerly on the Fabian Executive were: Harold Wilson, Prime Minister and First Lord of the Treasury; Lord Gardiner, Lord High Chancellor; Patrick Gordon Walker, Secretary of State for Foreign Affairs; Denis Healey, Secretary of Defense; James Griffiths, Secretary of State for Wales; The Earl of Longford, Lord Privy Seal and Leader of the House of Lords; Douglas Houghton, Chancellor of the Duchy of Lancaster; Michael Stewart, Secretary of State for Education and Science; R. H. S. Crossman, Minister of Housing and Local Government.

[38] Cf., Dorothy Day, *The Eleventh Virgin*, (New York, A. & C. Boni, 1924).

behavior of prices or wages, salaries or other money incomes is in the national interest." [39] The bureaucrats still had the last word, and for the average Briton there could be no escape and no hiding place from the government's all-seeing computers.

True, there seemed to be something different about Her Majesty's opening address to the Parliament on November 3. She no longer spoke in the first person plural, but referred instead to "*My* Armies, *My* Ministers, *My* Government." Grammatically, at least, the Queen had been stripped of the royal prerogative in an apparent move to belittle the Monarchy. Reading the text prepared by Labour Party Ministers, she likewise found herself compelled to say: "My Government will initiate early action to reestablish the necessary ownership and control of the Iron and Steel Industry . . . ." [40]

Harrying the throne had been for some time an approved left wing blood sport in England, and there is no question that it was Fabian-instigated. During the fifties Malcolm Muggeridge, a privileged scion of Fabian Socialism's first family, specialized in taking potshots at royalty. He was a nephew of the autocratic Beatrice Webb and a former Moscow correspondent. He was also a former editor of *Punch* and a contributor to the *New Statesman* as well as more highly paid weeklies in Britain and America. While he denied being a Fabian, he was frequently advertised in *Fabian News* as a speaker at the Society's meetings and weekend schools. [41]

In the sixties the Queen and her circle became the target of two sharply critical Fabian tracts. [42] With that intellectual snobbery so characteristic of the Socialist elite, it was asserted that the Court lacked appreciation of the finer things of life. Somehow those attacks on the Establishment culminated in a scheme for "integrating" the historic public schools of England into the State-controlled educa-

[39] *British Record,* Political and Economic Notes Issued by British Information Services. Supplement to British Record No. 19, (December 22, 1964).

[40] Text of Her Majesty's Most Gracious Speech to Both Houses of Parliament, (November 3, 1964), British Information Services.

[41] *Fabian News,* (April, 1963), reported that Malcolm Muggeridge, son of H. T. Muggeridge, a leading early Fabian, had contributed an article to London's *Sunday Times* entitled "Follies of the Fabians." There he stated that: "the Fabians' aloof benevolence and sublime certainties have worked on the corrupt minds of demagogic politicians to produce the telly-watching, bingo-playing, hire-purchasing democracy we have today." Nevertheless, in the same year he also contributed an article of amiable reminiscences about his family to the fiftieth anniversary issue of the *New Statesman.*

[42] John Vaizey, *Education in a Class Society. The Queen and Her Horses Reign, Fabian Tract No. 342,* (London, The Fabian Society, January, 1962).

Howard Glennerster and Richard Pryke, *The Public Schools,* Young Fabian Pamphlet, No. 7, (London, The Fabian Society, November, 1964).

tional system, at an estimated cost to public funds of 15 million pounds. The project was eagerly seconded by the incoming Labour Party Government and promised high priority on its schedule of things to come.

Britain's so-called public schools were, of course, private and independently financed boarding schools, where many of the men who contributed to England's past greatness had received their early training. If it was true, as the Duke of Wellington remarked, that the Battle of Waterloo was won on the playing fields of Eton, a future Red Napoleon should have nothing to fear from coming generations of English schoolboys. What a leading Fabian educator calls the "bad characteristics" of such schools—namely, their "emphasis on leadership and character" [43]—will presumably be eliminated by making them tuition-free and by offering their admittedly superior classroom facilities to "children who have had the least opportunities in life." [44]

According to John Vaizey of the Fabian Executive and the London School of Economics, entry to the better schools where places are scarce must be distributed on the same principle as food rationing. And he asked significantly, "Is not this the better English tradition?" [45] So despite all predictions of plenty made by Fabian orators in the 1964 election campaign, the principle of rationed scarcity was elevated to the status of an enduring tradition!

Undismayed by the slimness of his parliamentary majority, the Right Honorable Harold Wilson, M.P., Prime Minister, First Lord of the Treasury and Vice Chairman of the Socialist International,[46] announced he would proceed without delay to implant full-scale Socialism in Britain—and eventually in the world. If anyone misunderstood him, it really was not Wilson's fault.

Like his predecessors of the postwar era, Wilson's initial move was to raise four billion dollars abroad, nominally to strengthen the British pound but, in fact, to finance his government's elusive schemes for what it termed the "social democratic revolution." The first billion came from the International Monetary Fund, providentially set up twenty years earlier by Lord Keynes and described by a Socialist International spokesman as being "in essence a Socialist conception." [47]

[43] Vaizey, *op. cit.*

[44] Glennerster and Pryke, *op. cit.*

[45] Vaizey, *op. cit.*

[46] Another Vice Chairman of the Socialist International, former Foreign Minister Giuseppe Saragat, was elected President of Italy in December, 1964.

[47] Hilary Marquand, "The Theory and Practice of Planning," *Economic Development and Social Change,* (London, Socialist International Publication, no date—1962 or 1963), p. 28.

The remaining sum was contributed by eleven sympathetically minded governments, chief among them being the United States which proffered a cool billion.

Visiting Washington to confer with the newly elected President Johnson, Wilson solemnly told White House correspondents that the theme of these discussions was "interdependence." What at first blush might have seemed no more than a classic bit of Fabian impudence, was spoken in deadly earnest. For the route of "interdependence," taken in the literal sense and pursued to its logical conclusion, leads in the end to World Government: a goal to which Harold Wilson and his colleagues are profoundly pledged.

In that centennial year of the Socialist International, a Fabian Socialist clique had assumed control of the Mother of Parliaments, whether briefly or enduringly. The Labour Party Platform, which Fabians drafted and on which they stood, stated clearly: *"For us World Government is the final objective . . . ."* [48] It was no coincidence that the platform of the Socialist International, approved two years before in Oslo, proclaimed the same objective and designated the United Nations as an interim medium for achieving it. Nor was it purely wishful rhetoric when *Socialist International Information* declared that the British Labour Party's victory marked "a renaissance of the power and influence of democratic Socialism throughout the world." [49] The nineteenth century dream of Socialist World Government, which some called a specter, seemed closer to becoming a reality than ever before.

From the first, the strongest obstacles to fulfillment of that conspirators' dream had been the two great English-speaking nations. It was to capture those twin citadels of personal liberty and private initiative that the Fabian Socialist movement had originally been founded, seeking to accomplish by patient indirection what quite obviously could not be done by frontal attack. After eighty years, with Britain apparently won, all that remained was to persuade the mightiest of her erstwhile colonies to renounce independence without a struggle. And then . . . .

What deterred the Fabian tortoise from striking, and striking hard, was the slight matter of a parliamentary majority—and the abiding

[48] *The New Britain. The Labour Party's Manifesto for the 1964 General Election.* (London, The Labour Party, Transport House, 1964), p. 22. (Italics added.)
[49] "The Significance of the Labour Party's Victory," *Socialist International Information,* (October 24, 1964), Vol. XIV, No. 23.

common sense of the British people. With Churchill lingering on his deathbed, Englishmen were moved somehow to remember their fighting heritage and to ignore the counsels of submission. They may also have been influenced by the fact that in less than one hundred days of the Wilson government, the price of virtually every household article had soared—due in part to the new 15 per cent tax on imports, in part to the weakness of the pound sterling. Capital was in flight, and who could blame it?

Thus when Patrick Gordon Walker stood again for a presumably safe seat in Parliament, for the second time he suffered an inglorious defeat. The Labour Party's margin in Parliament was by then reduced to three, with four safe Conservative seats yet to be filled. Nine Liberals in the House had already served notice that they would not vote with Labour on the issue of steel nationalization. Unless a miracle occurred, or unless Wilson could manage to sidestep every controversial issue, it looked very much as if he would be forced to call another general election in a matter of weeks—or months.

Meanwhile, Patrick Gordon Walker resigned as Foreign Secretary. The post went to Michael Stewart, recent Secretary of State for Education and Science—another professor, like Wilson and Gordon Walker. Young Anthony Crosland of the Fabian Executive moved up from a lesser spot in the Treasury to be Secretary of State for Education. And for the first time since October there was gloom at 10 Downing Street. The Prime Minister no longer whistled as he polished his boots.

In the face of all the portents, however, Wilson was grimly determined to hang on. The appointment of Michael Stewart as Foreign Secretary was further proof that the Prime Minister did not propose to trim his Socialist sails. Though Stewart was described by press correspondents as a relative unknown, this only meant his background was relatively unknown to the public. In Fabian Socialist circles he was very well-known indeed.

Ten years older than Wilson, Michael Stewart began his career as a young Fabian Socialist official in the Royal Household during 1931. Some years later he stood for the House of Commons, becoming a parliamentary secretary in the Labour Government from 1945 to 1951. He and his wife Mary were another of those high-level Fabian husband-and-wife teams, comparable in spirit if not in productivity to the Webbs or the Coles. In 1962-63 Mary Stewart served as chairman of the Fabian Executive; while Michael owed his ideas on foreign affairs to years of service with the Fabian International Bureau and its important directing committee.[50] He was the author of *Fabian Tract No. 296*, published in 1955 by the International Bureau: *Policy and Weapons in the Nuclear Age*.[51]

In January, 1958, Michael Stewart approvingly reviewed Professor Blackett's book, *Atomic Weapons and East-West Relations*,[52] in which the theory of the "minimum deterrent" was advanced. "It is hard to dispute the main contention," wrote the future Foreign Secretary in a properly defeatist vein, "that an attempt to keep world peace by striving for a permanent Western superiority in science and technique is bound to fail . . . ."

Whether or not the Fabian-packed Labour Party Government was able to hang on, Britain's Fabian Socialist movement would remain a formidable and destructive power in the future as it had proved to be in the past. Its connections and its influence are world-wide; it has demonstrated more than once that it can be as dangerous in defeat as in victory. Following a political failure at home in 1931, it proceeded to develop really effective plans and means for the greatest coup of its history: the penetration and transformation of the United States of America. And with the help of American admirers, Fabians were returned to office some years later in England. The wealth and power of the largely unsuspecting United States is still the Fabian Society's trump card.

Certainly no tears were detected in official circles in Washington when Wilson's Labour Party was handily reelected on March 30, 1966, winning a substantial parliamentary majority. This victory empowered Wilson to move forward along Socialist lines as rapidly as he could do so without alienating the Commonwealth countries or embarrassing his American friends. It also seemed to assure Fabian control in Britain for a full five years to come. By the end of that time, who knows? In the words of an old, sad song, "It may be for years, or it may be forever."

---

[50] *Fabian Society 75th Annual Report, 1957-58*, p. 20. Under the heading, "Members of Main Committees," Michael Stewart is listed as a member of the International Bureau Committee. *Fabian Society 80th Annual Report, 1962-63*, p. 4, announces the election of Mary Stewart as chairman of the Fabian Executive.

[51] With Rex Winsbury, a past chairman of the Young Fabian Group, Michael Stewart was also the author in October, 1963 of *Fabian Tract No. 350, An Incomes Policy for Labour*. Stewart was described as "an economist and prospective parliamentary candidate for Folkestone and Hythe."

[52] "Grim but Enthralling," *Fabian News*, (January, 1958).

II

THE UNITED STATES

9

The Fabian Turtle Discovers America

SHORTLY after the New Year in 1888, a shy, frail and previously undiscovered young American awoke to a new life. For the next ten years—until his death at the age of forty-eight—he was not only to experience the rewards of literary success but to be acclaimed as the lay prophet of a new and fashionable political cult. His name, Edward Bellamy, would soon be known from Massachusetts to California, and even in such world capitals as London, Paris and Berlin. The reason? One of the most ingenious manuscripts ever received by Benjamin Ticknor of the Boston publishing firm, Lee and Shepherd, had just been published over Bellamy's signature, and it proved to be the best-selling American novel since *Uncle Tom's Cabin*.

Edward Bellamy was a former editorial writer and book reviewer who appeared to have been something of a drifter. Son of a New England minister, he had studied for a few terms at Union College in Schenectady and then spent a year in Dresden, Germany, where he pursued an already awakened interest in Socialism.[1] Everything he started seemed to be cut short either by illness or his own restless temperament; for Bellamy suffered intermittently from tuberculosis, that plague of early America.

Returning from Europe Bellamy prepared for the bar, but practiced only briefly. Instead he went to New York City with a letter of recommendation from Colonel Thomas Wentworth Higginson, the well-known Abolitionist and latter-day Socialist, and began writing for the New York *Evening Post*. When he was only twenty-two, Bellamy

[1] Sylvia E. Bowman, *The Year 2000—A Critical Biography of Edward Bellamy*, (New York, Bookman Associates, 1958), pp. 97-98.

delivered a lyceum address on the "barbarism" of competitive industry and the beauties of a socialized system, which apparently resulted in his leaving New York and joining the staff of the Springfield *Union.*

Poor health made regular work difficult; but an early retirement brought Bellamy the fame that had so far escaped him. Though he had published some two dozen short stories in respected American magazines of the day, his circle of admirers was small. Settling down in the little cotton-mill town where he was born and fortifying himself with generous infusions of whiskey and black coffee, he produced several novels that gained him but slight attention. At last he wrote *Looking Backward,* the tale of an American utopia and a singularly effective piece of propaganda for a non-American doctrine.

Like many another popular novel, it was not destined to become a classic. By now it remains little more than a literary curiosity, buried in libraries throughout the world and resurrected only occasionally. A briefer edition, reprinted in the nineteen-thirties,[2] gives hardly a clue to its original impact. When the book first appeared, however, it was noted for its novelty and for the fact that it was a socialist romance which never once mentioned Socialism.

A book review of March 29, 1888, in *The Nation* (then owned by the New York *Evening Post,* where Bellamy had been a contributor) did not hesitate to mention the proscribed word. Hailing the work as a "glowing prophecy and gospel of peace," the anonymous critic added that even if Bellamy's schemes for solving the land question "ought theoretically to have restored the society of ancient Peru instead of bringing about the millennium, . . . Mr. George himself would rejoice in a realized ideal of Socialism such as this."

The "Mr. George" referred to was, of course, Henry George, author of *Progress and Poverty,* who had run unsuccessfully for mayor of New York City less than two years before and polled the surprising total of 67,000 votes—7,000 more than a muscular young Republican named Theodore Roosevelt. As *The Nation's* reviewer noted, the brand of Socialism offered in fiction-coated form by Bellamy was stronger medicine than any prescribed by Henry George, who urged a Single Tax on land as the remedy for humanity's ills. *Looking Backward* predicted that America's golden age would be achieved not merely

---

[2] Modern Library Edition, New York, Random House, no date, with a foreword by Heywood Broun. A new British edition of *Looking Backward* was published in 1948 and advertised in *Fabian News,* shortly after the Communist Party issued a directive on reviving "native Communism."

by making real estate unprofitable, but by making all other investments equally unprofitable.

This marvel was to be wrought, presumably by peaceful means, through "the national organization of labor under a single direction." For like its predecessor, *Uncle Tom's Cabin*, which had sparked anti-slavery agitation in New England, *Looking Backward* was Abolitionist in spirit. In the most polite and indirect way, it preached to the questing Puritan conscience the abolition of "wage slavery."

There was nothing accidental about it, as some biographers assert today. In the same year that Edward Bellamy began writing his long-projected utopian novel, Karl Marx's daughter Eleanor—George Bernard Shaw's Dark Lady[3]—toured the United States, noticed a great deal of "unconscious Socialism," and announced that some day "the *Uncle Tom's Cabin* of Capitalism would be written." [4] A mutual friend, Laurence Gronlund, transmitted the word to Bellamy, with a further specification that the book should be designed to attract persons of "judgement and culture." Five other utopian novels were published in 1888; but Bellamy's was the only one to be promoted by a clique of Socialist-tinged intellectuals even then in the process of formation. Though its popularity waned as fashions in fiction changed, the long-range movement it served to launch has persisted in various related forms for some three-quarters of a century.

Julian West, the hero of *Looking Backward*, was a properly well-to-do Bostonian of the type Bellamy and Gronlund hoped to reach. In 2000 A.D. Julian awoke from a long, hypnotic sleep to find that the United States had evolved painlessly into something called the Cooperative Commonwealth, where everyone was happy, comfortable and behaved like an angel. Looking backward, he was able to detect many flaws in the society of his birth and to perceive that they had all been corrected by the new collectivist system. It was, as the British social evangelist, William Morris, rather snobbishly remarked, "a cockney Paradise" which he personally would not care to inhabit.[5]

Sweetened by a sentimental love-interest, this optimistic fantasy appealed to America's kindly, culture-hungry middle class, in an era when the routine of daily life was brightened by the Lend-a-Hand Clubs and the Chatauqua Circles. For a time *Looking Backward* sold

[3] Hesketh Pearson, *Bernard Shaw*, (London, Methuen & Co., Ltd., 1961), p. 120.

[4] Bowman, *op. cit.*, pp. 116-117.

[5] E. P. Thompson, "William Morris," *Monthly Press Review*, (New York, 1961), p. 632. Letter from Morris to Glasier, May 13, 1889.

at the then fantastic rate of a thousand copies a day. Total sales in the United States eventually topped half a million and in England reached nearly half that amount. As a result, Edward Bellamy became the figurehead and symbol of an American Fabian Socialist movement, whose future pattern of growth he could not foresee in detail. British Fabians, however, and their disciples in the United States were available to guide its development, from the eager beginnings to the grim conclusion which a veteran American Socialist, Upton Sinclair,[6] assures us blithely was never closer than it is today.

Lee and Shepherd, original publishers of *Looking Backward*, were promptly besieged with questions about its unknown author. Among others, Frances E. Willard, then heading the very respectable National Council of Women in Washington, D.C., wrote to a friend employed by the firm: "Have been reading Edward Bellamy's *Looking Backward* and think it's a revelation and an Evangel. Who and where is he? . . . What manner of man is he in private?" To which she received the reply: "We do not know, except that his letters are mailed from Chicopee Falls, Massachusetts."[7] Three weeks later Frances Willard, ever an ardent advocate of women's causes, wrote to say, "Some of us think that Edward Bellamy must be Edwardina —that a big-hearted, big-brained woman wrote the book. Won't you please find out?"

As the moving spirit of the International Women's Christian Temperance Union, Frances E. Willard was a lifelong intimate of English temperance leader Lady Henry Somerset and a perennial house guest at her country estate. Like a number of early American feminists and reformers, Frances Willard also joined the Fabian Society of London.[8] Though disappointed to learn that the author of *Looking Backward* was no female, her enthusiasm for the novel was not diminished. Frances Willard quickly brought it to the attention of British friends and claimed credit for introducing the book to students at Oxford, besides commending it to her many lecture audiences in America. In a face-to-face discussion, Bellamy even persuaded her that references to after-dinner wine and cigars in the year 2000 were permissible,

---

[6] In a television interview with Upton Sinclair by Paul Coates, originating at Station KTTV, Los Angeles, May, 1962.

[7] Frances E. Willard, "An Interview with Edward Bellamy," *Our Day*, Vol. IV, 1889.

[8] William A. Clarke, "The Fabian Society," *New England Magazine*, (March, 1894), p. 91.

since by then the curse of intemperance would have been safely removed.

In private life, Edward Bellamy was addicted to stronger beverages than wine;[9] but his frequent inability to appear in public was usually ascribed to "dyspepsia." He was no less guarded about revealing the origins of his Socialist creed. In a letter to William Dean Howells, the silver-haired New England poet and essayist, he stated: "I have never been a student of Socialist literature, or have known more of Socialist schemes than any reader of newspapers might." This careful denial may be doubted, for Bellamy was a voracious reader of German as well as English books. In his lyceum address of 1872, he had already shown more than a bowing acquaintance with Socialist doctrines.

To others, he "confessed" that he learned all he knew of "scientific Socialism" from a little volume by Laurence Gronlund, a Danish-American lawyer then living in Philadelphia. It was called *The Co-operative Commonwealth*—a term that modern Socialists still use interchangeably with the term "industrial democracy," given currency some years later by Sidney and Beatrice Webb. Published in 1884, also by Lee and Shepherd, *The Cooperative Commonwealth* was the first book deliberately to present the doctrines of Marxian Socialism in non-Marxist terms for American readers. Four years later Gronlund ordered his own work withdrawn from circulation, in order to help promote the sales of his friend Bellamy's novel—a rare example of literary altruism.

Educated in Europe, Laurence Gronlund was already a full-blown Marxist when he emigrated to the United States. As a lawyer, teacher and would-be labor organizer in this country, he had come to the conclusion that neither European methods nor an alien terminology could ever succeed in making Socialism acceptable to the great majority of Americans.[10] Social revolution must be disguised. It must be a gradualist movement for social reform. Perhaps it was not purely by coincidence that a similar idea occurred at precisely the same time to the founders of the London Fabian Society. This idea coincided with the long-term plan for England and America of the two tireless arch-conspirators, Karl Marx and Frederick Engels, from whom modern Social Democracy stems.

As early as 1872 Karl Marx, speaking in Amsterdam, had intimated

[9] Bowman, *op. cit.*, pp. 149-150.
[10] Richard T. Ely, *Socialism and Social Reform*, (Boston, T. Y. Crowell & Co., 1894), p. 102.

that social revolution might be accomplished by peaceful means in England and America—that is, by taking advantage of libertarian traditions and free institutions to subvert them. Both countries were well-known to Marx and had treated him kindly. London was his home during years of exile. There he set up the First International, known as the Workingmen's International Association, on September 28, 1864 at a public meeting in St. Martin's Hall, Long Acre. While Marx never visited the United States, the weekly five dollars which he received as a special correspondent for the New York *Tribune* was for a time his chief source of income.[11] He sent articles on the Crimean War to that newspaper, whose editor, Horace Greeley, likewise called himself a Socialist—although Greeley seems to have perceived little difference between the utopian farm colonies inspired in antebellum America by Charles Fourier and Robert Owen and the "scientific socialism" of a Karl Marx.

The father of modern Social Democracy believed that in certain respects the United States held the key to world revolution. In the preface to Volume I of *Das Kapital,* Marx wrote: "As in the eighteenth century, the American War of Independence sounded the tocsin for the European middle class, the American Civil War sounded it for the European working class."

Following the collapse of the Paris Commune which he had backed after its formation, Marx ordered the headquarters of his First International transferred to New York City in 1872, under the direction of a trusted aide, Friedrich Adolph Sorge. Seventy years later a grandson of that selfsame Sorge headed a Communist spy ring in Tokyo, whose intrigues precipitated the Japanese decision to strike southward at Pearl Harbor and brought the United States into World War II in time to save Communist Russia.

In his lifetime, Karl Marx freely deplored the fact that his Socialist followers in the United States were no more than a displaced group of angry trade unionists—refugees from the revolutions of 1848 and 1870. Their meetings were held and minutes were written in German. Socially, politically and psychologically, they were not only isolated from the main current of American life, but for years they rebuffed attempts by English-speaking Socialists to join them. Laurence Gronlund; his friend Charles Southeran, the biographer of Horace Greeley; and Florence Kelley, who translated Engels' *Condition of the Work-*

[11] John Spargo, *Socialism,* A Summary and Interpretation of Socialist Principles, (New York, The Macmillan Company, 1913), p. 210.

ing Class in England in 1844 (pristine Marxists, all), were expelled in turn from America's Socialist Labor Party for being unorthodox—and non-German.

A British Fabian Socialist and charter member of the London Fabian Society, Edward R. Pease, once observed tartly that the early Social Democrats in the United States resembled some small dogmatic sect whose every action required a Marxian text to sanctify it.[12] For years, this remained the characteristic mood of working-class Socialism in America. Though the General German Workingmen's Union and the Socialist Labor Party made some temporary headway in centers of immigrant population—notably New York City, where the slogan "Down with German Socialism and German *lager!*" became a war cry of Tammany Hall—Engels remarked in a private letter to Sorge that the disappearance of the stubborn, unruly old German comrades would be a healthy thing for the Socialist movement in America. Revolutions and barricades, dynamite and rifles were all the talk among the German-American Marxists of the eighties, and anybody who suggested anything else was unworthy of the name of Socialist.

The decade had been a stormy one for the comrades. In Russia, social revolutionaries conspired to kill grand dukes and ministers of state, and in 1882 had actually succeeded in assassinating the Czar. In Chicago three German-American Anarchists and one native American, Albert Parsons, were hanged in 1887 for complicity in the Haymarket Square bombings the year before. Socialist protests against these executions had led the American public to believe that Socialists and Anarchists were identical—and in some instances, they were, as persistent Anarchist infiltration of the First International and the Socialist Labor Party demonstrated.

To the average American of the eighties, as Edward Bellamy said, the very word Socialism brought to mind ideas of atheism, revolution and sexual novelties. Visits to the United States in 1884 by Frederick Engels and in 1886 by Wilhelm Liebknecht, a co-founder of Germany's Social Democratic Party, did nothing to dispel that impression. Engels' godless views on religion and marriage, as expressed in his *Origin of the Family*, were widely publicized. Wilhelm Liebknecht, who prophesied the future triumph of Socialism in the United States

[12] Edward R. Pease, *History of Socialism*, (London, A. & C. Black, 1913), p. 339.

one Sunday afternoon at Brommer's Park in New York City,[13] was accompanied by Eleanor Marx and her common-law husband, Edward Aveling, translator of *Das Kapital* into English. During a fifteen week lecture tour as guests of the Socialist Labor Party, the couple's un-conventional union provoked a public scandal. Here, it seemed, was living proof that Socialists favored free love and flouted family ties; and the topic was revived at intervals long after the unhappy Eleanor Marx, in England, had committed suicide as a result of Aveling's desertion.

Abhorred by native American workingmen and members of the urban middle class, Socialist ideas nevertheless began in the middle eighties to exert a certain fascination in learned circles. They were spread by professors and students of a new, somewhat occult science known as Political Economy. Foremost among these campus sooth-sayers was Professor Richard T. Ely of Johns Hopkins University—later of the University of Wisconsin, where, notably, he influenced the thought of a future governor of Wisconsin and Progressive Sena-tor, Robert M. La Follette, Sr. It was Professor Ely who took the initiative in organizing the American Economic Association, which convened for the first time on September 9, 1885, at the fashionable United States Hotel in Saratoga, New York.[14]

Minutes of this historic meeting show that the Socialist-minded element at once captured a majority of the Association's elective offices. Professor Ely, who served as chairman, was voted general secretary of the organization. Two like-minded colleagues, Professors H. C. Adams of Cornell and E. J. James of Pennsylvania, were elected first and second vice presidents; and Professor E. W. Bemis (later on the faculty of the University of Chicago) attended as secretary of the Connecticut branch. Included among the several hundred charter members, not yet a recognized authority, was the future Professor John R. Commons of Indiana and Michigan Universities, whose out-line of political economy became a standard textbook for several generations of college students throughout the country.

Those five were the main leaders of academic socialism,[15] which in their day cast a shadow no larger than a man's hand. They argued privately, and sometimes publicly, for the municipal or national owner-

---

[13] *The New York Times*, (September 21, 1886).

[14] *Minutes of the American Economic Association*, Vol. I.

[15] W. D. P. Bliss, *A Handbook of Socialism*, (London, Sonnenschein, 1895), p. 146.

ship of what they termed "natural monopolies," but for the time being did not profess to the full Socialist program of nationalizing all land and capital.[16] The new learned society provided a dignified sounding board for their doctrines, as it does for their modern counterparts. It is interesting to note that the American Economic Association very soon published over its imprint two essays by an amateur economist who also happened to be the chairman of the London Fabian Society —the emerging Sidney Webb.

Lending the authority of the cloth to the Association's original meeting were the Reverend Lyman Abbott and the Reverend Washington Gladden, both to become prominent in the Christian Socialist movement. There was also Dr. E. R. A. Seligman of Columbia, the Association's first treasurer, who became something of a power behind the scenes in national politics as well as in the academic world. Member of a wealthy German-American banking family in New York and privately tutored as a lad by Horatio Alger of the rags-to-riches precepts, Dr. Seligman was usually regarded as a conservative; yet throughout a long lifetime he condoned every heterodoxy in the name of academic freedom. The Reverend Abbott (a future editor of The Outlook) and Dr. Seligman were promptly named to the council of the American Economic Association together with a reserved, lantern-jawed young associate professor from Bryn Mawr College, Dr. Woodrow Wilson, who none suspected would one day be President of the United States.

Appointed to the Labor Committee was Woodrow Wilson's good friend, Dr. Albert Shaw, then editor of the Tribune in Minneapolis with its strongly German-Socialist population, and later chosen to edit the influential Review of Reviews. Dr. Shaw's personal contacts with British Fabians were established in the nineties, when he published a book entitled Municipal Government in Great Britain.

Other characters of incidental interest attending the founders' meeting of the American Economic Association were Thomas Davidson, who had inadvertently helped to found the Fabian Society of London, and F. H. Giddings, editor of the Springfield Union, where Edward Bellamy was employed for five years. It must be recorded that representation from the New England colleges was slight and not a single professor from Harvard was elected to office that year—an omission long since rectified. In those post Civil War years education was moving westward, along with the expanding economy.

At its annual meeting three years later, members of the same Asso-

[16] Ibid.

ciation listened to a paper by a solemn, bearded little Englishman wearing a beribboned pince-nez. It was Sidney Webb in person, appearing as an emissary of the British Economic Association (afterwards the Royal Economic Society) which a fellow-Fabian, George Bernard Shaw, had been instrumental in founding. Flanked by his faithful lieutenant, Edward R. Pease, Webb came to America for the first time in September, 1888, and remained for a full three months.[17] In his portmanteau he carried the manuscript of an essay, "The Historical Aspects of the Basis of Socialism"—shortly to be published as "Socialism in England" over the imprint of the American Economic Association, and later included in the *Fabian Essays*, for whose American edition of 1894 Edward Bellamy wrote a foreword.

In America of the late eighteen-eighties the cocksure young Londoner found a strange new world, pulsating and throbbing with gigantic economic forces that were producing fresh forms of wealth undreamed of by even the most utopian imagination;[18] but his conceit was equal to the challenge. He had no scruples in recommending the same gradualist tactics of revolution which he felt were destined to conquer England for Socialism. To Webb's calculating eye, it was plain that any frontal attack against the vast new citadel of capitalism was doomed to failure. In fact, owing to the furor already created by a handful of Anarchists and militant Socialists, the little Socialist movement in the United States faced the possibility of being outlawed by act of Congress unless it could speedily muster the support of a large body of respectable middle class opinion around the country.

For that purpose Edward Bellamy's well-contrived novel, which its author acknowledged was written "to convert the cultured and conservative classes," provided a practical springboard. New England with its close cultural ties to Old England and its susceptibility to New Thought of all kinds, seemed the logical place from which to launch a new and less vulnerable type of Socialist movement. Sentimental memories still lingered there of Brook Farm and other utopian communities, and the influence of the English Christian Socialists had lately made itself felt through the writings of Dr. Elisha Mulford and the Reverend Washington Gladden. Theosophy, which stressed the brotherhood of a fatherless humanity, was also winning converts. Bos-

---

[17] Edward R. Pease, *The History of the Fabian Society*, (London, A. C. Fifield, 1916), pp. 75-76.

[18] Max Beer, *Fifty Years of International Socialism*, (London, Allen & Unwin, 1937), p. 109.

tonians had heard of the beautiful Annie Besant, a leading British Theosophist who was likewise a member of the London Fabian Society.

When Sidney Webb and Edward Pease appeared in Boston during the autumn of 1888, armed with letters of introduction to literary folk, college professors, clergymen and assorted uplifters, no more than ten thousand copies of *Looking Backward* had been sold.[19] Enough to make it a best-seller at the time, but only a glimmering of what was to come! While literary promotion was not the Fabians' prime purpose, from first to last they have never objected to making the fortune of an author or a publisher, provided they could, in the process, create a cordial climate of opinion for Socialism. Chief beneficiary in this instance was the Houghton Mifflin Company,[20] which purchased the rights from Lee and Shepherd and, as a result of certain activities set in motion by the two English visitors, was able to develop Bellamy's book into a uniquely valuable property.

The previous June, a pair of Boston newspapermen had already written to Bellamy expressing their desire to form a club for the propagation of his ideas. They were Cyrus Field Willard, labor reporter for the Boston *Globe* and a relative of Frances E. Willard, and Sylvester Baxter, editorial writer for the Boston *Herald*, who had penned the first ecstatic review of *Looking Backward*. Both were Theosophists, devotees of Madame Blavatsky and Annie Besant. Since summer hardly seemed the best season for rounding up an organization of cultured Bostonians, Baxter seized the opportunity for making a trip to Germany with a stopover in London.

Meanwhile, several former army officers in Boston wrote to Bellamy on September 7 telling him of their own plan to found a club in his name. The leaders were Captain Charles E. Bowers and General Arthur F. Devereux, a Civil War hero who had made a name for himself at Gettysburg. Whatever their intention, it was certainly not to advance the cause of Socialism. In common with other thoughtful citizens, they viewed the sudden eruption of trusts and monopolies in the United States with concern. At the same time, they could not fail to be aware of the problems created by wave after wave of immigrant

---

[19] Edward Bellamy, *Edward Bellamy Speaks Again*, (Kansas City, Peerage Press, 1939), p. 206. This sales statement was made by Bellamy himself.

[20] Bowman, *op. cit.*, p. 115. A new edition subsequently issued by Houghton, Mifflin was based on the amended text prepared by Bellamy in 1888 for Rabbi Solomon Schindler of Boston, who translated *Looking Backward* into German.

labor pouring into a country largely unprepared to receive them, so that the newcomers were often victimized both by earlier arrivals from their own native lands and by chaotic new conditions of industry.

In establishing a club "for the elevation of man," General Devereux and his friends hoped to suggest the need for specific reform measures to both major political parties in America before the problems at hand became too acute for an orderly solution. On September 18 their little group, named the Boston Bellamy Club, held an initial meeting with twenty-seven charter members. At this point it began to look as if more patriotic elements had stolen a march on the Socialists. In haste, Edward Bellamy sent a letter from his retreat in Chicopee Falls, begging the military men to postpone further meetings and to unite with the group which Willard and Baxter still hoped to organize. The moment was a delicate one, calling for some diplomacy, and just then, as if by prearrangement, a master diplomat in embryo, Sidney Webb, appeared on the scene. Minutes of the British Fabian Society indicate that by September 21 Webb had already left London for the United States.

In October a conference was held, and the two factions agreed to combine. On December 6 a committee was named to draft a joint statement of policy quite unlike that previously adopted by the military group. Besides the two army officers and the two journalists, another voice was introduced on the committee. It was the voice of the Reverend W. D. P. Bliss, carefully prompted by Sidney Webb. Bliss was a local clergyman, soon to assume the duties of pastor at Grace Church in South Boston and to be dismissed a few years afterwards for his Socialist activities, Christian and otherwise.

Born in Constantinople of American missionary parents, Bliss was a frequent visitor to London where he fell under the Fabian spell. For some twenty years he proved himself an eager spokesman of Fabian Socialism in the United States and an exponent of the superior virtues of the London Fabian Society. As a writer, editor and organizer, he was almost abject in his adulation of Webb and Pease, who sometimes found themselves embarrassed by his misplaced zeal. Ousted from one church after another and unable to support himself by writing, he later secured a position with the United States Bureau of Labor— the first but by no means the last old Socialist to withdraw to that snug harbor.

The twelve weeks Webb and Pease spent in the United States during the autumn of 1888 coincided exactly with the period when the revised Boston Bellamy Club was in process of being formed. In certain respects the club was similar to the London Fabian Society, with a declaration of principles corresponding to the Fabian *Basis,* and subscribed to by members of the parent club and affiliates to be set up throughout the country. The name proposed for the new organization was typical of the Webb talent for compromise. It was to be called the Nationalist Club, a name which appealed on one hand to patriotic pride, and on the other hand suggested the club's final goal: namely, the nationalization of private industry. The purpose of the club was to "educate" the American people through lectures, books and publications in the reform measures and general ideas advocated by *Looking Backward,* and thereby to stimulate such political action as might ultimately lead to the establishment of the Cooperative Commonwealth—a polite synonym for the all-embracing State foretold in other terms by Marx and Engels.

The declaration of principles showed the imprint of Sidney Webb's hand, down to the use of the words "practical" and "practicability" which characterized so many impractical documents drafted by him over the years.[21] The statement is worth quoting at least in part, because of its devious nature and because of its subsequent acceptance by thousands of well-meaning, if ingenuous, Americans:

The principle of the Brotherhood of Humanity is one of the eternal truths that govern the world's progress on lines which distinguish human nature from brute nature . . . .

No truth can avail unless *practically* applied. Therefore those who seek the welfare of man must endeavor to suppress the system founded on brute principles of competition and put in its place another based on the nobler principles of association . . . .

We advocate no sudden or ill-considered changes; we make no war upon individuals who have accumulated immense fortunes simply by carrying to a logical end the false principles upon which business is now based.

The combinations, trusts and syndicates of which the people at present complain demonstrate the *practicability* of our basic principle of associa-

---

[21] See "Labour and the New Social Order," written by Webb and adopted by the British Labour Party Conference in June, 1918, which similarly denounces "the competitive struggle" and advocates "the socialisation of industry so as to secure the elimination of every kind of inefficiency and waste." It also refers to "practical programmes of the Labour Party often carelessly derided as impracticable."

tion. We merely seek to push this principle a little further and have *all* industries operated in the interests of the nation—the people organized— the organic unity of the whole people.[22]

At a meeting on December 15, 1888, where Edward Bellamy made one of his rare personal appearances and was elected vice president of the club, this declaration was approved by the leaders. Private papers of the president, General Devereux, reveal that a member of the Fabian Society of London, presumed to be Sidney Webb himself, attended *incognito*. The same statement was read and adopted by the general membership at the first public meeting of the Boston National- ist Club in Tremont Hall on January 18, 1889.

By that date Sidney Webb had returned to England, leaving behind a lively memento of his visit. Historically, it was only the first in a long series of informally linked undertakings to be promoted under Fabian Socialist tutelage in the United States. All have been marked by the same superficial candor and mildness, and an air of bland self-righteousness which seems to be the peculiar contribution of New England to the American psyche. And yet, from the very beginning, all these organizations were penetrated at the core by a Fabian So- cialist conspiracy to capture the mind of America and eventually the machinery of government, in the interests of a revolutionary future wholly alien to the American tradition.

[22] (Italics added.)

10

Putting The Silk Hat On Socialism

1.

FOR a few years, the Bellamy cult spread like a brush fire across the United States. By November, 1890, its leaders reported 158 Nationalist clubs in twenty-seven states. Sixteen of these clubs were located in New York and sixty-five in California, which Laurence Gronlund exuberantly judged to be more nearly ripe for the Cooperative Commonwealth than any other state in the Union. The movement bypassed former Confederate states and made few overtures to the Catholic church, generally viewed in the nineteenth century as an immigrant church—notwithstanding the fact that Catholic colonists in Maryland and Pennsylvania had fought almost to a man in the War of Independence.

According to Edward Bellamy, his new social gospel was to be spread "not by foreign malcontents, but by Americans descended from generations of Americans." In February, 1891, 165 chartered clubs existed throughout the country, a majority of them in the Far and Middle West. Fully fifty newspapers supported the Nationalist cause in whole or in part, and Sylvester Baxter declared you could not go into a major newspaper office in New York, Philadelphia or Boston without finding one or more Nationalists on the staff. Though the *Atlantic* remained aloof, other respected monthly magazines of the age opened their pages to Nationalist propaganda. Bellamy himself contributed a brief article to the *North American Review* on the "Progress of Nationalism in the United States." [1]

[1] Edward Bellamy, "Progress of Nationalism in the United States," *North American Review*, CL, (June, 1892), pp. 362-363.

The first issue of a brand-new periodical called *The Literary Digest,* launched in March, 1890, featured a lead article by General Francis A. Walker, president of Massachusetts Institute of Technology and original president of the American Economic Association. It was a critique, mildly critical but none the less friendly, of that much-reviewed novel, *Looking Backward.* Early numbers of *The Literary Digest* were loaded with references to Nationalism in America and Socialism in Great Britain, though no connection between the two was inferred. There were items on Nationalist clubs in California and elsewhere; as well as an article by one Angelo Majorama on "Socialism in England," reporting that "Socialism has invaded the Universities" and "in England is closely allied with religion." And the reelection of Annie Besant to the London School Board was politely noted.

Repeatedly, the middle class character of the Nationalist clubs was stressed—especially in their own club notes, printed in a short-lived official monthly, *The Nationalist.* Started in Boston with fifty members, the clubs attracted some rather well-known personalities of the day; and the movement as a whole was stamped with the hallmark of New England culture. The membership of the Boston club was a good deal more impressive, if less cohesive, than the London Fabian Society's had been at the time of its founding only five years earlier.

There was William Dean Howells, venerable and kindly dean of American letters;[2] the Reverend Edward Everett Hale, product of the Harvard Divinity School and scion of Mayflower Pilgrims, widely known as the author of that patriotic classic, *The Man Without a Country;* Hamlin Garland, writer of homespun tales from the midwestern prairies; and John Storr Cobb, a founder of the Theosophical Society in America. While subscribing to the club's Socialist program, most of these respectable gentlemen were apparently unaware of the Marxist philosophy that prompted it. Each in his own fashion was a prototype of the non-analytical do-gooder who has contributed so

[2] In February, 1898 William Dean Howells was quoted as saying: "It was ten years ago that I first became interested in the creed of Socialism. I was in Buffalo when Laurence Gronlund lectured there before the Fortnightly Club. Through this address I was led to read his book, *The Cooperative Commonwealth,* and Kirkup's article in the *Encyclopaedia Britannica.* Afterward I read the *Fabian Essays;* I was greatly influenced also by a number of William Morris's tracts. The greatest influence, however, came to me through reading Tolstoi. Both as an artist and as a moralist I must acknowledge my deep indebtedness to him." *The American Fabian,* (February, 1898), p. 2. Published in an article signed G. for Gronlund.

liberally ever since to the spread of what Eleanor Marx called "unconscious Socialism" in America.

Like the Fabian Society of London, the Nationalist clubs welcomed members of both sexes, a somewhat daring innovation in a nineteenth century politico-cultural movement. Active women who joined the Boston club included Julia Ward Howe, author of "The Battle Hymn of the Republic"; Frances E. Willard, reformer and temperance leader; Anne Whitney, the sculptress who made a bust of James A. Walker, president of Harvard University; Mary A. Livermore, editor and suffragette; and Lucy Stone, the feminist whose followers embarrassed three decades of hotel clerks by their insistence that married ladies should use their maiden names.

In Fort Dodge, Iowa, and Fall River, Massachusetts, it was said the best people in town attended Nationalist meetings. In San Francisco, a popular rabbi resigned from his synagogue to preach the tidings of Nationalism to Jew and Gentile alike. The Chicago club, which assembled by written invitation on May 6, 1889, in the gilt and plush elegance of the recently opened Palmer House, was composed of merchants, bank officers, lawyers and other presumably solid citizens. Nationalist groups, like their cousins of the British Fabian Society, always claimed to have the working man's welfare at heart, but apparently desired few personal contacts with him.

A handful of confirmed Socialists steered the organizational work and controlled policy statements. Besides Bellamy himself, they included Laurence Gronlund, the bridge from an earlier Marxism; Eltweed Pomeroy, owner of an industrial plant in New Jersey, who sponsored one of the country's first employee profit-sharing schemes; and the Reverend W. D. P. Bliss, Fabian apostle to the clergy, who spent much of his time trying to convince various Protestant churchmen and their flocks that Christianity and Socialism were compatible in practice—contrary to what they might chance to read in Papal Encyclicals.[3] On Manhattan Island, Percival Chubb, a charter member of the

[3] In three Encyclicals Pope Leo XIII traced the social rules to be followed by Christian democrats: 1) In "Quod Apostolici Muneris," December 28, 1878, he indicated that "the equality existing among the various members of society consists only in this: that all men have their origin in God the Creator, have been redeemed by Jesus Christ, and are to be judged and rewarded or punished by God exactly according to their merits or demerits." 2) In "Rerum Novarum," May 15, 1891, he affirmed that "the right of private property, the fruit of labor or industry, or of concession or donation by others is an incontrovertible natural right; and everybody can dispose reasonably of such property as he thinks fit."

London Fabian Society who sailed to America in 1888 and lived there till his death at the age of ninety-nine, proselyted cheerfully among the Ethical Culturists.[4]

In their delight at the movement's sudden growth, its organizers failed to follow the cautious example of the English Fabians, who refused to identify their Society with the fortunes of any political splinter party. As a result, the Nationalist clubs were quickly absorbed into the People's Party, which in the national elections of 1892 gleaned over a million votes and won twenty-two seats in the electoral college. William Dean Howells claimed that Edward Bellamy virtually founded the Populist Party, and indeed its platform clearly reflected the ideas of *Looking Backward*.

By the close of 1892, most of the Nationalist clubs had disappeared. By that time, also, Bellamy's much-vaunted Americanism had begun to ring a bit hollow, thanks to an editorial of his which appeared in the Boston *Globe* for July 4, 1892. There he proclaimed that "in the year 1992 . . . the Fourth of July will have ceased to be a popular holiday of much note." He predicted "another Declaration of Independence in America" which "in importance will quite eclipse the document (great in its way as that was) promulgated in Philadelphia a hundred and sixteen years ago." It would, he said, abolish distinctions between employer and employed, capitalist and proletarian, and put an end to economic inequality. Without specifying the precise day, month or year when this "newer and greater Declaration of Independence" would come, he announced: "I believe it will come and that society will be, *peaceably or forcibly*,[5] conformed to its terms within the expectations of men now middle-aged."

Those explosive remarks were made in an era when "the Glorious

---

3) In "Graves de Communi," January 18, 1901, he pointed out that "Totally different from the movement known as 'Social Democracy,' [Christian democracy] has for its basis the principles of Catholic faith and morals—especially the principle of not injuring in any way the inviolable right of private property." These views of Leo XIII were specifically reaffirmed by his successor, Pope Pius X, in the "Motu Proprio on Popular Christian Action" given at Rome, December 18, 1903. Quotations cited above are from that document.

[4] Percival Chubb was for many years Director of Education at the Ethical Culture High School in New York City. He retained his interest in Socialism and his membership in the Fabian Society of London to the end. In the August, 1923 issue of *Fabian News* the following personal note appeared: "Percival Chubb, who was the first secretary of the Fellowship of the New Life on its formation in 1883, is on a visit to London from America where he has resided since 1888. He would like to be remembered to any old friends still in the Society."

[5] (Italics added.)

Fourth" was celebrated with picnics, parades and firecrackers every-where in the United States, and when the day itself was regarded by adults and children alike as being only second in importance to Christmas. While Bellamy's editorial was greeted with cheers by all convinced Socialists, including a close-knit group of upperclassmen and recent alumni of Harvard University who had succumbed to the Nationalist lure, it offended public opinion in Boston and the country as a whole. His prediction that society would be *peaceably or forcibly* transformed within a relatively few years rather deflated the claims made by Bellamy admirers, then and since, to the effect that he was "one of the most peaceful and humane revolutionists who ever lived."

Partly because of this incident, partly because the novelty of the whole thing had worn thin, the Nationalist movement was soon ex-tinct, despite efforts of Bellamy and his friends to revive it. Neverthe-less, it accomplished the one practical purpose for which it had been so hastily launched. When the Congress of the United States, impelled by the violence-scarred Homestead and Pullman strikes, passed a law in 1894 declaring Anarchism illegal, Socialism escaped the prohibition.

Having caught the fancy, however fleeting, of many middle class folk in urban communities throughout the United States, Socialism had acquired some veneer of respectability. As Edward Bellamy noted in his introduction to the 1894 American edition of *Fabian Essays,* Nationalism was, chiefly, the form in which "scientific Socialism" had thus far been brought to the attention of the American people. Older, more literal Marxists were impressed in spite of themselves and agreed with something like relief that Bellamy had succeeded in "putting the silk hat on Socialism in America."

To a number of younger men and women, Nationalism also pro-vided the starting point for future careers in other Socialist-dominated enterprises to come. Along with the aging Colonel Thomas Went-worth Higginson, such youthful sprigs as Mary Livermore and Mary Austin of the Boston Nationalist Club in time became pillars of the Intercollegiate Socialist Society (ISS), afterwards the League for Industrial Democracy. So did Florence Kelley of the New York club, who had studied Marxism in Switzerland. She became a self anointed crusader against child labor, and as chairman of the National Con-sumers League lobbied incessantly throughout the country for state and federal control of wages and working conditions.

William J. Ghent, a fellow member of New York's Nationalist Club, and Algernon Lee of the Milwaukee club, became successive directors of the controversial Rand School of Social Science. From the Chicago club came Clarence Darrow, dramatic defender of the McNamara brothers and other accused dynamiters, and a charter member of the ISS; and Henry Demarest Lloyd, author of *Wealth Against Commonwealth* and an inspirer of the Public Ownership League of Chicago which eventually fathered the Tennessee Valley Authority. Lloyd's son, David Demarest Lloyd, followed in his papa's footsteps, becoming Director of Research and Legislation in the Fabian-instigated Americans for Democratic Action[6] and serving just prior to his death in 1951 as a White House speech writer for Fair Deal President Harry S. Truman. By that time the Fabian technique of "penetration" had developed into a fine art in America.

2.

For the time being, however, a good many budding radicals of Anglo-American stock and middle class education found that with the collapse of the Nationalist movement they had no place to go. When the need for a helping hand became evident, William A. Clarke of the London *Chronicle* and a member of London's Fabian Executive was dispatched to assist those drifting American intellectuals who still dreamed of achieving a gradual and bloodless revolution in their native land. For the March, 1894, issue of *The New England Magazine*, highly rated in academic and literary circles, Clarke wrote an article simply entitled, "The Fabian Society."

An able journalist and propagandist, William Clarke was well qualified to pen an official apology for the British Fabian Society in the United States. Almost casually, he brushed aside the view "still expressed sometimes in American newspapers, that the Socialist movement is largely made up of cranks and scoundrels." On the contrary, he said, "In Marx, Lassalle, Rodbertus and others, the Socialist movement has been served by some of the best brains of our century . . . . I know the inside of the Socialist movement well, and it certainly numbers among its adherents the ablest men I know. The Fabian Society contains not a few of these men . . . . At present, almost all callings are represented in the Fabian Society of London and its forty-eight provincial societies . . . . Lawyers, artists, journalists, doctors, workingmen; clergymen, teachers, trade union leaders; literary people, shopkeepers, and persons of no occupation . . . . No millionaires . . .

[6] To be treated in detail in a later chapter.

but quite a few well-to-do people. A large proportion are bright young men, and there are not a few bright and active women."

This seems to have been the first public image of the London Fabian Society to be formally unveiled in America by one of its own leading spokesmen. The Society was falsely depicted as being no more than a mild-mannered reform movement—"not looking for the millennium or any perfectly blissful earthly paradise." Its ultimate revolutionary aims, as expressed in the *Basis*, were not stated. What the article sought chiefly to convey was an impression that most Fabian Socialists were "educated, intelligent, of sweet disposition . . . people who enjoy books and music and the theater and good society. . . . The Socialist movement . . . has taught them there is a great suffering world beyond the four walls of home to be helped and worked for." Clarke's artful press agentry was not only a timely prelude to the American edition of *Fabian Essays*, which appeared the same year, but served in a general way to whitewash the Fabians and their friends at home and abroad.

Somehow he contrived to suggest that the still youthful London Fabian Society was a solid, long-established British institution: one that could serve (although he tactfully refrained from saying so) as a model for Socialist intellectuals aspiring to develop a similar leadership group in America. Just as soon as it became evident that Socialist activities in the United States were not going to be declared illegal, William Clarke offered his personal services in helping to found an American Fabian Society in Boston, with branches in other cities.

Early in 1895, the irrepressible W. D. P. Bliss—stimulated by a recent visit to London, where he had mingled happily with the Fabian masterminds and arranged for the publication by Sonnenschein of his own *Handbook of Socialism*—assumed the editorship of a new monthly journal, *The American Fabian*. Published by the Fabian Educational Company of Boston, it was to become the organ of a projected American Fabian League, as soon as such a body could be formed. Subscriptions were solicited from erstwhile Nationalists and other Socialist sympathizers on or off the university campuses, at the modest price of fifty cents a year—eighty cents if ordered jointly with *The Dawn*, a Christian Socialist sheet started by Bliss in 1889. Headquarters of the Fabian Educational Company were located at 241 Tremont Street by arrangement with the People's Party Club of Boston.

A twenty-page monthly, more pretentious in format than the slim but durable little *Fabian News* of London, *The American Fabian* first saw the light of day in February, 1895. Disarmingly, the front page of its inaugural issue carried a photograph and profile of the British utopian philosopher, William Morris, who believed in embellishing social reform with art, poetry and other cultural adornments. The masthead featured a quotation from Mazzini, the Italian Anarchist: "The next great word is Association"—a seemingly innocent word which the Nationalists had employed in their platform as a synonym for nationalization.

On an inner page a new, long-term revolutionary objective of the journal's founders was succinctly stated. It was not merely to rewrite the Declaration of Independence, as Bellamy had once suggested; but *to effect a series of basic changes in the Constitution itself that would make possible the introduction of State Socialism step by step in the United States.* With all the valor of inexperience the editors announced, more boldly than most of their modern counterparts would care to do today:

We call our paper "The American Fabian" for two reasons: we call it Fabian because we desire to make it stand for the kind of educational Socialist work which is so ably done by the English Fabian Society . . . . We call our paper "The *American* Fabian" because our politics must in a measure differ from those of the English Fabians. England and America are alike in some things; in some things they are utterly unlike. England's [un-written] Constitution readily admits of constant though gradual modification. Our American Constitution does not readily admit of such change. England can thus move into Socialism almost imperceptibly. *Our Constitution being largely individualistic must be changed to admit of Socialism, and each change necessitates a political crisis.* This means the raising of *great new issues* . . . .[7]

Such far-reaching calculations were not wholly the fruit of American thinking, as can be deduced from the fact that the very next issue of *The American Fabian* printed the text of the London Fabian Society's *Basis.* The "need" to alter the Constitution of the United States as a preliminary to radical social change was reaffirmed just three years later by the British Fabian Socialist, Ramsay MacDonald. Returned from a trip to America, he gave a talk on the United States at the London Fabian Society's headquarters in Clement's Inn. "*The great bar to [Socialist] progress [in the United States],*" said he, "*is the written constitutions, Federal and State, which give ultimate power to a law court.*" This assertion by a future Socialist Prime Minister of

[7] (Italics added.)

England was made on January 14, 1898;[8] and there is no reason to presume he or his Fabian associates in Britain and America ever deviated from that view.

To subvert the underlying principles of the United States Constitutions, Federal and State, which upheld the right to own and operate private property as a corollary of the Natural Law, was a project of real magnitude. When proposed in *The American Fabian,* most Americans deemed such a thing to be impossible—just as it seemed impossible that a handful of "gentle" Fabian intellectuals in England could seriously shake the foundations of the British Empire. Confession of intent to revise the Constitution in America of the eighteen-nineties appeared more visionary than alarming. If it was ever to be accomplished, it would have to be done obliquely, secretively and gradually over a period of years by a Socialist elite schooled to take advantage of every local and national crisis for their own covert ends.

The first step was to develop a leadership group and a receptive body of public opinion, through the organized promotion of Socialist thought and study. To that end, the April, 1895, issue of *The American Fabian* offered a tentative constitution for an American Fabian League. It was to be a federation of clubs, with national executive and publication committees but without other national officers. Any club working in any way to spread Socialist ideas or to advance any Socialist measures could join the American Fabian League by applying to the secretary of the Executive Committee.

The various local clubs or societies were free to organize in any manner they wished and choose their own special objectives, methods of work, and time of meetings. They could use any name they preferred, and could exercise full autonomy over their own members, who might or might not be outright Socialists. One thing, however, was essential: the American Fabian League constitution specified that in any club *only those persons who communicate in writing to the Secretary of the Executive Committee their acceptance of the principle of ownership and conduct of industry by the community shall have a right to hold office in the National Executive Committee, or to vote in the National League . . . ."* [9] The Publications Committee would draft a program of "measures or subjects for the federated clubs to consider and study or agitate upon, month by month, in order to produce systematic concerted action."

[8] *Fabian News,* (February, 1898).
[9] (Italics added.)

Here was the blueprint for a semi-secret national organization whose sole visible link with its members was *The American Fabian*. It is noteworthy that the magazine during its five-year existence printed few names except those of publicists already well-known. Club officers and personnel of the Executive Committee were not identified, and no membership figures were announced. Articles were generally unsigned, or signed with only an initial, except when reprinted from other periodicals. In fact, it was several years before *The American Fabian* ventured to print a list of its own contributing editors—all Socialists and former Nationalists. As of February, 1898, they were: Edward Bellamy, W. D. P. Bliss, Helen Campbell, Eltweed Pomeroy,[10] Henry Demarest Lloyd, Prestonia Mann, Professor Frank Parsons,[11] and Charlotte Perkins Stetson.

The Christmas issue of 1895 displayed a Nativity scene, captioned "The Birth of the First Socialist," on the same page with a brief biography of the profoundly anti-religious Karl Marx. It also contained the following modest organizational items: "The Kensington Fabian group meets every Tuesday evening. Mr. Bliss is giving his course of lectures and the hall is filling up . . . . The Philadelphia group meets every Saturday at 1305 Arch Street . . . . The New York Society (formerly the Altrurian Society) meets every Wednesday evening at 10 East 33rd Street. It has weekly discussions and debates, and on January 8 will have a supper."

No attempt was made to conceal the fact that the American movement maintained close ties with the British Fabian Society. A note in the same issue stated: "Mr. E. R. Pease, secretary of the London Society, writes us that if secretaries of American Fabian Societies will send him their names and addresses, he will send them the *Fabian News* and tracts as they appear. Let us accept this generous offer and bind the English and American movements together. We need not and should not copy the English movement, but surely we may learn from the older and parent movement."[12]

Besides establishing direct contacts between the London Executive and key individuals in American Fabian groups throughout the country, the generous offer made by Pease had other uses. Both the *Fabian News* and the tracts issued by the British Society, which

[10] Eltweed Pomeroy was also president of the National Direct Legislation League.
[11] Of Boston University.
[12] *The American Fabian*, (December, 1895), p. 5.

appeared to the general reader to have a purely informational and propagandist content, could be construed by the faithful as providing quiet but unmistakable directives from the fountainhead of Fabian Socialism in London. A full set of selected Fabian tracts for Americans was advertised at seventy-five cents in *The American Fabian,* bolstered by an admiring quotation from the *Review of Reviews* which said: "The peculiarity of the Fabian tracts is that every fact and statement in them has been verified [sic]."

The American Fabian League was not planned as a mass organization. Its avowed purpose was to unite all existing reform movements in America under the leadership of individual Socialists, who in turn received their instructions from a single national Executive Committee. The original program included planks on sound currency, a national eight-hour law, women's suffrage, state employment bureaus and aid for the unemployed, and control over the sale of alcoholic beverages. Most of these proposals, since enacted into law, were not in essence Socialist. They simply made it easier for individual Socialists to penetrate labor, women's and temperance groups, with a view to winning mass support for other, more far-reaching Socialist objectives outlined by the League's Executive Committee.

Americans today may be surprised to find that the same Fabian program advocated a *severely graduated income tax* and a *heavy and graduated inheritance tax,* as well as *a tax on land values.* It also called for *proportional representation,* which aimed to give left wing splinter parties a voice in government, local and national; the initiative and referendum, which would permit legislation to be initiated outside of the legislatures; and "any Constitutional amendments that might be needed" to legalize the Fabian Socialist plan for America.

A strictly *non-partisan* approach to Socialism was recommended for the American Fabian League. This would leave individual Fabians free to join any political party, Socialist or otherwise, and work inside it to promote Socialist legislation. When W. D. P. Bliss, in his capacity as editor of *The American Fabian,* came out strongly for Bryan and free silver in 1896, he was rebuked by Edward R. Pease for committing the American Fabian movement to the platform of a political party.

Prestonia Mann, a well-to-do bluestocking who aspired to become the Madame Récamier of a Socialist salon, inherited the editorship of *The American Fabian* from Bliss. She had heartily endorsed the stand taken by Pease. "The British Fabian Society," she wrote in a letter of

December 30, 1896, to Henry Demarest Lloyd, "owes most of its strength to its steadfastness in standing by its determination not to be beguiled into becoming a political party . . . . We must follow the example of British Fabians."

In April, 1898, *The American Fabian*, whose editorial offices had been transferred from Boston to New York, reported briefly: "Sidney and Beatrice Webb, the distinguished authors of a *History of Trade Unionism* and *Industrial Democracy*, arrived in New York last week. They will remain in the country for a few months, returning to London about Christmas by way of New Zealand and Australia." Sydney Olivier, of the original Fabian Big Four, traveled with them as far as Washington on business for the British Colonial Office,[13] lending a spuriously official aura to their journey.

The Webbs encountered none of the disagreeable publicity which had attended the tour of Wilhelm Liebknecht and Eleanor Marx a dozen years before and which marked the visit of the Russian Socialist, Maxim Gorki, several years later. For one thing, they were properly married and acceptable in good society. For another, they shunned the limelight. With the caution and worldly wisdom that always characterized their personal behavior, they spoke at no mass meetings, made no conspicuous public appearances or political pronouncements. They lectured only to small groups of serious thinkers or handpicked audiences on university campuses, and mingled with leading lights of the American Economic Association whose books were regularly advertised in *The American Fabian*.

In New York City, they dined with Prestonia Mann, at whose summer place in the Adirondacks and town house in Manhattan upper-class Socialists met and mingled. The Webbs established the pattern for future visits to the United States by British Fabians, in which social diversion and Socialist purpose were discreetly combined.

In Chicago the Webbs stayed at Hull House as guests of the very ladylike spinster, Jane Addams, whose beautifully modulated voice and great, inscrutable dark eyes masked a defiant and firebrand spirit. Beatrice Webb recalled the event long afterwards in her diary[14]— failing to mention, however, that thereafter almost every British Fabian who visited the United States included a stop at Hull House on his schedule. Founded in 1889 and modeled after Toynbee Hall in

[13] *Fabian News*, (April, 1898).

[14] Beatrice Webb, *My Apprenticeship*, (London, Longmans, Green & Co., Ltd., 1919), p. 40.

London where so many members of the London Society made their first carefully limited contacts with slum dwellers, Hull House launched the social-settlement phase of the Socialist movement in America which afterwards spread to other cities. Like the earlier gospel missions, it combined the occasional soup kitchen and the supervised playground with indoctrination in a new gospel of "social reform." It preceded by some fifty years the enactment of legislation creating politically administered city, state and federal welfare agencies; and, in addition to its many incidentally charitable aspects, it served as an early experimental laboratory for the Fabian-invented "social sciences." By now the golden legend of Hull House has been so assiduously cultivated in book and story by friends and former residents that any attempt to expose its persistent Socialist connections would be viewed as a sacrilege.[15]

And yet, as a sympathetic historian records, the doors of Hull House were always open to social and economic "reformers" and political radicals.[16] There the Social Democratic Party was organized by Eugene V. Debs in 1898, to replace what American Fabians termed the "barbarous"[17] Socialist Labor Party headed by the Curaçao-born and German-educated Marxist, Daniel De Leon—subsequently professor of International Law at Columbia University. Like future Socialist splinter parties, the short-lived Social Democratic Party sought to win working-class votes under the guidance of Socialist intellectuals; but in no sense represented the full spectrum of intellectual Socialism's activities and aims in the United States.

A sudden upsurge of patriotic feeling in America preceded the outbreak of the Spanish-American War. In that atmosphere of hostility to all types of European penetration of the Western Hemisphere, it was once again obvious to sophisticated observers that no movement in the United States could survive which acknowledged foreign inspiration and leadership. Laurence Gronlund raised the question, saying he preferred to be known as a collectivist rather than a Fabian. So did

---

[15] On February 3, 1945, Robert Morss Lovett, president for nearly twenty years of the Fabian-affiliated League for Industrial Democracy and a long time resident of Hull House, sent a telegram on the occasion of the League's fortieth anniversary, saying: ". . . I always regard my connection with the League as one of the happiest of my life—perhaps next to Hull House." *Forty Years of Education,* (New York, League for Industrial Democracy, 1945), p. 53.

[16] Howard Quint, *The Forging of American Socialism,* (Columbia, University of South Carolina Press, 1953), p. 320.

[17] Papers of Henry Demarest Lloyd. Letter of Prestonia Mann to H. D. Lloyd, December 30, 1896. (University of Illinois, Urbana, Illinois).

the former Altrurian Society of New York, which had objected to the name Fabian because "it seemed English" and "because a successful Socialist movement in this country should be distinctly American."[18] Evidently the Webbs reached a similar conclusion, and their tour of 1898 signaled the beginning of the end for *The American Fabian—though not for the movement it had helped to form.*

In the fall of that year John W. Martin—graduate of London University, former vestryman from Hackney and member of the Fabian Executive from 1894 to 1899—followed the Webbs to America. Nominally, he was to deliver a series of lectures arranged for his benefit by branches of the American Fabian League.[19] Additionally, his mission was to liquidate *The American Fabian* and to serve as a personal link between the surviving Executive Committee of the American Fabian League and the Fabian Executive of London. With Prestonia Mann, Martin edited the last issues of the journal under the joint pseudonym of "John Preston." The final issue appeared in 1899, approximately a year after the death of Edward Bellamy.

Following the example of his London confrères—like himself of lower middle class origin—who improved their fortunes and social position by wedding women of property, John W. Martin duly married the energetic Prestonia Mann. Settling in New York, he dabbled in local school board politics and enjoyed the status derived from authorship of an occasional unpopular book. After gaining some slight notoriety in World War I as a financial backer of the *Liberator* magazine, he became, in his latter days, a consultant on international affairs at Rollins College. Martin and his wife appear to have remained lifelong Fabians, maintaining contacts with high-level Fabian Socialists, British and American, both in New York and at their ultimate retreat in Winter Park, Florida.[20]

Though the official organ of American Fabianism folded in 1899,

[18] *The American Fabian*, (April, 1895), p. 5.

[19] *The American Fabian*, (May, 1898), p. 12. Under the heading, "Proposed Fabian Lecture Tour," it was announced: "Mr. John W. Martin, a member of the London Fabian Executive Committee, intends visiting this country this fall, if a sufficient number of lectures can be arranged for him . . . . Here will be an excellent opportunity for American groups or individuals to assist in propagating the faith by securing Mr. Martin for one or more lectures. Application for further information should be sent to Mr. J. W. Martin, 49 Downs Roads, London, N.E., or to Edw. R. Pease, Secretary of the Fabian Society, 276 Strand, London, W.C."

[20] *Fabian Society 73rd Annual Report, July, 1955-June, 1956,* contains a notation (p. 17) regarding "the death overseas of Dr. John Martin, who served on the Executive from 1894 to 1899 and founded the American Fabian Society [sic]—itself, alas, no more."

the movement itself lived on in many seemingly disconnected small reform clubs across the nation. A Bellamy Memorial Meeting of June 7, 1898, presided over by William Dean Howells and described in *The American Fabian,* had been sponsored by a Fabian group calling itself The Social Reform Club. In September, 1898, W. D. P. Bliss was reported to be organizing a Union Reform League on the Pacific Coast, with tracts being prepared by Professor Commons of Syracuse University, Professor Frank Parsons of Boston University, Professor E. W. Bemis of the University of Chicago, and Dr. Charles B. Spahr of *The Outlook.* Already the name Fabian and even the name Socialist were being discarded as a matter of procedure—though as late as 1919 local groups calling themselves Fabian Societies were revived in Boston and Chicago.[21]

The brief public appearance of an American Fabian League in the eighteen-nineties coincided with what has been called the London Society's first blooming. Just as some persons still aver that the Fabian Society of London—which not only dominates the British Labour Party today, but the Socialist International as well—died at the turn of the century; so it is misleadingly claimed that Fabian Socialism died long ago in America, at the time when the American Fabian League dropped out of sight. A conveniently premature death notice found its way into American encyclopedias—confirmed with tongue in cheek by such an authority on Socialist affairs as the late Morris Hillquit, himself a leading member of more than one Fabian-affiliated organization.[22]

The long-range objectives of Fabian Socialism in the United States were clearly and permanently defined in *The American Fabian.* Techniques for achieving them had still to be developed, along with the openings for putting those techniques into practice. From the first, it was recognized that the difficulties of organization in the United States were very great. Such difficulties were variously attributed to the size of the country; the diversity of races, religions and national origins; the patriotic spirit innate in the majority of Americans; the opportunities for self-improvement offered by an expanding capitalist

[21] *Fabian News,* (April, 1919). Letter from Stuart Chase.

[22] *Fifty Years of Education, 1905-1955,* (New York, League for Industrial Democracy, 1955). Morris Hillquit is listed as having served from 1908-15 as treasurer of the Intercollegiate Socialist Society, later called the League for Industrial Democracy, which British Fabian Margaret Cole, *The Story of Fabian Socialism,* (London, Heinemann Educational Books, Ltd., 1961), p. 347, designates as a connection of the London Fabian Society.

system. To this the secretary of the London Fabian Society, Edward R. Pease, who had no love in his heart for America, added contemptuously: "European countries with their great capitals have developed national brains. America, like the lower organisms, has ganglia for various purposes in various parts of its gigantic frame." [23] The task of Fabian Socialism in America was to discover means of transmitting self-destructive impulses to those hidden ganglia.

By announcing its own apparent demise and voluntarily going underground at a well-chosen moment, the Fabian Socialist movement in America, steered and manipulated with cold-blooded determination by British Fabians, has succeeded in outliving its founders and in becoming an integral, potent and progressively more deadly tool of the international Socialist movement. The future was forecast by William Dean Howells in words that seem more ominous today than when they were spoken. Asked "What are the prospects for Socialism in America?" Howells replied: "As to that, who can say? One sees the movement advancing all around him, and yet it may be years before its ascendancy. On the other hand, it may be but a short time. A slight episode may change history. A turn here or a turn there, and we may find our nation headlong on the road to the 'ideal' commonwealth." [24]

Howell's statement was made in February, 1898. History has proved that Fabian Socialism in America, wearing the silk hat of respectability, did not end there. It was only the beginning.

[23] Edward R. Pease, *History of Socialism,* (London, A. & C. Black, 1913), p. 341.
Max Beer, *Fifty Years of International Socialism,* (London, Allen and Unwin, 1935), pp. 108-115. This book is dedicated to Fabian Professor R. H. Tawney.
[24] *The American Fabian,* (February, 1898), p. 2.

11

The Professor Goes To Washington

FAR from the noise of popular celebrations which hailed the hopeful opening of the twentieth century, a small but crucial event occurred in England that seemed straight out of *Alice in Wonderland*. Sidney Webb induced the Royal Commission of London University to declare economics a science—and once declared so by that august body, it was assumed to be so! On February 20, 1900, Beatrice Webb confided to her diary, "This divorce of economics from metaphysics and shoddy history is a great gain," that is, for the advancement of scientific Socialism in the English-speaking world. She admitted blandly that the coup had been achieved by trickery, through successfully packing the University of London Commission.[1]

In those days science was a word to conjure with and the Webbs were gifted at legerdemain. While attracting little general notice, the Royal Commission's pronouncement went a long way toward establishing the authority of research and teaching methods pursued with political intent by British Fabians—not only at the little London School of Economics[2] where they ruled supreme, but also at the larger universities of England and America where they were making converts.

[1] Beatrice Webb, *Our Partnership*, (London, Longmans, Green & Co., Ltd., 1948), p. 195.

[2] In 1895, five years after its founding, the London School of Economics, then occupying two rooms in Adelphi, boasted exactly eight registered students and two lecturers. One of these instructors was the Director, W. A. S. Hewins, who voiced conservative views on economics but faithfully followed Sidney Webb's lead in matters of organization. The other was the radical Graham Wallas, whose field was politics. Max Beer, *Fifty Years of International Socialism*, (London, Allen & Unwin, 1935), pp. 82-83.

145

Soon other types of social inquiry were invested with the lofty title of "social science" and presumed by a guileless public to be as free as the physical sciences from subjective or doctrinal bias. Thus professors who happened to be Socialists could present propagandist conclusions as though they were laws of nature, determined by "impartial" research. No wonder the British Fabian Socialist, John Atkinson Hobson—who wrote *Free Thought in the Social Sciences*, pointing out the uses of social psychology as a tool for manipulating the masses —could assert so confidently, if somewhat after the fact, *that the future secret weapon of strategy would be the university professor!*

More speedily than in England, Hobson's dictum proved true in the United States, where professors as well as students aspired to become the future rulers of America. All across the continent at the turn of the century, little clusters of college professors had begun studying Socialism in secret, because an open avowal of such interest might have led to their dismissal. Recalling his youth as an instructor at the University of California, Dr. Harry L. Overstreet—long a professor of Philosophy at the City College of New York and sponsor of many Socialist causes—said: "We were studying Socialism [at California] and didn't want anyone to know we were doing it." [3]

At the Philadelphia University Extension, a group of self-styled liberals gathered around Woodrow Wilson, professor of Jurisprudence and Political Science at Princeton University. Most of them held regular positions elsewhere, as Wilson did, commuting to Philadelphia[4] to lecture in their free time as a means of augmenting their incomes and improving their extracurricular contacts. Some, like Professor Henry C. Adams and, at a later date, Professor Richard T. Ely, were the acknowledged leaders of academic Socialism in their day.

Others belonging to the Wilson circle were Dr. Albert Shaw, of the *Review of Reviews*; Professor William Graham Sumner, who explained morality in terms of folkways and tribal taboos, and who helped blur the distinctions between primitive and civilized man to an extent still reflected today in United States foreign policy; and the Reverend

[3] *Forty Years of Education*, (New York, League for Industrial Democracy, 1945), pp. 46-47.
[4] From 1893 to 1898 the Nationalists continued to maintain their "Bureau of Nationalist Literature" in Philadelphia, which distributed Bellamy's speeches and *Looking Backward*, and Professor Frank Parsons' *Public Ownership of Monopolies* and *Philosophy of Mutualism*—all known to Woodrow Wilson. Sylvia E. Bowman, *The Year 2000—A Critical Biography of Edward Bellamy*, (New York, Bookman Associates, 1958), p. 136.

William Bayard Hale, editor and correspondent, who had gone to Oxford in 1895 and returned to write *The Eternal Teacher*, advocating a species of Christian Socialism akin to that of W. D. P. Bliss. They contributed to the *University Extension World*, which became the *American Journal of Sociology*; and they brought to the group, if nothing more, an awareness of the municipal politics of Sidney and Beatrice Webb.

With other American intellectuals of British ancestry, they attended summer meetings at Oxford announced in *The Citizen* (1895-1901), a publication of the Philadelphia University. British extension-type lecturers such as J. Hudson Shaw (better known as Broughman Villiers) and the arch-Fabian Graham Wallas—both of whom also taught at summer sessions in Philadelphia and New York—addressed the visiting scholars. The ancient halls and towers of Oxford provided a mellow setting for spokesmen from the London School of Economics still in its somewhat unpromising infancy. It is remarkable, and certainly a tribute to the Fabian talent for impressing Americans, that so small and ill-favored a nursling, which the London School continued to be for some years, had already gained so large a reputation among leaders of liberal thought in the United States.

Even after he became president of Princeton University in 1902 and could no longer participate actively in the work of the Philadelphia University Extension, Woodrow Wilson continued to take a lively interest in that little backwater of academic ferment. New personalities appeared there from time to time whose interest in national politics was undisguised. Among them were William T. Harrison, United States Commissioner of Education under Theodore Roosevelt, and Columbia University's chief political economist, Dr. E. R. A. Seligman, one of the earliest to perceive the presidential possibilities of Woodrow Wilson.

There was also Lincoln Steffens, who wrote "The Shame of the Cities" for *McClure's Magazine*—a series purporting to expose corruption and poverty in American cities and suggested by the Fabian tract, "Facts for Londoners." An early article in the *New England Magazine* (June, 1894) by the migrant British Fabian William A. Clarke had quoted the poet Shelley as saying, "Hell is a city very much like London," and remarked that Shelley was unfair to Hell. The same Manichean spirit pervaded Steffens' work, though expressed in the astringent journalistic style, known as muckraking, then coming into vogue. For a dozen years Fabian-type "fact finding" in a popular vein—practiced not only by outspoken Socialists like Lincoln Steffens and Upton Sinclair, but by such skilled reporters as Ray Stannard Baker and Ida Tarbell, who only leaned toward Socialism—enjoyed a field day in the American press.

In a period when Fabian Socialists were devoting themselves to penetration and permeation of the Liberal Party in England, a mixed bag of professors and publicists who had borrowed the liberal label prepared the way for a similar parasitic development in the United States. To a greater or lesser degree, they had been touched by Socialist ideas—a condition unsuspected by the general run of Americans. Within a surprisingly short time, Dr. Woodrow Wilson, the professors' choice, became the Democratic Party's candidate for the Presidency of the United States. He was elected due to a split in Republican ranks, fomented in part by old-fashioned patriots, in part by Eastern liberals and Midwestern progressives.

Immediately after Wilson's election, the United States Department of Labor was established. It absorbed the old Bureau of Labor, now the Bureau of Labor Statistics. The Bureau furnished, like the factory inspectors' reports in England, facts and figures Socialists have utilized to advantage for agitation and propaganda purposes. The Bureau of Labor Statistics is known today chiefly as the oracular source of the monthly *Consumer Price Index*, to which the "escalator-clause" in many modern union contracts is tied and which assures an overall, if gradual, inflationary spiral.

That move to consolidate Federal labor agencies in Washington had been promoted by the Fabian W. D. P. Bliss, who became a Bureau of Labor investigator in 1907, the first of a flock of Socialist bureaucrats who have quietly roosted in the Department of Labor ever since. The wide and variegated connections enjoyed by Bliss were evident in the list of contributors to his *New Encyclopedia of Social Reform*, published by Funk and Wagnalls in 1908. There the names of well-known British Fabians (Percy Alden, M.P., Right Honorable John Burns, Sidney Webb, Edward R. Pease) and leading American Socialists of the day (Professors E. W. Bemis and F. H. Giddings, Morris Hillquit, Robert Hunter, Upton Sinclair) appeared side by side with names of such eminent non-Socialists as Samuel Gompers, Honorable Oscar Straus, Booker T. Washington and Cardinal Gibbons.

Under the Wilson Administration still another long-desired Fabian Socialist objective became a reality: the income tax, which was superimposed on the older and kindlier American tradition of indirect taxation. Originally proposed by Karl Marx in the *Communist Manifesto*, a heavily graduated income tax had been urged by American Fabian Leaguers as well as by their mentors of the London Fabian Society. Twice branded unconstitutional by the United States Supreme Court, it was finally legalized by pushing through the Sixteenth Amendment to the Constitution after the outbreak of World War I— at a time when distracting questions of foreign policy were uppermost in the public mind. The income tax became law in 1916, just in time to help pay for the war, a war out of which Woodrow Wilson had vowed to keep the country. Feather light at the beginning, like the "Old Man of the Sea" it has proved a progressively heavier burden upon the shoulders of an entire people—as well as a subtle political device for altering the basic economy and social structure of the nation.

While Woodrow Wilson could not actually be named a Socialist, he was the first Chief Executive of the United States to accept Socialist-minded intellectuals as aides and advisers and to present Fabian Socialist programs as his own. His book, *The New Freedom*, was an early attempt to equate the Democratic Party with a strange new concept of democracy which mirrored the Industrial or Social Democracy of the British Fabians. As he admitted in the preface, with a frankness seldom matched today, he did not write the book at all.[5] It was compiled by a former colleague of the Philadelphia University Extension days, the Christian Socialist William Bayard Hale, on the basis of Wilson's 1912 campaign speeches.

From first to last, *The New Freedom* denounced capitalism as being contrary to the interests of the common man. Justice, not charity, was its theme. Somewhat quaintly, it identified the captains of industry of the day with the trustees of Princeton University who seemed to have given Dr. Wilson a hard time during his presidency of that institution. Opening with the bleak assertion (reiterated by Wilson's political successors during half a century of unparalleled industrial growth) that the American economy was stagnant and individual opportunity was dead, it stated:

We stand in the presence of a revolution—not a bloody revolution, America is not given to spilling of blood—but a silent revolution, whereby America will insist upon recovering in practice those ideals which she has always

[5] Woodrow Wilson, *The New Freedom*, A Call for the Emancipation of the Generous Energies of a People, (New York, Doubleday, Page & Co., 1913), p. vii.

professed, upon securing a government devoted to the general and not to special interests.[6]

And it concluded with the premature but eerie prediction:

. . . We are just upon the threshold of a time when the systematic life of this country will be sustained, or at least supplemented, at every point by government activity. And we have now to determine what kind of governmental activity it shall be; whether, in the first place, it shall be direct from the government itself, or whether it shall be indirect, through instrumentalities which have already constituted themselves and which stand ready to supersede the government.[7]

The instrumentalities referred to by Wilson were large industrial and financial concerns, headed by the United States Steel Corporation and J. P. Morgan and Company, which according to the Socialist demonology of the period constituted a kind of invisible government. Whatever instrumentalities may stand ready to supersede the American Government today are internationalist in character and Fabian Socialist-directed; and it was in Wilson's time that such left wing groups made their first tentative efforts to grasp power in the United States by exerting influence over the Chief Executive.

As Bellamy had done, *The New Freedom* called for "a new declaration of independence." [8] It deplored the system of checks and balances in government, devised by well-meaning but sadly outdated Founding Fathers, and demanded an "evolutionary" interpretation of the Constitution, as well as sweeping changes in the Judiciary. "Development" and "evolution" were the "new scientific watchwords." [9]

Having been a teacher of law in its political aspects, Wilson found the judicial outlook of Louis D. Brandeis, Harvard Law School professor, highly congenial. Brandeis was the author of the historic "Brandeis Brief," which ushered in a whole new phase of constitutional law based more on sociological than legal interpretations. He was a frequent caller at the White House during the first Wilson Administration, when others found it difficult to see the President. Together with the Progressive Senator La Follette of Wisconsin, he plied Wilson liberally with advice and information.[10]

[6] *Ibid.,* p. 30.
[7] *Ibid.,* p. 217. (Italics added.)
[8] *Ibid.,* pp. 48-49.
[9] *Ibid.,* pp. 42-47.
[10] Ray Stannard Baker, *An American Chronicle,* (New York, Charles Scribner's Sons, 1945), p. 276. Wilson later excoriated Senator La Follette as one of "a little group of wilful men" for his continued opposition to United States participation in World War I, even after war had been declared.

Brandeis had read and greatly admired *Wealth Against Commonwealth* by Henry Demarest Lloyd of the American Fabian League.[11] In fact, it was through Lloyd that Brandeis was asked to serve on a panel of lawyers to present the miners' case before Theodore Roosevelt's Anthracite Coal Commission of 1902. For a time, American Fabians and their "liberal" satellites had hoped to advance their cause through the "New Nationalism" of the first President Roosevelt. But they found that Roosevelt's interest in genuinely needed regulation and reforms stopped short of tampering with the Constitution.

The Harvard jurist was a close friend of Florence Kelley, of the National Consumers League,[12] whose activities in behalf of working-class women and children demonstrated dramatically how middle class Socialists in the early nineteen-hundreds managed to capture the momentum of legitimate reform drives for their own far-flung ends. Brandeis was for years a neighbor of Elizabeth Glendower Evans, Socialist hostess and financial angel with whom Florence Kelley's daughter lived while studying at Radcliffe. When the Oregon Ten Hour Law for Women was due for a test before the Supreme Court, Florence Kelley enlisted the services of Brandeis.

His niece, Josephine Goldmark—aide and biographer of Florence Kelley—has described the circumstances under which the now-famous Brandeis Brief was prepared in 1907.[13] For two hectic weeks Josephine Goldmark and Florence Kelley assembled and sifted a huge mass of statistics, reports and precedents from foreign lands, hastily supplied by Socialist researchers. The result was something new in legal presentations, with a mere page and a half of legal argument attached to many pages of carefully slanted social and economic research, which the honorable Justices were scarcely equipped by training or experience to evaluate. Termed revolutionary at the time, this method (based on a novel concept of "juridical notice") has by now become

[11] Josephine Goldmark, *Impatient Crusader*, Florence Kelley's Life Story. (Urbana, University of Illinois Press, 1953), p. 153.

[12] Florence Kelley, who called herself a Marxist, had been a Nationalist and an American Fabian. She later served as president of the Intercollegiate Socialist Society, and vice president of the League for Industrial Democracy, affiliates of the London Fabian Society. See Appendix II.

[13] Goldmark, *op. cit.*, pp. 143-159. On page 159, Miss Goldmark states: "The Brandeis Brief in the Muller case, reprinted together with Judge Brewer's opinion, was in great demand from law schools and universities as well as from labor unions and libraries . . . *Gone was the deadening weight of legal precedent.*" (Italics added.)

standard practice and serves, at least in part, to explain some otherwise baffling Supreme Court decisions of recent years.

Significantly, Woodrow Wilson named Louis D. Brandeis, nominally a Progressive Republican, to the Supreme Court in 1915, where he continued to work for liberalization of the Constitution. His appointment was bitterly contested in the Senate, along with the appointment of a former Harvard Law School instructor and fellow Progressive, George Rublee, to the Federal Trade Commission. Born in Wisconsin, Rublee was a polished product of both Groton and Harvard. His vacations in Cornish, New Hampshire, dated from an era when visitors to Washington, who had tried and failed to reach the President, complained: "Wilson stays in Cornish and communes with God." [14] During the summer of 1914, Wilson occupied the spacious red brick home of the American novelist, Winston Churchill, in Cornish, while the chief presidential adviser, Colonel Edward M. House, resided in nearby Manchester.

Members of the discreet summer colony which developed in Cornish and survived for decades included Edward Burling, Sr., Rublee's colleague on the World War I Shipping Board, and his partner in a Washington law firm that specialized in hiring Harvard alumni who had been law clerks in Justice Brandeis' office. Cornish familiars also included Philip Littell, later an editor of the liberal-Fabian weekly, the *New Republic*; and the very personable Professor Robert Morss Lovett, who was to serve as the leading front man for revived American Fabian Socialist organizations after World War I.[15] Some wintered at the Turtle Bay colony in Manhattan.

All had been honor students at Harvard together in the late eighteen-eighties and early eighteen-nineties when Bellamy's Nationalism, adorned with touches of John Ruskin and William Morris, captivated young campus intellectuals. The old school tie endured, and in a rarefied, profitable and mysterious fashion, certain of its wearers permeated the highest circles in Washington politics and New York finance—particularly after a third partner in the Burling-Rublee law firm, Dean Acheson, became Under Secretary of the Treasury and Secretary of State in later Administrations.

Still another member of that long-lived Harvard group was Thomas W. Lamont, Sr.—affectionately known to old college chums as

---

[14] Baker, *loc. cit.*, p. 276.
[15] To the end of his life, Professor Lovett was the house guest of Edward Burling, Sr., when visiting Washington.

"Tommy"—who never ceased to be impressed by the superior wisdom of George Rublee, an upperclassman when Lamont was a sophomore. From financial reporter on a New Jersey newspaper, Lamont rose to become a senior partner of J. P. Morgan and Company, in the dismantlement of which he eventually assisted. In 1933 Lamont signed the so-called *Bankers' Report* advocating diplomatic recognition of Soviet Russia.

As President of the United States, Woodrow Wilson did not hesitate to name outspoken Socialists to obscure but critical posts in government. A case in point was Fred C. Howe, Wilson's Commissioner of Immigration at the Port of New York. A writer and lecturer by profession, Howe resigned after a congressional investigation into alleged neglect of duty, in connection with his unauthorized action in releasing alien radicals held for deportation by the Department of Justice.[16] Both before and after the incident, he figured prominently in a number of Socialist-dominated organizations.[17]

Wilson had also sent the Christian Socialist William Bayard Hale[18] as his special representative to revolution-torn Mexico in 1913-14, instituting a species of presidential diplomacy which has since become almost routine. In Mexico Wilson received private reports both from Hale and from another erstwhile lecturer at the Philadelphia University Extension, Lincoln Steffens, who was in Vera Cruz to attend a Socialist conference in 1914. Those reports helped to effect some curi-

---

[16] *Record of the Sixty Sixth Congress,* (Washington, U.S. Government Printing Office, 1919), pp. 1522-23.

[17] *Railway Review,* Chicago, (January 27, 1923). "Fred C. Howe, New York City; National Committee, American Civil Liberties Union; special writer, Federated Press; . . . chairman, committee on resolutions and member of National Council, Peoples' Legislative Service; contributing editor, *Labor Age;* Defense Committee, I. W. W.; organizer, School of Thought, Siasconset, Nantucket, Mass." Howe was also a director of the League for Industrial Democracy. See Appendix II.

[18] A telegram of June, 1916, from the German Ambassador in Washington to the German Foreign Office, furnished by the United States Department of State and presented by Bruce Bielaski testifying before the Senate Subcommittee on the Judiciary on December 6, 1918, revealed that *from the outset of World War I* William Bayard Hale held a contract extending until June 23, 1918, *as a confidential agent of the German Foreign Office* at a salary of $15,000 per year. Subsequently he went to Germany as correspondent for an American press service which, as the telegram also reveals, was not aware of Hale's connection with the German Government. He returned to America following the entry of the United States into World War I. Senate Document No. 62, 66th Congress. *Report and Hearings of the Subcommittee on the Judiciary, United States Senate,* (Washington, U.S. Government Printing Office, 1919), Vol. II, pp. 1393-94.

ous results, including support and eventual recognition of the *junta* of General Venustiano Carranza, at a time when the latter controlled no more than ninety square kilometers in all Mexico and when his councils were deeply infiltrated by agents of German Military Intelligence.

In 1940-41 the writer of this book was permitted to examine the Woodrow Wilson Papers in the Library of Congress. A folder relating to Mexico contained a personal letter from Secretary of State Robert Lansing commenting on Wilson's preference for soliciting amateur advice often contrary to the observations of seasoned and responsible officials.

Recent hearings before the Senate Subcommittee on Internal Security disclosed that, in a more recent Latin American crisis, diplomatic policies of the United States, which placed and have maintained Fidel Castro in power, were similarly instigated by reports from a "liberal" journalist, Herbert L. Matthews, of *The New York Times*. Meanwhile, well-founded advance warnings by professional diplomats, concerning Castro's long-standing Moscow ties, were ignored or suppressed.[19] Compounding that folly, plans for the ill-starred Bay of Pigs invasion were entrusted to amateurs under presidential supervision rather than to military technicians. So, from all indications, history repeats itself; and the same brand of Socialist-suggested ineptitude as practiced by President Wilson, has once more invited penetration of the Western Hemisphere by a European military power.

[19] *Hearings before the Subcommittee to Investigate the Administration of the Internal Security Act and Other Internal Security Laws of the Committee on the Judiciary, United States Senate.* (Washington, U.S. Government Printing Office, 1962), 87th Congress, Part 5, (January 9, February 8, 1961. February 2, 1962). Testimony of William Wieland, pp. 485-681, *Part 13*, (July 13, 1962). Testimony of Whiting Willauer, pp. 861-888.

12

The Perfect Friendship

1.

BY FAR the most influential of Woodrow Wilson's advisers (who always disclaimed responsibility, however, for any errors in Mexican policy) was a gray, neat, quiet, almost wraith-like little man, with luminous blue eyes and receding chin, Edward M. House of Texas. He held the honorary title of Colonel, conferred on him by Governor Hogg, one of two Texas "reform" governors he had propelled into office. In disgust, House gave the gold-braided uniform and regalia that went with the title to his Negro coachman, preferring to be addressed simply as "Mister."

He was a potent but anonymous figure in Democratic Party councils and knew politics from the grass roots up. His support, pre-convention strategy and adroit instructions to floor lieutenants insured Wilson's nomination at Baltimore in 1912. So confident was House about the outcome that he felt no need to watch the proceedings and sailed for Europe the day the convention opened. Without his help Wilson could not have been nominated—nor without the Texas delegation and its resounding "Forty Votes for Woodrow Wilson of New Jersey," repeated throughout 46 ballots.

Since 1902, the very year Woodrow Wilson became president of conservative and Presbyterian Princeton University, House had waited patiently for this moment. He was looking for a fail-proof candidate to replace William Jennings Bryan, perennial Democratic candidate for the Presidency. A brilliant orator, the Great Commoner thundered

155

against the trusts, "the interests" and the gold standard,[1] and deified labor and the common man. Bryan held audiences spellbound, but he could not win elections and would not stop running. What House wanted was a candidate who might be trusted to carry out a program fully as radical but more systematic than Bryan's—quietly and without alarming the public.

A southerner born and bred, who had migrated to the North and captured the governorship of an important industrial state, Woodrow Wilson seemed the ideal candidate—in fact, almost too good to be true. He was a respected scholar who had been exposed since 1885 to Fabian Socialist views on economics and the social sciences; he was a specialist in American history and constitutional law who wanted to see the Constitution revised; and to top it all, he was a perfect model of decorum and schoolmasterly rectitude. From Sidney Mezes—the brother-in-law whom House elevated by political leverage to the presidency of the University of Texas—and from other professorial friends, House heard about the battles waged by Dr. Wilson at Princeton in the interests of academic "liberalism."

During what he sometimes referred to as his twilight years from 1902 to 1911, House made a point of cultivating key persons in the academic world. Even President Charles W. Eliot of Harvard was numbered among his friends. As one who had failed to meet the entrance requirements at Yale and barely squeezed through a few years at Cornell, it gave House a good deal of quiet satisfaction to move among the academic mandarins—and even be able through his political connections to name the heads of certain city and state universities. At a later date he arranged to have his brother-in-law made president of the City College of New York, where Mezes instituted a regime of hospitality towards radical professors and students.[2]

From afar House watched Wilson's progress as governor of New Jersey, previously a Republican stronghold, where the former professor was being educated for still higher things. When the two men finally met in 1911 through publisher Walter Hines Page of *World's Work*, afterwards Ambassador to England, an immediate bond of sympathy was established. It was the beginning of what Woodrow

---

[1] Bryan's famous Cross of Gold speech proclaimed, "You shall *not* crucify mankind on a cross of gold!"

[2] See Appendix II for names of professors at the City College of New York who were student-leaders and/or valued "cooperators" of the Intercollegiate Socialist Society and its successor, the League for Industrial Democracy.

Wilson called "the perfect friendship," one of the strangest friendships in American political history.

Of his second meeting with Wilson, House said: "It was remarkable. We found ourselves in agreement upon practically every one of the issues of the day. *I never met a man whose thoughts ran so identically with mine.*" And a few weeks later, when Woodrow Wilson again visited him, House could not resist saying as his caller rose to go: "Governor, isn't it strange that two men, who never knew each other before, should think so much alike?"

Wilson answered: "My dear fellow, we have known each other all our lives!" [3]

Edward M. House has been described by another friend, who actually did know him for more than twenty-five years, as being "highly conventional in the social sense" and "highly radical, more than liberal, in the politico-social sense." [4] House believed the United States Constitution, creation of eighteenth century minds, was "not only outmoded, but grotesque" and ought to be scrapped or rewritten.[5] As a practical politician, he realized this could not be done all at once, given the existing state of popular education; so he favored gradual changes which, in the long run, would produce the same results.

A similar point of view was expressed in Woodrow Wilson's campaign speeches, afterwards printed as *The New Freedom.* Previously it had been voiced by both American and British Fabians. Perhaps the voters who read or heard Wilson's speeches at the time dismissed the point as mere campaign oratory; but it was one of those basic issues on which Wilson and House found themselves in full agreement, having reached identical conclusions by alternate routes. As a man who never held an official position, though for nearly seven years he was to wield extraordinary power, the Texas Colonel was technically free to subscribe to any ideas he chose. One cannot help wondering, however, by what superior intellectual process President Wilson was able to reconcile such convictions with the oath he took on March 4, 1913, to uphold and defend the Constitution of the United States.

The political and social credo of Colonel House, in which Wilson so warmly concurred, was unveiled in fictional form shortly after the

[3] Arthur D. Howden Smith, *Mr. House of Texas,* (New York, Funk and Wagnalls, Co., Inc., 1940), p. 43.

[4] *Ibid.,* p. 23.

[5] *Ibid.,* pp. 23; 93.

presidential election. Late in the fall of 1912 there appeared a curious novel entitled *Philip Dru, Administrator*. It was published by B. W. Huebsch, a favorite publisher of the Left and for many years a valued collaborator of American Fabian Socialist groups.[6] Though the book was anonymous, some people surmised that House was the author, and he confessed as much to intimates. The Colonel had written the first draft in December, 1911, while in Austin, Texas, recovering from an illness.

Its radical ideas attracted a degree of attention unwarranted by the book's literary merits, or lack of them. Philip Dru was a young West Pointer who led an armed rebellion against a tyrannical and reactionary government in Washington subservient to the privileged "interests." He became the ruler of America and by a series of Executive decrees proceeded to remold the mechanics of administration, revise the Judiciary, reshape the laws affecting labor and capital, revamp the nation's military forces, and arrange to set up an international body or league of nations.

More specifically, the Administrator appointed a *board of economists* to work out a tariff law leading to "the abolition of the theory of protection as a government policy." He also instructed the board *to work out a graduated income tax*. Philip Dru further called for "a new banking law, affording a flexible currency bottomed largely on commercial assets"; and proposed to make corporations "share with the government and states a certain part of their earnings."[7] The former foreshadowed the Federal Reserve Bank; the latter, the corporation income tax.

Labor, said Dru, should "no longer be classed as an inert commodity to be bought and sold according to the law of supply and demand." The Government would give employment to all who needed it. Dru "prepared an old-age pension law and also a laborers' insurance law," and provided for certain reforms "in the study and practice of medicine." Finally, he "incorporated in the Franchise Law the right of labor to have one representative on the boards of corporations and to share a certain per cent of the earnings above wages, after a reason-

---

[6] In 1922, B. W. Huebsch was a member of the Executive Committee of the American Civil Liberties Union, a Socialist-inspired organization; and in April, 1961 he was one of the sponsors of a rally in New York City to abolish the House Un-American Activities Committee.

[7] *The Intimate Papers of Colonel House*, Charles Seymour, ed., (Boston, Houghton Mifflin Co., 1926), pp. 152-159.

able per cent upon the capital had been earned." In return, labor was to submit all grievances to compulsory arbitration.

When the newly installed Democratic Administration announced the legislative program it wished enacted, House's novel aroused even more pointed comments. Cabinet members remarked on the similarity between Dru's program and the legislation requested over the years by Woodrow Wilson. "All that book has said should be, comes about," wrote Franklin K. Lane, Wilson's Secretary of the Interior, in 1918 to a personal friend. "The President comes to Philip Dru in the end." [8]

Among the junior officials who read the novel and took it to heart was a handsome young Assistant Secretary of the Navy. His name was Franklin Delano Roosevelt, and his doting mother, Sara Delano Roosevelt, was then and always a close friend of Colonel House. The Texas Colonel was the first important Democrat to support Roosevelt's nomination for the Presidency in 1932.[9] Whether House presented a copy of *Philip Dru, Administrator* to the dowager Mrs. Roosevelt or to her son,[10] its contents unquestionably played a part in the political education of still another American president. It even recommended "fireside chats."

Few works of fiction have so deeply affected, for better or worse, the trends of contemporary life in the United States. In effect, *Philip Dru, Administrator* became a kind of handbook or Cooke's Guide for Democratic presidents, who proceeded to throw away the old book of presidential protocol spelling out the Chief Executive's relation to the Congress, the Judiciary and the military. Those tried and true precepts had been honored by every American president, irrespective of party, until Woodrow Wilson and, whatever the personal inadequacies of the incumbent, had served to hold the country together along constitutional lines and preserve it from the dangers noted by de Tocqueville as inherent in any democratic system of government.

Strongly opposed to the division of powers prescribed in the Constitution, Edward M. House was one of the first Americans to foresee the possibility of evading constitutional safeguards by Executive decree and to perceive the vast power to be derived from control over the mechanics of administration—two lush possibilities further explored by other White House advisers since 1932 on a scale un-

[8] Smith, *op. cit.*, pp. 49-50.
[9] Arthur Willert, *The Road to Safety*, (London, Derek Verschoyle, 1952), p. 172. From a letter of Sir William Wiseman to Lord Grey of Falloden.
[10] Smith, *op. cit.*, pp. 366-367.

imagined by Colonel House. In 1963, a Chief Executive even induced the Congress to convey its traditional and long-cherished tariff-making authority to his office, with hardly a voice throughout the country raised in protest.

There was nothing so very mysterious about the source of Woodrow Wilson's radicalism, which he preferred to call "liberalism." It developed (and in his case was perhaps deliberately fostered by far-seeing associates) in an academic atmosphere already tinged with Socialist thinking, where the "scientific" approach to economics and sociology was being extended to history and to the law. From John Stuart Mill, whom Wilson admired, it was not such a far cry to Sidney Webb, who claimed Mill had died a Socialist. The real mystery is how a man like Edward M. House, product of the Old Frontier and the pistol-packing politics of the Southwest, happened to become a vehicle for ideas and programs that were plainly Socialist in origin. For some reason, this has never been explained.

Two years younger than Wilson, House was born in Houston, Texas, in 1858. Reared in an era of gunplay, Comanche raids and rule-of-thumb law in the wild Southwest, he was soft-spoken and courteous; but to the end of his life, prided himself on his skill with a pistol. His father, Thomas William House, was an Englishman who had gone to Texas to fight under General Sam Houston and stayed on to make a fortune there. The elder House often remarked that he wanted to raise his sons to "know and serve England."

Thomas William House acted as an American agent for London banking interests, said by some to be the House of Rothschild, which had invested in Texas rice, cotton and indigo from 1825. At any rate, he was one of the few residents of a Confederate state to emerge from the Civil War with a handsome personal fortune in cotton, land and private banking.[11] He gave his seventh son, Edward, the middle name of Mandell, after a Houston merchant who was a family friend. In later years, this gave rise to a rumor that Edward Mandell House, who became a friend and ally of Kuhn, Loeb and Company in New York City, was of Jewish origin—which was not the case.

As a small boy, Edward attended school for several years in England. Much of his youth and adult life was spent in the British Isles, which he regularly revisited. Like his well-cut suits and proper boots, the radical views he affected so unobtrusively from early manhood were made to order for him in London. Being his father's son, he was

[11] *Ibid.*, pp. 8-11.

readily accepted into those prosperous middle class circles that voted traditionally for a Liberal Party which was increasingly penetrated, after the turn of the century, by Fabian Socialists. Concerning the period from 1895 to 1911 in Britain, a distinguished European visitor, Professor Francisco J. Nitti of Milan, observed:

Indeed, in no country of the world are the middle classes so much inclined towards Socialism as in England, where eminent men of science, dignitaries of the Church and profound thinkers tend more and more towards Socialist doctrines.[12]

Personally, House preferred the company of authors, playwrights and professors, of which the British Fabian Society boasted a noteworthy assortment. Among other connections, Edward M. House formed a lasting friendship with the journalist, George Lansbury,[13] a lifelong pillar of the Fabian Society, who for some years represented its more outspokenly radical wing inside the Independent Labour Party and finally became Parliamentary Leader of the Labour Party. Lansbury's biographer tells how he once persuaded the American soap millionaire, Joseph Fels (a member of the London Fabian Society, thanks to the prodding of Mrs. Fels, née Rothschild[14]), to lend five hundred pounds sterling to underground Russian Social Democrats including Lenin and Trotsky, when they were stranded in England.[14a] From 1912 to 1925 George Lansbury was the editor of the London *Daily Herald*, organ of the Fabian-dominated Labour Party until it ceased publication in 1964.

Though few historians mention it, the medical history of Edward M. House accounts in part for a career that might otherwise seem a marplot's dream. An attack of brain fever in boyhood, followed by a severe sunstroke, had permanently impaired his health. House lived

---

[12] Francisco J. Nitti, *Catholic Socialism*, (London, Sonnenschein, 1895; New York, The Macmillan Co., 1911), p. 312.

[13] Smith, *op. cit.*, pp. 35; 102.

[14] *Fabian News*, (March, 1905), in an article entitled "New Farm Colonies," refers to Joseph Fels as "one of our members." Beatrice Webb, in her diary during May, 1904 quoted by Margaret Cole, *Beatrice Webb*, (New York, Harcourt, Brace, 1946), p. 189 confirms the fact that both Joseph and Mary Fels belonged to the Fabian Society of London. A descendant, Joseph Fels Barnes, currently on the editorial staff of a New York publishing house, was in Moscow on a Rockefeller fellowship during 1931-32, where he was warmly received in deference to his family history.

[14a] Raymond Postgate, *The Life of George Lansbury*, (New York, Longmans, Green and Company, Ltd., 1951), pp. 69-70.

to be nearly eighty, but only by taking precautions not to over exert himself. His preference for remaining in the shadow of large events he had helped shape was due, in the first instance, to a physical inability to endure strong sunlight or heat. He could never spend a summer in Washington.

Passionately interested in politics, domestic and international, House faced the fact as a very young man that he could not hope to withstand the strain and stress of public office. After his father's death, he arranged matters so as to be assured of a regular income of $25,000 a year—an amount he judged suitable to support him comfortably throughout a lifetime of anonymous and unsalaried "public service." A similar notion of Socialist "public service," subsidized by capitalist dividends, was popular among leading British Fabians of Victorian and Edwardian days, notably Sidney Webb, and has its modern counterpart in the support received by outstanding Fabian Socialists from private foundations in the United States.

It is hard to say just when House conceived the bold plan of penetrating America's Democratic Party at the apex and molding the policies of a sympathetic Chief Executive in the interests of a Socialist program to change the face of America. Whether the idea was his own or inspired by Fabian friends in Britain, every step he took over the years appeared to be directed toward its fulfillment. Though it involved years of obscure political chores and patient waiting, in the end House came closer to achieving his purpose than England's Fabian Socialists were ever able to do within the framework of the Liberal Party. His career was a living example of Socialist gradualism at work.

With the election of Woodrow Wilson, House became a power at home and abroad. From then until their final break at Paris in 1918, the President relied on House, trusted him completely and never made a move without consulting him. While previous Presidents had their confidants, nothing quite like the association between House and Wilson had ever been seen before in America. The understanding between them was based on ideology as well as affection. It was as if they shared a mutual secret not to be divulged to the American people.

As Bernard Baruch said, and he had reason to know, "the Colonel's hand was in everything"—from Cabinet appointments to decisions affecting war and peace. The small apartment Colonel House had rented in an unfashionable block on East Thirty-fifth Street in New York City became a nerve center of the nation. There was a switchboard with direct telephone lines to the White House and the State, War and Navy Departments, and a constant stream of callers. People came to House, as they had been doing all his life, because he was too fragile in health to go to them; and this merely enhanced his importance. Even the President visited him incognito, almost as often as the Colonel visited the White House.

From the time the United States declared war on Germany, the apartment above Colonel House's was occupied by Sir William Wiseman, wartime chief of the British Secret Service in America, whose functions included counterespionage as well as high politics. Introduced to the President by House, the young and enterprising Sir William had already become a great favorite with Wilson, who naively used him as a personal emissary on various confidential missions to London and Paris. When the war ended, Sir William Wiseman remained in the United States and joined the firm of Kuhn, Loeb and Company.

Just after the United States broke diplomatic relations with Germany as a preliminary to declaring war, an episode involving Sir William occurred, which shows the partiality that highly placed American liberals felt for the outbreak of revolution in Russia. In New York City Leon Trotsky—then employed as an electrician at the Fox Film Studios—was the leader of a Russian revolutionary group with headquarters at 63 West 107th Street.[15] Wiseman was interested in this group principally because its activities were financed by a German-language newspaper in New York known to be receiving funds from German Government sources. Following the Kerensky Revolution, Trotsky sailed for Russia with a group of associates on March 27, 1917, via the Norwegian American Line. He was carrying a substantial amount of money.

When the vessel stopped at Halifax, Nova Scotia, Canadian authorities picked Trotsky off the ship and held him.[16] From Petrograd the gentle Social Democrat, Kerensky, cabled Woodrow Wilson asking

[15] Willert, op. cit., p. 29.

[16] On the night before his departure, Trotsky had made a speech before a joint meeting of German and Russian Socialists at Harlem River Park Casino in New York City. Speaking in both German and Russian, he said: "I am going back to Russia to overthrow the provisional government and stop the war with Germany and allow no interference from any outside government." A report on this meeting had been submitted to Colonel Van Deman and General Churchill of United States Military Intelligence. Senate Document No. 62, 66th Congress, *Report and Hearings of the Subcommittee on the Judiciary, United States Senate,* 1919, Vol. II, p. 2680.

the latter to intervene. Colonel House informed Wiseman of the President's desire that Trotsky be allowed to proceed. Wishing to oblige its new and powerful Ally in what did not appear to be a very important matter, London instructed the Canadians to send Trotsky on his way—leaving Sir William Wiseman, who had forwarded the President's request, technically blameless.

So Washington and London innocently furthered the plans of German Military Intelligence, which at about the same time passed Lenin in a sealed railway car through Germany to Russia, there to assume with Trotsky the leadership of the Bolsheviki. Together, Lenin and Trotsky soon overthrew Kerensky, pulled Russia out of the war, and freed German armies on the Eastern front to fight Allied troops in the West. The release of Trotsky was a prime instance of the dangerous results of high-level civilian meddling in wartime;[17] as well as a classic demonstration, the first in history, of how Socialism opens the door to Communism.

This remarkable episode has been preserved for posterity by the usually well-informed Sir Arthur Willert, London *Times* correspondent in Washington, who worked closely with Sir William Wiseman. Willert was distressed by what he called the "deplorable" tendencies of a good many British lecturers and travelers who roved the United States during the earlier part of the war "saying whatever their politics and prejudices dictated."[18] Conspicuous among them was Mrs. F. W. Pethick-Lawrence, distaff member of a well-known British Fabian husband-and-wife team, who waged an energetic "peace campaign" in America after her own country was at war.

Mrs. Pethick-Lawrence stayed at Hull House in Chicago, rallying feminists, social workers and college professors and receiving the wholehearted backing of Jane Addams and her many Socialist friends.[19] Jane Addams, an American Fabian Socialist and an eventual Nobel Peace Prize winner, became a world celebrity as a result of her

[17] Willert, *op. cit.*, p. 29. Based on information obtained from the private papers of Sir William Wiseman.

[18] *Ibid.*, p. 89.

[19] *Revolutionary Radicalism, Its History, Purpose and Tactics*. Report of the Joint Legislative Committee Investigating Seditious Activities, filed April 24, 1920, in the Senate of the State of New York, (Albany, J. P. Lyon Co., 1920), Vol. I, p. 974. Report by Louis P. Lochner, January 18, 1915: "Almost coincident with Mme. (Rosika) Schwimmer, (a German agent) came a noted Englishwoman, Mrs. Pethick-Lawrence of London, England. For several weeks she was a guest of Miss Addams, and came before many organizations with her Woman's Movement for Constructive Peace."

pacifist activities, which continued throughout the war. Even Colonel House had conferred with her before departing for Berlin on his own peace mission preceding the outbreak of hostilities in 1914.[20] In June, 1915, on her way to the Hague Conference as a leading representative of the "neutral women," Jane Addams was the admired guest in London of Sidney and Beatrice Webb, who had visited her at Hull House seventeen years before.[21]

What troubled Willert and other more or less official British observers was the fact that so many of these self-styled peace movements were also fostered by representatives of the German Foreign Office,[22] eager to deter the United States at any cost from joining the war on the side of the Allies. Among the groups supporting Mrs. Pethick-Lawrence was the Organization of American Women for Strict Neutrality, founded by a Miss L. N. Miller of Roland Park, Baltimore. Supposedly an independent movement, this organization received monetary and other aid from German Government sources and had branches in many American cities.[23] It was reported that the Chicago membership list included Nina Nitze, wife of a University of Chicago professor.

Nina Nitze's brother, Paul Hilken[24] of Roland Park, Baltimore, was later discovered to have served as the chief paymaster for German saboteurs in the United States, who on instructions from the *Dritte Abteilung* in Berlin set off the notorious Black Tom and Kingsland explosions.[25] Her son, Paul Nitze, has risen in our own day to become Secretary of the Navy in the Kennedy and Johnson Administrations and a spokesman for civilian as opposed to military defense planning —which only goes to show how neatly World War I memories have been swept under the rug.

[20] Smith, *op. cit.*, p. 102.

[21] Cole, *Beatrice Webb*, p. 40.

[22] *Senate Document No. 62*, 66th Congress. Extensive testimony and exhibits to this effect are presented throughout Vol. I and Vol. II. See especially Vol. II, pp. 1394-95; 1791-1795.

[23] *Ibid.*, p. 1792.

[24] A special Act of Congress was passed compelling Paul Hilken to testify concerning his World War I dealings with German sabotage agents. This testimony became a part of the Mixed Claims Commission Record, now preserved at the National Archives in Washington. It was reviewed in Justice Owen D. Roberts' report on his decision of October 30, 1939, rendered as Umpire for the Commission.

[25] The *Dritte Abteilung*, or Section III of German Military Intelligence, planned for and recruited volunteers for sabotage and terrorist acts abroad. See Records of the Mixed Claims Commission, National Archives, Washington.

2.

In March, 1916, Sir Arthur Willert wrote to his editor in London: "We ought to make it impossible for people like ——, ——, —— or —— to find here the hearing they are refused in England. It is really extraordinary how the country is being penetrated by the wrong sort of Englishmen . . . . I imagine there are plenty of German Social Democrats who would be only too glad to come over here from Germany and air their views. But they do not come for obvious reasons; and I cannot see why our own precautions should be so patently inferior to those of Germany." [26]

As a result of this pointed suggestion, some official steps seem to have been taken. Soon Willert was pleased to report a "different" type of British lecturer and traveler coming to the United States. Among the "right sort," he guilelessly listed Emmeline Pankhurst, the suffragist; Granville Barker, the playwright; G. M. Trevelyan, the historian; and S. K. Ratcliffe, author and editor.[27] Ironically enough, they too all belonged to the London Fabian Society which, like American Socialism, was divided on the war issue. S. K. Ratcliffe was a member of the Fabian Executive and its chief wartime courier to the United States. He was an editor of the Fabian-controlled *New Statesman*[28] and became the London representative of the *New Republic*, a so-called liberal weekly which had been founded in New York in 1913-14 as an opposite number to the *New Statesman*.

Financed by Dorothy Whitney Straight, whose brother was a J. P. Morgan partner, the *New Republic* was staffed in the beginning by a number of talented, ambitious and socially acceptable young Socialists from Harvard, who dropped the Socialist label but not its program soon after graduation. Among them was the pundit and

[26] Willert, *op. cit.*, p. 89.

[27] *Ibid.*, p. 93.

[28] In the Jubilee Issue of the *New Statesman* (April 19, 1963, p. 543) the editor, John Freeman, stated: "We were founded in April, 1913, by a group of Fabians, among whom Beatrice and Sidney Webb, Bernard Shaw and J. C. Squire were most closely concerned. Clifford Sharp was the first editor. He was succeeded in 1931 by Kingsley Martin, who occupied the editorial chair for 30 years." In the same issue, R. H. S. Crossman, a former chairman of the Fabian Society, stated (p. 551): "During 50 years the fortunes of the *New Statesman* and the Labour Party have been more intimately linked than either side would care to admit. Why have successive editors and successive Party Leaders deliberately underestimated this intimacy?"

columnist, Walter Lippmann, who had joined the Fabian Society of London in 1909.[29]

The British Marxist and Fabian, Professor Harold J. Laski, teaching at Harvard from 1915 to 1919, was a frequent wartime contributor, though his articles were discreetly signed H. J. L. The *New Republic*[30] supported Woodrow Wilson and continued to support him throughout the war—in contrast to its more overtly radical sister weekly, *The Nation*, which maintained a pacifist and anti-war stand, idolized conscientious objectors like Eugene V. Debs and Scott Nearing, yet did not blanch at bloody revolution in Russia.

Always limited in circulation, the *New Republic* catered to an intellectual and professional elite rather than to the perfervid mass of Socialist sympathizers in New York City. Apparently, it was in high favor with key personages in the Wilson Administration, especially Colonel House. By what Lippmann prudently calls "a certain parallelism of reasoning," the *New Republic* often suggested policies that President Wilson followed. In those years the paper enjoyed a kind of mysterious importance which it never quite equaled again, not even under the New Frontier.

During the winter of 1916 young Lippmann had several interviews, "such as any journalist has," with the President; but he denied that his personal relations with Wilson were ever close. Thereafter, Herbert Croly, senior editor of the *New Republic*, and Walter Lippmann *met about once every fortnight with Colonel House* to discuss problems "relating to the management of neutrality" prior to the reelection of President Wilson in 1916.[31] With S. K. Ratcliffe commuting from London to attend editorial luncheons at the *New Republic*, the Fabian circuit was complete.

Following the example of top-level British Fabians, *New Republic* editors moved in good society and were considered eminently respectable. Penetration and permeation were their tasks. Like the Webbs

---

[29] *Fabian News,* (October, 1909)

[30] In addition to Lippmann, the original staff of the *New Republic* included Herbert Croly, author of *The Promise of American Life*, who secured the financial backing; Philip Littell, Walter Weyl, Charles Rudyard and Francis Hackett. Soon Charles Merz and Alvin Johnson, later to head the New School for Social Research, joined the board of editors. In 1922 Robert Morss Lovett became its book review editor.

[31] Walter Lippmann, "Notes for a Biography," *New Republic,* (July 16, 1930).

and other worldly-wise leaders of the London Fabian Society, they accepted the war as inevitable and concentrated on planning for the New Order, which all good Socialists felt sure must emerge from social unrest anticipated after the war.[32]

It was no accident that the Fabian Socialist Walter Lippmann, while on the staff of the *New Republic*, was named by Colonel House in 1917 as executive secretary of a confidential group to formulate war aims and postwar policy for President Wilson. There the famous —or infamous—slogan, "Peace Without Victory" was born, to be revived in a more literal sense many years later during the Korean War.

That postwar planning group, dubbed The Inquiry (or Enquiry), was headed by Dr. Sidney Mezes, president of the City College of New York and brother-in-law of Colonel House. On the pretext that any publicity might give rise to rumors that the United States was preparing to accept a negotiated peace, the existence of the group was kept secret. Meetings were held in the New York headquarters of the National Geographic Society at 156th Street and Broadway by courtesy of Dr. Isaiah Bowman, a director of the Geographical Society and longtime president of Johns Hopkins University. According to Lippmann, some 150 college professors and other "specialists" (who included the Reverend Norman Thomas, later head of the American Socialist Party) were recruited to collect data for eventual use at the Peace Conference. Since no government funds were provided in those days for such lofty projects, the working expenses of the group were privately paid—presumably by President Wilson himself, although he was not a wealthy man.

Eight memoranda, the so-called territorial sections of the Fourteen Points, were prepared by The Inquiry. This document, with several additions, was given by the President to Congress and to a waiting world on January 8, 1918. One impromptu addition was some kind words uttered by President Wilson about the "sincerity of purpose" of the Russian Bolsheviki—though the same might also be said of any forthright thug. While the implications of the Fourteen Points, wrapped as they were in high-flown verbiage, were not generally understood, the document was widely applauded by members of President Wilson's own party in Congress as well as by Progressive

---

[32] In 1919, the Reverend Lyman P. Powell, President Wilson's old friend, edited a two volume symposium published by The Review of Reviews Company, entitled *Social Unrest*. It contained articles by many well-known British and American Fabian Socialists, as well as some non-Socialists.

Republicans and Socialists—and, of course, by the college professors whose thinking was guided by the *New Republic*.[33]

Since then, it has sometimes been said that Walter Lippmann "wrote the Fourteen Points for President Wilson," a claim Lippmann has taken pains to disavow. Obviously, he assisted at the birth in more ways than one. When a clarification of the Fourteen Points was asked by Allied Prime Ministers in November, 1918, thirteen of the fourteen interpretive sections were written by Walter Lippmann at the request of Colonel House. The fourteenth (relating to the League of Nations) was written by Frank Cobb, editor of the Pulitzer-owned New York *World*, where Lippmann was subsequently employed as chief editorial writer. The demands outlined in the Fourteen Points, however, did not originate with Lippmann nor with The Inquiry. They were conceived by Sidney Webb and the Fabian Society of London.

In December, 1917, a statement of war aims, prepared by Fabian members of the International Socialist Bureau in London, had been laid before a special conference of the British Labour Party and Trades Union Council. Its authors were Camille Huysmans, a Belgian Socialist, then secretary of the International Socialist Bureau; British Fabians Arthur Henderson and Sidney Webb; and the alleged "ex"-Fabian, Ramsay MacDonald. Sidney Webb, whose skill in drafting memoranda has rarely been equaled, did the actual writing. Promptly published as *Labour's War Aims*, it was the first general statement of British Fabian Socialist policy in world affairs and was designed to be copied by Socialists in other countries and to establish the primacy of the Fabian Society within the postwar Socialist International.

Labour's War Aims antedated the Fourteen Points and included every item covered in the later document: universal "democracy"; an end to imperialism and secret diplomacy; arms limitation, and abolition of profits from armaments; plans for settling such thorny issues as Alsace-Lorraine, Poland and Palestine, and for the self-determination of subject nationalities in the Austro-Hungarian and Ottoman Empires; economic controls and an international commission for reparations and war damage. Moreover, it called for collective security, a supranational authority, an international court of justice and international legislation on labor and social matters,[34] in what its Fabian authors fondly hoped might soon be an all-Socialist world.

[33] John Dos Passos, *Mr. Wilson's War*, Lewis Gannett, ed., (New York, Doubleday & Co., 1962), p. 307.
[34] Margaret Cole, *The Story of Fabian Socialism*, (London, Heinemann Educational Books, Ltd., 1961), pp. 169-171.

These were the high-sounding aims which afterwards became the stock in trade of liberal-Socialist and Socialist-labor groups in every Allied country. Somehow, Woodrow Wilson, the President of the United States, became a mouthpiece for the selfsame demands. Walter Lippmann, always gifted at double-talk, would doubtless attribute the resemblance to "a certain parallelism of reasoning." It hardly seems necessary, however, to invoke extrasensory perception when such well-placed physical facilities existed for transmitting the original Fabian program verbally and textually to the President. How far Woodrow Wilson was aware of his debt to the British Fabian Socialist planners, we may never know; but it seems impossible that the alert, omniscient Colonel House, who shortly before the New Year, 1918, carried all documentary material relating to the Fourteen Points to the White House, could have failed to be informed of or to connive in the transmission.

That view is confirmed by the curious mission on which Ray Stannard Baker, the former muckraker who became press chief at the Paris Peace Conference, was sent by House in February, 1918. Baker was to "report fully for the information of the President and the State Department on the state of radical opinion and organization, *especially the attitude of labor in England,* and later possibly in France and Italy." [35] He was given confidential introductions to various left wing leaders in Great Britain and instructed to send his letters via Embassy pouch and his cabled reports in secret code. At House's suggestion that it would be better if Baker were not known to be an agent of the government, he was accredited as a correspondent of the *New Republic* and the New York *World*—though he never sent dispatches to either.

The first person Baker met in England was Professor Gilbert Murray, an Asquith Liberal of long-standing Fabian sympathies. Murray told him that the Asquith faction, opposing Prime Minister Lloyd George, was prepared to accept Wilson's leadership and program of action, and in this was supported by nearly all of the labor groups, including the Labour Party. The next Englishman he saw was Graham Wallas, one of the original Big Four of the Fabian Society, who had delivered the Lowell Lectures at Harvard and dedicated his book, *The Great Society,* to young Walter Lippmann. A further list of the persons interviewed by Baker reads like a *Who's Who* of the London

[35] Ray Stannard Baker, *An American Chronicle,* (New York, Charles Scribner's Sons, 1945), p. 306. (Italics added.)

Fabian Society—G. M. Trevelyan, Arthur Ponsonby, Philip Snowden, H. W. Massingham, George Lansbury, Arthur Henderson, Bertrand Russell and Mary Agnes Hamilton, to mention only a few.

Though he met several Lords of the Round Table group, who backed Lloyd George and the Empire, Baker felt they had outlived their time. His real enthusiasm was reserved for the Fabians; although he did not appear to be aware of the existence or function of that discreet Socialist Society. To him the Fabians were merely "thoughtful intellectuals" and Labourites. Finally, at the invitation of the playwright, Granville Barker, he lunched with Sidney and Beatrice Webb —and pronounced it one of the great experiences of his life to sit between them and be instructed in the laws of economic affairs. Baker found the Webbs "great admirers of President Wilson, and anxious for a better understanding between the 'democratic' groups of England and the United States." [36]

Even now, almost half a century after the fact, it is humiliating for an American to find an emissary of the White House displaying such worshipful admiration for the leaders of a foreign secret society, anxious only to utilize the world-wide prestige of the President of the United States to further their own radical intrigues at home and abroad. Yet Baker's abject performance was praised by House's man in the State Department, the then-Counselor, Frank Polk. And much later, Wilson himself told Baker, "Your letters at that time helped me." [37] Ray Stannard Baker was the individual finally chosen by Wilson to be his official biographer.

As Sidney Webb's honored guest, Baker was present at the fateful conference of June, 1918, when the British Labour Party was formally constituted under Fabian Socialist control and adopted Webb's blueprint for chaos, *Labour and the New Social Order*, as its permanent platform. Baker appraised that managed conference as being quite the most revealing exhibit of British opinion he had yet seen. In a lyric report to Washington he described the new Party as "the most precious and vital force in British life today"—differing sharply with America's wise old labor chieftain, Samuel Gompers, who said the Labour Party in England did not really represent the rank-and-file of the British working class.[38]

The confidential reports sent by Baker were calculated to persuade

[36] Baker, *op. cit.*, p. 339.
[37] *Ibid.*, p. 355.
[38] *Ibid.*, pp. 343-345.

President Wilson that labor in Britain, as well as on the Continent, regarded him as a man of supreme vision, called by destiny to unite the forces of "true liberalism" throughout the world. Slightly reversing the true order of events, Baker assured Wilson that British labor was not only in sympathy with his "democratic" policies, but "indeed, had incorporated them in its own statement of War Aims!" At the same time, Baker's letters warned that "Mr. Wilson can never hope for whole-hearted support upon the reconstructive side of his program from those *at present in power,* either here or in France." Thus the ground was prepared for the Peace Conference, even before the blood-shed had ended; and seeds of personal prejudice were planted in the President's mind against the Allied statesmen, representing old-line Liberal Parties, with whom he would be obliged to deal.

Such advice from a trusted source naturally tended to strengthen Wilson in his determination to hold out for unconditional acceptance of the Fourteen Points as a basis for peace, and to insist that the League of Nations be considered an integral part of any peace treaty. The first American version of a "convention" for a League was drafted by the President's friend, Colonel House, on July 13 and 14, 1918, in his summer home at Magnolia, Massachusetts, with the aid of Professor David H. Miller of The Inquiry group. Colonel House did not undertake this task until after he received a copy of the British Government's draft plan, which was forwarded to him, unread, by the President.[39] It was by no means the first plan for a supranational authority, purporting to be a preventive against war, that had come to the Colonel's attention.

Fully three years earlier the Fabian Research Department in London, then shepherded by Beatrice Webb, had prepared two reports of its own on the subject, together with a project by a Fabian Committee for an international authority along Socialist lines. Bearing the signature of Leonard Woolf, it was printed in 1915 as a special supplement of the *New Statesman* and hailed with rapture by Herbert Croly's *New Republic.* Under the title *International Government,* this Fabian Socialist document was published the following year by Brentano's in New York.

The draft so speedily produced by Colonel House on two summer days in Massachusetts bore a striking resemblance to the Fabian proposals, whose Socialist authors were not otherwise in a position to impose their ideas on the British Foreign Office. House's twenty-three

[39] Smith, *op. cit.,* pp. 259-260.

articles formed the basis for the President's tentative draft, which adopted all but five of those articles and became the first official American plan for a League of Nations. Eventually the so-called Wilson plan was incorporated with a revised British Government version for presentation to the League of Nations Commission at the Paris Peace Conference.

From such motley materials the Covenant of the League was stitched together. And yet, when it was finally completed, Woodrow Wilson considered it so peculiarly his own that he was willing to invite personal and political defeat, to sacrifice the fortunes of his Party and his own far from robust health rather than allow a single line of it to be changed. To a practical politician like Colonel House —who had long since learned, as Sidney Webb also had, the necessity for graceful compromise when no better recourse offered—Wilson's attitude must have seemed fantastic as well as suicidal.

The perfect friendship of Woodrow Wilson and Edward M. House ended as abruptly as it began. All the world knows that the break between the two men, predicted annually for seven years by newsmen, occurred at the Peace Conference in Paris. No two historians agree on the reasons, and the principals have never divulged them. Certain facts, however, are evident. Public sentiment in America had turned against the President and his internationalist views. In November, 1918, he lost the Congress and with it any hope of securing rubber-stamp approval for the Treaty or the League. House attributed this, in part, to Wilson's own indiscretion. For Wilson, House had lost his political magic.

In December, 1918, Woodrow Wilson went to the Peace Conference in Paris, a defeated man too unfamiliar with defeat to recognize it. Such authority as he enjoyed was derived from popular acclaim in Europe and was largely ceremonial. Though hailed as a savior by millions, his power was strictly limited. He was a president nearing the end of his second term who had forfeited his support at home— and every politician in the world knew it. While he might persuade, he could not command.

Shrewdly, House had advised Wilson to make no more than a brief appearance and a few speeches in Europe, and return to pull strings from the White House. The Colonel also recommended sending a bipartisan committee of Congress to the Peace Conference. But their relationship had already changed: Wilson no longer listened to anything so unflattering as common sense. As Sir William Wiseman cynically remarked, the President was drawn to Paris as a debutante is entranced by the prospect of her first ball.

In those days it was a generally accepted fact that the treaty-making power of the United States resided not merely in the President, but in the President *with* two-thirds of the Senate present and voting. The Constitution said so; and as yet no techniques had been devised by faceless bureaucrats or Executive aides for diverting or assigning that power, or preempting it piecemeal. *Philip Dru, Administrator,* was not yet in the saddle—Yalta and Teheran were still undreamed of—and nobody in America except a handful of Socialist intellectuals and foreign-born radicals wanted any part of International Government. So Wilson, the bitter-ender, went home to failure and collapse; while House, the gradualist who never stopped trying, remained in Paris, attempting to salvage by negotiation whatever fragments of his program could still be saved. As it had been from the beginning, their real quarrel was still with the Constitution, and on that rock they foundered separately.

The first attempt by Fabian Socialists to penetrate and permeate the Executive branch of the United States Government failed in the end. But they would try again, and go on trying, until fortress America was leveled, or until their own long-range subversion was definitely exposed. Colonel House was only one man, where a multitude was needed. He had set the pattern and outlined goals for the future, and he still had a scheme or two in mind. In particular, he foresaw it would be necessary for the Fabians to develop a top-level Anglo-American planning group in the field of foreign relations which could secretly influence policy on the one hand and gradually "educate" public opinion on the other. His experience in Paris had shown him that it must be a bipartisan group.

To the ambitious young Fabians, British and American, who had flocked to the Peace Conference as economists and junior officials, it soon became evident that a New World Order was not about to be produced at Paris. Most of the younger men in whom House placed his hopes for the future of liberalism and a positive foreign policy in America had already departed—Walter Lippmann, Felix Frankfurter, and above all, young Franklin D. Roosevelt. The few American intellectuals still remaining in Paris, who clustered around Professor James T. Shotwell, were young men of still undefined political affiliations and excellent social standing—such as John Foster and Allen Dulles, nephews of Wilson's Secretary of State, Robert Lansing; Christian

Herter, and Tasker Bliss, the political general who did not get along well with Pershing.

For them, Colonel House arranged a dinner meeting at the Hotel Majestic on May 19, 1919, together with a select group of Fabian-certified Englishmen—notably, Arnold Toynbee, R. H. Tawney and John Maynard Keynes. All were equally disillusioned, for varied reasons, by the consequences of the peace. They made a gentlemen's agreement to set up an organization, with branches in England and America, "to facilitate the *scientific* study of international questions." As a result two potent and closely related opinion-making bodies were founded, which only began to reach their full growth in the nineteen-forties, coincident with the formation of the Fabian International Bureau. The English branch was called the Royal Institute of International Affairs. The American branch, first known as the Institute of International Affairs, was reorganized in 1921 as the Council on Foreign Relations.

Edward M. House, the lifelong radical whose name was listed in the New York *Social Register,* in his quiet way had set the wave of the future in motion.

13

Left Hands Across The Sea

1.

ORGANIZATIONALLY, Fabian Socialism struck roots in the United States with the founding of the Intercollegiate Socialist Society (ISS) in 1905. Earlier attempts to establish Fabianism in America, which for a time seemed so promising, had proved impermanent—possibly because they tried to cover too much ground too fast. Fabian gradualists had not yet discovered how to make haste slowly *in America*.

After nearly twenty years of experimenting with utopian front-organizations, social-reform clubs and secret study circles in ivied halls—of proselyting among writers, preachers, suffragists, settlement workers, university professors and assorted intelligentsia—the Fabian Socialist movement in the United States of 1905 was no more than a sprinkling of disconnected groups and scattered individuals. Robert Hunter, who became a member of the Executive Committee of the ISS but in the end renounced his ties with Socialism, has described the situation as he knew it in those early days:

When I was a resident at Hull House in Chicago, at Toynbee Hall in London, and at the University settlement in New York, I was drawn by some bond of sympathy into close association with the labor and socialist leaders of the three great cities. For many years at home and abroad, I passed from one group to another in a world little known at the time—a world almost exclusively occupied with social problems and their solutions. The groups in America were small and without influence; but in Europe the leaders were in Parliament, and lines were forming in preparation for the class conflicts which followed the World War.[1]

[1] Robert Hunter, *Revolution*, (New York, Harper & Brothers, 1940), p. 6.

176

Over the years, a certain number of Americans had discreetly joined the Fabian Society of London, partly because of its snob appeal, partly because there did not seem to be any comparable organization at home. In Britain, the Fabian Society taught manners to raucous partisans of revolution and made university-trained men and women the spokesmen for a type of Socialism that to many seemed a substitute for or an adjunct of religion.

In America, a new Socialist Party, formed in 1902 by Eugene V. Debs and Morris Hillquit,[2] had polled a total of 400,000 votes in the presidential elections of 1904. When analyzed, much of that vote was found to have come from Russian-Jewish immigrants in the New York needle trades, who had streamed to America in the eighties and nineties, bringing with them European ideologies of revolt;[3] and from the remnants of outlawed Anarchist labor groups in the West who flocked into Big Bill Haywood's newly organized Industrial Workers of the World. Despite an impressive showing at the polls, in the light of America's election laws there was little prospect that Socialism could ever really come to power in the United States through a third party. For most of those who had voted the Socialist ticket, revolution was still the goal and violence was by no means abjured.

It was not by political platforms and programs, but as an alleged "educational" movement that Fabian Socialism gained a lasting foothold in the United States. Lessons in leftism for college students proved to be the magic formula that unexpectedly opened the door to future influence and respectability. Under the pretext of satisfying young peoples' "normal desire" for information on the nature of Socialism, the ISS—which in 1921 changed its name to the League for Industrial Democracy (LID)—was able to establish itself unobtrusively as an American outpost and affiliate of the London Fabian Society.

Having endured more than half a century, it is today the oldest continuing Socialist society in the country—the deceptively mild and

[2] Morris Hillquit, New York; national secretary, Socialist Party of America; joint publisher, *The Call*; instructor, and lecturer, Rand School of Social Sciences; national council, League for Industrial Democracy; national committee, American Civil Liberties Union; one of original founders, Intercollegiate Socialist Society; contributing editor, *Labor Age;* chairman, Committee on Organization and Finance, Conference for Progressive Political Action. *Railway Review*, Chicago, (January 27, 1923).

[3] Mark Starr, "Garment Workers: 'Welfare Unionism'," *Current History*, (July, 1954), Reprint by International Ladies Garment Workers Union. No page numbers.

beneficent mother society from which a whole swarm of destructive activities and organizations has sprung. The LID in 1956 even supplied a chairman for the Socialist International.[4] At a succession of latter-day anniversary dinners, graced by an imposing array of higher educators, theologians, industrial union czars and public officials, the tale of its modest beginnings has been told and re-told.

Late in the afternoon of September 12, 1905, a hundred-odd dissatisfied adults and two college students gathered in a loft above Peck's Restaurant in New York's famed fish market district. Of the ten who signed the original call to the meeting, all but the youthful Jack London and Upton Sinclair had been moving spirits in the American Fabian League.[5] Some, like Colonel Thomas Wentworth Higginson and Clarence Darrow, had even helped to launch the first Bellamy Nationalist clubs, demonstrating a continuity in the Fabian movement, from its beginnings in this country, that persists to the present day. It is a species of profane apostolic succession, traceable directly to the first high priest of Fabian Socialism, Sidney Webb, and beyond him more mysteriously to the author of all Social Democracy—the diabolically inspired Karl Marx, seated in his London study with half a dozen black cats climbing up his arms and shoulders.[6]

Not only the signers of the call but those who responded to it were confirmed advocates of Socialism in quest of a following. Among them were such characters as William Z. Foster, Elizabeth Gurley Flynn and Ella Reeve Bloor, who at a later date became leaders of the Communist Party in the United States. Their presence at the founders' meeting of the ISS testified to the essential unity of all professing the Social Democratic faith, despite some differences on method, procedure and dogma which became increasingly acute during World War I and after the Russian Revolution.

[4] The late Bjaarne Braatoy, a former president of the League for Industrial Democracy and a World War II staff member of the Office of Strategic Services, became chairman of the Socialist International in 1956. He died of a heart attack in 1957.

[5] Signers of the original call were: Colonel Thomas Wentworth Higginson, Clarence Darrow, Charlotte Perkins Gilman, J. G. Phelps Stokes, B. O. Flower, Leonard O. Abbott, Oscar Lovell Triggs, William English Walling, Jack London and Upton Sinclair.

[6] Max Beer, *Fifty Years of International Socialism*, (London, Allen & Unwin, 1935), p. 137. Account of an interview with Maltman Barry, a contributor in the eighteen-seventies to the London *Standard*, who frequently visited Karl Marx at home.

This basic sympathy serves to explain certain otherwise mystifying features in the society's subsequent history. Namely, its intensive efforts during the nineteen-twenties to furnish legal aid and subsistence for the then-illegal Communist Party of the United States; and the visible determination of ISS members, individually and collectively, since 1917 to insure the survival of the Socialist Fatherland, notwithstanding the fact that their organization ultimately took steps to bar known American Communists from its ranks.

From that first enthusiastic gathering at Peck's Restaurant, the ISS was born. The object of the new venture was discreetly understated —a departure from previous techniques—yet broad enough to embrace many Socialist factions. It was declared to be purely "for the purpose of promoting an intelligent interest in Socialism among college men and women, graduate and undergraduate . . . and the encouraging of all legitimate endeavours to awaken an interest in Socialism among the educated men and women of the country." Membership in the Socialist Party was *not* a prerequisite for membership in the ISS.

Jack London, flushed with his recent success as the novelist of the great outdoors and the darling of the conservationists, was the unanimous choice for president. J. G. Phelps Stokes and Upton Sinclair were elected vice presidents and Owen R. Lovejoy, reformer and Ethical Culturist, was treasurer. Morris Hillquit, Katherine Maltby Meserole, George Strobell and the Reverend George Willis Cooke were named to the Executive Committee. On the plea that the Executive of a collegiate society ought to include at least one undergraduate, Harry Laidler, then a student at Wesleyan, was added as an afterthought.

In various fumigated accounts of the Intercollegiate Socialist Society's formation, one point is passed over lightly if not wholly suppressed. Nominally, the new organization existed chiefly to stimulate an interest in Socialism among undergraduates, who were to be organized in campus chapters or clubs under a centralized leadership. Yet only a few of its hundred or more founding members were primarily involved in collegiate activities. What, then, was the function of the ISS with reference to its adult founders and to the successive generations of college alumni who remained so firmly attached to it over the years?

Not for more than fifty years was its true purpose officially dis-

closed. By that time a substantial number of its trainees and "cooperators" had achieved influential posts in education and in government.[7]
Others controlled the expenditure of multi-million dollar labor union
funds. Their combined influence was widespread, and their personal
respectability was assured. Only then was it considered safe to admit,
in literature designed for student recruitment, that the ISS had actually been *founded as an American Fabian Society*[8]—a secret society
of intellectuals, that would provide the leadership for a Fabian Socialist movement devoted to gaining political power in America, directly
or indirectly. Just as in the London Fabian Society, individual members were expected to be politically active in their chosen spheres,
while the ISS itself remained aloof from public controversy on electoral and policy matters.

Because British Fabians of the day gave top priority to the formation of student groups at Oxford and Cambridge, their American
understudies now stressed the importance of recruiting bright and
ambitious adolescents. Here, again, the ISS preferred to mask its
motives. For years ISS spokesmen continued to protest that their intention was *not to indoctrinate.* To an attack in *Collier's*, Colonel
Thomas Wentworth Higginson replied wittily but far from truthfully:
"The primary aim of the society was to create students of Socialism,
not to produce Socialists, and any who criticized this object must be
classed with those medieval grammarians who wrote, 'May God
confound thee for thy theory of irregular verbs!' " [9] There is a marked
similarity between his argument and the grounds sometimes given
today for inviting Communist Party speakers to address campus audiences.

By way of further dissembling their proselyting zeal, student chapters of the ISS even adopted the practice of inviting an occasional
speaker opposed to Socialism. In the organization's *Bulletin* for 1912,
Professor V. Karapetoff of Cornell University explained: "From an
educational point of view, this is an excellent training for analysis
and debate." As a result, university administrations did not seriously
interfere with the "peaceful activities" of the student chapters. At the
same time, such undergraduate groups provided a buffer for Socialist

---

[7] See Appendix II.
[8] From a prospectus of 1959-60 issued nationwide for the Students' League for
Industrial Democracy, under the masthead of the League for Industrial Democracy. (Italics added.)
[9] (Italics added.)

professors, who had previously feared, with good reason, to expose themselves.

It was a full half century before the ISS finally conceded that from the first its intent had been fiercely and fervently missionary. In a fiftieth anniversary commemorative booklet,[10] inscribed to Dr. Harry Laidler "for a lifetime of dedicated service," Mina Weisenberg acknowledged that the organization had always aimed *to capture the heads and the hearts of the nation's future leaders*.[11] True, one did not need to be a Socialist in order to join a college club; but somehow—as in the earlier American Fabian League—only convinced Socialists were accepted as officers of campus chapters or were welcomed after graduation into the parent society.

On the proverbial shoestring, the ISS began its work among the colleges within a few months after its formation. Unlike European universities, which had long been breeding-places for student Socialism, the undergraduate field in America was still largely a virgin one. Before the Intercollegiate Socialist Society arose, only two Socialist study groups for college students were known to exist in the United States. One had been started at the University of Wisconsin by William Leiserson, ultimately a chairman of the National Mediation Board, and Dan Hoan, future Socialist Mayor of Milwaukee. Both men became enduring members of the new Socialist Society.

The other group had been experimentally launched at the University of Chicago by William English Walling, who gained some prominence during his lifetime as a writer on labor politics and a member of the Labor Delegation to the Versailles Peace Conference. An ardent Socialist of the gradualist persuasion, Walling likewise became an inspirer and founder in 1909 of the National Association for the Advancement of Colored People. In that enterprise, which during more than half a century has swelled to formidable dimensions, Walling was associated with W. E. B. Dubois, a Negro alumnus of Harvard (1890), who joined the ISS as an adult, became a well-known educator and eventually attached himself to the Communist apparatus.[12]

Walling's chief claim to posthumous fame, however, derives from his book, *American Labor and American Democracy*, published in 1926 with an introduction by Professor John R. Commons. There he

---

[10] Reprinted in full in the *Congressional Record* of October 12, 1962.

[11] (Italics added.)

[12] Bela Hubbard, *Political and Economic Structures*, (Caldwell, Idaho, Caxton Printers, Ltd., 1956), p. 111.

advanced a plan *for effecting State Socialism in the United States under cover of the traditional two-party system,* rather than through a third party. That his plan was of interest to British Fabians is evident, since he lectured in 1929 at a Fabian Summer School in England.[13] William English Walling is generally regarded as a precursor of the present-day school of "democratic" action in American politics. He was among those who signed the original call leading to the founding of the ISS.

Another patriarch of "democratic" Socialism, Upton Sinclair, actively aided the ISS in its infancy. From his home at Princeton, New Jersey, in the fall and winter of 1905-06, Sinclair shipped out bundles of Socialist propaganda, Fabian-fashion, to inquiring students and professors.

Then twenty-seven years old, Sinclair had just spent nine years as a wandering graduate and undergraduate student in universities from California to New York and had written five unknown novels. Immensely facile, persistent and energetic, he aspired to become an American Emile Zola, but never quite achieved it. In those journeyman years he was a protégé and house guest of Elizabeth Glendower Evans, whose well-appointed Boston home was simultaneously frequented by Florence Kelley and Judge Louis D. Brandeis.

At the moment, Sinclair was engaged in completing still another novel, *The Jungle,* a subsidized exposé of conditions in the Chicago stockyards, which he wrote without ever having been in Chicago. His source was an early American Marxist, A. M. Simons, who had written a pamphlet, called *Packingtown,* six years before. Simons[14] did the "research" for Sinclair and served as a model for the election-night orator in the final pages of *The Jungle.* Because muckraking was just coming into style, and because President Theodore Roosevelt had a legitimate bone to pick with the meat packers dating from the beef scandals of the Spanish-American War, Sinclair's sixth novel proved a sensation, catapulting him into a long and profitable career as a Socialist muckraker.

When President Theodore Roosevelt invited Upton Sinclair to come to Chicago as one of a commission to investigate the stockyards, the latter prudently declined. In his place, he sent Ella Reeve Bloor, "the little nut-brown woman" later known to Communists as

[13] *Fabian News,* (July, 1929).
[14] William A. Glaser, "A. M. Simons: American Marxist." *Institute of Social Studies Bulletin,* Vol. I, No. 6, p. 67.

Mother Bloor, whose son, Hal Ware, was to found a Communist espionage cell within the United States Department of Agriculture in 1934. Sinclair's persistent connection with individuals who became well-known Communists eventually won for him a wide and enthusiastic audience in Soviet Russia, where his highly-colored literary cartoons of the American scene remained popular for decades after they were passé in America. In later life, he described such friendships with apparent frankness in memoirs that were serially published in the Rand School's *Institute of Social Studies Bulletin* for 1952-53.

The most spectacular event in the first two years of the ISS was Jack London's speaking tour of the colleges. This was something new in America, suggested by the British Fabian practice of having student clubs at Oxford and Cambridge sponsor visiting Socialist lecturers. The notion of expanding a single lecture into a coast-to-coast campus tour, however, was a distinctly American feature, which proved useful then and later to the new organization, since it allowed a single organizer, or at most a bare handful, to cover the country. In time, it would also provide income and outlets for peripatetic British Fabians—from S. G. Hobson in 1908 to Harold Laski in 1924-1949, to Herman Finer, John Strachey, Rebecca West, St. John Ervine, and a host of less well advertised English Socialists in more recent years.

So Jack London was merely the first in a long left-ward procession that to this day has never ended. Then at the peak of his literary popularity, a husky figure in an open-necked white flannel shirt, he looked as sturdily American as his native redwoods, although his mission was less indigenous. The day after his appearance at Yale University, the New Haven *Register* declared: "The spectacle of an avowed Socialist, one of the most conspicuous in the country, standing on the platform of Woolsey Hall, was a sight for God and man!" Unabashed by such comments, Jack London retorted by inscribing himself in various hotel registers, "Yours for the Revolution!"—a flamboyant gesture that appealed to his immature audiences and to the wealthy hostesses who vied with each other in lionizing him.

2.

During 1906, a number of student groups sprang up at Columbia, Wesleyan, Yale, Harvard and other colleges. Of these, the Columbia University crop proved in the long run to be of most direct service to the future "educational" work of the parent organization in New York City; while the Harvard club developed a top-level, largely under-cover elite, more closely resembling and intimately allied to its progenitors of the British Fabian Society.

Charter members of the Harvard Socialist Club included Walter Lippmann, Kenneth MacGowan, Lee Simonson, Nicholas Kelley, Osmond Fraenckel and Heywood Broun; with Sam Elliott, Hiram Moderwell, John Reed, Robert Edmond Jones and others soon joining up.[15] "If anyone taking a bird's-eye view of Cambridge at one o'clock in the morning were to see five or six groups of excited Harvard men gesticulating on various street corners, let him know that a Socialist club held a meeting that night," wrote young Walter Lippmann in the *Harvard Illustrated Review*.

There is no evidence that any of the individuals mentioned ever renounced their allegiance to Socialism—with the possible exception of the New York *World* columnist, Heywood Broun, first president of the American Newspaper Guild. After serving for years on the Board of Directors of the League for Industrial Democracy (LID) and developing close ties with the Communists,[16] Broun finally became a near-deathbed convert to Catholicism. John Reed, now buried beside the Kremlin wall, openly threw in his lot with the Communists after 1917, becoming an employee of the "international revolutionary propa-ganda bureau" in Moscow.[17] Reputedly the victim of a typhus epi-demic, John Reed left behind him a purported eyewitness account of the Russian Revolution, *Ten Days That Shook The World*—a potent piece of Soviet propaganda, now believed (like the Webbs' later work on Soviet civilization) to have been of composite authorship.

Others of the group found it preferable after graduation to mas-querade under the name of liberal. Nicholas Kelley sat from 1912 to 1933 on the Board of Directors of the Intercollegiate Socialist Society and the LID. Nevertheless, he became the liberal vice president and general counsel of the Chrysler Corporation[18]—first automobile com-

---

[15] *Forty Years of Education*, (New York, League for Industrial Democracy, 1945), p. 19.

[16] J. B. Matthews, *Odyssey of a Fellow Traveler*, (New York, Mt. Vernon Pub-lishers, Inc., 1938), p. 272.

[17] *Senate Document No. 62*, 66th Congress, Vol. III, p. 469. Testimony of Louise Bryant, wife of John Reed. According to Louise Bryant, Reed's chief in the propaganda bureau was Boris Reinstein of Buffalo, New York, afterwards Lenin's secretary.

[18] See Appendix II.

pany to capitulate in the industry-wide strike of the middle nineteen-thirties which was sparked by young Walter Reuther, who had been president of the Students' League for Industrial Democracy (SLID) chapter at Wayne University.

Lee Simonson and Robert Edmond Jones helped to found the Theatre Guild in New York City, which popularized the plays of George Bernard Shaw according to techniques borrowed from the Moscow Art Theatre. Kenneth MacGowan, president of the Harvard Socialist Club in 1910, became a professor of Theater Arts at the University of California and a motion-picture producer.

Strangest of all and hardest to unravel is the tangled web of Walter Lippmann's career—the lad who had seemed to be the brightest and most promising among the charter members of the Harvard Socialist Club and who gradually became so entrapped in his own obscurantism that in the end he found it difficult to express and maintain a plain-spoken position on any topic. Perhaps the case of Walter Lippmann best illustrates the secretive nature and frequently confusing surface manifestations of top-echelon Fabian Socialism in the United States.

Only son of well-to-do and cultured German-Jewish parents in New York City, the boy Lippmann was handsome, well mannered and remarkably but not offensively precocious. At Harvard he made a brilliant scholastic record, ingratiated himself with his professors, and joined a quantity of non-social clubs, being ineligible at that time for membership in the more exclusive Porcellian and Hasty Pudding Clubs. He did volunteer work at Hale House, a Boston settlement house where generations of young Harvard Socialists went to learn how the less fortunate lived.

With fellow members of the Harvard Socialist Club, Lippmann spent idyllic weekends at the country home of the Reverend Ralph Albertson, exponent of Christian Socialism and president of *Twentieth Century* Magazine. During the summer of 1909 the attractive, ambitious youth was received into the Fabian Society of London,[19] which watched over and promoted his subsequent career, judging him qualified for tasks of infiltration at the highest levels.

After graduation, Lippmann served briefly as aide to the Socialist mayor of Schenectady, New York. Thereafter he withdrew from the rough and tumble of Socialist Party politics to become a "liberal"

---

[19] *Fabian News*, (October, 1909).

interpreter of British Fabian Socialist policies—first to Democratic leaders in the Wilson Administration, later to financial pillars of the Republican Party. True, an uninstructed reader of Lippmann might find it difficult to form a clear picture of where he really stood. A painstaking analysis of his column, "Today and Tomorrow," from 1932 to 1938 finds him taking favorable, unfavorable and neutral positions in somewhat bewildering succession on identical issues of the day.[20]

During those years he was engaged in penetrating the upper ranks of the American business and financial community and gaining the good will of industrial statesmen. Having supported his World War I chief in the War Department, Newton D. Baker, against Franklin D. Roosevelt for the 1932 Democratic nomination, Lippmann recouped his error by becoming a columnist for the Republican New York *Herald Tribune* and the author of "liberal" Republicanism. It was not only his function to let the conservatives know what the "other half thinks," but also to let Socialists know what the conservatives thought and planned.[21]

Articles attacking him in the pro-Socialist weekly, *The Nation*, by LID members Amos Pinchot and Max Lerner merely aided him to win friends in other circles. (Pinchot variously called him "The Great Elucidator" and "The Great Obfuscator"!) Lippmann's trip to Europe in the middle nineteen-thirties with Thomas W. Lamont of J. P. Morgan and Company appeared to confer the final accolade upon him. It is unjust, however, to assume as many did that Lippmann had abandoned his Socialist faith. A chronological sampling of his books and articles to date reflects, in a more or less guarded fashion, the changing policies of British Fabian Socialism—from the Wilsonian Fourteen Points and League of Nations to the Atlantic Community and regional federations; from outright defense of the Socialist Fatherland to the tacit assumption that Communism is here to stay; from advocacy of direct government operation of the basic means of production and exchange to indirect political control of the nation's wealth through "cooperation" and voluntary renunciation of their historic role by leaders of private enterprise.

Forsaking any hope of political rewards at an early age, when the best he might have expected was to be named Ambassador to Turkey, Lippmann dedicated himself instead to reaching key persons in diplomacy, business and the academic world—and to benefitting unostentatiously from his private investments and an ample income derived from syndication of his column. Lippmann's social success, fiscal good fortune and unerring gift for restricting his contacts to persons of importance, have naturally provoked some ill-natured comments from Socialists of lesser status, not privy to his lofty role in what H. G. Wells in *The New Machiavelli* called "the open conspiracy." They fail to perceive his lifelong consistency as a penetrator and permeator par excellence, or to recognize his continuous service as a forecaster of Fabian fashions in thought and action. It must not be forgotten that Lippmann was the first American intellectual to advocate the use of applied psychology in promoting Socialism. He was also the first to introduce John Maynard Keynes to America, having helped to arrange for the publication in this country of Keynes' early and mischievous work, *The Economic Consequences of the Peace.*[22]

Above all, Walter Lippmann has been the chief literary practitioner in this country of a tactic which the British Fabian Sidney Webb developed to a fine art in politics and which Vladimir Lenin himself approved on occasion, describing it as "one step backward, two steps forward." This tactic was rediscovered and emulated in Washington in the early nineteen-sixties by both "liberal" Democrats and "modern" Republicans. *Life* magazine for March, 1961, reported that Walter Lippmann, rescued from apparently harmless desuetude, had become one of President John F. Kennedy's favorite columnists and informal advisers. He survived Kennedy, so many years his junior, to become an adviser behind the scenes to President Lyndon B. Johnson.

Toward the public at large, Lippmann's attitude does not differ materially from that which he expressed many years ago as president of the Harvard Socialist Club: "In a general way, our object was to make reactionaries standpatters; standpatters, conservatives; conservatives, liberals; liberals, radicals; and radicals, Socialists. In other words, we tried to move everyone up a peg. We preferred to have the whole mass move a little, to having a few altogether out of sight." [23] That year he circulated a petition requesting a course in Socialism, which was signed by three hundred students and which apparently bore fruit. In 1910 Professor Graham Wallas, one of the

---

[22] *Congressional Record*, (October 12, 1962), p. 22120.
[23] *Ibid.*

original Big Four of the London Fabian Society, was invited to deliver the Lowell Lectures at Harvard.

It was a time when American Fabian Socialism, still in the exploratory stage and unsure of its future, was seeking to discover techniques for moving the great mass of American public opinion in the direction of "peaceful" social revolution. The Harvard student group and its mentors, disturbed by press reactions to Jack London's cheerful rowdiness, were beginning to ask themselves earnestly, as G. D. H. Cole did much later in a jocular vein:

> How shall we educate the Americans
> To admire the Fabian Socialist elegance . . . ? [24]

To such questions, Professor Graham Wallas seemed in his day to be the answer incarnate.

Wallas had been one of the first two instructors at the London School of Economics, when the number of its students could be counted on the fingers of a single hand. Conversational in his manner of teaching, smiling, insinuating and attractive,[25] he made a lasting impression on many young people at Harvard and some of their elders as well. His field was politics, which he treated primarily as a problem in social psychology. More than any other person, he initiated the psychological approach to Socialism, by which widely disparate elements of the population could be led, step by step and almost unawares, to accept and foster radical changes in the social, economic and political spheres. For Graham Wallas, as he wrote in *The Great Society*, the aim of social psychology was "to control human conduct!"

Superficially, Wallas appeared to be just another free-lance professor, unfettered by organizational ties or loyalties. He had purportedly severed all connections with the London Fabian Society in 1904, after tilting publicly with Sidney Webb on tariff policy and on the matter of municipal aid to Catholic schools—of which Wallas disapproved. In fact, however, he had taken upon himself an isolated mission of key importance. America was truly a land flowing with milk and honey, which must be subjugated before British Fabians could hope to build their own peculiar version of Blake's Jerusalem in the New World as well as the Old. It was advisable, however, that any such schemes of conquest should not seem to originate with the London Fabian Society.

[24] *Fabian Journal*, (February, 1951).
[25] Max Beer, *op. cit.*, pp. 82-83.

In his time, Wallas was a one-man Fabian International Bureau, beamed directly at the United States, fully thirty years before such a bureau was officially created. At intervals he returned to teach in the London School of Economics and to be warmly welcomed by old comrades. Through the select contacts which he cultivated on both sides of the water, Wallas proved helpful in securing appointments, fellowships and emoluments for individual British Fabians, as well as money from American foundations for expanding the London School. He also appears to have exercised some influence on Socialist-minded individuals already holding, or soon to hold, policy-making posts in Washington.

Demonstrating that Anglo-American Fabians never ceased to treat Wallas as one of themselves, Harold Laski, a future chairman of the London Society then teaching at Harvard, wrote on March 11, 1918, to Justice Oliver Wendell Holmes: "A brief note came from Felix full of eagerness and a cry of joy about the general sanity and foresight of Graham Wallas. I wish he were back." [26] The "Felix" was, of course, the late Supreme Court Justice Felix Frankfurter, then counsel and secretary of President Wilson's Mediation Commission, which had just issued its *Report on Industrial Unrest.*

During 1919 Graham Wallas was lecturing at the New School for Social Research in New York City. The school had recently been founded by the *New Republic* editor, Alvin Johnson, as an adult education center for the well-to-do and a haven for lame duck professors of the Socialist persuasion. In a letter of December, 1919, Wallas told Laski that Sir William Beveridge, as director of the London School of Economics, had just written to inquire about the prospects of Harold Laski's working in London, and added: "I am suggesting to him that you should try to teach both at Oxford and in London." [27] Sidney Webb also wrote urging that a post be found for Laski at the London School—a sign that Wallas and Webb still saw eye to eye on matters of importance to the London Society.

In recommending the psychological approach to control of public opinion, Graham Wallas set the tone for several generations of Fabian Socialist activity in America. He bequeathed his literary style and intellectual mannerisms to Walter Lippmann, for whom Wallas cher-

[26] *Holmes-Laski Letters,* 1916-1935. With a foreword by Felix Frankfurter. De-Wolf Howe, ed., (Cambridge, Harvard University Press, 1953), p. 141.

[27] Kingsley Martin, *Harold Laski: A Biographical Memoir,* (New York, The Viking Press, Inc., 1953), p. 38.

ished high hopes that were only partially fulfilled. More significantly, the studied and carefully timed application of social psychology to practical politics, which furnished the impetus for Roosevelt's New Deal, Kennedy's New Frontier, and Johnson's Great Society, can be traced to the ideas first instilled among Harvard "liberals" by Graham Wallas. Such latter-day developments as the Institute for Advanced Behavioral Studies at Stanford University—where respectable Socialists like Bruce Bliven, erstwhile editor of the *New Republic*, have been sustained in their declining years—sprang from the seeds sowed by Wallas over half a century before.

Friends recall Graham Wallas as a kindly and cultured English gentleman with a natural sweetness of disposition,[28] a useful trait in any missionary endeavor. Even Beatrice Webb, ordinarily acid in commenting on the cronies of Sidney's bachelor days, described Wallas as "lovable." It is instructive to note that ever since Wallas made his appearance on the American scene, the Fabian Socialist leadership in the United States has recognized the value and enjoyed its share of "lovable" characters—from August Claessens to Harry Laidler and Norman Thomas; from Robert Morss Lovett to John Dewey and the venerable, omnipresent Dr. Reinhold Niebuhr, Director Emeritus of Union Theological Seminary, whom it seemed difficult to credit with any destructive purpose.

Testifying before a Congressional Committee in 1956, Harry Laidler, who for some fifty years administered America's counterpart of the London Fabian Society, suggested that the choice of such front personalities was deliberate. In a purely secular vein, Laidler cited the words of St. Francis de Sales: "You can catch more flies with one drop of honey than with a barrel of vinegar."

3.

Not only the taste of honey, but the newly organized opportunities for gaining prominence and/or success in their chosen fields captivated and held many gifted young intellectuals through the years. Continuity of membership, often handed down from father to son, and the steady acquisition of new blood well mixed with the old, proved to be as characteristic of the revitalized American Fabian

[28] Max Beer, *op. cit.*, pp. 82-83.

movement as of the London Society. Walter Rauschenbusch[29] and his son Stephen, the Arthur M. Schlesingers, Senior and Junior, are only a few of the more outstanding examples.

Husband-and-wife teams, following in the footsteps of the Sidney Webbs and their coterie, flourished this side of the water. Among them were J. G. Phelps Stokes, an early president of the Intercollegiate Socialist Society, and his wife; Richard L. Neuberger and his wife Maurine, who successively became United States Senators from Oregon on the Democratic ticket; Paul H. Douglas, who served as president of the American Economic Association in 1947 and was elected United States Senator (D.) from Illinois the next year, and his wife Emily Taft Douglas, a former Congresswoman; Melvyn A. Douglas and his wife, Helen Gahagan Douglas, former actress and Congresswoman; Avraham Yarmolinsky and his wife, Babette Deutsch, the poetess, whose son, Adam, became a key Defense Department official in the Kennedy Administration. Thus the American Fabian movement, re-launched under such modest circumstances in 1905, has survived and snowballed to the present day through the polite tenacity of individuals and families.

Like the Fabian Society of London, the membership of the ISS and its successor, the League for Industrial Democracy, consisted of a few hundred publicists and public figures usually better known for their activity in related organizations than in the parent group; plus a much larger group of industrious but less widely trumpeted associates whose connection with the parent organization remained constant but vague. Membership lists of the LID have never been published, but from first to last the membership appears to have been more numerous than is commonly believed.

In 1955, on the occasion of the ISS's 50th anniversary celebration, a "partial record of past and present collaborators" was officially made public by Mina Weisenberg. Inserted into the Congressional Record, this list provides a disturbing picture of persons in influential places,

---

[29] See Appendix II. Walter Rauschenbusch was from 1886 to 1897 pastor at the Second Baptist Church, New York City. There he read and was influenced by the works of Henry George, Tolstoi, Mazzini, Marx, Ruskin and Bellamy. In 1891-92 he spent some time abroad, studying economics and theology at the University of Berlin and industrial conditions in England. "There, through Sidney and Beatrice Webb, he became interested in the Fabian Socialist movement." *Dictionary of American Biography*, Dumas Malone, ed., (New York, Charles Scribner's Sons, 1935), Vol. XV, pp. 392-393.

up to and including the White House itself, committed to the gradual but ever more rapid achievement of a so-called Cooperative Commonwealth in America.[30] Here, among other things, is the key to the modern influx of Socialist-oriented university professors who have not only shaped the current philosophy of education in the United States but who—like Professors Alvin H. Hansen and Seymour E. Harris and a host of like-minded colleagues since 1932—have been called upon as Executive "consultants" to formulate and steer the policies of the United States Government.

It became a tacit tradition among native Fabians, open or covert, to promote not merely their friends and relatives but approved individuals often personally unknown to them yet known to the leadership of the American group. As trusty Fabian Socialists, frequently wearing the "liberal" or "progressive" label, established themselves gradually, firmly and increasingly in the professions, literature and popular journalism; in higher education and research; in reform movements, labor union leadership, politics and government service, they trained and carried their successors along with them. Thus the movement for "peaceful" social revolution in the United States expanded, becoming ever more diffuse and more difficult to pinpoint, until it assumed the aspect of a nationwide fraternity with a largely secret membership held together by invisible ties of ideology. Few outsiders realized this movement emanated always from a single center, whose unchanging aim was to supplant the constitutional American system of checks and balances with a collectivist state under Socialist International guidance.

It is noteworthy how many who subsequently became "valued leaders of thought in their respective fields," [31] started their careers as collegiate leaders of Socialist clubs and devoted the whole of their lives, directly or indirectly, to furthering the same destructive cause. By 1910, when Harry Laidler became the first paid organizer of the ISS, that society admitted it was holding lectures and discussions and distributing literature through its chapters in fifteen universities. Two years later it reported forty-three chapters,[32] and by the time of World War I the tally had risen to sixty.[33]

[30] This official list is printed in full in Appendix II and merits detailed study.
[31] *Forty Years of Education, op. cit.,* p. 20.
[32] Morris Hillquit, *History of Socialism,* (New York, Funk and Wagnalls Co., Inc., 1910 Edition), p. 355.
[33] *Social Democratic Herald,* (May 11, 1912).

Active officers of student clubs in that era, who became prominent in the intellectual ferment following the war, included: Inez Milholland, Mary Fox and Edna St. Vincent Millay, the bohemian poetess, of Vassar; Bruce Bliven of Stanford, who became a senior editor of the *New Republic*, and Freda Kirchwey (of Barnard) longtime editor of its sister left wing weekly, *The Nation;* Randolph Bourne, the essayist, Paul Douglas, the liberal Senator, and Louis Lorwin, the columnist, all of Columbia; Isadore Lubin, of Clark, who became a Labor Department official in the New Deal Administration, together with Edwin Witte and David Saposs of Wisconsin. From 1945 to 1952 Dr. Lubin represented the United States on the United Nations Economic and Social Council.[34]

Amherst produced Evans Clark, afterwards of *The New York Times* and the Twentieth Century Fund; Ordway Tead, writer and lecturer, who became Research Director of the LID and served as chairman of the Board of Higher Education in New York City; and the Raushenbushes, father and son.[35] The father strove to perpetuate Socialist dogmas among the clergy, while the son helped to found the National Public Ownership League, which spawned the Tennessee Valley Authority and other schemes for political control of electric power.

There were also Broadus Mitchell of Johns Hopkins; Abraham Epstein of Pittsburgh, sometimes called "the little giant of social insurance"; Theresa Wolfson of Adelphi, long a professor of Economics at Brooklyn College; Otto Markwardt and William Bohn, then instructors at Wisconsin, the latter to become an editor of the Socialist *New Leader;* and others, too numerous to mention, coming from Ivy League colleges as well as land-grant colleges. Harvard University, though an acknowledged leader in the production of Socialist intellectuals, was far from being the unique source.

In those pre-World War I years British Fabian lecturers were already roaming the campuses and cities of America. Fiction by British Fabian authors, whom few Americans recognized as Socialists, headed the best seller lists. The novels of H. G. Wells, Arnold Bennett and John Galsworthy, the published plays of George Bernard Shaw, became standard reading matter for literate Americans and were favored as high school graduation gifts to boys and girls preparing for college.

---

[34] Alice Widener, *Behind the U. N. Front,* (New York, The Bookmailer, 1962), p. 107.

[35] *Ibid.* The father spelled his name Rauschenbusch; the son dropped the Germanic *c.*

Immediately after the war, publication in this country of two works by two British Fabian economists, J. M. Keynes' *Economic Consequences of the Peace* and R. H. Tawney's *The Acquisitive Society*, helped to popularize Marxian critiques of the economic and social order, even though the name of Marx was not mentioned. The "social unrest" that a number of serious thinkers hopefully predicted would follow the First World War and usher in a new world order was seized upon by Wilsonian liberals in America, abetted by Christian Socialist divines, as a pretext for advancing piecemeal the program outlined in Sidney Webb's *Labour and the New Social Order*.

A generally tolerant attitude towards the Russian Revolution and a sophisticated indifference to its bloodier aspects, tempered by some public finger shaking, have characterized American Fabians from 1917 to the present day. The roots for this must be sought in the splintered history and joint Marxist-IWW origins of the Socialist movement in the United States. And for this movement the American Fabians, like their British tutors, attempted to provide intellectual leadership and direction behind a blandly respectable front.

14

The More It Changes . . .

1.

LESS than six weeks after the formation of the Intercollegiate Socialist Society, the Rand School of Social Science was born. It was named for Elizabeth Rand, who died in July, 1905, leaving a $200,000 trust fund to "carry on and further the work to which I have devoted the later years of my life." An ardent Abolitionist in girlhood, Elizabeth Rand became an equally ardent Socialist in her old age. Wealthy and openhanded, she had been a donor to many obscure Socialist publications and schemes in America.

Trustees of the fund created under Elizabeth Rand's will were her daughter, Carrie Rand Herron, and her son-in-law, George D. Herron, a deposed Congregationalist minister. Dr. Herron had been the first chairman of the Socialist Party of America, elected at its founders' convention in 1902; and he was one of two persons chosen to represent organized Socialist groups in the United States at the International Socialist Congress of 1902 in Brussels. Previously, he had been Professor of Applied Christianity at Grinnell College in Iowa, a unique chair endowed by the same Elizabeth Rand.

In 1901, Dr. Herron had obtained a divorce from his wife,[1] the mother of four children, and made Carrie Rand his bride in a poetic but unconventional ceremony recognized as binding under the common law of the State of New York. One Saturday evening in May, with the scent of flowers filling the room, George Herron and Carrie

---

[1] In 1892, Dr. Herron dedicated his book, *A Plea for the Gospel*, "to my wife, Mary Everhard Herron, who has been to me a living conscience."

Rand announced to a small circle of Socialist comrades and to the world at large the accomplished fact of their "spiritual union"—the long-standing "marriage of our souls." Next, the host of the evening, Dr. Charles Brodie Patterson, editor of *The Arena* and *Mind*, made a brief address. He was followed by the Reverend William Thurston Brown of Plymouth Church, Rochester, whose Annunciation Service was described by one listener as a "poem in prose." Each of the fourteen guests present, among them the romantic poet, Richard Le Gallienne, was invited to make a brief verbal offering to the consummation of this love union. William Mailly, national secretary of the young Social Democratic Party (soon to be merged into the Socialist Party), declared that the marriage meant, above all, a more complete consecration to Socialism! [2]

Uplifting as the event may have seemed to sentimental Socialists of the period, Dr. Herron's colleagues and neighbors back in Iowa found it both bizarre and shocking. Just ten days later the council of the First Congregational Church in Grinnell recommended that Dr. Herron be dropped from church membership rolls, deposed from the Christian ministry and removed from the teaching staff at Grinnell College, a church-sponsored institution.[3] While the Socialist press attempted to depict Dr. Herron as a martyr to his political beliefs, the circumstances of his divorce from a loyal wife, and his remarriage without benefit of clergy, were the actual reasons for his ouster.[4] Despite the great increase in divorce statistics since the turn of the century, grass roots reaction to such apparently carefree personal behavior on the part of religious or civic leaders remains much the same today as yesterday.

Taking a cue from Sidney and Beatrice Webb, with whom they had fraternized at the Brussels Congress, the Herrons decided to use the trust fund left by Elizabeth Rand to found a school designed as "an intellectual center for the Socialist movement in the United States." [5] The sum available was very much larger than the Hutchinson

[2] Leonard D. Abbott, "A Socialist Wedding," *International Socialist Review,* (July, 1901).

[3] *The Congregationalist,* (June 15, 1901).

[4] *Ibid.* Concerning Dr. Herron, the Reverend E. M. Vittum, pastor of the Congregationalist Church in Grinnell, wrote: "Any statement that he has been persecuted by his church on account of heresy or socialism is an absolute falsehood. For some time past there have been increasing suspicions of his moral character, culminating when a divorce, with custody of the children, was granted to Mrs. Herron."

[5] *Chicago Socialist,* (October 30, 1905).

Trust employed by Sidney Webb to launch the London School of Economics. Moreover, unlike the London School, the Rand School of Social Science was not connected with any accredited university and thus did not feel constrained to dissemble its Socialist aims. Its functions more nearly approximated those of the Workers' Educational Association in Britain, which offered courses in Socialism to working men and women and trained future Trade Union and Labour Party officials.

After a short while, the Herrons very considerately retired to spend the rest of their lives in Italy, where the scandal provoked by their common-law marriage could less readily be adduced by the general press to discredit the Socialist cause in America. Possibly anticipating their departure, the Herrons made Morris Hillquit a co-trustee of the Rand School Fund. Hillquit, born Mischa Hilkowics, was a canny labor lawyer in New York City who became a chronic aspirant to political office on the Socialist Party ticket. An inspirer and founder of the ISS, Morris Hillquit also helped to found the Amalgamated Clothing Workers Union, which acquired wealth and political power under his leadership and that of Sidney Hillman. Rand School of Social Science always maintained close ties with Amalgamated. To this day, Amalgamated officials still sit on the Board of the Rand School (now known as the Tamiment Institute) and serve as officers and directors of the League for Industrial Democracy.

The original Board of Directors named in the school's certificate of incorporation included Algernon Lee, Job Harriman, Benjamin Hanford, William Mailly, Leonard D. Abbott and Henry Slobodin.[6] All had formally declared themselves to be "in full accord with the principles and tactics of the modern Socialist movement in America."[7] Job Harriman, who was born on an Indiana farm and practiced law in Los Angeles, was to be at various times the Socialist Party's candidate for mayor and governor of New York, and vice president. Algernon Lee and Leonard D. Abbott, whose propaganda efforts dated from the era of the Bellamy Nationalist clubs, were among the founders of the ISS.

In addition, a three-man advisory committee for the school was appointed.[8] Members were Dr. P. A. Levine, later of the Rockefeller Institute, the first but not the last recorded Socialist to penetrate the

---

[6] Morris Hillquit, *Loose Leaves from a Busy Life*, (New York, The Macmillan Co., 1934), pp. 65-66.

[7] *Rand School Bulletin*, 1911.

[8] Hillquit, *op. cit.*, pp. 65-66.

great private foundation; Herman Schlueter,[9] Social Democratic editor of the *New Yorker Volkszeitung*; and Professor Charles A. Beard of Columbia, also listed as a "faculty sponsor" [10] of the ISS. Dr. Beard, a widely respected historian, eventually renounced the Marxian approach to history after a lifetime as a Socialist. By that time, however, he had already produced a number of influential books, written jointly with his wife, Mary, that portrayed the Founding Fathers as self-interested spokesmen for a propertied clique and deprecated the American Constitution as a class-inspired document.

In 1907 the Rand School gave desk space to the ISS in a brownstone house at 122 East 19th Street, in New York, site of its present headquarters.[11] Successive secretaries of the Rand School, William J. Ghent and Algernon Lee, served as titular secretaries of the ISS, and the school's trusted assistant secretary, Rose Laddon Hanna,[12] handled ISS correspondence—their salaries being paid from Rand School funds.

Plainly, the relationship between the two organizations was a family one, of shared ideas, facilities and personnel. Few observers realized that the seemingly mild and modest ISS, which for some time appeared to be almost a pensioner of the Rand School, was in reality the superior, policy-making body.

The school was the ISS link to revolutionary labor groups and Socialist Party politics, in which members of the ISS were prominent without involving the parent body. Every facet of American Socialism's high-strung, contentious political history during the first two decades of the twentieth century was reflected in the Rand School, where the atmosphere was often more emotional than intellectual. Its cooperative cafeteria advertised, "Every bite a nibble at the foundations of capitalism!"

Members of the ISS—including such noted Marxist ideologues as John Spargo and labor economist I. A. Hourwich, along with an ever increasing number of professors from Columbia University—taught

[9] Max Beer, *Fifty Years of International Socialism*, (London, Allen and Unwin, 1935).

[10] See Appendix II.

[11] *Forty Years of Education*, (New York, League for Industrial Democracy, 1945), p. 20.

[12] *Ibid.* After retiring from the school, Mrs. Hanna resided for some years at the Grand Hotel in Moscow, where as representative of the Open Road Travel Bureau she arranged tours of the Socialist Fatherland, chiefly for Russian-American labor groups, and helped bring millions in tourist dollars to the Soviet Union.

at the Rand School.[13] Over the years, the school offered lectures on a broad range of cultural subjects, to which a Socialist flavor was added. There were "courses" in psychology, literature, music, foreign languages and the arts, for which no formal academic credits were given. Algernon Lee, as Educational Director of the Rand School, stated flatly that the teaching work of the school fell into two parts:

1) That which offers general public opportunities to study Socialism and related subjects.
2) That which gives Socialists such systematic instruction and training as may render them more efficient workers in the Socialist Party, the Trade Unions, the Cooperatives.[14]

Rand School "students," largely immigrants and children of immigrants from Czarist Russia, played a lively part in the strikes and demonstrations of the garment workers in New York. They supported the dynamite-laden strikes of the Industrial Workers of the World (IWW), organized among miners and railroad men in the Far West and among the textile workers of Lawrence, Massachusetts, under the leadership of Big Bill Haywood. The Rand School in its early years sponsored Red Sunday Schools for children in various parts of the country and helped to establish local "labor schools" in a number of industrial cities. In the IWW-led copper strike of 1911-12, it set up a temporary training school for strike organizers in Albuquerque, New Mexico. Certainly the Rand School was far from being an ivory tower and in no way resembled the traditionally peaceful groves of academe.

With the coming of World War I the Socialist movement in the United States found itself sharply divided on the issue of American participation. A species of radical pacifism, more or less discreetly encouraged by some Fabian visitors from England and by agencies of the Imperial German Government, gained the upper hand within the Socialist Party. In May, 1915, just after the sinking of the *Lusitania*, the Party amended its national constitution to include the following provision:

[13] *Rand School Bulletin*, 1911. A partial list of Rand School teachers for that year named Professors Franklin H. Giddings, D. S. Muzzey, Charles A. Beard, Columbia; Professor William Noyes; Professor I. A. Hourwich; Professors Vida D. Scudder and Emily Balch Green, Wellesley; Charlotte Perkins Stetson Gilman; William N. Leiserson; George R. Kirkpatrick; Algernon Lee; Robert W. Bruere, afterwards president of the Morris Plan Bank; John Spargo; Morris Hillquit; W. J. Ghent; Benjamin C. Gruenberg; Florence Kelley.
[14] *American Labor Yearbook*, 1919-20, p. 207.

Any member of the Socialist Party elected to office who shall in any way vote to appropriate moneys for military and naval purposes, or war, shall be expelled from the Party.[15]

Through the Socialist Propaganda League, Scott Nearing and Eugene V. Debs, perennial Socialist Party candidate for the Presidency, of the United States, attempted to spread their gospel of noncooperation to American labor in wartime. In 1918 Debs preached pacifism to three million members of the American Federation of Labor and received a ten-year prison sentence, later commuted. In February, 1919, the Federal Government tried Scott Nearing and the Rand School for publishing, writing and circulating a pamphlet, *The Great Madness*, during the war. Though Nearing was acquitted, the Rand School was fined $3,000. Yet in 1955 Mina Weisenberg frankly described Debs as having been a "cooperator" and frequent lecturer of the ISS, and she listed the wife of Scott Nearing as a director of the LID in 1923.[16]

Many other members of the ISS were identified, first or last, with the pacifist agitation and anti-patriotic intrigues of the World War I era. Still the ISS itself—like the Fabian Society of London—denied any responsibility for the actions of its individual members and refrained from taking a public stand on the controversial issue of the war. A telegram of January 27, 1919, from Harry W. Laidler, then secretary of the ISS with offices at 70 Fifth Avenue, to the chairman of a U.S. Senate Investigating Committee, asserted disingenuously:

In the list of alleged pacifists and radicals submitted by the Military Intelligence Bureau to the Senate Committee, the names of several college professors are included, and after their names the words Intercollegiate Socialist Society. In most instances, the only connection that these men have had with the society has been as endorsers of the society's stated object to promote an intelligent interest in socialism among college men and women. The society is an educational, not a political propagandist organization, having been organized to throw light on the worldwide movement towards industrial democracy known as socialism, in the belief that no intelligent collegian can afford to be ignorant of the movement, and that no one can intelligently support or intelligently oppose socialism unless he understands its ideals and aims.[17]

Not long afterwards, by order of President Wilson, himself a former

---

[15] *Revolutionary Radicalism, Its History, Purpose and Tactics.* Report of the Joint Legislative Committee Investigating Seditious Activities, filed April 24, 1920, in the Senate of the State of New York. (Albany, J. P. Lyon Company, 1920), Vol. II, pp. 1777 ff.

[16] See Appendix II.

[17] *Senate Document No. 62*, 66th Congress, Vol. III, p. 2857.

college professor, the Military Intelligence Bureau was instructed to destroy its card files on subversives during World War I—a loss described as irreparable by Thomas M. Johnson, author of *Our Secret War*, an account of United States intelligence operations in the First World War.

2.

With the outbreak of revolution in Russia, which Socialists everywhere believed to be the forerunner of world revolution, the excitement in American Socialist circles was intensified. To comprehend the attitude of international Socialism towards the Bolshevik seizure of power, it should be recalled that Vladimir Lenin had long been the leader of a minority faction in the Russian Social Democratic Party, a branch of the prewar Socialist International. With the same topsy-turvy use of language practiced today by Soviet spokesmen, it called itself the majority (or Bolsheviki).

Prior to 1917, Lenin had attended congresses of the Socialist International in person or by proxy, and his militant tactics were privately condoned by a good many Social Democrats in other countries as being justified by internal conditions peculiar to Czarist Russia.[18] He was one of the Socialist family, the wayward son who made good. The entire clan was impressed, even though it might sometimes be annoyed at his high-handed methods.

In the coup of October, 1917, Lenin was joined by Leon Trotsky, previously a member of the majority faction inaccurately dubbed the Mensheviki (or minority) in the Russian Social Democratic Party.[19] During the premature revolution of 1905 in Russia, Trotsky had been closely associated with a Russian-born Socialist and international mystery man named Israel Helfant, who took his doctorate in finance at a Swiss university and thereafter acted as a fiscal agent for various international Socialist enterprises. Better known by his cover name of "Parvus," Helfant made a personal fortune in the Balkans and Turkey during the years just preceding and after the outbreak of World War I. Returning to Germany in 1915, he founded a Socialist newspaper, *Die Glocke*, supporting the Social Democratic majority in the German party. He was frequently consulted on Russian affairs by the Imperial German Government.[20]

[18] Max Beer, *op. cit.*, pp. 144-159.
[19] *Ibid.*
[20] *Ibid.* After 1919, Max Beer was employed by Helfant as editor of *Die Glocke*.

It is an interesting sidelight on the shadowy origins of the Bolshevik Revolution to know that "Parvus"-Helfant was the man who advised the German Government to pass Lenin through Germany en route from Switzerland to Russia in 1917.[21] He was also responsible for bringing Lenin and Trotsky together, as joint leaders of the revolution. All this might seem remote from events in the United States, if it were not for the fact that Trotsky had spent several years in New York just prior to the October revolution. His former associates there were delighted when he suddenly emerged as commandant of the Red Army and co-leader of the Bolshevik coup in Russia. Theoretical differences were overlooked in the general rejoicing.

Personally, Trotsky enjoyed a considerable following among Russian American labor groups in New York who formed the bulwark of the Rand School and the American Socialist Party. In 1915 the latter Party had advocated use of the general strike as a political weapon.[22] Its members and sympathizers were naturally interested when British Socialists threatened to call a general strike in support of Trotsky's Red Army, stalled at Warsaw in August, 1920, on what had appeared to be the start of a triumphal sweep through Europe.

In its heyday the Socialist Party of America had some 150,000 dues-paying members.[23] It more nearly resembled Britain's Independent Labour Party, led by the maverick Fabian, Keir Hardie (for whom the Intercollegiate Socialist Society staged a big Carnegie Hall rally), than the present British Labour Party which came to prominence after World War I.

By 1920 the American Socialist Party, an affiliate of the Socialist International, had succeeded in electing more than one thousand of its members to political office, published hundreds of newspapers, secured passage of a considerable body of legislation, won the support of one-third of the American Federation of Labor membership, and was instrumental in organizing the Industrial Workers of the World.[24] While it offered no serious electoral challenge to the two major political parties, its influence was far from negligible.

Because of the Socialist Party's international ties and the strong sympathy so many of its members, themselves of Russian origin, displayed for the Bolshevik Revolution, there was some fear that

[21] *Ibid.*

[22] *Revolutionary Radicalism,* Vol. II, pp. 1777 ff.

[23] Ira Kipnis, *The American Socialist Movement, 1897-1912,* (New York, Columbia University Press, 1952), p. 422.

[24] *Ibid.,* p. 5.

Socialist elements would take advantage of the industrial unrest predicted after World War I to organize politically inspired strikes and disorders in America. Even college boys, too young to vote, were being infected with the idea of radical social change.

In the *Intercollegiate Socialist* for April-May, 1919,[25] a bimonthly edited by Harry W. Laidler under the imprint of the ISS, the Reverend John Haynes Holmes, pastor of the Community Church in New York, urged that college youth be prepared to play a part in the stirring events anticipated for the postwar era. "The times call for a fearless and comprehensive statement of the Socialist message," Reverend Holmes declared. "Furthermore, this should be especially directed at the minds of our young men and women everywhere, for the Great War has prepared these minds for the sowing of the seed of radical social change."

The same issue of the same publication contained an article entitled "Two Years of the Russian Revolution" by Alexander Trachtenberg, member of the executive committee of the ISS and director of Labor Research at the Rand School of Social Science. On page 32, Trachtenberg wrote, heatedly:

Menaced by foreign military forces, the work of social and economic regeneration is now endangered. *The Russian Revolution is the heritage of the world.* It must not be defeated by foreign militarism. It must be permitted to develop unhampered. It must live, so that Russia may be truly free, and through its freedom blaze the way for *industrial democracy* throughout the world.[26]

In August, 1920, the Fabian Socialist-dominated Labour Party of Great Britain set an example to the American brethren of revolutionary action aimed at ending the threat of Allied military intervention in Soviet Russia. At a joint conference held August 9 at the House of Commons by the Parliamentary Committee of The Trades Union Congress, the National Executive of the Labour Party and Labour Party Members of Parliament, it was resolved:

That this joint Conference . . . feels certain that war is being engineered between the Allied Powers and Soviet Russia on the issue of Poland, and declares that such a war would be an intolerable crime against humanity. It

[25] Later the *Socialist Review.*
[26] Trachtenberg later became a member of the Central Committee of the Communist Party, USA. In 1945 he was in charge of all the Party's national and Moscow-obtained literature. Louis Francis Budenz, *This Is My Story,* (New York, McGraw-Hill, Inc., 1947), pp. 230, 305. (Italics added.)

therefore warns the Government that the whole industrial power of the organized workers will be used to defeat this war.

Executive committees of affiliated organizations throughout Britain were summoned to proceed to London for a national conference. Meanwhile, they were advised to instruct their members to be ready to "down tools" if and when the conference gave the word. On August 13 the assembled national conference pledged itself "to resist any and every form of military intervention against the Soviet Government of Russia." It demanded:

1) an absolute guarantee that the armed forces of Great Britain shall not be used in support of Poland, Baron Wrangel, or any other military and naval effort against the Soviet Government;
2) the withdrawal of all British naval forces operating directly or indirectly as a blockading influence against Russia;
3) the recognition of the Russian Soviet Government and the establishment of unrestricted trading and commercial relationship between Great Britain and Russia.[27]

Although the British Labour Party at its annual conference in Scarborough two months before had voted by a large majority against affiliation with the Communist Third International, still Labour Party leaders were prepared to take extreme measures, far beyond the bounds of parliamentary propriety, to defend and preserve the Socialist Fatherland. The meaning was spelled out in a speech by J. H. Thomas, described as a relatively moderate British labor leader of the day, who said:

Desperate as are our measures, dangerous as are our methods, we believe the situation is so desperate that only desperate and dangerous methods can provide a remedy. These resolutions do not mean a mere strike. Do not make any mistake. They mean a challenge to the whole Constitution of the country.[28]

Whether that widely publicized threat mirrored the actual sentiments of British labor, then about 70 per cent organized in trade unions;[29] or whether it was merely a well-engineered bluff based on Fabian Socialist control of Labour Party and trade union machinery,[30] will never be known. If it was a bluff, the reigning Liberal Party Government of Great Britain did not venture to call it—and any

[27] *Revolutionary Radicalism*, Vol. II, pp. 1599 ff.
[28] *Ibid.*
[29] Max Beer, *op. cit.*, p. 228.
[30] In the British elections of 1920, the Labour Party was so far from obtaining a majority of the working class vote that one wonders how much popular support it could have mustered and held for a general strike.

prospect of Allied military action against Bolshevik Russia speedily collapsed. Lloyd George could not take the risk of even a short-lived general strike in an election year. No wonder Sidney and Beatrice Webb, whose long and patient maneuvers had made all this possible, were received with royal honors during their visit to Moscow in 1932.

On August 14, 1920, the London *Daily Herald*, organ of the British Labour Party edited by Colonel House's old friend, George Lansbury, reported: "Labour's National Conference yesterday made the dramatic decision to vest in the Council of Action full authority to call at its discretion an immediate national strike to enforce the demands of the Conference. After the main resolution was passed, the delegates stood silent a full minute, then broke into the strains of the 'Red Flag.'" It may or may not be noteworthy that the *Herald* used the expression, "All Power to the Council [the Soviet]!"

This historic meeting was attended by at least one American observer, Professor Henry Wadsworth Longfellow Dana, formerly of Columbia University and then a lecturer at the New School for Social Research. His glowing account of it appeared on November 14, 1920, in *The Call*, then the leading New York Socialist newspaper, under the heading, "Three Revolutionary Trades Union Congresses." In 1920 Professor Dana, grandnephew and namesake of the revered New England poet, was vice president of the Intercollegiate Socialist Society.

Signs of intimacy between British and American Socialists, and the apparent readiness of both to place the survival of Soviet Russia above any domestic concerns, led the New York State Legislature to expel five Socialist Assemblymen-elect in the spring of 1920. They were disqualified on the strength of their pledges to the Socialist Party, as well as their own personal acts and statements. Legislators complained that the Socialist Party was not properly a political party at all, because it admitted minors and non-citizens to its councils, and because its constitution prohibited members from voting funds for military purposes.

Unlike some State legislatures, which are narrowly political, the New York body once maintained an extremely high level of brains and legal talent. Its 1920 report on Socialist activities—sometimes referred to as the Lusk Report, and mockingly disparaged by Socialist-minded publicists and historians[31]—is a classic document that could

[31] The textbook on American history by David Saville Muzzey, long used in many high school classes, reflects Socialist opinion about the Lusk Committee.

serve even now as a model for Congressional investigators. Published under the title, *Revolutionary Radicalism*, it sounded the first sober warning of the danger that international Socialism portended for the future of America.

Among the ousted Socialist Assemblymen was that fun-loving old German-American revolutionary, August Claessens, who in addition to his duties as a Party agitator also taught at the Rand School of Social Science. Some of his best friends had joined the Communist Party, which split away from the Socialist Party in 1919 and for a time was the object of Department of Justice raids indignantly protested by radicals of every hue. In a speech delivered early in 1919 at the Brownsville Labor Lyceum and reported in *The Call*, Claessens was quoted as saying:

There is little real difference between the Socialist Party and the Communists. We want to get to the same place but we are traveling different roads. The reason they are being raided and we unmolested is not because we are considered more conservative, but because we are more powerful than those little groups.[32]

The power to which Claessens referred was the voting strength of the big needle trade unions in New York City, which from their inception had voted en bloc for the Socialist Party. The Socialist role of those unions is reflected in the dramatic history of the *Jewish Daily Forward*, described by one of its own editors as "a powerful instrument of Socialist persuasion."[33]

At its national convention of May, 1920, the Socialist Party showed itself to be of two minds. One group, led by prominent instructors in the Rand School, insisted the Party should not mislead the public, but instead should boldly proclaim its revolutionary principles and aims. Another group, led by Morris Hillquit, favored Fabian tactics of delay and compromise, and advised modifying the Party's constitution to meet the technical objections raised by the New York State Assembly. Shrewd and worldly-wise as Sidney Webb himself, Hillquit judged that the United States was not yet ripe for revolution, and that there was nothing to be gained by forcing the issue.

More clearly than many of his foreign-born associates, Hillquit

---

Dr. Muzzey, who taught at Columbia University, lectured regularly at the Rand School and was listed as a "cooperator" of the League for Industrial Democracy in 1955. See Appendix II.

[32] *Revolutionary Radicalism*, Vol. I, p. 587.

[33] J. C. Rich, "60 Years of the *Jewish Daily Forward*," *The New Leader*, Section Two, (June 3, 1957).

recognized the essentially conservative temper of the American people. He foresaw the widespread resentment, especially among returning servicemen, that any direct attack on American institutions would provoke. Moreover, as a lawyer he perceived the legal obstacles to undertaking a frankly anti-constitutional program.

Since the purpose of the Socialist convention was, after all, to draft an election program, Hillquit argued that the Party could not win independent voters with a blanket statement of destructive aims. It must appeal to discontented elements throughout the country on a purely parliamentary basis. Had not Lenin only recently recommended parliamentary action for British labor and warned against imitating too closely "the first forms of the revolution in Russia"? [34]

Denounced by old comrades as an opportunist, Hillquit was stung into making a public profession of his own radical faith. "We have never at any time changed our creed," he protested. "Never, certainly, to make ourselves acceptable to any capitalist crowd . . . . *As international Socialists, we are revolutionary, and let it be clearly understood we are out to destroy the entire capitalist system.* The capitalist system . . . must come to an end!" [35]

While that rousing pronouncement hardly justifies the label of right wing Socialist which is sometimes applied to Hillquit, in practice his counsel of caution won the day. The Party's constitution was amended, and the five expelled Assemblymen were duly permitted to take their seats in the New York State Legislature. In the Presidential election of 1920 the Socialist Party chalked up nearly a million votes for its candidate, Eugene V. Debs, who directed his campaign from a prison cell; but it never again conducted a major national campaign. By 1921 its membership had dropped to a mere 13,500: only a few thousand more than when the Party was founded. Whatever the future of Socialism in America, as a Columbia University historian remarked, obviously it no longer lay with the Socialist Party.[36]

[34] According to a report by Haden Guest, joint secretary of a British Labour Delegation to Russia in 1920, Lenin had told the delegates: "The Left Communists in England are making blunders because they are too much copying the first forms of the revolution in Russia. I am in favour of Parliamentary action. We had 20% of Communists in the Constituent Assembly and this was enough for victory. In your country 15% might be enough for complete victory . . . . I hope Henderson comes into power with the Labour Party. It will be a lesson to the workers." *Revolutionary Radicalism,* Vol. II, pp. 1599 ff.

[35] *Ibid.,* p. 1789.

[36] Kipnis, *op. cit.,* p. 429.

15

. . . The More It Stays The Same

1.

IN THE future as in the past, the continuing leadership of the Socialist movement in the United States resided in America's Fabian Society,[1] the polite but persistent Intercollegiate Socialist Society, which changed its name but not its nature in 1921. Discarding the Socialist title, that by now had become a liability, it called itself the League for Industrial Democracy—the name under which it survives today.

This alias implied no break with the destructive philosophy and goals of international Socialism. It was rather a device for pursuing them more discreetly, at a temporarily reduced speed. Few outsiders connected the term Industrial Democracy with those archetypes of Fabian Socialism, England's Sidney and Beatrice Webb, who had used it as the title for one of their earliest propaganda books. The slogan adopted by the LID, "Production for use and not for profit," originated with Belfort Bax, another vintage British Socialist. It was a handy formula for expressing Marxist aims in non-Marxist language.

Although most of its members and friends now described themselves publicly as liberals, basically the American society remained the same. As ever, its self-appointed function was to produce the intellectual leaders and to formulate the plans for achieving an eventual Socialist State in America. Like its British model, the LID proposed to operate from the top down and meet the working masses halfway. Voting

[1] *Forty Years of Education*, (New York, League for Industrial Democracy, 1945), p. 56. A telegram to the League on its fortieth anniversary from Mandel V. Halushka, a Chicago schoolteacher, read, "Birthday greetings to America's Fabian Society!"

power and financial support would come from labor, which was to be organized as far as possible into industry-wide, Socialist-led unions.

As the Lusk Committee only vaguely surmised,[2] British Socialists, not Russian nor German, had set the pattern for gradual social revolution to be followed in America and other English-speaking countries. The development of an elite, and research for planning and control purposes, were its primary tasks. Penetration and permeation of existing institutions, indirect rather than direct action, were its recommended procedures.

Owing to the greater expanse and complexity of the United States as compared to England, and to the wide variety of opinions due to the varied national origins of its people, special emphasis had to be placed on the formation of opinion-shaping and policy-directing groups at every level—particularly in the fields of education, political action, economics and foreign relations. While as yet such groups existed only in embryo, and Socialist programs were in public disrepute, sooner or later the opportunity for a breakthrough would come. The way of the turtle was slow but sure.

Superficially, some changes in LID operations were made in deference to the times. Adults were now frankly admitted to membership in an organization which they had always dominated. Student chapters, disrupted by the war, had almost disappeared; but until 1928 no direct effort was made to revive them in the name of the Students' League for Industrial Democracy. For the moment, it seemed more prudent to operate through the new Intercollegiate Liberal League, formed in April, 1921, at a Harvard conference attended by 250 student delegates from assorted colleges.[3]

Keynote speakers at this conference included such trusty troupers

---

[2] Only two direct references to the Fabian Society occur in the Lusk Report, and the first is misleading:

"In England during the '80's the Fabian Society was formed which remains an influential group of intellectual Socialists, *but without direct influence on the working man or Parliament.*" *Revolutionary Radicalism*, Vol. I, p. 53. (Italics added.)

"We have already called attention to the Fabian Society as an interesting group of intellectual Socialists who engage in a very brilliant campaign of propaganda." *Ibid.*, p. 145.

Obviously, the Lusk Committee underestimated both the current and potential influence of the Society.

[3] *Depression, Recovery and Higher Education.* A Report by (a) Committee of the American Association of University Professors. Prepared by Malcolm M. Willey, University of Minnesota, (New York, McGraw-Hill, Inc., 1937), p. 317.

of the old Intercollegiate Socialist Society as Walter Lippmann, Henry
Mussey, Charlotte Perkins Gilman and the Reverend John Haynes
Holmes[4]—all billed as liberals rather than Socialists. The objectives
of the organization, as stated in the prospectus, were even more carefully understated than those of the former ISS. They were: *The cul-
tivation of the open mind; the development of an informed student
opinion on social, industrial, political and international questions.*[5]
Due to the reassuring tone of the prospectus and the psychological
appeal of the word liberal, three presidents of leading Eastern colleges actually consented to address the organizing conference.[6]

In his speech on that occasion, the Reverend Holmes invited students to "identify themselves with the labor world, and there to martyr
themselves by preaching the gospel of free souls and love as the rule
of life." Vaguely, he predicted a revolution and added, "If you want
to be on the side of fundamental right, you have got to be on the
side of labor." A militant advocate of pacificism during the war,
Reverend Holmes had frequently been under surveillance by Federal
agents. Intelligence sources reported that his speeches were used as
propaganda material by the German Army in its efforts to break down
the morale of American troops.

Subsequent meetings of the Intercollegiate Liberal League dealt
with what British Fabians of the period often referred to as "practical
problems of the day." Speakers were provided through the cooperation
of the *New Republic*, whose literary editor, Robert Morss Lovett,
was also president of the LID. Both English and American Fabian
Socialists responded to the call. In January, 1923, the *Fabian News*
of London announced:

W. A. Robson has gone to America for about six months, as a member of a
small European mission which will lecture at the leading universities under
the auspices of the Intercollegiate Liberal Union [sic].

Evidently a touch of Fabian elegance was needed, for the Liberal
League's Socialist slip was already showing. In 1922, that outspoken
American Socialist, Upton Sinclair, making a tour of the universities,
had delivered several lectures sponsored by the Intercollegiate Liberal
League[7]—and very nearly succeeded in exposing its Socialist origin.

[4] *Ibid.*
[5] (Italics added.)
[6] *Ibid.*
[7] At other colleges and universities Upton Sinclair's lectures were sponsored
by local units of the Cosmopolitan Club—an organization similar in character
and inspiration to the Intercollegiate Liberal League.

Concerning such incidents, a committee of the American Association of University Professors reported tolerantly: "The Intercollegiate Liberal League suffered from misinterpretation, and somewhat at the hands of 'heresy hunters.'"[8] In 1922, it merged with the Student Forum and its membership numbered a select 850 on eight college campuses.

Like the young people whom it was schooling in duplicity, the parent LID cultivated a liberal look and an air of candid innocence. This pose was rendered more credible by the fact that certain troublesome "cooperators" had voluntarily withdrawn from the ISS. Gone but not forgotten were firebrands like Ella Reeve Bloor, Elizabeth Gurley Flynn, William Z. Foster and Robert Minor, who had been active in the violent IWW-led strikes of other years and who later became top functionaries in the Communist Party.

No suspicion of Communist ties could be permitted to cast its shadow upon the League for Industrial Democracy, on which the future of the Socialist movement in America depended. Yet individual members and even ranking officers, acting independently or through subsidiary organizations, continued to display a puzzling solicitude for the well-being of illicit Communists. To an outsider it sometimes looked as if the chief concern of open-minded League members in the nineteen-twenties was to procure the survival of the illegal Communist Party, then calling itself the Workers' Party, with whose methods they were officially in disagreement.

In this connection, it may be pointed out that the role of the renovated LID was from the start a defensive one. After 1917, both public officials and the American public at large regarded Communism very much as Anarchism had been viewed in the eighteen-eighties and nineties. Since virtually all members of Communist parties here and abroad were former Socialists, and since a good many avowed Socialists[9] had now one foot in the Communist camp, the average American could hardly be expected to make much distinction between them. A respectable front was urgently needed.

Like the Bellamy clubs of a previous era, the LID was called upon, not only to make Socialism acceptable under other names, but to

---

[8] *Ibid.*

[9] Algernon Lee, author of *The Essentials of Marxism*, said: "A large proportion in the early nineteen-twenties went Communist, and of these only a few have found their way back." Quoted in August Claessens' autobiography, *Didn't We Have Fun?* (New York, Rand School Press, 1953), p. 20.

preserve the whole social revolutionary movement in this country from possible extinction. "Left can speak to left"—a principle later voiced by the British Fabian, Ernest Bevin, at Potsdam—was its undeclared but pragmatic rule of action.

There is no doubt that radicals of every kind were highly unpopular in the United States after World War I—and no doubt there were good reasons. Information had been received linking a number of left wing publications in this country with the Communist International's propaganda headquarters in Berlin. As a result, the Department of Justice launched an all-out drive to immobilize centers of seditious propaganda in America. A series of raids was conducted in 1919-20 by order of Attorney General Mitchell Palmer, which led four Harvard Law School professors headed by Felix Frankfurter to file a protest with the Justice Department.[10] Socialist-liberal writers—enjoying themselves hugely, as Walter Lippmann recalls—joined forces to taunt and harass the earnest if unsophisticated officers of the law.

When steps were also taken in 1919-20 to close the Rand School of Social Science on grounds that it harbored known Bolsheviks,[11] there was some fear that even the Intercollegiate Socialist Society itself might soon be exposed to summary action. Not only August Claessens, but a whole flock of ISS valued "cooperators" were listed as instructors and lecturers at the Rand School in June, 1919,[12] when the New York State Legislature appointed a committee headed by Senator Clayton R. Lusk to investigate radical activities. The Senator's methods were of a classic simplicity. He issued a search warrant and called for State Troopers to escort the investigators who descended suddenly on the Rand School, impounding records and files.

On the basis of evidence so obtained, the Committee took steps to close the school by court injunction and throw it into receivership.

[10] Helen Shirley Thomas, *Felix Frankfurter: Scholar on the Bench*, (Baltimore, Johns Hopkins University Press, 1960), p. 19. Distributed in England by the Oxford University Press.

[11] *Who's Who in New York* for 1918 lists A. A. Heller as a director of the Rand School. Treasurer and general manager of the International Oxygen Company, which had benefitted from wartime contracts, the Russian-born Heller served as commercial attaché of the unofficial "Soviet Embassy," whose chief, Ludwig Martens, left the United States under pressure.

[12] In 1919, instructors and lecturers at Rand School included: Max Eastman, Charles Beard, Elmer Rice, Oswald Garrison Villard, John Haynes Holmes, Harry Laidler, Lajpait Rai, Joseph Schlossberg, August Claessens, Harry Dana, Henrietta Epstein, E. A. Goldenweisser, James O'Neal, Eugene Wood, A. Philip Randolph, I. A. Hourwich, Henry Newman, Harvey P. Robinson and Joseph Slavit. *Bulletin of the Rand School*, 1918-19. See Appendix II.

With the help of Samuel Untermeyer, a prominent New York attorney whose brother, Louis, taught Modern Poetry at the Rand School, the injunction was lifted and the school's records were returned. Thereupon the so-called Lusk Laws were passed,[13] requiring all private schools in New York State to be licensed. The purpose was to close the Rand School on grounds that it did not meet the necessary qualifications.

Here the hidden source of Socialist power in New York, hinted at by August Claessens, suddenly revealed itself. The attorney for the Rand School, Morris Hillquit, was backed by the mass indignation and voting power of the Amalgamated Clothing Workers and other Socialist-led trade unions. Prudently the Lusk Laws were vetoed in 1920 by that happy warrior, Governor Alfred Emanuel Smith, in what has been described as the most brilliant veto message of his career. The episode is significant because it marked the first step in an unholy alliance between the New York State Democratic organization and the Socialist-led needle trades unions: an alliance that was to put Franklin D. Roosevelt into the Governor's mansion and eventually into the White House, and bring "democratic Socialists" into the highest councils of Government.

Governor Smith's veto of the Lusk Laws also offered a striking example of the uses of Fabian Socialist permeation in America—the technique recommended so warmly by Beatrice Webb, explained so clearly by Margaret Cole[14] and employed so successfully by British Fabians operating inside the Liberal Party in England. It is a technique of inducing non-Socialists to do the work and the will of Socialists. No one supposes for a moment that Governor Al Smith was himself a Socialist; nor does anyone imagine he drafted that very brilliant veto message personally. Besides being an astute politician of the Tammany Hall stripe, Smith was a devout Catholic layman. To reach him required not only permeation at first hand, but permeation at second hand as well.

In this instance, it may be noted that one of Governor Smith's counselors on matters involving "social justice" was Father (later

---

[13] The year that the Lusk Laws were passed and vetoed by Smith, 1920, the School heard Louis Lochner on Journalism, Gregory Zilboorg on Literature, Leland Olds on American Social History, Frank Tannenbaum on Modern European History, and James P. Warbasse on the Cooperative Movement. *Bulletin of the Rand School,* 1919-20. See Appendix II.

[14] Margaret Cole, *The Story of Fabian Socialism,* (London, Heinemann Educational Books, Ltd., 1961), pp. 84 ff.

Monsignor) John Augustin Ryan of the National Catholic Welfare Council,[15] who in 1915 founded the Department of Social Sciences at the Catholic University of America. In an objective analysis entitled *The Economic Thought of John A. Ryan,* Dr. Patrick Gearty has revealed that much of Father Ryan's thinking on social and economic matters was derived from John Atkinson Hobson, the British Fabian Socialist philosopher and avowed rationalist.

In 1919, Father Ryan had already unveiled the draft of a postwar "reconstruction" plan, in an address delivered in West Virginia before the conservative Knights of Columbus. The Ryan plan has since been known by the somewhat misleading title of "The Bishops' Program of Social Reconstruction," because it was printed over the signatures of four Bishops who formed the National Catholic Welfare Council's Executive Committee. It was reprinted in 1931, just prior to the election of Franklin Delano Roosevelt as President.

An illuminating fact about the plan was that it took special note of "the social reconstruction program of the British Labor Party"—a program written by Sidney Webb and published as *Labour and the New Social Order.* Father Ryan specifically cited the "four pillars" of the Webb opus. Concerning them, he stated, "This program may properly be described as one of immediate radical reforms, leading to complete socialism . . . . Evidently *this outcome* cannot be approved by Catholics." [16] True to Catholic orthodoxy, "complete Socialism" must be rejected; but not the bulk of the ill-begotten Fabian "reform" program. Illogically, Father Ryan praised the means while rejecting the end. Although his views certainly cannot be regarded as typical of the Catholic leaders of his day, he left disciples behind him and founded a school of thought which has since come to be accepted unquestioningly by many otherwise devout Catholic teachers and students of the social sciences.

More concretely, Father Ryan defended in speeches and articles the right of the five expelled Socialist Assemblymen to be seated in the New York State Legislature. In 1922, his name appeared on the letterhead of the Labor Defense Council, a joint Socialist-Communist construct, set up to obtain funds for the legal defense of illegal Communists arrested at Bridgman, Michigan, whose attorney of record was Frank P. Walsh.

[15] Renamed in 1923 The National Catholic Welfare Conference.
[16] (Italics added.)

Although controversial Catholic clerics of conservative economic views have occasionally been silenced, somehow John Augustin Ryan contrived to do very much as he pleased. At a later date he was frankly known as the padre of the New Deal; and for services rendered was honored in 1939 with a birthday dinner attended by more than six hundred persons. The guests included Supreme Court Justices Frankfurter, Douglas and Black, Secretary of Labor Frances Perkins, Secretary of the Treasury Henry A. Morgenthau, Jr., plus a liberal assortment of left wing trade union leaders, progressive educators and New Deal congressmen.

There is no question that the moral influence of Father Ryan, coupled with considerations of practical politics, led Governor Smith in 1920 to intervene on behalf of the Rand School. In other respects, also, Smith anticipated that tolerance for Socialist programs and personalities which characterized his successor, Franklin D. Roosevelt. During Smith's campaign for the Presidency in 1928, most of his eager supporters scarcely noticed it when he announced "over the radio" that he favored "public ownership of public power."

The Lusk Laws were briefly revived in 1921 under Governor Nathan Miller, but the Rand School continued to operate happily without a license. It even collaborated in opening a summer school at Camp Tamiment vaguely patterned after Fabian Summer Schools in Britain. There *New Republic* regulars George Soule and Stuart Chase, Mary Austin, Evans Clark and other LID pundits[17] tutored the humbler Rand School rank-and-file in Socialist politics, economics and general culture.

With time and patience, the school settled its legal difficulties and has survived to the present day as a teaching, research, publishing and propaganda center of "peaceful" Marxism known as the Tamiment Institute. It has lived to enjoy 40th, 45th, 50th and 55th anniversary dinners, complete with souvenir booklets celebrating old times and old-timers. During its lifetime, it has been regularly favored with visits by leading British Fabians: from Bertrand Russell, John Stra-

---

[17] The year after the Lusk Laws were repassed in 1921 marked the opening of Camp Tamiment. Evans Clark taught Political Science, William Soskin, Modern Theatre, Mary Austin, American Literature, Otto Beyer, Industrial Problems. Robert Ferrari lectured on Crime, Taraknath Das on the Far East. The roster of lecturers also included Clement Wood, Arthur W. Calhoun, George Soule, Joseph Jablonower, Norman Thomas, Solon DeLeon, Jessie W. Hughan and Stuart Chase. *Bulletin of the Rand School,* 1920-21. See Appendix II.

chey, M.P. and Norman Angell to Margaret Bondfield, M.P., Margaret Cole and Toni Sender,[18] representative of the International Confederation of Free Trade Unions at the United Nations. While no change in the Rand School's outlook has ever been recorded, so far has Socialism been rehabilitated, that the present Taminent Institute now wears an aura of respectability in some academic circles.

In the same year that the Lusk Laws were revived and every known radical organization in the country seemed to be under fire, the LID chose Robert Morss Lovett, professor of English at the University of Chicago, as its president, a post he was to hold for seventeen years. He was a man of keen intelligence, quiet charm and unfailing courtesy, with a thorough knowledge of nineteenth-century English prose sometimes called the literature of protest. To paraphrase Henry Adams, Lovett had been educated for the nineteenth century and found himself obliged to live in the twentieth, a situation to which he was never quite reconciled.

Born on Christmas Day to thrifty, pious New England parents, he came of pilgrim stock but never referred to it. He had graduated summa cum laude from Harvard in the days when Bellamy-type Socialism, adorned with touches of John Ruskin and William Morris, was attracting young Cambridge intellectuals; and he made connections there that lasted until his death at the age of eighty-four. During the eighteen-nineties, Lovett went to Chicago to assist University President John Rainey Harper in bringing culture and scholarship to the booming Midwest. Soon he became a sort of campus legend by virtue of his wit, audacity, kindly disposition and practically unshakable aplomb. An inveterate diner-out and something of a bon vivant, he was punctual in keeping appointments and punctilious in meeting his commitments, academic or social. Because of a certain engaging simplicity of manner, all his life people were eager to protect him and insisted he was somehow being taken advantage of—though the fact was that he invariably did as he chose, without excuses or explanations.

Through his wife, a close friend of Jane Addams and Florence Kelley, Lovett was drawn into the circle of settlement workers, social reformers, pacifists, American Socialists and visiting British Fabians that revolved around Hull House. Due to his own pacifist activities during World War I, he became a scandal to patriots and a hero

---

[18] Toni Sender's salary was partially paid by the AFL-CIO, an item regularly reported in its annual budget.

to Socialists. The event that transformed the rather aloof university professor into a public figure was a mammoth peace meeting in Chicago which ended in a riot.

The circumstances under which Lovett happened to preside at that gathering shed some light on his subsequent career. At the last minute, the original chairman of the meeting failed to appear, and other possible substitutes evaporated. Nobody of prominence could be found willing to take the responsibility for an event almost sure to provoke a public scandal. Obligingly and with a certain amused contempt for the absentees, Lovett agreed to act as chairman, thereby inaugurating a long and tangled career as front man for a legion of left wing organizations and committees. At moments when no one else of established reputation cared to expose himself, Lovett was always available. After the heat was off, others were pleased to take over.

In 1919, Lovett was invited to New York to become editor of *The Dial*, a literary monthly attempting to endow radicalism with a protective facade of culture and to provide an outlet for the talents of young college-trained Socialists then beginning to throng to the great city. Among his youthful staff assistants on *The Dial* were Lewis Mumford,[19] who has since become something of an authority on civic architecture and city planning, and Vera Brittain, who later married Professor George Catlin, a prime architect of Atlantic Union. In a year or two, Lovett was made literary editor of the *New Republic*, a position he occupied six months of the year while retaining his chair at the University of Chicago. He was also named to the Pulitzer prize fiction awards committee. These vantage posts not only provided liberal cover for a confirmed Fabian Socialist, but enabled him to promote the new literature of protest, with its emphasis on "debunking" American institutions, that became popular in the nineteen-twenties and thirties.

Through S. K. Ratcliffe, the *New Republic's* long time London representative, and through that magazine's opposite number in Britain, the *New Statesman,* it was easy enough to keep regularly in touch with the fountainhead of Fabian Socialism. So many eminent British Fabian authors and educators were busily traveling back and forth across the Atlantic, to share in the wealth of a country whose crassness they deplored, that they passed each other in transit on the high seas. Scarcely a one missed being entertained at the *New Republic's* weekly

[19] See Appendix II.

staff luncheons, and Lovett and his associates were helpful in booking many on the lucrative university lecture circuit. As he confided to friends, Lovett longed to visit England; but was blacklisted by the British Foreign Office because he had aided some Hindu revolutionaries, only incidentally financed by German agents, during the war. Thus contacts between the Fabian Society of London and the titular head of its American affiliate necessarily remained indirect. For the time being, perhaps it was better so.

2.

Throughout the nineteen-twenties—while the United States was enjoying a giddy whirl of industrial growth and paper profits, and the outwitting of Prohibition agents became a major national pastime —there was always that same small, close-knit core of studious men and women bent on remaking the country according to a more or less veiled Marxist formula. Bitterly disappointed that world war had not produced a world-wide Socialist commonwealth, they still found much to console them in the international picture. The predominance of the Social Democratic Party in Germany; the existence of a somewhat crude but frankly all-Socialist State in Soviet Russia; and the emergence of the Fabian Socialist-controlled Labour Party as the second strongest political party in Britain: these developments gave them hope of being able some day to bring the unwilling United States to heel.

True, the Socialist movement in America still seemed a comparatively small affair, foreign to the great majority of average Americans. Its appeal was still confined chiefly to social workers, rebel college professors and students, a handful of ambitious lawyers and wealthy ladies, and a few militant Socialist-led unions that were far from representing a majority in the ranks of American labor. The postwar scene, however, was enlivened by the addition of many college-trained young people, cut adrift from family discipline and religious moorings, who found companionship, a faith and ultimately well paid careers within the reorganized Socialist movement. The prestige of British Fabian authors in New York publishing and book review circles helped to open doors for their liberal brethren in the United States. Superficially, the American version of the British Fabian Society almost looked, as it had in England, to be a species of logrolling literary society.

Political power, however, was the prize for which it secretly yearned, insignificant as its efforts in that direction might appear at the moment to be. Socialist intellectuals already aspired to influence the military and foreign policy of the United States and continued to plan quietly for the creation of a Socialist State in America within a world federation of Socialist States. Their postwar aspirations had been foreshadowed in a "Wartime Program" issued early in 1917 by the American Union Against Militarism: a program that in a small way echoed the British Fabian Socialist plan contained in Leonard Woolf's *International Government*. The "Wartime Program" stated:

With America's entry into the war we must redouble our efforts to maintain democratic liberties, to destroy militarism, and to *build towards world federation*. Therefore, our immediate program is:

To oppose all legislation tending to fasten upon the United States in wartime *any permanent military policy based on compulsory military training and service*.

To organize legal advice and aid for all men conscientiously opposed to participation in war.

To demand publication by the Government of all agreements or understandings with other nations.

To demand a clear and definite statement of the terms on which the United States will make peace.

To develop the ideal of internationalism in the minds of the American people to the end that this nation may stand firm for world federation at the end of the war.

To fight for the complete maintenance *in wartime* of the constitutional right of free speech, free press, peaceable assembly and freedom from unlawful search and seizure. With this end in view the Union has recently established a Civil Liberties Bureau . . . .[20]

Founders of the organization issuing that statement were described as "a group of well-known liberals."[21] Closer inspection, however, reveals that virtually every member of its founders' committee was a long-standing "cooperator" of the Intercollegiate Socialist Society, later the League for Industrial Democracy.[22]

[20] David Edison Bunting, *Liberty and Learning*. With an Introduction by Professor George S. Counts, President, American Federation of Teachers. (Washington, American Council on Public Affairs, 1942), p. 2. (Italics added.)

[21] *Ibid.*, p. 1.

[22] This committee was composed of Lillian D. Wald, of the Henry Street Settlement; Paul U. Kellogg, editor of *Survey Graphic*; the Reverend John Haynes Holmes; Rabbi Stephen S. Wise; Florence Kelley, president of the Intercollegiate Socialist Society and head of the Consumers League of America; George W. Kirchwey; Crystal Eastman Benedict; L. Hollingsworth Wood, a prominent

When it became evident after the war that the Union's dream of world federation must be postponed, the LID remained the directive and policy-making body behind a gradual Socialist movement soliciting public support on a variety of pretexts. Its aims were promoted through a handful of closely related organizations, invariably staffed at the executive level by directors and officers of the League. Chief among them were the American Civil Liberties Union (ACLU), the Federated Press, and the American Fund for Public Service, also known as the Garland Fund, a self-exhausting trust which helped to forestall deficits in the other organizations and even contributed charitably to the subsistence of masked Communist enterprises.

Through such organizations, the Socialist movement maintained discreet contacts with illegal Communist groups in the nineteen-twenties. William Z. Foster, identified then and later as a leader of the Communist Party, was both a director of the Federated Press and a trustee and indirect beneficiary of the Garland Fund. As late as 1938, four acknowledged Communists served on the national committee of the ACLU.[23]

While the LID stood aloof, taking no responsibility for the actions of its subsidiaries, their unity was visibly confirmed by the fact that Robert Morss Lovett held top posts in all four organizations. He was not only president of the LID, but a director of the ACLU and the Federated Press, which served a number of labor papers and left wing publications, both Socialist and Communist. Lovett also sat on the board of trustees of the Garland Fund, and he chaired a host of ephemeral committees. In fact, he appeared in so many capacities at once that he was sometimes compared to the character in W. S. Gilbert's ballad who claimed to be the cook, captain and mate of the *Nancy* brig plus a number of other things.

Obviously, Lovett could not really have directed all the organizations and committees over which he presided in the twenties and after. The administrative and editorial work of the League was handled by Harry Laidler, aided after 1922 by the former clergyman Norman Thomas in the sphere of Socialist politics and by Paul Blanshard as LID organizer. Paul Blanshard later directed the Federated Press.[24]

Quaker attorney; Louis P. Lochner, afterwards of *The New York Times* Bureau in Berlin; Alice Lewisohn: Max Eastman; Allen Benson and Elizabeth G. Evans. *Ibid.* See Appendix II.

[23] *Ibid.*, p. 10. See chart of political affiliations of national committee, American Civil Liberties Union.

[24] Paul Blanshard was a contributor to the official 1928 Campaign Handbook

More recently, he has been identified with an organization known as "Protestants and Other Americans United for the Separation of Church and State," dedicated to expunging all references to God from public schools and public life in America. He anticipated G. D. H. Cole, the president of the London Fabian Society, who smilingly advocated "the abolition of God"!

Though Lovett's actual duties—aside from his work as an editor, teacher and public speaker—always remained somewhat mysterious, he appears to have acted mainly as a liaison between top-level Socialists and Communists as well as academic and moneyed groups. During the Socialist movement's period of temporary regression, he was in his glory. His contacts were numerous, and his personal amiability, combined with discretion, made him acceptable to all. "Let one hand wash the other" and "recoil, the better to spring forward" (*Reculer pour mieux sauter*) were the private maxims that guided him on his variegated rounds. It was hard to believe that so delightful and considerate a dinner guest, as Felix Frankfurter has described in his autobiography, and so informed and sober a classroom figure could be so dangerous a radical.

Yet an old friend, who never shared his political views, still recalls how the normally serene Robert Morss Lovett once remarked with sudden intensity: "*I hate the United States!* I would be willing to see the whole world blow up, if it would destroy the United States!" His startled companion dismissed the incident as a momentary aberration —and refrained from mentioning to Lovett that his words were much the same as those of Philip Nolan in *The Man Without a Country*.

Most conspicuous of the postwar organizations manned by League for Industrial Democracy members was the American Civil Liberties Union. Like the LID, the ACLU has survived to the present day, acquiring a patina of respectability with the passage of time and the decline of old-fashioned patriotism, for which both bodies cherish an ill-concealed contempt.

Formed in January, 1920, the ACLU was a direct outgrowth of the wartime Civil Liberties Bureau, a branch of the American Union Against Militarism. The Bureau assumed "independent" life in 1917

of the Socialist Party, entitled *The Intelligent Voter's Guide* and published by the Socialist National Campaign Committee. Other contributors were: W. E. Woodward, Norman Thomas, Freda Kirchwey, McAllister Coleman, James O'Neal, Harry Elmer Barnes, James H. Maurer, Lewis Gannett, Victor L. Berger, Harry W. Laidler and Louis Waldman. All were officials of the League for Industrial Democracy. See Appendix II.

when a young social worker from St. Louis named Roger Baldwin moved to New York to direct the work of its national office.[25] During the war, it furnished advice and legal aid to conscientious objectors, thus gaining the support of some quite reputable Quakers. When it was reorganized on a permanent basis after the war as the ACLU, Roger Baldwin, who had just finished a prison term for draft-dodging, returned as its executive officer. For all practical purposes, he ran the organization for approximately forty years.

While the ACLU was still in the process of formation, Baldwin wrote in an advisory letter: "Do steer away from making it look like a Socialist enterprise. We want also to look patriots in everything we do. We want to get a good lot of flags, talk a good deal about the Constitution and what our forefathers wanted to make of the country, and to show that we are really the folks that really stand for the spirit of our institutions." [26] Such deceptive practice was in the classic Fabian tradition—symbolized by the wolf in sheep's clothing that decorates the Shavian stained-glass window at a Fabian meetinghouse in England. Promptly adopted by Baldwin's associates, this tactic has succeeded in deluding not a few well-intentioned Americans.

The immediate function of the American Civil Liberties Union in 1920 was to combat the postwar flurry of arrests, deportations and court actions against Communists and other seditionists, many of whom were foreign born. Baldwin had previously described such individuals "as representing labor and radical movements for human welfare," and contended they were being "insidiously attacked by privileged business interests working under the cloak of patriotism." [27] Twin weapons of the quasi-forensic ACLU were legal aid and a species of propaganda designed to arouse public sympathy for the "victims" of the law—an expedient normally frowned upon by the American bar.

If it was Roger Baldwin who defined the propaganda line, another founder of the ACLU,[28] Harvard Law Professor Felix Frankfurter, provided the legalistic approach. In his protest of 1920 to the Department of Justice; in his argument as *amicus curiae* before a federal court in Boston, where he assured the right of habeas corpus to criminal aliens awaiting deportation;[29] and earlier, in two reports

[25] Bunting, *op. cit.*, p. 2.
[26] *Revolutionary Radicalism*, Vol. I, p. 1087.
[27] Bunting, *op. cit.*, p. 3.
[28] Thomas, *op. cit.*, p. 21.
[29] *Ibid.*, p. 19.

submitted as counsel for President Wilson's Mediation Commission, Frankfurter initiated the mischievous practice of invoking the Constitution for the benefit of its avowed enemies.

Perhaps more than any other American, Frankfurter helped to establish the fiction that it is somehow unconstitutional and un-American for the United States to take measures to defend itself against individuals or groups pledged to destroy it. His reports on the Preparedness Day bombings and the Bisbee deportations won him a sharp rebuke from that forthright American, former President Theodore Roosevelt, who wrote in a personal letter to Frankfurter:

I have just received your report on the Bisbee deportations . . . . Your report is as thoroughly misleading a document as could be written on the subject . . . .

Here again you are engaged in excusing men precisely like the Bolsheviki in Russia, who are murderers and encouragers of murder, who are traitors to their allies, to democracy and to civilization . . . and whose acts are nevertheless apologized for on grounds, my dear Mr. Frankfurter, substantially like those which you allege. *In times of danger nothing is more common and more dangerous to the Republic than for men to avoid condemning the criminals who are really public enemies by making their entire assault on the shortcomings of the good citizens who have been the victims or opponents of the criminals* . . . . It is not the kind of thing I care to see well-meaning men do in this country.[30]

One of the more sensational events in which early leaders of the American Civil Liberties Union took a hand was the case of the "Michigan Syndicalists." The circumstances leading up to it were peculiar, to say the least. In August, 1922, a Hungarian agent of the Communist International, one Joseph Pogany, alias Lang, alias John Pepper, arrived illegally in the United States. Having assisted in setting up the short-lived Bela Kun Government in Hungary, he was presumed to be something of a specialist in the bloodier forms of revolutionary behavior. Pogany brought with him detailed instructions for organizing both legal and illegal branches of the new Communist Party USA. Those instructions were to be divulged by him at a secret Communist convention, held at a camp in the woods near Bridgman, Michigan, which was duly raided by the authorities.

As a result, seventeen Communists—including William Z. Foster, then editor of the *Labor Herald*—were arrested and arraigned under Michigan's anti-syndicalist laws. At his trial in Bridgman, Foster, who

---

[30] *Roosevelt to Frankfurter, December 19, 1917, The Letters of Theodore Roosevelt*, Manuscript Division, Library of Congress, Washington, VIII, 1262. (Italics added.)

later openly headed the Communist Party, testified under oath that he was not a Communist, thereby escaping conviction. Many others attending the conclave had prudently slipped away the night before the raid, leaving a mass of records and documents behind. In sifting this material, it was discovered that several of the delegates were connected with the Rand School of Social Science. Some, like Rose Pastor Stokes and Max Lerner, have since been listed as "cooperators" of the LID.[31]

Max Lerner, a bright young intellectual who had been a student leader of the Intercollegiate Socialist Society at Washington University in St. Louis, was among the seventeen persons arrested in or near Bridgman. Like Foster, he claimed to have attended that secret convention in an editorial capacity. What his other motives may have been are not recorded, since from that time forward Lerner appeared to operate strictly within the framework of the Fabian Socialist movement. For years he continued to write articles for *The Nation, The Call* and *The New Leader,* and to lecture on economics at the Rand School, the New School for Social Research and more conventional institutions of learning. He was a lifelong admirer of the self-proclaimed Marxist, Harold Laski, who found Lerner's political outlook close to his own.[32]

When Laski was quoted in 1945 by the Newark *Advertiser* as condoning bloody revolution, he sued for libel in a London court—and lost the case. It was Max Lerner (together with Harvard Professor Arthur M. Schlesinger, Sr.) who took the initiative in collecting an American "fund" for Laski,[33] to help defray the latter's court costs of some twelve thousand pounds. More recently, we find an unreconstructed Max Lerner writing a widely circulated column for American newspapers. In an article sent from Switzerland in August, 1963, he deftly exploited the malodorous Stephen Ward pandering case (forced into prominence by the Fabian Harold Wilson, M.P.) as a means of promoting sympathy for Socialism.[34]

[31] See Appendix II.

[32] Kingsley Martin, *Harold Laski: A Biographical Memoir,* (New York, The Viking Press, Inc., 1953), p. 86. "Among the younger men, including, for instance, Max Lerner, he [Laski] found intellectuals whose political outlook was close to his own."

[33] *Ibid.,* p. 168.

[34] San Francisco *Examiner,* (August 11, 1963). "We underestimate," writes Lerner, "how deeply most people need a rebel-victim symbol. There is a lot of free-flowing aggression in all of us, and one of the functions of a *cause célèbre* is to give us a chance to channel some of it . . . . This brings us back to Ward as the rebel against society, and the victim of its power-groups."

The pained outcry that the Bridgman case evoked in the twenties from Socialist-liberal writers and publicists was symptomatic of a curious phenomenon never explained by medical science: Wound a Communist, and a Socialist bleeds! A circular letter of April 6, 1923, soliciting funds for the legal defense of the arrested Communists, described them plaintively as a "group of men and women met together peacefully to consider the business of their party organization." This letter appeared on the stationery of the Labor Defense Council, whose national committee included the names of well-known Communists. It was signed by eight equally well-known members of the LID and/or ACLU.[35] At about the same time, Robert Morss Lovett persuaded the wealthy wife of a University of Chicago professor, to post securities valued at $25,000 as bond for the Bridgman defendants. The securities were subsequently forfeited when several of the accused jumped bail and fled to Moscow.

A more enduring cause *célèbre*, in which both Socialist- and Communist-sponsored "defense" organizations battled jointly to reverse the course of justice, was the Sacco-Vanzetti case. Nicola Sacco and Bartolomeo Vanzetti were Italian immigrants of admitted Anarchist views[36] who were arrested in 1920 for the robbery and murder of a paymaster and paymaster's guard in South Braintree, Massachusetts. Found guilty and sentenced to die, they were finally executed in 1927. Since several million words have already been written about the case in the form of legal briefs, editorials, articles and books, it

[35] Signers of this letter were: Freda Kirchwey, editor of *The Nation*; Norman Thomas, leader of the Socialist Party; The Reverend John Nevin Sayre; Mary Heaton Vorse, contributor to *The Nation* and the friend and inspirer of Sinclair Lewis; Roger Baldwin, director of American Civil Liberties Union; The Reverend Percy Stickney Grant: The Reverend John Haynes Holmes; Paxton Hibben, director and solicitor of funds for the "Russian Red Cross" in the United States. All are listed by Mina Weisenberg as "cooperators" of the League for Industrial Democracy. See Appendix II.

[36] In this connection, it is interesting to note that in June, 1919, the first issue of *Freedom*—a paper published by the Ferrer group of Anarchists at Stelton, New Jersey—stated editorially: "It may well be asked, 'Why another paper?' when the broadly libertarian and revolutionary movement is so ably represented by Socialist publications like the *Revolutionary Age, Liberator, Rebel Worker, Workers' World* and many others, and the advanced liberal movement by *The Dial, Nation, World Tomorrow* and to a lesser degree, the *New Republic* and *Survey*. These publications are doing excellent work in their several ways, and with much of that work we find ourselves in hearty agreement." (*Author's note*: One of the founders of the Ferrer School, Leonard D. Abbott, was also a founder of the Intercollegiate Socialist Society. He was associate editor of *Freedom*. Members of that short-lived paper's editorial staff were teachers at the Rand School.)

would be superfluous to review the matter in detail. Some $300,000 was contributed for the legal defense of those "two obscure immigrants about whom nobody cared"—as Arthur M. Schlesinger, Jr. has described them sentimentally in *The Age of Roosevelt.*

Left wing leaders had apparently promised Sacco and Vanzetti they would be saved at any cost, and a mighty effort was made to that end. All the available propaganda stops were pulled out. The whole spectrum of leftist literary lights, from Liberal to Socialist to Communist, was brought into play. Academic Socialism's foremost figures were enlisted to dignify the campaign, and student organizations were rounded up. Among the legal scholars who helped to prepare documents on the case was Harvard Law Professor Francis B. Sayre, son-in-law of Woodrow Wilson and a relative of the Reverend John Nevin Sayre.[37] The Brandeis family became so emotionally involved in the cause of the two allegedly persecuted immigrants that Justice Brandeis felt obliged to disqualify himself when the question of reviewing the case reached the Supreme Court.

For several years the Harvard campus was split down the middle on the issue of Sacco and Vanzetti's guilt or innocence. Professors Felix Frankfurter and Arthur M. Schlesinger, Sr. rallied the innocence-mongers. They were supported by Roscoe Pound, Dean of the Law School and a disciple of Brandeis in the field of sociological law. On the other hand, University President A. Lawrence Lowell urged moderation and suggested that some credence be placed in the good faith and common sense of Massachusetts' judges and law enforcement officers. So vehemently did Felix Frankfurter denounce his academic superior that it was suggested the little law professor resign. "Why should I resign?" asked Frankfurter, adding insolently, "Let Lowell resign!" When it was all over, the long-suffering President Lowell wrote in mild exasperation to Dean Pound that he thought "one Frankfurter to the Pound should be enough."

Not only *The Nation* and *New Republic*, but at least two respected New York dailies, insisted to the end that Sacco and Vanzetti were the blameless victims of a Red scare or public witch hunt. So impassioned and so confusing was the public debate that some Americans today are still under the impression that Sacco and Vanzetti were somehow "framed" or "railroaded" to their death. Only recently a final confirmation of their guilt has come to light. It was contained

---

[37] The Reverend John Nevin Sayre was a founder of the ACLU and signed the appeal for funds in the Bridgman case.

in a quiet announcement by Francis Russell, a man who has spent the better part of his life seeking to demonstrate Sacco and Vanzetti's innocence.

In the June, 1962, issue of *American Heritage* Russell told how he finally traced the long-missing bullets found in the body of the paymaster's guard, Berardelli, to a police captain, now deceased. Two ballistic experts, using modern techniques, analyzed the bullets and testified they had unquestionably been fired from the .32 caliber pistol which Sacco was carrying at the time of his arrest. Thus Francis Russell was forced to conclude that Sacco wielded the murder weapon and that Vanzetti was at least an accessory.

Oddly enough, a similar conclusion based on less objective evidence was made public by Upton Sinclair in 1953. In a memoir published serially in the Rand School's quarterly *Bulletin of International Socialist Studies*,[38] Sinclair quoted Fred A. Moore, an attorney for Sacco and Vanzetti, as saying he believed Sacco to be guilty of the shooting and Vanzetti to have guilty knowledge of it. Sinclair further relates how Robert Minor, a Communist Party official, telephoned him long distance in Boston and begged him not to repeat the attorney's opinion. "You will ruin the movement! It will be treason!" cried Minor.

From that indiscreet telephone call, it is inferred that Sacco and Vanzetti may have robbed and killed to fill the Party's underground treasury, as Stalin and his Bolshevik comrades are known to have done in Russian Georgia during 1910-11. At any rate, the missing payroll funds, amounting to nearly $16,000, were never recovered. A third man, reported by witnesses to have assisted at the South Braintree crime, vanished coincidentally with the cash. This, however, is not the "legacy" referred to by Professor Arthur M. Schlesinger, Sr., who in 1948 wrote the introduction to an emotion-packed volume perpetuating the martyr legend of "the poor fish-peddler and the good shoemaker." [39] As of 1962, Schlesinger's son, Arthur, Jr., was a member of the national committee of the American Civil Liberties Union, which had handled the appeals and coordinated the propaganda in the historic Sacco and Vanzetti case.[40]

[38] Upton Sinclair, "The Fishpeddler and the Shoemaker," *Bulletin of International Social Studies,* (Summer, 1953).

[39] Cf. Louis G. Joughlin and Edmund M. Morgan, *The Legacy of Sacco and Vanzetti.* With an introduction by Arthur M. Schlesinger, (New York, Harcourt, Brace & Co., 1948).

[40] *Freedom Through Dissent,* 42nd Annual Report, July 1, 1961 to June 30, 1962, American Civil Liberties Union, New York, 1962. (List of officers, directors, national committee members, etc. Page not numbered, opposite p. 1.)

16

By Any Other Name

1.

DESPITE some disillusioning experiences, the Socialist-inspired American Civil Liberties Union has never to this day ceased its efforts in defense of the catastrophic Left. Such consistent activity in behalf of the militants and expendables of the revolutionary movement has naturally exposed the ACLU to what its friends term "misinterpretation." During the nineteen-twenties it was occasionally described by opponents as a legal branch of the Communist Party.[1] In 1940, it finally barred "totalitarians" from membership, a decision resulting in the protest-resignation of Dr. Harry F. Ward, its original chairman. At a later date, the ACLU took further steps to neutralize criticism by denouncing as legally untenable the principle of "guilt by association."

In view of its origins and history, one might reasonably doubt the depth of ACLU devotion to the Flag and the Constitution. It does

[1] In 1928 Roger Baldwin, longtime Executive Director of the ACLU, stated flatly: "*I believe in revolution*—not necessarily the forcible seizure of power in armed conflict, but the process of growth of class movements determined *to expropriate the capitalist class and to take control of all social property*. Being a pacifist—because I believe non-violent means best calculated in the long run to achieve enduring results, I am opposed to revolutionary violence. *But I would rather see violent revolution than none at all*, though I would not personally support it because I consider other means far better. *Even the terrible cost of bloody revolution is a cheaper price to humanity* than the continued exploitation and wreck of human life under the settled violence of the present system." Roger Baldwin, "The Need for Militancy," *The Socialism of Our Times*, edited by Harry W. Laidler and Norman Thomas, A Symposium. (New York, The Vanguard Press, Inc., 1929). For the League for Industrial Democracy, (based on a Conference of the League for Industrial Democracy held at Camp Tamiment in June, 1928), p. 77. (Italics added.)

not necessarily follow, however, that preservation of the Communist Party is the main purpose of the ACLU. In protecting the shock troops of social revolution it has successfully deflected or blunted any incipient attack on the big guns in the rear: the intellectual leaders of the Socialist movement in America, a number of whom served on the original board and national committee, and whose modern counterparts still serve there today.[2]

This tactic of defense in depth has been employed with little or no variation from the experimental beginnings of the ACLU in 1920 to its more smoothly organized operations of the present day. In a tear sheet circulated with its 35th Anniversary appeal, the ACLU outlined its mid-century program as follows:

Against those indiscriminate federal, state and local measures which, though aimed at Communists, threaten the civil liberties of all Americans; to make an effective civil rights program the law of the land; against both governmental and private pressure group censorship of movies, plays, books, newspapers, magazines, radio and television; to promote fair procedures in court trials, congressional and administrative hearings.

Acting on the novel premise that good citizens are imperiled whenever sedition is curbed or obscenity is discouraged, the American Civil Liberties Union often finds itself in the position of defending both subversion and pornography on narrowly technical grounds. At the same time, it seeks a broad interpretation of the Constitution in the area of civil rights. In its Annual Report for 1961-62, the organization applauds decisions which underscore *the power of the Federal Courts to impose change*[3]—a power not visibly allotted to the Judiciary by the United States Constitution.

Of late years, the American Civil Liberties Union has also enlarged the range of its propaganda to admit lobbying by approved private pressure groups. Moreover, a certain emphasis on its own highly specialized concept of civil liberties appears to have crept into the field of mass entertainment. Wizard television lawyers, who seldom (if ever) lose a case, dramatically "sell" the ACLU point of view to nationwide audiences without identifying it.

A liberal sampling of its latter-day activities discloses that the ACLU, while extending itself geographically and greatly multiplying its routine tasks, has never veered from its original course. In 1950,

---

[2] See Appendix IV.

[3] *Freedom Through Dissent*, 42nd Annual Report, July 1, 1961 to June 30, 1962, (New York, American Civil Liberties Union, 1962), p. 51. (Italics added.)

the Pittsburgh branch of the ACLU upheld the right of Communists to serve on grand juries.[4] In 1951, the national office announced its intention of challenging all future cases brought under the Smith Act, which required Communist Party officials to register.[5] In 1961, while protesting its opposition to Communism, the organization filed a brief as a friend of the court in the Communist Party's appeal under the McCarran Internal Security Act.[6]

Public support for repeal of the McCarran Act itself was solicited by the counsel for American Civil Liberties Union in Southern California. Speaking at the First Unitarian Church in Los Angeles, he flayed the McCarran Act as being the gravest danger to the Bill of Rights in the nation's history.[7]

At about the same time, the chairman of the Marin County chapter —one of twenty-four Civil Liberties branches in California—questioned the legality of a Christmas crib on the courthouse lawn in San Rafael, suggesting it violated the principle of Church-State separation.[8] On the spiritual front, the ACLU's Niagara Falls chapter also backed a test case in Federal court on behalf of the Black Muslims, who claimed that their "right to practice their religion" was obstructed in Attica State Prison; and the St. Louis ACLU Committee investigated a charge that prisoners were being denied the right to buy anti-religious books and pamphlets.[9] After praising the Supreme Court's decision which held the nonsectarian Regents' Prayer in New York schools to be unconstitutional, the ACLU's Annual Report for 1961-62 predicted: "We are confident that when more sectarian religious practices (in the schools) are brought to the Court's attention, they . . . will be declared unconstitutional . . . Christmas and Chanukah observance, Bible reading, recitation of the Lord's Prayer and baccalaureate services." [10] With the aid of ACLU lawyers, that impious hope has since been fulfilled.

As might also have been predicted, the ACLU filed a friend-of-the-court brief in behalf of Dr. Robert Soblen, the convicted Soviet spy, who for years had headed New York State's largest public mental-

[4] *Daily Worker*, (April 20, 1950).
[5] *Ibid.* (December 13, 1961).
[6] *The Worker*, (July 16, 1961).
[7] *Ibid.* (December 17, 1961).
[8] *The Wanderer*, St. Paul, Minnesota, (December 14, 1961).
[9] *Freedom Through Dissent*, 42nd Annual Report, July 1, 1961 to June 30, 1962, (New York, American Civil Liberties Union, 1962), p. 26.
[10] *Ibid.*, p. 22.

health institution. It appealed a Federal District Court decision holding that American-born Herman Marks had forfeited citizenship rights by serving in the Cuban rebel army of Fidel Castro.[11] In February, 1962, it petitioned the Senate's Post Office and Civil Service Committee to reject an amendment to the postal-rate bill, banning the distribution of Communist propaganda.[12]

While upholding freedom of agitation for Communists and even for crypto-Nazi *agents provocateur*, the ACLU sought to deny military commanders the right to arm their personnel against the fallacies of Communist propaganda, though the lack of such instruction had caused an undisclosed number of soldiers and junior officers to yield to brainwashing by Chinese Communists during the Korean War. In March, 1962, the civil liberties group submitted a memorandum to the special preparedness committee of the Armed Services Committee, asserting that restriction of free speech for the nation's military leaders "raises no civil liberties issue." [13]

Many of the ACLU's views sooner or later have found expression in political action. On August 17, 1963, for example, members of ACLU college chapters, acting jointly with the Students for Democratic Action, induced the Western States Conference of Young Democrats in Berkeley, California, to pass a resolution calling for repeal of the McCarran Internal Security Act.[14] It is noteworthy that in California alone, branches of the ACLU existed in 1962 at the University of California, California Institute of Technology, Long Beach State College, Los Angeles City College, Los Angeles State College and San Diego State College.[15] These are among the long-term fruits of the organizing Committee on Academic Freedom, one of its most significant and least publicized activities.

The Committee on Academic Freedom was formed in 1924, at a time when teachers and college professors were being urged to express themselves openly about the Sacco-Vanzetti case and to participate in Progressive Political Action. The original statement of the Committee was prepared by Dr. Harry F. Ward, chairman of the ACLU, and Dr. Henry R. Linville, president of the Teachers' Union.

[11] *Ibid.*, p. 58.
[12] Los Angeles *Times*, (February 12, 1962).
[13] Associated Press dispatch, (March 5, 1962).
[14] San Francisco *Chronicle*, (August 19, 1963). This Conference also passed resolutions calling for diplomatic and trade relations with Castro's Cuba.
[15] *Freedom Through Dissent*, 42nd Annual Report, July 1, 1961 to June 30, 1962, (New York, American Civil Liberties Union, 1962), p. 80.

Nominally created to aid teachers and college professors threatened with dismissal for unorthodox views, this committee progressively opened the way for the free and ever freer dissemination of radical ideas in schools and colleges. Through its ties with the American Federation of Teachers, the American Association of University Professors and various "progressive" educational bodies, it was eventually able to exert a potent influence not only on the formulation of academic policies but on the type of individuals accepted for employment.

By 1938 the members of this committee were described as being "among the outstanding leaders in American education." [16] The Committee included three college presidents—of Vassar, Wisconsin and Mt. Holyoke. All but one of the group were listed in *Who's Who in America* or *Who's Who in New York*. A biographical breakdown by Dr. David E. Bunting, Dean of the University of Tampa, revealed that the typical committee member was then fifty-eight years old, had a doctor's degree, and was a full professor in a major American university. Though economically comfortable, he was not wealthy. Politically, he either voted "independently" or for the Democratic Party. He belonged to at least four organizations espousing a "liberal" point of view, was a member of the Progressive Education Association and (usually) of the American Federation of Teachers. He was the author of at least three books, either on education or branches of the social sciences. Obviously, he was neither an average American nor an ordinary teacher, but a recognized expert in his chosen field, whose opinions were listened to with respect.[17]

What Dr. Bunting failed to mention was that fully half of the Committee's twenty-eight members were also long time "cooperators" of the League for Industrial Democracy,[18] the key organization for the ad-

[16] David Edison Bunting, *Liberty and Learning*, (Washington, American Council on Public Affairs, 1942), p. 11.

[17] *Ibid.*

[18] Members of the Committee on Academic Freedom were: Edward C. Lindeman,* chairman, New York School of Social Work; Ellen Donohue, secretary, Ethical Culture School, New York; John L. Childs,* Columbia University; Morris R. Cohen,* City College of New York; George S. Counts,* Columbia University; Charles A. Elwood, Duke University; Frank P. Graham,* University of North Carolina; Sidney Hook,* New York University; Horace M. Kallen,* New School for Social Research; William H. Kilpatrick,* Columbia University; K. N. Llewellyn,* Columbia University; A. O. Lovejoy, Johns Hopkins University; Kirtley F. Mather, Harvard University; Alexander Meiklejohn,* University of Wisconsin; Felix Morley, Haverford College; Alonzo F. Meyers, New York University; William A. Neilson, Smith College; Reinhold Niebuhr,* Union Theological Seminary; James M. O'Neill,* Brooklyn College; Frederick L. Redefer, Progressive Educa-

vancement of Fabian Socialism in America. They subscribed and/or contributed to the publications of the American Council on Public Affairs, which "encouraged properly qualified scholars to give greater attention to the background, analysis and solution of contemporary problems." [19] Thus social, economic and political views considered acceptable by the League for Industrial Democracy and the American Civil Liberties Union were transmitted indirectly to the nation's educators, who were "encouraged" to apply them not only as teachers but also in the field of public affairs.

Unobtrusively, the Committee on Academic Freedom in New York, working intimately with the LID-sponsored Council on Public Affairs in Washington, also promoted and accelerated a movement to bring "properly qualified scholars" into Washington, as well as into State and municipal governments—there to steer as far as possible the affairs of the nation. As the British Fabian philosopher, John Atkinson Hobson, had foretold, the university professor would become the secret weapon of Socialist strategy on a broader scale than ever before. The Doctor of Philosophy, with a certified "progressive" and "democratic" outlook, was being groomed to invade the administrative branches of government, no longer singly but *en masse*.

The specialized meaning concealed in such terms as "progress" and "democracy" was disclosed by Roger Baldwin, chief spokesman for the ACLU, who now addressed himself with increasing frequency to academic audiences. In his book, *Civil Liberties and Industrial Conflict*, written jointly with C. B. Randall and published by the Harvard University Press, Baldwin admitted frankly that while many persons regarded civil liberties as ends in themselves, he believed them to be *"means for non-violent progress."* [20] Progress, he said, meant "the extension of the control of social institutions by progressively larger classes, until human society ultimately abolishes the violence of class conflict." [21] If not quite orthodox Marxist doctrine, this was a mere variation on it in terms of the fluid classes existing in American society.

---

tion Association; Vida D. Scudder,° Wellesley College; L. L. Thurstone, University of Chicago; Mary E. Wooley, Mt. Holyoke College. Bunting, *op. cit.* (Starred names are cited by Mina Weisenberg as League for Industrial Democracy stalwarts. See Appendix II.)

[19] Statement of American Council on Public Affairs, 1942.

[20] R. N. Baldwin and C. B. Randall, *Civil Liberties and Industrial Conflict*, (Cambridge, Harvard University Press, 1938), p. 3. (Italics added.)

[21] *Ibid.*

Speaking at the 1936 Spring Conference of the Eastern States Association of Professional Schools for Teachers, Baldwin had also explained that by "progressive" he meant "the forces working for the democratization of industry by extending public ownership and control, which alone will abolish the power of the comparatively few who own the wealth." [22] "Real democracy," he stated on another occasion, "means strong trade unions, government regulation of business, ownership by the people of industries that serve the public." [23]

That, of course, was not at all what "progress" and "democracy" implied to the average American. But Roger Baldwin was no average American, nor were the educators whom he was educating. They belonged to a rapidly expanding, carefully controlled intellectual elite, who by habitually using familiar terms to convey something quite different to each other than these terms meant to the general public, would guide America unawares along the road to that cooperative commonwealth which British Fabians also called Industrial Democracy.

2.

Imitative in matters of basic policy, the League for Industrial Democracy outstripped its British Fabian tutors in techniques of deception. For more than half a century, the Fabian Society of London had solemnly required every member to subscribe to the *Basis*. When that strange document was finally replaced by a modern constitution, the first line of the latter still read: *"The Fabian Society consists of Socialists."* [24]

True, the Society also had its prized semi-undercover collaborators —among others, such personages as Sir William Beveridge and John Maynard Keynes, who retained nominal membership in a virtually extinct Liberal Party. Nevertheless, anyone known to belong to the Fabian Society of London or its affiliates could automatically be termed a Socialist.

For reasons of expediency, this relatively forthright practice was abandoned by the Fabian Society's American counterpart, the LID.

[22] R. N. Baldwin, "Freedom to Teach." *Proceedings of the 1936 Spring Conference of the Eastern States Association of Professional Schools for Teachers,* (New York, Prentice-Hall, Inc., 1936), p. 324.

[23] Roger N. Baldwin, "What Democracy Means to Me." *Scholastic* (December 18, 1937), Vol. XXXI, p. 27.

[24] (Italics added.)

Members were not only encouraged to conceal the fact of the LID's British Fabian inspiration (as though it were a bar sinister) but even to deny publicly that they were Socialists, if in doing so they could more effectively promote Socialist policies. As Upton Sinclair noted, some old-timers were displeased when the organization ceased in 1921 to call itself a Socialist Society.[25] Yet the advantage of that fraudulent gesture became increasingly apparent as individual members of the LID were propelled to eminence in their chosen fields.

Climbers, as well as those who had already arrived, were shielded by the League's failure to publish annual membership lists. Confronted with evidence that he had once held office in the Intercollegiate Socialist Society or the Students' League for Industrial Democracy, a public figure often dismissed it blandly as a folly of youth, long since outgrown. That convenient loophole has been employed by such widely disparate characters as Walter Lippmann and Walter Reuther, president of the United Automobile Workers union and a vice president of the AFL-CIO; as well as by a number of equal and lesser luminaries. A glance at the record, however, demonstrates that remarkably few of the persons admitted to the League's charmed circle of social and professional benefits have actually fallen away. The complacent truism, "Join for one year, join for fifty," has proved to be as true of the League for Industrial Democracy as of its senior partner the London Fabian Society.

In 1943, the League modified its constitution, not solely for reasons of tax exemption but also for the sake of improved wartime camouflage. Its purpose was now asserted to be *education for increasing democracy in our economic, political and cultural life.* Knowledgeable insiders, of course, understood *democracy* to mean what Roger Baldwin and others had already defined it to mean. Namely, government regulation of business leading eventually to public ownership and/or control of industry, chiefly accomplished through the pressure and voting power of strong Socialist-controlled unions. Socialism was the "true democracy," to be attained by anesthesia rather than violence. What final *consolidation* might mean was another matter, never mentioned. If anyone was deceived by the new terminology, it was only the general public.

Somewhat indiscreetly, however, British Fabians still continued to acknowledge the LID as the leading Socialist society in America. In

[25] *Forty Years of Education,* (New York, League for Industrial Democracy, 1945), p. 15.

Fabian Society Annual Reports of 1925-1930, it was even patronizingly referred to as "one of our provincial societies." As late as 1962, Margaret Cole, while carefully minimizing its importance, recognized the LID to be among the principal overseas affiliates of the Fabian Society.[26] Its value in complementing the plans of British Socialists was indicated by Norman Thomas, head of the American Socialist Party, when he stated in a pamphlet published by the LID in 1953: *"Britain's problems admit no solution on a purely nationalist level."* [27]

Past or present, it thus becomes difficult for the LID to deny its relationship with the leading Socialist Society of Great Britain. Files of *Fabian News* reveal that for years League members attended or lectured at Fabian Summer Schools. Articles by LID publicists have consistently appeared in Fabian periodicals. When a League official enhanced his prestige by joining the Fabian Society of London, the item was occasionally reported in England, if not in America. Over thirty years ago, for example, Clarence Senior, long a national director of the LID and from 1961 a White House consultant on Latin American affairs, was received into the London Society. *Fabian News* innocently reported the event in its issue of July, 1929. Lately, however, the Society has refrained from printing the names of American members or even guests, because this tends to brand them *ipso facto* as Socialists.

To the LID's 45th Anniversary event, Lady Dorothy Archibald, Fabian Socialist member of the London County Council, sent the following cautious tribute:

. . . I have come to the conclusion that there are no short cuts to *progress*, but that the long and arduous road of *education* is the only certain way. This is the road you have followed for forty-five years and, knowing your country a little, *I feel that your work is as necessary as is the work of the Fabian Society in this country.*

When I was directing a Fabian Summer School this last year, I had the great pleasure of having several young Americans as students. Their contribution to the School was outstanding and I was happy to discover that they were members of the L.I.D.

It is my profound hope that the field of your work may extend every year so that the younger generation in America may receive an education in real *democracy.*[28]

[26] Margaret Cole, *The Story of Fabian Socialism,* (London, Heinemann Educational Books, Ltd., 1961), p. 347.

[27] Norman Thomas, *Democratic Socialism,* A New Appraisal, (New York, League for Industrial Democracy, 1953), p. 4. (Italics added.)

[28] *Freedom and the Welfare State.* A Symposium by Oscar R. Ewing, Herbert

"Greetings from Home" on the same occasion included telegrams from Senator Hubert Humphrey and the then Congressman Jacob K. Javits, Harry A. Overstreet, Upton Sinclair, Robert Morss Lovett and the Reverend John Haynes Holmes.[29] Leading all the rest, however, was a wire from Eleanor Roosevelt. As a long-standing "cooperator" and sponsor of the LID, she could hardly have failed to be familiar with its definition of "democracy." Her message, though confounding to purists in political science, was readily grasped by persons attending the League's anniversary luncheon. It read:

I hope you will have a successful conference and will stress the need for making *democracy* work for all people as a *form of government* and a *way of life*.[30]

To the day of her death, Eleanor Roosevelt supported the League for Industrial Democracy and half a dozen closely related organizations, a fact which she never troubled to conceal. She was introduced to it through her good friends Florence Kelley, Paul Kellogg of *Survey* magazine and Lillian Wald of the Henry Street Settlement, all of whom served as officers and/or directors of the organization. As her telegram suggests, Eleanor Roosevelt's attachment to the LID was based on practical as well as idealistic considerations.

Through another close friend and early social worker, Frances Perkins, who had served as Governor Roosevelt's New York State's Commissioner of Labor, Eleanor Roosevelt was well informed about the potential ability of the needle trades unions in New York City to deliver the margin of victory in State elections. Top officials of both the Amalgamated Clothing Workers of America and the International Ladies Garment Workers Union served routinely as officers and directors of the LID. Delegates to the 1944 Democratic Party convention in Chicago still recall the cryptic remark attributed at that time to Franklin Delano Roosevelt: "Clear it with Sidney." Sidney, of course,

---

H. Lehman, George Meany, Walter P. Reuther and others. Harry W. Laidler, ed. On the Occasion of the 45th Anniversary of the League for Industrial Democracy (New York, League for Industrial Democracy, 1950), p. 34. (Italics added.)

[29] *Ibid.*, p. 35. Among others sending greetings or serving as sponsors, in addition to the LID's Board of Directors, were: Premier Einar Gerhardsen of Norway, Norman Angell, Stuart Chase, Helen Gahagan Douglas, Senator Paul H. Douglas, David Dubinsky, Quincy Howe, William A. Kilpatrick, Henry Morgenthau, Jr., Franklin D. Roosevelt, Jr., Mary K. Simkhovitch, Channing H. Tobias and Jerry Voorhis. *Ibid.*, p. 37.

[30] *Ibid.*, p. 35. (Italics added.)

was Sidney Hillman, then president of the Amalgamated Clothing Workers.

Survivors of the Roosevelt era will also remember Joseph Lash, a controversial young protégé of Eleanor Roosevelt, whom she invited occasionally to the White House and aided in obtaining a military commission during World War II. Few are aware, however, that Joe Lash was a leader of the Students' League for Industrial Democracy[31] (SLID) in the nineteen-thirties, when it boasted over a hundred chapters and collaborated with Communist-led youth groups. It published a magazine called *Revolt*, later known as *The Students' Outlook*. Nominally, SLID was working for "peace." To that end, it opposed Reserve Officers Training Corps drill in high schools and colleges and urged severe limitations on military preparedness.

In those years the Students' League also urged its members to aid professed anti-fascist movements in Europe and agitated actively in favor of what it termed "civil rights" for American strikers. Student chapters assisted the LID Emergency Committee for Strikers' Relief, whose chairman was Norman Thomas and whose secretary was theologian Reinhold Niebuhr, with John Herling, present-day labor columnist for the Washington *Daily News*, serving as their assistant.[32]

Among the more promising junior Leaguers of that day were two sons of an old-fashioned Marxian Socialist of German extraction who had settled in the American Midwest. The boys were Walter and Victor Reuther, potent names in American labor today. As president in 1932 of the SLID chapter at Wayne University, red-haired Walter led a student delegation on the picket line at the Briggs Body plant in Detroit. In 1933, the two eager young Socialists spent a summer running errands for the anti-Hitler underground in Germany and then were employed for about eighteen months at the Ford automobile plant in Soviet Russia, sending back glowing reports on the Workers' Fatherland.

Schooled in the newer techniques for capturing union leadership, Walter and Victor returned home in time to help lead the Automobile Workers Industrial Union (originally a part of the Red trade-union

---

[31] Joseph Lash, together with Monroe Sweetland, later editor of the *Oregon Democrat*, and George Edwards, a future member of the bench in Detroit, were named by Mina Weisenberg in *The League for Industrial Democracy: Fifty Years of Democratic Education* (New York, League for Industrial Democracy, 1955), as leaders of the SLID during that period.

[32] *Congressional Record*, House of Representatives, (October 16, 1962), pp. 22124-22125.

apparatus) into the Congress of Industrial Organizations (CIO). The reorganized and expanded mass union, known as the United Automobile Workers union[33] (UAW), subsequently ejected the better known Communists from its midst; and control of that increasingly powerful labor body passed into Socialist hands. The only difficulty then was and still is that no one has ever been sure how many of those undercover Socialists still remained Communists at heart.[34]

The maneuver was not generally understood at the time, and is less understood today. When it became obvious even to the Communists that American working people would not accept Communist direction, but might follow social democratic leaders as long as they did not frankly call themselves Socialists, younger men carefully trained for such a contingency took over. The Reuther brothers, who always had a foot in the Socialist camp, were ideally prepared for the role. They have been long time collaborators and directors of the adult League for Industrial Democracy and at present hold membership in a number of its loftier latter-day offshoots.

From 1933, SLID cooperated with various "direct action" youth groups and in 1935 merged openly with them to form the American Student Union (ASU). According to Mina Weisenberg, a historian and director of the LID, the ASU "became [sic] deeply infiltrated with Communists." After five years, the Students' League split away, not because it had any real quarrel with the Marxist philosophy of its associates, but because—as Mina Weisenberg states—it found some difficulty in justifying the Soviet Union's invasion of Finland.

Owing to the red cloud which had dimmed its name, SLID did not publicly reestablish its college chapters until after World War II. The paid staff then included James E. Youngdahl, a nephew of the liberal Republican Washington jurist who dismissed the Owen Lattimore case, and James Farmer,[35] who went on to become national director of the Negro Council on Racial Equality (CORE). It was not until 1947 that the Students' League took the precaution of barring known Communists from membership. Throughout the entire decade

[33]Now the United Automobile, Aircraft and Agricultural Implement Workers Union of America, with a membership said to exceed 1,000,000.

[34] *In Left Communism, an Infantile Disease*, V. I. Lenin advised his followers: "It is necessary to agree to any sacrifice, to resort to all sorts of devices, maneuvers and illegal methods, to evasion and subterfuge, in order *to penetrate the trade unions, to remain in them* and to carry out Communist work in them at all costs." (Italics added.)

[35] As recently as 1963, James Farmer was a member of the board of the adult League for Industrial Democracy.

of the nineteen-forties, however, a six-week summer course, resembling certain Fabian Summer Schools in England, was held annually by the League for Industrial Democracy, to train young college people for organizing and for other union work.

According to official League historians, SLID had allegedly acted against the advice of the senior body, when it merged with the National Student Union in 1935 and for five years appeared to have severed its connection with the adult LID. Actually, SLID members were only following the example of their elders, many of whom drifted farther and farther leftward during the same period—as their Fabian counterparts in Britain were likewise doing in the nineteen-thirties. A singular predilection for Communists was evinced in that era of the united front. It was confirmed by the fact that many high ranking LID officials lent their names to organizations and committees since identified as Communist controlled.

The very amiable Robert Morss Lovett, who personally aided the National Student Union in his final years as president of the League,[36] is alleged to have held membership during his lifetime in some fifty Communist front organizations. A. Philip Randolph, long time LID official and a Socialist leader in the present-day agitation for Negro civil rights, has been connected with numerous organizations (or their ad hoc committee offshoots) which were cited as Communist fronts by Federal authorities and/or state or territorial investigating committees.[37]

In the cloud cuckoo-land of Fabian Socialism's many cooperative ventures, individuals later cited in connection with Soviet espionage were also recruited, among others, Frederick Vanderbilt Field.

[36] Although a National Student Association report of September, 1953, stated that the Students' League for Industrial Democracy was defunct, an official League brochure published in 1955, *The League for Industrial Democracy At Mid-Century*, reported that in June, 1954 the Students' League held a conference on "The Patterns of Social Reform in North America" at the International Center of the Carnegie Endowment for International Peace in New York. There a Canadian Member of Parliament addressed them from the same rostrum as C. Wright Mills, sociology professor from Columbia; Daniel Bell, labor editor of *Fortune* magazine; Felix Gross, sociologist from Brooklyn College and Mark Starr, labor educator. (Speakers cited are listed by Mina Weisenberg as "collaborators" of the adult League.)

[37] See *Investigation of Un-American Propaganda Activities in the U.S.* Special Committee on Un-American Activities, 78th Congress, Second Session. (Appendix, Part IX, *Communist Front Organizations*.) (Washington, U.S. Government Printing Office, 1944); also, *Cumulative Index to Publications, 1938–1954*, (January, 1955); *Supplement to Cumulative Index, 1955–1960*, (June, 1961).

Undeniably united front activities, in which Communists, Socialists and an undetermined number of innocents were involved, flourished in America as in Britain prior to the outbreak of World War II. By some irony of fate, however, it proved a saving grace for the LID that certain outstanding figures in its New York City chapter decided at the same time to champion the cause of the exiled and subsequently murdered Leon Trotsky. This very vocal group included John Dewey, professor of Philosophy at Columbia University; Sidney Hook, chairman of the department of Philosophy at New York University; officials of the International Ladies Garment Workers Union (ILGWU); editors of the Social Democratic *New Leader,* and others. By virtue of being anti-Stalinist, they were presumed to be anti-Marxist and pro-American. As late as 1952, some of them were regarded as allies and editorial outlets by supporters of the late Senator Joseph McCarthy. Once again, as in the bygone twenties, the LID was able to sidestep unwelcome notoriety and avoid being stigmatized as the effective leadership group of international Socialism in America.

The radical nature of the League for Industrial Democracy should have been obvious from the start, since its original officers and directors included such well-known early Socialist Party leaders as Morris Hillquit, August Claessens and Eugene V. Debs. In the 1924 national elections, however, the majority of LID members and friends promoted the Conference for Progressive Political Action and supported the Presidential candidacy of Senator Robert M. La Follette. Since 1928, they have thrown their weight behind the Democratic Party's top candidate in New York State, and, from 1936, they have done the same for the national ticket. Nevertheless, the Socialist Party continued to run a nominal candidate for the Presidency, who was invariably a permanent officer of the LID.

In six national elections, that token candidate was Norman Thomas, a former Protestant clergyman, who had once headed the LID student chapter at Princeton. A native American of Anglo-Saxon stock, Thomas possessed a mellow voice, a booming laugh, and a sophisticated low-pressure approach which proved highly attractive to educators and professionals. While he never entertained the faintest hope of being elected, Thomas had reasons for keeping his name on the ballot. Among other things, his position as titular head of the Socialist Party carried with it the right of representation in the Fabian-dominated Socialist International.

Until his "retirement" in 1962, it was usually Norman Thomas who headed United States delegations to congresses of the Socialist International, and transmitted the ensuing directives to interested groups in the United States. The "restatement" of Socialist aims emerging from the International's Frankfurt Congress in 1951—which found expression in the *New Fabian Essays* in Britain—was duly interpreted for Americans by Norman Thomas in a significant pamphlet entitled *Democratic Socialism*. Published in 1953 by the LID, his statement served as a lodestar for all domestic Fabian Socialists, avowed or unavowed.

For the edification of any innocents who still persist in regarding Norman Thomas as a true-blue American, distinguished for his apparently selfless advocacy of a broad program of social reform,[38] it may be noted that he declared in this pamphlet:

My definition of modern socialism . . . accords with the socialist statement on "Aims and Tasks" which was adopted by the Congress of Socialist Parties at Frankfurt, Germany, in 1951. It closely parallels "Socialism, a New Statement of Principles," presented in 1952 by the British Socialist Union.[39]

Like the British comrades, Thomas frankly advocated *"the social ownership of such key industries as steel"*—while "refusing to discuss democratic socialism in such misleading terms as *total* social ownership vs. *total* private ownership." [40] He explained that some followers of Karl Marx—for example, Karl Kautsky—"never insisted on the need for social ownership of *all* means of production and distribution." [41] Neither, as a matter of fact, did the Fabian *Basis*. The Machiavellian foresight of Sidney Webb, disclosed long before in *Labor and the New Social Order*, was tacitly reflected in Thomas' declaration:

. . . We have learned that it is possible to a degree not anticipated by *most* earlier Socialists to impose desirable social controls on privately owned enterprises *by the development of social planning*, by proper taxation and labor legislation, and by the growth of powerful labor organizations.

[38] See statement at the League's 40th Anniversary dinner by the Hon. Newbold Morris, President, New York City Council. *Forty Years of Education*, (New York, League for Industrial Democracy, 1945), pp. 39-40. In this speech Morris said: "Norman Thomas is a Socialist. Yet I don't believe that there are very many principles which would remove Norman Thomas from a liberal in any party, and I suppose he chose the hard way . . . . He might have climbed the ladder by enrolling in either one of the major parties and going from Alderman to Sheriff, to Borough President, to Congressman, to United States Senator and so on all the way up . . . . There are a lot of others around here who have chosen the hard way and I admire them for it."

[39] Thomas, *op. cit.*, p. 5.

[40] *Ibid.*, p. 8. (Italics added.)

[41] *Ibid.*, p. 8. (Italics added.)

Still more significantly, Thomas added:

> For some years American Socialists have been fairly well agreed that "social ownership should be extended to the commanding heights" of our economy, which include our natural resources, our system of money, banking and credit, and certain basic industries and services . . . . I have already argued the specific reason for public ownership of the steel industry. It meets all the tests which I have earlier suggested.[42]

An identical program for Britain was urged at virtually the same time by the late Parliamentary Leader of the British Labour Party, Hugh Gaitskell, in *Fabian Tract No. 300, Socialism and Nationalisation*.[43] It has since been reaffirmed by his successor, Harold Wilson, who pledged himself to carry out the policies of Gaitskell.

In defining the relationship of "Democratic Socialism" to Communism, Norman Thomas made a plea for "non-orthodox" Marxism—especially in the United States, where "we still have a middle class in a true economic sense, while those who think of themselves as belonging to the middle class are even more numerous."[44] Pointedly, he criticized Russian Communism as being "a betrayal of Socialism" and *a subversion of true Marxism.* He condemned "statism" and questioned "the necessity of a dictatorial elite in Russia"—without referring to the invisible Socialist elite in America that proposed to utilize the outward forms of democracy in order to impose a gradually tightening system of centralized controls. While deploring Soviet deceit and violence, at no point did Thomas recommend hostility towards Communism.[45] "Other *associations* of men," said Thomas, improving on the Natural Law, "have an *inherent* right to exist."[46]

Conscious, however, of the adverse effect which identification with an unpopular cause might have on Socialists in America, Thomas uttered a clear warning to followers and friends. Russian Communism, said he, "in its march to power has so successfully claimed Marx for its own, it has so persuaded men that Lenin and Stalin are the true successors of Karl Marx, that *the socialist who rests his case upon Marx, as upon a Bible, has to fight an uphill battle. Marxist orthodoxy*

---

[42] *Ibid.*, pp. 28-29. (Italics added.)

[43] Hugh Gaitskell, M.P., *Socialism and Nationalisation*, Fabian Tract No. 300, (July, 1956). In the foreword, Gaitskell states he wrote the essay in 1953 (the same year that *Democratic Socialism* appeared) but did not publish it until 1956.

[44] Thomas, *op. cit.*, p. 10.

[45] *Ibid.*, p. 9.

[46] *Ibid.*, p. 34. The Natural Law, implicit in the United States Constitution, recognizes the inherent right of human creatures to exist. Associations, being man-made, have no inherent rights and only exist permissively. (Italics added.)

does not give the democratic socialist the best vantage point for his struggle." [47] Almost verbatim, Thomas echoed the sentiments expressed by Karl Marx and Frederick Engels during their lifetime, concerning the most effective way to social revolution in the United States.

Through Norman Thomas the past and present leaders of international Socialism spoke to the New World. Thus the importance of his remarks cannot be measured in terms of the trifling vote which he commanded as the American Socialist Party's candidate. One apparent reason for keeping that Party alive has been to mislead the American public as to the true strength of the Socialist movement in the United States, by conveying the impression it is far too tiny to represent a serious threat. Even Thomas himself admitted as recently as July 13, 1963, in a television interview with Paul Coates carried over California stations, that Socialists in this country who do not vote for the Socialist Party "have usually found it better to vote Democrat." Many are so-called independents, committed to a program rather than a party, who forever tease aspiring Republicans with the hope they can be wooed and won.

Nor should the influence of Thomas' statement be gauged by the limited size of the League for Industrial Democracy, which circulated the pamphlet. While the official membership of the adult LID never claimed more than four or five thousand at any time, like the Fabian Society it was a pilot organization, whose members already commanded the heights in many sectors of American life—political, educational, religious, trades union and cultural. Bishop Francis J. McConnell, for example, a former president of the Federal Council of Churches,[48] who signed the so-called Bankers' Report of 1933 advocating recognition of Soviet Russia, was long a vice president of the League.

As vice president of Union Theological Seminary, the patriarchal Dr. Reinhold Niebuhr had also helped to shape the social thinking of generations of young seminarians. Former president of the LID New York chapter and former treasurer and board member of the national body, Niebuhr probably lent his name to more Socialist-inspired committees and organizations than any other living American. Nor did age diminish the old master's skill in attracting highly placed sym-

---

[47] *Ibid.,* p. 9. (Italics added.)
[48] Later The National Council of Churches, and affiliated today with the World Council of Churches.

pathizers. As late as September, 1963, Attorney General Robert Kennedy announced that one of the ten books he would take with him, if going to the moon, would be Reinhold Niebuhr's book with the oddly Manichean title, *Children of Light and Children of Darkness* —an unusual choice for a Catholic! [49]

In the field of labor, the League's officers and national directors have included some of the most commanding figures in recent industrial union history: among others, David Dubinsky of the International Ladies Garment Workers; Jacob Potofsky of the Amalgamated Clothing Workers; Walter Reuther of the Automobile Workers; Arthur J. Hayes of the Machinists; James Carey, erstwhile head of the Union of Electrical, Radio and Machine Workers; A. Philip Randolph of the Pullman Car Porters; and Boris Shishkin, former educational director of the American Federation of Labor.[50] William Green and his more liberal successor, George Meany, president of the AFL-CIO and recipient of a League award, seldom ventured to refuse an invitation to address LID conferences. While LID control of trade union machinery was not all-embracing, and was certainly far less obvious, than that of the Fabian Society in Britain, at least it provided a firm base of political and financial support for internationally derived Socialist programs in several key electoral states, notably New York, New Jersey, Michigan, Pennsylvania and Illinois.

A small galaxy of United States Senators has been listed among the LID veteran collaborators. That senior legislative group includes: Paul H. Douglas of Illinois, Wayne Morse of Oregon, Hubert Humphrey of Minnesota, the late Richard Neuberger and his widow, Maurine Neuberger of Oregon, the late Herbert Lehman of New

---

[49] Hearst Headline Service dispatch by David Sentner. Published September 1, 1963. *Children of Light and Children of Darkness*, published in 1945, is a collection of the West Foundation lectures delivered by Dr. Reinhold Niebuhr at Stanford University in 1944. It is an argument for the "mixed economy" and "the open society," regarded by Socialists as a transitional stage to Socialism. Only ten years earlier, in *Reflexions on the End of an Era*, (New York, Charles Scribner's Sons, 1934). Dr. Niebuhr had said that the sickness of capitalism was "organic and constitutional"—rooted in "the very nature of capitalism . . . in the private ownership of the productive process." He predicted that "the end of capitalism will be bloody rather than peaceful," and considered Marxism "an essentially correct theory and analysis of the economic realities of modern society." (See *Reinhold Niebuhr: His Religious, Social and Political Thought*, edited by Charles W. Kagley and Robert W. Bretall, (New York, The Macmillan Co., 1956), p. 137.)

[50] See Appendix II. See also annual lists of League for Industrial Democracy's officers and board of directors.

York, and Jacob K. Javits, who as a congressman was for years a regular and applauded speaker at League conferences. It was Senator Lehman, however, who distinguished himself at the League's 45th Anniversary symposium on "Freedom and the Welfare State" by saying:

A hundred and seventy years ago the welfare state concept was translated into the basic law of this land by the founders of the republic . . . . The founding fathers were the ones who really originated the welfare state.[51]

An astounding misuse of the measured phrase in the Preamble to the Constitution, "to create a more perfect union and to promote the general welfare"—all the more so, because the definition of "welfare" has suffered several changes since 1787!

The weight exerted to this day by individual LID members and their trainees in education, government administration, the United Nations, and the private "research" foundations, is subject matter for separate study. A whole chain of interlocking organizations, aspiring to mold the outlook of public opinion makers and to draft the policies of United States Government agencies, has quietly come into being, each with a solid core of LID elder statesmen and their younger disciples. By no means have all of the League's tried and true supporters found it necessary to choose "the hard way."

In adapting the tactics and programs of British Fabianism to our native scene, the small, once struggling and always reticent League for Industrial Democracy fulfilled its mission of penetrating and permeating the fabric of American life. Its peculiarity stemmed from the fact that it was from first to last a Socialist creation. Although the accent might be American, its voice was the voice of international Socialism controlled by British Fabians.

3.

The surprising thing is that anyone should ever have doubted the Socialist intentions of the officers, members and conscious collaborators of the League for Industrial Democracy. Successive presidents,

[51] *Freedom and the Welfare State*, (New York, League for Industrial Democracy, 1950), pp. 7 ff. British Fabian speakers on that occasion included Corley Smith, Economic and Social Counsellor, United Kingdom Delegation to the United Nations; Margaret Herbison, M.P., Under Secretary for Scotland; Toni Sender, Representative of the International Confederation of Free Trade Unions to the United Nations. G. D. H. and Margaret Cole and Morgan Phillips of the Socialist International sent greetings.

from Robert Morss Lovett to Nathaniel M. Minkoff, have made no secret of their radical beliefs. There was the venerable philosopher John Dewey, father of Progressive Education, who was said to have inherited the pragmatic mantle of William James, yet permitted himself to be identified with the Trotskyite or Lovestoneite wing of American Marxism.

Next president of the LID was Elizabeth Gilman, wealthy and socially prominent spinster, a leader of the Urban League and perennial chairman of the Socialist Party in Maryland. She was followed by Bjaarne Braatoy, former professor of Government at Haverford College, who served in the World War II Office of Strategic Services, working intimately all the while with the Fabian International Bureau. At war's end he was employed as tutor and "technical assistant" to the German Social Democratic Party and thereafter became world chairman of the Fabian-dominated Socialist International.

Not least, there was Mark Starr, British-born and Fabian-bred, a pet pupil of G. D. H. and Margaret Cole. For some thirty years he proved to be a strong, indisputable link between the New Fabian Research Bureau in London, where the modern leadership of the Fabian Society was centered, and the Fabian Socialist movement in the United States. No product of ivied halls, Mark Starr nevertheless became president and board chairman of the foremost society of intellectual Socialists in America. From 1935 to 1961 he also served as educational director of the ILGWU—perhaps the most internationally minded labor union in America, with a membership of 450,000 and declared assets of some 425 million dollars (as of June, 1962).

Through Mark Starr, the G. D. H. Cole brand of Marxism tinged with Syndicalism was transmitted to a potent sector of American labor. It was Starr who institutionalized a good many of the Coles' special ideas on labor politics, labor education and politico-labor research in the United States. As late as 1952, he asserted that *education for the abolition of private profit* was the prime purpose of all education.[52] In 1949, according to a report issued over his own signature by the ILGWU educational department, Mark Starr "wrote *Labour Politics in the U.S.A.* for the British Fabian Society, and a pamphlet for the United World Federalists." [53] Published by the Fabian Society-Victor

[52] Mark Starr, "Corruption in a Profit Economy," *A Moral Awakening in America*, A Symposium, (New York, League for Industrial Democracy, 1952), p. 22.
[53] *Report of Education Department*, ILGWU (June 1, 1948–May 31, 1950), p. 15. During that period, Mark Starr also helped to revise a new edition of *Labor In America*, a senior high school text, *ibid.*, p. 15.

Gollancz in England, *Labour Politics in the U.S.A.* was issued as a fifty-six page pamphlet by the LID.

Son of a miner, Mark Starr had worked in the coal mines as a boy and served during World War I as local officer of the South Wales Miners Federation. Referring to his origins, Starr remarked many years later in a personal letter that if he had not been a radical, he "would have been a moron." Possibly this view was colored by the fact that from the age of fourteen he was educated at Fabian-operated workers' schools and the London Labour College.

Before emigrating to America in 1928, Starr was for seven years a division officer of the National Council of Labour Colleges in Britain. He belonged to the little Independent Labour Party, headed by some of the more stridently left wing Fabians and openly sympathetic to the Communist cause. During that period he was also associated with Margaret Cole—a founder of New Fabian Research who was elected president of the Fabian Society in 1963 and who took a lively interest in promoting a species of Socialist indoctrination for working people broadly termed "further education." [54]

On reaching New York, Starr was promptly hired to teach at Brookwood Labor College, which between 1925 and 1928 had received an outright grant of $74,227 from the Garland Fund.[55] Soon he was placed in charge of Brookwood extension courses. Despite his

[54] "Adult education" was a field in which Margaret Cole and her husband were active for years. It became her chief public function in 1951-1960, when she was chairman of the Further Education Committee of the London County Council. *Fabian News*, (January, 1963).

[55] *Report of the American Fund for Public Service*, popularly called the Garland Fund, 1925-28, states, "For the three-year period covered by this report, the enterprises to which we have given outright the largest amounts of money were: Vanguard Press, $139,453; Brookwood Labor College, $74,227; Rand School, research department, $16,116; League for Industrial Democracy, $10,500." Cf. testimony of Walter S. Steele before the House of Representatives, Special Committee to Investigate Communist Activities in the United States, *Report of Committee*, (December, 1930), p. 226.

Steele's testimony continues, as follows: "The Vanguard Series, issued by The Vanguard Press, was organized and financed by the American Fund for Public Service, Inc. and distributed by the Rand Bookstore. (The Vanguard Press was set up by the communist-socialist controlled American Fund for Public Service, Inc. It publishes communist-socialist literature for distribution. Its publications are also distributed by the Rand Press.)"

Authors listed in the Steele testimony include: Karl Marx, V. Lenin, Peter Kropotkin, Franz Oppenheimer, Henry George, Benjamin R. Tucker, Robert Blatchford (British Independent Labour Party), Clarence L. Swartz, James Peter Warbasse, Jesse W. Hughan, Alexander Berkman, Charles H. Wesley, Coleman Hayes-Wood, A. S. Sachs, Scott Nearing, Robert W. Dunn, Upton Sinclair.

own very sketchy academic background, in 1941 Starr became vice president of the American Federation of Teachers. In 1944, he was appointed labor consultant to the Office of War Information, whose Director, Elmer Davis, was once a fellow director of the LID.[56] By that time, of course, Starr had taken out American citizenship—though he preferred to consider himself a "citizen of the world"—and in March, 1949, organized an ILGWU symposium on "World Government." [57]

In 1948, President Truman named Mark Starr to the United States Advisory Commission on Educational Exchange, where he remained until 1952. This commission was authorized under Public Act 402 to *advise the State Department and the Congress on the operation of information centers and libraries maintained by the United States Government in foreign countries,* as well as on the exchange of students and technical experts. In June, 1949, Starr headed the U.S. delegation to the first Adult Education Conference organized by UNESCO at Elsinore, Denmark,[58] where the shades of Marx, Engels and Kautsky rather than the ghost of Hamlet's father stalked. A month later he was lecturing at a British Labour Party Summer School in Durham, England.[59] That year the New York City Board of Education conferred its annual Adult Student's Award on Mark Starr as their prize specimen of an adult student who had made good.[60]

As educational director of the ILGWU, Starr helped to instill the Fabian Socialist approach in a labor union whose early history had been marked by episodes of physical violence and the politics of left wing revolt. He advised that "instead of arousing antagonism, as the old-time agitator had to do, now the union leader must be capable of skillful negotiation and *of winning over public opinion to support the claims of his organization.*" [61] In cooperation with the Federal Council of Churches and other religious bodies, he arranged visits to garment shops and union headquarters for groups of clergymen and presented them with an adroit propaganda pamphlet, *What the Church Thinks of Labor.*[62]

Through LID connections and the Public Affairs Committee which

[56] See Appendix II. Also annual lists of LID officers and directors.
[57] *Report of Education Department,* ILGWU, (June 1948–May 1950), p. 28.
[58] *Ibid.,* p. 30.
[59] *Ibid.,* p. 29.
[60] *Ibid.,* p. 30.
[61] *Ibid.,* p. 25. (Italics added.)
[62] *Ibid.,* p. 15.

he chaired in 1949, Starr also developed fruitful contacts between the ILGWU and liberal professors throughout the country—but particularly at the Harvard School of Business Administration. Speaking with a lingering trace of a Welsh burr, Starr delivered the Ingliss lecture at Harvard on "Labor Education." In August, 1949, the *Harvard Business Review* carried an article by Willard A. Lewis of the ILGWU legal department,[63] and in 1952 Starr addressed the Harvard Business School Club.

It is interesting to note that in April, 1953, Starr's department organized an ILGWU panel discussion, where the subject of "Planning and Personal Freedom" was discussed by such "eminent experts" as Dr. George Soule of Columbia University and the *New Republic,* and Dr. J. Kenneth Galbraith and Dr. Seymour E. Harris of Harvard[64]—the latter pair to become controversial figures seven years later as advisers to the Kennedy Administration. In 1951 Clarence Senior—another future Kennedy adviser—addressed a weekend institute at Hudson View Lodge on the Puerto Rican problem.[65] During such sessions, the learned gentlemen both received and imparted instruction, as preliminary grooming for the future demands of public life.

University and public libraries were generously supplied by Starr with union literature. In one case, a pamphlet giving the union's view on *Trends and Prospects in the Garment Industry* was sent to the economics departments of 650 colleges. Labor attachés of United States Embassies abroad, in whose selection union endorsement often played a part, were furnished on request with union-produced pamphlets, phonograph records and propaganda films; and similar "assistance" was given to Occupation Forces in Japan and Europe.[66] All "educational" material distributed by the union was based, directly or indirectly, upon the Fabian Socialist premise formulated by G. D. H. Cole and promoted by Mark Starr as "dean of American labor educators." Namely, that "education must build new incentives other than those of private gain!"

Under the watchful eye of Starr, research and political activities of the ILGWU were vastly expanded. Both departments were headed and staffed by trusted officials of the LID. Throughout that period of mutual growth, the ILGWU's research director was Dr. Lazare Teper,

[63] *Ibid.,* p. 31.
[64] *Report of Education Department,* ILGWU (June 1951–May 1953), p. 14.
[65] *Ibid.,* p. 26.
[66] *Report of Education Department,* ILGWU (June 1948–May 1950), p. 18.

who had joined SLID at Johns Hopkins and served for years as a
director of the adult LID. In 1951 and after, Dr. Teper lectured at
the Industrial College of the Armed Forces, evoking no protest whatever from the Socialist Party or its allies.[67]

Political director of the ILGWU under Starr's command was Gus
Tyler, a product of SLID at City College of New York.[68] According
to an article in *The New York Times,* it was Tyler who in 1949 introduced political stewards or "commissars" into union locals.[69] That
same year he gave a course on politics at the City College of New
York, and in 1950 conducted a course in Political Action at the New
School for Social Research. Since 1961, Gus Tyler has been overall
educational director of the ILGWU, succeeding Mark Starr but following loyally in his footsteps. Starr's permanent secretary was the
Russian-born Fannia M. Cohn, nominally responsible for arranging
"panel discussions." Veteran member of the LID from the days when
it was known as the ISS, she served on the executive committee of
the League's New York chapter.

Through the combined efforts of such "democratic" Socialists, the
ample research facilities of the ILGWU were made available in a
more or less guarded fashion to the LID. Thus, from 1935, the
ILGWU's research department stood in somewhat the same relation
to the LID as the New Fabian Research Bureau did to the British
Fabian Society.[70] At Starr's invitation, the redoubtable Margaret Cole
herself often flew from London to address union groups[71] and presumably to synchronize "research" operations with those of the British
comrades.

Even today, when the widely diffused "research" activity of the
Fabian Socialist movement in America is parceled out among various

[67] *Report of Education Department,* ILGWU (June 1951–May 1953), p. 27.
(See also report, *The Ultra Right and the Military Industrial Complex,* published
by the Socialist Party-Social Democratic Federation and submitted with a covering letter by Norman Thomas to the Special Preparedness Subcommittee of the
Senate Committee on Armed Services. *Hearings before the Subcommittee,* Part 6,
1962, pp. 3016 ff. In this document, Socialists protest against permitting conservative speakers to address the Armed Services.)
[68] See Appendix II.
[69] *Report of Education Department,* ILGWU (June 1948–May 1950), p. 30.
[70] *Loc. cit.,* pp. 58-64. (See account of functions of New Fabian Research Bureau
in Part I, *Fabian Freeway.*)
[71] *Report of Education Department,* ILGWU, (June 1948–May 1950), p. 10.
Numerous other visits by Margaret Cole and members of the London Fabian Executive are unrecorded in union publications.

specialized fringe organizations, as well as university centers for "advanced study," the research department of the International Ladies Garment Workers Union continues to function as a control center and guiding force in the politico-labor field. Allegedly it is acting for the benefit of its members and those of sister unions, domestic and foreign, which it aids.

During Mark Starr's prolonged and well-paid term as educational director, the union probably became better known abroad than any other American labor organization. More and more, its New York headquarters were a port of call for labor delegates coming from Germany, Japan, Italy, Korea, and especially from Latin America.[72] Educational assistance and political advice were freely given to budding labor unions, all the way from Ireland to New Zealand, from Ghana to Chile and Brazil. In some instances, the freshly organized unions actually preceded the establishment of industries in which they hoped to set labor standards. Nevertheless, they provided bases for political agitation in backward countries seeking to install Socialist-oriented governments, and in new nations emerging from the Fabian-shattered remnants of once-flourishing colonial empires.

Starr's services to Fabian Socialism on a world-wide scale appear to date from 1948, when his opportunities as a member of an official government commission dovetailed neatly with his union duties. That was the same year David Dubinsky, freewheeling president of the ILGWU, helped to launch the International Confederation of Free Trade Unions (ICFTU),[73] labor adjunct of the Socialist International. In 1949, Dubinsky addressed the Fabian Society in London while attending the first annual meeting of the Confederation.[74]

Effective organizer of the Free Trade Union Committee in America was Jay Lovestone, international director of the ILGWU. A brilliant, if mercurial character, Lovestone had received his baptism in Socialism as student president of the ISS chapter at the City College of New York. Veering leftward, he became a top functionary of the Communist Party but was expelled for "left deviationism." Thereafter, he headed a group of American Marxists who supported the exiled Leon Trotsky and his doctrine of permanent revolution. As such, Lovestone was welcomed back into the Fabian Socialist fold and entrusted with far-flung international missions in the name of labor. Together with his

[72] *Ibid.*, p. 15.
[73] *Ibid.*, p. 26.
[74] *Ibid.*, p. 32.

assistant and faithful shadow, Irving Brown, he has since visited trouble spots in Europe and the Orient on all-expenses-paid union tours as a labor statesman and traveling inspector general.

If anyone wonders what possible influence such an international labor body could have on domestic events in the United States, at least one example can be cited. On March 11-13, 1963, the Railwaymen's Section Committee of the International Transport Workers Federation met in Brussels. According to the *International Trade Union News* of April 1, 1963, issued fortnightly by the ICFTU:

> The Committee expressed deep concern at the very serious position in which railwaymen of many countries in all parts of the world found themselves, as the result of transport policies directed against the railways or the ruthless rationalization plans of management, or both. These developments were jeopardizing the livelihood of many railwaymen, and in some cases the obstinate attitude of the employers was *forcing the railway unions to take militant action* . . . .[75]

Based on "research" by a Fabian Socialist-controlled international labor group, decisions were reached in Brussels identical to those leading to the renewed call for a nationwide railroad strike in America not many weeks later.

Just as the Transport and General Workers Union in Britain has long been the chief bulwark of the London Fabian Society, so the ILGWU and the closely related Amalgamated Clothing Workers Union have been twin pillars of strength to the LID. From 1935 to 1952, the ILGWU donated 21 million dollars to alleged worthy causes,[76] including political campaigns. From 1951 to 1953 alone, its benefactions exceeded five million dollars[77]—of which the greater part was extracted from the pay envelopes of working people and spent at the discretion of union officials. With financial angels of such stature in the offing, it is little wonder that the Fabian Socialist movement in America prospered and that its influence grew out of all proportion to the modest size of its directive body: the League for Industrial Democracy.

At the present time, the LID enjoys the position of an elder statesman, having delegated many of its more active functions to kindred organizations colonized and steered by certified Socialist "collabora-

---

[75] (Italics added.)

[76] *Report of Education Department*, ILGWU, (June, 1951–May, 1953), p. 27. (In this connection, *Herald Tribune* article of January, 1952 is cited.)

[77] Mark Starr, "Garment Workers: Welfare Unionism," *Current History*. July, 1954. Reprint by ILGWU, pages unnumbered.

tors," past and present. Its own list of officers and directors for 1963 discloses a stable handful of old-timers plus a number of youthful newcomers, among them children and grandchildren of original members. For the moment, the League appears to be hardly more than an appendage of the needle trades unions, as it once seemed a mere pensioner of the Rand School. Nevertheless, it is still the senior body of Fabian Socialism in America, from which future dictates on Socialist fashions may be expected to issue. At any desired instant, it can spring to new life again, even though its current status may appear to some to be that of a has-been. Like the Fabian Society of London, the League for Industrial Democracy has always been one of the most underrated Socialist leadership groups in the world.

The fact is that the LID has been preparing ever since the end of World War II for what seems to be virtual retirement. Its star studded anniversary meetings of the nineteen-fifties were a series of premature swan songs. Already every one of those successor organizations had been founded and activated that were to adapt Fabian Socialism to the grandiose dimensions of the space age. These would transport the United States, by fast freeway, toward a shimmering goal which present-day Socialists call "total democracy" but which earlier, undisguised Marxists admitted was world-wide social revolution.

Appropriately, the LID conferred its 1963 award for distinguished service upon the aged Upton Sinclair, last surviving member of the group that issued the original call to the ISS in 1905. With his usual happy faculty for letting the radical cat out of the bag, it was Upton Sinclair who on another occasion revealed the tried-and-true route by which Fabian Socialism must travel to power in the United States. Experience had already shown, said he, that it would be done via the two-party system, rather than through any third party. "So I know," announced Sinclair, *that it will be the Democratic Party and not the Socialist Party which will bring this great change to America. It will not be called socialism; its opponents will insist that it is communism, while its friends will know that it is industrial democracy.*" [78]

---

[78] *Forty Years of Education,* (New York, League for Industrial Democracy, 1945), p. 16. (Italics added.)

17

Fabian Face Cards In The New Deal

1.

"IT MAY be called by some other name!" Those words run like a refrain through the literature of Fabian Socialism, from the movement's modest beginnings to the present day. Again and again they recur in the writings and speeches of Fabian publicists, from George Bernard Shaw to Harry W. Laidler[1] to Upton Sinclair to Mark Starr[2] to Arthur M. Schlesinger, Jr. Meeting the identical statement so many times over, one can hardly fail to realize that it is a clue to Fabian tactics, past and present. So clear a warning, so frequently repeated, is obviously designed to alert friends of the movement to the stealthy procedure of encroaching Socialism—on the assumption that, like any other oft-announced plan of attack, it will be ignored or discounted by the prospective victims.

In 1932 a seemingly impromptu but in fact carefully researched program for advancing social revolution by peaceful means was called

[1] Harry W. Laidler and Norman Thomas, Editors, *The Socialism of Our Times.* A Symposium by Harry Elmer Barnes, Stuart Chase, Paul H. Douglas, Morris Hillquit, Harold J. Laski, Roger N. Baldwin, Paul Blanshard, H. S. Raushenbush and others. (New York, The Vanguard Press, Inc.—League for Industrial Democracy, 1929). "Introduction," by Harry W. Laidler, pp. xi ff. *"It may be called by some other name."* (Italics added.)

[2] Mark Starr, "Cheer Up Comrade Cole!" *Institute of Social Studies Bulletin,* Rand School, (Summer, 1952), p. 68. Starr wrote: "As Socialism, collectivism, public ownership and control become necessary in the United States, they will be adopted in specific instances and cases. *It may be called by some other name,* but, as in the case of the Tennessee Valley Authority, public ownership will be applied after appropriate discussion and debate if the need is demonstrated; and there will be no quibbling about whether Marx, Stalin or Cole would okay that action." (Italics added.)

255

The New Deal. Both the name and the program were first unveiled in a book by Stuart Chase entitled *A New Deal*. Never very widely circulated and soon conveniently buried, it was meant for a select coterie of prospective public servants—and for the eyes of one man in particular, Franklin Delano Roosevelt. For all practical purposes, this volume soon replaced the moderate 1932 platform of the Democratic Party, which pledged thrift and a curb on Federal spending.

Appearing in a critical election year, its publication like that of other books by Stuart Chase was financed by the Twentieth Century Fund, an allegedly educational foundation set up for purposes of "public service" by Edward A. Filene of Boston. Director of the Twentieth Century Fund from 1928 to 1953 was Evans Clark, a former president of the Intercollegiate Socialist Society and vice president of the League for Industrial Democracy.[3] In 1920 Clark had been employed as Director of Information for Ludwig Martens, the unofficial Soviet ambassador who was expelled for conspiratorial activities.[4] Both Clark and his wife, Freda Kirchwey,[5] long time editor of the leftist weekly, *The Nation*, were intimates of the British Fabian Socialist and avowed Marxist, Harold Laski, whose articles were featured from time to time in *The Nation* and whose ideas strongly influenced certain leaders of the incoming administration.

Stuart Chase had graduated from Harvard in 1910 and joined the Fabian Society of London the same year. He was a certified public accountant and an equally certified Socialist, with a flair for popularizing borrowed ideas in a smooth and painless style. In Boston he was one of the circle revolving around Mrs. Glendower Evans, which included Florence Kelley, Louis D. Brandeis and Upton Sinclair. During World War I he worked from 1917 to 1919 as an official of Wilson's War Food Administration in Chicago. There he became vice president of the Socialist-sponsored Public Ownership League, an organization dedicated to promoting public ownership of electric power and related industries. Moving to New York, he served as treasurer of the LID, was a frequent lecturer at the Rand School, an editor of the *New Republic* and a featured contributor to *The Nation*.

[3] See Appendix II.

[4] According to testimony given in 1952 before the Reece Special Committee of the House of Representatives to Investigate Tax-exempt Foundations.

[5] See Appendix II. For Freda Kirchwey's friendship with Laski, see Kingsley Martin, *Harold Laski: A Biographical Memoir*, (New York, The Viking Press, Inc., 1953), p. 128. "Freda Kirchwey, editor of the New York *Nation*, an old friend . . . whose political opinions had developed on similar lines to his own [Laski's]."

Admittedly, Chase sympathized with the idea of violent revolution as a cure for social ills, holding it to have been absolutely "necessary and inevitable" in Russia. "It may some day be inevitable in this country," he warned, and added coolly: "I am not seriously alarmed by the sufferings of the creditor class, the trouble which the church is bound to encounter, the restrictions on certain kinds of freedom which must result, nor even by the bloodshed of the transition period. A better economic order is worth a little bloodshed. But I am profoundly disturbed by the technological aspects of this method of solving the problem of distribution in a highly mechanized society such as ours. In the attempt, production might be shattered beyond repair." [6]

Except as a last resort, Chase did not advise catastrophic action in the United States. In the long run, said he, similar collectivist results could be achieved through national planning, regulation and control by government agencies operating more or less within the framework of the Constitution. To that end, he outlined a broad program—based in part on Sidney Webb's *Labour and the New Social Order* and in part on the monetary nostrums of John Maynard Keynes—guaranteed to lead in due time to a nonprofit system. For the next few years, he proposed merely three major steps:

1. A managed currency, to prevent accidental inflation and deflation.
2. Drastic redistribution of the national income, through income and inheritance taxes.
3. A huge program of public works, to become a continuing program especially in the fields of housing and rural electrification. [7]

All three of these prescribed remedies were adopted in 1933, and after, by the Roosevelt Administration, whose program became officially known as the New Deal.

Undeniably, Socialism's first major, Fabian-planned opportunity in the United States came about through the Democratic Party's landslide victory in 1932. It followed in the wake of a financial panic of unprecedented severity, provoked by the stock market crash of October, 1929. Few Americans alive today recall that the Great Depression, which somehow lasted longer in America than anywhere else, was a world-wide phenomenon of European origin, touched off by the failure of the *Creditanstalt* bank in Vienna. Through their contacts with

[6] Stuart Chase, *A New Deal*, (New York, The Macmillan Co., 1932), pp. 155-156.
[7] *Ibid.*, pp. 190-193.

foreign Socialists, American Fabians were able to predict the impending day of doom in the United States with some certitude, and they were prepared to take advantage of it.

Some months before the crash H. Stephen Raushenbush—secretary of the Socialist-fostered committee on coal and giant power—referred to a period of low wages, high prices and general unemployment as if it were already a fact.[8] He viewed the prospect optimistically, saying, "We can see more clearly the function which liberals and socialists—both those who are essentially scholars and students and those who are politicians—can have in changing the social order." [9] Raushenbush invited young Socialists graduating from college to enter the Government service, especially the Interior and Treasury Departments, as a means of developing techniques and obtaining necessary information for gaining control over private industry. And he asserted confidently: *"Within the next ten years we are going to have a chance such as we have not had in the last forty."* [10]

Within the next few years private American investments previously valued at 93 billion dollars shrank to a mere 14 billion dollars. The unemployed in the United States were estimated to number twelve to fourteen million. For the first time in its existence, the nation cried out for a political savior. He descended like a god from the machine and he offered the people something that, with a flash of psychological insight, was cleverly termed "relief."

As A. Susan Lawrence, M.P.—member of the Fabian Executive and friend of Frances Perkins, Jane Addams and Eleanor Roosevelt —reported at a Livingstone Hall lecture in London: "By one of history's strangest freaks, the elaborate system of checks and balances devised in the American Constitution, has resulted for the moment at any rate, in the complete personal ascendancy of Franklin Roose-

---

[8] H. S. Raushenbush, "Some Measures in Transition," *The Socialism of Our Times.* A Symposium. Harry W. Laidler and Norman Thomas, eds., (New York, The Vanguard Press, Inc.—League for Industrial Democracy, 1929), p. 42.

[9] *Ibid.,* p. 40. "Yet the problem of government officials is a major problem of immediate socialism. In Germany, after the revolution, the bureaucracy was nationalist and nearly sabotaged the republican government until it had been replaced. One good man with his eyes, ears and wits about him, inside the department—whether it be the Interior where the oil scandal started and the Boulder Dam Bill received most active support, or the Treasury where the taxation scandals breed and the government tax policies originate—can do more to perfect the technique of control over industry than a hundred men outside."

[10] *Ibid.,* p. 45. (Italics added.)

velt." [11] On that occasion, the chairman was Helen Keynes, sister of the left wing financial oracle, John Maynard Keynes who had contributed so liberally to the strange new fiscal policies of the Roosevelt Administration. Helen Keynes stressed the "supreme importance," for the "survival of democracy," of what was happening in the United States. Susan Lawrence dwelt upon the practical opportunities it offered for Socialism and Socialist-led labor groups.

The dramatic emergence of Franklin Delano Roosevelt at that precise moment in history was neither as providential nor as fortuitous as it may have seemed to the general public. On the contrary, it had been painstakingly planned and prepared far in advance. Almost twenty years before, as a crisp young Assistant Secretary of the Navy under Woodrow Wilson, Franklin Roosevelt had been briefed on the career of *Philip Dru, Administrator*—that fictional personage who devised a formula for centering power in the administrative branch of government, as a means of imposing sweeping social changes. At least as early as 1920, Roosevelt was marked for future greatness by Philip Dru's creator, Colonel Edward Mandell House.

It is noteworthy that in a lifetime of political observation Colonel House backed only two candidates for the Presidency. The first had been Woodrow Wilson. The second was Franklin Roosevelt, whose family name and humanitarian pretensions could be counted upon to rally such leftward Progressives of the defunct Bull Moose Party as Senators La Follette, Norris and Hiram Johnson and Governor Gifford Pinchot of Pennsylvania; while his own record of Democratic Party regularity rendered him acceptable to old-line Democrats. The timely support Roosevelt had given Al Smith, whose name he placed in nomination at the 1928 Democratic Convention, gained him the governorship of New York and the uncritical good will of Irish and Italian voters throughout the country.

At the same time, Roosevelt's experiments in "social reform" at Albany, where he appointed former social settlement workers to administer his new unemployment and emergency relief programs, recommended him to professional liberals everywhere. As Governor, he activated the State Employment Service along lines which American Fabians had been urging since the eighteen-nineties and he made other innovations likely to find favor with the leaders of New York

[11] "Livingstone Hall Lectures." *Fabian News*, (May, 1934).

City's garment workers. True, his old classmates at Groton and Harvard—while conceding that Franklin was a gentleman—rated him something less than a mental giant; but even this might be viewed as an advantage in politics, where the too conspicuous exercise of brainpower did not necessarily insure popularity.

To compensate for any possible cerebral shortcomings, he was thoughtfully provided with a "brain trust"—a term of British Fabian origin—whose traveling expenses to Albany were reputedly paid by the Twentieth Century Fund. Among others, Felix Frankfurter, whom Roosevelt had known ever since the former served on Wilson's War Labor Policy Board, and such polite former Wilsonian Socialists as Stuart Chase and Fred C. Howe met with the Governor both before and after his nomination as President. Once in office, he could be expected to put into practice plans that Woodrow Wilson had merely been able to foreshadow.

A no less vital factor in the progressive education of the President-select was his energetic and ambitious wife, Eleanor. While Franklin served his country during World War I from a desk in the Navy Department, Eleanor had joined the National Consumers League in New York.[12] Inspired and directed by the Quaker-Marxist, Florence Kelley,[13] the Consumers League was a prime medium through which American Fabians captured the leadership of social reform activities during the first three decades of the twentieth century. Ostensibly it crusaded against sweatshops, child labor and excessive hours of work for women, and lobbied for standards of industrial safety. Many public-spirited citizens were naturally moved to support such worthy and emotionally appealing causes. In fact, Newton D. Baker, Secretary of War under Woodrow Wilson, once served as president of the Consumers League without suspecting its long-range Socialist objectives.

The Consumers League was only the first in a long list of Socialist-inspired organizations with which Eleanor Roosevelt was to affiliate herself during a long and active life. Through it she was introduced to that curious demi-world of social settlement workers, left wing labor organizers and assorted academic, literary and political crusaders that Robert Hunter has described. Their channels of communi-

[12] Frances Perkins, *The Roosevelt I Knew*, (New York, The Viking Press, 1946), p. 18.
[13] In 1920 Florence Kelley was also president of the Intercollegiate Socialist Society, and after 1921 a vice president of the League for Industrial Democracy.

cation extended from Toynbee Hall in London to Hull House in Chicago to the Henry Street Settlement in New York and Hale House in Boston.

Thus Eleanor came to know Lillian Wald, Jane Addams and Frances Perkins who, like Florence Kelley, had spent some years at Hull House. Through these and other new friends, Eleanor Roosevelt met and fraternized with female leaders of the Fabian Society on post-World War I trips to England. She had been educated in England as a girl, and in the nineteen-twenties she had attended and lectured at Fabian Summer Schools there. The genteel, high-minded tone of British Fabian Socialism impressed her, as well as the fact that it had achieved political power in the name and with the support of labor.

After 1921 Eleanor brought two New York organizers of the Women's Trade Union League—now the International Ladies Garment Workers Union—to see her husband and to tutor him in the theory and background of the trade union movement as they knew it.[14] One was Rose Schneiderman, a red-haired firebrand who had organized the shirtwaist workers in bygone days and who in 1920 became, with Felix Frankfurter, a founder of the Civil Liberties Union and a member of its board of directors.[15] The other was Maude Schwartz, an Anglo-Irish woman, active in the Fabian-led British labor movement for many years before coming to this country.

Both were practicing Socialists, adept at winning converts through heart-appeal rather than dogma. They told their host about the English cooperatives, developed with the help of Socialist trade unions, which had their imitators in some sections of America thanks to the early efforts of James Warbasse.[16] They fired his sympathy with tales of ancient wrongs corrected as a result of union action and stirred his mind with the practical possibilities of an expanded and political-ized trade union movement in America. The seeds they sowed, in the course of various sickroom visits during the early nineteen-twenties, later bore fruit in the National Recovery Act, the purpose of which was not only to raise wages and prices according to a Keynesian formula, but also to foster the growth of labor organizations bound to Roosevelt by ties of personal loyalty.

Never a serious student, Franklin Roosevelt had been accustomed since boyhood to deriving his ideas from conversations with trusted

[14] Perkins, *op. cit.*, pp. 30-32.
[15] See Appendix IV.
[16] See Appendix II.

intimates and members of his family circle, while retaining a superficial air of jaunty independence. It was not surprising, therefore, that his mother's old friend, Colonel House,[17] should have been the very first Fabian planner to perceive that young Franklin was a rare jewel, to be polished, placed in the proper setting and flashed with dazzling effect upon the world at an appropriate moment.

Above all, House recognized that Roosevelt possessed a certain adaptability, both personal and political, which the unbending Woodrow Wilson had lacked. The Squire of Hyde Park—inclined as a young man to look down his nose through his pince-nez at ordinary folk—had succeeded in developing a genial, outgoing personality, marked by high good humor, which would enable him to adjust the most arrant Socialist novelties to the realities of machine politics. "Mr. Sinclair, I cannot go any faster than the people will let me," he told the admiring Upton Sinclair in an interview soon after his election.[18]

Even an infantile paralysis attack in 1921 that left him a cripple failed to disqualify Franklin Roosevelt for the historic role he had been chosen, possibly unawares, to fill. A fine head, a triumphant smile, and a golden voice on the air, with radio just then becoming a potent political factor,[19] could be deployed to distract popular attention from the fact that he had suffered physical impairment. As Frances Perkins, his devoted associate for many years, pointed out, one political advantage of his infirmity was that it obliged him to suffer bores cheerfully. He could no longer walk away from them, as he had been apt to do in his more impatient youth.

In 1932 Colonel House lived just two blocks from the Roosevelt home on East Sixty-fifth Street in New York City. Early that year, the small gray master-marplot slipped in and out of the Governor's town house almost daily to proffer advice and tactical suggestions. Despite his advanced age—he was then seventy-four—House still had a national network of politically influential friends who

---

[17] House was responsible for naming young Roosevelt, as Assistant Secretary of the Navy, to the Advisory Interdepartmental Committee. There Roosevelt's friendship with Felix Frankfurter, then counsel for the War Labor Policy Board, seems to have begun.

[18] *Forty Years of Education*, (New York, League for Industrial Democracy, 1945), p. 16.

[19] In her Livingstone Hall lecture, reported in *Fabian News* of May, 1934, A. Susan Lawrence, M.P. said that, while the tone of the New York press was comparatively critical, an "American expert" (who was evidently a Briton) had remarked to her: "The Wireless can whip the Press all the time."

knew what was happening in State politics and could sway the votes of State delegations. And despite his own depression-shrunk fortune, he was said to be one of four men who contributed $10,000 to Roosevelt's pre-convention campaign. The others were: Jesse I. Straus of Macy's, who had originally headed the Governor's emergency relief organization in Albany and who was afterwards named Ambassador to France—a precedent-shattering appointment; William Woodin, who became Roosevelt's first Secretary of the Treasury; and Frank Walker, later Postmaster General, an anti-Smith Catholic from the Midwest who had just sold a chain of motion picture houses to Paramount and who, like another early Roosevelt backer, Joseph P. Kennedy, enjoyed the confidence of West Coast movie moguls.

In those months, the radical-minded Colonel proclaimed to still solvent Wall Street acquaintances that the capitalist system as they had known it was finished and that Franklin Roosevelt was the man picked by experts to salvage the remains. For services rendered, House was modestly rewarded by being permitted to choose Roosevelt's first Ambassador to Britain, Judge Robert Worth Bingham of Louisville, Kentucky—whose son, Barry Bingham, in 1947 became a founding member of the Americans for Democratic Action.[20]

The Colonel's own days of White House authority were over, never to be revived. Somewhat wistfully, he saw his former guest room privileges and direct telephone wire conferred on younger favorites whose radical bias was as unsuspected by the electorate as his own had been. He had set the stage, however, for a new breed of informal Presidential advisers—more potent, more elusive and more definitely committed to policies of Fabian Socialist origin than any mere Kitchen Cabinet of the past. The extra-constitutional method devised by House for relieving a Chief Executive from the burden of independent decision has become accepted practice today.

Other leading pre-convention strategists were Roosevelt's former New York State campaign manager, Louis M. Howe, and U.S. Senator Cordell Hull. As a congressman, Hull had written the first Federal Income Tax Law of 1913, as well as the revised Federal Income and Inheritance Tax Laws of 1916—omitting to place a permanent ceiling on either of them. It is unlikely that the homespun statesman from the Tennessee hills ever dreamed that the rather moderate bills he drafted might provide a basis at some future date for a "redistribution of the

[20] See Appendix V.

national income," as proposed by Fabian Stuart Chase in 1932—and as included since 1918 in the Fabian-dictated program of the British Labour Party.[21] The fact that an old-line southern Democrat had been induced to sponsor the basic legislation so ardently desired by all spokesmen of gradual Socialism was an early and notable example of success for the Fabian technique known as *permeation.*

Personally conservative but politically regular, Hull was appointed Secretary of State by Roosevelt at a moment when brain trusters did not regard that department as of primary importance to their plans. Just then the sole foreign policy issue that stirred them was the diplomatic recognition of Soviet Russia, a project in which American as well as British Fabian Socialists took a lively interest.

As in Britain, this move was described as offering vast foreign trade possibilities—if sufficiently lenient long-term credits could be arranged for the nearly bankrupt Russians. The Soviets' well-publicized intent to purchase huge quantities of cotton in the southern United States (a promise that came to little) helped win Hull's consent to the establishment of diplomatic relations with that Ishmael among nations. It was the first outstanding misstep of the Roosevelt Administration in the field of foreign policy.

At a later date—as *The New York Times'* well-informed Washington bureau chief, Arthur Krock, reported—Hull's authority was repeatedly circumvented by assistants having a direct pipeline to the White House. Many of his policy-making functions were also preempted by specially appointed presidential envoys and by Roosevelt's preference for acting as his own Secretary of State in crucial negotiations. That type of personal diplomacy, originally commended to Woodrow Wilson by Colonel House and enthusiastically practiced by each succeeding Democratic President, tended to nullify the advisory roles of the Senate and the Cabinet as defined in the Constitution.

Instead, something vaguely resembling the British Privy Council system came into being—the difference being that the Washington version was unsanctioned by custom or law or tradition, and that the

[21] A sharply graduated system of income and inheritance taxes had been advocated by the American Fabian League in the eighteen-nineties. In 1928 it was still a plank in the official program of the American Socialist Party. Members of the Socialist National Campaign Committee, which issued the 1928 handbook containing that program, were listed on the cover as follows: "W. E. Woodward, Norman Thomas, Freda Kirchwey, McAllister Coleman, Paul Blanshard, James O'Neal, Harry Elmer Barnes, James H. Maurer, Lewis Gannett, Victor Berger, Louis Waldman." All, without exception, have been officers and/or directors of the League for Industrial Democracy.

identity of the White House counselors was often unknown to the general public and subject to change without notice. If bystanders wondered why Cordell Hull, an old style American in the mold of Andrew Jackson, submitted so long to such indignities, they concluded charitably that he remained at his post some twelve years in order to avert a mass invasion of the State Department by hungry New Dealers and One Worlders—as occurred, in fact, after his retirement.

From the outset, however, Secretary Hull was obliged to tolerate the presence of a select number of Harvard-trained Frankfurter protégés in key State Department positions. On his arrival, Hull found Herbert Feis already ensconced in the economic section. Feis was assisted from 1933 to 1935 by Professor Alvin H. Hansen, public speaker and occasional pamphleteer of the LID, the first of the older Harvard economists to embrace the doctrines of John Maynard Keynes.[22] Alger Hiss, who had begun his career as the law clerk of Supreme Court Justice Holmes, rose to become director of the State Department's Political Affairs Section and secretary of the Postwar Policy Planning Committee.

Secretary Hull evidently disliked having members of the Frankfurter coterie foisted upon him and managed to divest himself of some from time to time. But, apart from an occasional delaying action engineered by his supporters on Capitol Hill, there was not a great deal he could do to stem the tide of encroaching Socialism—or to discourage its covert Communist beneficiaries.

2.

Soon after his election to the Presidency in 1932, Franklin Roosevelt met privately in Washington with a group that included Felix Frankfurter, Fred C. Howe and some dozen members of Congress. With the notable exception of Congressman Fiorello La Guardia of New York City, the legislators came chiefly from the western states. Strangely enough, they did not belong to the Democratic Party, but styled themselves Progressive Republicans. All had bolted to Roosevelt in 1932 and sought assurances that their aid would be suitably requited.

Politically, they were a hybrid species. The elders among them, Senators George C. Norris of Nebraska and Hiram Johnson of California, dated from the Bull Moose era, as did Frankfurter and Howe.

[22] Seymour E. Harris, *John Maynard Keynes. Economist and Policy Maker,* (New York, Charles Scribner's Sons, 1955), p. 208.

After helping to split the Republican Party in 1912, they threw their weight behind the Wilson Administration. From 1924, they had enjoyed the somewhat eccentric backing of the Conference for Progressive Political Action, precursor of the modern-day Americans for Democratic Action. "Conservation of natural resources" was the high-sounding slogan by which these solons maintained themselves in office and justified their emancipation from such routine concerns as party loyalty. They joined or supported the Public Ownership League of America,[23] nominally a nonpartisan organization,[24] whose perennial secretary and guiding spirit, Carl D. Thompson, was a former national campaign manager and information director of the Socialist Party.[25]

As early as March, 1924, Senator Norris had introduced a bill providing for a nationwide government-operated system of electric power. Admittedly, it was conceived by the Public Ownership League and promoted at a so-called superpower conference held on January 16-17 at the Hotel Hamilton in Washington, D.C.[26] Senator Norris registered at the opening session and addressed the conference, pledging all-out support. A committee was named to assist him in drafting a superpower bill. Heading that committee was Father John A. Ryan,[27] later known as the padre of the New Deal—and once identified by the Washington *Star*, in a renowned typographical error, as chairman of the "Socialist Action Committee" of the National Catholic Welfare Conference.[28]

The original Federal power bill (S-2790) was a bold one, clearly transcending mere government ownership and distribution of electric

[23] *Public Ownership*. A Monthly Journal Published by the Public Ownership League of America. Carl D. Thompson, Editor. (Chicago, December, 1923), p. 53. Eleven members of Congress, including Senator Norris and Congressman Fiorello La Guardia, were named as supporting the Public Ownership League. The same journal stated in June, 1935, p. 72: "The Public Ownership League now has some ten or fifteen members of Congress who are also members of the Public Ownership League."

[24] *The Call Magazine*, (July, 1917), p. 7. This magazine, a Socialist publication, described the Public Ownership League as "strictly non-partisan," and added: "Many noted and prominent members of the Socialist Party, including two members of the present Executive Committee, are members of the League."

[25] The name of Carl D. Thompson appeared on Socialist Party letterheads and campaign leaflets from 1912 to 1916.

[26] *Public Ownership*, (February, 1924), pp. 54-55.

[27] *Ibid.* Other members of the committee included: James P. Noonan, International President of the Electrical Workers; Ben Marsh, Executive Secretary of the National Farmers' Council; Jennie Buell, Michigan State Grange; Charles K. Mohler, consulting engineer, Chicago.

[28] Washington *Star*, (November 8, 1931).

power. As Carl Thompson had stated from the first, the purpose of the Public Ownership League was not only to secure public owner-ship of utilities but also Federal control of railroads, coal and *"all industrial forces depending upon electric power for their successful operation."* [29] As if by some process of thought transference, the intro-duction of America's first public power bill coincided with a move in England to electrify the railroads,[30] and with proposals initiated by British Fabian Socialists to install the grid system of public power. In Russia, Lenin's mammoth (and even now only partially completed) scheme for electrification of all Soviet industries and farms under State control had just been announced.

At that date, as might have been expected, the public superpower bill failed on Capitol Hill. So did a subsequent bill (S-2147) of 1926 providing for a Tennessee Valley Authority (TVA) and a joint reso-lution (SJ-163) the following year—both filed by Senator Norris at the request of the Public Ownership League. By that time, however, the true mastermind of the public ownership movement in America, H. Stephen Raushenbush, second-generation Fabian Socialist and one-time secretary of the LID, had developed a more cautious plan for what he termed "encroaching control" designed to lead to "ultimate abolition of the profit system." [31] Champions of direct revolutionary action complained that his "Program for the Gradual Socialization of Industry" [32] resembled the formula for achieving chastity a little bit at a time prescribed by Leo Tolstoi in *The Kreutzer Sonata*. In the booming United States of 1927, both methods appeared equally un-likely to succeed.

The central feature of the Raushenbush program was a government-operated Power Authority, a term he seems to have coined. It was to serve as a "yardstick" for private industry and, by demonstrating superior virtue, lead to the eventual extinction of the private sector. From a book entitled *The Public Control of Business* by Keezer and May,[33] Raushenbush unearthed a pertinent item, namely, that there

[29] *The Call Magazine*, (July, 1917), p. 7. (Italics added.)

[30] *Public Ownership*, (February, 1924), p. 58.

[31] H. Stephen Raushenbush, "Cataclysmic Socialism or Encroaching Control," *New Leader*, (March 5, 1927).

[32] H. Stephen Raushenbush, "Program for the Gradual Socialization of Indus-try," *New Leader*, (March 12, 1927).

[33] Dexter M. Keezer and Stacy May, *The Public Control of Business*. A Study of Anti-Trust Law Enforcement, Public Interest Regulations, and Government Participation in Business, (New York, Harper & Brothers, 1930 edition).

appeared to be no constitutional obstacle to the Government's operating a business or industry, provided such action was declared to be in the public interest. Indeed, as numerous court decisions seemed to confirm, it was easier for the Government to go into business than to "regulate" existing enterprises. That handy loophole, publicized by Stephen Raushenbush, provided the legal sanction for a whole series of business ventures soon to be undertaken by the New Deal Administration—not only in the field of electric power production, but also in housing, rural electrification, farm mortgages and agricultural products, storage, insurance and general banking.

With the onset of the Great Depression, the Public Ownership League's scheme for a so-called Tennessee Valley Authority was once more revived. This time, however, it was offered on the pretext of providing employment and stimulating recovery. Electric power was not so much as mentioned in Senator Norris' TVA bill of 1933. Other features were added piecemeal through a series of supplementary bills, until at last the plan emerged full-blown. In March, 1935, David Lilienthal, director of the TVA, finally felt it safe to announce: "These dams are not being built for scenic effect, these millions of dollars are not being spent merely to increase business activities in this area. These dams are power dams, they are being built because they will provide electric power." [34]

It was not until 1937, however, that the actual scope of the TVA was disclosed to the American public. The assembled blueprint, showing a whole chain of dams linked together under the grid system to form a gigantic nationwide public power complex,[35] closely resembled the original sketch drafted by the Public Ownership League between 1923 and 1925. Both the plan itself and the gradual means by which it was achieved illustrate the strategy of Fabian Socialism more clearly than any other of the numerous schemes which devotees of that revolutionary faith have launched in this country.

Begun on a small local scale, its slow encroachment mirrors the origins and progress of the Fabian Socialist movement in the United States. It would seem, therefore, a coincidence that the first municipally owned power plant in America should have been established in 1896, at a time when British instigators of the American Fabian

[34] Chattanooga *News*, (March 1, 1935).
[35] *The New York Times*, (June 6, 1937). "Our Dreams Come True. Our Plan for a Public Power System for the United States Slowly but Surely Being Realized," *Public Ownership of Public Utilities*, (September, 1937).

League were actively promoting municipal ownership of public utilities at home; and that America's first city-owned electric plant was located in Chicopee Falls, Massachusetts[36] home town of Edward Bellamy!

Over a quarter century of patient penetration and permeation was required before the public-power movement was able to entrench itself in the national government, securing the potent aid of Federal tax money. At the time, only a handful of non-Socialist observers discerned the implications. One was *The New York Times'* ever-vigilant Arthur Krock. On December 21, 1933, Krock reported that the TVA, "while not very expensive as things go under President Roosevelt," had spent over forty millions of a fifty million dollar appropriation in less than a year of initial activity. And he commented shrewdly, "It is, even more than NRA or AAA, a social and economic laboratory." With the great mass of Americans numbed by the hurricanelike effect of the Depression and a Socialist camarilla riding high in Washington, such discreet warning passed largely unnoticed.

The TVA has now been in operation some thirty years, quietly but steadily expanding its empire and accepted almost as a natural phenomenon by a new generation. The ultimate step, total control over all key industries, appears to have been necessarily postponed. But not forever. TVA was and still remains, as Norman Thomas revealed,[37] the enterprise nearest and dearest to the hearts of American Fabian Socialists and the one most central to the accomplishment of their long-range plans for making (and taking) over America.

3.

President-elect Franklin D. Roosevelt's meeting with Felix Frankfurter, Fred C. Howe and Republican Progressives in Congress preceded by only a few months the revival of the Tennessee Valley Authority project, disguised as an anti-depression measure. It was one of the earliest bills to be rubber-stamped for passage under the New Deal, and there is no reason to suppose its intent was unknown to the President. Naturally, its champions wished to be assured in ad-

---

[36] *Public Ownership of Public Utilities,* (September, 1937), p. 76.

[37] Norman Thomas, *Democratic Socialism: A New Appraisal,* (New York, League for Industrial Democracy, 1953), p. 6. "Of recent years, the majority of American Socialists have been—I think correctly—insistent that the model for what is socially owned is not the Post Office Department but the Tennessee Valley Authority, with provision for direct representation of workers and consumers on it."

vance of the incoming Executive's blessing, as well as to be certain they would have a voice in naming officials charged with the administration of TVA and allied programs.

From that meeting of minds, there emerged a novel type of patronage, based more on ideology than constituencies, which for a time baffled political experts and continues to trouble many loyal Democrats today. Several seemingly mysterious Cabinet appointments, announced soon afterwards by Roosevelt, were traceable to recommendations by Republican Progressives. Felix Frankfurter, who had organized the Progressives-for-Roosevelt, became a kind of one-man employment service for placing liberal lawyers and economists in the Executive departments and agencies. The new order of precedence provoked Alfred E. Smith in 1936 to a pained and picturesque outburst. "Who is Ickes?" he cried. "Who is Wallace? Who is Hopkins, and in the name of all that is good and holy, who is Tugwell and where did he blow from? . . . If La Guardia is a Democrat, then I am a Chinaman with a haircut." [38]

A little field research along the sidewalks of New York might have given Al Smith a clue. For in 1934, two years after Roosevelt's election, several persons influential in the formation of the New Deal were listed as teaching at the Rand School of Social Science, which Al Smith once helped inadvertently to preserve. They were Stuart Chase, Rexford G. Tugwell and Raymond V. Moley.[39] In 1930 and 1931, institutes on unemployment, social insurance and public power had been held at the Rand School to prepare the Socialist faithful for the shape of things to come. The superpower movement, which claimed Governor Smith as a supporter,[40] acted in close understanding with leading British Fabians—as indicated by a letter of November 13, 1930, printed in *Fabian News*, from the Public Ownership League's Carl D. Thompson to Alderman A. Emil Davies, later chairman of the London Fabian Society.[41]

[38] Quoted in the *New Republic*, (September 15, 1958).
[39] *Rand School Bulletin*, 1934-35.
[40] *Public Ownership*, (December, 1923), p. 53.
[41] Other issues of *Fabian News* show Davies to have been a frequent visitor to the United States in the nineteen-thirties. His biography in *Who's Who* describes him as follows: Alderman and past Chairman of the London County Council; Fellow, Royal Economic Society; former lecturer in Economics, University of Leeds; Member, Permanent Bureau International Union of Cities; Chairman, City and Commercial Investment Trust, London, England. In 1923 his son, Ernest Davies, who succeeded his father on the Fabian Executive, worked for the New York *Globe*.

It would have shaken quite a few unsuspecting Democrats to know how many major and minor officeholders under the New Deal had been connected for years with organizations pledged to further the programs of Fabian Socialism in America. Such attachments ranged from the Rand School and the League for Industrial Democracy to the American Civil Liberties Union, the National Consumers League, the Public Ownership League, the New School for Social Research, the National Association for the Advancement of Colored People (NAACP), the Government Planning Association, the Public Affairs Council and other social democratic concoctions—up to, and including, the Fabian Society of London. If the great majority of officials who formed the intellectual core of the New Deal were Democrats, in the sense that the average American understood the term, then Al Smith certainly was a "Chinaman with a haircut!"

Of course, Smith must have known that Henry Agard Wallace, the New Deal Secretary of Agriculture who later became Vice President and in 1944 only missed by a phone call becoming a future President, had supported his (Smith's) candidacy in 1928. Wallace was the son of Henry Cantwell Wallace, a leading midwestern Republican who had been Secretary of Agriculture under Presidents Harding and Coolidge. He was the grandson of still another Henry Wallace, a member of President Theodore Roosevelt's Country Life Commission. Henry the third, however, was a Republican Progressive who had jumped early aboard the Democratic bandwagon.

As editor of the family newspaper, the Iowa *Farmer*, young Henry by his articles and speeches helped to carry the traditionally Republican Corn Belt for Franklin Roosevelt. In that campaign Wallace was aided by the Socialist-led National Farmers Council, whose organizer, Ben Marsh, openly supported the aims of the Public Ownership League.[42] For eighteen months before the election Wallace had also been calling for a reduction in the gold content of the dollar, combining the old dream of the Bryan bimetallists with John Maynard Keynes' seductive vision of a managed currency. Though a country boy, Wallace was not unsophisticated.

While he cultivated a dreamy and mystical air and a friendship with the well-known Irish poet, "A. E.," who brought news of the Fabian-led British cooperative movement to American farmers,[43] Wal-

---

[42] *Public Ownership,* (February, 1924), p. 55.
[43] A. E.'s real name was George William Russell. Born an Orangeman in Lurgan County, Ireland, he discovered Theosophy in 1898 and the Fabian Society

lace also had a taste for scientific experiment. In his spare time he had developed a special strain of hybrid corn which made possible higher crop yields. Through its American grain agent, Dr. Joseph Rosen (who had himself crossbred a new and hardy variety of rye seed), the Soviet Government during the nineteen-twenties displayed an interest in Wallace and his hybrid corn experiments.

The communications and transactions that ensued, in turn, aroused Wallace's friendly interest in what American liberals used to call the Soviet experiment—where a surplus of foodstuffs has never been a political problem. Given the tolerant attitude toward Russian Communism that Wallace took with him to Washington, it is not surprising that the Department of Agriculture became in 1934 under Harold Ware the center of the first identified Communist cell in the United States Government.[44]

By 1936 many sober citizens were inclined to agree with Fabian Socialist Stuart Chase that "Henry Wallace had lifted American agriculture bodily out of the free market system . . . ."[45]

Wallace's chief lieutenant in Agriculture was Rexford Guy Tugwell, another poetaster and rapt observer of the Soviet economy. In 1915, at the age of twenty-four, he had published a Whitmanesque effusion that read:

> We begin to see richness as poorness; we begin to dignify toil.
> I have dreamed my great dream of their passing,
> I have gathered my tools and my charts;
> My plans are fashioned and practical;
> I shall roll up my sleeves—make America over.

A free verse paraphrase of the Victorian quatrain so popular among early British Fabians, those lines expressed the credo that was to guide Tugwell and his friends through life. "Why should Russians have all

---

soon afterwards. In 1930-31 he spent a year in the United States lecturing on agricultural cooperatives to farmers from Maine to California. In 1934 he made another lecture tour, linking the New Deal's rural electrification schemes with his own cooperative farm propaganda. He contributed to *Commonweal, Catholic World, The Nation, The New Republic, etc.* See *Biography of Twentieth Century American Authors,* (New York, Appleton-Century-Crofts, 1954).

[44] Harold Ware was the son of Communist Ella Reeve Bloor. He had previously been decorated with the Order of Lenin for his work on State farms in the USSR. Members of the original cell included Alger Hiss, Lee Pressman, John Abt and Nathaniel Weyl, according to testimony given before the Internal Security Subcommittee of the Senate Judiciary Committee.

[45] Stuart Chase, *Rich Land, Poor Land,* (New York, McGraw-Hill, Inc., 1936), p. 246.

the fun of remaking a world?" wrote his Rand School colleague, Stuart Chase, in *A New Deal*.[46]

Tugwell blew into Washington from the economics department of Columbia University, having previously taught at the University of Pennsylvania and Washington State. One of the first Socialist-minded economists allowed to translate his theories into government practice, he made the most of the opportunity. There was little in the application of the early New Deal in which Tugwell did not have a finger. Besides abetting Wallace in a forlorn attempt to transform abundance into scarcity by ploughing under crops and killing suckling pigs, Tugwell also sat on the Housing Board, the Surplus Relief Administration, the Public Works Board, the President's Commercial Policy Committee and other newly created bodies. He fathered the thought, seconded by the President's Commercial Policy Committee, of grading all industries according to their efficiency and utility and denying tariff protection to those judged a "burden" on the United States.

It was Tugwell who proposed that consumers be represented, in addition to labor unions and employers, on the twenty-seven industry boards to be set up under the National Recovery Act. The object of this seemingly benevolent move was to cut prices and profits, while increasing wages—a prelude to the disappearance of the profit system, which a number of early New Dealers believed to be close at hand. Like some other impatient neo-Fabians, Tugwell was chagrined at the New Deal's failure to abolish the profit system at once; and like Wallace, he moved leftward with the years. His last fling in public office was as Governor of Puerto Rico from 1945 to 1948, during a period when thousands of islanders were being airlifted via nonscheduled planes to New York City,[47] there to find themselves enrolled on the public welfare and registered as voters for the Communist-line Congressman, Vito Marcantonio.

Hand in hand with Tugwell, two other early New Deal enthusiasts pushed through the scheme for giving consumers' groups the decisive voice in fixing wages and prices under the National Recovery Act. They were Fred C. Howe and Mary Harriman Rumsey. Still a Fabian Socialist at sixty though calling himself a Progressive, Fred Howe was a relic of the old muckraking era and a veteran member of the

[46] Stuart Chase, *A New Deal*, (New York, The Macmillan Co., 1932), p. 252.
[47] R. L. Martin, *American Aviation*, (May, 1948). First report of that curious population movement appeared in *American Aviation*. Its scope and purpose were revealed in a subsequent investigation by the New York *World Telegram*.

League for Industrial Democracy.[48] Named to the Agricultural Adjustment Administration (AAA), he soon moved to the NRA Consumers Advisory Board where Mary Rumsey flourished. One of the wealthiest women in America, Mary Rumsey was the sister and mentor of W. Averell Harriman, Administrator of the NRA in 1934-35.[49]

An intimate of Eleanor Roosevelt and Frances Perkins, Mary Rumsey shared their social outlook, having veered a good deal toward the Left since her debutante days when she founded the Junior League. Frances Perkins described her fondly as "a convinced and advanced liberal." [50] The Rumsey estate in the fox hunt country near Middleburg, Virginia became a happy hunting ground for spokesmen of cooperative agriculture and nonconformist economics. Mary Rumsey had struck up a close friendship with the Irish poet-economist, "A. E.," the London Fabian Society's gift to American farmers; and she was fêted in top level Fabian-Labour Party circles on her periodic trips to England. Long a supporter of the National Consumers League (NCL), Mary Rumsey saw to it that the so-called consumers' representatives appointed to NRA boards were drawn from lists approved by the NCL. A two-to-one vote against industry was normally the result.

Outstanding among the lady politicos who stamped their features and foibles indelibly on the New Deal was Secretary of Labor Frances Perkins. A professional social worker, Frances Perkins had been trained at Hull House in Chicago, merely transferring the views and enlarging the contacts acquired there when she moved on to New York. Her first assignment in Albany was as a lobbyist for the National Consumers League and the Women's Trade Union Council.[51] She specialized in reforms having an emotional appeal for intellectuals and a vote-getting appeal among labor organizations.

As Industrial Commissioner of New York State under Franklin D. Roosevelt, she had imported a promising young LID economist, Paul H. Douglas, from Chicago to draft the Governor's unemployment and relief program.[52] Commissioner Perkins proved so useful in gaining

[48] See Appendix II.

[49] W. Averell Harriman has held many diplomatic and administrative posts under the Roosevelt and Truman Administrations. He was Governor of New York from 1955 to 1959. In the Kennedy and Johnson Administrations he has served as Assistant Secretary and Under Secretary of State for Far Eastern Affairs, and finally Roving Ambassador.

[50] Perkins, op. cit., p. 206.

[51] Ibid., p. 10 ff.

[52] Ibid., pp. 104-105.

the support of New York City's garment workers and other Socialist-led labor bodies, that FDR took her to Washington as the first female Cabinet member in history—an appointment warmly urged by Eleanor Roosevelt, Felix Frankfurter and the fast-fading Colonel House. Her personal influence with the President was exceeded only by that of her bosom friend, Eleanor Roosevelt, and her protégé and fellow social worker, Harry Hopkins. Certainly, her quiet but adroit contribution to the labor politics of the New Deal was highly prized.

Secretary Perkins' twelve-year tenure in the Department of Labor was marked by an influx of Socialist-recommended economists, analysts, statisticians, investigators and legal experts that to this day has never ceased. They were following the advice of Stephen Raushenbush to infiltrate government offices at every level. Some were so reticent and mouselike that their entry into the Federal service was tantamount to a disappearing act, and a full-dress congressional investigation would have been required to discover them. One of the more prominent examples, however, was Dr. Isadore Lubin, a lifelong collaborator of the LID, who served his apprenticeship as president of the Intercollegiate Socialist Society at Clark and Missouri.[53] Provided with some protective coloration by a recent tour of duty at Brookings Institute, Dr. Lubin was triumphantly ushered into the Department of Labor by Frances Perkins.

There, with immense industry and true Socialist zeal, Lubin reorganized the Bureau of Labor Statistics whence official indices on employment and unemployment still issue, often at moments best calculated to create political effects. Dr. Lubin developed the oracular *Consumer Price Index,* which remains a constant but invisible factor in the inflationary spiral—although its underlying assumptions have seldom been questioned and never checked. He is one of the few Americans who could claim to have improved on the statistical methods of the British Fabians.

Dr. Lubin's talents were not restricted to his job as Commissioner of Labor Statistics. In May, 1940, when FDR revived the National Defense Council in the confident anticipation of America's entry into World War II,[54] the President insisted on naming Sidney Hillman, LID official and president of the Amalgamated Clothing Workers, as the labor member of that council. Roosevelt asked Secretary Perkins to help her old friend Hillman; so she loaned him Dr. Lubin's services.

[53] See Appendix II.
[54] Perkins, *op. cit.,* p. 355.

Thereafter, Dr. Lubin became a kind of resident statistician to the White House, incidentally conveying to the President his own and Hillman's views on preferential aid to Russia. From 1940 Isadore Lubin was "constantly available and incalculably valuable . . . in checking every decimal point" [55] on figures used in the President's speeches and presentations. Since Lubin's staff had access to the files and conferences of business people throughout the country, he was also able to keep the White House informed on the most private thoughts of management. A personal note from Lubin to Hopkins in 1941 read:

I thought you might be interested in the following statements which are the summary of the report of one of my men who attended the recent meeting of the American Management Association . . . [56]

Frances Perkins sparked the Administration's move for nationwide unemployment insurance and old age pensions. At FDR's request, she headed a behind-the-scenes committee to draft the Social Security Act, whose title was a masterpiece of applied psychology. [57] Like TVA this was a project designed for permanence though pushed through under the impact of the Depression. It was part of a long-range program particularly cherished by the Secretary and her chums. Early in 1933, visitors to the White House reported that Eleanor Roosevelt was urging all and sundry to read a book called *Prohibiting Poverty*, by Prestonia Mann Martin, then an old lady in semi-retirement but once the angel of the American Fabian League.

Even before his inauguration, Franklin Roosevelt had agreed to take steps toward setting up a system of compulsory social insur-

---

[55] Robert Sherwood, *Roosevelt and Hopkins,* An Intimate History, (New York, Harper & Brothers, 1948), p. 216.

[56] *Ibid.,* p. 286. (*Author's Note:* Isadore Lubin was posted after the war to the United Nations. As U.S. Delegate to the UN Social and Economic Council in 1951, he joined British Socialist delegates in pushing through a resolution to set up the Ad Hoc Committee on Restrictive Business Practices. This would have exposed American firms doing business abroad to surveillance and prosecution by a proposed International Trade Organization operating under the Havana charter, which accepted State owned monopolies and cartels as benign. It was not until 1955 that the U. S. Delegation ceased officially to collaborate in this project. As of 1962, Dr. Lubin was listed as Professor of Public Affairs at Rutgers University.)

[57] The lengths to which research in Applied Psychology, as a means of molding public opinion, was being carried at that time can be inferred from an article appearing in the *Journal of Social Psychology,* (February, 1934). Written by A. D. Annis and N. C. Meier, it was solemnly entitled: "The Induction of Opinion Through Suggestion, by Means of Planted Content."

ance.[58] It reflected proposals which the English Fabian Socialist, Sidney Webb, had written en bloc into the 1918 platform of the British Labour Party and which American Socialists had been urging ever since. In Britain that plan was eventually presented to the electorate as an overall scheme to abolish poverty by fostering dependence on State-operated agencies. Undertaken ten years earlier in America, however, it could not conveniently be offered in package form.

Thus the pattern of the welfare state, which England's Fabian Socialists[59] frankly describe as "the transition from capitalism to Socialism," was not immediately revealed to Congress or the public. As in the case of TVA, it unfolded a little at a time, through a series of gradual but cumulative measures. By now the Social Security Act has been expanded to include death benefits, widows' pensions and some disability features. Its payments are based not upon need but upon "right." With the addition of public medical care for the aged (which, in Russia at least, helps to speed the demise of elderly pensioners) and eventual bonus payments for childbearing, the cradle-to-grave cycle of public benefactions will be complete.

Although the New Deal's welfare program was largely derived from British Fabian sources—having been transmitted to this country by American Fabian Socialists and such allies as Father John A. Ryan—Roosevelt chose to regard it as peculiarly his own idea. Not long before his death, he complained to intimates that England's much touted Beveridge Plan should by rights have been called the Roosevelt Plan.[60] He pointed out that Sir William Beveridge had visited him in Washington in 1934. Like the Fabian leaders of the British Labour Party, FDR never scrupled to use welfare for electioneering purposes. Indeed, he once begged Secretary Perkins and her group to speed their initial work on the Social Security Act, saying he could not otherwise go before the voters in 1936.[61]

The legal difficulties involved in preparing the bill were considerable. There was no precedent for such action in America and no apparent justification for it under the Constitution. Help came, however, from an unexpected quarter. At a dinner party in Washington, Secretary Perkins found herself seated beside Justice Harlan F. Stone,

[58] Perkins, op. cit., p. 278.
[59] Michael Stewart, M.P., "Labour and the Monarchy," Fabian Journal (March, 1952).
[60] Perkins, op. cit., pp. 283-284.
[61] Ibid., p. 294.

then classed with Brandeis and Cardozo, as a liberal on the Supreme Court Bench. She confided to the Justice that she was trying to work out some plan for social insurance but could discover no way of doing so that would be approved by the Court. Significantly, he whispered to her: *"The taxing power of the Federal Government, my dear; the taxing power is sufficient for everything you want and need!"* [62]

So Secretary Perkins advised her committee that the taxing power could be used as a means of building up funds for future unemployment and old age payments. She told no one, except the President, the source of her superior legal wisdom. Yet, somehow, the intelligence so liberally volunteered by Justice Stone ran like quicksilver throughout the Administration, rapidly becoming a part of its operational philosophy. While the propriety of Stone's conduct may be questioned, his informal words proved more potent than any official opinion he ever penned. They furnished the key to that magic New Deal formula which enabled Roosevelt to remain in office for the rest of his natural life and which was described in a phrase attributed to Harry Hopkins as "tax and tax, spend and spend, elect and elect!" [63]

To head the new Social Security Administration, which Congress ruled must be bipartisan, Secretary Perkins proposed John Gilbert Winant, former Governor of New Hampshire. He was one of the first important Republicans from the Eastern seaboard to be invited into the New Deal-Fabian Socialist parlor, and he stayed there to the bitter end. A year or two later, after Secretary Perkins had prevailed on Secretary Hull and congressional leaders to support a bill permitting the United States to join the International Labor Organization, she succeeded in having Winant made director of that body.

There the craggy man from the Green Mountains was exposed to the tutelage of such adroit Socialist diplomats of labor as W. Stephen Sanders and Philip Noel-Baker, [64] pillars of the London Fabian Society at Geneva. He displayed so much willingness to learn, that the British Fabian Socialist leader, Harold Laski, finally suggested to President

---

[62] *Ibid.*, p. 286.

[63] Frank R. Kent of the Baltimore *Sun* claimed Hopkins had made this statement to a mutual friend, Max Gordon, at the Empire racetrack in New York. Hopkins naturally disavowed it.

[64] The late Philip Noel-Baker, a recipient of the Socialist-controlled Nobel Peace Prize, was a Quaker who succumbed to the lure of Fabian "peace" propaganda. As a youth he attended Haverford College in Pennsylvania, and until his death continued to cultivate many friendships in the United States.

Roosevelt that Winant be appointed wartime Ambassador to the Court of St. James.[65] In this capacity, "Gil" Winant kindly consented to address a Fabian Society Luncheon[66] and entertained the Executive of the British Labour Party at the Embassy well before that party came to power. He allowed the charming but undeniably radical Laski to write speeches for him, recommend reading matter and personal contacts, and generally "set him straight." [67]

The International Labor Organization (ILO), through which Winant was able to attain those social and diplomatic heights, had been set up under the League of Nations charter, pursuant to a resolution introduced by British Fabian-Labour Party delegates at Versailles. Since that time, British Fabian Socialists have played a dominant part in its deliberations, both directly and indirectly via the Socialist International. Through the ILO machinery officials of many countries, who could not afford to be openly linked either with the Fabian Society or the Socialist International, were able to maintain discreet contacts with both. The measure of Secretary Perkins' prestige in such circles can be inferred from the fact that she was able to get her protégé, "Gil" Winant, elected director.

Surviving the League of Nations that spawned it, the ILO operates today from Geneva under the banner of the United Nations. Labor, government, and "employer" delegates from the Soviet Union and the satellite nations as well as from the so-called free world attend its congresses, where labor and government representatives jointly vote down the representatives of free enterprise with somewhat monotonous regularity. There unheralded spokesmen of the Socialist International and the Cominform can meet and mingle unobtrusively; and there British Fabian Socialists and their allies, Scandinavian, French, Belgian and others, are seen to be in command. For that reason, United States business has refused for several years to send representatives to ILO gatherings. While the actual role of the ILO remains obscure at this point in world history, the suggestion has been made that its Geneva offices may well provide a discreet point of contact

[65] Kingsley Martin, *Harold Laski: A Biographical Memoir*, (New York, The Viking Press, Inc., 1953), p. 139.

[66] "Luncheon to the American Ambassador," *Fabian News*, (October, 1941).

[67] Martin, *op. cit.*, pp. 139-141. Following the Allied victory in Europe, Winant served on the European Advisory Council, being himself advised by George F. Kennan and Philip E. Mosely. Winant was later reported to have died a suicide.

between the apparently hostile but mutually complementary Socialist and Communist Internationals.[67a]

4.

There were only two members of Roosevelt's Cabinet who remained from the first to the last day of his extended reign: Frances Perkins and Harold L. Ickes. Secretary Perkins has told how the President-elect, before moving to Washington, called her to his home on Sixty-fifth Street to apprise her of her new estate. Ushered into his study, she found him talking to a stocky, fair-haired man with the blunt features of a Pennsylvania Dutchman. "Frances, do you know Harold?" asked FDR. That was her introduction to Harold L. Ickes, variously known to historians as the strong man, the hatchet man and the curmudgeon of the New Deal.

If Frances and Harold did not know each other, they had friends in common in Felix Frankfurter, Jane Addams and Paul Douglas. During the campaign—then just passed—Ickes had served on the national committee of the Progressive League, whose chairman was Senator George C. Norris, chief spokesman on Capitol Hill for TVA. The League's secretary was Fred C. Howe and its national committee included Felix Frankfurter, Henry Wallace and Donald R. Richberg, a former law partner of Ickes and later named counsel for the NRA. Formed in September, 1932,[68] just two months before the national elections, the Progressive League could only have hoped to exert a decisive influence at the polls by attracting so-called independent voters and by splitting the Republican Party through an appeal to its liberal wing. With a Roosevelt landslide seemingly in the offing, the Progressive League was also prepared to snatch the fruits of victory from the triumphant Democrats. It contrived to secure for those "progressive" elements—who had been faithful, in their fashion, to the aims of the London Fabian Society and its provincial offshoots in America[69]—a controlling voice and hand in the new administration.

[67a] In June, 1966 George Meany led an AFL-CIO labor delegation out of the International Labor Organization, because a Polish Communist had been elected that year to head the ILO. Meany had never protested in other years, however, when international Socialists were chosen to fill the same post.

[68] Helen Shirley Thomas, *Felix Frankfurter: Scholar on the Bench* (Baltimore, Johns Hopkins University Press, 1960), p. 23.

[69] Under the heading, "Provincial Societies," *Fabian Society Annual Reports* for 1925 through 1930 listed "the League for Industrial Democracy of New York." Organizations like the Civil Liberties Union, the National Farmers Council, and the Public Ownership League were in turn offshoots of the ISS-LID.

Harold Ickes, technically a Democrat since 1928, boasted a long and unsuccessful career in progressive politics. A Chicago attorney, scrappy and embittered, he had won scant distinction in his profession. Instead, he made a living of sorts as a fundraiser and campaign manager for a whole series of defeated "reform" candidates, local and national. He ran the losing mayoralty campaigns of John M. Harlan in 1905 and Professor Charles E. Merriam in 1911. From 1912 to 1914, he was Bull Moose chairman for Cook County. During the next two years he was chairman of the Bull Moose's organization in Illinois and a member of the Progressive Party's national committee. In 1920 and 1924 he handled the bids of Senator Hiram Johnson for the Republican Presidential nomination, then backed the elder La Follette in his third-party effort. In 1926 he managed the Illinois campaign of a defeated "independent" Republican candidate for the U.S. Senate.

Since his student days at the University of Chicago, where he graduated in 1897 and took his law degree ten years later, Ickes had been involved with a group of scholarly reformers and academic planners headed by Professor Charles E. Merriam—afterwards a potent figure in the councils of the big tax free foundations. This group read the early publications recommended by the American Fabian League and the London Fabian Society on municipal government, public ownership of public services, and city and national planning. Its leaders conferred solemnly with Sidney and Beatrice Webb in 1898 when that oddly matched couple visited Jane Addams in Chicago. Thereafter, on the pretext of battling graft and corruption in government—always a handy issue in Chicago—a number of its members permeated civic and national organizations with a view to promoting Fabian Socialist objectives, but avoided direct identification with the American Socialist Party.

Thus Ickes, from the turn of the century, had been active in the nationwide conservation movement. He helped organize the Illinois League of Municipalities, which after 1917 supported the program of the Public Ownership League. In the natural course of events he came to know Alderman A. Emil Davies, a regular postwar visitor from London who was a charter member of the International Union of Cities as well as an honorary vice president of the Public Ownership League of America. From 1931, Ickes also belonged to an elite corps calling itself the Government Planning Association,[70] which drafted the

---

[70] Reorganized in 1934 as a quasi-official body, it was later called the National Planning Association.

tentative blueprint for the New Deal in consultation with a Fabian-sponsored group in London known as PEP (Political and Economic Planning).

Recommended by Senator Hiram Johnson to be chief of the Bureau of Indian Affairs, Ickes surprisingly walked away with what left-wingers of his time considered the prize post in the Cabinet. As Secretary of the Interior, he had the major responsibility for coordinating and enforcing the Public Ownership League's superpower program. Ickes also persuaded Roosevelt to place the huge Public Works Administration under the Interior Department, arguing that he was an old hand at discouraging graft. Thus Ickes had the rare pleasure during his first year as Secretary of being authorized to spend $3,300,-000 on public works, then the largest sum ever handed over to any Federal department in peacetime. And it was only the beginning!

Written into the Public Works Act by the Department of the Interior's legal wizard, Benjamin V. Cohen, was a provision giving "cities, counties, districts and other political subdivisions" a free gift of 30 per cent (later 45 per cent) towards the cost of building publicly operated electric plants. To speed distribution of this largesse, Ickes created a special three-man Power Board to review applications. In 1935, he appointed Carl Thompson, secretary of the Public Ownership League and erstwhile Socialist Party official, to the Power Review Board.[71] He named H. Stephen Raushenbush, philosopher of "encroaching Socialism" and chairman of the Socialist-sponsored coal and giant power Committee, to a spot in the Bituminous Coal Division, later making him "coordinator of compliance." In 1941, Raushenbush was quietly transferred to the Economics and Statistical Branch of the Interior Department's Division of Power, retiring as chief of that strategic service in 1947.[72]

First or last, a rather remarkable array of well-known and lesser known advocates of gradualist Socialism turned up on the Interior Department payroll. Ickes sent Ernest Gruening to Alaska and Robert Morss Lovett to the Virgin Islands—two of many LID notables with whom the Secretary shared his tax-supported good fortune. He put John Collier, who later wrote a pamphlet for the Fabian International

---

[71] *Public Ownership*, (June, 1935). In 1939-1941 Carl Thompson was employed as a consultant to the Bonneville Power Administration, according to testimony given by its director at hearings before the Subcommittee on Appropriations, 76th Congress, Third Session.

[72] Washington *Post*, (January 16, 1947).

Bureau, in charge of the Bureau of Indian Affairs, with Felix Cohen of the LID as Assistant Solicitor. Ickes' own testy speeches and writings, which gained him a reputation for mordant wit and enabled him to wage a one-sided vendetta with the stricken business community of the thirties, were reputedly the work of Saul Padover, an angry young man who in after years became a founding member of the Americans for Democratic Action.[73]

Endowed with the power to allot large chunks of Federal money for public construction in cities and states, Ickes dispatched a small army of scouts from Washington (sometimes referred to as Harold's Gestapo) to spy out the land. Obviously, they were in a position to exert substantial pressure on city, state and county political organizations, which duly returned the New Deal to office in four successive national elections. It would be naive to suppose that Ickes, an old campaigner tasting the sweets of power at last, failed to take full advantage of his opportunities. Apart from personal loyalty to Roosevelt, Harold loved his job and was determined to make both the New Deal and himself permanent fixtures in Washington. He was the first member of the Cabinet to greet FDR's suggestion of a third term with eager approval, challenging an unwritten law respected since the days of George Washington.

Nearly a billion dollars from Ickes' original public works appropriation—and more at later dates—was diverted by President Roosevelt to temporary works-projects, set up to provide direct Federal relief for the nation's unemployed.[74] As an emergency measure, this unconventional step might be justified by the real and widespread human need existing in 1933. There is evidence, however, that the temporary emergency was unnaturally prolonged by other administration policies which delayed industrial recovery. Three and a half years and six billion dollars later, unemployment relief was still being administered on an emergency basis—with the most vocal pressure groups, organized by Communist unemployed councils, getting a disproportionate share. While consumer industries revived somewhat, mining and manufacturing, which constituted the real strength of the country, declined. It was not until the outbreak of war in Europe, when the United States was called upon to fill military orders for the French and British, that America's basic industries were finally able to restore production lines on a nationwide scale.

[73] See Appendix V.
[74] Sherwood, *op. cit.*, p. 52.

The man whom Roosevelt placed in charge of distributing Federal unemployment relief was one of the oddest bits of human flotsam to be washed up by the Great Depression on the shifting sands of American history. Harry Hopkins was a courtier from the Corn Belt. In later years he had the look of an emaciated scarecrow in a battered gray fedora. His great talent lay in pleasing and impressing just the right people in his chosen sphere. Nominally devoted, during most of his career, to improving the condition of the poor, he escaped as often as possible to the diversions of racetracks, theaters and nightclubs and showed a marked preference for the company of the fashionable, the rich, the powerful[75]—providing they were "liberally" inclined.

No king's almoner of old ever had access to such resources as were placed at Harry Hopkins' command, nor more freewheeling liberty of action in dispensing them. Whether it was love of spending, personal ambition, a fanatical devotion to "the Chief," a Socialist creed, or some strange combination of all these that impelled him, even his best friends agree that patriotism was not his ruling passion. Frances Perkins once described him as "a shrewd man who had become acquainted with a lot of Democratic politicians while administering relief and the WPA." [76] So well acquainted, indeed, had Hopkins become with them that (though not even an official delegate) he was placed in charge of Roosevelt headquarters at the rigged 1940 Democratic Convention where FDR was nominated for the third time.

The pragmatic principle which guided Harry Hopkins as director of Federal Emergency Relief, afterwards called the Works Progress Administration, was expressed by his principal aide, Aubrey Williams, speaking at a relief conference in Washington: *We must stick together. We must keep our friends in power.*" [77] When seeking the approval of a Senate Committee in January, 1939 to his appointment as Secretary of Commerce, Hopkins admitted that statement had been made; but pleaded a man's right to "one indiscretion." [78] For American Fabian Socialists, as for their comrades in Britain, power was the goal!

Harry Hopkins, who ultimately acquired a degree of personal power second only to the President's, began his career as a social settlement

[75] *Ibid.*, p. 5.
[76] Perkins, *op. cit.*, p. 128.
[77] Williams has been identified as a Communist before congressional committees; but denies this.
[78] Sherwood, *op. cit.*, p. 109.

worker at a salary of $5 per month—and disbursed over $5,000,000 during his first two hours as a Federal official.[79] With a kind of inverse snobbery, he liked to refer to himself as the son of an Iowa harness-maker; though the truth was, the elder Hopkins applied himself for only a few years to that fast-failing trade. While Harry was growing up the family subsisted mainly by selling candy, magazines, soft drinks and sundries to college boys from the nearby Grinnell campus.

As a student at Grinnell College, Hopkins was deeply influenced by two of his teachers, Dr. Edward A. Steiner and Professor Jesse Macy. Dr. Steiner, Austrian-born and a convert from Judaism, had once visited Leo Tolstoi in Russia and written a book about it. At Grinnell, Steiner occupied the chair of Applied Christianity endowed by Elizabeth Rand and held not many years before by Dr. George Herron, original chairman of the American Socialist Party. Professor Macy, who taught one of the first political science courses in America, had spent some time in England during the formative years of the London Fabian Society. He had imbibed its social and economic outlook and regaled his pupils at Grinnell with firsthand recollections of Sidney and Beatrice Webb.

After Hopkins' graduation, Steiner found an opening for the young man on the staff of a small social settlement house in New York. Though not much attracted to social work as a calling, Harry took the virtually unpaid job because it afforded him a chance to get to the big city.[80] Once there, he stayed and did what was expected of him, moving as rapidly as possible, however, into the administrative realm of organized charity. By 1924 he was Executive Director of the New York Tuberculosis and Health Association, which had built up a reserve of $90,000 and which Hopkins left with a deficit of $40,000.[81] His political leanings can be inferred from the fact that he voted the

[79] *Ibid.*, pp. 23; pp. 44-45.

[80] *Ibid.*, pp. 21-22.

[81] *Ibid.*, p. 27. (*Author's Note:* Hopkins remained some seven years with the New York Tuberculosis and Health Association. As late as September 8, 1932 (*ibid.*, p. 32) he wrote his brother, Lewis, that he was still being carried on the organization's staff. Robert Sherwood, Hopkins' biographer and friend, says (*ibid.*, p. 28) that Hopkins greatly increased the Association's income, principally through the sale of Christmas seals. Soon after Hopkins resigned, a letter from New York City Health Commissioner to *The New York Times* of June 8, 1932 stated that not one penny of the funds raised from the sale of Christmas seals ever went to the relief of a person with tuberculosis or to an institution for his care. It was subsequently charged that "all its money had been expended for salaries and overhead.")

Socialist Party ticket in 1917, and in 1924, like many Socialist intellectuals, went progressive with La Follette.[82]

During the summer of 1928, Hopkins took an expense-paid trip to London to study municipal health administration. This was a field long preempted by British Fabian Socialists operating through the London County Council, and his field trips inevitably brought Hopkins into touch with members of the Fabian Society. To his wife he wrote that he found the British program superior to anything in America. Hopkins' meteoric rise, that began soon after his return from England, is suggestive of the manner in which the London Society rewards its approved and faithful permeators. From the autumn of 1928, Hopkins came more and more to the attention of Governor Franklin D. Roosevelt's intimates, especially Eleanor Roosevelt,[83] interested as always in the social welfare approach to politics.

In 1931, the merchant prince Jesse I. Straus invited Hopkins to Albany to assist in administering a program of State unemployment relief. A year later Straus withdrew, leaving Hopkins in full charge. At Albany, as later in Washington, Hopkins introduced a species of work relief first suggested in this country by Father John A. Ryan in his so-called *Bishops' Report* and based on proposals made by a Quaker group in England after World War I. Actually, the idea of work relief for the unemployed had been developed in Britain at the turn of the century by Joseph I. Fels, the American soap magnate who joined the London Fabian Society. Fels' experiments were reported by the American Fabian Socialist, W. D. P. Bliss,[84] in his *New Encyclopedia of Social Reform in* 1908.

To win approval of New York labor organizations for his work relief scheme, Hopkins was obliged to work closely with Frances Perkins, Industrial Commissioner for the State. In less than two years he supervised expenditures of some 60 million dollars from bond issues, without scandal and with evident benefit to Roosevelt in the campaign of 1932. The new State relief agency received sympathetic press treatment from such Harvard alumni as Heywood

[82] *Ibid.*, p. 109.
[83] *Ibid.*, p. 30. (*Author's Note:* Hopkins' contact with Eleanor Roosevelt was initiated through Dr. John A. Kingsbury of the Association for Improving the Condition of the Poor, who had known Eleanor Roosevelt for years as a co-member of the Association for Labor Legislation. Dr. Kingsbury had befriended Hopkins from the time of the latter's arrival in New York and had employed him as an assistant. Hopkins subsequently took Dr. Kingsbury to Washington as one of his own assistants on WPA.)
[84] *Ibid.*, p. 148.

Broun, then a popular columnist on the New York *World* and always a warm friend of Hopkins.

Within a remarkably short time Hopkins had endeared himself permanently to Eleanor Roosevelt, who adopted him into the family and sponsored him in every future endeavor. Soon after being elected to the Presidency, FDR also received an exceptional commendation of Hopkins from Jane Addams, dean of social welfare workers in America. That is how a harness-maker's son from Iowa, with a private taste for high living, managed to get to Washington in May, 1933.

There he dispensed a total of nine billion dollars in direct Federal relief over five years, until new laws were finally written and the Works Project Administration was abolished. Though such sums have come to seem almost routine today, at that date they were rated astronomical. Hopkins' activities as Federal Relief Administrator won the unqualified approval of so ardent a Fabian Socialist as Stuart Chase, who observed hopefully that historians of the future might very well regard Harry Hopkins as one of the world's greatest administrators.[85]

While it lasted, the WPA was easily the most controversial agency in government, not only because of its informal bookkeeping methods, but because it became a sounding board for much radical propaganda of the period. That was the decade of the so-called Popular Front against Fascism, in which Socialists and Communists throughout the world collaborated openly. In 1934, the eminent British Fabian Socialist and pacifist, Sir Norman Angell,[86] visited Washington and toured the country as a member of "le comité mondiale contre la guerre et le fascisme," [87] the world-wide Popular Front organization headed by Henri Barbusse, renowned French novelist and identified Communist. Youth, professional and cultural groups were its special targets, and its success was conspicuous in branches of the WPA that catered to such groups.

Some critics were inclined to blame Hopkins' principal aide, Aubrey Williams for the fact that left wing agitators flourished on WPA time, notably in theater, motion picture, art and writers' projects. There is evidence, however, that Williams was encouraged by persons more

[85] Stuart Chase, *Rich Land, Poor Land,* (New York, McGraw-Hill, Inc., 1936), p. 328.

[86] *Fabian News,* (December, 1934).

[87] Sir Norman Angell, *After All: Autobiography of Sir Norman Angell,* (New York, Farrar, Straus and Young, 1951), p. 264.

highly placed than himself. Far from being reproved, he was made director of the National Youth Administration. In July, 1941, Williams joined Eleanor Roosevelt, Justice Felix Frankfurter and Librarian of Congress Archibald MacLeish in sponsoring the American Youth Congress at Campobello.[88] This congress was organized on the initiative of the British Fabian Socialist, Betty Shields-Collins, secretary of the London Fabian Society's Anglo-American group and prewar secretary of the World Youth Congress movement.[89] Prominent at the Campobello rally was the perennially youthful Joseph P. Lash—a particular pet of Eleanor Roosevelt—who had been a leader of the Student League for Industrial Democracy and had also confessed to Young Communist League affiliations.[90]

A dangerous by-product of the tolerance towards Communists which top-level American Fabian Socialists practiced as consistently as their British brethren, was disclosed some years later. After long and painstaking inquiry, the Senate Subcommittee on Internal Security concluded that the National Research Project of the WPA had served "as a kind of trapdoor through which underground Communists gained access to the Government" in the middle nineteen-thirties.[91] A number of individuals since identified as Communist agents entered the Federal service through that handy trapdoor, some rising to posts of major responsibility under the Roosevelt and Truman Administrations. Transferring from department to department by a kind of mutual aid agreement with like-minded colleagues, they were not only able to supply information but also to affect the policies of government itself.[92]

Eleven persons linked with Communist spy rings were discovered by the Senate Subcommittee on Internal Security to have entered the

---

[88] Perkins, *op. cit.*, p. 110. (Illustration.)

[89] *Fabian News*, (November, 1941). In this issue it was announced that Betty Shields-Collins, just returned from America, would lecture November 17 at an International Affairs Group "snack luncheon meeting" on "The U.S.A. and the U.S.S.R." She was described as "General Secretary to the World Youth Congress Movement until the outbreak of war; has visited America both before the war and since; is secretary to the Society's Anglo-American group; organized the recent International Youth Rally."

[90] Martin Dies, *The Martin Dies Story*, (New York, The Bookmailer, 1963), pp. 150-151.

[91] *Interlocking Subversion in Government Departments, Report and Hearings of the Subcommittee on Internal Security of the Committee on the Judiciary.* U.S. Senate, 83rd Congress, (Washington, U.S. Government Printing Office, 1953-54), p. 10.

[92] *Ibid.*, pp. 10-14 ff.

Federal Government via the WPA. An overall total of eighty persons in Federal service, thirty-seven of whom attained posts of high importance, were unmasked by the Subcommittee as connected with Communist spy rings. All were directly or indirectly linked with the group in the WPA. It has since been confirmed that appropriate authorities, up to and including the White House itself, were duly apprised of the facts by the Federal Bureau of Investigation; but continued to protect and promote the offenders.[93] As a result, a small but well-placed network of covert Communists in Federal service enjoyed a field day which lasted for years, rifling the most secret files with impunity and "sharing all that we have and are"[94] with Soviet Russia.

Incredible as it seems, the lenience that made such things possible originated at the uppermost level of government. Franklin Roosevelt's personal attitude was revealed when he ignored repeated warnings from FBI and other sources concerning Communists in the U.S. Government. In 1942, in wartime, he blocked removal from merchant ships of radio operators "whose only offense was in being Communist."[95] The President's stand was officially conveyed by Secretary of the Navy, Frank Knox, at a meeting with naval officers on May 19, 1942. According to the minutes of that meeting:

. . . The Secretary then spoke and said that he held no brief for the activities of the Communist Party; but that the President had stated that, considering the fact that the United States and Russia were allies at this time and that the Communist Party and the United States efforts were now bent towards winning the war, *the United States was bound not to disapprove the activities of the Communist Party, and specifically not to disapprove the employment of any radio operator for the sole reason that he was a member of the Communist Party or that he was active in Communist Party affairs.* The Secretary further stated that this was an order and must be obeyed without mental reservations.[96]

Soon afterwards a Naval Intelligence Unit in New York City, set up to control Communist espionage and propaganda, was dissolved

[93] Associated Press dispatch, November 6, 1953. Chicago speech by Attorney General Herbert Brownell. (See also testimony of J. Edgar Hoover before Senate Subcommittee on Internal Security, November 17, 1953.)

[94] *The New York Times*, (June 23, 1942). This phrase is from a speech delivered by Harry Hopkins at a Russian Aid Rally in Madison Square Garden, June 22.

[95] Robert Morris, *No Wonder We Are Losing*, (New York, The Bookmailer, Eighth Edition, 1961), pp. 38-45. Memorandum for the Secretary of the Navy, signed FDR, quoted on p. 41.

[96] *Ibid.*, pp. 43-44. (Italics added.)

by the Bureau of the Budget,[97] which had been transferred from the Treasury to the White House by an historic Executive Order of 1939. Instructions were issued requiring Army Intelligence to destroy its files on Communists, similar to the demand made by Woodrow Wilson after World War I. Only prompt action by members of Congress saved the Army records from destruction in World War II.

If some members of Roosevelt's wartime Cabinet held no brief for the Presidential policy of being kind to Communists, and if most government officials were either unaware of it or accepted it with mental reservations, the same could not be said for the President's more intimate circle. FDR's strict concept of personal loyalty required that any individual whom he fully trusted must see eye to eye with him on matters he considered basic. And once having adopted an idea, he regarded it as peculiarly his own, often forgetting the source from which it came.

Roosevelt believed, for instance, that by giving Stalin everything he asked for during the war, no matter how excessive the request, the proletarian dictator would be bound by some principle of *noblesse oblige* to cooperate loyally in setting up a postwar world of peace and plenty. How did FDR know this? He had a hunch! And besides, Harry "The Hop" Hopkins had told him so.[98]

This is not to say that Roosevelt was himself a Communist, as has sometimes been loosely suggested. Having been trained and dominated for a good many years by Fabian Socialist advisers, perhaps he simply demonstrated the same protective attitude towards Soviet Russia and its agents as did those British Fabians whose road in the end has always led toward Moscow. Only convinced Fabian Socialists and liberals at the very pinnacle of political power in Washington could do for the Soviet Communists what they were unable to do for themselves, both at home and abroad.

Hitler's invasion of Russia on June 22, 1941 had aroused intense but mixed emotions among Anglo-American Fabians. If it restored fraternal bonds previously strained by the Stalin-Hitler pact, the joy of feeling together again[99] was shadowed by anxiety for the future of the Soviet Union. As usual, American liberals and progressives, who

[97] *Ibid.*, pp. 45-46.
[98] *Life* magazine, (June 30, 1949). Report of conversation with FDR by former Ambassador to Moscow, William C. Bullitt.
[99] Margaret Cole, *The Story of Fabian Socialism*, (London, Heinemann Educational Books, Ltd., 1961), p. 270.

shunned the Socialist name while faithfully playing the game, echoed the sentiments of their British tutors with a special urgency of their own. They could hardly wait to pour out the products of American industry and skill in defense of the threatened Socialist Fatherland.

On July 27, FDR dispatched Hopkins as his confidential messenger to Stalin with an immediate offer of Lend-Lease aid, even though Soviet Russia was not yet an Ally of the United States. At that time public opinion in America was strongly opposed to this country's entering the war, and few persons outside the President's official family realized the extent of his private commitments, not only to Churchill but also to Stalin. Less than a year before, Roosevelt had won election for the third time by virtue of his promise to the mothers and fathers of America: "I am not going to send your sons into any foreign war." That meant he could not ask the Congress to declare war against the Axis powers, *unless the United States were attacked.* In such case, as FDR pointed out to intimates, it would no longer be a "foreign" war!

Hard upon Hitler's invasion of Russia, the New Deal Administration proceeded to exert such diplomatic pressure on Japan as could hardly fail to provoke an open breach. It is interesting to find that Vice President Henry Wallace, by then an outspoken friend of Soviet Russia, took the initiative of writing to his Chief: "I do hope, Mr. President, you will go to the absolute limit in your firmness in dealing with Japan." [100] By November, 1941, if not before, it was apparent to such informed persons as Harry Hopkins that war in the Pacific would come at the convenience of the Japanese[101]—the only question being where and when. Soviet Russia, it has since been learned from captured Japanese police records, thoughtfully arranged to help bring about the required incident.

Through the intrigues of a Dr. Richard Sorge, Red Army Intelligence operative, Japanese militarists were persuaded, during the summer and fall of 1941, to strike southward at American, French, Dutch and British possessions, instead of northward at Soviet territory.[102] Sorge, a German citizen but a member of the Russian Com-

[100] Robert E. Sherwood, *Roosevelt and Hopkins*, (New York, Harper and Brothers, 1948, 1950), p. 357. Letter from Wallace to FDR.

[101] *Ibid.*, pp. 426-427. Testimony of Commander L. R. Schulz to Joint Committee on the Investigation of Pearl Harbor.

[102] Cf. *The Sorge Spy Ring.* Section of CIS Periodical Summary No. 23, December 15, 1947, Department of the Army, (Washington, U.S. Government Printing Office).

munist Party,[103] had managed to entrench himself as press attaché at the Nazi Embassy in Tokyo. Because his nine-year old spy ring also had contacts with influential and high-ranking Japanese, he succeeded in engineering the desired coup.

On October 15, just a day or two before his arrest in a general police roundup, Sorge was able to radio Moscow that his mission had been accomplished and that Japan would strike to the South. The blow fell at Pearl Harbor on December 7. More than two thousand Americans lost their lives, the U.S. Pacific Fleet was crippled, and the United States became an Ally of Soviet Russia.

Thereafter aid unlimited would flow from America to the Workers' Fatherland. In a letter of March 7, 1942 to United States war agencies, Roosevelt ordered that priority in munitions be given to the Russians above all other Allies and even above the armed services of the United States. Technically, the Lend-Lease Act of 1941 had stipulated that war matériel could only be sent abroad if the Army and Navy Chiefs of Staff certified it was not required for American military forces. This posed no problem, however, for the Commander-in-chief or his personal Lend-Lease representative, Harry Hopkins. According to Hopkins' biographer, General George C. Marshall expressed the belief that he originally owed his appointment as Army Chief of Staff to Harry Hopkins.[104]

From beginning to end, it was Hopkins to whom Roosevelt entrusted the task of dispensing weapons, equipment, machinery and raw materials to our overseas Allies on a scale never seen before in history. Comparatively, the amounts that had been expended on the WPA were mere small change. Under the impetus of the war emergency, 60 billion dollars worth of assorted supplies were freely given away, with little if any ever refunded or expected to be. "Let's forget the silly, foolish old dollar sign!" President Roosevelt gaily told the American people in one of his more famous "fireside chats."

Of the total, a recorded 11 billion dollars went to Soviet Russia, though the real value has never been accurately assessed. Such munificence not only insured the salvation of the Bolshevik Government, whose pact with Adolf Hitler had touched off World War II. It also

[103] *Ibid.*, (Sorge's sponsors to the Russian Communist Party included Dimitri Z. Manuilsky, member of the Central Committee of the Communist Party of the Soviet Union, and more recently a representative to the United Nations from the Ukraine.)

[104] Sherwood, *op. cit.*, p. 101.

made possible those secret postwar stockpiles[105] which enabled the Red Army to annex its Baltic and Balkan neighbors as well as Hungary, Poland, Czechoslovakia and East Germany in the years immediately following World War II.

By contrast, only a trickle of warplanes went to Chiang Kai-shek's China, ostensibly an Ally, whom we should aid, at a time when the capital, Chungking, was being bombed daily, on a twelve-hour schedule. Of the matériel that did reach Chiang Kai-shek, some lacked spare parts and some was unfit for combat use.[106] Hopkins never found time to get to Chungking himself, though he made several trips under almost equally hazardous conditions to London and Moscow. For the most part, he left the mangled details of China aid to his assistant, Lauchlin Currie—later named by Elizabeth Bentley testifying before the Senate Subcommittee on Internal Security as a "full-fledged member of the Silvermaster [Communist] group" [107] and a prime collaborator of wartime Soviet espionage groups in Washington.

As the undisputed czar of Lend-Lease, operating sometimes with and sometimes without portfolio, Hopkins was in his element. Temperamentally, there was nothing he enjoyed more than spending money, and no one ever had more to spend. Caring little for titles or personal wealth, he was entranced by the perquisites and the sense of power—a point of view that he seems to have shared with many Socialist and Communist leaders.

Warned by the experience of an earlier White House confidant, Colonel House, Hopkins was careful not to overplay his hand. Prudently he described himself as no more than an office boy, and he displayed such intense devotion to the President that newsmen remarked that Hopkins would have jumped off the Washington Monument if FDR had happened to suggest it. Yet in the area of wartime produc-

---

[105] *Hearings Regarding Shipments of Atomic Materials to the Soviet Union During World War II,* House of Representatives Committee on Un-American Activities, (Washington, 1950), U.S. Government Printing Office, pp. 947-950. Testimony of Major General Leslie R. Groves, "I am sure," said General Groves, "if you would check on the pressure on officers handling all supplies of a military nature during the war, you will find the pressure to give to Russia everything that could be given was not limited to atomic matters . . . . That particular plant was oil refinery equipment, and in my opinion was purely postwar Russian supply, as you know much of it was."

[106] Sherwood, *op. cit.,* p. 406 ff.

[107] *Interlocking Subversion in Government Departments. Report and Hearings of the Subcommittee on Internal Security of the Committee on the Judiciary,* U.S. Senate, 83rd Congress, (Washington, U.S. Government Printing Office, 1953, 1954).

tion and distribution, Harry Hopkins was in effect the Deputy President of the United States, a function quite unforeseen by the framers of the Constitution.

In matters of the gravest consequence, he was both intermediary and adviser to the President, making his headquarters at the Executive Mansion and actually residing for several years in the Lincoln bedroom. Chronically ill with a nutritional ailment following an operation for stomach cancer, Hopkins summoned from some mysterious reserve the energy to serve as expediter and hidden persuader for the duration of the war.

Besides the ever present Dr. Isadore Lubin, Hopkins' own preferred aides included Leon Henderson of the Office of Price Administration and Sidney Hillman and Robert Nathan of the Office of Production Management.[108] Of these, Lubin and Hillman were long time officers of the (Fabian Socialist) LID; while Henderson became a founding member of the postwar Americans for Democratic Action.

At the American Embassy in London, where John Winant reigned and Benjamin V. Cohen acted as wartime counsel, Hopkins could fraternize unseen with top British Fabian Socialists, among them Herbert Morrison, Home Secretary and Minister of Home Security in Churchill's coalition Cabinet.[109] As early as 1940, Hopkins had written to Roosevelt, "We must marshal our complete economic strength for the task of defense," adding in approved Fabian Socialist vein: "This means that instead of retreating from our social and economic objectives, we should push forward vigorously to *abolish poverty* from the land." [110]

It was through Hopkins that the apparently nonpolitical Dr. Vannevar Bush, then Dean of Engineering at Massachusetts Institute of Technology, felt constrained to submit his now famous memorandum to the President on new weapons research, notably in the field of atomic fission. Together with Hopkins, Dr. Bush prepared a letter of authorization for FDR's signature, setting up the organization that led to development of the atom bomb. In conversations at Casablanca during January, 1943, Winston Churchill discussed atomic matters with Roosevelt in Hopkins' presence. A month later Churchill initiated

[108] Sherwood, *op. cit.*, p. 287.
[109] *Ibid.*, p. 351. In 1941 Hopkins wrote a cordial note to Herbert Morrison: "I have your tin hat for La Guardia and shall give it to him with your warmest greetings. I much regretted not seeing you and having a discussion over a high-ball. We shall do that yet."
[110] *Ibid.*, p. 180. (Italics added.)

a lengthy cable correspondence on the subject with Hopkins. The Prime Minister protested because the United States had suddenly ceased pooling information on atomic research with its British Ally.[111]

The reason was that in December, 1942, at a secret laboratory located under the stands of the University of Chicago's Stagg Field, a team of American scientists had finally succeeded in splitting the atom. At this point the project moved from the research stage into the field of weapon design and construction, under control of the War Department. Dr. Bush spelled out the revised information policy in a memorandum of March 31 to Hopkins, which concluded: "To step beyond it would mean to furnish information on secret military matters to individuals who wish it either because of general interest or because of its application to non-war or postwar matters. To do so would decrease security without advancing the war effort." [112]

Clearly, Hopkins was one of a very few persons who were conversant from the start with the atom bomb project in America. He was also precisely informed on the policy called for by military security. If he chose to ignore or override such precautions, it could only be attributed either to an incurable lightness of mind or a well developed tendency to favor other interests above those of the United States.

Not until late in 1949 was it definitely proved, on the strength of reliable records and equally reliable United States Army witnesses, that wartime Federal agencies had shipped to Soviet Russia rare chemicals and minerals suitable for use in atomic research, along with miles of alloy tubing and pipe that could be used in construction of an atomic pile. At least three-quarters of a ton of uranium chemicals were found to have been delivered through Lend-Lease channels to Russia in March and June, 1943, and in June, 1944. It was further confirmed that 2.2 pounds of pure uranium was sent from this country to the Soviet Union at a moment when the entire American stock amounted to 4.5 pounds.[113]

Such forbidden items could not possibly have moved through the Lend-Lease pipeline without official United States certificates of release,[114] issued by order of Harry Hopkins. Responsible testimony

---

[111] *Ibid.*, pp. 154-155; 703-704.

[112] *Ibid.*, p. 704.

[113] *Hearings Regarding Shipments of Atomic Materials to the Soviet Union During World War II.* Testimony of Major George Racey Jordan, pp. 930 ff.

[114] *Ibid.*, p. 90. Major General Leslie R. Groves, in charge of the Manhattan Project, stated there was no way for the Russians to have gotten uranium prod-

was given to a committee of Congress indicating that Hopkins was not merely aware of these transactions but took a keen interest in pushing them through. In March, 1943, when information on atomic matters was apparently being withheld from Churchill, an official but apparently purloined map of the Oak Ridge atomic plant and a report on details of its construction went forward to Russia by plane via Great Falls, Montana. Clipped to the documents was a covering letter on White House stationery, signed simply H. H. and addressed to A. I. Mikoyan, then Soviet Deputy of Foreign Trade in charge of Lend-Lease at the receiving end.[115] Here was the supreme example of what Soviet Purchasing Commission employees in New York referred to ironically as Super-Lend-Lease!

The Fabian face cards in the New Deal have been exposed. For the first time in history a program of gradualist Socialism, backed by political power and perpetuated by every trick of applied psychology, was put into effect. Instigated by the foremost brains of the London Society, it was implemented by Fabian Socialist intellectuals and welfare workers in the United States who used many well-meaning or accommodating citizens as unconscious tools. Above all, its leaders had access to the apparently limitless industrial and financial resources of the greatest capitalist nation on earth. Thus the Fabian Socialist movements in America and England moved into a new phase, in which nomenclature did not matter and where dealings between governments were manipulated on instructions from International Socialists in London. Without the combined efforts of highly placed Fabian Socialists both in England and America, the apparently uneasy but none the less recurrent coalition of the Second and Third Internationals could never have come about.

---

ucts in this country "without the support of U.S. authorities in one way or another."

[115] *Ibid.*, p. 930 ff. Testimony of Major Jordan.

18

Secret Weaponry

1.

THERE was another secret weapon valued more highly than the atom bomb by Anglo-American Fabians of the New Deal era. Namely, the university professor, who, as the British Fabian Socialist philosopher, John Atkinson Hobson, had suggested was to be the future secret weapon of national strategy. A familiar of Justice Louis D. Brandeis and of the latter's protégé, Felix Frankfurter, Hobson merely pointed up a trend that had been gaining momentum in America since the turn of the century. With the Roosevelt Administration, the liberal-to-Left professor moved into his prescribed orbit as the planner and guide of national policies based on Fabian research, which officials and politicians would trigger.

A trio of university professors played a major part in shaping the seemingly impromptu social, fiscal, legal and diplomatic strategy of the Roosevelt Administration and other Democrat administrations to follow. Two were British nationals, closely identified with the Fabian Society of London. The third was an American citizen of European origin who had helped to found organizations in this country known to be affiliates of the (Fabian Socialist) League for Industrial Democracy,[1] and who had been rebuked by former President Theodore Roosevelt, for his radical bias, as displayed in a government report.

---

[1] Frankfurter was a founder and director of the American Civil Liberties Union; a legal counsel for the NAACP. He was also one of the original stockholders and contributors of the *New Republic* and a member of the board of Survey Associates, publishers of *Survey Graphic*. Helen Shirley Thomas, *Felix Frankfurter: Scholar on the Bench*, (Baltimore, Johns Hopkins University Press, 1960), p. 21.

All three were equally at home in the lecture halls of England and the United States; and though they held forth in many localities, all left a particular imprint on Harvard University. They were brilliant conversationalists, tireless letter writers and mental gymnasts of the first order, with a talent for gaining the ear of important persons and a calculated appeal to youth that has caused their influence to outlast their times. Their names were Felix Frankfurter, Harold J. Laski and John Maynard Keynes.

It has been admitted by New Deal insiders that FDR privately agreed, more than a year before becoming President, to sponsor the Tennessee Valley Authority project; the Agricultural Adjustment, Public Works and Conservation programs; Securities Exchange and Holding Company control; and something resembling the National Recovery Act.[2] He had also agreed to sponsor a system of social insurance leading to the welfare state.[3] If no hint of those intentions appeared in the Democratic Party platform of 1932, only the public was surprised by the rapid-fire developments following Roosevelt's accession to power. The original brain trusters, who trailed him from Albany to Washington, knew what to expect. Their immediate problem was to discover ways of writing the new program of encroaching Socialism into law.

For that purpose it seemed natural to turn to Felix Frankfurter, Byrnes Professor of Law at Harvard University, whose specialty was administrative law. Preeminent among FDR brain trusters, he was a tiny figure of a man, with a large head and keen, dark eyes behind gleaming spectacles. Endowed with exceptional brainpower and adroitness, he had championed many Socialist-approved causes at the intellectual level without ever descending into the pit of Socialist Party politics.

Born in Vienna, Felix was brought to New York City by his parents at the age of twelve, speaking only German and Hungarian. By the time he was nineteen he had mastered the English language and graduated third in his class from the City College of New York. In 1906 he took his law degree at Harvard University, tutoring less talented students to help pay expenses. That was the year when the Intercollegiate Socialist Society founded a club at Harvard, with

[2] Robert Sherwood, *Roosevelt and Hopkins*, (New York, Harper & Brothers, 1948), p. 47-48.
[3] *Ibid.*, p. 47.

Walter Lippmann as president. According to Lippmann's biographer, in 1909 Frankfurter often joined the club members for happy, discursive weekends at the Chestnut Hill home of Dr. Ralph Albertson, a leading Christian Socialist of the day.[4] Characteristically, Felix Frankfurter was never named as having been a member of the club in anniversary speeches and publications of the LID.

Only a few years later, however, he was intimately associated with Walter Lippmann as a co-founder of the *New Republic*—the liberal weekly designed as an American opposite number of the British Fabian Socialist *New Statesman*. In that capacity, Frankfurter made the acquaintance of the chief stockholder of the *New Republic*, Dorothy Whitney Straight, who married Leonard K. Elmhirst and moved to England in 1925. As Mrs. Elmhirst, she helped to endow a Fabian Socialist-sponsored front organization in England called Political and Economic Planning or PEP, which was organized as a "charitable trust" in 1931 and helped to devise plans for the New Deal in advance of FDR's election.

Between 1916 and 1922 Frankfurter filed briefs in several important cases involving hours of labor and minimum wages. He gave legal advice in the famous Scopes trial defended by the Socialist attorney, Clarence Darrow; in the 1926 case of the Patterson, New Jersey silk mill strikers; and in the still more controversial Sacco and Vanzetti appeals of 1927. Frankfurter used, advocated and taught the technique initiated by Justice Louis D. Brandeis before the latter's ascension to the Supreme Court. Known as the Brandeis Brief, it involved amassing a volume of factual, historical and/or pseudo-philosophic material and presenting it with the shortest possible legal argument. Prudently, Frankfurter disclaimed any strict adherence to Brandeis' sociological approach to the Law, leaving that reputation to his colleague and bosom friend, Dean Roscoe Pound of Harvard Law School.

Instead, he professed a deep concern for procedural regularity, a difficult point with which to take issue. By invoking the Olympian names of Brandeis and Holmes as often as possible and discoursing in the loftiest philosophic vein, he almost succeeded in diverting attention from his own radical associations and purposes. Yet, as late as 1930, Frankfurter wrote that *through the use of due process the*

[4] David Elliot Weingast, *Walter Lippmann* (*A Study in Personal Journalism*), (New Brunswick, Rutgers Press, 1949), p. 10.

justices could read their own economic and social views into the neutral language of the Constitution.[5] As a Supreme Court Justice, he was to lean heavily on the same due process clause precisely because of its flexibility, proclaiming it "the most majestic concept in our whole constitutional system." [6]

Although he lacked practical experience in drafting legislation, for years Frankfurter had advised his students to familiarize themselves with the legislative process. With their assistance he duly became the legal progenitor of the New Deal. At FDR's request, Frankfurter supplied his own handpicked former students for every key legal post in the new Administration so that he controlled, in effect, both the writing and interpretation of the new legislative measures. It almost seemed as if he had been preparing for such a contingency ever since his appointment to the Harvard Law faculty in 1914, and when the moment came, he was ready.

Believing that the past is prologue and that changes in juristic concepts must be initiated through the law schools, Frankfurter had always selected his pupils with care. His classes, according to the Harvard University catalogue, were "open only to students of high standing with the consent of the instructor." The most promising were invited on Sunday evenings to the Frankfurter cottage on Brattle Street for extracurricular discussions on law and life. For the chosen few, Frankfurter's supervision went far beyond the classroom and into their future careers.

Each year two honor graduates of Harvard Law School had been assigned, largely on Frankfurter's recommendation, as secretaries to the liberal Supreme Court Justices, Louis D. Brandeis and Oliver Wendell Holmes. In 1933, at least eight of those erstwhile prodigies quickly became prominent in the New Deal Administration. Brandeis' former secretaries included Dean G. Acheson, who served briefly as Roosevelt's Under Secretary of the Treasury and at Frankfurter's urging was later installed in the State Department; James M. Landis, Federal Trade Commissioner and co-author, with Benjamin V. Cohen, Thomas G. Corcoran and Frankfurter himself, of the Securities and Exchange Act; William Sutherland, counsel to the Tennessee Valley

---

[5] Felix Frankfurter, "The Supreme Court and the Public," *Forum* magazine, (June, 1930), pp. 332-333. (Italics added.)

[6] *Joint Anti-Fascist Refugee Committee vs. McGrath,* 341 U.S. 123, 174 (1951). The Joint Anti-Fascist Refugee Committee is cited on the Attorney General's list of subversive organizations.

Authority; and Paul Freund, a lawyer in the Reconstruction Finance Corporation, who returned to teach at Harvard. Holmes' former secretaries accounted for Thomas G. Corcoran of the RFC; Lloyd Landau and Donald Hiss of the Public Works Administration; and Alger Hiss of the Agricultural Adjustment Administration, who went on to the State Department, the Carnegie Foundation—and ultimate disgrace. All were Frankfurter's "boys."

When the Tennessee Valley Authority was set up and needed an executive who was also a clever lawyer, Frankfurter produced David Lilienthal, whom he had previously placed with Wisconsin's utilities control commission in training for just such a job.[7] To Agriculture, Frankfurter sent the aggressively liberal Jerome L. Frank; to Interior, he sent Nathan R. Margold; and to Labor, he sent Charles E. Wyzanski, Jr., more recently a trustee of the Ford Foundation and a member of the Council on Foreign Relations. In those days it was said—apparently with good reason—that no New Deal department nor agency would hire a lawyer unless he was on Frankfurter's "White List."

The professor's influence, however, was not limited to supervising legislation and selecting legal personnel. He was consulted on every major administrative move and Presidential statement. For some six or eight months after Roosevelt took office, Frankfurter commuted each week to Washington from Cambridge, Massachusetts. The White House door was regularly open to him, and no official doors were closed. Within the first "hundred days" most of the basic New Deal legislation had been written and passed—a task that would clearly have been impossible in so short a time if not partially mapped out in advance.

With America's first Socialist-inspired government program staffed and operating, Frankfurter left to spend a year as visiting professor at Oxford University in 1933-34—an invitation conveniently arranged by Fabian admirers in England. His parting words to exuberant New Dealers reflected the mood of the Fabian tortoise. "Go slowly," he warned, "go slowly." In particular, Frankfurter advised *delaying as long as possible* a Court test of the National Recovery Act, whose constitutionality he doubted. This was strange advice from a man whose

---

[7] Frankfurter's personal interest in public ownership of public utilities dated from 1914, when he was a member of the board of trustees of the National Bureau of Public Utilities Research.

own highest ambition was to sit on the Supreme Court, and on any grounds of principle the advice seems hard to justify.[8]

By a telltale coincidence, Frankfurter's words were echoed before the year was out by a minor British financier, Israel M. Sieff, long regarded as one of the Fabian Society's more able permeaters. On May 3, 1934, Congressman Louis T. McFadden of Pennsylvania told the U.S. House of Representatives that a certain Israel Moses Sieff of London, England had recently declared in a public speech: "Let us *go slowly* for a while, until we can see how our plan works out in America." [9] Sieff belonged to the British organization, Political and Economic Planning or PEP, *and the plan to which he referred was the New Deal.* Why on earth, the Congressman wondered, should a British national living in London refer to the New Deal as "our plan"? Unintentionally, Sieff had revealed a relationship between Fabian Socialist planners in England and in the United States.

Political and Economic Planning (PEP), of which Sieff was a founder, sponsored social, industrial and political "studies," apparently with a view to influencing official action as well as "opinion-forming" groups. Some of its findings were eventually published and some were not. Its method of work, which has never varied, was described in a prospectus, *About P.E.P.*, distributed in 1956 by the organization itself:

The method of work is to bring together as a group a number of people who are concerned professionally with one or another aspect of the problem under discussion, as well as a few non-specialists who can ask the fundamental questions which sometimes escape the experts. This technique enables P.E.P. to bring to bear on a problem the combined experience of men and women working in different spheres including *business, politics, the Government and local authority services, and the universities.* The groups are assisted by *a paid research staff, who act as their secretaries and drafters. The names of those who form the groups are not disclosed* and the results of their work are published on the authority of the organisation as a whole. *This rule was adopted deliberately from the first* and has proved of great value. *It enables people to serve who would not otherwise be able to do so;* it ensures that members can contribute freely to discussion without being bound by the official views of any body with which they may be identified . . . .

For the convenience of working members, a club was also formed in 1931 with rooms in the building at Queen Anne's Gate. The P.E.P. Trust and

[8] Thomas, *op. cit.*, p. 29.
[9] *Congressional Record*, House of Representatives, (May 3, 1934), pp. 8042-43. (Italics added.)

the P.E.P. Club are separate institutions, although there is naturally a large common membership . . . . As regards the subjects for study, the Council of Management tries to pick those which seem likely to have reached the forefront of public discussion at about the time when the work has been completed and the findings published . . . . The aim throughout has been to maintain a balanced programme of social, industrial and general economic studies, chiefly in order that the work of particular groups may be guided by an understanding of national needs and resources as a whole.

. . . income is derived in roughly equal proportions from donations (given mainly by firms in industry and commerce); subscriptions to the broadsheets; grants from educational foundations. Many of the donations are made under covenant, thus enabling P.E.P. to claim refund of income tax paid by the donors.[10]

The rule of secrecy, governing the activities of PEP from the start, not only concealed its sources of inspiration, but allowed American planners to participate without attracting any special notice. It also made possible an exchange of ideas and personnel with the New Fabian Research Bureau, which was organized at about the same time. Prominent members of the organization over the years have included Sir Julian Huxley, Israel Sieff, E. M. Nicholson, Kenneth Lindsay, Thomas Jones, Jack Pritchard, A. D. K. Owen, Richard Bailey, J. B. Priestley—all identified more or less intimately with the Fabian Society, which by its own definition "consists of Socialists."

One of PEP's first and most faithful donors was the American-born Dorothy Elmhirst, whose British spouse was to serve from 1939 to 1953 as director of the organization. At her Devonshire estate, Dorothy Elmhirst welcomed Professor Felix Frankfurter, who had visited her on Long Island with Herbert Croly during the formative days of the *New Republic*. Frankfurter was greeted no less warmly in 1933-1934 by his roommate of World War I years in Washington, Lord Eustace Percy, as well as by old friends at the *New Statesman*, the London School of Economics and the New Fabian Research Bureau. All exemplified for Frankfurter "those civilized standards of English-speaking people" which he was so eager to apply in America.

Political and Economic Planning was evidently conceived as a polite transmission belt for ideas and plans originating in the New Fabian Research Bureau. That is not to say its membership or donors' lists were 100 per cent Fabian. On the contrary, a number of honestly liberal or conservative business firms and individuals were persuaded, at one time or another, to lend their names and to contribute funds

---

[10] (Italics added.)

to PEP projects. Whether they hoped to improve their own public image or were merely seeking information, they were charmed by the urbane manner, discreet privacy and studious pretensions of Political and Economic Planning. While their presence lent weight to PEP pronouncements, such persons still remained outsiders. They had little to do with selecting the subjects for survey, and no voice in the conclusions reached. For all practical purposes, the internal operations of the group were controlled by the Management Council and the permanent, paid office staff.

Political and Economic Planning was one of the earliest Fabian Socialist front organizations to employ the device of bringing together business men, public officials and professional intellectuals for planning and propaganda purposes. A forerunner of that mixed society which was to effect a "humane" transition to Socialism, the organization served the Fabians as an instrument of peaceful permeation and penetration, both in government and private industry. Its initial object was to secure coordination between Socialist planners in the United States and the United Kingdom, leaving emulation on an Empire-wide scale to come later.

A PEP document issued in 1931, under the title *Freedom and Planning*, had recommended setting up National Councils in Agriculture, Transport and Coal Mining—resembling the industry-wide councils afterwards set up in the United States under the National Recovery Act. The manufacturer was to be regulated through national planning. Waste in distribution was to be eliminated through a system of department and grocery store chains. The individual farmer would be told just what and how much he could plant. Large tracts of land were to be acquired by the Government, and publicly-owned electric power plants were to be administered by a government utilities trust. It was such recommendations, contained in PEP's *Freedom and Planning*, that obviously emboldened Israel M. Sieff to refer to the New Deal as "our plan."

Both in form and method of work, Political and Economic Planning was a pilot organization. Aside from the influence it boasted of exerting on the architects of the New Deal, the organization also became the model for a whole series of similar and related organizations in this country which by now have acquired almost mystic prestige. Some of the group's present-day American offshoots specialize in economic and social studies; some in foreign affairs; some in world government schemes. All aim to affect national policy and to shape public opinion, while remaining immune from public control.

An immediate American counterpart of PEP was the National Planning Association, quietly reorganized in 1934 after Felix Frankfurter's return to the United States. The new organization was reputedly financed by grace of Dorothy Elmhirst. It included New Deal officials, trade union leaders, business men and publicists, with a solid core of League for Industrial Democracy regulars.[11] Israel M. Sieff kept in touch during frequent trips to America. Sometimes he was accompanied by Leonard K. Elmhirst long time chairman of PEP.[12] A lineal descendant of both PEP and the National Planning Association is the Committee for Economic Development founded in 1941.

The National Recovery Act was duly declared unconstitutional in 1935 by unanimous decision of the Supreme Court. The Bituminous Coal, Agricultural Adjustment and National Labor Relations Acts suffered a similar fate by majority vote. A fresh legislative approach to the question of planned Federal control over industry and agriculture was urgently needed to salvage the main features of the New Deal program. It was supplied through the novel application of a provision in the Constitution empowering the Federal Government to regulate interstate commerce: an application that in its manifold effects is a far cry from any intention entertained by the Signers.

For this ingenious advice, FDR was obligated to Felix Frankfurter who continued to make himself available in a supernumerary capacity. Somewhat against his own better judgment, the little law professor also supported Roosevelt's ill-fated attempt to pack the Supreme Court —though Frankfurter felt that time and new appointments could be depended upon to provide justices more nearly subservient to the Executive will. For service rendered, he was finally rewarded in 1938 with the fulfillment of his heart's desire: a seat on the Supreme Court.

In that sheltered eminence Frankfurter could enjoy the prerogatives

[11] Among those who have been named as members of the National Planning Association were: Frank Altschul, Chester Bowles, James Carey, Harry Carman, Norman Cousins, Felix Frankfurter, A. J. Hayes, Eric Johnston, Laird Bell, James G. Patton, Walter Reuther, Elmo Roper, Beardsley Ruml, H. Christian Sonne, Clarence E. Pickett, Wayne C. Taylor, L. S. Buckmaster, Harry A. Bullis, J. D. Zellerbach, Jacob Panken, Randolph S. Paul, George Soule. Many of these individuals later joined the Committee for Economic Development.

[12] Elizabeth Edwards, *The Planners and Bureaucracy*, (Liverpool, K. R. P. Publications, no date), p. 22. From internal evidence, this pamphlet appears to have been written in the middle nineteen-forties.

for which he had apparently yearned. Making some obvious concessions to the traditional aloofness of the Supreme Court, he appeared
less frequently at the White House and proffered less direct advice;
but when he did speak, he was listened to! [13] It was on Frankfurter's
recommendation that FDR dispatched Harry Hopkins to England
even before the Lend-Lease Act had been passed.[14] And it was invariably Frankfurter who took a final, critical look at President Roosevelt's major policy speeches and "fireside chats" before they were delivered. Frankfurter's lifelong friendship and daily morning strolls
with his Georgetown neighbor, Dean Acheson, whose rise in the State
Department hierarchy he sponsored, are credited with having had a
profound effect on American foreign policy—especially during those
years when Presidents Roosevelt and Truman were delivering the
hegemony of a large portion of the globe to Soviet Russia and Communist China.

Officially, the Supreme Court remained Frankfurter's prime field of
concentration until his retirement in 1961—as it had been the chief
subject of his studies and published articles prior to his elevation to
the Supreme Court. During his tenure, the quality and temper of that
once-august body altered visibly, and its "law-making" function was
emphasized at the expense of the legislative power of the Congress.
Though Frankfurter's role was conveniently veiled by the secrecy governing the Supreme Court's deliberations, it has been a potent one.
There he could contribute obliquely, whether by his own action or his
influence on less learned colleagues, to the gradual decline of that
separation of powers inherent in the Constitution, which has been
recognized since 1898 by British Fabians as the most serious obstacle
to the advance of Socialism in America.

2.

Among the self-proclaimed liberals and progressives clustered
around FDR, most of whom dissembled their Socialist purpose for
reasons of practical politics, Harold J. Laski was a bird of gaudier
plumage. He was the popular image of the Red Professor, who could
never resist airing his views in or out of season. Laski made no secret
of his Marxist beliefs and openly advocated social revolution, whether
by consent or by violence. Anyone who adopted him as a pet, solicited
his articles, promoted him as a teacher of American youth, or listened

[13] Sherwood, *op. cit.*, p. 230.
[14] *Ibid.*, pp. 230 ff.

seriously to his ideas on national or international policy, at least had no illusions as to where Laski stood. Possibly the only fact about him not fully advertised was his connection after 1940, with the Fabian International Bureau.

Precocious child of a middle class merchant in Manchester, England, Harold Laski joined the Fabian Society at Oxford and to the end of his life remained one of its most vocal members. Declared unfit for military service in World War I, he took a teaching post at McGill University in Canada. There he was speedily discovered by Norman Hapgood, a Hearst magazine editor of Socialist leanings, who made a special trip from Toronto to Montreal to meet Laski. Hapgood described this "extraordinary, brilliant young man" to Felix Frankfurter, who obtained an instructorship for Laski at Harvard in 1915 and became his closest friend. The following summer, to supplement a minute income, young Laski was also provided a job in Philadelphia cataloguing the papers of the deceased soap magnate, Joseph I. Fels.

During the four years he taught at Harvard, Laski edited the Harvard *Law Review,* devoting a whole issue to Duguit, the father of Soviet law, and began studies for a doctorate which he never completed. He contributed articles frequently to the *New Republic;* flashed like a comet across the Left Wing intellectual scene in Boston and New York; and wrote a rather pretentious book, *Authority in the Modern State,* which he dedicated jointly to Felix Frankfurter and Justice Oliver Wendell Holmes. Laski's May-and-December friendship with the aging Holmes has been widely publicized. Disingenuously, Laski once advised him to read the *History of the Fabian Society* by Edward R. Pease—"rather a pleasant book in its way." [15]

Tired, bored and seeking mental diversion, Holmes took "great pleasure" in the "dear boy's" companionship and phenomenal display of learning. Laski, like Sidney Webb, had a photographic memory. It enabled him to quote whole passages from the most recondite works, even citing the pages on which they appeared. An inveterate name-dropper, he also had a lifelong tendency to recall meetings with the great that never happened—and in which, of course, he figured to advantage. Since he told a good story, and since he actually did know a surprising number of distinguished persons for one so young, his admirers condoned that harmless mythomania.[16]

[15] *Holmes-Laski Letters,* Mark DeWolfe Howe, ed., (Cambridge, Harvard University Press, 1953), p. 141. (Laski to Holmes, March 11, 1918.)
[16] Kingsley Martin, *Harold Laski: A Biographical Memoir,* (New York, The Viking Press, Inc., 1953), pp. 45-46.

When he went to teach at Harvard, Laski was just twenty-two. Frail, undersized and looking even smaller in his dark English suits, he had the air of a preternaturally wise child, mostly head, eyes and round horn-rimmed glasses. Appearing anything but dangerous, he still managed to attract an immoderate amount of attention, as he was destined to do all his life. This was not only because of his conspicuous gifts, but also because of the opinions he felt called upon to impart on a wide range of controversial topics—particularly, the Russian Revolution.

While he had his defenders, Laski provoked a good deal of spontaneous resentment among the general student body, which devoted an entire issue of the Harvard *Lampoon* to attacking him. He won notoriety in Greater Boston by getting himself involved in the police strike of 1919. Though never officially asked to leave Harvard, even his best friends agreed at the time it might be wiser for him to move on.

Leading lights of the Fabian Society made a concerted effort to find the proper niche for Harold at home. His sponsors included Graham Wallas, then lecturing in New York at the New School for Social Research; Sidney Webb, supreme pontiff of the Fabian Society; and Lord Haldane, a governor of the London School of Economics, who had just allied himself publicly with the Fabians and the British Labour Party.[17] With their backing, Laski was offered a place at the London School, and in a very few years inherited Graham Wallas' chair of Political Science. To qualify for the promotion Laski wrote a massive tome, *The Grammar of Politics*, which started by taking gradualist Socialism for granted and ended with a frankly Marxist position. Praised by Sidney Webb, it became a standard university textbook, replacing nineteenth century texts on political science just as it has since been replaced by more fashionable Socialist works.

Laski's highly personalized method of teaching—a technique similar to G. D. H. Cole's in England and Felix Frankfurter's in the United States—gained him fervent followers among the young people who flocked to study under him. They came not only from the United Kingdom but from Asia, Africa and America, in the decades when Rockefeller Foundation grants were helping to build the London

---

[17] *Ibid.*, pp. 38-40. Lord Beveridge in his autobiography *Power and Influence*, (New York, The Beechhurst Press, Inc., 1955), p. 181 also states: "One of my first appointments (i.e. to the faculty of the London School) was Hugh Dalton. Another was Harold Laski, urged on me by Graham Wallas to rescue him from an uncomfortable position at Harvard.")

School of Economics into a world center of Socialist instruction. Laski's classes were filled to overflowing with students of every hue and color, and they stood in line outside his office waiting to consult him.

Consciously he strove to instill his own Marxist doctrines in future leaders of revolutionary movements from outposts of the Empire which he hoped and schemed to dissolve. Tom Mboya of Kenya's African National Union Party and the saturnine Krishna Menon of India were among the pupils whose contact with him outlasted their university days. At one time, it was said, most of the senior civil servants in Nehru's government were former students of Laski's. Of the young men indoctrinated by him at the London School, not a few occupy top posts in their own countries today—especially in the so-called developing nations.

Outside of the classroom he agitated ceaselessly in public lectures, periodicals and personal correspondence for one burning global issue after another—Freedom for India, Ethiopia, the Spanish Loyalists— and generally urged cooperation between Liberals, Socialists and Communists. He served with Leonard Woolf and John Strachey as a director of the strongly pro-Soviet Left Book Club. Though the director of the London School, Sir William Beveridge, expressed some fear that Laski's outspoken hostility to the capitalist system might discourage the flow of contributions, such fears proved groundless. A total of $3,000,000 for buildings, research and general expenses was donated by the Laura Spelman Rockefeller Memorial Fund and the Rockefeller Foundation to the London School from 1924 through 1949, while Harold Laski served in its department of Political Science.

Like G. D. H. Cole—an equally avowed Marxist, and a pedagogue whose influence on the coming generation of Fabian Socialist leaders rivaled Laski's—he frankly aimed to mold the minds of future government officials at home and abroad. Britain's post World War II Foreign Minister, Socialist Ernest Bevin, who did not always see eye to eye with Laski, once told a Labour Party Conference: "If it's the universities that are to be criticized, well, put up a vote of censure on Harold Laski, because it's the product of the universities I have got to accept!" [18]

Laski's influence on alumni of the mines, shipyards and factories in Britain was also considerable. Despite his reputation for intel-

---

[18] Francis Williams, *Ernest Bevin*, (London, Hutchinson & Co., Ltd., 1952), p. 237.

lectual snobbism, a number of trade union officials who rose to government office with the British Labour Party regularly turned to him for advice. Emanuel Shinwell of the Miners' Union, for example, who enjoyed quite a reputation as a revolutionary agitator, wrote in his autobiography: "My mind was finally made up after a conversation with my late friend, Harold Laski . . . I lifted up my telephone and spoke to Attlee. I told him I would accept the Secretaryship of State for War." [19]

While Laski never aspired to nor accepted political office himself, he remained an audible offstage presence, irritating at times to the old pros of the Parliamentary Labour Party but impossible to ignore. In 1932, he joined a little group of militants inside the Labour Party who called themselves the Socialist League; and, in 1937, he signed their Unity Manifesto urging a united front in Britain between Labour and the Communist Party against Fascism. Significantly, most of the Labour Party members signing that petition were intellectuals and outstanding figures in the Fabian Society. [20]

After the Popular Front movement in which he was active had been forcibly dissolved, Laski still argued in 1939-40 for a friendly attitude toward Soviet Russia, no matter how badly that country had behaved in Finland, Poland and the Baltic States. [21] In February, 1941, he initiated a correspondence with Herbert Morrison, Fabian Socialist Home Secretary in the coalition Cabinet of Winston Churchill, to make sure that the "civil rights" of Communists in wartime Britain were being protected. Following Hitler's invasion of Russia, Laski was one of the first and most ardent spokesmen for all-out aid to the Soviet Union, with a view to securing Russian cooperation in a postwar Socialist world. [22]

From 1939, Laski sat on the Executive of the British Labour Party. Under the prevailing system of rotation, he automatically became its chairman in 1945—the year in which the Party rode to power on the strength of its deceptive promise to abolish poverty. Chairman of the Labour Party's campaign committee and policy subcommittee in

[19] Emanuel Shinwell, *Conflict without Malice*, (London, Odhams Press, Ltd., 1955), p. 187.

[20] Williams, *op. cit.*, p. 210. Labour Party members who signed the Unity Manifesto included Stafford Cripps, Harold Laski, Aneurin Bevan, John Strachey, William Mellor. It was also signed by such leaders of the British Communist Party as Harry Pollitt, William Gallacher, James Maxton, Tom Mann.

[21] Martin, *op. cit.*, p. 130.

[22] *Ibid.*, p. 131.

that critical election year was Herbert Morrison, by then on exceedingly close terms with Laski.

Following the Party's victory at the polls, Professor Laski made an astounding proposal to Clement Attlee, its Parliamentary Leader since 1935. He invited Attlee to abdicate and allow the incoming parliamentary majority to elect a leader—presumably Herbert Morrison, to whose campaign aid a number of the newly elected Labour M.P.'s owed their seats and who, in Laski's opinion, would have made a much better Prime Minister than Attlee. While not unconstitutional under British law, a more inept suggestion has rarely been offered by a political pundit.

Curtly, Attlee replied, "Dear Laski, I thank you for your letter, contents of which have been noted." [23] When Ernest Bevin, boss of the powerful Transport Workers' Union, learned of the "chicanery," he moved promptly in Attlee's behalf and no more was heard of the matter. Needless to say, this bit of backstage business did not endear Laski to Prime Minister Attlee or Foreign Minister Bevin, and effectively precluded him from becoming personal adviser-in-chief to the Labour Party Government as he so ardently longed to be.

For all that, Laski could neither be ignored nor suppressed. From 1946 to 1948 he was voted chairman of the London Fabian Society, which supplied the plans, legislation and key personnel for the Labour Government in Britain and to which over two-thirds of its parliamentary majority belonged. Moreover, Laski was idolized by foreign Socialists, a number of whom held cabinet rank in their own countries after the war—especially in France, Belgium, the Scandinavian countries and in Czechoslovakia, where Laski advised the Beneš Government to cooperate with the Communists. Followers of Pietro Nenni in postwar Italy hailed him as "a figure comparable with Marx in the intellectual history of Socialism." Despite his ineptitude in practical affairs, to the end Harold Laski remained a symbol of the International Socialist Professor, who used his connections *abroad* to affect the course of British policy when deterred from doing so at home.

Never admitting that a man cannot serve two masters, Harold Laski often referred to the United States as his second country. Few Americans even in his own time realized how large a part of his adult life was spent in the United States, or how deep a swath he cut in both educational and governmental circles in America. Of his thirty-odd year teaching and advisory career, it is estimated that almost one-

[23] Williams, *op. cit.*, pp. 238-239.

third was spent in North American colleges and universities, either as a visiting professor or special lecturer.

Following his early fiasco at Harvard, Laski was to return to this country again and again as a paid and fêted guest. He gave a series of formal lectures at the Universities of North Carolina and Indiana; taught for a semester in 1939 at Columbia University Teachers' College; lectured more briefly at Yale and at Princeton's bicentennial, and at the State Universities of Washington, Oregon, California and Colorado; and in 1946 Laski debated Senator Robert Taft at Kenyon College in Ohio. Of course, he made numerous appearances at the New School for Social Research in New York City where he helped to organize a group of Socialist refugee professors.

After World War II he spent some time at Roosevelt University in Chicago where his disciple from the London School, Professor Herman Finer, also held forth. Laski's final tour in the United States was made under the auspices of the Amalgamated Clothing Workers, to deliver the Sidney Hillman Memorial Lectures, jointly sponsored by that Socialist-directed union and local institutions of higher learning from coast to coast.

More frankly Marxist in doctrine than some other members of the London Fabian Society, Laski's lectures and writings conveyed a revolutionary message not necessarily couched in Marxist jargon. If it was true, as his friend Louis Fischer once wrote unkindly, that Laski lived increasingly in an "intellectual ghetto" on his visits to the United States, geographically the area was widely dispersed. Across the years he developed connections in the academic life of America enjoyed by few other foreign professors, and he recruited an army of followers among faculty and students. Though Laski seemed to cause only a passing furore at womens' clubs and university pink teas, in the long run he built up a serious network of Socialist propagandists and Soviet sympathizers, many of whom are still active in education and politics today. In falling heir to Graham Wallas' chair at the London School, Harold Laski also inherited Wallas' function as the London Fabian Society's foremost missionary to America's colleges and universities.

In 1929, Laski contributed a significant article to *The Socialism of Our Times,* the symposium edited by Harry W. Laidler and Norman Thomas and issued by the League for Industrial Democracy.[24] Some

[24] *The Socialism of Our Times.* A Symposium. Harry W. Laidler and Norman Thomas, eds. (New York, The Vanguard Press, Inc.,—League for Industrial Democracy, 1929), pp. 131 ff.

of the points contained in that article had previously appeared over his signature in *Harper's* magazine for June, 1928, and subsequently reappeared more concretely in the programs of the New Deal.

Specifically, Laski urged Socialists to take the initiative in sponsoring an eventual Federal program of "social insurance" leading, as always, to the welfare state. He supported municipal ownership of public services, such as gas and electricity, street railways and savings banks, "to demonstrate the superiority of collectivism to the average voter." He advocated for the courts in America, "reform" such as his good friend, Felix Frankfurter, was then attempting on a state-wide scale for Governor Franklin Roosevelt of New York. Above all, Laski advised Socialists to agitate endlessly in favor of taxation for social—not merely administrative—uses. "Pressure for higher taxation on unearned and larger incomes is vital," he wrote, [with] "amounts so raised to be used as *grants in aid to the States for social purposes*." [25] What Laski did not say, was that the lion's share of any funds raised for such purposes would still have to come from the pockets of the working people—since taxes on the rich, however punitive, would never suffice to pay for the program.

In conclusion, he stated: "I feel strongly the impossibility of American political institutions today, from the angle of a movement toward Socialist measures. *The separation of powers is the protective rampart of American individualism*." [26] This is interesting in view of Laski's prolonged intimacy with Felix Frankfurter, who became a Justice of the Supreme Court of the United States. Laski was a periodic house guest of Frankfurter in Cambridge and later in Washington, and for a quarter century carried on a voluminous correspondence with his "dearest Felix" that kept the latter constantly informed on the Fabian Socialist outlook in London. Those letters, profusely quoted in Laski's biography by Kingsley Martin, editor of the *New Statesman*, also included comments and recommendations on American policy which Frankfurter was in an unrivaled position to transmit to President Franklin D. Roosevelt.

Professor Laski's politico-social fellowship with Felix Frankfurter and Evans Clark of the Twentieth Century Fund cannot be discounted as a merely personal association. For Laski, like G. D. H. Cole, Graham Wallas and the Webbs, was first, last and always a professional revolutionary of the gradualist school. Every private

---

[25] (Italics added.)
[26] (Italics added.)

contact he cultivated and virtually every line he wrote in his micro-
scopic handwriting, no matter how heavily coated with endearments,
was as charged with political intention as a telegraph cable is charged
with electricity.

His intimacy in America with members of the original Roosevelt
brain trust in Albany, plus his close connections in London with
Israel Sieff and the founders of PEP, gave him a matchless opportunity to synchronize the ideas of British and American Fabian Socialists in formulating plans for the New Deal. Inevitably, he was
aware that FDR would be pushed as the Democratic Party's candidate for the Presidency, long before the American public had any
knowledge of it.

Laski was in the United States in 1928-29 following FDR's election
as Governor of New York, and again in 1931, returning to deliver a
Kingsway Hall lecture in London on "The American Collapse." [27]
He was in America during the fateful first "hundred days" of 1933
and reported his observations briefly at a Fabian Society evening
social.[28] Soon after the National Recovery Act was declared unconstitutional by the Supreme Court, Professor Laski spoke at a Fabian
Society Friends' Hall lecture on "The Failure of the American Experiment." He flayed the United States Constitution as a class document, calling it "Capitalism's strongest safeguard on earth today"; and
added that Roosevelt was America's sole bulwark "against the Fascist
form of Capitalism." What was needed both in America and England,
he claimed, was a united front of all liberal and left wing groups
(including the Communists) to "save Democracy." Either Capitalism
or Democracy would prevail, he said, in America as in Europe—a
strange species of political science, equating democracy with the
Socialist commonwealth.[29]

Precisely when, where or how Professor Laski first met Franklin D.
Roosevelt is not recorded by their official biographers. Evidently the

[27] *Fabian News*, (October, 1931). Announcement of forthcoming lecture on
Thursday, November 19, 1931 by Professor H. J. Laski.

[28] "The Fabian Social," *Fabian News*, (June, 1933). This item states: "The
Social evening party held at the Livingstone Hall on Thursday, May 4 was very
successful. About 200 members and friends assembled and an enjoyable evening
was spent. Short speeches were given by Sir Stafford Cripps, K.C. M.P., G.
Bernard Shaw, Professor H. J. Laski and S. K. Ratcliffe, the last three having just
returned to this country from America."

[29] "Friends Hall Lectures," *Fabian News*, (December, 1935). Review of Professor H. J. Laski's speech of November 14 on "The Failure of the American
Experiment."

two were introduced by a trusted mutual friend—generally believed to have been Felix Frankfurter—under casual and informal circumstances. Their original encounter could have taken place during any one of Laski's frequent trips to the United States in the late nineteen-twenties or early nineteen-thirties. Eleanor Roosevelt was not present, for she stated in 1956 [30] that she had never met Laski but believed he was "honest"—a characteristic *non sequitur!* Nevertheless, it is recorded that the honestly Marxist professor paid a number of calls on FDR at his office in the White House; was acquainted with the Roosevelt daughter, Anna; and was the recipient of warm and approving personal letters from the President himself.

The extent to which Professor Laski and his ideas were persona grata at the White House from the very outset of the Roosevelt Administration can be gauged by the fact that Joseph P. Kennedy, Sr. sent his two eldest sons to study under Laski at the London School of Economics. No Marxist himself, the senior Kennedy was already several times a millionaire. The stock market crash of 1929 and the ensuing depression had shaken Kennedy's confidence, however, in the durability of the capitalist economy, although he suffered no serious financial loss and was even reputed to have made money by selling short on the market.

During 1932 Kennedy, Sr. was quoted as saying that he would gladly sacrifice half his fortune in order to save the other half for his children—a pledge which he was, happily for him, never called upon to fulfill. In that frame of mind, he traveled aboard the original Roosevelt campaign train and contributed generously to FDR's election. While waiting to succeed James M. Landis, Dean of the Harvard Law School, as head of the Securities and Exchange Commission, Kennedy père offered up his firstborn as an ideological hostage. During 1933-34, in the interval between his graduation from Choate School and matriculation at Harvard, Joseph P. Kennedy, Jr. was sent to study political science at the London School. He made the grand tour to Moscow under the chaperonage of Professor and Mrs. Laski.[31]

According to the Harvard College De-cennial Report on the Class of 1938, Joe's year at the London School,

was a tremendous experience, as it was under Professor Laski that young Joe developed his dominant ambition to devote himself to a career in public

[30] In a personal letter from Eleanor Roosevelt to M. P. McCarran.
[31] Mrs. Laski was a well-known advocate of birth control clinics in England.

service. Indeed, referring to Joe's interest in politics, Professor Laski speaks of "his determination to be nothing less than President of the United States." It was this interest that was to guide his studies at Harvard . . . and which dominated his whole life after graduation in 1938.

In 1940, as a junior member of the Massachusetts delegation to the Democratic National Convention, young Joe resisted the pressures for a third term "draft" of President Roosevelt and bravely cast his vote for James M. Farley. Though he may not have realized it at the time, that vote ended Joe Kennedy, Jr.'s hopes for a political career via the Democratic Party almost as effectively as his subsequent tragic demise in a World War II bomber over Germany.

There was a second Kennedy son, however, who did almost everything that Joe did, being the understudy of his admired older brother. In 1934-35 he, too, went to learn about politics from Professor Laski in London. Imitatively he was no less affected by the experience than Joe, Jr. had been, even though he did not complete the full scholastic year owing to an attack of jaundice. When Joe, Jr. was killed in action during World War II, it was Jack who stepped into his brother's shoes and achieved his brother's hoped-for political role. Thus Professor H. J. Laski, British Fabian Socialist and self-proclaimed Marxist, had the rare distinction of helping indirectly to select and to educate two Democrat Presidents of the United States: Franklin D. Roosevelt and John F. Kennedy.

Probably Laski's most prized contribution to the domestic policies of the New Deal was the idea of using Federal tax-moneys as *grants in aid to the States for social purposes*. Eagerly adopted by New Deal strategists and never legally challenged to this day, Laski's suggestion proved remarkably useful to FDR in perpetuating both himself and the Democratic Party in office.

As the apparent author of that handy device, Laski became a special favorite of President Roosevelt. In a letter of January 10, 1939, FDR wrote Professor Laski that he would be "honored and happy to have you dedicate the little book to me." [32] The book in question was a series of essays entitled *The American Presidency*. Three weeks later the American President again wrote to Laski, then in Seattle, thanking him for a reprint of one of the essays and saying: "Come and see me as soon as you get East." [33] The book was published in 1940, the year when Roosevelt ran for a third term in defiance of all previous Presidential tradition.

[32] Martin, *op. cit.*, p. 114.
[33] *Ibid.*, p. 114.

Complaints about Laski, no matter how valid, never reached the American people, entranced as they were by the beneficent father-image of FDR that New Deal psychologists had created. On January 14, 1941, Congressman Tinkham of Massachusetts read into the House *Record* a warning by Amos Pinchot, disillusioned former Socialist and brother of Pennsylvania's liberal former Governor. Somewhat belatedly, Pinchot pointed out that Laski and other English radicals were working on President Roosevelt with the object of introducing Socialism into the United States. He stated boldly: "Many young Socialists declare that what is generally called the Roosevelt Program is in reality the Laski Program, imposed on New Deal thinkers, and finally on the President, by the London Professor of Economics [sic] and his friends."

Still the great voting public in America remained unaware of Laski's existence: he was caviar for the intellectual elite. After Roosevelt's death, Congressman Woodruff of Michigan published an extension of remarks in the House *Record* of February 6, 1946, denouncing Laski and to a lesser extent Lord Keynes. The Congressman declared that Professor Laski had for some time "had a backdoor key to the White House." And he added, "a surprising number of us, Professor, have begun to think it is time to change the lock."

Such rare observations, while correctly assessing the general influence of British Fabian Socialists on the New Deal and its successor, the Fair Deal, were weakened by a lack of corroborative detail. They failed to note that a number of the ideas advanced before 1940 by Professor Laski and his friends originated in the New Fabian Research Bureau, and after 1940 mirrored programs of the Fabian International Bureau and the Socialist International. Moreover, patriots of an earlier day were hampered by not having access to the Laski-Frankfurter and Laski-Roosevelt letters—which have since been quoted in part by the Professor's friendly biographer, Kingsley Martin, although never revealed in their entirety.

Even Robert Sherwood's heavily documented volume, *Roosevelt and Hopkins,* which appeared in 1948, omitted any mention of Harry Hopkins' talks with Laski during Lend-Lease trips to England. Himself a New Deal henchman, Sherwood scrupulously avoided pointing out that Hopkins' views on wartime aid to Russia coincided with the opinions expressed by Professor Laski both in letters and in print.[34]

[34] Cf. articles by H. J. Laski, *New Statesman,* July 5, 1941 and September 13, 1941.

In fact, Harold Laski's name was not even listed in the index of the Sherwood opus. Yet President Roosevelt, replying to a letter from Laski after America's entry into World War II, wrote: "Dear Harold, So good to hear from you again. *Hopkins has already told me of his visit with you, and everything reported to me checks with the many things you told me.*" [35]

Again and again during World War II, Laski asserted that it was the duty of a popular leader to lay the foundations for postwar Socialism.[36] In that way, social revolution might be brought about by popular consent—perhaps simultaneously in many countries.[37] This Fabian Socialist design also involved preserving, *at any price and any sacrifice*, the friendship of Soviet Russia; for the kind of postwar world that Laski envisioned presumed something more than superficial coexistence with the USSR. The question of Allied war aims became the main burden of his articles in both British and American publications, as it was of his private correspondence.

After Hitler's invasion of the USSR, Laski argued that the future depended on America's and Britain's ability to convert a temporary wartime alliance with the Soviet Union into a lasting postwar partnership. No guarantees of good faith were required from the Soviets. The immediate program of wartime assistance must be such as to convince Communist leaders that the capitalist nations were their loyal allies, and that they would only make peace on terms acceptable to Soviet Russia.[38]

The long-range program of cooperation to follow the war was more subtle. Laski contended that Soviet Russia and the Western powers might learn a great deal from each other.[39] While the USSR was more advanced in Socialist organization, possibly she could be induced

[35] In his letter to President Roosevelt, Laski had expressed gratitude for the "noble appointments" of John Winant and Benjamin V. Cohen, as Winant's adviser at the U.S. Embassy in London. He had also written: "[It is] exhilarating . . . when you believe that the two nations, after we've won, hold the fate of the world in their hands. If liberal America makes England speak the right words and *do the right acts,* even this may in the end be worth the blood and tears that have been shed." Martin, *op. cit.,* p. 141. (Italics added.)

[36] *Ibid.,* p. 141. (Footnote)

[37] Cf. President Roosevelt's Message to Congress of January 6, 1941.

[38] Martin, *op. cit.,* pp. 141-142.

[39] Apparently this has become a standard Fabian Socialist cliché. "We saw much and learned much," wrote John Parker in *Fabian News* for October, 1963, describing a recent Fabian Society tour to Russia which he conducted. A long time member of the Fabian Executive, John Parker has been making "educational" visits to the USSR since 1932, when he accompanied Margaret Cole and the original New Fabian Research Bureau delegation on a study trip.

to see the advantage of practicing a little more social and religious tolerance. The eternal hope of Fabian Socialists that the Soviet Union would "mellow" as a result of contacts with the West was still being echoed as recently as 1963 by spokesmen of the New Frontier, and was announced as a presumptive fact in the *Fabian News* of August, 1963.

About six months after Pearl Harbor, Professor Laski received a cordial invitation from Eleanor Roosevelt to address the International Students' Congress to be held in Washington during September, 1942. Eleanor Roosevelt wrote that she would be "particularly happy" if Laski could be there to speak to the young people, and she invited him to stay at the White House—"as I know it would give my husband as well as myself a great deal of pleasure to have an opportunity to see you." [40]

If Laski had quietly applied for a visa in the routine way, he would probably have received it. Filled with a strong sense of his own importance, however, he took the unusual step of asking Churchill's permission. Since Laski had for months been publicly critical of Churchill, as possessing an anti-Socialist outlook and "eighteenth century mentality," the Prime Minister quite reasonably declined to grant him an opportunity for airing such sentiments in Washington. [41] So Eleanor Roosevelt never had the pleasure of seeing him—and Laski seems naively to have lost his only chance for a face-to-face discussion with FDR concerning the shape of the postwar world to come.

He could still wield a potent pen, however, and he proceeded to do so until the end of the war. Since mail to and from the President of the United States or a Supreme Court Justice was classed as "privileged" by Allied censors, Laski could be assured of privacy when writing to Roosevelt and Frankfurter. If he preferred, he could always send letters or articles to the Washington *Post* and the New York *Nation* via the U.S. Embassy pouch. Soon after Christmas in 1942 he wrote to FDR: ". . . above all, I hope you will teach our Prime Minister that it is the hopes of the future and not the achievements of the past from which he must draw his inspiration." Though Roosevelt and Frankfurter both reproved Laski for his increasingly sharp attacks

[40] Martin, *op. cit.*, p. 145.
[41] On March 25, 1942 Churchill had written Laski: "I certainly should think it very undemocratic if anyone were to try to carry socialism during a party truce without a parliamentary majority."

on Churchill, privately they enjoyed his comments—especially FDR, who according to eyewitnesses found personal amusement in forcing Winston to play second fiddle to himself and Stalin at Big Three conferences.

Essentially, Laski's wartime mission with reference to the United States resembled Ray Stannard Baker's at the end of World War I. In private letters, destined to be read by the President or retailed to him, Laski discoursed on the state of the nation and the state of mind of the "common man" in England. Hints on postwar aims and "some sort of world organisation" to follow the war were interwoven with human anecdotes and the political gossip that Roosevelt loved.

Just as Baker had done, Laski reported that America's President was the only hope of the working masses in Britain—and everywhere else—for a better life after the war. By nourishing Roosevelt's messianic delusion, which was no less pronounced in its way than Woodrow Wilson's had been, Laski encouraged the President to take a stand on postwar matters that coincided with the views of the Fabian International Bureau. Often it involved preferring the interests of Soviet Russia over those of the British Empire or the United States itself.

As early as December, 1941, Laski had written to Felix Frankfurter:

At present the masses of Britain have, I think, three clear convictions. (i) Churchill is a grand war leader. (ii) The U.S.S.R. shows it has roots in popular opinion more profound than any other system. (iii) The only man who can define purposes which prevent collapse and chaos after the war is the President. Whether he will have his chance in time, whether he can find a successor to continue his policies, these are things we endlessly discuss in common, not I fear, too hopefully.[42]

This was no simple outpouring of private hopes and fears. Coming from a member of the Fabian Executive and addressed to FDR's foremost privy councillor, it had the quality of a succinct and far-reaching policy directive. It sheds new light on the peculiar urgency of Harry Hopkins, Frankfurter's nominee for Lend-Lease powers, to give the USSR more than enough of everything to carry her through the fighting phases of the war; and helps to explain Hopkins' insistence on regarding Soviet Russia rather than Britain as the "decisive factor" to be considered.[43] Moreover, it provides a clue to the otherwise

[42] Martin, op. cit., p. 143.
[43] Sherwood, op. cit., pp. 748-749. Sherwood states that Hopkins had with him at the Quebec Conference, which set the stage for the Teheran Conference of 1943, a document that contained the following estimate: "Russia's post-war po-

inexplicable Big Three conferences, where the United States was committed to satisfying the Soviet Union's territorial and geographic postwar aims. Historically, secret covenants between nations have sometimes preceded a war; *but never before has a superior power rushed to award the fruits of victory to the greediest and most impoverished of military partners while a war was still in progress!*

Fear that President Roosevelt, a willing Fabian Socialist captive, might fail to succeed himself in 1944, or might not physically survive World War II, supplied a motive for the premature concessions granted to Soviet Russia at Teheran and Yalta. The Teheran Conference of 1943, which preceded the cross-Channel invasion of Europe desired by Stalin and opposed by Churchill, in effect assured the USSR of a free hand in Eastern Europe plus confirming her hold on Poland and the Baltic countries. Roosevelt's obviously failing health in 1945 hastened the Yalta Conference that delivered Manchuria to Soviet forces and enabled them to furnish the Chinese Communist armies with enough captured Japanese military matériel to insure Communist control over the mainland of China.

Thus a President of the United States, acting in his Supreme Court-affirmed capacity of absolute military Commander-in-chief, circumvented the postwar treaty-making powers of the Congress by presenting it with a series of accomplished facts. Even the format of the postwar United Nations was agreed upon at Teheran. The Fabian Socialist allies of Bolshevism had learned a lesson from Woodrow

---

sition in Europe will be a dominant one. With Germany crushed, there is no power in Europe to oppose her tremendous military forces. It is true that Great Britain is building up a position in the Mediterranean vis-à-vis Russia that she may find useful in balancing power in Europe. However, even here she may not be able to oppose Russia unless she is otherwise supported.

"The conclusions from the foregoing are obvious. Since Russia is the decisive factor in the war, she must be given every assistance and every effort must be made to obtain her friendship. Likewise, since without question she will dominate Europe on the defeat of the Axis, it is even more essential to develop and maintain the most friendly relations with Russia.

"Finally, the most important factor the United States has to consider in relation to Russia is the prosecution of the war in the Pacific. With Russia as an ally in the war against Japan, the war can be terminated in less time and at less expense in life and resources than if the reverse were the case. Should the war in the Pacific have to be carried on with an unfriendly or negative attitude on the part of Russia, the difficulties will be immeasurably increased and operations might become abortive."

This remarkable document, headed "Russia's Position," was alleged to have been quoted from "a very high level United States military strategic estimate." It reflected with singular fidelity estimates published in the Fabian Socialist *New Statesman* by that high level nonmilitary expert, Professor H. J. Laski.

Wilson's experience after World War I, and were determined not to risk a repetition. On the strength of these events it has since been alleged, with reason, that in modern times the most effective foreign agents of the Soviet Union operate as Fabian Socialists.

Before leaving Washington for Yalta, Franklin D. Roosevelt on January 16, 1945, dictated and signed what must have been his last personal letter to Harold Laski. From the broken, almost illegible handwriting that appears in the signature, one seeing it could deduce that the author was a very sick man.[44] Besides mentioning the forthcoming meeting with Marshal Stalin and Prime Minister Churchill, and FDR's own hope of visiting England and seeing Laski in the summer to come, the letter contained this meaningful assurance: *"Our goal is, as you say, identical for the long range objectives . . . ."* [45]

3.

Men whose goal is revolution, whether subtle or violent, have often made use of inspired charlatans—soothsayers, astrologers, numerologists, cultists of one kind or another, who could convey a revolutionary message in high-flown double talk. During the decades culminating in the French Revolution, for example, there arose a whole line of magnificent imposters, "who posed as initiators of the occult sciences, as possessors of the Great Secret and the Grand Magisterium; and there in consequence, the Higher Mysteries . . . They took root and flourished, developing an hundred splendors of romantic legends, of sonorous names and titles." [46]

Of these the most splendid and the most successful was a self-ennobled Italian barber known as Count Cagliostro. Practicing alchemy, occultism and the healing arts, he bewitched a cultivated public in half a dozen tongues, as well as in a private jargon that had meaning for the initiate alone. Forecasting the future was his specialty. Even now, almost two centuries later, there are still scholars prepared to debate the point as to whether he was a savant or a rogue.

Cagliostro was the sensation of Paris and Strasbourg, where respectable bankers vied with one another to take advantage of his prognostications and to supply him with funds. At one time his patron was a Prince Royal, the brother of Louis XVI, sometimes called

---

[44] Martin, *op. cit.*, This letter is reproduced on the page opposite p. 135.
[45] (Italics added.)
[46] William R. H. Trowbridge, *Cagliostro* (*Savant or Scoundrel?*) (New Hyde Park, University Books, 1961), p. x.

Philippe Egalité—leader of that liberal wing of the nobility who sympathized with the first stages of the French Revolution and most of whom subsequently went to the guillotine. Cagliostro's elaborate intrigues played a well-known part in hastening the fall of the established order in France.[47] Who would have suspected him, in his heyday, of harboring such a purpose?

Spiritual heir and latter-day facsimile of that darling of the eighteenth century Enlightenment, was a Cambridge University don named John Maynard Keynes. He, too, was a magnificent figure: six feet three, and superbly tailored; an authority on wines, fine foods and beautiful women; patron of the arts, and master of the English language which he only distorted by design. He, too, posed as the possessor of elusive secrets, key to the Higher Mysteries of economics and public finance. More fortunate in his origins than Cagliostro, Keynes' final role was as bursar of King's College, Cambridge. There he studied the dietary habits of pigs with a view to improving the breed on the college-owned farm; and he ruled over the Political Economy Club, where his followers were made privy to the master's techniques for apprehending and controlling future events.

An alchemist who succeeded in substituting paper for gold, a mystifier who claimed that money multiplied itself in the spending, Keynes compelled bankers to do his bidding and imposed his schemes on the highest personages in an age of political unreason. In the long run, his inspired economic gibberish and esoteric fiscal panaceas did more to promote the insolvency of English-speaking nations and speed the timetable of world-wide social revolution than any forthright revolutionary arguments could have done. It is a commentary on the moral and intellectual fiber of the times that, while Cagliostro died in poverty and disgrace, John Maynard Keynes ended his days as a self-made millionaire and authentic peer of the realm, mourned by a school of professional disciples pledged to perpetuate and update his more destructive fantasies.

The same question can be asked about Keynes that is asked about Cagliostro: Was he charlatan, adventurer, trickster, or the friend of humanity he claimed to be? Was Lord Keynes a highly polished secret weapon of the Fabian Socialist conspiracy to weaken the capi-

---

[47] Cagliostro is best known for having engineered the notorious affair of the Diamond Necklace, in which a Cardinal and a Queen of France were unwittingly entangled. The scandal touched off by that incident rocked the country and helped bring about the end of the monarchy.

talist system progressively by consent of its beneficiaries—at the same time retaining its productive machinery intact for the benefit of the heirs? Or was he the good physician dedicated to prolonging life? The plain answer has long been obscured by the circumstance that Keynes' reputation[48]—like the currencies he strove to manage—was systematically inflated through the efforts of a fervent Fabian Socialist claque on both sides of the Atlantic, while his ideas were usually represented as being too profound for the ordinary man and woman to grasp.

The story of his life, told by followers and friends, in some details approaches the fabulous. Dr. Seymour Harris—professor of Economics at Harvard's Littauer School of Business Administration, who became Senior Consultant to the United States Treasury Department in 1961 [49] —gravely reaffirms that Keynes was fascinated by the theory of compound interest before he was five years old.[50] While such Gargantuan precocity can be doubted, it is true that Keynes was born to an assured future in left wing economics. His father, John Neville Keynes, was a professor at Cambridge, who published a book in 1890 entitled *The Scope and Method of Political Economy*. For its strictures against the free enterprise system, therein called *laissez faire*, the book was approved by early leaders of the London Fabian Society. It was also included on reading lists of Socialist-slanted works recommended by *The American Fabian* magazine to its public.

The younger Keynes was educated at Eton and King's College, Cambridge, which qualified him almost automatically for entry into the British Civil Service. Though he took no scholastic honors at the university, somehow he acquired a reputation for brilliance due to his

[48] In an editorial note, *The New York Times* (Western edition) of September 9, 1963 stated concerning Keynes: ". . . the greatness of his reputation is *unassailable*."

[49] Dr. Seymour E. Harris worked with Presidential candidate Adlai Stevenson on his press campaign and two-day seminars in 1954. He was also a member of his task force on the economy. Harris has served as consultant to a dozen federal departments. As of 1962, he was Senior Consultant to the Secretary of the Treasury and to the Council of Economic Advisors; a member of the National Academy of Sciences, the National Research Council, the Committee on Textile Research, and the Public Advisory Committee on Area Development. Seymour E. Harris, *The Economics of the Political Parties*, With Special Attention to Presidents Eisenhower and Kennedy. (New York, The Macmillan Co., 1962). Dedication reads: "For Arthur M. Schlesinger, Jr. and John Kenneth Galbraith," p. vii Introduction.

[50] Seymour Harris, *John Maynard Keynes: Economist and Policy Maker*, (New York, Charles Scribner's Sons, 1955), p. 19.

conversational talent and his cool insolence in debate. Moreover, as he was prompt to point out, the name Keynes properly pronounced rhymed with "brains." His gifts of persuasion were apparent to undergraduate friends who nicknamed him Pozzo,[51] after a Renaissance mercenary noted for skill in courtly intrigue as well as in administering slow poisons.

Campus political organizations gave Keynes an opportunity to test his fine Italian hand. As a freshman he joined the Liberal Club, a youthful adjunct of the Liberal Party that came to power in England not many years later. As a sophomore he also became a member of the Fabian Society's student chapter at Cambridge[52] guided by Professor G. Lowes Dickinson, whose adepts were enjoined to capture the Liberal Club by penetration. Keynes' college circle included Bertrand Russell and Leonard Woolf, both well-known in later life for their propaganda services to Fabian Socialism; and the poet, Rupert Brooke, whom some Fabians still claim as their own, even though he discovered the meaning of patriotism before he died as a soldier in World War I. Keynes himself—in common with many British and American Socialists—was to file as a conscientious objector.[53]

Two of his father's associates, Professors Alfred Marshall and A. C. Pigou, groomed young Keynes for a career in economics; but even with their help, he placed no better than twelfth in his final examination. It is amusing to find Marshall and Pigou, both classified in their day as Fabian Socialist sympathizers, dismissed by present-day Keynesians as "classical economists"—[54] along with any others who preceded or failed to accept the vision of revealed economic truth ultimately vouchsafed to the world by John Maynard Keynes.

The sympathetic Professor Marshall rescued Keynes from a minor clerkship in the Colonial Office, bringing him back to lecture on economics at Cambridge University. Later the joint patronage of Marshall, Pigou and Sidney Webb (himself escaped from bondage in the Colonial Office, to become the high priest of Fabian Socialism) was responsible for making Keynes editor of the *Economic Journal* in 1911, and secretary of the Royal Economic Society in 1913. These posts established the young hopeful as a presumably serious economist and

---

[51] R. F. Harrod, *The Life of John Maynard Keynes*, (New York, The Macmillan Co., 1951), p. 180.

[52] *Ibid.*, pp. 60-61.

[53] *Ibid.*, p. 63.

[54] Seymour E. Harris, *John Maynard Keynes: Economist and Policy Maker*, (New York, Charles Scribner's Sons, 1955), p. 5. *et al.*

lent him the prestige so necessary to his future policy-making role. The Fabian Research Department, organized in 1912, was available to supply statistics and to prepare articles on request.

After the outbreak of World War I, Keynes took refuge in the British Treasury Department, where he diverted himself in spare moments by working out a foolproof method of stock market speculation. All his life he enjoyed gambling[55]—bridge, poker, roulette; but like most people, he preferred a sure thing. When the war ended, he found an opportunity for putting his system of mental wagers into practice. Beginning in 1919 with a moderate stake of four thousand pounds (less than $20,000), he parlayed it by 1937 into a neat fortune of 506,000 pounds (about 2.5 million dollars). A goodly share of his winnings resulted from the lowered interest rates that he promoted so assiduously in official quarters, and that caused the list prices of certain common stocks to rise.[56] Throughout the thirties he also speculated profitably in foreign exchange and public utilities stocks.

During the nineteen-twenties Keynes headed an investment firm in London, in partnership with former Treasury colleagues, and displayed what appeared to be an uncanny faculty for predicting politico-economic trends likely to affect the stock market. To selected clients, he gave the benefit of his insight. These included his future bride, a beauteous Russian ballerina of the Diaghilev troupe, whose investments he offered to handle and whom he married in 1925—the same year that he made a trip to Soviet Russia. It has been reported by informed sources that stock market tips, originating with Keynes, paid the expenses of the unofficial and official Soviet embassies in London from 1924 to 1932. At that period he was tireless in his demands that the British Treasury provide fuller statistics on national investment and foreign exchange.

Keynes' international bent owed much to a friendship renewed in London with his old Fabian Socialist college chum, Leonard Woolf. Throughout his long bachelorhood (he married at forty-two) the lanky and personable Keynes was identified with the so-called Bloomsbury group revolving about Leonard Woolf and his wife, Virginia. It was composed of highly educated and magnified[57] upper middle class bohemians, talented and successful practitioners of literature or the

---

[55] *Ibid.*, p. 23.
[56] *Ibid.*, p. 24.
[57] Cf. L. Frank Baum, *The Wizard of Oz.* ("The Highly Magnified Woggle-bug, H.E.")

arts. They were addicted to group-opinions and to a superficially critical, but none the less protective, attitude towards Soviet Russia.

An apparent point of difference with Russian Marxism was their belief that collectivist-minded intellectuals—rather than what Keynes called "the boorish proletariat"—were destined to become the professional rulers of an ideal future world. Bertrand Russell once described the Bloomsbury Fabians as a passionate mutual admiration clique of the elite; and there is no doubt they contributed greatly to the myth of Keynes' unique mental powers.

It may be recalled that from 1915 Leonard Woolf was also the London Fabian Society's leading amateur of international affairs; the author of *International Government*, which supplied the first blueprint for the League of Nations; head of the New Fabian Research Bureau's international committee; a founder and for ten years chairman of the Fabian International Bureau. Woolf's views on World Government and German reparations were faithfully reflected by John Maynard Keynes, when the latter attended the Versailles Peace Conference as a member of the British Treasury delegation.

There, as one of the younger dissidents, British and American, grouped around Colonel E. M. House, Keynes established long-lasting ties with Walter Lippmann and with Felix Frankfurter who represented the Zionist cause at the Peace Conference.[58] Returning from Paris, Keynes expressed their mutual dissatisfactions in his first book-length work, *The Economic Consequences of the Peace*. Lippmann and Frankfurter helped arrange for its publication in America, where it was touted and officially distributed by the League for Industrial Democracy as it was by the Fabian Society in Great Britain and the Colonies.[59] Here Keynes announced frankly that capitalism in Europe was doomed.

Not directly active in politics, Keynes retained a nominal affiliation with the Liberal Party and avoided declaring himself a Socialist. Inevitably, he sided with the Asquith Liberals, who were instrumental in handing over the reins of government to the Fabian-led Labour Party in 1924. During the election year, he delivered a famed anti-capitalist lecture at Cambridge, published in 1926 as *The End of Laissez Faire*. There—like his father before him—he identified modern capitalism with the early nineteenth century foreign trade doctrine known as *laissez faire*, based on earlier and cruder forms of

[58] Thomas, *op. cit.*, p. 17.
[59] *Fabian News*, (March, 1920).

industrial production. Professor David McCord Wright of McGill University, Montreal—himself an admirer, in some respects, of Keynes —has noted that the "day of judgment" which Keynes predicted recurrently for capitalism was in reality purest milk of the Marxian word.[60]

In 1923, Keynes bought a controlling interest in *The Nation and Athenæum*, placed it under the editorship of the well-known Fabian Socialist, Kingsley Martin; and utilized it as a vehicle of personal opinion and aggrandizement for himself and his friends. His widely-publicized attacks on the gold standard, appearing there and elsewhere, eventually persuaded the British people and certain Treasury officials as well, that the use of gold as a basis for monetary value was the chief cause of unemployment in England and the only begetter of the Great Depression. When Keynes complained in 1932 that for twelve years he had exercised no influence whatever on British Treasury policy, there was more than a touch of poetic license in his lament.

In 1929, he was named by Philip Snowden, Fabian Socialist Chancellor of the Exchequer, to an official Committee of Inquiry into Finance and Industry; and from 1930 he served on the MacDonald government's economic Advisory Council. The unprecedented attack and public humiliation to which he subjected Sir Montagu Norman, Governor of the Bank of England, as a witness before the Macmillan Committee in 1931, set the stage for Great Britain's abandonment of the gold standard, so strongly advocated by Keynes.

Fiscal and economic plans of the Labour Party Government from 1929 to 1931 echoed a Keynesian formula by now grown familiar to Americans. It was estimated that a government-financed public works program, designed to increase employment by 5 per cent, would "increase" the Treasury's income by one and one half per cent via taxes. This windfall, *supplemented by a 7 per cent cut in defense expenditures,* would serve to launch the Labour Party's welfare program. Deficit spending and a managed currency, both implied in these recommendations, were not stressed in the public announcement.

When politics intervened to prevent application of such a plan in England, it was exported to the United States, where it provided a basic pattern for New Deal budgets of the nineteen-thirties. The idea of "paying" for politically profitable welfare programs by stripping the defense establishment was a long-cherished Socialist scheme that

---

[60] David McCord Wright, "Mr. Keynes and the 'Day of Judgment'," *Science*, November 21, 1958, Vol. 128, No. 3334, p. 1259. Published by the American Association for the Advancement of Science.

proved agreeable to Franklin D. Roosevelt. In consequence, U.S. Army recruits hastily called up after Pearl Harbor were discovered to be drilling with dummy rifles made of wood. Shelved for almost twenty-five years thereafter, the double-barreled Fabian Socialist scheme to procure funds for the "war against poverty" by a gradual process of military disarmament was suddenly revived by the Johnson Administration in 1964, as if it were a new invention.

First public intimation that British Fabian Socialists meant to foist their largely untried fiscal remedies upon the United States Government came on December 31, 1933. On that date, *The New York Times* printed an open letter from John Maynard Keynes to President Franklin D. Roosevelt which filled the better part of a page in the Sunday paper. The advice it contained was at once so paradoxical and so remote from the preoccupations of the average citizen that relatively few readers took it seriously. Only a handful of New Deal insiders, long allied with the London Fabian Society and its American offshoots, realized that Keynes' open letter laid down guidelines for financial policy which the keepers of the United States Treasury would observe for years to come.

In October, the Roosevelt Administration, following the Keynes-inspired example of the British Government, had abandoned the gold standard and adopted the device of a managed currency. To avoid serious fluctuations in the value of the dollar, Keynes now advised the United States Treasury to go into the business of buying and selling bullion. He also stated flatly that a *permanent* program of government "investment" in public works should be contemplated to supplement the inadequacies of private investment in creating employment. As aids to economic recovery, he recommended higher wages and higher prices—the latter to be achieved through a policy of cheap money and lower interest rates, touched off by lowered interest rates on government loans.

Above all, Keynes warned the President against "that crude economic fallacy known as the quantity theory of money!" This was a delicate way of suggesting that a government's spending need not be limited to the amount of its income, actual or anticipated. By inference, cheap money could always be borrowed to meet any threatened day-to-day deficits—leaving the long-range Government deficit a mere item of Treasury bookkeeping. In retrospect, it is obvious that every proposal made by Keynes in his open letter was subsequently adopted by the New Deal Administration.

For whatever reason, vast and still vaster sums were "invested" in public works. The United States Treasury proceeded to buy and sell silver as well as gold, at immense cost to taxpayers yet unborn and profit to the knowledgeable few. Through increased gold and silver purchases from Mexico in 1938, the New Deal Administration compensated the Mexican Government almost to the penny for loss of oil royalties incurred as a result of the latter's expropriation of American and British-owned oil leases and related properties—a maneuver attributed to Keynes' great friend, Harry Dexter White, then Assistant Secretary of the U.S. Treasury.

Between 1932 and 1953, "liberal" Democratic Administrations in Washington performed the remarkable feat of borrowing 250 billion dollars at steadily declining rates of interest, accomplished in part by pressure on the banks to absorb ever-larger quantities of government bonds. While each individual bond issue was repaid as it fell due, somehow the total remained on the Government books as an ever-mounting public debt. It was frenzied finance—a prescription for hand-to-mouth government operation, via a system of double entry bookkeeping.

Keynes paid a triumphal visit to the United States in June, 1934, one of numerous visitations. At that time, he was frequently consulted by many key persons in the Government, all eager for his comments and suggestions.[61] According to Secretary Perkins, he pointed out that in every respect the New Deal was doing exactly what his own theories called for. This was not surprising, in view of the fact that Keynes had cooperated closely with the British Fabian Socialist planners of PEP in drafting the preliminary plans for the New Deal, which were transmitted to Roosevelt via Felix Frankfurter, Stuart Chase, Harry Hopkins and Frances Perkins herself. When relief and public works appropriations were cut in 1937, Keynes warned of an economic recession—as did, in fact, occur, though not entirely for the reasons he alleged.

In 1934, Keynes was personally received by President Roosevelt, who wrote to their mutual friend, Felix Frankfurter, "I had a grand talk with K. and liked him immensely." [62] To Frances Perkins, however, the President confided: "I saw your friend Keynes. He left a whole rigamarole of figures. He must be a mathematician rather than

[61] Frances Perkins, The Roosevelt I Knew, (New York, The Viking Press, 1946), p. 225.
[62] Harrod, op. cit., p. 448.

a political economist." [63] On the whole, Keynes' invitation to a higher, wider and handsomer program of government spending proved a pleasant prospect to the President, even if the attempt to justify it mathematically did not. Roosevelt's own uncomplicated attitude toward money was best revealed in a mock-serious reproof to one of his secretaries who tended to be over-generous in her use of punctuation marks: "Grace, how often must I tell you not to waste the taxpayers' commas?" [64] Dollars or commas, they were much the same to FDR: if anything, he was more averse to wasting commas!

Following his interview at the White House, Keynes took the precaution of stopping in to see Secretary Perkins at the Department of Labor. After remarking ruefully that he had "supposed the President to be more literate, economically speaking," he rehearsed his famous theory of "the multiplier" in simple terms. The "multiplier" was actually an invention of Richard F. Kahn,[65] one of Keynes' clever students, which the "master" appropriated as his own.

As reported by Frances Perkins (on whose economic literacy he failed to comment), Keynes said that a dollar spent on relief was a dollar given in turn to the retailer, the wholesaler, and finally to the farmer—which, as any American farmer can testify, never happens! "With *one dollar*," Secretary Perkins enthused, "you have created *four dollars* worth of national income!" [66] And she added, "I wish Keynes had been as concrete when he talked to Roosevelt instead of treating him as though he belonged to the higher echelons of economic knowledge!" [67] Keynes shrewdly surmised that Secretary Perkins would convey his simplified explanations to the President. In consequence, Roosevelt soon afterwards requested—and received—a 4 billion dollar appropriation for public works from the Congress.[68]

It was not necessary to be a serious student of Keynes in order to put his preachings into practice. Marriner Eccles, chairman of the Federal Reserve Board under Roosevelt, for instance, definitely helped to promote policies based on Keynesian economics. These, as Professor Seymour Harris has mentioned approvingly, included: printing-press money, unbalanced budgets, attacks on thrift, a redistribution of national income; all leading to increased production, especially in

[63] Perkins, *op. cit.*, p. 225.
[64] Sherwood, *op. cit.*, 217.
[65] Harris, *op. cit.*, p. 51.
[66] (Italics added.)
[67] Perkins, *op. cit.*, p. 226.
[68] T. R. B., "Washington Letter," *New Republic*, (June 17, 1934).

consumers' industries, and to a larger volume of retail sales. Yet Eccles himself declared in 1951, "I have never read Keynes' writings except in small extracts to this day." [69]

Evidently Eccles derived his ideas from secondary sources, including some of his own assistants who were ardent Keynesians—among them, Lauchlin Currie. It may be useful to observe that Keynes' views were officially derided by Soviet economists, who declared with unexpected veracity that his recipes could not possibly save capitalism in the long run. Nevertheless, individuals since disclosed as agents of the Soviet conspiracy in Washington, such as Lauchlin Currie and Harry Dexter White, were among the most active promoters of Keynesian measures. That circumstance alone might lead one to suspect his policies did not coincide with the best interests of the United States.

With the appearance in 1936 of his *General Theory of Employment, Interest and Money*, the various anti-depression remedies advanced by Keynes were codified and elevated to the status of an economic doctrine. For its influence on men and events to come, publication of the *General Theory* has been held comparable only to that of Karl Marx's *Das Kapital*. Despite a difficult style quite unlike Keynes' lucid journalistic prose, the burden of the work is a simple one. Employing a strange vocabulary and an authoritative manner, the *General Theory* undertakes to demonstrate that public investment (or government spending) must be indefinitely prolonged to correct the "deficiencies" of private capital.

It is based on two major assumptions, both of Marxist origin and both open to serious question. First, that a government is in duty bound to provide "full employment" for its citizens: a condition only attained in the past under slave-economies. Second, that periodic slumps are inherent in the "sick" capitalist system. Regular infusions of government aid, therefore, are prescribed to insure a perpetual boom. The cure-all is attractively packaged and easy to swallow, even though the aftertaste may be bitter. If the patient eventually weakens and dies—well, that is bound to happen some day, and by then the hopeful physician will be out of reach. In the long run, as Keynes remarked, not too originally, we are all dead.

For devotees of pure English or uncluttered logic, reading Keynes' *General Theory* is a painful experience. The text abounds in such

[69] Marriner Eccles, *Beckoning Frontiers*, (New York, Alfred A. Knopf, 1951), pp. 37-39; 78-79; 132.

stock terms as "durable consumer goods"—though clearly, nothing consumed can properly be called durable. The word which Keynes used most assiduously, however, and to which he attached the most variable meanings, is a word reminiscent of the stock market speculation: namely, "marginal." Thus he speaks of "marginal tendency to consume"; the "marginal utility[70] of labor"; the "marginal efficiency of capital," by which he really means "inefficiency." All of these singular factors are measured percentage-wise and their effect on the national economy is computed.

"Liquidity preference" is the horrid phrase used by Keynes to describe the normal human impulse to keep some ready cash on hand, instead of spending or investing it at once. This, says Keynes, should be discouraged, because it takes money out of circulation. Saving is equated with hoarding, like the gold in the French peasant's sock— even though modern savings banks often play a very useful role in private investment. In that Keynesian wonderland of topsy-turvy verbiage and distorted logic, one notes a gradual but implacable trend toward shutting off all the sources which are the lifeblood of private investment—including a campaign to dishearten the long-term investor by ever lower interest rates. Thus, in an artificially stimulated economy, which Keynes visualizes as constantly expanding, the role of private capital must inevitably shrink in proportion to the always more dominant public or government sector, until initiative fails at last and free enterprise gives up the ghost without a struggle.

Though Keynes is usually regarded, quite correctly, as the father of deficit spending, the implications of his *General Theory* are more far-reaching than the average American who is not "economically literate" might suppose. Public investment—so called because it allegedly reaps dividends in the shape of larger tax returns, even if the original capital outlay is never recovered—involves a great deal more than the mere act of spending.[71] It means "planning" of the nation's economic life by invisible government planners; it means political supervision of private industry to measure its "social utility" and "efficiency" in providing jobs; it means a manipulated currency, to make certain that real wages do not rise too rapidly and that the only

---

[70] A term borrowed from Jevons and used as a replacement for the Marxian theory of surplus value.

[71] Some followers of Keynes assert that if sufficiently large sums are invested by government, the entire amount will return in taxes—thanks to the operation of the "multiplier." To date, this phenomenon has not occurred.

benefit of last week's wage raise will be a bigger tax deduction. In other words, it means Big and Bigger Government.

Total employment itself calls for higher and higher levels of production, presumably to absorb the labor of a growing population. It means Big Industry and Big Labor, both increasingly subservient to Big Government. Moreover, total employment demands total consumption—that is, continuous and frantic personal spending without thought for the future. Whatever is not spent returns as taxes to the Government, which will care in some fashion for its carefree citizens in old age, sickness and other contingencies. The society evolving from all this combines the philosophy of the grasshopper with the community life of the ant—a synthesis never imagined by LaFontaine, that innocent of the *ancien régime!*

The revolutionary nature of Keynes' New Economics was, of course, unnoticed by and unknown to the great American public. Its inner meaning was divulged only to the illumined few and has never to this day been generally acknowledged. Leaders of the international Socialist movement, however, were quick to grasp the point. The first enthusiastic review of Keynes' *General Theory* by any professional economist came from the pen of G. D. H. Cole,[72] avowed Marxist, lifelong foe of the profit system and foremost Fabian Socialist doctrinaire of his time.

Whether Keynes himself remained an overt or covert member of the British Fabian Society is a purely academic question. Born, bred and nourished in the Fabian creed, he is not known to have ever forsaken it. Most of his relatives and close friends were openly connected with Fabian Socialist organizations. In 1922, his sister, Helen Keynes, revived the Fabian Educational Group, a "liberal" women's group founded during World War I. Years later his niece, Polly Hill, became a staff member of the New Fabian Research Bureau, employed at her uncle's request.

Although Keynes declined to join the New Fabian Research Bureau except as an Associate Member, his refusal caused no rancor and his views on economics were reflected in a majority of the forty-two "solid research pamphlets" published by the Bureau between 1933 and 1938. It was understood that his gesture had been prompted by a desire to avoid compromising his policy-making role as financial adviser to liberal statesmen abroad and Coalition governments at home. For

[73] Seymour E. Harris, *John Maynard Keynes: Economist and Policy Maker,* (New York, Charles Scibner's Sons, 1955), p. 206.

years he continued to draw overflow crowds at lectures sponsored by the London Fabian Society. If he was not formally a member of the Society, he was still its most conspicuous ornament—and most effective secret weapon.

To disarm non-Socialist critics and to convey his true purpose to a Socialist elite, the author of the *General Theory* described himself blandly as an "economic nationalist." [73] Though the term mystified many, others recognized it as a reference to the nationalism of Edward Bellamy, early prophet of the cooperative commonwealth, whose novel, *Looking Backward,* Keynes had read as a boy in Cambridge, England. Memories of the Bellamy Nationalist clubs, America's first Fabian Socialist-inspired political movement, still survived in Cambridge, Massachusetts, where Keynes' influence was to become a potent latter-day force. Elsewhere he stated delicately: "The Republic of my imagination lies on the extreme left of celestial space." [74]

Keynes' views on the nationalization of basic industries were more candidly disclosed in a private letter of February 1, 1938, to President Franklin Delano Roosevelt. There he wrote:

. . . If I was in your place, I should buy out the utilities at a fair price in every district where the situation was ripe for doing so, and announce that the ultimate ideal was to make this policy nationwide. But elsewhere I would make peace on liberal terms, guaranteeing fair earnings for new investment and a fair basis of valuation in the event of the public taking them over hereafter.

That there should be no misunderstanding, he added: *"I accept the view that durable investment must come increasingly under state direction."* [75]

The system promulgated by Keynes, as even his most loyal disciples admit, was in reality no system at all. It was a rationale and a tool for achieving total political control, at a gradually increased tempo, over the economic life of a nation. Specifically designed to affect public policy, it adapted the once-pedestrian methods of Fabian Socialism to an age of high-powered mass production. More than any other contrivance, Keynes' New Economics performed the feat of lifting the Fabian tortoise off the back roads and byways, and putting it on a

---

[73] In his later years, Keynes also described himself solemnly as a "mercantilist" —referring to the eighteenth century mercantile theory, when foreign trade was under State control!

[74] *Nation and Athenæum*, (February 20, 1926).

[75] Franklin D. Roosevelt, *Papers, Keynes to Roosevelt,* (February 1, 1938). Franklin D. Roosevelt Library, Hyde Park, New York. (Italics added.)

modern freeway in a fast car supplied by its own willing victims.

Many years earlier—back in 1909, when the British Empire was strong enough to enforce peace throughout the world—spokesmen for the Conservative Party of Great Britain had asserted that Fabian Socialists would never be able to achieve their declared aim of non-violent social revolution—because the free enterprise system would never consent meekly to its own destruction.[76] To that taunt John Maynard Keynes, who became Lord Keynes of Tilton, supplied a delayed but deadly answer. He furnished a formula for the peaceful transition to Socialism and helped mightily to induce the United States, greatest industrial nation on earth, to adopt it as an official policy.

Dealing in broad generalities based on equally broad assumptions, the *General Theory* was merely a framework to which Keynes' acolytes and heirs could add such refinements or excrescences as their fancy dictated. It bred a new scholasticism, rather than objective study: for there could be no tampering with the basic concepts. Moreover, the macro-economics of Keynes, being primarily designed to influence public policy, implied that its adepts alone were qualified to plan the economic and fiscal destiny of nations. Thus the keys to the future were delivered into the hands of an intellectual elite trained to interpret the New Economics. This perhaps was the secret of its profound appeal to students and professors of political economy, intoxicated by the vistas of power and influence which their monopoly of the Keynesian technique conferred.

In academic circles the success of the *General Theory* was prompt and lasting. The young took it up and their elders followed, one of the first "older" economists to promote it being Professor Alvin Hansen of Harvard and the LID. A Keynesian school of thought arose, a close-knit fraternal entity whose members supported and advanced each other professionally. As Harvard Professor A. J. Schumpeter explained, this was a well-organized group professing "allegiance to one master and one doctrine," with "its propagandists, its watchwords, its esoteric and popular doctrine." [77] Linked to it was a wider ring of sympathizers in public and private life, and beyond these a still wider

---

[76] *The Case Against Socialism, A Handbook for Speakers and Candidates.* With prefatory letter by the Rt. Honourable A. J. Balfour. (London, George Allen & Sons, 1909), p. 90.

[77] *The New Economics: Keynes Influence on Theory and Public Policy,* A Symposium, Seymour E. Harris, ed., (New York, Alfred A. Knopf, 1947), p. 339.

ring of persons who had absorbed, consciously or unconsciously, some phases of the Keynesian mystique.

Harvard University, where Keynes lectured in person, appears to have been the first influential center from which those widening smoke rings of modern Fabian Socialist doctrine were wafted. Its glowing core was the Department of Economics which, by affiliation with the School of Business Administration, was even able to extend the Keynesian outlook into the industrial and managerial field. A proud example of this permeation process was Robert S. McNamara, who, after serving as an assistant professor of Business Administration at Harvard from 1940 to 1943 and flying a desk for several years in the Army Air Force, became an executive of the Ford Motor Company— and ultimately civilian czar of the United States Department of Defense. His role, as professional army men have pointed out, was to devise and execute a series of nonmilitary actions for encirclement of the military.

Anyone who studied at a leading American or British university in the middle nineteen-thirties remembers how all at once the whole character of political economy seemed to change; along with such allied subjects as sociology, history and political science. Every previous approach was suddenly found to be outdated, and the New Economics of John Maynard Keynes became the harbinger of a New Social Order. Actually, the New Economics was not quite so new as its name. It borrowed something from Jevons, the nineteenth century Briton applauded in the original *Fabian Essays*, and much from minor Scandinavian economists engaged in applying a type of Socialism which has been called the Middle Way. The only major economic prophet, however, whose teachings the new doctrine did not wholly contradict, was Karl Marx; for Keynes discreetly left some things unsaid.

Paul Sweezy, known today as a "brilliant" Marxist as well as an ardent Keynesian, still recalls the electric excitement, the tingling sense of power and opportunity unlimited, that swept the campus in his student days.[78] Even a nonprofessional economist like the late John F. Kennedy, who was a Harvard undergraduate in the years when the Keynesian revelation first dawned, could hardly have avoided being impressed by the newly fashionable economic gospel. Many years later, by way of a practical testimonial, President Kennedy

[78] *Ibid.*, p. 106.

invited a number of his old teachers to Washington to aid him in planning policies for the nation and the world. His own talk was rich in such Keynesian catchwords as the gross national product, the balance of payments, and especially National Growth, which seemed vague but full of promise to a largely untutored popular audience.

It is generally agreed today that there is hardly a political economist of prominence in America who—even when he appears critical of Keynes—has not been influenced by the Keynesian method.[79] If he had resisted seriously, it is safe to say he would not be prominent. So strong and widespread is the influence of the Keynesian School, as exerted through the American Economic Society, the American Academy of Political Science, the American Association of University Professors and other respected bodies—not to mention the League for Industrial Democracy and the Americans for Democratic Action.

A graduate student in economics at a major American university who was bold enough to attack the Keynesian method as the intellectual fraud of the century and the product of an inspired charlatan, would be surprised to receive a doctorate—and would probably have difficulty in securing either an academic or government post, or the publishing outlets needed to rise in the profession. So dominant and so exclusive has the New Economics become, that the posthumous authority of Keynes is even greater than it was in his lifetime, when he framed international monetary policy and dictated postwar trade policies for England and the United States.

For some thirty years the New Economics launched by Keynes has been potent political medicine in Washington. Deficit budgets and grandiose spending became the hallmarks not only of the New Deal, but also of its liberally permeated successors, the Fair Deal and the New Frontier. Public "investment" in public works was superseded by Lend-Lease in World War II, to be followed by the multiple forms of foreign aid and civilian-planned defense in the postwar era. A reversion to the early New Deal emphasis on welfare and public works, with some added global overtones, was evident in President Johnson's first State of the Union message.

One of the questions that appears to have escaped Keynes, as even the faithful Professor Harris admits, was: How high can a national debt rise without resulting in national bankruptcy?[80] Spurred by ad-

---

[79] Seymour E. Harris, *John Maynard Keynes: Economist and Policy Maker,* (New York, Charles Scribner's Sons, 1955), p. 208.
[80] *Ibid.,* p. 214.

vice from John Maynard Keynes and macro-economists of the Keynesian School, the architects of the official public debt of the United States caused it to soar to 305 billion dollars by July 1, 1963—some 25 billion dollars more than the combined public debts of the other 112 nations of the world. Yet the Government was still borrowing money to finance a permanent program of foreign aid, on which a substantial part of our domestic production and employment seemed to depend. Even now there are Keynesians in the United States and England who *complain that our annual deficits are not high enough to assure prosperity for all!*

Although Lord Keynes died peacefully in 1946 and was interred with all the pomp an admiring Labour Party Government in Britain could provide, the mischief he compounded lives on. If his influence was vast during his lifetime, it has been enormously magnified since his death. In the pantheon of Fabian Socialism, even a demigod is not irreplaceable: there are always trained heads and hands prepared to push his theories, with appropriate variations, to their unnatural conclusion.

The cult of national suicide, initiated by Keynes and known as the New Economics, is not only preserved but expanded by his sophisticated followers, operating through the twin channels of politics and higher education with the blessing of the Socialist International. An entire generation of political economists has been reared in Keynes' image; and Keynesian clichés have become the debased tender of intellectual exchange from Washington and London to Calcutta and Damascus. As *The New York Times* proclaimed in a banner headline on September 9, 1963: "Once revolutionary, the economics of Keynes now is orthodox." [81]

Almost imperceptibly, John Maynard Keynes became the "prophet of the new radicalism," as a current spokesman of that radicalism, Arthur M. Schlesinger, Jr., has confessed. Since its goals do not differ noticeably from those of the old radicalism, little public mention is made of ultimate aims. The technical expedients for achieving them at ever-accelerated speed are stressed. Thus the methodology of Keynes has inspired a whole series of new high speed techniques and new forms of penetration for effecting a tacit transition to Socialism under the somewhat bewildering conditions of the post World War II atomic era.

[81] *The New York Times,* (Western edition), (September 9, 1963). Article by British economist George Schwartz.

Far from being defunct today, the Keynesian approach has become almost unassailable by virtue of time and repetition. The deceptively innocent slogan of "full employment," for instance, was embodied in a Resolution passed in 1952 by the International Labor Organization in Geneva.[82] The same slogan reappears in the present-day programs of Socialist-directed trade unions and political organizations in the United States.

The Keynesian promise of a perpetual boom maintained through government spending—modern version of the Greek myth of the miraculous pitcher—was dished out as a basis for the Democratic Party's national election campaign of 1964. In the shape of dazzling and generally unsubstantiated statistics, it has been rewarmed and served up to an uncritical public through popular magazines,[83] daily columnists[84] and news releases from official sources. All presage, often without realizing it, a transition to that Socialist way of life which the London *Sunday Times* once defined as "competition without prizes, boredom without hope, war without victory and statistics without end."

The time-honored Fabian Socialist tenet, reaffirmed by Keynes, of indirect rule by an academic elite, was echoed as recently as 1963 in the Godkin Lectures delivered at Harvard by Clark Kerr, President of the University of California. The role of the professor in government, he noted, is no longer confined to Washington, but extends more and more into the fields of state and local administration as well. With the proliferation of the Federal-grant universities, that role seems destined to increase still further. Today, as never before, the campus is being drawn to the city hall and the state capitol. As Dr. Kerr explained it, the politicians need new ideas to meet new

[82] The Resolution referred to included the following significant sentence: "The Conference draws attention to the possible advantages of an international Convention which would provide for *the assumption by Governments to accept full employment as a primary objective of social and economic policy*, and to establish or designate appropriate national authorities which would be responsible for studying continuously the evolution of the employment situation and for making recommendations concerning the action to be taken to maintain full employment." (From a Report on the 34th Conference of the International Labor Organization, by William L. McGrath, Adviser to Charles P. McCormick, Employer Delegate on the United States delegation, p. 10). (Italics added.)

[83] See special Report: "$50 Billion Worth of Good News," *Life* magazine, (January 10, 1964).

[84] See nationally syndicated column by Sylvia Porter, published January 23, 1964 in the Riverside, California *Daily Enterprise*.

problems and the agencies need "expert" advice to handle the old problems. The professor, he asserted, can supply both.

By way of authority, he quoted the concluding sentences of Keynes' *General Theory*: ". . . 'the ideas of economists and political philosophers, both when they are right and when they are wrong, are more powerful than is commonly understood. Indeed the world is ruled by little else . . . . I am sure that the power of vested interests is vastly exaggerated compared with the *gradual encroachment of ideas*.' As, for example, the ideas of Keynes." [85]

[85] Clark Kerr, *The Uses of the University*, (Cambridge, Harvard University Press, 1963). Chapter III, "The Future of the City of Intellect," p. 116. (Italics added.)

19

Power And Influence

1.

THREE times in the twentieth century, American Fabian Socialists on advice of their principals in London have formed a new leadership group to meet the challenge of a new era. In each case this occurred during a period of change and dislocation following a victorious war. Invariably, too, it was at a moment when agents of more direct revolutionary action had so outraged public opinion that the future of radicalism in America seemed threatened and a protective front of more or less untarnished respectability was needed.

Following the Spanish-American War and coincident with the 1905 revolution in Russia, the Intercollegiate Socialist Society was founded upon the remnants of still earlier Fabian bodies. It was reorganized after World War I in the wake of various ill-starred Bolshevik intrigues, and became the League for Industrial Democracy, which supplied personnel and plans for the New Deal. Each leadership group in its day sparked a flurry of satellite organizations, committees and publications, longer or shorter lived as events might dictate. Thus the continuity and expansion of international Fabian Socialism under new names and fresh faces was assured, with the old goal of worldwide social revolution unchanged but unavowed. Psychologically, the process was adapted to what modern market research describes as the American taste for novelty, whether in the field of ideas or consumers' goods.

Not long after World War II another key organization appeared, known as Americans for Democratic Action. It emerged out of the vapors and confusion that afflicted Socialist groups in the immediate

342

postwar period. Directly descended from older Fabian Socialist elite bodies, ADA was more narrowly political in character than the ISS or LID, without actually being a political party. Just as a parasite vine can climb faster and higher by entwining itself around some previously rooted object, ADA would attach itself to one or both of the traditional political parties in the United States—with a view to imposing its program and its preferred candidates for national, state and local offices.

Like the original London Fabian Society, ADA's limited size, modest budget and announced object of social reform for the voting masses offered no clue to the scope of its ambitions or the revolutionary nature of its long-range goals. Unlike the London Society, however, whose constitution states flatly that "the Fabian Society consists of Socialists," Americans for Democratic Action has for reasons best known to itself usually chosen to deny its lineage and to disclaim its Socialist purpose.

Few contemporary Americans knew or cared that on January 3, 1947, a collection of men and women met at the Willard Hotel in Washington, D.C., to set up what has properly been called a political action arm of the American Fabian Socialist movement. Though not a large crowd, its precise size is difficult even now to determine. Informed estimates vary from more than 400 to a founders' list of 152 persons.[1] Nominally, they had responded to a "call" from the Union for Democratic Action to reorganize the "liberal" forces in the United States, at a time when the prestige of such forces was conceded to be at low ebb.

Since the day, almost two years before, when Franklin D. Roosevelt was laid to rest in the rose garden at Hyde Park, the political fortunes of the liberal Left had declined. Dazed New Deal Cabinet members and their aides relinquished their posts without a murmur.

[1] William E. Bohn, veteran American Socialist who was there, estimated the crowd at " a couple of hundred." *New Leader,* (April 15, 1957), p. 9.

Clifton Brock, a sympathetic historian, states it numbered "more than 400." Clifton Brock, *Americans For Democratic Action: Its Role in National Affairs.* Introduction by Max Lerner, (Washington, Public Affairs Press, 1962), p. 51.

Appearing before a House Committee in 1950, former Attorney General Francis Biddle, then national chairman of ADA, agreed to submit a founders' list of 350 names, as of January 7-9, 1947. This list, when submitted and published in the record of the Hearings, contained exactly 152 names. *Lobbying, Direct and Indirect.* Part 6 of Hearings before the House Select Committee on Lobbying Activities, House of Representatives, 81st Congress, Second Session, (Washington, U.S. Government Printing Office, House Document 66193, 1950). "Americans for Democratic Action," July 11, 12, 1950, pp. 19-23.

One by one, the wartime agencies with their wage-price-production controls, which left-wingers had hoped to retain as instruments of postwar policy, were folding. So-called liberals and progressives were being separated by the hundreds from the Federal payroll. Only the Department of State had succeeded in absorbing on a permanent basis any substantial number of the temporary wartime employees who could be relied upon to further assorted leftist aims.[2]

Access to the Presidential power, that made possible the attainment of so many Socialist schemes under Democratic Party auspices in the New Deal era,[3] was no longer a "liberal" perquisite. The new White House occupant, Harry S. Truman, was a product of Missouri's Pendergast machine, which could claim closer ties with the underworld of organized crime than with the ideologists of organized labor's Socialist wing. Henry Wallace—long the white hope of those Progressives who backed him instead of Truman for the Vice Presidential nomination in 1944—appeared to have thrown caution to the winds, and was now reputed on good authority to be negotiating with U.S. Communist leaders to form a Third Party.[4]

The Cold War—a concept never fully accepted by Fabians—had replaced the starry-eyed wartime alliance with Soviet Russia and its agents in the United States. Slowly and painfully, the activities of Communists who had been employed indiscriminately since 1934 by Liberal-Democrat administrations in Washington were beginning to come to light. In June, 1945, the Federal Bureau of Investigation had arrested six persons associated with *Amerasia*, an obscure leftist periodical that maintained connecting offices in New York City with the

---

[2] *Interlocking Subversion in Government Departments*, pp. 26-29. (See Bibliography). Testimony of J. Anthony Panuch, former Deputy Assistant Secretary of State, concerning the absorption in large numbers of "un-screened personnel" by the Department of State at the close of World War II. "I would say," stated Mr. Panuch (p. 29), "that the biggest single thing that contributed to the infiltration of the State Department was the merger of 1945. The effects of that are still being felt, in my judgment.

[3] Harry W. Laidler, *Socialism in the United States*, (New York, League for Industrial Democracy, 1952), p. 16. "Then came the New Deal legislation," wrote Dr. Laidler. "Roosevelt and his followers adopted immediate demand after immediate demand from the platform of the Socialist Party . . . in the light of these developments many labor progressives and radicals swung their support from the Socialist Party to the New Deal. The socialist movement found itself in the curious position of having collectively and through individual Socialists, greater influence in molding legislation than ever before, while finding it increasingly difficult to obtain a large membership and following as a party."

[4] Brock, *op. cit.*, p. 72.

then widely known and respected Institute of Pacific Relations. Incident to those arrests, the FBI recovered a staggering total of seventeen hundred top secret, secret and/or confidential documents relating to the Far East, all stolen from U.S. Government files.

In January, 1946, the defection of Igor Gouzenko, code clerk at the Soviet Embassy in Ottawa, led to the discovery of other widespread Communist espionage in Canada and the United States, aimed at undermining America's postwar control of atomic weapons. Failure of the Truman Administration to prosecute the *Amerasia* case convincingly,[5] or to act energetically on information conveyed by Canadian authorities, furnished a natural campaign issue for the Republicans, who won control of the Congress in November, 1946, for the first time in years. Sadly the left wing *Nation* proclaimed in an election postmortem: "Let us not fool ourselves in this hour of appraisal. The progressive forces in America have been routed."

For the *Nation* and its friends, however, there was still comfort in the fact that a Fabian-dominated Labour Party Government held power in postwar England. Pledged to liquidate the Empire overseas and the private enterprise system at home, rulers of that new Socialist stronghold were engaged in nationalizing Britain's basic industries and regimenting her traditionally independent people along welfare state lines, on the strength of a spurious campaign promise to "abolish poverty." "Now American progressives, temporarily out of power, have much to learn from Britain," wrote David C. Williams in the *Fabian Journal*, monthly organ of the London Fabian Society. "As issues such as Palestine move toward solution, there will be growing attention to England's domestic programme and an increasing tendency to put English experience to use in America."[6]

For the time being, the Labour Party Government's lavish deficits

---

[5] Among six persons arrested, only three were indicted. Of those three, one pleaded guilty and was fined $2,500; another entered a plea of *nolo contendere* and was fined $500; Justice Department attorneys dropped an airtight case against the third. Overwhelming evidence obtained by the FBI was suppressed. As recently as 1962—according to the Department of State's *Biographic Register* for 1961-62—one of the six, John Stewart Service, was serving as U.S. Consul in Liverpool, England. He has since been honorably retired on Government pension . . . . Hearings held by a House Committee in 1946, confirming the guilt of all six persons arrested, were withheld from publication for four years. They were finally printed in the *Congressional Record*, Vol. 96, Part 6, 81st Congress, Second Session, (May 22, 1950), pp. 7428 ff.

[6] David C. Williams, "Labour Britain and American Progressives," *Fabian Journal*, (March, 1947), p. 9.

were being underwritten by the United States. A multibillion dollar "reconstruction" loan to Britain, negotiated by the late lamented John Maynard Keynes, had been approved by a Democratic Congress in the spring of 1946; but more aid would unquestionably be needed to keep British Fabian Socialists in office for an indefinite term. To assure sympathetic cooperation at the highest official levels, it was essential for American Fabian Socialists, temporarily in eclipse, to improve their own situation at the earliest possible date.

This necessity was emphasized by a visit from the Honourable Patrick Gordon Walker, Labour M.P. and special emissary of the Fabian International Bureau. Soon after the November elections in America, he was dispatched on a lecture tour of the Eastern United States by David C. Williams, then directing the London Bureau of the Union for Democratic Action. Avowed reason for Gordon Walker's trip was to rally America's liberal Left in support of the Socialist Government in Britain.[7] His arrival in January, 1947, was timed to synchronize with a conference at the Willard Hotel called by the Union for Democratic Action.

That two-day conference in the nation's capital marked the birth of Americans for Democratic Action (ADA). Sometimes described as a New-Deal-in-exile, ADA's primary aim irrespective of high-sounding declarations was to recapture for its supporters the power and influence that individual Socialists (according to Dr. Harry Laidler) had enjoyed under the New Deal. In a keynote speech delivered at the opening session of the conference, Governor Chester Bowles of Connecticut[8] urged the delegates by implication to disassociate themselves from past united front activities and to "organize a progressive front divorced from Communist influence." After scoring "illusions about a Third Party," he denounced Republicans and conservative Democrats with impartial fervor. "But the fact remains," he concluded, "that we have no practical alternative. *All our efforts, all our ingenuity must be thrown into the struggle to establish liberal [sic] control of the Democratic Party.*"[9]

Next day at a caucus composed of the more influential delegates, it was agreed that the Union for Democratic Action, boasting at most ten thousand members throughout the country, would merge with a new organization to be called Americans for Democratic Ac-

---

[7] Williams, *op. cit.*, p. 10.
[8] More recently Under Secretary of State and Ambassador to India in the Kennedy-Johnson Administration.
[9] Brock, *op. cit.*, p. 51. (Italics added.)

tion. Among those taking part in the caucus were Eleanor Roosevelt, Presidential widow; David Dubinsky of the AFL and Walter Reuther of the CIO; Joseph Rauh, Jr., Washington attorney, subsequently known as "Mr. ADA"; Marquis Childs, newspaper columnist and author of *Sweden: The Middle Way*, an apologia for Scandinavian Socialism. Predetermined conclusions reached by this policy-making group were reported back to the conference on the very same day by Eleanor Roosevelt, who also stressed the view that the handiest vehicle for immediate advancement of the new organization's program was the Democratic Party.[10] A carefully pruned statement of ADA principles was released to the press by Barry Bingham, editor and publisher of the Louisville *Courier-Journal*.

To anyone schooled in the ways of American Fabian Socialism, operating behind a mask of liberal reformism and addicted to creating over the years new organizations with continuously interlocking memberships, the founders' conference of ADA was merely a repetition of history. True, the Willard Hotel was a long way from the loft above Peck's Restaurant, where founders of the Intercollegiate Socialist Society had met in response to a similar "call" more than forty years earlier. A larger number of the mid-century conferees could be classed as "opinion-formers," having already achieved national prominence in their respective fields of politics, labor, education, religion and journalism; while others freely aspired to public office. Still there was an odor about the proceedings reminiscent of the old Fulton Street Fish Market district—although the sole surviving founder of the defunct Intercollegiate Socialist Society to attend was Dan Hoan, former Socialist Mayor of Milwaukee.

There was more visible evidence of kinship with the League for Industrial Democracy, successor to the ISS and still a going concern in its own right. In fact, the tie with LID was secured by a double knot. The Union for Democratic Action, which officially fathered ADA, had been launched on April 28, 1941, shortly after passage of the Lend-Lease Act and just before Hitler's anticipated attack on Russia.[11] Formed to "help the Allies win the war," it was summoned

[10] *The New York Times*, (January 5, 1947).
[11] The date for Hitler's invasion of Russia was originally set for May 15, 1941. It was postponed six weeks, until June 22, apparently as a result of General William Donovan's trip to Yugoslavia undertaken at the request of Britain's Secret Service chief in the United States, William Stephenson. These facts were known at the time to top U.S. as well as Russian officials.
H. Montgomery Hyde, *Room 303*, (New York, Dell Publishing Co., 1964), (re-

into being by a committee whose officers and members consisted almost to a man of seasoned LID "collaborators." [12] A number of the selfsame individuals afterwards turned up as founders, officers and/or hard-core members of ADA.[13]

In his semi-official history of Americans for Democratic Action, an ADA Book Club selection in 1962, Professor Clifton Brock remarked by way of exculpation: "The UDA, ADA's predecessor organization, was a splinter group spun off the Socialist Party. Very few UDA members remain in ADA today." [14] The statement is both vague and misleading. In the first place, the announced aims of Union for Democratic Action and Americans for Democratic Action have never conflicted noticeably—as Brock's use of the term "splinter group" would imply—with the aims of the little American Socialist Party or the larger Socialist International. Second, UDA disbanded when ADA was founded; but former UDA members joined the new organization en bloc, forming the nucleus of its day-to-day activities until age or political office made it preferable for them to retire to the sidelines. Moreover, ADA—in common with the London Fabian Society—has never laid undue stress on formal membership, once an identity of ideas and aims has been established.

At least three former UDA activists were to serve for years as rotating officials of ADA. These were: James Loeb, Jr., called the "organizing genius of UDA"; James Wechsler, editor-columnist of the New York *Post*, a confessed former Communist who embraced the Middle Way; and Joseph Rauh, Jr., termed the "lodestar" of ADA, who in his zeal for civil liberties has consistently served as counsel for individ-

---

print), p. 62. An authorized account of British Secret Service in the United States during World War II. Previously published in 1962 by Farrar, Straus and Co., and published in England under the title, *The Quiet Canadian*.

[12] Officers of the committee issuing the "call" to UDA were listed in *The New York Times* (April 29, 1941). Chairman: Reinhold Niebuhr. Vice chairmen: John L. Childs, Professor of Education, Teachers' College, Columbia University; Franz Daniel, General Manager of the Laundry Workers' Joint Board, Amalgamated Clothing Workers, CIO; Robert Bendiner, editor of *The Nation*. Secretary: Murray Gross, Complaint Manager, Dressmakers Union, ILGWU. Treasurer: Freda Kirchwey, Managing Editor of *The Nation*. (See Appendix V for names of full committee.)

All but one of the above-named officers, and a majority of the committee members appear on the official list of League for Industrial Democracy "collaborators" and student chapter-heads, published by Mina Weisenberg. (See Appendix II.)

[13] See Appendix V for official list of ADA founders.

[14] Brock, *op. cit.*, p. 216.

uals suspected of giving aid and comfort to Communists, from William Remington to Sidney Lens.[15]

These three—Loeb, Weschler and Rauh—are sometimes said to have been the "real founders" of ADA, which is not literally true. They could more accurately be described as expendables and front-runners of Americans for Democratic Action—a semi-secret political society whose membership lists have never been made public and whose alleged sympathizers frequently seem as effective in its behalf as any dues-paying member. All three were present at the ADA's founding conference. James Loeb, Jr.[16] was promptly named secretary-treasurer of a national organizing committee, jointly headed by Leon Henderson, former director of the Office of Price Administration, and Wilson Wyatt, former housing expediter, who became campaign manager for Adlai Stevenson in 1952.

The converging bloodlines of ADA were exemplified in the person of Dr. Reinhold Niebuhr, presiding at the Willard Hotel conference. He was not only national chairman of the Union for Democratic Action; but also former president of LID New York chapter and a seemingly permanent member of the LID national board of directors. Leading theologian of the liberal Left,[17] Dr. Niebuhr's doctrines like his politics were "progressive." Originally an advocate of the "Social

[15] William Remington, wartime U.S. Department of Commerce official, was convicted of perjury for denying Communist Party connections and for denying he had given information to a Communist espionage agent. His counsel was Joseph Rauh, Jr.

Sidney Lens—sometime director of United Service Employees Union Local 329, AFL-CIO, whose name appears on the masthead of many latter-day Socialist publications—was questioned on February 15, 1963 by the Senate Subcommittee on Internal Security regarding alleged connections with the Fair Play for Cuba Committee; as well as with Communist-sponsored organizations cited at the time on the Attorney General's list. To most of the questions, he pleaded lapse of memory. Asked if he had ever belonged to a Trotskyist organization, he took the Fifth Amendment. His attorney was Joseph Rauh, Jr.

[16] James Loeb, Jr., publisher of a small newspaper in upstate New York, later served briefly as Ambassador to Peru in the Kennedy-Johnson Administration. He was recalled at the request of Peruvian authorities, for alleged interference in that country's national elections, and has since been sent as Ambassador to Guinea.

[17] Other socially conscious clerics who attended the Willard Hotel Conference and are inscribed as ADA founders were: Rt. Rev. William Scarlett, Episcopal Bishop of St. Louis; Dr. A. Powell Davies, pastor of All Souls Unitarian Church, Washington, D.C.; Rabbi Milton Steinberg of the Park Avenue Synagogue, New York City; Reverend (now Monsignor) George Higgins of the Social Action Committee of the National Catholic Welfare Conference; Bishop G. Bromley Oxnam, retiring president of the Federal Council of Churches. (See Appendix V.)

Gospel," he had progressed by 1934 to a doctrine which he styled "Christian Radicalism."

At that point—as his young friend and co-founder of ADA, Arthur M. Schlesinger, Jr. has noted—Niebuhr rejected the Sermon on the Mount for pragmatism, even declaring that the choice between violence and nonviolence in social change was purely a matter of expediency.[18] In his *Reflections on the End of an Era*, published in 1934, Niebuhr saw "the sickness of capitalism" as something organic, rooted in its very nature and "in the private ownership of the productive process." He declared Marxism—which by definition is godless—to be "an essentially correct theory and analysis of the economic realities of modern society" and predicted "the end of capitalism will be bloody rather than peaceful." [19]

By 1944, when he delivered the West Foundation lectures at Stanford University, Dr. Niebuhr had progressed far enough to perceive the expediency of the Keynesian approach. Published the following years as *The Children of Light and the Children of Darkness* (a book Senator Robert Kennedy would take with him to the moon!), that lecture series was a plea for the "mixed economy" and the "open society" according to the gospel of John Maynard Keynes.[20] In 1947, as a top figure in UDA, Niebuhr professed himself a "pragmatic liberal," opposed to every dogma and dedicated to gradual, piecemeal social reform, very much as the early British Fabian Socialists had contrived to represent themselves to the public. That was the image, above all others, which ADA hoped to convey to the American people.

An outsider, witnessing those deliberations at the Willard Hotel that spawned the ADA, might easily have supposed he had wandered into some anniversary function of the League for Industrial Democracy. So many of the old familiar faces were there! The usual blue chip speakers and greeters at annual LID conferences and dinners—with the exception of such proclaimed Socialists as Norman Thomas or Harry Laidler—were in evidence on the platform and the floor.

Eleanor Roosevelt, who was to receive an LID award in 1953 as "First Woman of the World," was free at last to proclaim her organi-

[18] *Reinhold Niebuhr: His Religious, Social and Political Thought.* A Symposium. Edited by Charles W. Kegley and Robert W. Bretell, (New York, The Macmillan Co., 1956), p. 135.

[19] *Ibid.*, p. 137.

[20] As far back as 1926, Keynes had written: "The next move is with the head, and fists must wait." John Maynard Keynes, *Essays in Biography*, (New York, Harcourt, Brace & Co., 1933), p. 91.

zational ties with the liberal Left. She was accompanied by her son, Franklin D. Roosevelt, Jr., who as a Congressman would roll up a 100 per cent voting score in favor of ADA-approved bills, and who was to become Under Secretary of Commerce in the Kennedy-Johnson Administration. In Eleanor Roosevelt's entourage were her ever-controversial protégés, Joseph P. Lash and Aubrey Williams. Lash has been listed as an early LID collaborator. Williams, an editor of the *Southern Farmer* and deeply involved in the budding "civil rights" movement, was to serve on the national committee of the American Civil Liberties Union,[21] a League for Industrial Democracy affiliate.

Such veteran LID "collaborators" as Senators Herbert Lehman, Richard Neuberger and Frank Graham, sometime president of the University of North Carolina, were prominently on hand, along with senators-to-be Hubert Humphrey and Paul Douglas. Also present was Congressman Andrew Biemiller, another old regular of the League, later to serve as a congressional lobbyist for the united AFL-CIO. David Dubinsky of the ILGWU, Walter Reuther of the United Auto Workers, James Carey of the Union of Electrical, Radio and Machine Workers and other left wing union chieftains cited as stable collaborators of LID, attended in person, flanked by their lawyers and lieutenants. Directly or indirectly, they offered the electoral and financial backing of Socialist-led unions grown to giant size in World War II.[22]

Editors and journalists long true to LID hastened to place their skills at the disposal of ADA. They included Robert Bendiner of *The Nation;* William Bohn, an old Socialist warrior of the "80 per cent Socialist" *New Leader;* Monroe Sweetland of the Molalla, Oregon *Pioneer,* afterwards on the campaign staff of Presidential candidate John F. Kennedy; and, of course, James Wechsler of the New York *Post.* Other old LID-ers were columnist Edgar Ansell Mowrer and long time Soviet apologist Louis Fischer. Ironically enough, two new-

[21] See Appendix IV. As of 1964, Aubrey Williams was also national chairman of the Committee to Abolish the House Un-American Activities Committee.

[22] In 1961 the three—the UAW, the UEW and ILGWU—were announced to be among the ten wealthiest labor unions in the United States, according to a list made available for the first time by the U.S. Department of Labor. Ranking second and third in annual income were the Electrical Workers and the Auto Workers, with annual incomes of $62,273,000 and $50,668,000, respectively. Fifth on the list was the ILGWU, with an annual income of $21,702,000 . . . . United Steelworkers of America, which topped them all with an income in excess of $65,000,000 was also represented at the ADA founders' conference; but withdrew its support a few years later because of alleged ADA radicalism.

comers better known for their social graces than Socialist leanings, the brothers Joseph and Stewart Alsop, headed the alphabetical list of ADA charter members.

At its inception, Americans for Democratic Action appeared to be little more than a body of self-anointed political leaders in search of a following, and a program in search of a party. Convinced that no third party could win practical power in the United States, ADA's initial task was to detach misguided progressives from the third party movement then being organized by Henry Wallace with the backing of American Communists. For the moment, what Professor Brock cynically calls "the utility of enemies on the Left" was doubly clear to ADA. By disassociating itself openly from domestic Communist Party leaders servile to Moscow (and subject, in any case, to being removed without notice), ADA insured its own respectability, as well as its ability to shield the more vulnerable elements of the Left in time of peril.

Apparently, ADA was the American version of that mysterious Third Force, often referred to by postwar European Socialists. The term was first used in Austrian Social Democratic newspapers, and given currency in the late nineteen-forties by the French Socialist leader, Leon Blum, to denote the end of the Popular Front. Deprecating Communist Party tactics on the one hand, and decrying conservatives as reactionary-fascist on the other, ADA sought to impose its own formula for achieving social change, via a series of New Deal-type "reforms," as the only reasonable alternative.

Toward the Soviet Union proper, ADA's attitude was marked by the same patience and helpfulness (though, naturally, "a little bit criticizing")[23] which always distinguished the London Fabian Society. Indeed, the original ADA program asserted: "We firmly believe in breaking out of the vicious circle of mutual distrust between ourselves and Russia. We favor a policy based on an understanding of the legiti‑ mate [sic] aspirations of the Soviet Union."

The function of this reborn organization was not solely to regain power and influence for its members and sympathizers, nor simply to repeat the experience of the New Deal. It was also to develop and speed new applications of the Keynesian method for a peaceful transi‑ tion to Socialism, in terms of the postwar era. Momentarily, econo‑

[23] *Hearings of the Subcommittee on Internal Security of the United States Senate Committee on the Judiciary,* pp. 44-45. Statement of Colonel Igor Bogolepov.

mists of the Keynesian school (represented at the ADA founders' meeting by Dr. Boris Shishkin of the ILGWU and LID, and Dr. J. Kenneth Galbraith of *Fortune* Magazine and Harvard University) were somewhat embarrassed. The big American depression they predicted so confidently would follow World War II had somehow failed to materialize. How could all-out deficit spending be justified, in a robust and expanding economy?

As things turned out, there was little need for philosophic justification. Even so frivolous a bit of Keynesian propaganda as Galbraith's book, *The Affluent Society*, proved largely superfluous, except as a morale builder for Keynesian professors. The utility of government spending as a lever for winning elections was already apparent to practical Democratic leaders and to legislators of both national parties —the more so, when pointed up by ADA-stimulated pressures from trade unions, minority groups and liberal intellectuals. One project after another for permanent Federal spending programs in the fields of housing, health, nutrition, education and general "welfare" would be concocted by ADA or its allies, and presented by its chosen legislators. Defeated in one session of Congress, such bills would be revived with variations in the next.

Increased government authority over bank credit and bank reserves would be urged. "Goals" in housing, health, education and related fields were to be set by administrative planners. "Full employment," keystone of the whole Keynesian economic structure, must be accepted as a responsibility of the Federal Government, with planning, supervision and controls over private employment implied but not stated. Government financing, and if necessary, government plants must be used to "provide more power, more steel and other vitally necessary raw materials." Finally, would arise, during an election year, the Area Redevelopment Administration Program. All these steps would be proposed successively in ADA platforms, and urged again and again on the Congress and the Executive, until accepted in whole or in part. Each would lead the country another step closer to total welfare state control, and expand the "public sector" of the economy as opposed to the "private sector."

Something new, however, was to be added in the new era: namely, uninhibited government spending in the international field. Means would be devised to transform the Marshall Plan—supposedly designed for temporary postwar reconstruction and eagerly supported by ADA—into a permanent, large-scale program of foreign assistance, direct and indirect. Even military spending at home and abroad would not be discouraged, providing the ultimate decisions were dictated by ADA-approved State Department officials. Until such time as international control of atomic energy (advocated in the original 1947 ADA program, and never abandoned) had been achieved, the threat of nuclear destruction could always be raised to generate that atmosphere of perpetual crisis needed to justify Keynesian spending policies. Membership cards of ADA announced its devotion to *"freedom and security for all people everywhere"* [24]—presumably at the expense of the United States.

It is hard to believe a handful of people, meeting privately at the Willard Hotel in 1947, could have contrived to spark so many of the measures which in less than twenty years have propelled the United States so far and so fast along the freeway to International Socialism. In fact, it might seem incredible, except for the undisguised evidence of what an even smaller group of Fabian Socialists—through penetration and permeation, through research, propaganda and persistence—has done to make a shambles of the former British Empire.

2.

Possibly because he was in England when the reorganization[25] took place, a key instigator and ever-faithful servant of Americans for Democratic Action was not included on its founders' list. He was David C. Williams, wartime representative in London of American trade unions and director of the London Bureau of the Union for Democratic Action Educational Fund. Concerning him, an editorial note in the *Fabian Journal* for March, 1947, (p. 7) stated authoritatively: "David C. Williams . . . is a member of the Fabian Society and of the St. Marylebone Local Fabian Society."

Recalling that normal procedure in the Fabian Society has always been "join for one year, join for fifty," there is no reason to suppose the foregoing statement is outdated—although the formalities of membership are not infrequently waived for individuals engaged in delicate overseas missions. David C. Williams, in particular, has been notable for his unswerving devotion to the cause of Fabian Socialism, by whatever name it might be called.

---

[24] (Italics added.)

[25] *Fabian Journal*, monthly organ of the Fabian Society, duly noted the formation of ADA. A footnote in its March, 1947 issue (p. 10), referring to the Union for Democratic Action, stated: "Recently reorganised under the title 'Americans for Democratic Action' it includes as officers and members many persons prominent in the New Deal, and in trade union and progressive organisations."

As ADA's Director of Research and Education[26] and as long time editor of the *ADA World*, he has had a major responsibility for transmitting and expounding the Fabian policy-line on selected issues to ADA supporters. For almost twenty years, indifferent to wealth or worldly success, this quiet American has served as an efficient, durable and self-effacing link between Americans for Democratic Action and its Socialist blood brothers in Britain.

Williams was an Ohioan by birth and a citizen of the world by choice. Son and namesake of a Unitarian clergyman who once headed the Intercollegiate Socialist Society's student chapter at Marietta College,[27] he qualifies as a second generation Fabian Socialist. Perhaps the most decisive fact in his life was that he went as an American Rhodes Scholar to Oxford, graduating in 1935. There he encountered a left wing political group operating on a scale then undreamed-of in the United States. For the first time, he saw labor politics practiced in public style by a student elite and was exposed to adult masterminds of a movement that was destined to provide him with a career.

It was a decade when Fabian influence, frustrated at the government level in Great Britain, rose to commanding heights in the universities. At Oxford G. D. H. Cole was "the great gazebo," while at Cambridge John Maynard Keynes personally taught his exciting new theory. The Left Wing political tradition, however, was more pronounced and more continuous at Oxford.[28] Many an American student less predisposed than Williams found the allure of Fabian tutors and companions overwhelming, and never recovered from that early infatuation.

University Fabian Societies transformed into Labour Clubs[29] flour-

[26] In the *Fabian International Review*, to which David C. Williams contributed an article on the 1956 national elections in the United States, the following item appeared in a column headed "Our Contributors": "David C. Williams is Director of Research and Education, Americans for Democratic Action." *Fabian International Review*, No. 12, (September, 1956), p. 15.

In an editorial box on page 3, the same issue of the same publication stated: "*Fabian International Review* was launched in January, 1953 to provide a serious socialist commentary of world events. Since then it has appeared every four months. It is with regret, therefore, that we announce this as our last issue.

"We have tried to maintain a good all-round quality and to contribute usefully to discussion among socialists . . . .

"The Fabian International Bureau will continue, of course, to publish pamphlets."

[27] See Appendix II.

[28] Margaret Cole, *The Story of Fabian Socialism*, (London, Heinemann Educational Books, Ltd., 1961), pp. 208-209.

[29] By 1924 all University Fabian Societies had become Labour Clubs, according to the *Fabian Society Annual Report*, 1924-25, p. 8.

ished almost beyond belief. The Oxford Labour Club in the thirties, for instance, boasted a thousand members and functioned virtually as a separate college within the university. It organized its own classes and lecture courses under its own touted professors and tutors, among them confirmed Fabian Socialists like G. D. H. Cole, A. D. Lindsay, Sir Arthur Salter and R. H. S. Crossman.[30] When the club held public meetings on questions of the day, it drew student audiences of two or three thousand. The speakers were such well-publicized personalities as Professor Harold Laski, John Strachey, Harold Nicolson, Herbert Morrison, Sir Stafford Cripps, all ranking members of the London Fabian Society.[31] Even the American Negro baritone, Paul Robeson, then attracting overflow audiences in London, gave a free concert at Oxford for the Labour Club.

Political theory was enlivened by some practical experience in politics, which involved organizing workers in nearby factory towns, sending delegations to Parliament and picketing the Ministries. Besides serving as a seed bed for future Fabian statesmen and civil servants, the Labour Club was also an agitational branch of the British Labour Party. Oxford students, transported to London by the busload, lent color and verve to mass demonstrations against the Government—a pattern now being commonly repeated in other countries around the world, sometimes with Communist assistance. More than one American joined the fun, although for visitors participation in British politics was strictly illegal. In 1938, Howard K. Smith—afterwards a foreign correspondent and television news analyst—became the first American Rhodes Scholar to head the Oxford Labour Club.[32]

British club members automatically held membership in the British Labour Party. Regardless of nationality, young Fabians of the inner circle that steered the Labour Club were elected as undergraduates into the parent London Fabian Society, according to a practice established since the turn of the century.[33] With reference to Americans,

[30] Howard K. Smith, *Last Train from Berlin*, (New York, Alfred A. Knopf, 1942), pp. 34-38. Though he could hardly have been unaware of the fact, Smith failed to mention that the teachers and speakers whom he named were all well-known Fabian Socialists.

[31] *Ibid.*, pp. 34-38.

[32] *Ibid.*, p. 38. *ADA World* for February, 1964, reporting Howard K. Smith's participation at a local ADA function, boasted he would be in charge of news coverage and analysis at the national party conventions for a nationwide TV network in 1964.

[33] Edward R. Pease, *The History of the Fabian Society*, (London, A. C. Fifield, 1916), p. 103. "In 1895," wrote Pease, "a University Fabian Society was formed at Oxford by and for undergraduates, but maintaining continuity by the assist-

the process appears to have moved into high gear during the nineteen-thirties—the decade of the Great Depression, the Spanish Civil War and the coming to power of Adolf Hitler. Not only the potential rulers of England,[34] but potential rulers of the United States as well, were to be groomed under Fabian supervision.

This was no mild academic joke; but a serious, long-range intention, pursued with patience and finesse, and backed by all the well-placed contacts at home and abroad that the Fabian Society could assemble. Young hopefuls tapped for future prominence usually rose with astonishing celerity in their chosen careers. They were the predestined recipients of fellowships, research grants, literary prizes and other awards, as well as choice posts in government and the professions. Since the Association of Rhodes Scholars made corresponding efforts on behalf of its members, in the long run the results were doubly gratifying.

Thus one finds Rhodes Scholars of the nineteen-thirties serving in the nineteen-sixties as senior officials or consultants in a number of Federal departments in Washington. Some have been in government service for years; others are retreads and/or recent appointees. A few are in position to wield great influence, and through their access to the White House itself, to be instrumental in promoting policies advocated by British Fabians—notably in the fields of international, military, disarmament and monetary policy.

Meanwhile, Britons who were once their contemporaries in the Oxford Labour Club have risen to leadership in the Labour Party, and speak with authority in the councils of the Socialist International. A conspicuous example is Harold Wilson, Parliamentary Leader of the British Labour Party and Vice Chairman of the Socialist International, who was a student and Fellow at Oxford in the nineteen-thirties. In a memorial to the late President John F. Kennedy—"one of the numerous tributes paid to . . . [him] by Socialists throughout the world"[35]—Wilson said: "I know a good number of his associates; some of them I have known for many years."[36]

---

ance of older members in permanent residence, such as Sidney Ball at St. John's. In 1900 there were four Fabian Societies at Oxford, Glasgow, Aberystwyth and Cambridge, and their members were always elected at once into the parent society in order that the connection may not be broken when they leave the University."

[34] Cole, *op. cit.*, p. 86.
[35] *Socialist International Information*, (December 7, 1963), Vol. XIII, No. 49.
[36] *Ibid.*, p. 715.

At least one effect of such long-standing camaraderie must be noted, which vitally affects the security and defense capabilities of the United States. On July 24, 1963, Harold Wilson attended a meeting of the Bureau of the Socialist International at Congress House in London. There a resolution was adopted concerning the Moscow Three-Power Conference on nuclear tests, which declared in part:

The Bureau of the Socialist International welcomes the prospect of an agreement ending nuclear tests in the atmosphere, in space and under water . . . . The Bureau hopes that this limited agreement will pave the way to an agreement covering all nuclear tests. *The Bureau pays tribute to the efforts of Mr. Harold Wilson who during his recent conversations with Mr. Krushchev suggested this limited agreement as the most fruitful means to achieve early progress.*[37]

Soon afterwards—despite a sober warning from General Curtis LeMay, then U.S. Air Force Chief of Staff—the United States Congress was persuaded to ratify the test ban agreement suggested to Khrushchev by that noted nonmilitary expert, Harold Wilson, and endorsed by the Socialist International. At a time when civilian planners in the Pentagon looked primarily to atomic missiles for the future defense of America, the pact prevented the United States from testing the efficiency of nuclear warheads on missiles still unproved! Some leading proponents of the test ban in administration circles were Secretary of State Dean Rusk (Oxford, 1934) and Walt Whitman Rostow (Oxford, 1937-38). Thus the old school tie, in shades of pink to red, spans the Atlantic.

How many American Rhodes Scholars have been enrolled in the London Fabian Society over the years, it would be difficult to say. No statistics on the subject have been released. The identity of such recruits has been closely guarded, apparently to avoid embarrassing those who hold or hope to hold positions of influence in their native land. Moreover, this particular type of recruitment might be construed by jurists as violating the intent of the Rhodes Trust, which, however singular, was anything but Socialist.

Cecil Rhodes, under whose last will the Trust was created,[38] had

[37] *Socialist International Information*, (August 3, 1963), Vol. XIII, No. 31-32. (Italics added.)

[38] Originals of seven wills written by Lord Rhodes between 1877 and 1899 may be found at Rhodes House at Oxford. The first five dealt with a world-wide secret society to promote the British Empire. The sixth, dated 1895, provided scholarships for "young collegians." The final will, drawn in 1899 and made public in 1902 after Rhodes' death, offered scholarships to American collegians. Rhodes' trustees simultaneously took steps to form the secret society proposed

been an impassioned English patriot and the most rugged of individualists. He looked forward secretly to a time when the United States would rejoin Great Britain, in a world federation of states steered from London. Superficially, his plans for international government, and for giving "young colonists" a political bias along with an Oxford education, might be said to resemble the Fabian Society's. Fundamentally, however, his purpose was diametrically opposed to that of Sidney Webb's select company.

Above all, Lord Rhodes was dedicated to the perpetuation and extension along classic capitalist lines of the British Empire, which Fabians schemed to dissolve. Obviously, he never intended that his fortune amassed in the gold fields and diamond mines of South Africa be used to train young Americans in Fabian Socialism; or to promote peaceful social revolution, under a cloak of learning and Old World culture, in a lost colony of the British Empire.

Of two thousand or more American Rhodes Scholars invited to Oxford since the Trust was formed, by no means did all succumb to the power of Fabian suggestion. There were men among them immune to Socialist blandishments, several of whom have found their careers in government abruptly terminated. Such patriotic and ill-rewarded Americans include Bryton Barron, former head of the State Department's Treaty Section, and Elvis J. Stahr, Jr., Secretary of the Army during the Kennedy-Johnson Administration, who resigned in protest against the "muzzling of the military."

There was also Stanley K. Hornbeck, Chief of the State Department's division for Far Eastern Affairs in the nineteen-thirties and political adviser on the Far East, who was dragooned, apparently in all innocence, into serving as a character witness for Alger Hiss.[39] Hornbeck was one of those who attempted without success to stem a tide in the conduct of United States foreign affairs, which in the middle forties delivered mainland China to Communist rule. As late as 1950, he made a valiant though futile effort to warn his successor,

---

by the old empire-builder. On July 24, 1902 the Pilgrims Society of Great Britain was founded, and six months later on January 13, 1903 the Pilgrims Society of the United States was organized. Thomas W. Lamont, Sr. was at one time chairman of the executive committee of the American Pilgrims.

[39] Alger Hiss, long a trusted and high-ranking State Department official, was identified as having been a secret member of a Communist cell and as having given confidential Government documents to agents of Soviet Intelligence. He was convicted of perjury and sentenced to prison.

Assistant Secretary of State Dean Rusk, against that perilous policy which covertly protected and preserved the Chinese Communists.[40] Presidential appointments of 1961-64, however, gave extraordinary prominence to American Oxonians of the same vintage as David C. Williams and Howard K. Smith, apparently holding mutually congenial views.[41] Among them were a Secretary of State; a Supreme Court Justice; several Under Secretaries, Assistant Secretaries and senior planners in areas directly concerned with formulating diplomatic, monetary, defense and disarmament policy for the United

[40] In a letter of June 7, 1950, Stanley Hornbeck wrote to Dean Rusk: "It was in the year 1945—and not before then—that the Government of the United States, first having taken action inconsistent with tradition and commitment in regard to China, embarked upon what became a course of intervention in regard to the civil conflict between the National Government and the Communists, in China . . . then and thereafter . . . the Government of the United States brought to bear pressures, pressures upon the National Government which were not against the Communists but were on their behalf." *The Institute of Pacific Relations.* Hearings before the Subcommittee to Investigate the Administration of the Internal Security Act and other Internal Security Laws, of the Committee on the Judiciary, 82nd and 83rd Congress, (Washington, U.S. Government Printing Office, 1951-52), p. 5363.

[41] A few of the former Rhodes Scholars appointed to high office during the Kennedy-Johnson Administration are:

Dean Rusk (Oxford, 1934), Secretary of State; sometime professor of Government at Mills College, and former president of the Rockefeller Foundation.

Byron E. White (Oxford, 1938-39), Assistant Supreme Court Justice, formerly Deputy Attorney General.

George C. McGhee (Oxford, 1937; University of London, 1937), Under Secretary of State for Political Affairs; once coordinator of the 400 million dollar aid program to Greece and Turkey.

Robert V. Roosa (Oxford, 1938-39), Under Secretary of the Treasury for Monetary Affairs; a Keynesian economist who has taught at Harvard and Massachusetts Institute of Technology.

Harlan Cleveland (Oxford, 1938), Assistant Secretary of State for International Organization Affairs, former chief of UNRRA's mission to China; former director of ECA's China program; former publisher of *The Reporter*, a "progressive" monthly.

Charles J. Hitch (Oxford, 1934), Assistant Secretary of Defense and Comptroller; wrote *The Economics of Defense in the Nuclear Age,* known as "the Bible" of Pentagon civilians.

Kermit Gordon (Oxford, 1938-39), director of the Bureau of the Budget, previously on the President's Council of Economic Advisers; Harvard professor of the Keynesian School; former director of the economic and administrative program of the Ford Foundation.

Walt Whitman Rostow (Oxford, 1936-38), counselor of the State Department and chairman of the Policy Planning Council; former deputy to the President's Special Assistant on National Security; former staff member, Center for International Studies, Massachusetts Institute of Technology.

States. Even the Director of the Budget, Dr. Kermit Gordon—who states that "growth" is the answer to deficits[42]—was one of them.

Based on an analysis of their writings, speeches and official acts, the collective opinions of those officials on basic issues can be rather simply tabulated:

Economics: post-Keynesian, that is, the greater the deficit, the greater the national growth; developed nations must expend their substance for the benefit of under-developed nations, on a government to government basis.

Welfare State: responsibility of the Federal Government to provide financial aid from tax monies to an ever-growing number of private citizens and institutions; pilot programs in medicare, public housing, rent subsidies, urban renewal, job training, aid to education, research and depressed areas, to be expanded year by year; more centralized control, as a result of Federal aid to states and municipalities; social security system to be used as a basis for collecting computerized Federal dossiers on the entire population.

Foreign Affairs: relaxation at any price of "tensions" with the Soviet Union; eventual admission of Red China and East Germany to the United Nations; economic aid "without strings" to satellite and neutralist nations, and subsidized "trade" with Soviet Russia.

Defense: long-range planning by civilian officials, in collaboration with the State Department; disregard of professional military advice, and downgrading of nonpolitical officers; elimination of "first strike" weapons, as designated by the Soviet Union; gradual obsolescence of the Strategic Air Force and various strategic weapons, through cessation of production and new development.

Disarmament: gradual, to reassure the American public; progressive, to reassure the Soviet Union; ultimately total, to assure "peace under World Law" and a World Police Force.

World Government: to be achieved as rapidly as possible through the United Nations, via "modernization" of the United States Constitution.

Implicit in all this but not openly stated, is the socialization of the United States through new forms of ownership and control of production, which must precede the application of any overall world plan.

Nearly all in the group are college professors who have served intermittently in government since World War II. In the years between, more than one has enjoyed the bounty of the great tax free research and educational foundations, where policy for government agencies and private institutions is often framed at the research stage. They

---

[42] *Hearings, Joint Economic Committee,* 88th Congress, First Session, (Washington, U.S. Government Printing Office, January 29, 1963).

include a former president of the Rockefeller Foundation; a former director of the Ford Foundation's economic and administrative program; and a former large-scale beneficiary of the Carnegie Foundation, Dr. Walt Whitman Rostow. All appear to have been well-schooled in post-Keynesian economics and a world outlook that tends to subordinate traditional interests of the United States to other considerations.

If, as the record would indicate, they have been affected since their student days at Oxford by Fabian Socialist ideas, they might be expected to render signal service to Americans for Democratic Action, whose international program closely parallels that of the Fabian Society. A sheltered and protected group of nonexpendables, those old Oxonians in the New Frontier seemed to have had little or no official contact with ADA—a possible exception being Assistant Secretary of State Harlan Cleveland, former publisher of *The Reporter*.[43] Like Harold Wilson, however, they can claim to have "known a good number" of its more eminent members and associates for years.[44] Several staunch supporters and/or founding members of ADA—Chester Bowles, G. Mennen Williams, J. Kenneth Galbraith, and W. Averell Harriman—have served with the group, sometimes in equally high government posts; but have apparently been expected to follow, not formulate official policy.

First and foremost in that Oxford group was Dr. Dean Rusk, named Secretary of State in the Kennedy-Johnson Administration. Placid, plump and singularly gifted at avoiding the public eye or the appearance of being personally responsible for controversial decisions, his record merits examination. During the middle nineteen-forties, he succeeded to the same Political Affairs and Postwar Planning posts in the State Department previously held by Alger Hiss—according to that peculiar sequence whereby a respectable crypto-Socialist often replaces an exposed Communist in administrative Washington.[45] Rusk was a member of the American Council of the Institute of Pacific

[43] Harlan Cleveland, Assistant Secretary of State for International Organization Affairs, formerly published *The Reporter*, a progressive monthly that normally followed the ADA line and to which ADA members often contributed. Editor of *The Reporter*, Max Ascoli, and his wife, the former Marion Rosenwald Stern, appeared for years on official ADA lists, as substantial and regular fund donors.

[44] For example, see the list of persons whose "generous assistance" is acknowledged by Walt Whitman Rostow in the Preface to his book, *The United States in the World Arena*, (New York, Harper & Brothers. 1960), p. xiii.

[45] Under Secretary of the Treasury for Monetary Affairs, Robert V. Roosa was appointed to a post comparable to that held by the late Harry Dexter White.

Relations, to which some highly reputable individuals and business firms with interests in the Far East innocently subscribed. Institute publications and propaganda are credited with having fostered those official United States policies which favored the Chinese Communists, deplored by Stanley Hornbeck and other concerned Americans.

Subsequently, the Institute of Pacific Relations was discovered by U.S. Government investigators to have been infiltrated by agents of Red Army Intelligence.[46] Yet Dean Rusk, a State Department official, still recommended Institute publications for use by the Chief of U.S. Military Intelligence.[47] Even in 1950, five years after the *Amerasia* case, he strongly supported the Institute's request for Ford and Rockefeller Foundation grants.[48]

That year, as Assistant Secretary of State for Far Eastern Affairs, Rusk delivered a memorable speech comparing the Chinese Reds to the American patriots of 1776. It was viewed in diplomatic circles as a prelude to recognition of Red China, contemplated by the State Department in 1950. Such action had already been taken by the Fabian-controlled British Labour Party Government of 1945-51, and was being urged in this country by ADA. The move was disrupted by the Communist invasion of South Korea, which the State Department accidentally invited through a widely circulated memorandum (evidently prepared in Dean Rusk's division) declaring Korea to be "outside the defense perimeter of the United States."

Dean Rusk demonstrated the same lenient attitude towards Communist troublemakers so characteristic of Fabian Socialists, as well as the classic Socialist function of opening the door to Communist con-

[46] In this connection a letter of February 13, 1934 from Edward C. Carter, director of the Institute, to Selsker H. Gunn of the Rockefeller Foundation may be of incidental interest: ". . . I don't think I told you that, when we saw Karakhan (then Assistant Commissar for Foreign Affairs) in Moscow in 1931, he told us that the Institute's researches in China and Japan would be equally valuable whether the Far East remained capitalist or became communist." *Institute of Pacific Relations. Hearings*, p. 5120.

[47] *Ibid.*, p. 2870. A letter confirming this statement was introduced into the record, but not printed.

[48] *Ibid.*, pp. 5023; 5026. A letter of September 16, 1950, (p. 5026) from William L. Holland, secretary-treasurer of the Institute to Dean Rusk stated: "May I make an urgent and probably irregular appeal to you to lend your weightiest support to the double IPR financial appeal which is to be considered by the Rockefeller Foundation on September 22 . . . . Your words of support for us to the Ford Foundation were very influential, even though action on that grant has been postponed pending the forthcoming appointment of a director for the foundation."

quest. During the Korean War he was instrumental in launching the fatal "No Win" policy, which persists to the present day. As President Harry S. Truman revealed in his *Memoirs,* it was Dean Rusk who took the first visible step towards establishing the principle of the "privileged sanctuary" in Manchuria, by agreement with Fabian Socialists then in control of the British Government at all levels.[49]

In a posthumously published interview with Bob Considine of the Hearst Newspapers,[50] General Douglas MacArthur stated he submitted a plan for victory that would have ended the Korean War in less than two weeks and eliminated Red China as a present or future military threat. Author of twenty victorious campaigns and conceded by experts to be one of the ablest military strategists of the century, General MacArthur was prevented by Fabian Socialist influence in our own State Department from putting his master plan into effect.

The reason alleged for the prohibition was that a clear-cut victory for American forces in the Far East might have touched off World War III. Owing to Soviet Russia's very limited nuclear and logistic capabilities at that date, "fears" of a world holocaust conjured up by the State Department are now recognized to have been unfounded—as they have been on every subsequnt occasion, thanks to the vastly superior power of American deterrents. This was no less true in the

---

[49] On November 6, 1950, Red Chinese troops and supplies were streaming into Korea, and Russian-built planes based in Manchuria were harassing American troops. MacArthur had ordered U.S. bombers to strike at the Yalu River bridges. A few hours before the American bombers were due to take off from their Japanese bases, an emergency meeting was called at the White House, attended by President Truman, Secretary of State Acheson, Secretary of Defense Lovett and Assistant Secretary of State Rusk. Regarding that meeting, President Truman wrote: "Assistant Secretary of State Dean Rusk pointed out that *we had a commitment with the British not to take action which might involve attacks on the Manchurian side of the river* without consultation with them. He also told Mr. Lovett that the State Department had presented MacArthur's report on Chinese Communist intervention to the United Nations and that an urgent meeting of the Security Council had been requested. At this meeting we would try to get a resolution adopted calling on the Chinese Communists to cease their activities in Korea . . . . Mr. Rusk also mentioned the danger of involving the Soviets, especially in the light of the mutual assistance treaty between Moscow and Peiping . . . . Then Lovett called the Air Force Secretary, Mr. Finletter (a staunch ADA man—ed.) and instructed him to *tell the Joint Chiefs what Mr. Rusk had set forth* and to tell them that he [Lovett] and Acheson both felt that this action should be postponed until they were able to get a decision from me." (Italics added.)

Next day some strictly limited action along the Yalu River was authorized; but the principle of the privileged sanctuary had been established. Harry S. Truman, *Memoirs,* (Garden City, Doubleday & Co., 1956), Vol. II, p. 374.

[50] Copyrighted by Hearst Headline Service, for release April 8, 1964.

more recent Cuban crisis than it was during the Korean War: the function of deterrents being, after all, to deter! As lately as April, 1964, General Thomas S. Power flatly declared that as long as the Strategic Air Force is maintained at peak efficiency and the Russians know it, *"there is no danger of a nuclear war."* [51]

The truth was that in 1950 Socialists everywhere—in America, in England and in the United Nations—displayed a quiet determination to protect and preserve Red China, whatever the cost in American or British casualties—just as Socialists of an earlier generation had moved in 1920 to preserve Soviet Russia. For the prolonged bloodletting in Korea and the final humiliating stalemate that so greatly damaged the American position in the Far East, Dean Rusk shared the responsibility to a degree not generally realized.

It hardly mattered that in 1952, when the damage had been done, Rusk delivered a verbal attack on the Red Chinese Government and spoke respectfully of Chiang Kai-shek; nor that he was chided for doing so by the British Fabian Socialist, Michael Lindsay, in a letter to the *New Statesman*.[52] This type of interplay only served to provide protective coloring for Dr. Rusk and to insure his availability for future service at a still higher official level.

As Secretary of State in the Kennedy-Johnson Administration, Dr. Rusk revived and enforced the principle of the privileged sanctuary in Southeast Asia. True, he talked bravely of victory in Vietnam. Yet at a cost of some 5 million dollars per day in United States economic and military aid, the jungle war in Vietnam was allowed to continue year after year under restrictions that made victory impossible. Once again the pretext was raised by the State Department (and echoed in the syndicated columns of such court favorites as Walter Lippmann, Marquis Childs, and Joseph Alsop) that the type of military action required to win in Southeast Asia would involve us in war with Red China—a war which that stricken country was neither economically nor militarily prepared to wage! *The fact is, that with Fabian-schooled officials and advisers dictating our foreign and military policies, the*

[51] From a speech delivered in Palm Springs, California by General Thomas S. Power, then commanding the Strategic Air Force. *The Daily-Enterprise,* (Riverside, Calif., April 18, 1964).

[52] A letter of 1952 from Michael Lindsay to the *New Statesman* and *Nation* stated: "Mr. Rusk's recent assertions that the Chinese Government was a Russian colonial regime and that the Kuomintang really represented the Chinese people have been widely criticized." *Institute of Pacific Relations, Hearings,* (See Bibliography), p. 5391.

United States has not been and never will be permitted to win a clear-cut military or diplomatic victory over Socialist/Communist forces.

As in Chungking long before, demands were made for instant social and political "reforms" in war torn Vietnam. Once again pressures were applied by the State Department, and seconded by docile aides in the Pentagon. Inevitably they led to the overthrow and death of President Ngo Dinh Diem, who—whatever his alleged shortcomings from the viewpoint of Western Democracy—gave every appearance of being a sincere patriot and devout anti-Communist. It was not the first time that assassination had been condoned by Rusk's State Department. With the same alacrity that they moved to recognize the killers of Diem, Dean Rusk and his subordinates hastened to extend diplomatic recognition to the transient administration of President Juan Bosch in the Dominican Republic, following the murder of General Rafael Trujillo. Eighteen million dollars in United States economic aid were rushed at record speed to Juan Bosch, whose accession was hailed in a congratulatory message from the Socialist International.[53]

Perhaps Rusk's smoothest service to the cause of Fabian Socialism was his participation in the Skybolt incident of 1963. Out of a clear blue sky his junior partner, Secretary of Defense Robert S. McNamara, cancelled production of the Skybolt missile, leaving the British Royal Air Force without a promised nuclear deterrent. This action was taken contrary to the advice of professional United States military experts. Unceremoniously announced to former Prime Minister Harold Macmillan at Bermuda, it was described at the time as the harshest blow inflicted in years on Britain's ruling Conservative Party. Similar action had previously provoked the fall of a Canadian Government, and the return to power of a Left liberal Premier known for his sympathy toward Socialist programs.

Some theorized that a more indirect result of *l'affaire Skybolt* was to convince General Charles de Gaulle of France that American pledges of atomic aid were unreliable and that he might just as well go it alone. Others theorize that de Gaulle has had a more sinister purpose all along. The impression that United States nuclear assistance was a Sword of Damocles, rigged for its effect on internal politics in allied nations, did not improve the position of the United States

---

[53] "Secretary's Report (September, 1961–July, 1963) to the Eighth Congress of the Socialist International, meeting in Amsterdam, 9-12 September, 1963," *Socialist International Information,* (August 24, 1963), Vol. XIII, No. 34-35.

in world diplomacy—a consideration of little moment to British Fabian Socialists, who were not concerned to preserve global confidence in the United States. Immediately after the Skybolt Conference so shocking to Prime Minister Macmillan, Opposition Leader Harold Wilson paid an unofficial but quietly triumphant visit to Washington, where he was greeted by men he had "known for years" as the presumptive Prime Minister of Britain.

While it was apparently Rusk's function to execute Fabian Socialist International policy at the uppermost level, the chief advance agent of such policy seemed for some years past to have been Dr. Walt Whitman Rostow. The so-called Millikan-Rostow Report was the fruit of a study conducted under his supervision at Massachusetts Institute of Technology's Center for International Studies. Published in 1957 as *A Proposal: Key to An Effective Foreign Policy,*[54] it foreshadowed what actually became United States foreign policy in the Kennedy-Johnson Administration. In *The Stages of Economic Growth,*[55] which appeared in 1960, Rostow sketched the first dim outlines of a world-wide New Deal to be supported by the United States along Keynesian lines.

Appointed deputy adviser to President Kennedy on national security matters, Rostow had a major voice in the preparation of a secret 286 page report on Basic National Security. Following a Moscow meeting in 1960 with Deputy Foreign Minister Kuznetsov, Rostow advised that the United States should abandon offensive or "first-strike" weapons, distasteful to the Soviet Union.[56] Notably, the B-70 bomber—deemed essential by the Strategic Air Command for our future safety, but cancelled by the Kennedy-Johnson Administration. By the same token, the Navy was denied permission to construct a nuclear-powered aircraft carrier and was restricted to building an obsolescent type vessel.

Moving to the State Department, as counselor and as chairman of its Policy Planning Council, Dr. Rostow continued to predict the shape of things to come. Reading his articles that appeared with remarkable frequency in the weekly Department of State *Bulletin,* the more perceptive division chiefs and foreign service officers could divine the attitudes they were expected to assume. In the February

[54] M. F. Millikan and W. W. Rostow, *A Proposal: Key to An Effective Foreign Policy,* (New York, Harper & Brothers, 1957).
[55] W. W. Rostow, *The Stages of Economic Growth,* (New York, Harper & Brothers, 1960).
[56] See article by Thomas Ross, Chicago *Sun Times,* (March 30, 1961).

17, 1964 issue, for example, Rostow launched a brand new slogan obviously designed to serve as a guideline for foreign policy: *Freedom and Diversity!* It was particularized in the March 16th issue of the same publication by Secretary Rusk, himself, in an article entitled "Why We Treat Different Communist Countries Differently." [57]

In an address to a group of business executives reprinted in the Department *Bulletin* of February 3, 1964, Rostow explained that the species of world-wide New Deal envisoned for underdeveloped countries will not wholly eliminate private business. While United States aid to those nations may give their governments control over the more basic forms of capital outlay, he pointed out kindly that such developments will create new mass markets for consumers' goods and simple agricultural tools, from which private manufacturers can benefit—at least for a while.

Prudently, Dr. Rostow refrained in that official publication from announcing the ultimate goal which he had already defined in other published works. Incredible as it might seem to most Americans, he actually looked forward to a day when the United States as a sovereign nation would cease to exist. If the question is raised as to where or how he might have acquired such ideas, it must be remembered that he, too, was a Rhodes Scholar at Oxford during the crucial nineteen-thirties.

In a somewhat unexpected fashion Walt Whitman Rostow fulfilled the desire expressed in Lord Rhodes' last will, to create in American students "an attachment to the country from which they sprang." Rostow's parents, as it happened, came from Russia. The fact that they named his elder brother, Eugene Victor Rostow, after the American Socialist Party leader, Eugene Victor Debs, leaves little doubt as to their political inclinations. Walt Whitman Rostow attended ancient Balliol, and can claim the distinction once ascribed to Lord Curzon:

[57] "Within the Soviet bloc," wrote Secretary Rusk hopefully, "the Stalinist terror has been radically changed. And within the Soviet Union, as well as most of the smaller European nations, there are signs—small but varied and persistent signs—of yearnings for more individual freedom. And there are practical reasons why men must be allowed freedom if they are to achieve their best." Department of State *Bulletin*, (March 16, 1964), p. 393.

Cf. Richard Loewenthal, "Freedom and Communism," *Socialist International Information,* (August 1, 1964), Vol. XIV, No. 16-17. This article by Loewenthal, of the London Fabian Society and the German Social Democratic Party, originally appeared as a supplement to *Berliner Stimme* early in 1964 and reflects the official foreign policy line of the Socialist International. Views expressed by Rusk and Rostow are similar.

". . . Of course, I went to Balliol College
And what I know not, is not knowledge."

Balliol was likewise the college of G. D. H. Cole, a mere tutor in Economics but an important wheel in the New Fabian Research apparatus, already recognized as performing the Society's most important function. Always eager to bring "new blood" into the movement, Cole and his wife invited students of radical tendencies to their Holywell home for weekly rounds of Socialist discussion.[58] A number of British Fabians, who became prominent in public life during the forties and after, were regular guests throughout their student years at the Coles' Monday evenings; as were some Americans who discarded the Socialist label under advisement.

Inevitably, Soviet Russia was a recurrent topic of discussion. Though admittedly not quite perfect, the Socialist Fatherland was regarded with affection and hope. Some collegians (like Howard K. Smith) even spent vacations in Moscow. No matter what the provocation, somehow those Fabian acolytes never lost hope of inducing Soviet leaders to alter their ways. The same schoolboy conviction, that Soviet Russia can eventually be persuaded to change its internal power structure and abandon its aim of world domination, suffuses the statements and positions of Walt Whitman Rostow; and in part through him, was incorporated into the foreign policy of the United States.

Rostow returned to England during World War II as a youthful Army Major attached to the U.S. Office of Strategic Services. In London he worked closely with various exiled Socialist leaders from Nazi-occupied countries, who had gathered under the sheltering wing of the Fabian International Bureau—and who hoped to assume power in their native lands at war's end. For his mysterious services, Major Rostow was awarded the Military Order of the British Empire, presumably through the good offices of Fabian Socialists in the Cabinet. Though just eight years out of college, he was invited in 1946-47 to lecture as Harmsworth Professor of American History at Oxford. In 1949-50 he was called to Cambridge University as Pitt Professor of American History.

During the two years that intervened between his teaching sessions at Oxford and Cambridge, Walt Whitman Rostow worked in Geneva as assistant to Dr. Gunnar Myrdal, then executive secretary of the United Nations Economic Commission for Europe. Myrdal was a

[58] Cole, op. cit., pp. 208-209.

Socialist and former Minister of Commerce in Sweden, who all but succeeded in wrecking his country's postwar economy. As wartime economic adviser to the Swedish Embassy in Washington, he had fallen under the spell of those American Keynesians who were certain the United States would suffer an even more severe depression after the Second World War than after the first.

Believing Sweden must hedge against the predicted world slump, Dr. Myrdal and his associates applied a number of inflationary Keynesian measures. These included cheap money and expansion of credit at home and raising the value of the *krone* abroad. Looking to Communist Russia for new trade opportunities, Myrdal personally engineered a billion *krona* (280 million dollar) trade agreement with the Soviet Union. The Swedish Government agreed to underwrite five-year credits in that amount to the Russians, who could buy directly from the manufacturers—an arrangement in some respects similar to the 1964 Soviet wheat deal with the United States.[59]

Although Sweden emerged from World War II in a very prosperous condition, the remedies prescribed by Dr. Myrdal had reduced the country, by 1948, to appealing for Marshall Plan aid. Meanwhile, Myrdal himself retired in style to Geneva, where he proceeded undisturbed to recommend economic policy for all of Europe. Fortunately, perhaps, his advice was not taken too seriously.

The reverence which Dr. Myrdal still inspires among Left liberals in the United States and England derives from a monumental fifteen hundred page work published in 1944, *An American Dilemma*. Despite his unconcealed Socialist affiliations, he was chosen by the tax free Carnegie Foundation to direct a $250,000 study of race relations in the southern United States. Since Sweden had never known a Negro problem, it was presumed Dr. Myrdal would be "unprejudiced." In his report, however, he acknowledged a debt to W. E. B. Dubois, a founder of the NAACP and an early promoter of Pan-Africanism.[60] Myrdal's repeated emphasis on the alleged tendencies to violence and

[59] The budget of Sweden's Socialist Government for 1964-65 included a 768 million dollar military appropriation, although little Sweden is traditionally a neutral nation. Informed observers have suggested Sweden's military forces anticipate assuming a key role in the world-police functions of the United Nations.

[60] Gunnar Myrdal (with the assistance of Richard Sterner and Arnold Rose), *An American Dilemma*, (New York, Harper & Brothers, 1944), (1483 pages), p. 601. (On July 6, 1966 Dr. Martin Luther King of the Southern Christian Leadership Conference received from the Swedish Consul General in New York a check for $100,000 which had been collected in Sweden for the benefit of his organization. Los Angeles *Times*, July 7, 1966).

disrespect for law, which *he* found innate in the American character, appears to have inspired, in some measure, the forms of later "civil rights" agitation in the United States.

By 1947, this massive and costly volume was already in its ninth edition. Used by NAACP lawyers, it furnished the so-called sociological background for the United States Supreme Court's school integration decision of 1954. Incidentally, it also contained some highly disparaging remarks about the United States Constitution. Referring to the "nearly fetichistic cult of the Constitution," Dr. Myrdal asserted that "the 150-year old Constitution is in many respects impractical and ill-suited for modern conditions . . . . Modern historical studies reveal that the Constitutional Convention was nearly a plot against the common people. Until recently the Constitution has been used to block the popular will." [61]

This was the man with whom Walt Whitman Rostow worked harmoniously for two years at Geneva—so much so, that on returning to England in 1949, he left his brother, Eugene Victor Rostow, to act as Myrdal's assistant. Eugene Victor Rostow, who later became Dean of the Yale University Law School, was reported in mid-1964 to be under consideration for an opening on the Circuit Court of Appeals in Connecticut as a preliminary to his eventual appointment to the United States Supreme Court.

Former students, who attended Dr. Walt Whitman Rostow's lectures in England and/or later in the United States, claim that his approach to American history is strictly geopolitical. Father of the alleged science of geopolitics was the British geographer, Sir Halford Mackinder, friend of early British Fabians at the University of London. Mackinder developed the theory of a pivot or "Heartland" area deep in Eurasia, and assigned a lesser role to all lands outside it. Since it stresses the relationship between physical geography and national behavior, geopolitics has aroused some interest among military strategists, armchair and otherwise.[62] Based on a materialistic view of

[61] *Ibid.*, pp. 12-13.
[62] As originally presented in 1904, Mackinder's theory seemed designed as a warning to the British Secret Service to block Czarist Russia's expansion in Asia. In modern times the same theory has been gratefully adopted by Soviet Russia to justify its own plan for world conquest. Rostow's geopolitical approach can therefore be interpreted as an indirect concession to Soviet Russia.

It is interesting to note that an article on geopolitics by the U.S. Department of State's official geographer contains the following pronouncement: "Whether we view Mackinder's theory as fact or fancy, the whole American concept of containment is bound up with his Heartland theory presented before the Royal

history, it has stirred the enthusiasm of both Socialist and national Socialist planners—and was utilized by military intelligence experts of the Black Reichswehr, notably Major General Ernst Haushofer, in drafting Adolf Hitler's blueprint for world conquest.

Adopting geopolitical jargon, Walt Whitman Rostow described America as a mere continental island off the greater landmass of Eurasia, comprising Europe, Asia and Africa. He explained the growth of the United States to greatness as being due to no inherent virtue in its own economic and constitutional system; but solely to divisions among Eurasian power blocs, which permitted such a circumstance to occur. By converse reasoning, a future union of Eurasian power blocs could either succeed in conquering the United States outright, or in forcing America's absorption into a globe-girdling federation of Socialist states, under a centrally controlled police force and planned economic system.[63]

Such absorption represents *the Fabian Socialist plan for peaceful world revolution.* It is demonstrated by the visible attempt, on one hand, to encircle the United States with a swiftly growing bloc of Socialist-ruled nations; and on the other, by an attempt to procure a permanent economic and political accommodation between the United States and Soviet Russia. This far-flung plan presupposes eventual world rule by an intellectual Socialist elite, backed by the mass electoral power of a world-wide Socialist Labor Confederation, whose docility will be guaranteed through the device of full, state-assured employment. For more than a decade, Dr. Walt Whitman Rostow appears to have been its veiled prophet in the United States.

Couched, like the theory of Keynes, in bland, semi-technical language designed to mystify the uninitiate, the overall plan is revealed by signs to an illumined few. With some effort, however, its outlines can be discerned by any normally intelligent layman who takes the trouble to read the voluminous and cloudy writings of Walt Whitman Rostow—just as the military intentions of Adolf Hitler might have been evident from 1922 to anyone perusing the equally cryptic works of Major General Ernst Haushofer.[64] Neither Rostow nor Haushofer

Geographical Society 60 years ago." G. Etzel Pearly, "Geopolitics and Foreign Relations," Department of State *Bulletin,* (March 2, 1964), p. 321.

[63] W. W. Rostow, *The United States in the World Arena,* (New York, Harper and Row, 1960), pp. 543-544.

[64] In 1940-41 the author of *Fabian Freeway* had the painful experience of reading the collected works of General Haushofer at the Library of Congress in Washington, D.C.

will ever be read for their pleasure-giving quality. Both convey the impression of talking over the reader's head to a special audience. Since it takes talent of a rare order, however, to remain totally unintelligible for hundreds of pages, there is always, somewhere, a moment of truth.

In Rostow's book *An American Policy in Asia*, for example, after a long, tortuous and frequently obscure argument, it finally becomes clear that Rostow advises granting Red China a seat in the United Nations, as well as diplomatic recognition by the United States. During the same year when this work appeared, *The New York Times* of October 2, 1955 reported:

A social scientist at Massachusetts Institute of Technology has undertaken to develop a new portrait of the United States in a world setting. Under the three year grant from the Carnegie Foundation of New York, Dr. Walt W. Rostow, a Professor of Economic History, is directing the study . . . . Dr. Rostow's project will examine our role in what he calls the "foreign policy revolution."

Similar collective labor brought forth still another book over the signature of Walt Whitman Rostow, *The United States in the World Arena*. After attributing the remarkable development of the United States during 150 years to luck and the more recent strides of the USSR to phenomenal ability, he wrote: "Now brutally and directly and in every dimension, the nation is caught up in a world where its military power, diplomatic influence and ideological conformation are explicitly, relentlessly under challenge from the Soviet Union." [65] The answer? America must "change its national style," while retaining its "operational vigor"—and even then success cannot be assured! "Will the United States," asks Rostow, "mobilize the strength, will and imagination to bring about the process of persuasion in the Communist bloc which, by denying all other alternatives, would permit without major war the gradual evolution and release of the forces for good in it?" [66]

The real break in the clouds, however, "so central to the author's judgments that it appears worthwhile to state it explicitly," [67] was reserved for the Appendix:

. . . the urgent imperative to tame military force and the need to deal with peoples everywhere on the basis of an accelerating proximity argue strongly

[65] Rostow, *op. cit.*, p. 537.
[66] *Ibid.*, p. 535.
[67] *Ibid.*, p. 543.

for movement in the direction of federalized world organization under effective international law. And, *should effective international control of military power be achieved, it might prove convenient and rational to pass other functions upward from unilateral determination to an organized arena of international politics.*[68]

Or, put in another way, says Rostow:

It is a legitimate American national objective to see removed from the United States the right to use substantial military force to pursue their own interests. Since this residual right is the root of national sovereignty and the basis for the existence of an international arena of power, *it is therefore an American interest to see an end to nationhood as it has been historically defined.*[69]

An end to nationhood will be achieved, said Rostow, when "the great conference has ended and the freely moving inspectors take up their initial posts from one end of the world to the other and the nightmare passes." [70] In a contrary vein, it may be pertinent to recall the laconic words of an old-style American who did not live to see the "No Win" policies in Korea, Vietnam and Cuba. "The United States," remarked Will Rogers, "never lost a war or won a conference!"

The "judgments" of Walt Whitman Rostow are not personal to him, nor confined to the close-knit group of high-salaried professors in government who enjoyed the benefits of an Oxford education in the same era as he. As previously noted, an official declaration approved by the Congress of the Socialist International at Oslo in 1962 stated plainly, "*The ultimate objective of the parties of the Socialist International is nothing less than world government . . . .* Membership of the United Nations must be made universal, so that all nations, including China, may be represented by their governments in power." [71]

The United States in the World Arena was published in 1960, and its contents (or at least, its conclusions) should have been a matter of public knowledge. Yet Walt Whitman Rostow was appointed only a few months later to an advisory post in the White House itself, and thereafter to a strategic position in the Department of State. With the great wealth of able, well-educated, and patriotic citizens available and willing to serve their country in an official capacity,

---

[68] *Ibid.*, p. 549. (Italics added.)
[69] *Ibid.*, p. 549. (Italics added.)
[70] *Ibid.*, p. 549-550.
[71] *The World Today: The Socialist Perspective.* A Socialist International Publication. (London, no date), p. 11. (Italics added.)

how does it happen that out of 170 million Americans a man was chosen who pursues objectives common to those of the Socialist International? One thing is certain: it did not happen by accident. A domestic political group able to deliver a substantial bloc of votes and a domestic lobby of substantial weight in Washington were required to assure the predominance of such officials in the Kennedy-Johnson and Johnson-Humphrey Administrations. Both requirements were met by Americans for Democratic Action, political arm of the Fabian Socialist movement in the United States.

20

More Power And Influence

1.

LIBERAL historians have been pleased to remark that the Holy Roman Empire was not Holy nor Roman nor an Empire. Similarly, it might be said today that Americans for Democratic Action is neither American nor Democratic; and there would be more truth than humor in the statement. Although the proof must at times be sought in a variety of obscure publications never meant for mass consumption, there is ample evidence that the inspiration for the organization was both British and Fabian Socialist; that its leaders have maintained close ties with leaders of the London Fabian Society; and that its emergence coincided narrowly with the post World War II revival of the Socialist International, whose declarations are echoed in ADA programs.

In that connection, it will be useful to sketch the relationship between the London Fabian Society and the Socialist International where the Society has been represented in one way or another since its early years. In 1896, George Bernard Shaw attended the London Congress of the Socialist International as a Fabian delegate.[1]

Founded in London in 1864,[2] the First Socialist International, whose honorary corresponding secretary for Germany and effective creator

[1] Max Beer, *Fifty Years of International Socialism*, (London, Allen and Unwin, 1935), p. 90.

[2] *Yearbook of the International Socialist Labour Movement*, 1956-1957. Edited by Julius Braunthal, Secretary of the Socialist International. Under the auspices of the Socialist International and the Asian Socialist Conference. (London, Lincolns-Prager, 1956), pp. 26-36.

was Karl Marx, had been dissolved at Hoboken, New Jersey in 1876. The Second Socialist International was reconstituted in Paris in 1889, on the one-hundredth anniversary of the storming of the Bastille. It survived until 1914, dominated largely by the German Social Democratic Party.[3] During World War I, social democratic splinter groups in Allied countries were utilized for subversive purposes by a special division of German Military Intelligence.

An open split among Socialist parties and societies of the world occurred during and after World War I. Following the Bolshevik Revolution in Russia, the Third or Communist International (called the Comintern) was formed in Moscow in 1919. The Comintern was nominally dissolved in 1940-41 and renamed the Cominform, and several of its leading ideologues have since held posts in the United Nations. Dimitri Manuilsky and Otto Kuusinen, prominent figures of the Communist International, have served as Soviet representatives in the crystal Tower of Babel on the East River in New York City.

Efforts of the British Labour Party, spearheaded by Fabian Socialist Arthur Henderson, failed to restore the old Socialist International in 1921, because a number of member parties demanded an organization that would unite both Socialists and Communists. Still, the British Labour Party persisted. On their own initiative, executives of the Second and Third Internationals met at Paris in February, 1922, but apparently failed to reach a firm agreement. The new Labor and Socialist International finally assembled in May, 1923 at Hamburg, Germany, where Arthur Henderson was elected president of the executive committee. From 1923 to 1938 the British Labour Party [under Fabian Socialist leadership] dominated the Socialist International[4] —and continues to do so today. This Party has been considered for decades to be the most important Socialist labor party of the world, and has sent labor organizers to many English-speaking countries, including the United States.

From the start, both the Socialist and the Communist Internationals have claimed to be the modern-day heirs of Karl Marx, by a kind of profane apostolic succession. Neither has ever forsaken the hope of uniting world-labor in one fold, a chief point of dispute being the identity of the secular shepherd. While the Communist Parties are more vociferous in denouncing the Socialists and in prac-

[3] Walter Theimer, *The Encyclopedia of Modern World Politics*, (New York, Rinehart & Co., 1950), pp. 341-342.
[4] *Ibid.*, pp. 341-342; 379.

tice suppress Socialist Party activities within the Communist bloc, Communist governments do not hesitate to accept practical aid from Socialist leaders abroad—and, in fact, rely heavily upon it.

Leaders of the Socialist International and its affiliates, impelled by a pluralist outlook, have never relaxed their patient efforts to persuade the Communist leaders, individually or collectively, to adopt a more "practical" point of view at home. As recently as the winter of 1964, Zigmunt Zaremba, Socialist and former member of the Polish Parliament and chairman of the Socialist Union of Central Eastern Europe, declared: *"Nobody wants to deny Communism the right to exist but, equally, Communism cannot deny this right to Socialism!"* [5] To more impartial observers, these rights are by no means self-evident.

Under the impact of World War II the Second International, whose Bureau was in Zurich, once more fell apart. During the war years, as has already been noted, the Fabian International Bureau served as host in London to a number of the Socialist International's exiled leaders. In 1946 the old International was formally dissolved at a conference of delegates from nineteen countries held at Clacton-on-Sea and Bournemouth, England; and an International Socialist Bureau was set up in London. At a congress held in Zurich on June 7-9, 1947, a resolution was passed stating the time was ripe to consider reestablishing the Socialist International.

Meanwhile, affairs of the International from November, 1947, were handled by the Committee of the International Socialist Conference, known as COMISCO, which held its first session in London during March, 1948. Under the chairmanship of the veteran British Fabian Socialist, Morgan Phillips, COMISCO took an active hand in setting up the labor arm of the Socialist International, the Confederation of Free Trade Unions. COMISCO likewise undertook to revitalize the more overt affiliates of the Socialist International, among others,[6] the International Organization of Socialist Youth.

Through Socialists of many nationalities accredited to the United Nations, COMISCO aided the International Organization of Socialist Youth in obtaining consultative status on various inter-governmental

---

[5] Zigmunt Zaremba, "Socialist-Communist Collaboration: A Discussion," *New Politics*, A Quarterly, (Winter, 1964), Vol. II, No. 1, p. 75. (Italics added.)

[6] Other integrated affiliates of the Socialist International are: the Asian Socialist Conference; the International Council of Social Democratic Women; the Socialist Union of Central-Eastern Europe; the International Union of Social Democratic Teachers.

bodies.[7] These included UNESCO and the United Nations Economic Commission for Europe, represented by Gunnar Myrdal and Walt Whitman Rostow. Young Socialists, who were not always in their first youth, were pledged to work for a new world order "to replace capitalism by a system in which the public interest takes precedence over the interest of private profit."[8] The Students' League for Industrial Democracy, whose adult board included leading members of ADA, was officially listed in 1956-57 as belonging to the International Organization of Socialist Youth.[9]

Formal rebirth of the Socialist International occurred at the Frankfurt Congress of 1951, after which a permanent headquarters was established in London. At that congress the term "Social Democracy" was made interchangeable with "Democratic Socialism," a distinction without a difference. A second congress held in October of the same year at Milan issued a Declaration of Socialist Policy for Underdeveloped Territories—whose effects are still evident today in the policies of the United Nations and the foreign aid policies of the United States. After explaining that technical and financial aid must be tendered in such a way as to avoid embarrassing the recipient governments or committing them to anything whatsoever, the International declared coolly: "It is the primary task of Socialists [in the developed countries] to create a public opinion favorable to active participation in a program of assistance to underdeveloped countries, *even if this effort should entail sacrifices from the peoples of the more advanced countries.*"[10] Both as publicists and public officials, ADA supporters have been intensely active in promoting long-term aid "without strings" to newly constituted governments of backward nations, some barely emerged from cannibalism.

---

[7] Other inter-governmental organizations in which the International Organization of Socialist Youth enjoys consultative status are: the U.N. Economic and Social Council; the U.N. Economic Commission for Asia and the Far East; U.N. Economic Commission for Latin America; U.N. Food and Agricultural Organization; International Labor Organization; World Health Organization; High Commissioner for Refugees; Council of Europe; Conference of Consultative Non-Governmental Organizations, World Federation of United Nations Associations; International Student Movement for the United Nations; coordinating Secretariat of the National Unions of Students; European Youth Council. *Yearbook of the International Socialist Labour Movement*, 1956-1957, p. 106. (See Bibliography).

[8] *Ibid.*, p. 109.

[9] *Ibid.*, pp. 105-106.

[10] *Ibid.*, p. 51. (Italics added.)

Decisions of the Frankfurt Congress were transmitted to the United States by Norman Thomas, one of the few open and avowed Socialists still to be found in this country—the others claiming to be liberals or progressives. Yet in the January, 1953, issue of *The Progressive,* a Left liberal monthly that boasted of having been founded in 1909 by the elder La Follette, the League for Industrial Democracy advertised three pamphlets for sale. They were: *Democratic Socialism,* by Norman Thomas; *National Health Insurance,* by Seymour E. Harris; and *World Labor Today,* by Robert J. Alexander. Endorsers, sponsors and contributors of the magazine at that time included endorsers, sponsors and/or prominent members of ADA.[11] In the same issue, *The Age of Suspicion* by James Wechsler of ADA, was offered gratis with subscriptions to *The Progressive* and membership in the Political Book Club. Book Club judges were Gerald W. Johnson, formerly of the Baltimore *Sun,* Michael Straight of the *New Republic,* and the durable Professor Max Lerner—intimate of Harold Laski, of the old British Left Book Club.

The September, 1954, issue of *The Progressive* featured a debate between Norman Thomas and Robert R. Nathan, then chairman of the ADA executive committee. It dealt with alleged defects and virtues of Americans for Democratic Action, Thomas taking the negative side. In "The Trouble with ADA," Norman Thomas reproached the organization for not insisting that the United Nations be strengthened to a point where it could enforce world disarmament.

On that issue, Thomas seems to have been premature, and the attitude of ADA was soon vindicated by higher authority. At its congress of July, 1955, in London, held jointly with the Asian Socialist Conference, the Socialist International declared: "This repeated emphasis on the need for world disarmament *prior to the establishment of a fund for the underdeveloped nations* is most unfortunate." [12]

---

[11] Among them were: Chester Bowles, Ralph Bunche, Adlai Stevenson, Edward R. Murrow, Walter Reuther, and Alain Locke, then the only American Negro former Rhodes Scholar; as well as Senators Paul Douglas, Estes Kefauver, Ralph Flanders, Wayne Morse, Richard Neuberger.

[12] *Yearbook of the International Socialist Labour Movement,* 1956-1957, p. 54. (See Bibliography). (Italics added.) "The Special United Nations Fund for Economic Development (SUNFED): Joint Statement adopted by the Fourth Congress of the Socialist International and the Asian Socialist Conference." This statement also declared (p. 53): "The policy of the borrowing countries . . . is definitely to restrict the influx of further private capital. Private investment cannot, therefore, be relied upon as the main source for the capital requirements of the underdeveloped countries. The Socialist parties in particular would not con-

Extolling "The Value of ADA" in *The Progressive*, Robert Nathan prudently confined himself to aspects of domestic politics. Admitting ADA had from the first been "torn between the political present and the Fabian future," he said that he expected ADA "to serve as a broker between ideas and their political implementation"—an argument for the art of the possible. Personally, continued Nathan, he was for "pragmatism with a philosophy of liberalism," and he insisted that he, for one, repudiated Socialism!

An obvious reason for the "debate," always a favorite Left liberal device, seems to have been to give Nathan the opportunity of confronting a notorious American Socialist and denying that ADA was a Socialist-oriented body. The utility of such denials can be inferred from the fact that Robert R. Nathan,[13] a senior official of the organization, was still able in 1963 to mingle amicably with top executives of private industry, as a trustee of the Committee for Economic Development.[14]

To exploit the classic Fabian techniques of permeation and penetration, it was important for ADA spokesmen to quash any allegation of Socialism, even before it was raised. Caution was further imposed upon the small but increasingly powerful organization by a profound popular distrust of foreign "isms" still extant throughout the country. If ADA and its chosen instruments were generally recognized to be part of a world-wide Socialist movement seeking to liquidate the United States by easy stages, they would be repudiated by the great majority of the American electorate, *including the bulk of organized labor.*

Nobody was more alert to that danger or more patently eager to avert it than Walter Reuther, president of the United Automobile Workers Union, and presently heading the Industrial Union Divi-

---

template with equanimity an increase in private investors' control over the economy of these countries.

"This leaves public investment as the real main source of external capital requirements." (Italics added.)

[13] Previously Robert R. Nathan held high Government posts in the Roosevelt and Truman Administrations. During World War II he was chairman of the Planning Committee of the War Production Board and deputy director of the Office of War Mobilization and Reconversion. With ADA backing, he became a consultant to the President's Committee on Economic Security, and was named economic adviser to France, Burma and the United Nations' Korean Reconstruction Agency.

[14] *Committee for Economic Development, Report of Activities in 1963,* from Thomas B. McCabe, Acting Chairman.

sion of the AFL-CIO. From 1951, Reuther had been a perennial vice chairman of Americans for Democratic Action, and his Washington attorney, Joseph L. Rauh, Jr., has held a series of executive posts in ADA. Asked on the *Face the Nation* broadcast for March 16, 1958, if he was ever a Socialist, Reuther replied, "Yes, but that was thirty years ago when I was very young and very foolish, and I got over it very quickly, for which I am very thankful." Thirty years earlier, the Dies Committee was hearing testimony about Reuther's postgraduate education in the Soviet Union and his presence at union caucuses of the Communist Party USA.[15] At that time, it hardly occurred to investigators to ask if he was also a Socialist.

Only three years before the *Face the Nation* broadcast, however, Walter Reuther had served on the committee for the 50th Anniversary Dinner of the League for Industrial Democracy—a Fabian Socialist organization with which, except for a brief interruption, he had been connected since his college days. In 1949, he had been invited to address the London Fabian Society on its native heath.[16] If, as Reuther said, he "got over" being a Socialist, there seems to be some confusion as to just when his reformation took place.

Adepts of social psychology since the days of Graham Wallas, the modern torchbearers of the American Fabian movement reacted swiftly against any public charge of foreign entanglements. When it was reported in Washington at the mid-century that ADA was somehow connected with Fabian Socialist leaders of the British Labour Party, the suggestion was protested with a vehemence that seemed excessive. Carey McWilliams, editor of *The Nation*, denounced it as the invention of black reactionaries bent on destroying the children of light. Going further, he ascribed it to "paranoid delusions, of which our reactionaries are the victims." [17]

Yet in a foreword to the volume in which those rash statements appeared, McWilliams acknowledged his own "deep indebtedness to Dr. Alexander Meiklejohn, with whom I had the honor to collaborate in a brief submitted to the U.S. Supreme Court in the case of the Hollywood Ten." Dr. Meiklejohn, once president of the University of Wisconsin, was a long time collaborator, official and board member of

[15] *Investigation of Un-American Propaganda in the United States.* Hearings before a Special Committee, House of Representatives, 75th Congress, (Washington, U.S. Government Printing Office, 1938), Vol. III, pp. 2188 ff.

[16] *67th Fabian Society Annual Report,* (July 1949-June 1950), p. 5.

[17] Carey McWilliams, *Witch Hunt: The Revival of Heresy,* (Boston, Little, Brown & Co., 1950), pp. 323-324.

the LID, acknowledged affiliate of the London Fabian Society. Since factual refutation seemed impossible, name-calling, slander and charges of mental ill-health were the standard retort of American Fabians to any outsider seeking to link them with their British brethren.

Referring to Senator Jenner's speech in 1949 about an ADA booklet advertising summer study-tours to Britain, Clifton Brock said plaintively, "Thus the initial tactic in the campaign to destroy ADA's reputation was to associate it with Britain's Labour Government." [18] Whatever the Senator's motive may have been, the connection to which he pointed was an inescapable and enduring fact. As late as 1960, the *Fabian News*, in its roster of local events, announced *a joint meeting of the Central London Fabian Society with Americans for Democratic Action*, held on July 13 at Conway Hall, Red Lion Square, London, W.C.1.[19]

With rare indiscretion, the *Fabian Society Annual Report* for 1949-50 had also announced two receptions held by the Society for its American associates:

A reception for James Loeb and some members of the Americans for Democratic Action was addressed by Austin Albu, M.P., who spoke on the history and work of the Fabian Society. Patrick Gordon Walker, M.P. acted as host, and *other delegates to COMISCO attended.*[20]

The second reception was for the United States delegation to the first conference of the International Confederation of Free Trades Unions of the World. The guests were received by the Rt. Hon. James Griffiths, M.P., and speeches on behalf of the guests were made by Walter Reuther (CIO) and David Dubinsky (AFL). Both of these receptions were organized in conjunction with the Director of the London Bureau of Americans for Democratic Action.

From the foregoing, it appears that James Loeb, Jr., then National Executive Secretary of ADA, and his unnamed companions were delegates to COMISCO, the Committee of the International Socialist Conference. Their host at the reception, Patrick Gordon Walker, became the British Labour Party's chief spokesman on foreign affairs, and in October, 1964, was named Foreign Secretary following a narrow Labour Party victory at the polls. The Director of the London Bureau of ADA, who arranged both receptions, has been identified as David

---

[18] Clifton Brock, *Americans for Democratic Action*, (Washington, Public Affairs Press, 1962), p. 135.
[19] *Fabian News*, (July, 1960). (Italics added.)
[20] (Italics added.)

C. Williams[21]—former Rhodes Scholar and member of the Fabian Society, who had sent Patrick Gordon Walker to the United States when ADA was in process of being organized.

In April, 1952, according to *Fabian News*, David C. Williams addressed a meeting of Members of Parliament on America's Point Four program for aid to underdeveloped nations. An article by Williams on the same subject appeared in the November, 1952, issue of *Venture*, organ of the Fabian Commonwealth Bureau. There Williams faithfully followed the line laid down by the Socialist International at its Milan Conference in 1951, and anticipated some points in the International's 1955 declaration on SUNFED.[22] He assured his readers, for instance, that the United States would not use the "power of the purse" to influence recipient nations, and said that private American capital—except for oil interests—was reluctant to invest in the program. Since such "investment" was supposed to be on a virtually nonprofit, no-return basis, it is not astonishing that private investors failed to find it attractive.

Other articles by ADA keynoters continued to appear in official British Fabian publications, never known to give space to any writer not affiliated in some way with the international Socialist movement. In May, 1954, *Fabian International Review* published "Eisenhower and Foreign Policy," by Arthur M. Schlesinger, Jr., then national co-chairman of ADA. *Fabian News* for the same month advertised it as an "important article," a clear hint that all members of the Society should read it. The article was important for non-Fabians, too, because it announced with a candor quite unlike ADA's more guarded pronouncements at home, the intention of Left liberals to gain control over both the foreign and military policies of the United States.

Its author was a second generation Harvard professor, whose father was a lifelong crony of Felix Frankfurter. Schlesinger, Jr. had been brought up to believe that Sacco and Vanzetti were saints, and that all who denied it were devils, and that radicalism was really Americanism. He graduated in 1938 from Harvard, a classmate of Joseph P. Kennedy, Jr. Though a non-Catholic himself, Schlesinger, Jr. chose for his senior honors essay to write a life of Orestes A. Brownson,

---

[21] In August, 1949 *The Progressive* printed an article by David C. Williams, "Labor Under a Labor Regime," an account of the British Labour Party in power. A biographical note described Williams as "London representative of Americans for Democratic Action," adding that "his articles have appeared in *The Nation, Labor and Nation* and the *New Leader.*"

[22] SUNFED-Special United Nations Fund for Economic Development.

a brilliant nineteenth century convert to Catholicism. It was published the following year and became a selection of the Catholic Book Club. Some say the subject was suggested to him by Harold Laski, an old family friend and frequent house guest. Laski had been Joe Kennedy, Jr.'s teacher at the London School of Economics, and being convinced that young Joe had a great future in American politics, he may have wished to bring the two young men together on a basis acceptable to the elder Kennedys. As things turned out, it was Jack Kennedy to whom Arthur M. Schlesinger, Jr. attached himself in later years, both as a campaign aide and White House adviser.

Fluent, intelligent and supremely self-assured, Schlesinger, Jr. attended Cambridge University in 1938-39 as a "Henry fellow." [23] Known since infancy to Harold Laski, young Arthur was warmly received in British Fabian circles and treated as a member of the Society. Toward the end of World War II, he had an opportunity to renew those contacts when he went overseas for the Office of Strategic Services, being employed in a clerical capacity in London, Paris and Germany. At that time—as he states wryly in Who's Who in America—Schlesinger, Jr. "attained the high rank of corporal" in the Army of the United States, just as Adolf Hitler had done in the World War I Austrian Army—a circumstance which hardly qualified either of them to formulate overall military policies for their nations.

In his article for Fabian International Review, Arthur M. Schlesinger, Jr. pointed out that control of military policy by Left liberals in the United States was only a preliminary step to gaining control of foreign policy. Discussing demands of American "liberals" at the time for a larger defense budget, he explained to his Fabian readers that from the "liberal viewpoint" the Eisenhower budget was "not a security budget, but a fiscal budget"—that is, motivated not by calm consideration of defense needs, but "by a fanatical passion to reduce taxes and move toward a balanced budget." He added:

I suspect that the drift of this argument has carried me outside the orbit of many British Socialists. The hard fact of the matter is that, where in Britain the left appears to want to cut the defense budget, in the United States the most effective liberals are opposed to the Eisenhower Administration's policy of cutting defense spending [that is, as of 1954].

Schlesinger suggested that American "liberals" had their own fiscal motivation—a strictly Keynesian one. They favored large defense outlays for the moment, not so much because of actual defense needs,

[23] Who's Who in America, 1964-65, (Chicago, A. N. Marquis), p 1771.

as because this imposed a policy of large-scale public "investment" and deficit spending. *"Above all,"* Schlesinger concluded, *"it has become evident that liberals could not hope to control foreign policy unless they were ready to try and control defense policy . . . . .* Military power becomes the master of foreign policy, not when there is too much of it but when there is too little." [24]

Apprised of those weighty considerations, the Fabian-steered Congress of the Socialist International in its SUNFED Declaration of 1955 ordered the disarmament question to be temporarily soft-pedalled by international Socialists, and aid to backward nations stressed instead. It stated:

. . . The trend of discussion at the U.N. has encouraged the belief that the creation of SUNFED might be made dependent on progress in disarmament . . . A world-wide agreement on disarmament would be extremely helpful; but we need not and should not wait for it, doing nothing in the meanwhile about economic plans. In fact, economic development in underdeveloped areas may itself lead to a decrease in world tension and may expedite talks on disarmament. Anyway, economic development is of sufficient importance to be considered on its own merits.[25]

There followed in 1956 the Millikan-Rostow Report, submitted to the National Security Council in Washington and advocating among other things what Senator Hubert Humphrey of ADA enthusiastically termed the SUNFED philosophy. The Report proposed a lump sum appropriation up to 12 billion dollars, to be dispensed by the United States Government over a period of five years in the form of long-term, low-interest loans to underprivileged nations. At the close of the first five-year plan, a second five-year plan of equal magnitude was envisioned, whether or not the original funds were repaid.

In fact, as the Millikan-Rostow Report (p. 79) loftily remarked, "The narrow criterion of whether a project can repay from its own revenues is at best irrelevant and at worst misleading." [26] Most of this fantastic proposal was embodied in the U.S. Development Fund Loan Bill, presented to the United States Congress in 1957. Although the amount was trimmed before passage and placed on an annual appropriation basis, the spirit of the International's declaration was preserved.

[24] (Italics added.)
[25] *Yearbook of the International Socialist Labour Movement,* 1956-1957, p. 54. (See Bibliography).
[26] "The Millikan-Rostow Report." *U. S. A.,* (September 28, 1956), Vol. III, No. 19.

To induce the United States Government to adopt—even piecemeal and unawares—a program of the Socialist International, and to persuade the Socialist International to adjust its own timetable in accordance with the plans of Left liberals in America, was no small accomplishment. It presumed a more systematic interchange than was revealed in occasional articles by ADA keynoters, and occasional summit meetings between American Fabians and foreign Socialists. Regular and dependable communications were required between the political arm of the American Fabian movement and the Fabian policy planners of the British Labour Party, who dominated the Socialist International.

Obviously, the simplest control-measure was to assign a reliable agent of the Fabian Society to an obscure but central position in ADA. From the start, this function appears to have been entrusted to David C. Williams, a man of many hats in ADA. By temperament, training and connections he was well-qualified for such duty. Unlike other Rhodes Scholars of his circle at Oxford, Williams aspired to no public eminence, but was content to work industriously and almost anonymously within the confines of the Fabian Socialist movement. He was a transparency, through which the light emanating from New Fabian Research—where the policy-making operations of the Society resided —was transmitted to the American faithful for adaptation to home usage.

Following his graduation from Oxford, Williams had returned for a few years to Ohio, where he engaged in teaching, engineering research and organizational work for the Teachers' Union. He became secretary of the Ohio Federation of Teachers, at about the same time that the British-born Mark Starr was climbing to national office in the organization. As secretary of the Ohio joint AFL-CIO legislative committee Williams lobbied for organized labor at the State Capitol, and in 1944 attempted (and failed) to obtain a seat in the Ohio Legislature.

During the final year of World War II he returned to London, where he represented the Union for Democratic Action and both the American Federation of Labor and the Congress of Industrial Organization—despite the fact that the AFL and CIO did not formally merge until ten years later. Williams also managed the Union for Democratic Action Educational Fund, a somewhat mysterious tax free foundation which survived at least until 1954. That year ADA, according to its own financial statement, "borrowed" $500 from the Fund.

David Williams was in London during 1945 and saw the Fabian-controlled Labour Party sweep to power. It is reliably reported that he participated in the operation, and certainly his sympathies were deeply involved. The suggestion has been made that Williams' office was the channel through which substantial sums were routed by Socialist-led trade unions in America, to insure the Labour Party's victory in the 1945 British elections—this in return for a promise of an early solution to the Palestine question, diplomatically referred to by Williams in his *Fabian Journal* article of 1947.

Knowledgeable persons regard David C. Williams as the true begetter of Americans for Democratic Action, and almost always a reliable clue to its operational policy. His articles, published by left wing journals in America and England, are not mere expressions of personal bias meant to exemplify that "freedom of discussion" on which ADA, like the Fabian Society, prides itself. They reflect the approved ADA line of the moment, as does the *ADA World* he has edited for years. More than any other person, Williams helped to shape that homogenized viewpoint on political, economic and social questions which marks ADA followers, for all their tendency to be critical of individuals, including each other.

Since 1947, *ADA World* has employed the device of the Congressional Score Card, previously used by the Union for Democratic Action. Originally, UDA collaborated with Michael Straight—publisher of The *New Republic* and son of its long time financial angel, Dorothy Whitney Straight Elmhirst—in issuing a rundown on members of Congress from the Left liberal point of view. Entitled "A Congress to Win the War," it was first published as a supplement to The *New Republic* of May 18, 1942, and thereafter widely circulated in pamphlet form among academic and professional groups. Each legislator was given a plus or minus mark, according to whether his vote on selected issues was for or against the views of UDA.

As adapted by *ADA World*, the Score Card graded members of Congress percentage-wise for their voting record on bills rated important to the success of the ADA Fabian Socialist program. Issued annually as a Congressional Supplement, the Score Card not only alerted ADA followers to the stand they were expected to take on specific issues; but also warned legislators of impending reprisals in forthcoming election campaigns. Its effects were first demonstrated in the 1948 campaign, when 79 congressmen, 5 senators and 4 governors who had been endorsed and backed by ADA were elected to office.[27] Among those newly elected senators were two ADA leaders, Paul Douglas and Hubert Humphrey, the latter becoming first Democratic Party whip in the Senate and then Vice President of the United States. A former midwest field director of ADA, Richard Bolling, was sent to the House from Missouri.

Though ADA claimed a national membership of only twenty-eight thousand at the time, its strength was swelled by the campaign efforts of the CIO-Political Action Committee, whose judgments coincided almost invariably with those of ADA. This was not surprising, since the CIO-Political Action Committee's stand on individuals and issues was largely dictated by the Reuther brothers, Walter, Victor and Roy —all devout supporters of ADA. Similarly, an army of International Ladies Garment Workers and their families marched in regimented ranks to the polls, to register approval or disapproval of political candidates as rated by ADA—according to precepts and principles originating in New Fabian Research.

With the merger of the AFL and CIO in 1955, the functions of the Political Action Committee were taken over by the joint Committee on Political Education, known as COPE, a more potent and even more adequately financed body, for which ADA supplied both candidates and ideology. It was a setup similar to that envisaged long before by George Bernard Shaw, in which labor was to provide the money and votes for election campaigns—and Socialist intellectuals were to supply the leadership, programs and political jobholders at local, state and national levels. Labor furnished the real lobbying power behind ADA programs in Washington, where Americans for Democratic Action confessed to having only one registered lobbyist receiving the modest salary of $9,000 per year. Meanwhile, ADA continued to produce a stream of "expert" witnesses for Congressional committees—virtually "running an underground railway" between Capitol Hill, Harvard University and Massachusetts Institute of Technology.

Potency of the combination can be inferred from the fact that ADA made at least one-third of their proposed policies effective in Congress from 1947 to 1960.[28] This analysis does not disclose the relative importance of the policies put over by ADA, nor take into account partial ADA victories. Deprecated by ADA spokesmen as a frustrating performance, falling far short of their own high hopes, it

[27] Brock, *op. cit.*, p. 102.
[28] *Ibid.*, p. 124.

actually denoted an alarmingly high rate of progress for a small Socialist-inspired organization claiming a national membership of at most forty thousand persons and an annual budget of some $130,000.

A possible weakness in the ADA power structure, seldom mentioned by ADA publicists or their opponents, is the fact that only a small executive fraction of organized labor has been consciously involved in such maneuvers. While it is true that the so-called educational propaganda prepared by COPE reaches millions of Americans, via broadcasts, television, union newspapers and syndicated ADA columnists, its actual operations are controlled by a few powerful and sophisticated union chieftains. They represent the Socialist-minded minority, not the majority of union labor. Notably, they are leaders of the United Auto Workers and the International Ladies Garment Workers.

By coincidence, these are the very unions which have contributed most regularly and faithfully to the support of ADA national headquarters, even when other unions fell away. An estimate based on ADA's own fiscal statements shows the total amount given directly by the ILGWU from 1947 through 1958 as $231,000, and the UAW total as $165,000.[29] To avoid conflict with the law, since 1951 such funds have been paid into ADA's "nonpolitical" account—if anything connected with that organization can properly be termed nonpolitical. Possibly the services of Joseph L. Rauh, Jr., and the frequent sums "in excess of $100" donated by him and members of his immediate family to ADA, may be reckoned as an indirect UAW contribution.

ADA spokesmen, while admitting that in its early years one-third of the organization's income came from labor unions,[30] point out that by 1960 a mere one-tenth of its annual budget was derived from union sources. This recalls the old story of the girl who had the baby out of wedlock, and excused herself by saying, "It was such a little one!" Whether such contributions were authorized by vote of the rank-and-file union membership is not recorded.

---

[29] These figures are based on average annual contributions of $21,000 from the ILGWU and $15,000 from the UAW over a period of 11 years. A list of contributions to ADA, in excess of $100, is filed annually with the Clerk of the House of Representatives under terms of the Corrupt Practices Act. It does not include donations to local and state branches of ADA or its affiliates. The same source also reveals that from 1951 to 1958 fourteen labor unions contributed a grand total of $350,546.40 to the national headquarters of ADA.

[30] Brock, *op. cit.*, p. 164.

The ILGWU and the UAW have donated larger amounts of their members' hard-earned cash to finance world-wide activities of the International Confederation of Free Trade Unions. Moreover, it is in great part due to the leaders of those two globally-oriented American labor unions that the AFL-CIO has been induced to contribute an annual one million dollars since 1955, to support the labor arm of the Socialist International.[31] In July, 1963, Walter Reuther, president of the United Auto Workers and heir-presumptive to the presidency of the AFL-CIO, took an expense-paid trip to Harpsund, Sweden, to attend what proved to be a joint meeting of various European leaders of the Socialist International and the Confederation of Free Trade Unions.[32]

Reuther was accompanied by Senator Hubert Humphrey, another pillar of ADA. Though the two Americans were prudently described as "observers," one wonders why they could not have found something in the whole wide world of a less officially Socialist character to observe.

Twelve months later that rustic conclave at the country home of Sweden's Socialist Prime Minister, Tage Erlander, was repeated, with very many of the same personages attending. On July 4, 1964, it was announced in *Socialist International Information* that "the following have been invited, among others: Willy Brandt, Harold Wilson, Jens-Otto Krag, Giuseppe Saragat, Senator Hubert Humphrey and Walter Reuther. The meeting will be held in private, as was a similar meeting in Harpsund last year." With refreshing candor, this front-page item was headlined "Socialist Leaders to Meet in Harpsung!" The meeting was scheduled for August 1-2, when Hubert Humphrey was already the Democratic Party's candidate for the Vice Presidency of the United States.

---

[31] Lester Velie, *Labor U.S.A.*, (New York, Harper & Brothers, 1958-59), p. 237.

[32] *Socialist International Information*, (August 3, 1963), Vol. XIII, No. 31-32. The item states, "Among those present were: Eric Ollenhauer, Herbert Wehner, and Willi Brandt (the Chairman and Vice-Chairman of the German Social Democratic Party), Harold Wilson (Leader of the British Labour Party), Niels Matthiassen (Secretary of the Danish Social Democratic Party), Tryggve Bratteli (Vice-Chairman of the Norwegian Social Democratic Party), Tage Erlander (Prime Minister of Sweden and Chairman of the Swedish Social Democratic Party), the leaders of the Swedish, Norwegian and German Trades Union Congresses, Arne Geijer, Konrad Nordahl and Ludwig Rosenburg, Hubert Humphrey (American Senator) and Walter Reuther (Leader of the American Automobile Workers Union.)"

2.

If Americans for Democratic Action in some ways belied its name, at least nobody could deny that (to paraphrase Max Beerbohm) it stood for action with a capital H. Its members were frenetically busy people who never stopped trying to promote their programs and, incidentally, themselves. Chiefly they consisted—as one ADA sympathizer said—"of academic intellectuals, the more socially conscious union leaders and members, municipal reformers, and other assorted groups and individuals of liberal [sic] political and economic inclinations." [33]

Because of its volubility and persistence, the organization made a good deal more noise than its size seemed to warrant. Moreover, ADA had a tendency to arrogate to itself a monopoly on civic virtue and public interest legislation. This irritated well-meaning citizens who happened to believe that desirable reforms need not invariably be achieved by the enlargement of Federal powers. Undeterred by occasional setbacks which they mourned publicly but from which they usually managed to extract some advantage, ADA's followers continued to spread their influence, via education and political action, into many high and otherwise sacrosanct places.[34]

In 1950, when only three and a half years old, ADA claimed to have 123 chapters in thirty states with a membership of nearly thirty-five thousand. Already it could boast of having made inroads into the Democratic Party machine. Eight major planks of the Fair Deal platform on which President Truman campaigned in 1948 coincided with ADA objectives—including the controversial civil rights plank which ADA delegates, led by Mayor Hubert Humphrey of Minneapolis, forced on the Democratic National Convention.

A number of President Truman's key administrative appointments (though perhaps not so many as ADA would have wished) went to ADA members and friends after 1948. This was the pay-off for contributions, electoral and fiscal, made to Truman's surprise victory by ADA labor leaders Dubinsky, Reuther *et al.* ADA announced that their role in political campaigns was to supply "the margin of victory:" a formula by which a minority claims the credit for swinging narrowly-won popular elections.

[33] Brock, *op. cit.*, p. 11-16.
[34] *Lobbying, Direct and Indirect. Hearings before the Select Committee on Lobbying Activities.* House of Representatives, Second Session, 81st Congress, (Washington, U.S. Government Printing Office, 1950), Part VI, p. 7.

By the time the next national elections rolled around, Americans for Democratic Action had gathered enough intra-Party strength to sway a majority of delegates at the Democratic National Convention. In 1952, ADA was able to name a presidential candidate, Adlai Stevenson. Old pros of the Democratic Party suspected that no matter whom the Democrats ran that year, he was bound to lose. The country definitely wanted a change, and General Eisenhower with his World War II laurels and his heart-warming grin seemed an unbeatable popular candidate—as ADA had recognized four years earlier, when it tactlessly tried to persuade Eisenhower to enter the Democratic primary against his titular Commander-in-chief, President Truman.[35]

It was not necessary that ADA leaders supposed Dwight D. Eisenhower to be a Socialist or even a Left liberal. They regarded him as a political general who owed his spectacular rise in the armed forces to the New Deal and General George C. Marshall, and who was never known to have clashed with either—not even when ordered to halt American troops outside Berlin, so that Russian armies were the first to enter the city. While in London during World War II, Eisenhower had mingled affably though not intimately with Fabian Socialists in the British wartime Cabinet;[36] and apparently they concluded he might be amenable to management as a future President of the United States. General Eisenhower, however, proved cold to ADA's 1948 proposition. He waited and received a more proper bid for 1952 from a group of Eastern Republicans.

Adlai Stevenson, whom ADA in its political wisdom chose to run against Eisenhower in two consecutive elections, was a candidate of another stripe. By his own statements, Stevenson was committed body and soul to ADA's welfare state and One World goals. With minor reservations, he had been charitably inclined toward the Soviet Union ever since he visited Moscow in 1926, as a cub reporter for his family's newspaper, the Bloomington *Pantagraph*. Stevenson had a barbed wit and a cultivated charm seemingly irresistible to Left liberals, who applauded him as madly in defeat as if he were a victor.

The *ADA World* in November, 1948 had mentioned Adlai Stevenson as "one of the original founders of ADA in Chicago." As late as February, 1952, the same house organ referred to him as "a charter member of ADA." Yet Stevenson wrote that very year in a letter to the late

---

[35] Brock, *op. cit.*, pp. 91-95.
[36] Few Americans recall today that Clement R. Attlee was Churchill's Deputy Prime Minister during World War II.

Senator Pat McCarran: "As for ADA, I have never been a member of it." [37] Skeptics pointed out that Adlai was notoriously absentminded. Undeniably he owed his election as Governor of Illinois in 1948, to efforts of the Independent Voters of Illinois, an ADA affiliate and a regular donor to ADA's national headquarters fund. Since the Independent Voters of Illinois, however, had retained its corporate independence, members of that organization could still state with legal accuracy that they did not belong to ADA.

At best it was a transparent subterfuge, deceiving nobody but the general public. Both politicians and personal admirers knew Adlai as ADA's boy. For his 1952 campaign manager, he chose Wilson Wyatt, founder-member and first national chairman of Americans for Democratic Action.[38] Arthur M. Schlesinger, Jr.—member of ADA's national board, chairman of its Massachusetts chapter and secretary of its foreign policy commission[39]—was Stevenson's special assistant on campaign issues and tactics. Only a few years before, ADA executive secretary James Loeb, Jr. had remarked complacently: "If ADA has any short range liability, it has been its insistence on political integrity." Under the Kennedy-Johnson Administration Adlai Stevenson, that paragon of political integrity, became United States Ambassador to the United Nations.

The repeated candidacy of Adlai Stevenson had more value for ADA than it did for the Democratic Party. Even as a loser, he provided a national sounding board for ADA's Fabian Socialist propaganda, within the respectable framework of the two party system. More important still, as titular leader of the Democratic Party for eight years, Stevenson was able to deliver its national machinery into the hands of his ADA backers and associates.

Thus Americans for Democratic Action, during a period of apparent defeat, was able to solidify its influence not only on the Democratic National Committee, but also on local and state Democratic committees in virtually all states outside the Solid South. It had a bigger voice than ever in selecting congressional candidates, and it concen-

---

[37] Washington *Post*, (August 30, 1952).

[38] As of 1964, Wilson Wyatt was Lieutenant Governor of Kentucky, having previously failed to win the race for a seat in the U.S. Senate. He illustrates the tendency of ADA followers to settle for state or local offices, when blocked in their quest for national office.

[39] These were the posts held by Schlesinger in 1950, according to former Attorney General Francis Biddle. *Lobbying, Direct and Indirect*, p. 30. (See Bibliography).

trated on winning congressional elections. The results were visible in the increased number of ADA-approved candidates sent to Capitol Hill in 1956 and after. For the first time in history, dedicated if unavowed agents of international Socialism gained effective control over the mechanics and patronage of a major political party in the United States. Not even Franklin D. Roosevelt had been able to change the pattern of the Party's operations so completely.

This situation prevailed in April, 1960, when Chester Bowles of Connecticut, a founder of ADA, and the late Philip Perlman of Maryland, U.S. Solicitor General under Truman and long an ADA sympathizer,[40] were named chairman and vice chairman of the Democratic Party's election year platform committee. Both belonged to the Democratic Advisory Council, a Left liberal caucus within the Party. Bowles held regional platform hearings in ADA strongholds like Philadelphia, St. Louis and Detroit, at which local ADA leaders aired their views. At least four other ADA members were named to the platform committee, including Joseph Rauh, Jr., sworn enemy of loyalty investigations and advocate of enlisting the Executive power to impose a *de facto* merger of racial elements in the United States. Rauh was the busiest single member of a subcommittee appointed to draft the Party platform.

In all but wording, the final document approved by the Democratic Convention in Los Angeles and ironically entitled "The Rights of Man," was a replica of the platform adopted by ADA at its own annual convention.[41] Besides a provocative civil rights plank, openly

[40] Brock, *op. cit.*, p. 179.

[41] On July 7, 1960 Joseph Rauh, Jr. apprised the full platform committee of ADA's stand on "the single most important issue," namely, "civil rights." His statement read, in part:

We believe the Democratic Party must be unmistakably committed to a program of federal action which will result in the eradication of segregation and other forms of discrimination from *all aspects of American life*.

Such a program would pledge that the next President, if he is a Democrat, will use the tremendous resources of his office to make desegregation a reality as quickly as possible . . .

In particular, he urged the following measures:

1. Enact Title III to empower the Attorney General to file civil injunction suits in cases involving denial of civil rights.
2. Support the Supreme Court's *decree* in the school desegregation cases and *provide assistance for school districts prepared to desegregate*.
3. Declare support for sit-in demonstrations.
4. Improve procedures in both Houses of Congress so that the will of the majority shall prevail and Congress will be a more responsive instrument of *our national purposes*.
5. Pledge vigorous enforcement of existing voting laws and enact additional

inviting civil disturbances, it contained a civil liberties plank dictated by Rauh that might, if enacted into law, seriously impede the FBI in collecting evidence on cases of espionage or treason for prosecution by the U.S. Attorney General. Even so tolerant an observer as Professor Brock has described the 1960 Democrat platform as the most radical ever adopted by a major political party in this country. Far from being discarded at a later date as mere campaign oratory, it became the visible operating program of the Kennedy-Johnson Administration.

In the field of higher education, Students for Democratic Action (SDA) had been established by 1950 on 100 colleges and campuses. Its revolving membership was described merely as "exceeding 3000." [42] Based on the same arithmetic, it can be computed that within ten years quite a few thousands of those anonymous trainees held positions in government, private industry, research foundations and the teaching profession. Normally, the better positions were obtained on the strength of superior college grades and recommendations supplied by liberal professors and deans.

A true-life Horatio Alger story of the Left may be seen in the career of Theodore Sorensen, once a model SDA member at the University of Nebraska. Sorensen's father had been campaign manager for Senator George Norris—original sponsor of TVA and one of those Progressive Republicans known in their day as the sons of the wild jackass. While still in law school, young Ted lobbied at the State Legislature for a Fair Employment Practices Act. He registered with his local draft board as a conscientious objector, following the pacifist example set by his parents.

At the age of twenty-three, Ted Sorensen went to Washington, poor and apparently friendless. There he found work with the Government in a series of routine jobs; but continued dutifully to attend ADA conventions. He soon attracted the notice of powerful patrons. Less than two years after arriving in the nation's capital, he was recom-

---

legislation to protect the right to vote, including, if necessary, *direct federal control and operation of registration and elections.*
6. Promulgate an executive order forbidding segregation and other forms of discrimination based on race, religion or national origin in all federal or federally aided programs.
7. Enact a federal fair employment practices law to establish and enforce equal job opportunity in all employment in or affecting interstate commerce. (Italics added.)

[42] *Lobbying, Direct and Indirect,* Part VI, p. 7 (See Bibliography).

mended by Senator Paul Douglas of ADA for the position of legislative aide to the newly elected and very wealthy junior Senator from Massachusetts, John F. Kennedy. After interviewing his prospective employer to make sure the two of them were "not too far apart on basic policy," Sorensen took the job. Eight years later he accompanied his boss to the White House, in the capacity of confidential assistant.[43]

From conversations with several hundred present-day college students in various parts of the country, it is evident to this writer that a strong reason for the appeal of Left liberalism to aspiring youth has been the diligence of adult ADA members in acting as an unofficial placement service. At the same time, Left-leaning professors—whose own tenure is assured by the joint ADA-Civil Liberties Union battles for so-called academic freedom—can threaten conservative students with failure and loss of credits for giving "wrong answers" in opinion-forming courses.[44] Thus traditional American values are reversed, with Left liberalism becoming entrenched as the current status quo.

Like members of the Fabian Society who took positions with the Federation of British Industries, ADA members entering industry or public service usually renounced any formal connection with ADA. They became part of a diffused but growing army of ADA non-members advancing that organization's ideas in ever-widening areas of American life. While ADA's official membership figures remained in the vicinity of thirty-five to forty thousand, the range of its contacts expanded progressively throughout the apparently frustrating fifties.

In 1957, Americans for Democratic Action convened to celebrate its 10th anniversary, meeting once more for sentimental reasons at the Willard Hotel in Washington. Twelve hundred delegates attended from all parts of the country. Old-timers of the League for Industrial Democracy were still very much in evidence. Speakers included the perennial Senators Douglas, Humphrey and Neuberger, with Wayne Morse of Oregon added to the list.[45] (Senator Morse's melodramatic

---

[43] Victor Lasky, *JFK: The Man and The Myth*, (New York, The Macmillan Co., 1963), p. 163-165.

[44] An inquiry conducted from 1962 to 1964 in one California school district showed similar pressures operating in high schools and even grade schools. Parents feared to protest, because those who did so found their children penalized with bad marks and loss of credits needed to graduate.

[45] In 1950 former Attorney General Biddle had named the following Senators as members of ADA: Humphrey, Lehman, Graham, McMahon, Douglas, Murray and Neely, all Democrats. *Lobbying, Direct and Indirect*, p. 30. (See Bibliography). While the ADA Score Card shows a very much larger number of Senators and Congressmen now winning high marks by ADA standards, no offi-

move from the Republican to the Democratic side of the Senate aisle did not alter the fact that he was first and foremost a Socialist both in words and deeds.) Walter Reuther, James B. Carey, A. Philip Randolph spoke for the unions, some of which after straying away had returned that year to the fold.[46] Arthur M. Schlesinger, Jr., Harvard historian, composed a not unflattering history of ADA for the occasion.

Conspicuous among the newer recruits was the towering figure and booming voice of Governor Theodore Roosevelt McKeldin of Maryland,[47] who had placed the name of Dwight D. Eisenhower in nomination at the Republican National Convention of 1952. Governor McKeldin's presence indicated that during the past decade ADA had also made some slight progress in permeating the Republican Party. Theoretically, it was the purpose of ADA to work inside both major parties, in order to gain dual support for its own Fabian Socialist programs. In July, 1950, former Attorney General Francis Biddle, testifying before a Congressional Committee as national chairman of ADA, reaffirmed this intention, while disclaiming any Socialist bias. *"My thought,"* said Biddle, *"is that we operate 90-some per cent in the Democratic area and a very small per cent in the Republican— and oh! that the Republican area were larger!"* [48]

At that time Biddle was asked, "Have you [in the ADA] ever supported any Republican candidates?" He replied, "Yes, in the New York Mayoralty election we supported Newbold Morris against O'Dwyer." (Newbold Morris, it may be recalled, addressed the LID's 40th Anniversary Dinner in 1945, and there uttered warm words of praise for Norman Thomas.) Biddle further noted that ADA had backed Congressmen Richard Hoffman of Chicago and Jacob Javits of New York.

Since the price of ADA endorsement is support of its policies, the path pursued by its favorites can be surmised. During eight years as a Republican Congressman, Jacob K. Javits voted the ADA way on

cial list of ADA members on Capitol Hill is available. Senator Joseph S. Clark of Pennsylvania, is a former State Chairman of ADA and contributes to *ADA World.* Senators Pat McNamara and Philip Hart of Michigan regularly follow the ADA-UAW line.

[46] Reports for 1957 listing "Contributions of $100 and over" and filed by ADA with the Clerk of the House of Representatives under the Corrupt Practices Act, show twelve labor unions contributing that year to ADA's "Non-Political Account," for a total of $47,677

[47] William E. Bohn, "Americans for Democratic Action Celebrates Its Tenth Birthday," *The New Leader,* (April 15, 1957), p. 9.

[48] *Lobbying, Direct and Indirect,* p. 15. (See Bibliography).

82 of 87 roll calls and earned a rating of 94 per cent on its Score Card.[49] Despite his fidelity Javits failed to get official ADA backing when he ran for the office of New York Attorney General in 1954. The alleged reason was that his rival, former Congressman Franklin D. Roosevelt, Jr., had a pluperfect ADA voting record. While some of Javits' friends professed to regard this as base ingratitude, it is unlikely Javits saw it that way. For the first time in his life, he needed conservative upstate votes to win.

Born and bred on New York City's lower East Side, a cherished speaker for years at LID[50] functions and those of the International Ladies Garment Workers Union, Javits required no printed endorsement to carry Manhattan, the Bronx and much of Brooklyn. He could hardly have lost the garment workers' vote if he had tried. On the other hand, a public announcement of ADA support, confirming rumors of his radical ties, might have been the kiss of death for Javits in suburban and upstate districts. A shrewd and accomplished campaigner, he could manage very well without such endorsement. From the apparently disinterested regularity with which he has voted for ADA programs ever since, it was obvious he harbored no grudge. As the senior senator from New York State in 1963, Javits still scored 94 per cent by ADA standards[51]—higher than any other senator on the Republican side of the aisle. Of course, he firmly denies being a Socialist.

[49] Brock, op. cit., p. 22.
[50] Title of a League for Industrial Democracy Round Table in which Congressman Jacob Javits participated in 1952 was: "Needed: A MORAL AWAKENING IN AMERICA." Corruption in business and in politics was discussed; but corruption in labor unions was not mentioned. Others who took part in the program with Javits included: Walter Reuther, James B. Carey, John Haynes Holmes, Charles S. Zimmerman, Sidney Hook, Mark Starr, Helen Gahagan Douglas, Abraham Lefkowitz, Gus Tyler, Leland Olds, George Catlin, James Farmer, August Claessens, and Samuel H. Friedman, reading a statement from Norman Thomas, then in Japan. Nancy Adams, Chief Woman Officer of the British Trades Union Congress, expressed the appreciation of the British labor movement for Marshall Plan aid. Clarence Senior, alleged expert on Latin American affairs and long time member of the London Fabian Society, presided over the Round Table. Harry W. Laidler, Editor, Needed: A MORAL AWAKENING IN AMERICA. A Symposium, (New York, League for Industrial Democracy Pamphlet, 1952). Samuel Friedman, National Vice Chairman and Executive member of the token Socialist Party, USA, was listed in 1964 as one of four delegates from the United States to the Council and Congress of the Socialist International in Brussels. Socialist International Information, Congress Issue, (September 19, 1964), Vol. XIV, No. 20-21.
[51] United Press International dispatch, (December 29, 1963).

ADA and labor union endorsements of political candidates are often separate but identical, especially if the union in question is the ILGWU. As the British-born Socialist, Mark Starr, explained, however, the complexion of the minority groups composing the ILGWU's rank-and-file has altered over the years. A large proportion of the membership—which remains numerically stable, despite a heavy turnover in individual members—now consists of Negro, Puerto Rican and Mexican women.[52] The sole political issue that really engrosses them is civil rights; so in a sense, the fate of the ILGWU leadership may be said to hinge on that issue.

The old immigrant garment-maker from Eastern Europe is no more —except for a little group of laborites, whom David Dubinsky is said to have "rescued from the Nazis in Poland" during World War II, and brought to this country.[53] One of the latter, Henoch Mendelsund, today heads the ILGWU's potent Joint Dress Board. As for the children and grandchildren of older European radicals who founded the garment workers union, they have prospered under the American system and many are today doctors, lawyers, college professors and civil servants. Far from becoming what the old-style unionist contemptuously referred to as "alrightniks," a number of them are now the backbone of the Fabian Socialist ADA.

The present-day ILGWU not only endorses candidates, but also instructs its four hundred thousand plus members, their families and friends how to vote. It organizes union participation in political campaigns, to an extent not permitted by law even in Britain. In New York City the ILGWU, acting jointly with the Amalgamated Clothing Workers, has organized a private political party: the so-called Liberal Party, which elects its own captive congressmen and also has an important voice in the City and State governments. Elsewhere the ILGWU adapts its political activities to the local scene.

An official report of the General Executive Board to the ILGWU convention, meeting in May, 1962, at Atlantic City, told how the union "played a critical part in four important contests throughout the nation, aside from the national election of the Kennedy-Johnson ticket in November, 1960." In San Antonio, Texas, for example:

. . . former ILGWU staff member Henry Gonzales won a special election to fill a vacancy. Gonzales is the first American of Mexican background to

---

[52] Mark Starr, "Garment Workers: 'Welfare Unionism'," *Current History*, (July, 1954), (Reprint by ILGWU.)

[53] *Report of the General Executive Board to the 31st Convention*. (New York, International Ladies Garment Workers Union, 1962), p. 96.

be elected to Congress from Texas. For years he was a vigorous champion of civil rights as a member of the Texas State Senate. Several minutes after taking his oath as a Congressman, he handed the clerk of the House a bill calling for abolition of the poll tax. Within 48 hours after his election, Gonzales, after visiting with Pres. Dubinsky in the General Office, pitched into a 12-hour whirlwind drive throughout New York City in behalf of Mayor Wagner's candidacy.[54]

Gonzales gained some newspaper notoriety in 1963, reportedly for slugging a fellow-congressman who had referred to him as a radical.

Like Americans for Democratic Action, the ILGWU has occasionally supported Republicans in city or state elections—or else has appeared to give them an even break. Two contests in New Jersey involving Republicans were mentioned in the report of the Executive Board:[55]

The peculiar feature of the New Jersey election in November, 1961 was the fact that two men classified as liberals were in a contest for the office of governor. The Republican candidate, former Secretary of Labor James P. Mitchell, had won the nomination in a primary contest against a conservative opponent.
He then faced the liberal Democratic nominee, Richard Hughes. Because both candidates were broadly "liberal," ILGWU units made their own choices in endorsements. It was apparent from the results which, despite contrary predictions, brought victory for Hughes, that garment workers and others clearly perceived the difference in his favor.
In this instance, the ILGWU followed an earlier precedent: In 1960, Jersey ILGers, acting on the basis of Republican Senator Case's liberal record, endorsed both him and Democratic candidate Lord. Case won re-election.[56]

Senator Case in 1963 rated a high 88 per cent on the ADA Score Card.

For the Presidency and Vice Presidency, ADA and its allies have supported none but Democratic Party candidates to date. They have often been accused, however, of seeking to influence pro or con the Republican Party's choice of nominees. Aside from the fact that left wing labor groups have been known to work in Republican primaries for the defeat of conservative candidates, and that ADA publicists always offer the Republican Party a great deal of unsolicited and somewhat suspect advice, evidence of ADA intervention is purely

[54] *Ibid.*, pp. 17-18.
[55] *Ibid.*, p. 18.
[56] Mitchell's opponent in the primary was Robert Morris, former counsel for the Senate Subcommittee on Internal Security. Observers reported that ILGWU workers and their associates, after assuring the defeat of Morris in the primary, failed to support Mitchell in the general election.

circumstantial. The case most frequently cited is that of the Republican Advance, a high level caucus of Eastern Republicans believed to have long since faded away.

Early in July, 1950,—just before former Attorney General Biddle on July 7, 1950, confessed to a House Committee ADA's deep desire to extend its influence in Republican circles—Republicans from ten Eastern states held a week-long meeting and formed the Republican Advance Committee. Its declared object was to develop a program for the Republican Party that could compete successfully with the New Deal-Fair Deal program. A less advertised purpose was to select a Republican standard-bearer for 1952 other than Senator Robert Taft of Ohio, Republican leader on Capitol Hill.

Among political figures involved in the Advance, before or after its creation, were: Governor Thomas E. Dewey of New York, titular head of the Republican Party, and his close associate, Herbert Brownell, who became Attorney General in the Eisenhower Cabinet; Senator Henry Cabot Lodge of Massachusetts, later Ambassador to the United Nations, and his brother, Governor John Lodge of Connecticut, later Ambassador to Spain; Senator Ralph Flanders of Vermont; and New Hampshire's Governor Sherman Adams of unhappy memory. It was this group which invited General Eisenhower to run for the Presidency in 1952, and which steered him into the White House.

Financial backers of the Republican Advance were reported to include Nelson A. Rockefeller, who became Under Secretary of Health, Education and Welfare in the Eisenhower Administration, and Sidney J. Weinberg, a partner in the Wall Street firm of Goldman, Sachs and a member since 1933 of the Business Advisory Council of the Department of Commerce, now called the Business Council. Only persons in the Advance group visibly associated with ADA were Russell Davenport,[57] an editor of *Fortune* magazine, and Governor McKeldin of Maryland.

---

[57] *Lobbying, Direct and Indirect*, p. 16. (See Bibliography). Following is a fragment of pertinent testimony:

Mr. Brown: "Have you [ADA] become more active in the Republican Party recently, your organization?"

Mr. Biddle: "No—we have not, except—well in this sense. Our influence has been rather striking. I do not know if you have noted the organization of a similar movement in the Republican Party; I do not think they have a name for it—led by Russell Davenport."

Mr. Brown: "You mean Republican Advance or something like that?"

Any part ADA may have played in instigating the Republican Advance is not susceptible of proof. It can merely be pointed out that the Fabian technique of permeation, as defined by Margaret Cole, envisaged persuading nonmembers of the Society to carry out, often unconsciously, the work and the will of Fabians. This has been the technique most often used by Left liberals of the United States in attempting to gain a foothold in Republican councils—as contrasted with their more direct and widespread penetration of the Democratic Party. It can also be said that in some respects the original aims of the Republican Advance were not displeasing to ADA.

Admittedly, ADA had a prime interest in blocking the Presidential nomination of Senator Taft, a man of strongly defined conservative principles. Labor's Political Action Committee had denounced him for his joint authorship of the Taft-Hartley Act, since invoked by Democrat and Republican Presidents alike in moments of threatened national crisis. Yet Taft always carried his own heavily unionized state of Ohio by large majorities. For many months before the Republican Convention of 1952, ADA's ever-growing corps of news commentators, political pollsters and syndicated columnists assisted in spreading the lethal rumor: "Taft can't win!" A somewhat comparable situation arose in 1963-64, when political seers throughout the country united as if with one voice to downgrade the popular appeal of Senator Barry Goldwater.

In 1959, an ADA publicist engaged once more in the gratuitous sport of trying to pick a future Republican Presidential candidate. *The Progressive* for February, 1959, carried an article entitled "Rockefeller in Washington," by David C. Williams, editor of the official *ADA World* and voice of the Fabian Society in America. Williams compared Nelson A. Rockefeller's "blinding charm" to that of President Franklin D. Roosevelt. He explained that Rockefeller, by virtue of a long record of collaboration with New Deal-Fair Deal programs, had personally succeeded in "transcending" the traditions of his party. Finally, Williams suggested that if Nelson Rockefeller were able to

---

Mr. Biddle: "Something like that. I thought it might be called Republicans for Democratic Action, but that did not seem quite appropriate . . . ."
Chairman: "Did the national organization [ADA] actually take a position for Eisenhower for President?"
Mr. Loeb: "For Eisenhower or Justice [William O.] Douglas . . . The position taken at the Board meeting in Pittsburgh in April, 1948 was for Eisenhower or Douglas."

"escape the limitations of his own party" and "tap fresh sources of power" he might make an acceptable President by Left liberal standards.[58]

Variously referred to in British Fabian Socialist literature as international director and research-and-educational director of Americans for Democratic Action, David Williams had stated in an earlier work, *The Intelligent Socialist's Guide to America:* "ADA is not a political party. It operates very much as the early Fabian Society did seeking to permeate the existing parties." In advising Left liberals that Nelson Rockefeller was a promising medium for permeating the Republican Party at the top, Williams was merely perpetuating a time-honored tactic of American as well as British Fabian Socialists. Fabians had long concentrated on "educating" the offspring of prominent families —partly, perhaps, with a view to traducing famed conservative names.

Nelson Rockefeller seems to have been exposed to such psychological seduction since childhood. As a boy he attended the experimental Lincoln School, together with three of his brothers, Winthrop, Lawrence and David. The Lincoln School was operated by Columbia University's School of Education, then dominated by the ideas of John Dewey, father of so-called Progressive Education and a president of the Fabian Socialist LID. There a sense of personal guilt for all the world's ills was instilled into young scions of wealth, who were simultaneously reminded of their duty to help fashion a new and better social order.

In his adult years, Nelson Rockefeller often referred to the New Order that was bound to come. As late as 1962, he was praised by Left liberals as the author of a book called *The Future of Federalism.* It has been described by Supreme Court Justice William O. Douglas as a "plea for a 'new world order' with the United States taking the lead in fashioning a new federalism at the world level." In other words, Rockefeller called openly for a type of World Government similar to that urged by Walt Whitman Rostow and others—where the independence of the United States, as we have known it, will be abolished.[59] Reviewing Rockefeller's book for the Washington *Post,* Justice Douglas wrote, rather strangely for one entrusted with preserving the United States Constitution:

[58] David C. Williams, "Rockefeller in Washington," *The Progressive,* (February, 1959), pp. 11-13.
[59] Cf. Nelson A. Rockefeller, *The Future of Federalism,* (Cambridge, Harvard University Press, 1962).

He [Rockefeller] does the nation great service when he propounds the theme of this book . . . . It is bold in conception and sets America's sights high.[60]

Summoned to Washington during World War II with other Republicans whom FDR had recruited in the name of national unity, "Rockefeller surrounded himself," says David C. Williams, "with forward-looking staff members, whose ideas he eagerly solicited and put to use." [61] Others have noted that the wartime agency which Rockefeller headed, as Coordinator of Inter American Affairs, contained an inordinate number of Communist fellow-travelers and assorted Left liberals. Rockefeller reappeared in Washington in 1950, as chairman of Truman's International Development Advisory Board, assigned to draft plans for United States aid to underdeveloped nations. Through the Rockefeller Brothers' Fund, he issued a report, *Partners in Progress,* "calculated [as Williams says] to make a maximum impact on public opinion."

The happy if unbusinesslike idea of an equal partnership between rich and poor nations was of British Fabian Socialist origin. The *Fabian Journal* for June 7, 1952, (pp. 20 ff.), carried an unsigned article, "Advance to Democracy: A Report to the Fabian Colonial Bureau on the Implications of 'Partnership' in Multi-Racial Societies." Ernest Davies, Fabian Member of Parliament and son of the former Fabian Society chairman, A. Emil Davies, was among the chief spokesmen for this radical interpretation of "Partnership."

It may be recalled that Ernest Davies worked in New York City during the nineteen-twenties as a newspaper reporter. Davies was the presiding officer in 1954 and 1955 of the first and second London Parliamentary Conference on World Government, which evolved two schemes for revision of the United Nations charter looking toward the creation of a World Government. According to letters received from participants, the second Conference decided to set schemes of World Government aside temporarily, in favor of a World Development Program. It is significant that the slogan of "Partnership" [62]—

---

[60] Quoted in an advertisement for Rockefeller's book, which appeared for nine successive months on the back page of *Freedom & Union* magazine, edited by Clarence K. Streit.

[61] Williams, *op. cit.,* p. 11.

[62] *ADA World* for May, 1955 announced a booklet, *Partnership for Freedom, Proposals for World Economic Growth,* published by the Union for Democratic Action Educational Fund. It was described as a 52 page booklet proposing a "new look" in American overseas aid. Sponsors of this booklet included: Eleanor Roosevelt, Reinhold Niebuhr, James G. Patton, Arthur M. Schlesinger, Thomas

like the term "Fair Shares," which in America became Truman's Fair Deal—originated in a Fabian Socialist bureau in London.

As a private citizen, Rockefeller organized a National Conference on International Economic and Social Development in 1952. He criticized the limited aid given by the Truman Administration to backward countries and urged that such aid be continued on a more lavish scale under the Eisenhower Administration. In particular, he called it "disastrous" to have made economic aid an adjunct to military aid under the Mutual Security Act.

While it may be questioned whether Rockefeller realized he was serving the interests of the Socialist International more effectively than the interests of the United States, some members of his "forward-looking" staff were probably very aware of the implications. No doubt he also had a certain mundane interest in opening up new lands for oil exploration and new markets for Standard Oil products—never suspecting that opportunities for private enterprise were due to be severely limited, under the Socialist International's plan for World Development.

As Under Secretary of Health, Education and Welfare in the Eisenhower Administration, Nelson Rockefeller insisted that all "security" cases be routed to him for review.[63] David Williams remarked approvingly that Rockefeller "was consistently liberal in his judgment on borderline cases—and his New Deal background was such that the appearance of the names of liberal [sic] organizations in a civil servant's file did not alarm him, as it did many others . . . ." Among those others was the Secretary, Oveta Culp Hobby, a peppery and patriotic lady from Texas who once headed the Women's Army Corps. For one reason or another, Rockefeller soon found himself forced to resign, but he persuaded Sherman Adams, presidential major domo, to create for him the novel post of special assistant to the President for foreign affairs.

David Williams makes much of the fact that Nelson Rockefeller— who was elected Governor of New York State in 1958 and 1962— worked serenely with the New Deal-Fair Deal in Washington, but was unhappy under the Eisenhower Administration. Williams suggests that Rockefeller's basic mistake in politics has been the wrong choice of party. Apparently, an attempt was made in the forties to enroll him

---

K. Finletter, Michael Straight, Robert R. Nathan, Stanley Andrews, Benjamin V. Cohen, Elmer Davis, Quincy Howe, Isadore Lubin, Paul R. Porter, Victor G. Reuther, Willard L. Thorp.

[63] Williams, *op. cit.*, p. 12.

in the Democratic Party—like another born Republican of vast wealth, considerable social charm and none too profound intelligence, W. Averell Harriman, who had joined the Democrats long before. In spite of all temptations, Rockefeller remained for utilitarian reasons a Republican. Among the reasons he has given for doing so, perhaps the most interesting as well as the most cynical is quoted by David C. Williams:

"Liberal Republicans and liberal Democrats often advocate the same programs," said Nelson Rockefeller, "but the Republicans have the advantage that they can execute them without destroying the confidence of business . . . ." [64]

[64] *Ibid.*, p. 13.

21

The Commanding Heights

1.

THE 1960 election campaign in the United States marked the first successful attempt of Left liberals, by then firmly lodged in the Democratic Party organization throughout the country, to regain such unobstructed access to the power of the Presidency as they enjoyed in the Roosevelt era.[1] That, after all, was an initial reason for founding Americans for Democratic Action, as some of its best friends have pointed out.

Three choices were offered in the Democratic primaries, with Adlai Stevenson a sentimental fourth, although he seemed to have little serious desire to run again in the grand national handicap. It looked like a genuine horse race for the nomination; but in retrospect is discovered to have been what sports fans call a "boat race." No matter which of the aspirants won, ADA would collect on the ticket. Even Lyndon Johnson, billed as the white hope of southern conservatives, had in fact been sired by the New Deal. Moreover, there were enough fiscal and electioneering irregularities in his background to guarantee his docility in the unlikely event that he gained the 1960 Presidential nomination.

Supposedly, a primary in the United States is wholly the personal affair of the candidates, with the party organizations coming into play only after the nomination has been made. Since ADA was not a political party, however, but merely a fraction within the Democratic

[1] Clifton Brock, *Americans for Democratic Action*, (Washington, Public Affairs Press, 1962), p. 82.

Party, it appears to have acted from the start to control the selection of the nominees.

In the primary race, Senators Hubert Humphrey and John F. Kennedy ran as an entry, with the former serving as the unwitting pacemaker. Both were led to the post by trusty ADA grooms. David C. Williams took leave from the *ADA World* to write his friend Humphrey's campaign speeches, insuring their impeccable Fabian Socialist color. Senator Kennedy, generally considered an "outsider," had a larger and more vigilant stable crew. It numbered at least three ADA founders: Gardner (Pat) Jackson, an old New Dealer hired for young Kennedy by his father; Monroe Sweetland, of the League for Industrial Democracy; and that improper Bostonian, Arthur M. Schlesinger, Jr.

At a later date this circle was enlarged to include another ADA founder, the Canadian-born Professor J. Kenneth Galbraith, an authority on the evils of affluence; the socially acceptable Paul Nitze, an adviser on military policy and the nonexistent missile gap; and Littauer Professor Seymour E. Harris, grand master of the mysteries of Keynesian economics and finance. Harris was also the co-author of an ADA-sponsored pamphlet on Medicare, and in 1962 would produce a study on the costs of higher education, which he judged should exceed 9.2 billion dollars annually by 1969-70.[2]

Meanwhile former Student ADA-ers Theodore Sorenson and Larry O'Brien served as legmen and exercise boys, recruiting swarms of crisp, crew cut assistants for every local headquarters. A well-schooled ADA member, Professor James MacGregor Burns of Williams—who had taken a special course of study at the London School of Economics[3] in 1949—was to write Kennedy's official campaign biography. Despite his own and his family's great wealth, Senator Kennedy did

---

[2] Cf. Seymour E. Harris, *Higher Education: Sources and Finance*. (Result of a Study Sponsored by the Ford Foundation. Dedicated to McGeorge Bundy.) (New York, McGraw-Hill Inc., 1962).

[3] Concerning the London School of Economics, Margaret Cole, president of the Fabian Society, wrote in 1963: "The argument which Webb might quite honestly have used but apparently did not—that the study of economic and social facts would of itself produce Socialist converts—turned out to be largely true. Whatever the political bias of its lecturers, the LSE retained (and deserved) for many a long day the reputation of being a manufactory of Reds." From a review by Margaret Cole of Sir Sydney Caine's book, *The History of the Foundation of the London School of Economics and Political Science, The Social Science Weekly*, (April 18, 1963), Vol. I, No. 29, p. 26.

not possess enough intra-Party strength of his own to afford the luxury of independence.

In the Wisconsin and West Virginia primary sprints Hubert Humphrey forced his younger rival, John F. Kennedy (not previously known for any consistent political philosophy) to equal and outstrip him in liberal sentiments. While Humphrey's campaign was brief and afflicted by money troubles, apparently he was not informed in advance of his pacemaking role: he desperately wanted to be President. At the Democratic National Convention—with tears in his eyes, for he tended to weep like a child under stress—Humphrey was finally persuaded by Joseph Rauh, Jr. to throw his support to Kennedy. As a consolation prize Hubert would be made Democratic whip of the Senate and permitted to name his former assistant, Orville Freeman, Secretary of Agriculture in the Kennedy-Johnson Administration.

A reliable tip on the primary results was volunteered, as early as March, 1960, by the knowing Arthur M. Schlesinger, Jr. To a sympathetic newspaperman, James Reston, he confided: "Nostalgically I am for Stevenson; ideologically I am for Humphrey; but realistically I am for Kennedy." From the moment the Democratic Convention opened in Los Angeles, it was clear to all but the most unrealistic observers that Kennedy was the predestined winner.

Despite his youth and less than distinguished performance in the Senate, he had many points to recommend him to a star-struck electorate. John F. Kennedy had the clean-cut, photogenic good looks of a motion picture hero, in addition to charm and breeding. In World War II he had served with the Navy's daredevil torpedo boat fleet in the Pacific and suffered enduring wounds. Having produced several best-selling books, he was considered an author and presumably an intellectual; yet he was actively interested in sports. Moreover, he had a devoted family, able and willing to spend an unlimited amount of money to put one of its sons in the White House. All this, and heaven, too: Kennedy was certain he could deliver the Catholic vote.[4]

With his family and religious background, who would ever believe John F. Kennedy was committed before his nomination to carrying out a Fabian Socialist program? Even Left liberals were incredulous. Did not Pope Pius XI declare in 1931: "No man can be at the same

[4] Victor Lasky, *JFK: The Man and the Myth*, (New York, The Macmillan Company, 1963), App. B, pp. 587-598. Text of the so-called "Bailey Report," analyzing the strength of the "Catholic vote" in the United States and circulated by Kennedy aides at the 1956 Democratic Convention. In 1960 the Gallup Poll reported that 78 per cent of U.S. Catholics had voted for John F. Kennedy.

time a sincere Catholic and a true Socialist?"[5] At the Los Angeles Convention Joseph Rauh, Jr., known as Walter Reuther's man, had some difficulty inducing bewildered ADA purists to cast their votes for Kennedy.

Rauh said he believed Kennedy to be a liberal,[6] and doubtless he had reasons. As ADA's key man on the platform committee, Rauh knew very well that the Democratic Party's radical platform was written months before the National Convention. By April, 1960, Kennedy had an opportunity to see it in nearly final form.[7] Far from objecting to its contents, Kennedy told Rauh that he wanted above all things to campaign on a liberal platform.[8] What else may have been said at the time is not reported. One thing, however, is sure. To win the affirmative backing of ADA's top brain trusters and of left wing union leaders trained to drive hard bargains—and through these, to gain the practical support of the Democratic Party organization—substantial assurances were required.

Perhaps the sharpest opposition to Kennedy within ADA came from its honorary president, Eleanor Roosevelt. Apparently, she nursed some resentment both on ideological and personal grounds against his father, former Ambassador Joseph P. Kennedy. Eleanor Roosevelt's chief reason, however, for mistrusting Senator Kennedy was his failure to have taken a stand against Senator Joseph McCarthy, bane of orthodox Left liberals and Communists in the fifties. From 1948, McCarthy had carried on what seemed at times to be a one-man campaign to alert the country to the dangers of Communist infiltration in government. In the process, he seriously alarmed Fabian Socialists who feared they might be the next to be exposed.[9]

Americans for Democratic Action waged a tireless vendetta against

[5] From the Encyclical *Quadragesimo Anno*, May 15, 1931.

[6] Brock, *op. cit.*, p. 181.

[7] *Ibid.*, pp. 181-182; p. 179.

[8] *Ibid.*, p. 182-184.

[9] That Communists have exploited such fears, and continue to do so, can be seen from the statement made in 1961 by U.S. Communist Party Leader, Gus Hall: "No matter what one's attitude may be towards the Communist Party, it must be recognized that the fight for its rights as a political party is a matter of defending the Bill of Rights and all democratic rights, and peace forces, and not of the Communists alone. This is an old lesson, but *sometimes it has to be learned anew.*" Gus Hall, "The Ultra-Right, Kennedy and the Role of Progressives," *Political Affairs*, (August, 1961), pp. 19-20. This was the article which— with that fine inconsistency for which Communists are noted—unleashed a general attack by all left wing and "liberal" forces in the United States against the "extreme right." (Italics added.)

McCarthy through every medium at its command, even publishing and selling thousands of copies of a Senate Subcommittee report on the Senator's personal finances.[10] In Britain the *New Statesman* and other Fabian Socialist-edited journals expressed shocked indignation at that man from Wisconsin who, according to them, was imperiling the American Bill of Rights—a document for which foreign as well as home-grown leftists often profess a touching concern. The agitation in educated circles on both sides of the Atlantic culminated in a resolution of censure against McCarthy by the U.S. Senate. ADA claimed and still claims today to have been primarily responsible for that propaganda coup. If so, it was surely one of the strangest cases of political lobbying in congressional history. Analysis suggests that the Senate's 1954 resolution against McCarthy was in the nature of a test vote, demonstrating ADA's dominance in the Democratic Party organization as well as its influence on liberal Republicans.

As a young congressman, Kennedy had originally represented a working-class district in Boston made up almost entirely of Irish Catholic voters. They abhorred Communism and idolized McCarthy, Republican though he was. In those days, Kennedy was outspokenly anti-Communist in foreign affairs; but voted affirmatively with the liberals on Federal spending and labor bills affecting his constituents. His father's hail-fellow-well-met friendship with McCarthy was a distinct asset to Kennedy in Massachusetts. To some degree, John F. Kennedy owed his own election as Senator in 1952 to McCarthy, who failed to go to Massachusetts that year and campaign for Kennedy's Republican opponent, Henry Cabot Lodge.

When the resolution to censure McCarthy came up two years later in the Senate, Kennedy's voice was not heard. Being hospitalized at the time, he could not be present—though he could, of course, have paired his vote. For this McCarthy's friends never forgave Kennedy, and neither did aggravated liberals like Eleanor Roosevelt. After his Pulitzer Prize winning book, *Profiles in Courage,* appeared in 1956, Eleanor Roosevelt is said to have commented that "Mr. Kennedy should show more courage and less profile"—an unkind reference to the rumor that the Kennedy nose, broken years before in football, had been quietly remodeled by plastic surgery during his long stay in the hospital.

Sensitive as he was to criticism, somehow it was the barbs from the Left that disturbed him most. "What did they want me to do, commit

[10] Brock, *op. cit.*, p. 146.

hara-kiri?" he asked a reporter. Apparently, the more practical politicians in ADA realized it would have meant political suicide in Massachusetts for Kennedy to speak out against McCarthy, and accepted his neutrality as a mark of deference to their side. Though Kennedy had been quoted in 1953 by the *Saturday Evening Post* as saying of Americans for Democratic Action, "I don't feel comfortable with those people," as time went on he learned to suffer them more gladly. In part, his increased cordiality seems to have been due to the discreet efforts of his aides, Theodore Sorenson and Lawrence O'Brien; in part, to his own discovery that ADA held the whip hand in the Democratic Party.

That uncomfortable fact was impressed upon Kennedy in 1956, when he tried and failed to win the Democratic nomination for the Vice Presidency. It was a fact to be seriously considered by a young man in a hurry, whose fond parents, brothers and sisters quite literally expected him to become President of the United States. In token of his improving relations with the liberal Left, the *New Leader* for May 18, 1957, printed a well-advertised book review by Senator John F. Kennedy. It gave favorable notice to a liberally slanted history of the U.S. Senate, written by a political commentator who later became an ardent apologist for the Kennedy-Johnson Administration.[11]

In September, 1959, when Kennedy had already begun to look like a serious Presidential contender, Allen Taylor, director of the New York State ADA, thoughtfully sent Ted Sorenson a long memorandum entitled, "Liberals' Doubts About Kennedy, and How to Handle Them."[12] Evidently Kennedy learned how; and it was a costly lesson. Not all the Kennedy family wealth, estimated at several hundred millions, could have paid for it. The price was his personal independence.

On January 20, 1961, John F. Kennedy was sworn in as the thirty-fifth President of the United States. He had achieved the heights; but he had done so by one of the slimmest popular margins ever claimed for a victorious candidate, a mere 119,000 votes, in an election still regarded as doubtful by sober historians. Kennedy's inaugural speech, for which he is perhaps best remembered, summoned the

---

[11] "Inside the Upper House," a review by John F. Kennedy, U.S. Senator from Massachusetts; author of *Profiles in Courage. The New Leader*, (May 13, 1957), p. 9. (The book reviewed was *Citadel*, by William S. White, New York, Harper & Brothers, 1957.)

[12] Brock, *op. cit.*, p. 185.

United States to "a long twilit struggle . . . against the common enemies of mankind . . . tyranny, poverty, disease and war itself." Surely
a noble sentiment, if pursued by Constitutional means and without
destruction of the country's internal order, or national sovereignty.

Fired by the drama of the occasion and the beauty of the youthful
President's rhetoric, few listeners asked by what means that global
struggle would be waged. As months went by, the inference deepened
that anyone who ventured to question the methods and underlying
aims of the new Administration was a cold-blooded advocate of
tyranny, poverty, disease and war. The questioners have now been
silenced by the tragic circumstance that John F. Kennedy was assassi-
nated less than three years after becoming President. Apparently he
was shot by a young assassin from the ranks of the Far Left whose
motives and connections have not yet been fully explained.

Exploiting the natural grief of JFK's widow and relatives, as well as
the emotions of a shocked American public, the same Left liberal
clique that helped put Kennedy in the White House endowed him
with a halo of martyrdom. For month after month leading to the
national elections of 1964, every form of heart-appeal that could be
devised by Fabian experts in mass psychology was utilized to keep
sorrowing voters faithful to the Party of JFK. The same elite corps of
Left liberal intellectuals, who had surrounded him as President, now
sought to perpetuate themselves or their alternates in power by perpetuating the memory of John K. Kennedy—not quite as he was, but
as a golden memory. *De mortuis nil nisi bonum.*

During the last years of his short but crowded lifetime, John F.
Kennedy was sometimes compared by informed observers to Britain's
leading Catholic Fabian, Lord Francis Pakenham. Both were Christian gentlemen of inherited wealth, secure social position and Gaelic
antecedents—although Pakenham came from a long line of Anglo-
Irish landlords, and Kennedy from Irish peasant stock. Both had style,
grace and good manners, though, of the two, Kennedy was far better
looking. They were frankly but not crudely ambitious. While they
might normally have been expected to find their habitat in conservative politics, both found they could go farther faster by allying themselves with the Fabian Socialist movement.

Pakenham became a convinced Marxist by joining the Oxford City
Labour Party of the middle thirties where, as he has said, the name
of Marx was on the tongue of every student and don.[13] Kennedy ab-

---

[13] Lord Pakenham, *Born to Believe*, (London, Jonathan Cape, 1953), p. 79.

sorbed the Keynesian outlook almost imperceptibly at Harvard College—after some desultory training at the London School of Economics, which his biographers usually took pains to minimize. Yet both were prominent Catholic laymen, Kennedy by birth and Pakenham by conversion. Neither seemed to perceive any conflict between the exercise of Catholic piety and the aims of international Socialism; even though one Papal Encyclical after another has affirmed that the right to own productive property and enjoy its fruits is among the natural rights of mankind. Both were adroit, quick-witted but not serious thinkers, and depended on others for ideas.

At the request of the Fabian Socialist Prime Minister, Clement Attlee, Pakenham was made a peer, Lord-in-Waiting and Privy Councillor, so that he could aid the Labour Party in the House of Lords. On being elevated to his new estate, he was received by the monarch, King George VI. It was a curious and moving encounter, the significance of which somehow escaped Lord Pakenham. He has told how the King looked at him long and penetratingly, and after a pause said suddenly: "Why did you . . . join them?" [14] The same question might have been asked about John F. Kennedy.

Historically, the Kennedy-Johnson Administration took office pledged to the most outspokenly radical program ever sponsored by an old-line political party in the United States. For publicity purposes the Administration was known as the New Frontier. The label was mystifying as applied to a casually elegant young man from Massachusetts, whose entourage was heavily weighted with doctors of philosophy from the Ivy League universities. Hardly anyone—except the oldest New Dealers, and a few scholars in the Anglo-American section of Fabian Research—remembered that the Progressive left-winger, Henry Wallace, once wrote a book called *New Frontiers.*

Published in 1934, *New Frontiers* restated in glowing terms the philosophy and objectives of the New Deal, where—as the veteran Fabian Socialist, Harry Laidler has affirmed—one Socialist demand after another was gratified. "We need now," wrote Wallace, "to re-define property rights in a way that will fairly meet the realities of today." [15] Americans, he said, must abandon the frugality, competitive spirit and individualism of the Old Frontier, where men, "whether Protestant or Catholic, accepted implicitly the Protestant ethic." [16]

[14] *Ibid.,* p. 159.
[15] Henry A. Wallace, *New Frontiers,* (New York, Reynal & Hitchcock, 1934), p. 268. (First printing, 50,000 copies.)
[16] *Ibid.,* p. 275-276.

On the New Frontier to come, Wallace said, "socially disciplined" men will work cooperatively to increase the wealth of the human race and apply their inventive skill to changing society itself. They will modify the governmental and political machinery, as well as the monetary and price system, to achieve "a far wider possibility of social justice and social charity" in the world. "So enlisted," wrote Wallace, "men may rightfully feel that they are serving a function as high as any minister of the Gospel. They will not be Communists, Socialists or Fascists, but plain men trying to gain by democratic methods the professed objectives of Communists, Socialists or Fascists . . . ." [17] Whatever its name, the imaginary New Frontier described by Henry Wallace sounded very much like old-fashioned Fabian Socialism.

There were at least two old New Dealers on Kennedy's campaign staff, Gardner Jackson and Monroe Sweetland, who had worked in the Department of Agriculture under Wallace and shared many of his views. Undoubtedly, they remembered his "vision" of the New Frontier. Arthur Schlesinger, Jr., who wrote a history of the Roosevelt era, might also have been expected to be familiar with the Wallace book. In searching for a label to use during the Kennedy campaign and after, which implied a Socialist commitment yet seemed merely picturesque to the general public, someone at Kennedy headquarters thought of borrowing the New Frontier tag from Wallace—on the chance that few would identify the source. If the matter ever came up, it could always be explained away as purely coincidental.

After presenting the new Administration with a name, a philosophy and a platform, ADA brain trusters took precautions to make sure their program would be carried out. In the interim between Kennedy's election and inauguration, appropriate steps were taken to staff the White House and the departments at every level with ADA members, past or present, and their Fabian-schooled allies. Less than three weeks after the Democratic Party's close victory at the polls, Professor Samuel H. Beer of Harvard, then national chairman of ADA, wrote to congratulate his personal friend, John F. Kennedy.

Beer, described editorially as "professor of Government at Harvard," had contributed an article to the November, 1956 issue of the British *Fabian Journal*, entitled "Labour Rethinks Its Policy. An American View." From this, it could at least be inferred that he enjoyed direct contacts with Britain's Fabian Socialists.

Beer suggested that the new President's first public acts should

[17] *Ibid.*, p. 276.

clearly demonstrate his intent to build a New Frontier for America, with the help of "forward-looking" and "imaginative" public servants. Characteristically, competence was not mentioned. Beer's letter to the President continued boldly:

ADA has no interest in individuals as such; however, we feel that the appointment to high office of such men as Chester Bowles, Orville Freeman, Adlai Stevenson and G. Mennen Williams will signify to the world your determination to shape your Administration in the image of your eloquent liberal campaign.[18]

The four individuals named by Beer, and many more ADA favorites, were appointed to serve in the Kennedy-Johnson Administration.

Alert Washington newsmen identified at least three dozen important officials, from Cabinet rank down, as past or present members of Americans for Democratic Action. Professor Brock, a friendly witness, not only confirmed the tally; but added that the number of ADA members serving in government posts, high and low, under the Kennedy-Johnson Administration was in reality much larger than even some of its keener critics knew.[19] "The extent of 'infiltration'," crowed Brock, "is greater than Senator Goldwater dreams." Just as every key post in the British Labour Party Government from 1945 to 1951 was admittedly held for some time at least by a member of the Fabian Society, American Fabian Socialists seemed to have achieved somewhat similar status under the Kennedy-Johnson Administration.

While this phenomenon of "infiltration" was frequently noted, in whole or in part, no one could say just how it occurred. Perhaps the simplest and most logical explanation is that the majority of Left liberal appointments were made through routine patronage channels. Anyone familiar with Washington realizes that a President is in somewhat the same situation as an author who receives some ten free copies of his book to give to personal friends and connections, the remainder being distributed in the routine order of business. For the most part, government appointments high and low—not excluding persons who have qualified for the higher civil service ratings—are cleared through the county, state and national committees of the Party in power.

That fact does not relieve a President of responsibility for appointments announced by the White House; but it does indicate the extent of ADA control over the Democratic Party machinery, that is,

[18] Brock, op. cit., p. 196.
[19] Ibid., p. 198.

an extent necessary to place so large a number of handpicked employees in all branches of the Federal Government. Evidently, the relationship of ADA to the Democratic Party in America approximated—if it did not quite equal—that of the London Fabian Society to the British Labour Party.

Most of the top Government spots had been filled by February 10, 1961, when ADA chairman Beer and three colleagues called to pay their respects in person to President Kennedy. For the first time since Truman's day, representatives of ADA were welcomed as such at the White House. In requesting the interview, Beer had written to the President's appointment secretary, "I want to make it clear that it is program, not jobs in which we are interested." After the conference, where economic policy and civil rights were discussed, Beer commented: "We felt that in both fields the President's objectives were ours, and that he was attempting and would attempt to pursue them just as far as he politically could." [20]

No public reference was made to mutual aims in the fields of foreign and military policy, relating to world development, cooperation with Communist nations, *de facto* disarmament and eventual federal union of all nations in a socialized world. Those delicate undertakings were left to selected, Fabian-trained officials and consultants manning the Government at strategic points, who could be depended upon to pursue their objectives systematically in consultation with social democratic officials abroad. White House ghost-writers—better versed in the Fabian classics than in simple arithmetic—even supplied the President with a space age version of the Independence Day comments made by Edward Bellamy in 1892.[21]

In a speech delivered at Independence Hall in Philadelphia (of all places), on July 4, 1962, President Kennedy "virtually proposed to repeal the Declaration of Independence in favor of a declaration of international *inter*dependence." [22] To a passive and somnolent audience, he declared:

But I will say here and now on this day of independence that the United States will be ready for a Declaration of Interdependence—that we will be prepared to discuss with a United Europe the ways and means of forming a concrete Atlantic Partnership—a mutually beneficial partnership between

[20] Brock, *op. cit.*, p. 200.
[21] Editorial by Edward Bellamy which appeared in the Boston *Globe*, July 4, 1892.
[22] *The New York Times*, (July 11, 1962). Quoted from an article by James Reston. (Italics added.)

the new union now emerging in Europe and the old American Union founded here 175 years ago . . . . Today Americans must learn to think continentally.[23]

These words were spoken on the 186th anniversary of the signing of the Declaration of Independence.

Other echoes of the Cooperative Commonwealth—foretold long ago by Edward Bellamy, father of the American Fabian movement— were revived by friendly Keynesian economists in anticipation of the 1964 election contest. No mention was made of their literary inspiration, which was obvious to Socialists but unknown to the average citizen—namely, Bellamy's Looking Backward, a novel depicting Socialist America in the year 2000. In March, 1963, a twenty-three man "research team" employed by an organization called Resources for the Future released a 987-page report. It described the material wonders that the common man in America would enjoy in the year 2000. Assuming, of course, that the Keynesian policies adopted by the Kennedy-Johnson Administration were continued indefinitely! Financial support for the "study" was supplied by the Ford Foundation at the expense of the American taxpayer.

By combining Keynesian theory with production and population statistics, and feeding the mixture into electronic computers, the young researchers came up with precise figures on what the year 2000 would hold. Any possibility of war, pestilence or bankruptcy was omitted from their calculations. Economic scarcity would no longer exist in that future America, where atomic reactors would supply only peaceful power, automobiles with wings would outnumber adult citizens, and the average family income would be $11,000 per year (without reference to purchasing power).

Apart from such attention-catching items, an interesting feature of this forecast was its assumption that Federal spending would increase in very much the same ratio as industrial production and Gross National Product. In short, an ever-expanding government would continue to appropriate an overall 20 per cent to 25 per cent of the nation's annual income. The miraculous pitcher would continue to pour milk and honey without interruption, while the tax pressures under which the average American operates today would simply be multiplied by five.

A demand for continuous economic "growth," which calls for pro-

[23] The New York Times, (July 5, 1962). Cf. also Harry A. Overstreet, A Declaration of Interdependence, (New York, W. W. Norton, 1937).

duction to rise each year like a supermarket's sales figures, was first voiced by New Frontier spokesmen in the 1960 Presidential campaign. It was based upon the latest post-Keynesian mystery: the Gross National Product, officially adopted as an index of prosperity by the Kennedy-Johnson Administration. Just how the Gross National Product itself is computed has never been clearly explained to the public. A clue to the process, however, was offered by Newton N. Minow, an early New Frontiersman who formerly headed the Federal Communications Commission.

At a 1963 symposium arranged in Los Angeles by the Center for the Study of Democratic Institutions—wayward grandchild of the Ford Foundation—Minow stated bluntly:

Nearly fifteen per cent of our national work force is already employed by the local, state or federal government, and *this represents almost a third of the gross national product.*[24]

So the Government can increase the Gross National Product at will, by the simple device of hiring more and more public servants— thereby increasing the ranks of an ADA-educated and chosen bureaucracy. A variation of this method of improving the nation's prosperity-image is to give frequent and substantial pay raises to government and state employees, especially in the higher brackets.

Two assumptions dangerous to the future of constitutional government in America are concealed in the tricky concept of the Gross National Product. First, the notion that government is entitled to take a fixed percentage of the rising national income each year, irrespective of national necessities. And second, that a government has the right to base its budget estimates on the private resources of individuals and companies. Recalling that the original purpose of Keynesian economics was to provide a method for a peaceful transition to Socialism in the United States, it becomes apparent that the economic policy adopted under ADA tutelage by the Kennedy-Johnson Administration, in effect, gives a green light to Socialism on the high speed Fabian Freeway.

Dissembling their joy at the trend of Administration policy, Left liberals outside the Government maintained a critical attitude and

[24] LeRoy Collins, Orville L. Freeman, Hubert H. Humphrey, Newton N. Minow, Hyman G. Rickover, and Thurgood Marshall on *The Mazes of Modern Government: The States, the Legislature, the Bureaucracy, the Courts. An occasional paper on the role of the political process in the free society.* (Santa Barbara, Center for the Study of Democratic Institutions, 1963), p. 21. (Italics added.)

continued to call for greater speed. For the most part, their grumbling was confined to their own special groups and house organs—while ADA commentators both on the air and in the daily press strove to rally broad popular support for the Kennedy-Johnson Administration. In the call to its annual convention in May, 1963, Americans for Democratic Action declared gravely that "the record of the Kennedy Administration so far has been one of accommodation to its critics of the right."

The *New Republic* commented editorially on June 1, 1963, that "in general the Kennedy performance is less impressive than the Kennedy style." It even charged the Administration with a lamentable tendency to yield to business pressures. "For example," said the *New Republic*, "the admirable goal of the Alliance for Progress (*in effect, U.S. sponsorship of a peaceful social revolution*)[25] has been compromised by the Administration's reluctance to tangle with influential business and property interests, both North and South American."[26] This type of needling by friendly critics was evidently intended to direct the Administration more firmly on the route international Socialism felt it should take.[27] At the same time, such comments helped to disarm conservative critics and to disguise the fact that the Kennedy-Johnson Administration was in reality a chosen instrument of Fabian Socialism.

While giving space to left wing complaints about the Administration, the *New Republic* (still considered the opposite number to Britain's Fabian-edited *New Statesman*) was usually careful to print an answer by some prominent ADA brain truster. In its issue of May 25, 1963, one Herbert Rowan had expressed the dissatisfaction of

[25] That is, in Latin America. (Italics added.)
[26] *New Republic*, (June 1, 1963)
[27] It is interesting to note that this rebuke coincided with the return to London on May 23, 1963 of a Socialist International mission to Latin America. An account of that mission, contained in the Secretary's Report to the Congress of the Socialist International, read as follows: "The Chairman of the Socialist International, Alsing Anderson died almost immediately after his return from the Interparliamentary Union Conference in Brazil, where he had done valuable contact work for the realization of the decision of the Oslo Council to send a mission to Latin America. The members, Max Diamant (Germany) and Yehuda Schuster (Israel), left London on 25 March and returned on 23 May, 1963. They visited the following countries: Puerto Rico, Dominican Republic, Mexico, Costa Rica, Panama, Venezuela, Colombia, Ecuador, Peru, Bolivia, Chile, Argentina, Urguay, Brazil, where they met leading representatives of the Socialist and Popular Parties." *Socialist International Information*, (August 24, 1963), Vol. XIII, No. 34-35.

certain Keynesian economists at President Kennedy's apparent unwillingness to spend more money and incur larger deficits. The following week Professor Seymour E. Harris[28] hastened to defend the Administration's record for liberality—pointing out that from 1953 to 1961 Eisenhower's annual expenditures rose by 7 billion dollars, while Kennedy's, in a mere three years, rose by 17 billion dollars! Harris explained in all seriousness that President Kennedy would have been glad to spend more, but was prevented by the temper of Congress from doing so.[29] Whether or not the sniping from the Left had an effect, the annual budget announced by the Kennedy-Johnson Administration nudged 100 billion dollars.

To the *New Republic's* Washington correspondent, who was disturbed about Kennedy's latter-day overtures to selected business groups,[30] Professor Harris replied that it is still important to maintain the confidence of businessmen. While government must be careful not to yield to their "demands," said he, there is no harm in speaking kindly to them. By way of authority Harris quoted the oracle of modern Left liberals, John Maynard Keynes, who once wrote in a letter to Franklin D. Roosevelt:

. . . It is a mistake to think that they [businessmen] are more *immoral* than politicians. If you work them into the surly, obstinate, terrified mood, of which domestic animals, wrongly handled, are so capable, the nation's burdens will not get carried to market . . . .[31]

This humane attitude, so reminiscent of the SPCA,[32] has inspired some false hopes among businessmen, as well as some unfounded fears among Left liberals. It was commended by Keynesian advisers to President Kennedy, as well as to his successor, President Johnson.

Less than six months later all criticism from the Left or the Right was abruptly hushed, when John F. Kennedy was suddenly and inexplicably struck down by an assassin's bullets. Before the Presidential

[28] In 1947, the year of ADA's founding, Harris was a member of its so-called Committee on Economic Stability. Other members of the Committee were: Chester Bowles, Chairman; Lauchlin Currie, William H. Davis, J. K. Galbraith, Richard V. Gilbert, David Ginsburg, Leon Henderson, Robert R. Nathan, Paul A. Porter, Joseph L. Rauh, Jr.

[29] Seymour E. Harris, "Kennedy and the Liberals," *New Republic,* (June 1, 1963).

[30] In May, 1963 Kennedy delivered what Professor Harris termed a "brilliant address" to the Committee on Economic Development.

[31] Seymour E. Harris, "Kennedy and the Liberals," New Republic (June 1, 1963).

[32] Society for the Prevention of Cruelty to Animals.

airplane left Dallas for Washington, carrying the casket of the slain Chief of State, the next Chief Executive had been sworn in. By an unexpected stroke of fate Vice President Lyndon Baines Johnson, whose hopes of reaching the White House appeared to have been permanently dashed in 1960, became the thirty-sixth President of the United States.

The panoply of the late President's state funeral, and the four-week period of official mourning that followed, veiled the inevitable maneuvers going on behind the scenes to procure continuance of the political status quo. Among the foreign dignitaries who flew to America to pay their final respects to John F. Kennedy was Harold Wilson, Parliamentary Leader of the British Labour Party and acting chairman of the Socialist International. Not unnaturally, Wilson took the opportunity to discuss the probable future with old and loyal friends of the London Fabian Society in Washington, including the aging columnist, Walter Lippmann. Puzzled news correspondents reported that on the return trip from Arlington Cemetery, where John F. Kennedy had just been interred, the new President, Lyndon B. Johnson, made an unscheduled detour. He stopped off for a forty-minute conference at the Georgetown home of Walter Lippmann.[33] From this oddly-timed gesture, the trend of the incoming Administration might have been foreseen.

2.

If anyone doubted that President Johnson meant to continue the Socialist-inspired policies, both foreign and domestic, of his Democratic Party forebears, such uncertainties were speedily resolved by his own public utterances. In January he told the nation: "We are going to take all the money that we think is being unnecessarily spent, and take it from the haves and give it to the have-nots." [34] Addressing the General Assembly of the United Nations, Johnson announced he wanted to see "the Cold War end at once" and especially to see "a New Deal on a world scale" come to developing nations just "as it came to America thirty years ago." [35] News photographers, who had been instructed that President Johnson's pictures were to be taken from the left profile only, perceived (as the Richmond News Leader remarked) that his image was better from the left than from the right.

[34] Human Events, (February 18, 1964). Quoted from the New York Daily News.
[33] Associated Press dispatch from Washington, (November 25, 1963).
[35] The New York Times, (December 18, 1963).

To the great American public, however, always eager to believe the best of an incoming President, the drift of Johnson's statements was not immediately apparent. Even more than John F. Kennedy (though for very different reasons) Lyndon B. Johnson, who had been so sharply attacked by Americans for Democratic Action in 1960, seemed an unlikely instrument of the Fabian Socialist world planners. A nonintellectual, whose reading matter for years had been confined to the daily papers, the *Congressional Record* and tales of early Texas history, he was surely no academic disciple of John Maynard Keynes.

As his biographers reveal, Johnson was a product of the New Deal school of spend-and-elect politics in which Franklin D. Roosevelt had been a past master. On the surface, he appeared to be merely a tall, hard-eyed professional politician from the Southwest, with a long record of wheeling and dealing on Capitol Hill. Johnson, however, revered power in every form and had displayed no hesitation about accumulating it as opportunities arose. Having begun his career as a poor but ambitious graduate of a small Texas teachers' college, he lacked the style and literary éclat of John F. Kennedy. Nevertheless, Lyndon B. Johnson and his helpmate, Lady Bird, were one of the wealthiest couples in their own right ever to occupy the White House.

Though he made no disclosure of personal assets on taking office, the joint worth of the Johnsons and their daughters was estimated to be no less than 9 million dollars[36] and possibly as much as 15 million dollars.[37] The business acumen of gentle Lady Bird Johnson has been credited with pyramiding a modest inheritance of $67,000 into a handsome fortune, during the twenty-three years her husband served, in an increasingly potent capacity, in Congress. If she was not the beneficiary of special favors incidental to her husband's position, she may be ranked with Hetty Green as one of the shrewdest women in American financial annals. White House aides insist President Johnson never intervened in his wife's business affairs, directly or indirectly. According to John Barton of the Washington *Star*, however, Texans who have had dealings with the Austin, Texas television station—which is owned 84.5 per cent by Lady Bird Johnson and her daughters—are prepared to state otherwise.[38]

Lyndon Baines Johnson first appeared on Capitol Hill in 1931, just before the New Deal dawned. He was employed on the staff of Con-

[36] Associated Press dispatch from Washington, (June 8, 1964).
[37] *Human Events*, (May 30, 1964)
[38] Washington *Star*, (June 8, 1964).

gressman Richard Kleberg, member of the family that owned the fabulous King Ranch, and a respected leader in south Texas. Although the Congressman was outspokenly critical of the Roosevelt Administration, somehow Johnson managed to inject himself into its good graces. Old inhabitants of Kleberg County and adjacent Texas counties still claim to have knowledge that Johnson betrayed his original benefactor, Dick Kleberg; but no details have ever been made public. At any rate, young Lyndon was appointed Texas director of the National Youth Administration in 1935 and was commended for rare efficiency by Aubrey Williams, its national administrator.

In 1937, Johnson was elected to the House of Representatives on a platform supporting FDR's Supreme Court packing plan. As a reward, President Roosevelt asked that the freshman lawmaker be assigned to the important Naval Affairs Committee, and thereafter seems to have taken a fatherly interest in his career. "Free Federal money" was invariably forthcoming for projects in Johnson's home district, assuring his election for five more successive terms. Johnson has since been quoted as saying sentimentally to political audiences, "Franklin D. Roosevelt was a second daddy to me."

Johnson ran for the United States Senate in 1948, on an anti-union labor plank, and was seated by a scant margin of 87 contested votes. One of his more zealous backers was George Parr of San Diego, Texas, known as the Duke of Duval County. Parr was the political boss and absolute monarch of several Spanish-speaking counties near the Mexican border, where a primitive, gun-toting style of politics prevailed. In the 1948 election, returns from Precinct 13 in Alice, Texas—county seat of Parr-ruled Jim Wells County—gave 765 votes to Johnson as compared to 80 for his opponent, *although only 600 ballots had been issued for that precinct.*

With a state wide count showing Johnson to be the loser by 113 votes, he made a victory statement on September 2, 1948. Next day a recount in Alice produced a new total of 967 votes for Lyndon, giving him his famous 87-vote victory. Inspection of the Alice polling list by a Texas Ranger and two former FBI agents disclosed that some 200 names had been added in a different shade of ink. Several of those individuals, when interviewed, testified they had not voted; others, not interviewed, were found to be deceased! As might have been expected, fraud was charged. An injunction was issued and a hearing ordered by Federal Judge T. Whitfield Davidson of the Northern District of Texas.

After several hasty appeals by Johnson to other courts had been denied, U.S. Supreme Court Justice Hugo Black obligingly set aside the Texas ruling, and no public hearing was ever held. The memory of those fateful events, however, lingers in the town of Alice. In spite of Parr's repeated and none-too-gentle attempts to lay the ghost of that disputed election, it has returned again and again to haunt Lyndon Johnson. The truth is, that even in his own home state Johnson was never a very popular figure. He was what might be called a politician's politician.

Undismayed, Johnson went to the Senate and was named Democratic Party whip in 1951. At approximately the same time, a former congressional page boy named Bobby Gene Baker was engaged as assistant Democratic Senate secretary. During Johnson's first term in the Senate, as the Washington *Star* [39] has noted, he served on the Commerce Committee which has jurisdiction over the Federal Communications Commission. The Commission, in turn, regulates and licenses all radio and television broadcasting stations—including the station owned by Lady Bird Johnson in Austin, Texas, whose worth has been enhanced by a notable lack of local competition. No questions were asked about the number of out-of-state business firms that bought advertising time on the Austin station, although they dispensed no products or services on the Texas market.

About a year after becoming whip, Johnson succeeded to the post of Democratic floor leader in the Senate. His young lieutenant, Bobby Baker, was promptly promoted from assistant to Democratic Senate secretary. With Republicans holding the Upper House, though only by a frail majority of one, Johnson still found it useful, beginning in 1952, to cooperate with the Eisenhower Administration. Although noisemakers in ADA attacked Johnson in 1955 for giving tacit support to "a Republican assault on liberalism," [40] he was vigorously defended by Senator Hubert Humphrey, former ADA national chairman. Ironically, much patronage flowed to Johnson during Eisenhower's two terms as President, particularly after the off-year election success of the Democrats in 1958 made Johnson majority leader of the Senate. His personal power and influence now extended into both parties; he was a man to be courted and feared. Bland or cajoling in his lighter moods, he was said to display a hair-trigger temper and an unrestricted vocabulary when crossed.

[39] Washington *Star*, (June 8, 1964)
[40] Brock, *op. cit.*, p. 157.

By applying what Capitol Hill veterans describe as a combination of the carrot and the stick, whose use was determined by an intimate knowledge of his colleagues' political problems or personal foibles, Johnson gained the reputation for being able to "get results" in Congress on practically any kind of legislation. In those operations, it has been suggested, the stack of bank notes kept on hand in the office of Democratic Senate secretary Baker may occasionally have played a part—as well as certain after hours gaieties organized by Baker that seemed more designed to entrap than to entertain. Bobby Gene was Johnson's enforcer and frequent go-between. One of the Senate's incorruptibles, the Honorable John R. Williams of Delaware, eventually forced the resignation of Baker by demanding an inquiry into the latter's far-flung business activities. It appeared that Bobby Gene had been selling everything but the Capitol dome, and had made side money for himself amounting to more than 2 million dollars.

Congressional circles were amused when Lyndon Johnson, then Vice President, issued a straight-faced denial that Bobby Baker was ever a protégé of his. The close association between Democratic leader Johnson and Democratic Senate secretary Baker had been a matter of common knowledge on the Hill. As late as 1960, while campaigning in South Carolina, Johnson told Baker's father, "Bobby Gene is my strong right arm, the last man I see at night, the first one I see in the morning!" It was hard to believe the shrewd and energetic majority leader did not know what his right arm was doing and had even forgotten that he had one! Lyndon Johnson was among the notables who attended the grand opening of Bobby Baker's motel in Ocean City, Maryland.

Called before a Senate committee, Baker calmly refused to answer 125 questions on grounds of possible self-incrimination. He could do so with impunity, thanks to a Supreme Court decision barring citations for contempt by congressional investigating bodies. Though a whitewash was charged, the inquiry was closed and Baker escaped without penalties. By then all direct communication between Johnson and Baker had ceased. It was remarked, however, that Bobby Baker's counsel at the Senate hearings was Abe Fortas, personal legal adviser to Lyndon Johnson and more recently a trusted member of the President's Kitchen Cabinet.[40a]

[40a] Justice Fortas now occupies the seat on the Supreme Court which Arthur Goldberg, an ADA founder and former counsel for the CIO, vacated to become Ambassador to the United Nations.

No rumors of corruption, but the fact that he had regularly voted against civil rights legislation, led the majority of ADA intellectuals to denounce Lyndon Johnson in 1960. Only a handful of specialists, known to the Fabian International Bureau, were aware that Johnson's dual role during the Eisenhower Administration had in reality helped to promote ADA-Socialist International programs of the nineteen-fifties—chiefly, in the fields of foreign aid and military spending.

Such policy was normally conveyed to the State Department as the fruit of "impartial research," via some high level, bipartisan organization like the Council on Foreign Relations or the American Assembly. Legislation required to finance it was passed without difficulty, as a result of Johnson's cooperative attitude in the Senate. Through the patronage made available to him by a grateful Republican Administration, a number of ADA-approved Democrats were quietly appointed to positions in the Departments of State[41] and Defense—the very areas where, as Arthur Schlesinger, Jr. had announced in the *Fabian International Review*, American Fabian Socialists intended to gain control.

Johnson could only have accomplished such feats by operating under at least nominally conservative colors, thus damaging his reputation among Left liberals. By voting with an influential group of southern Senators on domestic issues about which they felt strongly, he was able to win their support for other projects, where ADA spokesmen like Humphrey or Douglas would have failed. Since secrecy was necessary to avoid compromising delicate operations, Johnson resigned himself to incurring the wrath of most left-wingers —although, as he has since announced freely, he was always a New Deal liberal at heart.

It is not surprising, therefore, that otherwise well-informed ADA leaders expressed definite resentment against Johnson during and after the 1960 Democratic Convention. Joseph Rauh, Jr. has told of the dismay and sense of personal betrayal he felt, on hearing that Lyndon Johnson had been chosen as Kennedy's running mate in the 1960 campaign. Rauh's sentiments were echoed by David Dubinsky and other influential members of ADA. Some threatened to bolt the

---

[41] Frank L. Kluckhohn, former *New York Times* correspondent who served in the Department of State during the Eisenhower Administration, reports that of 126 political appointments in the Department, 107 went to Democrats—many of them recommended by Johnson. Frank L. Kluckhohn, *The Inside on LBJ*, (New York, Monarch Books, 1964), p. 33.

ticket or split their endorsement, but in the end were dissuaded from doing so.

John F. Kennedy had personally invited Johnson to be his running mate, reportedly calling him by telephone in the early morning hours. Previously, Johnson had declared he would refuse second place on the ticket. Not unnaturally, there was much speculation as to what led him to change his mind. One realistic account, attributed to a source close to Kennedy, went as follows: Johnson demurred at first, saying he would rather be majority leader of the Senate. To this Kennedy answered coldly and clearly: "What makes you think you'll still be majority leader?" After a thoughtful silence, Johnson yielded. He consented to run for the Vice Presidency, but reserved the right to run simultaneously for the Senate.[42]

It was generally assumed Kennedy's choice of Johnson, who had fought him so bitterly in the primaries, was dictated by political considerations. Apparently Kennedy did not think it safe just yet to write off the Southern vote, as Rauh and other ADA leaders urged him to do. Johnson's name on the ticket might be helpful in holding the South for the Democrats. That was the picture in 1960.

Four years later a somewhat more emotional explanation of Johnson's change of mind was circulated. Early in June, 1964, White House correspondents quoted President Johnson as saying that John F. Kennedy had had a premonition of death and deliberately chose Johnson to succeed him, explaining: "You are the man I'd want to be President, if anything happens to me." It was those words, Johnson claimed, which decided him to run for the Vice Presidency. If Kennedy said such a thing, it might have been intended more as an appeal to human vanity, than as a solemn intimation of his own end. Remembering that he had just been nominated and was wholly absorbed by the prospect of the political battles ahead, it is improbable he looked very far beyond the coming November. Moreover, he was young, strong and cheerful, not given to dark forebodings. Indeed, Johnson who was nearly ten years older and had already suffered one massive heart attack, might well have been expected to predecease him.

Far from being a serious contribution to history, the story released by the White House in June, 1964, seemed no more than a rather ghoulish bit of campaign propaganda. Calculated to impress superstitious persons, it gave the effect of an endorsement from the grave.

[42] Theodore H. White, *The Making of the President, 1964*, (New York, Atheneum, 1965), App. B, pp. 429-438.

In a sense, Johnson had begun campaigning for reelection within a day or so after he took the oath of office. On November 24, 1963— just two days after the assassination—the Los Angeles *Times* printed a feature about Johnson from Washington which said: "Mr. Johnson was trained deliberately for the Presidency *almost as if there had been a premonition in President Kennedy's mind."*

Superficially, there were changes when the Johnson family moved into 1600 Pennsylvania Avenue. Chic was replaced by folksiness; gilded youth by a fatherly air, which at times appeared slightly forced. In the anteroom to the President's office, the ten gallon hat took precedence over the homburg. As far as the staff was concerned, the changes were equally superficial. Of course, Johnson brought in his own long time personal aides to deal with the press and the public. Ted Sorenson and Arthur M. Schlesinger, Jr. departed. The former was replaced by speechwriter Sidney Hyman of the liberal Washington *Post;* the latter by Eric Goldman,[43] an old friend of ADA, who was asked to set up a screening service at Princeton to enlist a fresh supply of brain trusters and planners. ADA, it seemed, was playing a game of musical chairs.

Left liberal professors in the Executive Offices receded into the background, or returned to their accustomed haunts. Jerome Wiesner, who had headed the National Science Council, went back to MIT, and Walter Heller of the Council of Economic Advisers announced he would soon be leaving. The most prominent holdover was Mc-George Bundy, Harvard dean of Arts and Sciences, who as chief of the National Security Council now briefed the new President daily. For every Left liberal who vanished, however, another often less easily identified took his place. ADA infiltration, as Professor Brock had crowed, was so widespread both in the White House and the Departments, that a few changes really changed nothing at all.

It was to be expected that Johnson, offspring of the New Deal-Fair Deal, would turn to advisers of his own political generation. He preferred them to be nonofficial, rather than office fixtures: they aroused less comment that way. The new President's counsellors were prosperous attorneys of long residence in Washington, whom Johnson had known for years. Except for Clark Clifford, an accommodating practical politician who had served in the White House under Truman, all were known to lean to the Left.

[43] Since resigned. Due to be succeeded by Prof. John P. Roche of Brandeis University, past national president, ADA.

Senior member of Johnson's informal Cabinet was Dean Acheson, former protégé and lifelong friend of the New Deal's architect-in-chief, Felix Frankfurter. As Under Secretary and Secretary of State in the years following World War II, Dean Acheson had been instrumental in snatching defeat from the jaws of victory. He was identified with the school of diplomacy which had allowed Soviet Russia to occupy Eastern Europe and the Baltic States with no more than token protest and no resistance; delivered mainland China to Red rule; and launched the destructive "No Win" policy in Korea. He was the man who had refused to turn his back on Alger Hiss. To adult Americans who remembered the past, the return of Acheson had the eerie quality of a recurring nightmare.

Dean Acheson's role as a confidant of President Johnson seemed to guarantee the tenure of his former assistant, Dean Rusk, and the coterie of former Rhodes Scholars at the State Department. This, in turn, assured the continuance of a Fabian-inspired foreign policy which favored Socialist and even Communist nations, while demanding the progressive sacrifice of America's wealth, strength and prestige. William Bundy, brother of McGeorge, took over the post of Assistant Secretary for Far Eastern Affairs, once held by Rusk. Walt Whitman Rostow was assigned to steer the Alliance for Progress, apparently to speed the peaceful development of Socialism in Latin America, as a step toward achieving his declared goal of World Government.

Other informal advisers of President Johnson were James Rowe, Jr., a charter member of the Fabian ADA;[44] and Abe Fortas, of the firm of Arnold, Fortas and Porter, which had defended two generations of Communists and Left liberals in Washington. Once a Department of the Interior aide under Harold Ickes, Fortas was an expert in the political uses of public works—a talent which Johnson evidently proposed to utilize after his own reelection. Had not Arthur Schlesinger, Jr. once predicted that the United States would advance to Socialism through a series of New Deals? While Fortas was not directly identified with ADA, his law partner, Paul A. Porter, had been a member of its original Committee on Economic Stability.[45]

Johnson had promptly named Fortas to the commission, headed by Chief Justice Earl Warren, assigned to "investigate" the Kennedy

[44] See Appendix IV.
[45] *Report of the Committee on Economic Stability.* Published by Americans for Democratic Action, May, 1947. (See title page.)

assassination and "improve" on the massive report already submitted by J. Edgar Hoover. A lifelong advocate of civil liberties for Leftists, Fortas could be counted upon to help make sure that the assassination did not precipitate an unfavorable public reaction against Communists or Socialists.

Like Kennedy, Johnson was learning how to handle the liberals, or vice versa. The doubts expressed by so many ADA members a few years earlier were now converted into endorsements, as he threw his weight behind one New Frontier project after another. The subsidized wheat sale to Russia; the campaign year tax cut; the civil rights bill which, by implication, denied civil rights to service industries and promised a return to Reconstruction days in the South: all were dutifully, even vigorously backed by Johnson. In the area of national defense, he gave free rein to Secretary Robert McNamara, the former professor who personified the dictum of Mirabeau that "to administer is to rule." Once a spokesman for unrestrained military spending, Johnson now seconded McNamara's "economy" program, which involved a gradual phase out of the manned bomber by 1970, along with the progressive curtailment of nuclear weapons. To that end, Johnson himself issued an Executive Order stopping production of uranium and plutonium for military purposes.

President Johnson's unconditional surrender to ADA programs was perhaps the clearest testimonial to ADA's position of power in the Democratic Party; for power was one thing Johnson always recognized and respected. If he hoped to be reelected, he must have ADA support. Almost plaintively he reiterated in public statements that he really and truly was a liberal, and stressed his devotion to the memory of FDR. To Robert Spivak of the New York *Herald Tribune* Johnson remarked: "You say I am not a liberal. Let me tell you that I am more liberal than Eleanor Roosevelt and I will prove it to you . . . ." Presumably, the final proof of the pudding was to be postponed until after the 1964 national elections.

To ADA's annual Roosevelt Day dinners, President Johnson sent special greetings in 1964. Among other things the President's message said: "I was a Roosevelt man lock, stock and barrel. In many ways *he was my spiritual father*." [46] Reaction to this statement by members of the clergy attending the National Dinner in Washington is not recorded! The President also praised ADA for its "early advocacy of a test ban treaty, long before such support was popular."

[46] *ADA World*, (February, 1964). (Italics added.)

At the same time Johnson was cautious, ever-mindful of the perils of a campaign year. References to ADA as a left wing organization were stricken from the 1964 edition of his biography by Booth Mooney, a former Johnson staff-employee. A White House dinner for labor leaders and their wives, arranged by advice of David Dubinsky, was quickly followed by another dinner for handpicked leaders of business and industry. Both social events proved politically rewarding. The first resulted in an endorsement of Johnson by AFL-CIO brass at its Atlantic City convention; the latter in well-publicized pledges to vote for Johnson by a few prominent industrialists.[47] On May 4, he told a group of labor leaders:

The time has come for labor and Government and business to agree that we are going to achieve—and keep—full employment.[48]

One cannot help wondering if Johnson knew that the seemingly harmless phrase, "full employment," is the keystone of Keynesian economics, an invention of Fabian Socialists created to lure the United States towards full-scale Socialism.

Apparently Johnson, like Kennedy, was surrounded by Left liberal idea men and speechwriters who could not resist displaying their Fabian Socialist scholarship—thereby betraying their own origins. Searching for phrases to describe their bright new world of the future, like the dodo bird, they invariably looked backward. A commencement address, for example, delivered by President Johnson at the University of Michigan on May 24, 1964, invited the youth of America to join him in building "the great society." Anyone acquainted with the history of the Fabian Socialist movement knows that *The Great Society* was the name of a book by Graham Wallas, one of the original Big Four of the London Fabian Society.

First published in 1914, the 50th anniversary year of the Socialist International, *The Great Society* was based on lectures given four years earlier by Wallas as a visiting professor at Harvard. Wallas' course, Government-31, was a "must" for members of the Harvard Socialist Club of his day. An American edition of *The Great Society*

---

[47] It is a fact not generally known that the business leaders who made these endorsements of Johnson also happened to be trustees of the Committee for Economic Development, an organization which enjoys the benefit of "close consultation and discussion" with its Fabian-steered counterpart in Britain, known as PEP. *Committee for Economic Development. Report of Activities in 1963.* From Thomas B. McCabe, Acting Chairman, p. 6; pp. 15-18.

[48] *U.S. News and World Report,* (May 18, 1964).

(reprinted in 1920) had been dedicated to erstwhile Harvard Socialist Club president, Walter Lippmann—who in 1964 declared his intention to vote for Johnson. Somehow The Great Society became the "rallying cry" for Lyndon Johnson's 1964 campaign, replacing the slightly passé New Frontier. If Democrats resent the inference that their Party, their Administrations and their Presidents have been taken over lock, stock and barrel by a Fabian Socialist clique, why do they insist on borrowing their "rallying cries" from books and pamphlets written by well-known Fabian Socialists, British or American?

Further evidence of Democratic dependence on British Fabian Socialism—not merely for slogans, but for entire programs—was the Administration's "War on Poverty." Its source was officially disclosed by the British Fabian Socialist, Harold Wilson, Parliamentary Leader of the British Labour Party. Addressing the Eighth Congress of the Socialist International, which met in Amsterdam September 9 through 12, in 1963, Wilson said: "Ten years ago some of us in the Labour Party in Britain were moved to write a pamphlet called 'War on Want,' which led to a great movement in Britain and has gone far beyond our expectations . . . ." [49]

Strangely enough, the topic of the Socialist International Congress, where Harold Wilson spoke, was not poverty at all—or "want," as the British call it. The subject under discussion was: "The International Situation and the Struggle for Peace and Disarmament." The idea discreetly conveyed by Wilson was that disarmament might be achieved by popular demand in democratic countries, if funds normally allocated for national defense could be dramatically diverted into a war on poverty. While the movement might not succeed in abolishing poverty, it could certainly go a long way toward abolishing the armed forces of the Free World, and their weapons of the future.

Nearly ten years after the spark had been struck in Britain, the same idea was picked up and adapted to the American scene by a young man named Michael Harrington, a member of the executive committee of the American Socialist Party. Like so many other aspiring Socialists, he published a book. It appeared in 1962 as, *The Other America: Poverty in the United States*,[50] and it was an immediate

---

[49] *Socialist International Information*, (January 4, 1964), Vol. XIV, No. 1.

[50] According to *Socialist International Information* (March 14, 1964), "copies of Harrington's book, *The Other America*, are available in paperback for 95¢, from the Socialist Party, 1182 Broadway, New York, 1 N.Y. In Britain it has been published by Penguin Books—price 3/6."

sensation. This was not surprising, because all appropriate Fabian Socialist press and organizational contacts in the United States had evidently been primed to push the book and to promote the subject of poverty in general. Thus, a Saturday morning panel discussion at the 58th Annual Conference of the League for Industrial Democracy, held in May, 1963, was reminiscently titled, "Why Are the Many Poor?"—the title of *Fabian Tract No. 1*, first pamphlet ever printed by the London Fabian Society.[51]

President Kennedy is said to have read Harrington's book and to have been deeply impressed with it. Michael Harrington had made the astonishing discovery that there are thirty-five million Americans who are, by White House standards, poor, and presumably should have Federal help of one kind or another. Quite a lot of Federal funds could be absorbed rehabilitating thirty-five million people, even in a small way.

Michael Harrington himself was then not quite thirty-five years old. A graduate of Yale University, he had been a regular contributor to *The Reporter* and to *Commonweal*, a Catholic laymen's magazine of Left liberal leanings. For a time after leaving college, he was connected with the Catholic Worker movement—an independent but nominally Catholic movement of the Left, led by Dorothy Day, a convert from Communism. As recently as April, 1963, Miss Day—who had visited Castro's Cuba only the year before—attended a reception honoring the veteran Communist leader, Elizabeth Gurley Flynn. On that occasion Dorothy Day was quoted, perhaps erroneously, by a Communist newspaper as saying, "My association with Elizabeth Gurley Flynn will go on through my life, despite our basic religious differences" because "we can work together on economic and social questions." [52]

Possibly Miss Day, despite her fervor, was not familiar with the great Encyclical of Pope Pius XI, *Divini Redemptoris*, issued in 1937.

---

[51] Chairman of this panel session was Harry W. Laidler, Executive Director Emeritus of the LID. Panelists included: Jack Conway, Special Assistant to Walter Reuther; Martin Fleisher, faculty, Brooklyn College; Robert Lampman, President's Council of Economic Advisers; S. M. Miller, faculty, Syracuse University Youth Development Center; Oscar Ornati, faculty, New School for Social Research, author, forthcoming book on poverty; Michael D. Reagan, Director, Public Administration Programs, Syracuse University; Patricia Sexton, faculty, NYU.

[52] *The Worker*, (Sunday, April 7, 1963). Elizabeth Gurley Flynn, since deceased, was accorded a full-scale State funeral in Moscow's Red Square.

To Christians of the entire world the Holy Father uttered a warning, not merely for the moment but for all time: "Communism is intrinsically evil,[53] and no one desiring to save Christian civilization may cooperate with it in any undertaking whatever."

There is no evidence that Michael Harrington cooperates with Communism today. He is, however, a member of the Executive Committee of the little Socialist Party, USA openly affiliated with the Socialist International, which invariably acts to protect Communist nations and in many instances promotes cooperation with them at the world level. On March 28, 1964, the new slick paper edition of *Socialist International Information,* official organ of the International, featured an article by Michael Harrington reprinted from *New America,* U.S. Socialist Party publication. There Harrington explained why the "war on poverty" would speed the advance of Socialism in the United States. The reasons given by Harrington are worth noting: first, that the program *"is the assertion of a public claim on private resources";* and second, that *"it will necessarily involve an expansion of the public sector of American society."* [54] A previous issue of *Socialist International Information* had noted "Michael Harrington's contribution to Presidential thinking on 'The War on Poverty.'" [55]

Early in 1964, Harrington was called to Washington, along with other "specialists," to assist the Johnson Administration in drafting plans for its own anti-poverty campaign. Though the project was inherited from his predecessor, President Johnson had made it his own and announced the "war on poverty" as a major goal of his Administration. The campaign was frankly admitted to have been inspired by Michael Harrington's book. As a result, leading newspapers of the country threw open their columns to the young specialist on poverty, for by-line articles as well as interviews.

For an avowed official of the little U.S. Socialist Party[56] to be so

---

[53] The Latin word used in the Encyclical is *pravus,* root of the English word "depraved."

[54] (Italics added.)

[55] "Socialist Helped U.S. Map War on Poverty," Los Angeles *Times,* (March 22, 1964).

[56] Membership of the U.S. Socialist Party-Socialist Democratic Federation, an affiliate of the Socialist International, was officially listed as 3,000 in 1963. Numerically, it is one of the smallest Socialist Parties in the world, being outnumbered by the Luxembourg Socialist Workers' Party with a membership of 7,000. (Not all American Socialists necessarily belong to the Socialist Party, nor can be identified through such membership.—ed.) *Socialist International Information.* (August 24, 1963), Vol. XIII, No. 34-35, "Secretary's Report" (Sep-

cordially received in press and government circles was something new in America. Simultaneously, Harrington was treated like a younger brother by prominent members of ADA. As far as anyone could remember, nothing just like it had happened in this country before. It raised the interesting possibility that other American Fabian Socialists might decide in the not-so-distant future to drop their disguise and call themselves by their own true name. Presumably, they would only feel free to do so if convinced that the final victory of Socialism was at hand. Did they see in the "war on poverty" a decisive weapon for bringing their long, but not wholly uncomfortable struggle to an end?

Added to his other services, Michael Harrington represented a very serious and well-organized attempt to sell the Fabian Socialist conception of social justice and "social charity" to the Catholic hierarchy and Catholic laity. It was designed to undermine one last great obstacle to the sweep of Socialism throughout the world. In that strangely un-Christian effort, Harrington and his friends have been aided effectively, if not directly, by two British Fabian Socialist writers widely fêted in this country: Anne Fremantle, a niece of Beatrice Webb; and Barbara Ward (Lady Jackson), the latter described by a Washington news correspondent as one of President Johnson's favorite authors.[57]

To head his anti-poverty campaign, President Johnson initially chose Sargent Shriver, brother-in-law of the late President Kennedy and himself a member of an old and respected Maryland family. Sargent Shriver, had broken with family tradition by going to Chicago and becoming, in 1952, an eager supporter of Adlai Stevenson. Marrying a Kennedy sister, he became director of the Peace Corps in the Kennedy-Johnson Administration. Momentarily, his newer "poverty" post appeared to promise nothing more spectacular than a revival of Civilian Conservation Corps camps and similar half-forgotten projects dating from the New Deal. Its prospective importance was evident, however, from the fact that Adam Yarmolinsky[58] left his Pentagon

---

tember, 1961–July, 1963) to the English Congress of the Socialist International, meeting in Amsterdam September 9–12, 1963.

[57] In 1937 Barbara Ward was the co-author with Leonard Woolf of a volume entitled *Hitler's Road to Bagdad*. (Fabian International Section, The Fabian Society. London, Allen & Unwin, 1937). This book is not listed in recent biographies of Barbara Ward, circulated by her American publisher.

[58] Adam Yarmolinsky was the son of Avraham Yarmolinsky, long time head of the Slavonic language room at the New York Public Library, and the poetess,

post as Assistant Secretary for Defense for Personnel, to assist Shriver in launching the so-called war against poverty.

A young man of proper Socialist antecedents, of whom it had been rumored that he was being groomed by Left liberals to succeed J. Edgar Hoover, Yarmolinsky was no sacrificial lamb. He enjoyed the favor of leading ADA members, who regarded him as an authority on personnel practices measured by American Civil Liberties Union standards. Yarmolinsky's presence in Sargent Shriver's office could be taken as a virtual guarantee that the war against poverty would swell to boom proportions—after Johnson was reelected! That estimate was confirmed by a *New York Times* interview with Michael Harrington, which stated: "In Mr. Harrington's view, President Johnson's announcement of a war against poverty may be regarded as the staging phase for such a war rather than the beginning of one itself. The campaign can be started only when long-range plans that include *vast public works programs* are completed . . . ." [59]

Meanwhile, the political status quo was preserved without significant alteration. Keynesian economists were still in control of the Treasury and the Budget; agents of disarmament were in Defense. While Johnson talked of "frugality," as FDR had done to win election in 1932, he planned in terms of deficit budgets—"under 100 billion dollars" today, but who knows what tomorrow? President Johnson asked an initial sum just under one billion dollars to wage war on poverty; another 500 million dollars annually to raise salaries of Federal employees, many of whom had received pay raises only a short time before; while 3.5 billion dollars was asked and obtained for foreign aid—"no more than last year," but what of the years ahead?

The President promised "full employment"—and yet, by Executive Order, under the power relinquished to him by Congress, he proceeded to slash tariffs on imports priced to undersell American products, damage American industry and agriculture, and throw American citizens out of work. Subsidies were provided under the law for those

---

Babette Deutsch, a lifelong "collaborator" of the League for Industrial Democracy, who participated in many Socialist and United Front undertakings. A graduate of Harvard Law School, Adam Yarmolinsky headed the Fund for the Republic's Washington office in 1955, and thereafter was Secretary of the Fund. His superior was W. H. Ferry, who in 1962 issued a blast against J. Edgar Hoover and the FBI. Yarmolinsky's biography in *Who's Who in America* lists no investigative or personnel experience, prior to his appointment as Assistant Secretary of Defense for Personnel in the Kennedy-Johnson Administration.

[59] Quoted from *The New York Times* (no date) by *Socialist International Information*, (March 14, 1964). (Italics added.)

who were "harmed" by tariff reductions; so that, in effect, *the American taxpayer was subsidizing foreign industries.* Meanwhile, American manufactures and raw materials were being shipped abroad as free gifts. American industrialists, finding it harder to compete at home against the flood of foreign imports and obliged to seek government contracts, were compelled to submit more and more to government control and restrictions. Many of these things were the result of legislation which Johnson had originally spearheaded while in the Senate. He was now in a position to exert the power they conferred on a Chief Executive.

Foreign diplomats must have smiled behind their hands at America's pretensions of largesse, as the country's viable gold reserves in 1963 shrank to less than 4 billion dollars over the minimum required by law to remain in the vaults at Fort Knox. With other countries holding due bills against the United States for more than 22 billion dollars in gold and able to demand payment at will, America was, in effect, at the mercy of its foreign pensioners. At any desired moment, they could demand payment in gold and throw the United States into bankruptcy. Did they delay because of trade benefits offered by the President, now armed with tariff-making powers? Or were they waiting for a moment when, by common consent of its creditors, the gold-poor United States might be forced into some supranational world order which meant an end of its nationhood?

The American dollar was no longer as good as gold. Even sheiks and desert potentates of the Middle East refused to accept it, demanding payment in bullion. How was it, with such an alarming shortage of the precious metal in the United States, that a major American oil company could still arrange to pay for its Middle Eastern oil leases and concessions in gold? How was it that we were not ourselves mining it vigorously? What was the influence in Washington that made such gold payments without replacement possible, and what political favors were asked in return?

President Johnson insisted the country had never been so prosperous nor the economy so sound—and he quoted figures to prove it. Everything seemed to be moving; everything seemed to be booming; and everything was fearfully expensive. Private debt in the United States reached the astronomical total of 826 billion dollars by the end of 1963; while the public debt ceiling was raised a few months later to 324 billion dollars. The average citizen was caught in a vise between debt and taxes, from which the campaign year tax cut offered no noticeable relief; while state and Federal politicians voted themselves larger salaries and handsomer pensions at public expense.

Who could save for old age or a rainy day? Sooner or later, the Government, which in one way or another was already collecting over one-third of the average citizen's income, would have to pick up the tab for his medical and dental care, education, job-training and child rearing, in addition to unemployment insurance, old age pensions and burial costs. So the country went spinning along on wheels, faster and faster, down the non-stop Fabian Freeway that led to fiscal collapse—and a type of receivership sometimes known as Socialism.

This was how it had been planned, more than thirty years before, by a man named John Maynard Keynes and a small group of "respectable" Fabian Socialist conspirators in London, and by many others in other locales. They saw very plainly that the only way to capture the United States, and ultimately the world, for Socialism was by progressively weakening the financial system of this country to the point of total collapse. Once having reduced the two great English-speaking nations that were traditionally the bulwark of the free enterprise system and of liberty itself, Socialists would control the world— peacefully at first, perhaps later by force of Soviet arms. For when all is said and done, the Fabian Socialists have nowhere to go but to Communism.

By 1964, the United States had moved a great deal farther down the Fabian Freeway than most of its citizens knew. One final spurt of speed and power, and the total welfare state could be reached in a very few years. With the internal transition to Socialism apparently assured and external suasion applied at the psychological moment by a world-wide Communist-Socialist coalition, and possibly by a worldwide crisis calling for exceptional controls, the United States might be steered without conflict into the proposed World Federation of Socialist States. The rather simple legislation required for the purpose could be pushed almost imperceptibly through an ADA-controlled Congress.[59a] Was this the "fuller life" President Johnson's advisers had in mind for America when they revived Graham Wallas' dream of The Great Society in the one hundredth anniversary year of the Socialist International?

Lyndon Baines Johnson, former Democratic majority leader of the

---

[59a] On a single day in 1966, April 29, twenty nine resolutions looking towards the formation of an Atlantic Union regional Federal government were dropped into the Congressional hopper. (House Joint Res. 1089 through 1117.)

Senate and seasoned political manipulator, now seemed the man pre-ordained for the job. A ruthless hand at the controls was needed, where a softer nature might flinch. Was it true, after all, that Johnson had been deliberately chosen in case "something happened" to JFK—chosen not only by Kennedy himself, but also by those master planners of international Socialism and Communism whose agents surround any modern Democratic Party chief? Surely the final push would not be wholly entrusted to a willing but non-Socialist Chief Executive. He must have helpers, alert and well-schooled. Looking forward to the 1964 national elections, James MacGregor Burns, member of ADA and former pupil of London's Fabian Socialists, stated with clear and unmistakable intent: "Our need is not to win an election or a leader; we must win a government." [60]

That is exactly what happened on November 3, 1964, after an apparently monotonous political campaign marked by a good deal of sub-surface drama. It was no doubt a deep personal satisfaction for President Johnson to find that the nickname of Landslide Lyndon, with which his enemies had taunted him from 1948, was now apropos. But the victory was not his alone. For the first time in nearly thirty years Democrats held a better than two-to-one majority in both houses of the Congress; and a remarkably large number of them owed their seats to ADA-COPE support. More than ever the High Court could be depended upon, in the time-tested words of Mr. Dooley, to "follow th'iliction returns."

For all practical purposes, the constitutional separation of powers, seen by Anglo-American Socialists as the chief barrier to their conquest of the United States, had been reduced almost to the vanishing point. At long last a Socialist-schooled elite was in a position to exert unchallenged, if undeclared, control over all three branches of the Federal Government.

Obviously, the great majority of the American people was not aware of those circumstances, and would not knowingly have consented to them. Thus it seemed desirable for the Administration and its friends to keep the public guessing about Johnson's intentions as long as possible. The President himself must speak only in the broadest generalities, and news management of the strictest kind must be enforced. For the time being, it was important to preserve the image of LBJ as a moderate middle-of-the-roader, equally beloved by management

[60] James MacGregor Burns, *The Deadlock of Democracy*, (New York, Prentice Hall, 1963), p. 288.

and labor, and in his benign way acting wholly by popular consent.

Such considerations may explain the peculiar quality of the 1964 election campaign in the United States, where results were announced by television computers long before the votes had been counted. Organized labor and ethnic minority blocs were delivered almost intact to the Administration. Indeed, some experts claim the elections were actually won during the registration phase of the campaign, through the highly effective, if sometimes dubious, mass-registration techniques developed since 1958 by the industrial union branch of the AFL-CIO. Even in normally Republican areas Democrat registrars often outnumbered their rivals by as much as sixteen to one; and on election day were transformed into demon poll-watchers and vote-counters. One wonders whether even an Archangel Michael and his heavenly hosts would have sufficed to turn the tide, or to detect exactly what happened in 175,595 voting precincts around the country.

What the candidates said scarcely mattered. Their statements were transposed, interpreted and embellished by a practically solid phalanx of Left liberal press and TV commentators. Another unusual feature of the campaign was the vehemence of the overseas press in denouncing President Johnson's opponent—especially in editorial opinions from Scandinavia, Belgium, West Berlin, Italy, England, where Socialist Governments held office. Was this a preview of the inspired world press to be hoped for under a future World Government?

Organized pressure, to a degree never known before in the United States, was exerted on members of the business community, great and small—the purpose being, ironically enough, to convey an impression that the nation's businessmen were partial to President Johnson. Telephone calls from Washington warned that vital contracts might be forfeited. Credit was arbitrarily extended or denied. Federal and State agencies sent swarms of investigators to scrutinize the records of private companies and individuals. Well-timed offers of Area Redevelopment and other Federal funds were received in many smaller cities and towns. Even in the heyday of the New Deal, there had been nothing to equal this! Taking one thing with another, it was surprising that some twenty-seven million Americans were still found to have voted against Lyndon Johnson.

Tactics of the Johnson juggernaut were condoned by triumphant Washington insiders. In the excitement of victory, presidential favorite Walter Lippmann, who has seldom been known to make an unguarded statement, penned a more outspoken summary of the 1964 elections than any administration critic. "The campaign did not produce a debate about specific problems, and this was fortunate," wrote Lippmann in his syndicated column of November 8, 1964. "For the real business of the campaign was not to map out a course for the future. *It was to beat and crush a rebellion against the established line of domestic and foreign policy which was laid down in the generation which followed the great depression and the second world war.*" The statement speaks for itself—and for the gentle Fabians.

Epilogue:
The Moving Finger Writes

SWEET are the uses and perquisites of political office, even for those who declare their sole aim is to free humanity from its age-old burden of misery. In America, Hubert Humphrey, whose heart bleeds publicly for the poor of all nations, finds a $750,000 tax free mansion ordered for his vice presidential comfort by an ADA-controlled majority in the Congress. In Britain, Harold Wilson coolly invites the leaders of Socialist parties from fourteen countries, many like himself already holding top government posts, to meet at Chequers, traditional country home of British prime ministers.

With unintentional humor British newspapers hailed that event as a diplomatic coup—as if Harold Wilson, sometimes accompanied by Hubert Humphrey, had not been meeting on the Continent with the same Socialist leaders for years. Recognizing the revolutionary import of the new locale, *Socialist International Information* for May, 1965 headlined the conference "Socialist Summit at Chequers." Even the usually conservative *Times* of London commented in a leading article on April 26, 1965, "If Western Europe is to be led by Socialists, that may prove to have been a very useful beginning."

As international Socialism, open or disguised, moves steadily into positions of power, its chief spokesmen and political agents present an increasingly bland front to the world. This phenomenon was noted by Zigmunt Zaremba, chairman-in-exile of the Socialist Union of Eastern Europe and a Socialist member of the Polish Parliament before

444

World War II. Attending the Eighth Congress of the Socialist International at Amsterdam in 1963, he reported that "eminent party leaders, one after another, came to the rostrum to express, most cautiously, their parties' attitude toward important political questions, carefully skirting those questions which were 'premature.'"

"*The Congress*," wrote Zaremba in an article reprinted in the U.S. Socialist quarterly, *New Politics* (Winter, 1964), "*was clearly a gathering of those who held high office in their countries and those who hoped to do so shortly.*"[1] And he went on to say:

Only those questions on which there was already a consensus were brought to the floor for discussion and decision. These included disarmament and aid to the underdeveloped countries. Minor resolutions on France, Spain, Russian anti-Semitism, racism and civil rights struggles in the USA, and imprisonment of Socialist leaders by Communist-bloc countries were passed unanimously.

But behind the facade a whole series of questions was heatedly discussed. From the platform, only Guy Mollet [chairman of the French Socialist Party] touched on the question of the relationship of socialist and Communist movements in the present period. Behind the scenes, however, this question was the central issue of the discussions of the Central European Study Group and the Socialist Union of Eastern Europe.

For Socialist leaders, using the machinery of universal suffrage to gain and hold political power, special caution appears to be indicated as they round the bend heading toward an international federation of Socialist states. Because deep-rooted sentiments of patriotism, national honor and personal independence still animate a great many voters in a great many countries, every effort must be made by international Socialists to obscure the fact that the political and economic bases for such sentiments are being obliterated as rapidly as possible.

Just as a majority of citizens in the later Roman Empire never realized the Empire had fallen, because the outward forms of imperial government persisted several centuries longer; so the peoples of the so-called Free World are not to be made aware that their world is becoming progressively less free. "Socialism is about equality and freedom," insists Peter Townsend, chairman of the Fabian Society for 1965-66.[2] But George Bernard Shaw knew better. He knew the role

---

[1] (Italics added.)

[2] "Chairman's Message," *Fabian News*, (January, 1966). (The author of that Message is *not* the same Peter Townsend who was once Princess Margaret's suitor.)

that *coercion* must play in any Socialist scheme of things, and perhaps Peter Townsend does, too.

Meanwhile, whole populations are being conditioned to regard Socialist norms as normal, in preparation for a day when the leaders may more openly reveal their hands. Practical acceptance of many Socialist programs has been obtained, for the most part, by making shrewdly calculated appeals to the immediate interests of key groups and individuals, appeals which are invariably swathed in high humanitarian phrases. By now this technique has reached a point at which as one cynic observed, humanitarianism is the last refuge of the scoundrel.

Particularly in England and the United States where the public is indifferent to ideology, the psychological approach is used, as was suggested long ago by the British Fabian, Graham Wallas, in his book *The Great Society*. Developed in depth over the years by Fabian-inspired researchers, that method has been graded and refined with a view to reaching every level of modern society—labor, business, the professions, the bureaucracy, senior citizens, career-minded youth, even pre-school children. It calls for the permeation of colleges, universities, and religious seminaries by Fabian Socialist-oriented educators and administrators, as well as the introduction of uniform "standards" and "guidelines" into federally financed educational systems. For total effect, it requires total control of communications and entertainment media, a state of affairs already in being, if not in full force.

The professor is still the main channel through which the Fabian Socialist outlook percolates to society at large. As the venerable Walter Lippmann said, in a keynote speech opening "The University in America" Convocation at Los Angeles in May, 1966: "Professors have become in the modern world the best available source of guidance and authority in the field of knowledge . . . There is no other court to which men can turn and find what they once found in tradition and custom. Because modern man in his search for truth has turned away from kings, priests, commissars and bureaucrats, he is left, for better or worse, with the professor." [3] The gathering which Lippmann addressed that night included some 1,500 persons, among them presidents, deans and faculty members as well as bright students of the leading American universities. It was sponsored and steered by the

[3] Los Angeles *Times*, (May 8, 1966).

Center for the Study of Democratic Institutions—offshoot of an off-shoot of the Ford Foundation whose president was Professor Mc-George Bundy, former instructor and guide of American Presidents.

So the long-range plan, artlessly set in motion by a little group of serious thinkers meeting at 17 Osnaburgh Street, London, more than eighty years before and patiently pursued by three generations of respectable Fabian Socialists, moved smoothly toward its destined conclusion. With the clear-cut victory of the Fabian-led Labour Party in the 1966 British elections and the repeated success of the Johnson-Humphrey Administration in pushing one welfare state measure after another through the United States Congress, official cooperation between the two major English-speaking nations for the advancement of Socialism promised to reach new heights. The irony of it was, that as the *de facto* policies and actions of the heads of state leaned more and more strongly to the Left, their personal reputation for moderation soared.

Although Prime Minister Wilson's new government contained an even larger percentage of identifiable Fabians than before,[4] he was nearly always described in the general press as a right wing Socialist —really, hardly radical at all. Those hard-core Fabian Socialists who filled the Cabinet and the junior Ministries to the exclusion of simple Labourites presumably served as a kind of Loyal Opposition within the government they operated.

As if to confuse the picture still more, Peter Townsend's New Year's Message to the Society had warned the Wilson government against giving an impression of being bogged down by short-term problems at the expense of long-range Socialist objectives. He told Fabians that

---

[4] *Fabian News*, (April–May, 1966), announced there were 28 new Fabian Members of Parliament, and again printed a list of Labour Government appointments which identified present, though not past, members of the Fabian Society. It also listed, under the heading "New Fabian Appointments," the following:

Dick Marsh, a former member of the Executive Committee and an active member, of the Society's Trade Union Group, becomes the youngest member of the Cabinet at 38.

Eirene White, a former Chairman of the Society becomes the first woman Foreign Office Minister.

George Thomson, former chairman of the "Venture" Editorial Board, Summer School Director, etc., has been appointed Chancellor of the Duchy of Lancaster, with special responsibility for political negotiations for the entry of the country into the Common Market.

Reg Prentice, another former member of the Executive Committee has become Minister of Works.

"they will serve the Government far better as demanding, if sympathetic, critics than as captive apologists." [5] Since it would be decidedly awkward for members of the Government to take such a stand, one must infer that the chairman's message was addressed to rank-and-file Fabians in private life. They were urged to bring pressure on their coy leaders to do what the latter eagerly desired but preferred to do *as though yielding to popular demand.*

On the other side of the Atlantic, President Johnson fathered a whole flock of legislative acts, from Civil Rights to Federal-Aid-to-Education to Medicare, acts which had been plugged for years in both ADA and Socialist Party platforms. He pushed Keynesian-type deficit spending to breathtaking altitudes, and talked of extending the anti-poverty war—by then, costing well over one billion dollars a year at home—to the farthest corners of the earth. In matters of foreign trade and nuclear disarmament he offered fresh concessions to the Soviet bloc; while his alternately hot-and-cold Asian policy aided Moscow in its acrid and often deceptive dialogue with the Chinese Reds. Meanwhile, the "dialogue," blown up, by Leftist propaganda, to the stature of a "split," was something from which naive freemen could extract passing comfort.

In a paternal mood, Johnson even commended the United Nations Children's Fund for having transformed Halloween into "a program of basic training in world citizenship." [6] And yet Johnson was consistently referred to in the public prints as a moderate with conservative leanings, who basked in the support of the business community.

It is true that a select number of business executives had come to accept the Administration's post-Keynesian economics, in somewhat the same spirit as the New England transcendentalist, Margaret Fuller, once announced, "I accept the Universe!" Their conversion was due in part to the good offices of the Committee for Economic Development—an admitted affiliate of London's Fabian-inspired PEP (Political and Economic Planning), which now operated on a world-wide scale to secure the cooperation of management during the current period of peaceful transition to Socialism. Not unnaturally, such business leaders enjoyed Administration favor, and reciprocated with favors of their own in campaign season.

---

[5] *Fabian News,* (January, 1966).
[6] *Congressional Record,* (March 7, 1966), p. 4829.

This did not deter LBJ, however, from attempting to shift the blame for looming inflation, provoked by his Administration's prodigality, on his "friends" of the business community. Sternly the President told the U.S. Chamber of Commerce that if businessmen failed to keep rising prices down, they must expect to pay higher wages and higher taxes. It was the smoothest propaganda trick of a political year!

If in some respects, the President taxed the tolerance of his business supporters, his martial gestures in Vietnam proved no less a trial to his backers of the ADA. But they, too, remained sympathetic critics of LBJ, giving him credit for services rendered on the domestic front. In voting at their 1966 convention to disapprove the Administration's military policy in Vietnam, Americans for Democratic Action denounced the sin while continuing to love the sinner.

No one attending that convention and hearing Vice President Humphrey's pained defense of the Government's Vietnam policy doubted that he was really suffering, or failed to interpret his speech as a sacrifice on the altar of political necessity. Behind the scenes, it might well have been pointed out that two of the very same officials who had provoked the Korean War and then maneuvered it to a stalemate were once more directing U.S. Asian policy: Dean Acheson and Dean Rusk. Surely their skills could be relied upon to avert an American victory in Vietnam, if only by the simple device of sending too many troops to the scene and keeping military hardware in short supply.

Had not Rusk already intimated that a happy end-result of the bloodshed in Vietnam could be the eventual recognition of Red China, an event long and earnestly desired by the Fabian-begotten ADA? Although Arthur Schlesinger, Jr. gallantly volunteered to supplant Secretary Rusk as a presidential adviser, his offer was interpreted as a bit of high-level buffoonery—possibly designed to remind fellow-Fabians that any man is replaceable, if not expendable. Whether one graduate or another of the British Fabians' finishing school process was in charge, in the long run it made little difference, except perhaps to the individuals concerned.

Meanwhile Rhodes Scholars still manned the international ramparts in Washington. Walt Whitman Rostow of MIT's Center for International Studies (reputed to have been started with $300,000 worth of CIA money) was back at the White House again. Harlan Cleveland held forth as U.S. Ambassador to NATO. On the home front Nicholas deBelleville Katzenbach—who married a daughter of the Phelps Stokes clan, one of the founding families of the Fabian Socialist movement in America—had moved up to first place at the Department of Justice.

Like those other old Oxonians with whom he conferred from time to time in Washington, Britain's Prime Minister Harold Wilson claimed to support U.S. policy in Vietnam. But it hardly seemed more than lip service, in view of the fact that British merchant vessels docked regularly in North Vietnam ports and British companies engaged in trade with Hanoi. Though the Wilson government procured United Nations authority for the British Navy to seize and search ships *on the high seas* which were bound for Rhodesia, this privilege was not expected to apply to the Southeast Asian trade.

From the first, Harold Wilson appeared to favor negotiation as a means of ending the Vietnam conflict. His initial peace-feeler took the form of a visit to Hanoi by Harold Davies, M.P., a minor official in the Wilson government. Davies was an admirer of President Ho Chi Minh, who as far back as 1924 declared at a Communist International Congress, "I am a French colonial and a member of the French Communist Party." [7] On the same occasion Uncle Ho, falsely represented today in Leftist propaganda as leading a national independence movement like George Washington, stated plainly:

According to Lenin, the victory of the revolution in Western Europe depended on its close contact with the liberation movement against imperialism in enslaved countries and with the national question, both of which form a part of the common problem of the proletarian movement and dictatorship.[8]

Since those remarks were republished in Hanoi as recently as 1960, there is no reason to believe Ho Chi Minh has changed his stripes from that day to this.

Harold Davies, M.P. could look forward to a warm personal welcome in Hanoi, having written an enthusiastic article about the Northern Republic which appeared in the Left Wing French publication, *Horizons*, for December, 1957. It was quoted three years later in a little giveaway volume issued by Hanoi's Foreign Languages Publishing House and rather confusingly entitled *The Democratic Republic of Viet Nam, 1945-1960: Impressions of Foreigners* (p. 63).

[7] "Report on the National and Colonial Questions at the Fifth Congress of the Communist International," *Selected Works of Ho Chi Minh*, (Hanoi, Foreign Languages Publishing House, 1960), Vol. I, p. 143.
[8] *Ibid.*, pp. 143-144.

When his unofficial peace mission produced no visible results, Davies quietly returned to his post as parliamentary secretary to the Ministry of Pensions and National Insurance in London.[9]

So the question of the relationship between the Socialist and Communist movements in the present day—a question that only Guy Mollet of the French Socialist Party had ventured to broach publicly —becomes meaningful for Americans. While on the surface that relationship seems variable enough, its true nature and extent is still one of the best kept secrets of two highly secretive world organizations. Any public statements on the subject by leaders of the twin Internationals may be dismissed as inevitably misleading. Any inferences must be drawn from the facts of history itself, which records again and again the peculiarly protective attitude of the Socialists toward the Communist bloc nations and their agents and the great degree of sustained collaboration.

The Socialist and Communist world movements are like the two faces of a coin—not identical, yet inseparable. Sometimes one side appears uppermost, sometimes the other; but at the core they are still one. Which side of this counterfeit coin might face up at a given time, probably depends upon the circumstances of the moment. It is, of course, to the interest of every man, woman and child in America, desiring personal liberty in a free and sovereign nation, that the fraudulent nature of this coin be recognized and exposed so that we may be forever spared the necessity of making such a spurious choice.

One by one, the costliest and most highly prized nuclear secrets of the United States, on which the peace and safety of the whole Free World depend, have been delivered to the Soviet military clique, as a result of the consistently permissive temper of British and American Fabian Socialists toward Communist activists. Published hearings of the Subcommittee on Internal Security of the U.S. Senate Committee on the Judiciary demonstrate that today, as in the age of Roosevelt, the most elementary security precautions have been scrapped by a Fabian-dominated Administration indisposed to keep Communist operatives from entering the country or to deny them the privileges accorded to loyal American citizens.

At the popular level, it is evident that something resembling the United Front movement of the pre-World War II years has been

[9] Davies' name appears in this connection on the Government appointments lists released by the British Information Service as I. D. 702 (November, 1964 and April, 1966).

revived, to exert pressure on Socialist-oriented governments in matters of peace and disarmament. How broad this movement is may be gathered from an International Peace/Disarmament Directory compiled in 1962 by one Lloyd Wilkie of Yellow Springs, Ohio. Without claiming to include the names and addresses of all organizations working in one way or another for "peace," it lists more than six hundred groups and subgroups throughout the world and more than one hundred periodicals. They include academic, scientific, religious and merely agitational groups, ranging from end to end of the political spectrum.

Of course, the Women's International League for Peace and Freedom—founded long ago by the Chicago Socialist Jane Addams and conveniently used as a cover by illegal U.S. Communists in the nineteen-twenties—is there with all its branches. The Council on Foreign Relations is listed, as well as its opposite number in Britain, The Royal Institute of International Affairs. Both the Communist and Socialist Parties USA are named, as well as the ADA; but the two major American political parties are slighted. *The Catholic Worker* is cited, but the Vatican's peace efforts are discreetly overlooked.

The author explains he has played no favorites, and suggests that the inquiring reader learn the various shades of difference for himself, by getting in touch with as many of these groups and periodicals as he sees fit. To a casual observer, it is instructive to note how many of the national peace movements in foreign countries are affiliated with the World Council of Peace, chaired in 1962 by Professor J. D. Bernal, 94 Charlotte Street, London W-1. Even to reach the chairman of the Soviet Peace Committee, N. Tikhonov, whose local address was not available at press time, one was referred to the World Council of Peace in London.

While peace is undoubtedly wonderful, the motives of those who organize so-called peace movements and peace demonstrations of varied degrees of violence, are often suspect. In the past as in the present, pacifist groups have been used at critical moments to promote defeatism and to paralyze a nation's will to defend itself. One of the more striking historical examples was the so-called Bonnet Rouge Conspiracy, in which French Socialists participated during World War I, and which led one French regiment after another to lay down its arms in the face of an advancing enemy.

In the present atomic era the chief effort of international peace and disarmament groups seems to be directed at inducing the United

States to renounce its role as an atomic power, thereby leaving the Soviet Union supreme in the field. One can only speculate as to how far the veiled disarmament propaganda, purveyed by such high-level Fabian-inspired agencies as the Council on Foreign Relations and the American Assembly, influenced the nuclear pause proclaimed in 1961 by President Kennedy; or the decision of Secretary McNamara in 1964 to cancel the nuclear strategy of NATO without consulting his European Allies. In the final analysis, World Government under Socialist rulers becomes the pacific sea toward which all tributary movements flow.

With the end so nearly achieved, it seems more than ever unfair that the American people should not be permitted to know the identity of their betrayers. In almost every other country of the Free World, Socialism operates openly as a political party, and frequently is the ruling party. Here in America both the Socialist Party and the Socialist Labor Party are small and weak, and merely serve to delude the public into believing there is little to fear from that quarter. Yet the unseen and unacknowledged Fabian Socialist movement, whose American practitioners call themselves liberals or progressives, has access in the United States to greater sources of wealth and power than anywhere else on earth. It has penetrated multi-billion dollar tax free foundations, and manipulates the U.S. Treasury itself. Precisely because its leaders are not known for what they are, they occupy a great many key posts in government today and act invisibly in union with alien masterminds to dissolve the strength and substance of this nation.

Though the situation is acutely dangerous for a land that was liberty's true home, it is not necessarily hopeless. The answer was supplied by a relatively unschooled American, General Andrew Jackson, who fought in his own day to make America free and great. Perhaps it is only a legend, unknown to such sophisticated scholars as Arthur Schlesinger, Jr., but it became a tradition among professional military men of an earlier era.

Just before the Battle of New Orleans, we are told, an unusually dense fog descended on the fields outside the city, where General Jackson's army was to make its stand. As he rode out to inspect his ill-equipped troops, a young soldier spoke up.

"But General, sir," said the boy, "how can I fight and defend myself against an enemy I can't see?"

"Sooner or later, your enemy will show himself," replied the General, "and you will know what to do." Then, looking upward a moment as if for guidance, he added: "And in your future life, if you survive this—and by God, you will!—you will be confronted by many unseen enemies of your hard-fought liberty. But they will show themselves in time—time enough to destroy them."

APPENDICES

NOTE

The author here presents the names of many members and cooperators of the British Fabian Society and the British Labour Government as well as the names of members and cooperators and/or sponsors of American Fabian-type socialistic organizations such as the League for Industrial Democracy (LID); and of organizations which pose as "liberal," such as Americans for Democratic Action (ADA). The theme developed in the main body of the book is illustrated graphically as the lists conclude with the names of many ADA members who hold high positions in the Johnson Administration, today.

The reader's attention is called to the use of symbols (*) and (†) used for example to denote the presence of Fabian Socialists in the British Labour Government; and to denote members of ADA who are members or cooperators of the League for Industrial Democracy, and so forth. Thus the tie-ins, in terms of persons in both "liberal" and Socialist organizations, are shown.

A listing in certain of the following categories, does not of and by itself convict an individual as a Socialist. However, by an amassing of evidence of this kind, a persistent pattern appears and a movement convicts itself.

Here the mechanics are unveiled by which Socialism is transmitted from Great Britain and other countries to the United States. And here, in the United States, a Socialism is rapidly nearing completion for which International Communism is the only logical beneficiary. Americans who wish to change this tragic state of affairs are thus informed of the facts.

APPENDIX I

The following selective historical lists are offered as indicative of two things: 1) the continuity of the roster and of the Fabian Society; 2) the steady acquisition to Fabianism of new blood, always well-mixed with the old.†

It has become a fascination for the writer to read lists of names. They were gathered from the "Personal Notes," the "Women's Group," the Kingsway Hall Lectures, "Nursery," Meetings of the Society, Election Lists, London County Council election lists, Fabian Society Executive Committees and records of attendance thereof. Many names (at least two hundred) which did not appear at the historical level have become those of old friends. They testify to the unbroken existence and the steady functioning of the Society. Many turn up in news items, such as the study of the Institute of Pacific Relations made by a Senate Committee: Creech-Jones, Noel-Baker, R. H. Tawney, for example.

Individuals became Fabians by being proposed, sponsored, and elected; and were required to subscribe to the *Basis*. If the *Basis* made them English Socialists, the Society made them members of the Labour and Socialist International. MacDonald is not included after 1919; yet the Fabianism in his attitudes and those of his advisers is patent. Likewise, for all his close associations, Professor Gilbert Murray has not been listed here. Sir Stafford Cripps and Ernest Bevin like G. D. H. Cole and Ellen Wilkinson, swung to the far Left at times; but they are Fabians all—and Margaret Cole has made the old home in the Society comfortable for them all by enlarging the porch! John Scurr, a Catholic, belonged; but not John Wheatley. Arnold Bennett, J. B. Priestley, John Galsworthy are listed, although seldom; Patrick Braybrooke and St. John Ervine, often. The first three names are associated with *The Clarion* which consistently from 1929 to 1931 praised the artistry of Charles Chaplin and Paul Robeson. Reginald Pugh belonged, but up to 1950, not Arthur (now Sir Arthur) Pugh of Steel and Smelters trades.

A complete list of those who never came back to the Society even in spirit as Wallas, Wells, and Annie Besant did—while Chesterton, S. G. Hobson (*Pilgrim to the Left*), A. Orage (*New Age*), H. Slesser did not—would be significant. Although Clement Attlee credits much of Labour's strength

† Initials appearing occasionally after British names mean:

EC = Executive Committee
JP = Justice of the Peace
L.C.C. = London County Council
MP = Member of Parliament
NEC (LAB) = National Executive Committee, Labour Party
TUC = Trades Union Congress

to Irish Catholic workingmen, the latter are vastly unrepresented in the Fabian Society.

An estimated proportion of professed intellectuals to all others (also middle class) seems to be about three in eight. This includes those holding degrees, Bachelor of Arts (more usually, Bachelor of Science), Master of Arts, Doctor of Philosophy, and those recording their military rank for prestige, professors and—oddly—many medical doctors. Elsewhere is a list of Protestant ministers. Fabians often filled the position of Justice of the Peace, the office on which very much of local civics hinges. In 1945 local Fabian societies added 2,200 members to the Society. *Fabian Society Annual Report*, 1946, said, "Newly elected M.P.'s expected the Fabian Society to . . . provide them at short notice with policies, or with material for speeches."

Names like those of Ben Tillett, J. H. Thomas, J. R. Clynes, J. Wheatley, E. Bevin, A. Bevan, W. Citrine (now Viscount), John Hodges of the steel workers, Frank Hodges of the miners, and Frank Smith of the coal miners, were drawn into the field of gravity of the Society.

Margaret MacDonald, née Gladstone, died in 1911. She ranked with Mary MacArthur, Mary Middleton, Mrs. Bruce Glazier, Margaret MacMillan, to whose labors Socialism in Britain is heavily indebted; although, like Mrs. Glazier, they were inclined to confuse their Socialism with religion, leaving the philosophic propositions of Fabianism to Haldane, Joad, Russell, and Slesser (not to mention Wells and Shaw).

A sampling of names of Fabian Justices of the Peace in the nineteen-twenties and nineteen-thirties follows:

David Adams	F. W. King
R. Aldington	T. W. McCormack
G. Burgneay	H. J. May
Alderman H. Carden	Gwyneth Morgan
John Cash	Marion Phillips
Lilian Dawson	Mrs. C. D. Rackham
C. S. Giddins	E. Cubitt Sayres
G. M. Gillett	G. Thomas
M. W. Gordon	Mrs. G. Tiffen
Bart Kelly	A. G. Walkden

Some names represented prominent British families:

Oliver Baldwin	Lady Cynthia Mosley (née Curzon)
Sir Ernest Benn	Malcolm Muggeridge (nephew of
Anthony Wedgwood Benn	Beatrice Webb)
Arthur Creech-Jones	Philip Noel-Baker
Charlotte Haldane	John Ramage
Naomi Haldane (Mitchison)	Viscountess Rhonda
Lady Jowitt	Miss Sankey
Ishbel MacDonald	T. Drummond Shiels
Lady Melville	Lady Frances Stewart
Allen Moncrieff	C. Trevelyan
May Morris	

A sampling of speakers under Fabian auspices:

Viscount Bryce
Sir Walter Citrine (after 1045)
Hans Kohn (now in the U.S., listed as a member of the Society)
A. Duff Cooper (listed only once)
Herman Finer (now in the U.S., frequent lecturer and member of the
  Fabian Society)
G. P. Gooch
Professor Julian Huxley (now of UNESCO)
Father Vincent McNabb (listed but once)
S. de Madariaga (historian)
A. Allison Peers (listed but once)
A. J. Penty (guild socialist, usually criticized)
Evelyn Sharp
Wickham Steed
Arnold Toynbee
Freda Utley (listed but once)
John Winant (U.S. Ambassador, luncheon guest speaker)

Protestant ministers whose names appear in Fabian lists (often M.P.'s):

James Adderly
Ramsden Balmforth
G. C. Bynon
Henry Carter
John Clifford (deceased, 1923)
J. E. Hamilton
S. D. Headlam (deceased, 1923)

C. Jenkinson
James Kerr
Richard Lee
J. Massingham (non-practicing)
William Mellor (non-practicing)
Ben Spoor

A partial list of foreigners heard by the Society, mostly Social Democrats
(this list is not alphabetical; it falls into a sort of chronological order):

Count Karolyi (in 1919, he resigned the presidency of the new Republic of
  Hungary, when the Social Democrat regime led to that of Bela Kun)
Alfredo de Sordelli, Argentine writer
Herman Kantorowicz, German professor of Jurisprudence (once at Columbia)
Henri Gans
Baron Felix de Bethune (member)
Otto van der Sprenkel
Wolfgang Thiekuhl
Hans Kohn, German Social Democrat, now in the United States
G. Salvemini, Italian Social Democrat, Harvard professor
Carlo Rosselli, Italian anti-Fascist, Social Democrat, writer of *Socialisme
  Liberale;* his *Oggi in Spagna, domani in Italia* posthumously published with
  preface by Salvemini
A. H. Abbati (Swiss background)
J. B. Peixotto (member), American-born, cosmopolitan artist
K. Young (Chinese Consul General)
Sobei Mogi

D. J. Santilhano (Dutch), author of *Banking for Foreign Trade*
Prince Dimitri Sviatopolk Mirsky (1932)

Since 1940:

Dr. Alexander Baykov
Daw Saw Yin (of Burma)
Herta Gotthelf
Kudmul Shanti Rangarao (1947)
Anwar Iqbai Qureshi (Indian; 1947)
Kurt Schumacher (1947; reporting from Social Democratic contacts in Germany)
W. Sellers, of Nigerian Government
Stephen Drzcivieski
Professor Andre-Philipov (anti-Petain), September, 1942

Fabian names important in their avocations:

Sir Ernest Barker, political scientist
Patrick Braybrooke, lecturer, frequently in the United States, father of editor of *Wind and Rain*
Edward Carpenter, poet (one might say laureate of "the movement")
Colin Clark, economist
Victor Cohen, writer, lecturer at Fabian Summer Schools
M. H. Dobb, economist of London School of Economics, contributor to *Encyclopedia of the Social Sciences*
Denis Healey, appointed to "pursue a forward policy" in International Labour Organisation, Geneva (1946)
Julian Huxley (UNESCO)
H. W. Nevinson, writer
John Ramage, Scottish shipbuilder, contributor to *Labour Year Book*
Maurice Reckitt (and Eva C. Reckitt), contributor to *Labour Year Book*, author of *Faith and Society*, National Guildsman, Anglican Christian Socialist.
J. W. Robinson Scott, economist, editor *The Countryman*
W. E. Walling, U.S. labor economist

Fabians who have worked or are working on the American scene (incomplete list:

Herbert Agar
G. E. G. Catlin (Cornell)
Arthur Creech-Jones
A. E. Davies
Herman Finer (University of Chicago)
H. Duncan Hall
Herman Kantorowicz (Columbia)
Hans Kohn
Harold Laski (Harvard and Roosevelt)
Jenny Lee, invited by "forward" groups of John Hopkins and Columbia Universities
Michael Oakshott
Maurice Orbach
John Parker (Chicago; Roosevelt)
J. B. Priestley
D. N. Pritt

S. K. Ratcliffe, consistent visitor and reporter

W. Hudson Shaw (Oxonian), who came yearly to lecture in the University Extension Courses under auspices of Woodrow Wilson, in Philadelphia. They published *The Citizen*, 1895 to 1901. (Shaw, known as "Broughman Villiers")

R. H. Tawney

Graham Wallas

Barbara Ward, Catholic, but not lecturing under Catholic auspices (Lady Jackson)

A typical list of Fabians found in *Fabian News* and *Fabian Society Annual Report* in 1923-24:

F. G. Abbis	Izak Goller
David Adams	W. Graham
Percy Alden	A. Greenwood
Major C. Attlee	Mary Griffiths
W. J. Baker	C. H. Grinling
Elizabeth Banks	Dr. L. H. Guest
Mr. and Mrs. Granville Barker	Grace Hadow
E. Beddington Behrens	B. T. Hall
Marion Berry	Dr. S. Hastings
G. C. Binyon	W. Henderson
G. P. Blizard	Lancelot Hogben
Maeve Brereton	Lt. R. G. K. Hopp
Dr. Mabel Brodie	L. Isserlis
George Burgneay	Dr. Robert Jones
Noel Buxton	Hon. Arnold Keppel
Percival Chubb	James Kinley
Major Church	George Lansbury
J. D. Clarkson	Harold Laski
Mrs. Hansen Coates	H. B. Lees-Smith
Mrs. A. E. Corner	J. F. MacPherson
Morley Dainow	W. H. Marwick
Gilbert Dale	Sylvain Mayer
A. Emil Davies	Rosalyn Mitchell
Mrs. Boyd Dawson	Herbert Morrison
Dr. Percy Dearmer	Miss Pennythorne
F. Lawson Dodd	Reginald Pugh
H. Drinkwater	Amber Reeves
G. S. M. Ellis	W. A. Robson
Dr. J. W. Evans	W. Samuels
Dr. Letitia Fairfield	J. Scurr
M. Farrman	Hugh Shayler
Dr. Herman Finer	W. E. Simnet
F. W. Galton	Dr. Gilbert Slater
Joseph Gill	Captain Lothian Small
G. M. Gillett	N. A. Sprott
F. W. Gladstone	J. C. Squire

J. Stewart
Fred Tallant
Brig. Gen. C. B. Thomson
F. Thoresby
Mr. and Mrs. Joseph Tiffen
Ben Tillett

A. G. Walkden
D. W. Wallace
Col. T. B. S. Williams
Ernest Wimble
Ella Winter

Early Obituaries:

Arthur Clutton-Brock
Baron Felix de Bethune
G. H. Ellis
William Game
K. A. Hayland
Stewart Headlam

Maurice Hewlett
George Standring
Herbert Trench
George H. Underwood
Edmund H. Woodward

A list of names of Fabians from the *Fabian News* and *Fabian Society Annual Report,* 1929-31:

Albert Albery
Major D. Leigh Aman
Vera Anstey
A. Earle Applebee
Mabel Atkinson
Oliver Baldwin
Mrs. M. E. Beadle
Captain Hubert Beaumont
Sir Ernest Benn
Wedgwood Benn
William Bennett
J. D. Beresford
Theodore Besterman
G. P. Blizard
Constance Bloor
Patrick Braybrooke
Dr. W. H. Brend
Dr. F. G. Bushnill
Philip Butler
Ronald Chamberlain
Major Church
Anna Corner
Sir Stafford Cripps, K.C.
George Cruickshank
Hugh Dalton, D.S.C.
A. E. Davies
J. Percival Davies
Admiral Dewar
Dorothy Elliott
St. J. Ervine

J. L. Etty
Henry Farmer
Montague Fordham
J. A. Lovat Fraser
G. M. Gillett
Alban Gordon
Charlotte Haldane
A. Clifford Hall
J. E. Hamilton
Mrs. M. A. Hamilton
Mrs. M. Hankinson
J. Hazelip
A. Henderson
W. W. Henderson
Will Herron
Mrs. D. L. Hobman
F. E. Holsinger
F. W. Hooper
Daniel Hopkins, M.A., LL.B.,
    M.C.
George Horwill
Hubert Humphreys
S. B. Jackson
Lady Jowitt
Lt. Commander J. M. Kenworthy
Mrs. A. M. Lang
George Lansbury
Susan Lawrence
A. J. Lynch
Ishbel MacDonald

A. G. F. Machin
B. Skene MacKay
Margaret McKillop, M.A., M.B.E.
Miles Malleson
J. J. Mallon
S. F. Markham, B.A., B. Litt.
Henry May
J. B. Melville, K.C.
Mrs. H.C. Miall-Smith
Rosslyn Mitchell
Edith Morley
Herbert Morrison
Oswald Mosley
Joseph W. Neal
H. W. Nevinson
J. T. Newbold
Rt. Hon. Noel-Buxton
H. St. John Philby
Lord Ponsonby
Richard Pope
E. B. Powley
Mrs. H. M. Pulley
Mrs. C. D. Rackham
T. Ridpeth
J. Jones Roberts
H. S. Rowntree
Bertrand Russell
Miss Sankey
J. A. Sargent
John Scurr
John Sharman
Evelyn Sharp

Bernard Shaw
Dr. Drummond Shiels
Nicholas Size
C. M. Skepper
Dr. Gilbert Slater
Kingsley Smallie
Frank Smith
W. G. Smith
Harry Snell
Mrs. Snowden
Marion Somerville
Colonel Maurice Spencer
Leopold Spero
Jessie Stephens
Lady Frances Stewart
Mrs. H. M. Swanwich
D. Taylor
Norman Tiptaft
Mrs. R. Townsend
Ethel Turner
George Van Raalte
Gilbert J. Walker
Graham Wallas
William English Walling
Professor F. E. Weiss
James Welsh
Rebecca West
Ellen Wilkinson
F. H. Wiltshire
L. A. Wingfield
A. Young
Dr. Ruth Young

Obituaries:

Rev. G. S. Belasco
J. W. Buttery
Miss M. Gibson

J. H. Stobart Greenhalgh
Frederick Walter King
Mrs. M. Kirkwood

Fabian names from *Fabian Society Annual Report* and *Fabian News* in 1934-36:

A. H. Abbati
Jennie Adamson
Sir Norman Angell
A. E. Applebee
Wilcox Arnold
Major C. Attlee
Francis Bacon

Oliver Baldwin
Major Harry Barnes
J. P. Barter
H. L. Beales
L. A. Benjamin
Wedgwood Benn
Theodore Besterman

Mrs. G. P. Blizard
R. D. Blumenfeld, editor *Daily
Express*
Maud Bodkin
I. M. Bolton
H. N. Brailsford
Lionel Britton
C. Delisle Burns
Henry Carter
Professor G. E. G. Catlin
Mrs. Cavendish-Bentinck
Colin Clark
T. W. Coates
G. D. H. Cole
Dudley Collard
J. S. Collis
W. G. Cove
Ida M. Cowley
Philip Cox
A. Creech-Jones
Stafford Cripps
R. C. Crossman
Morley Dainow
Hugh Dalton
A. E. Davies, L.C.C.
J. P. Davies
Dr. Har Dayal
Barbara Drake, L.C.C.
A. R. Dryhurst
Mary Ellison
R. C. S. Ellison
St. John Ervine
Gordon Esher
Rowland Estacourt
Dr. Eric Fletcher
Dr. M. Follick
Robert Fraser
J. S. Furnivall
F. W. Galton
G. T. Garrett
Robert Gibson, K.C., LL.B.
Alban Gordan
Barbara Ayrton Gould
Dr. T. E. Gregory
Dr. L. Haden Guest
Captain Basil Hall
J. H. Harley
T. Driffield Hawkins

Arthur Henderson
Mrs. E. A. Hubback
Hubert Humphreys
Miss B. L. Hutchins
C. Jenkinson
Thomas Johnston
Sir William Jowitt
Mrs. R. Keeling
Helen Keynes
Dr. Hans Kohn
George Lansbury
Harold Laski
Richard Lee
H. W. Lewis
H. Light
Lord Listowel
Kingsley Martin
Mrs. C. J. Mathew, L.C.C.
Dr. Caroline Maule
Francis Meddings
Captain W. J. Millar
W. Milne-Bailey
Herbert Morrison, J. P., L.C.C.
H. T. Muggeridge
F. J. Osborn
F. W. Pethick-Lawrence
Miss E. Picton-Turberville
Major Graham Pole
Lord Ponsonby
Mrs. C. D. Rackham
John Ramage
S. K. Ratcliffe
Paul Reed
T. Reid
W. A. Robson
F. A. P. Rowe
Bertrand Russell
H. P. Lansdale Ruthven
Jocelyn Rys
H. Samuels
Captain W. S. Sanders
Amy Sayles
A. Luckhurst Scott
J. W. Robertson Scott
Dr. S. Segal
T. Drummond Shiels
Lewis Silkin
Arthur Skeffington

Lord Snell
Frank Soskice
Mrs. Arnold Stephens
F. L. Stevens
Michael Stewart
Professor J. L. Stocks
G. R. Strauss
Hubert Sweeny

R. H. Tawney
Ivor Thomas
Ernest Thurtle
Ben Tillett
Nanette Tuteur
Sir Raymond Unwin
R. McKinnen Wood
Leonard Woolf

Obituaries:

J. A. Fallows
A. Henderson (1937)
Walter Hudson
Mrs. R. B. Kerr
James Leakey

Dr. Robert Lyons
Fred Tallant
Alexander Wicksteed
George Francis Wilson

A specially selected list of names of Fabians from records of 1942 to 1947, showing continuity and prestige:

Clement Attlee
F. R. Blanco-White
H. N. Brailsford
Marjorie Brett
Frances Coates
Margaret Cole
Cecily Craven
A. Creech-Jones
Richard Crossman
Hugh Dalton
A. E. Davies
Barbara Drake
Dorothy Elliott
Lord Faringdon
Eric Fletcher
J. S. Furnivall
F. W. Galton
Agnes Gibson
Rita Hinden
Lancelot Hogben
C. E. M. Joad
William Jowitt

Harold Laski
George Lathan
A. Lewis
J. J. Mallon
Mrs. L'Estrange Malone
Kingsley Martin
C. Mayhew
Herbert Morrison
P. Noel-Baker
R. Postgate
R. A. Raffan
J. W. Raisin
John Ramage
W. A. Robson
Amy Sayle
Emanuel Shinwell
Arthur Skeffington
Reginald Stamp
Edith Summerskill
L. Woolf
Barbara Wootton

Obituaries:

Mostyn Lloyd
William Mellor (1942)
Lord Olivier (1943)

Beatrice Webb (1943)
Sidney Webb (1948)
Ellen Wilkinson (1947)

These names had long been listed; many through the thick and thin of the nineteen-twenties. They must have kept up their dues, for Margaret Cole made a clean slate of the paid up membership in her reorganization.

These names, old and new, of Fabians of the 1942 to 1947 group have taken on the hue and verve of ZIP and the New Fabian Research Bureau:

Austen Albu
Dorothy Archibald
Sir Richard Aucland
N. Barou
Barbara Betts
Aneurin Bevan
F. A. Cobb
Freda Corbett
E. F. M. Durbin
M. Edelman
Hugh Franklin
V. Gollancz
Frank Horrabin
Compton MacKenzie
Ian Mikardo
Ivor Montagu
George Orwell

John Parker
Morgan Phillips
Sybil Prinsky
D. N. Pritt (retained as counsel for "the Eleven" Communists on appeal before the U.S. Supreme Court)
Sir Hartley Shawcross
Stephen Spender
John Strachey
Ivor Thomas
Sybil Thorndike
Herbert Tracey
W. N. Warbey
G. D. N. Worswick
Lamartine Yates
K. Zilliacus

Last, but not the least, there follows a list of "empire" and "international" topics and the names of specially interested Fabians. These were taken from the *Fabian Society Annual Report* of 1945—1946, and which covers the election following the last year of war coalition when "Labour" formed a "Socialist" Government:

Fabian Colonial Essays, contributed by H. N. Brailsford, M. Fortes, J. S. Furnivall, Ida Ward, C. W. Greenidge, L. Woolf, Margaret Wrong, *et al.*, edited by Rita Hinden.

Newfoundland the Forgotten Island, by Lord Ammon.

The World Parliament of Labour, by R. J. P. Mortished: International Labour Organisation.

Africa, the West Indies, Palestine, India, and questions concerning the Post-War Settlement and dealing with education, resources, crops, unionism, politics, were treated by P. Noel-Baker, Wilfred Benson (ILO), E. E. Doll, A. Dalgleish, Lord Faringdon,* Captain Gammons, Frank Horrabin,* Julian Huxley, A. Creech-Jones,* Lord Listowel,* Harold Laski,* Professor W. MacMillan, John Parker,* Lord Rennel, Reginald Sorensen, L. Woolf,* K. Zilliacus.*

The names marked by asterisks are those of persons also serving on the Fabian Executive.

An International Farewell Gathering held in October, 1945, was presided over by P. Noel-Baker and sent greetings to French, Belgian and Italian "comrades" in letters signed by representatives of twelve countries and addressed to Daniel Mayer, Louis de Brouckere and Pietro Nenni, leading Social Democrats. Cf. *FSAR*, 1945, p. 15. In every *Fabian Society Annual*

Report, 1929 to 1950, the name of Margaret Cole appears in official, foreign and domestic connections.

As to the Webbs: Sidney (Lord Passfield) was on the Fabian Executive as late as 1934. From 1935 to 1939, while A. Emil Davies kept the Society together and the *Fabian News* coming out, the Webbs, having held up the publication of their book on Soviet Russia until after the Election of 1935, devoted themselves to receiving persons of "liberal" persuasion of every rank (including Maisky, the Russian Ambassador) and to propagandizing for Sovietism. They received a direct and negative reply to their rhetorical question: *Soviet Socialism: A New Civilisation?* from Pius XI in *Divini Redemptoris*.

Re: Fabian-inspired Brain Trust on U.S. Trade Union movement, see *Fabian News*, November, 1943. The following names are listed as participating:

Bryn Roberts, British TU Delegate to the United States.
Stanley Ceizyk (member of International Association of Machinists Unions, AFL).
Hugh T. Mahoney (member of the U.S. Steel Workers Union, CIO).
Sam Berger (Labor Advisor to U.S. Mission for Economic Affairs).
Ernest Davies, M.P., son of A. E. Davies and disciple of Laski; one time editor of *The Clarion*.

The following names are those of Fabians who may be characterized as "old-timers" of the nineteen-twenties and nineteen-thirties. These names were gleaned from the *Fabian News* and *Fabian Society Annual Report*. Many will be recognized as well-known in fields not usually characterized as "Fabian." These are marked with an asterisk.

* Dr. Addison; Elections (*FSAR*)
Herbert Agar; New Fabian Group, 1930
R. Aldington; Fabian parliamentary candidate, 1930, J.P.
* Rt. Hon. L. S. Amery; Livingstone Hall lecturer, 1933
* Lord Arnold; Summer School, 1933
Oliver Baldwin; Fabian parliamentary candidate, 1929, Personal Notes, 1932, 1935, 1937
Professor Ernest Barker; Personal Notes, 1925, Kingsway Hall lecturer, 1928
* H. Granville Barker; *Fabian Society Annual Report*, 1919
* Mrs. R. Cavendish-Bentinck; Appeal by Hon. Treasurer, 1936
* J. D. Beresford; Fabian Summer Schools, 1930-1933
Annie Besant; King's Hall lecturer, 1919, Obit., 1933
Amber Reeves Blanco-White; Personal Notes, 1923, Summer School lecturer, 1936
* Margaret Bondfield; King's Hall lecturer, 1920, parliamentary candidate, 1920; President of Trades Union Congress, 1923, Fabian Women's Group, 1931
* C. Delisle Burns; Meetings of the Society, 1927, Kingsway Hall lecturer, 1927, Obit., 1934, Personal Notes, 1933

* Rt. Hon. Noel Buxton, M.P.; Meetings of the Society, 1924, General Election, 1929
* Percival Chubb; Personal Notes, 1923
* Arthur Clutton-Brock; 1924
Alderman A. Emil Davies, L.C.C.; Executive Committee, 1924 (ret.), 3rd week Summer School, 1925 (chairman), Executive Committee election, 1934
O. V. der Sprenkel; Annual Meeting, 1925, Fabian Summer School, 1930
* R. C. K. Ensor; King's Hall lecturer, 1919, Personal Notes, 1933
* St. John Ervine; Kingsway Hall, 1927, Personal Notes, 1934
Rowland Estcourt; Obit., 1934
* Dr. Letitia Fairfield; Lectures, 1919, Executive Committee, 1924 (ret.)
Lovat Fraser; Annual Meeting, 1925
F. W. Galton; Executive Committee, 1924 (ret.), 1925-26 FAR; Executive Committee Election, 1934, Development Fund, 1946
Dr. G. P. Gooch; Meetings of the Society, 1924, Essex Hall lecturer, 1929, Livingstone Hall lecturer, 1938
* Rt. Hon. Arthur Greenwood, M.P.; General Election, 1924, Meeting of the Society, 1926, Kingsway Hall lecturer, 1929
Major Haden Guest, M.P.; Executive Committee, Council elections, 1919; 1924 (ret.), Kingsway Hall lecturer, 1924, General Elections, 1924, Summer School committee, 1925 (chairman), Fabian parliamentary candidate, 1934, Personal Notes, 1934
* Grace Hadow; Fabian Women's Group, 1924
Charlotte Haldane; Fabian Women's Group, 1929, Fabian Nursery Dance, 1938
Elizabeth Haldane; Fabian Women's Group, 1930
* Rt. Hon. Viscount Haldane; Obit., 1928, (OM)
Captain Basil Hall; Executive Committee, 1924 (ret.) 2nd week Summer School (chairman) 1925; Executive Committee Election, 1934, Fabian Summer School, 1934
* Professor Duncan Hall; Personal Notes, 1926
Mary Agnes Hamilton; Fabian Summer School, 1929, Fabian Women's Group, 1930, Personal Notes, 1933
* J. L. and Barbara Hammond; Personal Notes, 1926
* Professor Lancelot Hogben; Autumn lecturer, 1936, Summer School, 1942
Hubert Humphreys; (Not to be confused with the American Hubert Humphrey.) Caucus-Labour Party Conference, 1955
Helen Keynes; Summer School, 1927, Executive Committee Election, 1934, Livingstone Hall lecturer, 1937
Dr. Hans Kohn; Personal Notes, 1926, 1934, 1937; Fabian Summer School, 1933
* Rt. Hon. G. Lansbury; General Election, 1924, Personal Notes, 1930, 1935
Professor A. D. Lindsay; Kingsway Hall lecturer, 1926
Kenneth Lindsay; Summer School lecturer, 1928
Mrs. C. L'Estrange Malone; Executive Committee Election, 1933, Women's Group Meeting, 1942

S. F. Markham, M.P., B.A., B. Litt.; General Election, 1929, Personal Notes, 1930

Oswald Mosley, M.P.; Kingsway Hall lecturer, 1924, Livingstone Hall lecturer, 1931

H. T. Muggeridge; Fabian parliamentary candidate, 1934, Personal Notes, 1935

J. T. Walton Newbold; Personal Notes, 1929

J. F. Oakeshott, (father of Professor Michael Oakeshott, who is not a Fabian); Personal Notes, 1922

* Lord Olivier; Kingsway Hall, 1927, Personal Notes, 1933

E. R. Pease; Executive Committee, 1924 (ret.), Publicist, 1925, Annual Meeting, 1927

* Lord Ponsonby; Livingstone Hall lecturer, 1931, Summer School, 1935

H. S. Rowntree; Fabian parliamentary candidate, 1929

* Bertrand Russell; Kingsway Hall lecturer, 1924, 1926, 1930, 1934; Autumn lecturer, 1937

Sir Arthur Salter; Friends Hall lecturer, 1937

Professor G. Salvemini; FAR, 1929

John Scurr, M.P.; General Election, 1924, Personal Notes, 1925, 1930; London County Council Election, 1931, Obit., 1932

Clarence Senior; Personal Notes, 1929 (USA)

Harry Snell, M.P., L.C.C.; Executive Committee, 1924, (ret.), 1925-26, FAR, 1936, Executive Committee Elections, 1931, 1934, (Lord Plumstead)

* Wickham Steed; Autumn lecturer, 1936

F. L. Stevens; (Clarion) Personal Notes, 1930, Fabian parliamentary candidate, 1935

Hannen Swaffer; Summer School, 1931

Sir Raymond Unwin; Personal Notes, 1919, Autumn lecturer, 1935

Professor Graham Wallas; King's Hall lecturer, 1921, General Election, 1924; Kingsway Hall lecturer, 1930, Obit., 1932

William English Walling; Summer School, 1929

Rebecca West; Kingsway Hall lecturer, 1929

Ellen Wilkinson; Fabian Women's Group, 1930, Stop Press, 1947

* P. Lamartine Yates; Fabian Summer School, 1942

The following names are those of Fabians who in the nineteen-forties and nineteen-fifties contributed to the work of the Society notably enough to be reported in *Fabian News* and *Fabian Journal*, in *New Fabian Essays*, in pamphlets, lectures on the Colonial Bureau and the International Bureau.

Mark Abrams; Publicist, 1952,-53,-55, Summer School lecturer, 1951-54

Dorothy Archibald; Fabian May School, 1946, Election of the Executive Committee, 1946

Dr. Alexander Baykov; International Affairs Group, 1941

Anthony Wedgwood Benn, M.P.; Kingsway Hall lecturer, 1932, Friends Hall lecturer, 1937, Com. of the House 14-day work, 1956, Chairman, International Bureau, 1962-63

Helen C. Bentwich, L.C.C.; Livingstone Hall lecturer, 1938, "Recreation in a Machine Age" lecture, 1942

Geoffrey Bing, M.P.; Autumn lecturer, 1947

Professor P. M. S. Blackett; Jubilee lecturer, 1946, Retiring Executive Attendance Record, 1947

Don Bowers; T. U. C., Central London Fabian Society speaker

Christopher Boyd, M.P.; Local Societies Committee, 1954-55, (Retain death penalty)

Wilfred Brown; Co-oped to E. C., 1954, Publicist, 1956

W. A. Burke, M.P.; Trades Unions' Section, NEC (LAB) 1955

Lord Campion; Clerk of House of Commons, Easter School lecturer, 1955

Barbara Castle, M.P.; Summer School lecturer, 1953, Constituency Organisations' Section NEC, (LAB) 1955

A. J. Champion, M.P.; Summer School, 1953

Walter M. Citrine; Kingsway Hall lecturer, 1933

J. Cooper; Trades Unions' Section, NEC (LAB) 1955

Freda Corbett; Socialist Propaganda Committee, 1941

Geoffrey de Freitas, M.P.; Summer School, 1952, Director, 1953; New Year School Director, 1954

John Diamond; Hon. Treasurer of Fabian Society, 1952,-54,-55,-56, Finance and General Purposes Committee, 1952, 70th Anniversary Reception, 1954, Chairman, 1955

Rt. Hon. John Dugdale, M.P.; Colonial Advisory Committee, 1952,-54,-55, One day School, 1953

Andrew Filson; Stop Press, 1947, Research Programme, 1947

Herman Finer, D. Sc.; Personal Notes, 1924, Executive Committee Election, 1937, (Professor, University of Chicago)

Michael Foot, M.P.; Fabian Colonial Bureau Committee Debate, 1947

Hugh Franklin; Socialist Propaganda Committee, 1941

Tom Fraser; Committee of the Parliamentary Labour Party, 1956

Herta Gotthelf; International Bureau, 1948

C. W. W. Greenidge; Colonial Bureau, 1952,-54,-55

Anthony Greenwood, M.P.; Constituency Organisations' Section NEC (LAB), 1955

R. J. Gunter; Trades Unions' Section NEC (LAB) 1955

Margaret Herbison, M.P.; Women's Lecture Group, 1947, NEC (LAB) 1955

John Hynd, M.P.; Colonial Bureau Advisory Committee, 1952,-54,-55, Weekend School, 1952

Douglas Jay, M.P.; Elections, 1947, Autumn lectures, 1947

Sybil Jeger; Personal Notes, 1937, Local Societies and School and Socials Committee, 1952

Carol Johnson; Colonial Bureau Advisory Committee, 1952-1955

R. W. G. Mackay, M.P.; Summer School, 1949

Compton Mackenzie; Shaw Society, 1946

Hector McNeil; Socialist Propaganda Committee, 1941, Obit., 1955

G. R. Mitchison, M.P., Q.C.; Married to Naomi Haldane, Essayist, 1952

Fred Mulley, M.P.; Summer School lecturer, 1953, Local Societies Committee, 1954-55

B. Nicholls; Colonial Bureau Advisory Committee, 1954-55

Maurice Orbach; Middlesex Committee lecturer, 1947

Michael Pease; Publicist, 1949

Phillips Price, M.P.; Retain death penalty, 1956

Sybil Prinsky; Local Society News, 1947, Regional News, 1947

Dr. Victor Purcell; Speaker at International and Colonial Bureau Conference, 1952, Publicist

J. W. Raisin; Northwest London Fabian Societies, 1946, Local Societies Committee, 1952,-54,-55

Kenneth Rose; Annual General Meeting, 1954

Solly Sachs; Summer School, 1953

Eve Saville; Research and Publications Assistant, 1952

Hilda Selwyn-Clarke; Secretary of the Colonial Bureau, 1955, Assistant Secretary, 1953-1955

Sydney Silverman, M.P.; Easter School lecturer, 1956

F. W. Skinnard; Colonial Bureau Advisory Committee, 1952,-54,-55, Publicist, 1955

R. W. Sorensen, M.P.; Colonial Bureau Advisory Committee, 1952, Vice chairman, 1954-55

Jack Tanner; President of T. U. C., Speaker at 70th Anniversary Reception, 1954

Sybil Thorndike; Shaw Society, 1946

Evelyn Walkden, M.P.; Socialist Propaganda Committee, 1941

H. W. Wallace; Colonial Bureau Advisory Committee, 1952,-54,-55

W. N. Warbey, M.P.; Summer School, 1949

W. P. Watkins; Colonial Bureau Advisory Committee, 1954-55

A. Wedgwood-Benn; Autumn lecturer, 1935, Colonial Bureau Advisory Committee, 1954-55

D. Widdicombe; International Bureau Advisory Committee, 1952

Ronald Williams, M.P.; Colonial Bureau Advisory Committee, 1952,-54,-55; Summer School, 1954, Publicist, 1955

H. V. Wiseman; Summer School, 1952

G. D. N. Worswick; May School, 1946, European Recovery, 1949

Michael Young; Retiring Executive Attendance Record, 1947, Summer School lecturer, 1951, Easter School lecturer, 1954

AMERICAN PUBLICISTS MENTIONED WITH APPROVAL IN BRITISH FABIAN SOCIALIST PUBLICATIONS

Joseph and Stewart Alsop; 1956

Max Beloff; 1956 *American Foreign Policy*

Henry Steele Commager

Professor P. Sargent Florence

S. Glover

John Gunther; 1956

John Herling

Mark DeWolfe Howe

George F. Kennan; American Diplomacy, 1900-1950

Harry W. Laidler; Personal Notes, 1932

Dr. Margaret Mead; Weekend

Colonial Conference lecturer, 1942

T. A. Oxley; Travel slides on U.S.A., 1955

Eleanor Roosevelt

Arthur Schlesinger, Jr.; 1954

Rudolf Schlesinger; Weekend School lecturer, 1953

Joseph Schumpeter

Albert Schweitzer

D. C. Sommervell

Mark Starr; 1955 *Creeping Socialism*

Adlai Stevenson; 1955

Harry S. Truman; 1956

David Williams; 1947 *Fabian Journal*

John G. Winant; Luncheon, 1941

Elaine Windrich; 1956, Essayist, 1955

Ella Winter; Personal Notes, 1924

BRITISH PUBLICISTS MENTIONED WITH APPROVAL IN BRITISH FABIAN SOCIALIST PUBLICATIONS

Timothy Bankole; 1956, *Kwame Nkrumah*

Vernon Bartlett; 1955, Autumn lecturer, 1937

Professor Norman Bentwich; 1953

Aneurin Bevan; 1954, Autumn lecturer, 1942

Lord Beveridge; 1949

D. W. Brogan; 1955

Ivor Brown

Dean of Canterbury; *Eastern Europe in the Socialist World*

Lord Chorley; 1956, Essayist, 1954-55

Isaac Deutscher; Weekend School lecturer, 1953

Maurice Dobb; 1955

Arnold Forster; 1947

R. K. Gardiner; *The Development of Social Administration*

George Godfrey; 1955, Chairman of the Fabian Society of New South Wales

Michael Greenberg; *British Trade and the Opening of China*, 1952

Dr. John Hammond; International Bureau, 1943

John Hatch; Colonial Bureau Advisory Committee, 1954-55, Commonwealth Officer of Labour Party, 1956, Publicist, 1956

J. A. Hobson; 1954

Lord Ismay; 1955

James Avery Joyce; 1955

H. O. Judd; *The Development of Social Administration*

Michael Lindsay; 1947

Rene MacColl; *Just Back from Russia: 77 Days Inside the Soviet Union*

Jules Moch; *Human Folly: To Disarm or Perish?*

H. J. P. Mortishead; 1946

Malcolm Muggeridge; Easter School lecturer, 1955

D. L. Munby; 1953-54, Essayist, 1952

J. F. Northcott; 1953-1955

J. Boyd Orr

George Padmore; *Gold Coast Revolution*

Raymond Postgate; 1955, Retiring Executive Attendance Record, 1947

J. B. Priestley; 1947

Isobel Ryans

Viscount Samuel; *The Good Citizen*

W. H. Scott; 1955

Professor Hugh Seton-Watson; 1953, International Bureau Advisory Committee, 1954-55

Leo Silberman; 1956

Lord Simon of Wythenshawe; 1955

Derrick Sington; Essayist, 1953-1955

Stephen Spender; 1942 Weekend Education Conference

Leslie C. Stevens; *Life in Russia*

A. J. P. Taylor; 1955, Summer School lecturer, 1955

Morgan Thomson; Editor of *Forward*, Speaker, 1952

Peter Townsend; 1955-56, Home Research Committee, 1954-55

Arnold Toynbee; 1956, Kingsway Hall lecturer, 1926

Veronica Toynbee; Easter School lecturer, 1954, 70th Anniversary Reception, 1954

Barbara Ward (Lady Jackson)

Barbara Wooton; *The Social Foundations of Wage Policy*, Retiring Executive, 1942, 1954

The following members of the London Fabian Society were selected from about five hundred cards as representing Fabians who have given conspicuous service to the Society, judging by the citations in *Fabian News, Fabian Journal* and *Fabian Society Annual Report.*

Sir Richard Aucland, M.P.
 Livingstone Hall Lectures, 1937
 Guest of honor at luncheon, 1942
 Colonial Bureau Advisory Committee, 1952
 Speaker at Colonial Bureau Meeting, 1952
 Publicist
Brian Abel-Smith
 Essayist, 1955
 Executive Committee, 1954-55
 Weekend School lecturer, 1956
 Publicist, 1956
Austen Albu, M.P.
 Retiring Executive Attendance Record, 1946
 Summer School, 1949
 Essayist, 1952
 Finance and General Purposes Committee, 1952
 Publicist, 1953, 1954
 Chairman, Annual General Meeting, 1954
 Chairman, Society, 1954
 Executive Committee, 1952-1956
 Attended 70th Anniversary Reception, 1954
 Home Research Committee, 1955
 Speaker at Central London Fabian Society
Rt. Hon. Clement R. Attlee, M.P.
 Council Elections, 1919

Personal Notes, 1922, 1934
General Election, 1924
Jubilee Rally, 1946
Essayist, 1952
Publicist, 1954
Speaker at 70th Anniversary Reception, 1954
Leader of the Parliamentary Party, 1955
Resigned as Leader Parliamentary Labour, 1956
Dr. Thomas Balogh
 Fabian Weekend School lecturer, 1952
 Autumn School lecturer, 1952
 Executive Committee, 1952-1956
 Home Research Committee, 1952, 1954-55
 Publicist, 1954, 1956
 Essayist, 1956
 Economic Adviser to the Maltese Government, 1956
Dr. N. Barou
 Summer School, 1942
 Retiring Executive Attendance Record, 1947
 Current Publications, 1948
 Welsh Council of Fabian Societies, 1949
 Summer School, 1949
 Summer School lecturer, 1951
 Local Societies Committee, 1952

Weekend School, 1953 (Director)
70th Anniversary Reception, 1954
Publicist, 1953-1956
Speaker International Bureau Conference on German Rearmament, 1954
Essayist, 1955-56
Editor, *Fabian International Review*, 1955

Speaker at London Labour Party Conference Tea, 1955
Parliamentary Labour Party Committee, 1956
Konni Zilliacus
Meetings, 1942, 1949 (International Luncheon)
Executive Committee Elections, 1946
Summer School, 1949, 1952

[Copied from the Fabian Society Annual Report 1962-63]
EXECUTIVE COMMITTEE 1962/1963

The following are the results of the Annual Ballot certified to the General Secretary by the Chief Scrutineer:

Elected

A. Wedgwood Benn
B. Abel-Smith
P. Townsend
R. H. S. Crossman
Mary Stewart
H. D. Hughes
C. A. R. Crosland
A. Skeffington
J. Parker

T. Balogh
W. T. Rodgers
P. Shore
H. J. Boyden
John Hughes
R. Neild
Betty Vernon
S. Hatch

Co-Options

Under Rule 9 of the Society's Rules, the Executive Committee has co-opted the following five members: Jeremy Bray, M.P.; John Greve; John Vaizey; Rex Winsbury; Richard Bone.

Honorary Officers

The Executive Committee elected the following to serve for 1962/1963: Chairman, Mary Stewart; Vice Chairman, Brian Abel-Smith; Honorary Secretary, John Parker, M.P.

Mary Stewart, who is Chairman of the East London Juvenile Court and co-author of two Fabian pamphlets, has been a member of the committee for 13 years. Brian Abel-Smith has served continuously since 1955, and John Parker has been Honorary Secretary since 1954. John Diamond, M.P., was returned unopposed as Honorary Treasurer for the thirteenth time in the Annual Ballot.

THE LABOUR PARTY GOVERNMENT
AS OF OCTOBER, 1964.

This list appeared in the November-December, 1964 issue of *Fabian News*, with the following notation:

* A member of the Cabinet.
† A member of the National Fabian Society.

Agriculture, Fisheries and Food—Minister: *† Frederick Peart.
 Joint Parliamentary Secretaries: James H. Hoy, † John Mackie.
Aviation—Minister: † Roy Jenkins.
 Parliamentary Secretary: † John Stonehouse.
 Ministers of State: George Darling, † E. C. Redhead, Roy Mason.
 Parliamentary Secretary: † Lord Rhodes.
Colonies—Secretary of State: *† Anthony Greenwood.
 Under-Secretaries of State: † Lord Taylor, † Eirene White.
Commonwealth Relations—Secretary of State: *† A. G. Bottomley.
 Minister of State: Cledwyn Hughes.
 Under-Secretary of State: † Lord Taylor.
Defense—Secretary of State: *† Denis Healey.
 Deputy Secretary of State and Minister of Defense for the Army: † Frederick Mulley.
 Minister of Defense for the Royal Navy: †Christopher Mayhew.
 Minister of Defense for the Royal Air Force: Lord Shackleton.
 Under-Secretary of State for Defense for the Royal Navy: † J. P. W. Mallalieu.
 Under-Secretary of State for Defense for the Army: G. W. Reynolds.
 Under-Secretary of State for Defense for the Royal Air Force: † Bruce Millan.
Duchy of Lancaster—Chancellor: *† Douglas Houghton.
Economic Affairs—Minister: *† George Brown.
 Joint Under-Secretaries of State: † Maurice Foley, † W. T. Rodgers.
Education and Science—Secretary of State: *† Michael Stewart.
 Ministers of State: † Lord Bowden. † R. E. Prentice.
 Joint Under-Secretaries of State: † James Boyden, Denis Howell.
Foreign Affairs—Secretary of State: *† Patrick Gordon Walker.
 Ministers of State: Lord Caradon, Alun Gwynne-Jones, † G. M. Thomson, W. E. Padley.
 Under-Secretary of State: † Lord Walston.
Health—Minister: † Kenneth Robinson.
 Parliamentary Secretary: † Sir Barnett Stross.
Home Department—Secretary of State: * Sir Frank Soskice.
 Minister of State: Alice Bacon.
 Joint Under-Secretaries of State: Lord Stonham, George Thomas.
Housing and Local Government—Minister: *† R. H. S. Crossman.
 Joint Parliamentary Secretaries: † James MacColl, † R. J. Mellish.

Labour—Minister: *† Ray Gunter.
Joint Parliamentary Secretaries: † Richard Marsh, Ernest Thornton.
Land and Natural Resources—Minister: † Frederick Willey.
Joint Parliamentary Secretaries: † Lord Mitchison, † Arthur Skeffington.
Law Officers—Attorney-General: † Elwyn Jones.
Lord Advocate: George Gordon Stott.
Solicitor-General: Dingle Foot.
Solicitor-General for Scotland: James Graham Leechman.
Lord Chancellor: * Lord Gardiner.
Lord President of the Council: * Herbert Bowden.
Lord Privy Seal: *† Earl of Longford.
Ministers without Portfolio: † Eric Fletcher, Lord Champion.
Overseas Development—Minister: *† Barbara Castle.
Parliamentary Secretary: † A. E. Oram.
Paymaster-General: George Wigg.
Pensions and National Insurance—Minister: † Margaret Herbison.
Joint Parliamentary Secretaries: † Harold Davies, Norman Pentland.
Post Office—Postmaster-General: † Anthony Wedgwood Benn.
Assistant Postmaster-General: Joseph Slater.
Power—Minister: *† Frederick Lee.
Parliamentary Secretary: John Morris.
Public Building and Works—Minister: † Charles Pannell.
Parliamentary Secretary: Jennie Lee.
Scotland—Secretary of State: * William Ross.
Minister of State: E. G. Willis.
Under-Secretaries of State: Judith Hart, Lord Hughes, J. Dickson Mabon.
Technology—Minister: * Frank Cousins.
Parliamentary Secretary: Lord Snow.
Trade, Board of—President: *† Douglas Jay.
Transport—Minister: *† Thomas Fraser.
Joint Parliamentary Secretaries: † Lord Lindgren, † Stephen Swingler.
Treasury—Prime Minister and First Lord of the Treasury: *† Harold Wilson.
Chancellor of the Exchequer: *† James Callaghan
Chief Secretary: † John Diamond.
Parliamentary Secretary: Edward Short.
Economic Secretary: † Anthony Crosland.
Financial Secretary: † Niall MacDermot.
Lords Commissioners: G. H. R. Rogers, George Lawson, John McCann,
† Ivor Davies, † Harriet Slater.
Wales—Secretary of State: *† James Griffiths.
Minister of State: Goronwy Roberts.
Under-Secretary of State: Harold Finch.
Her Majesty's Household—Treasurer: Sydney Irving.
Comptroller: Charles Grey
Vice-Chamberlain: William Whitlock.
Captain of the Honorable Corps of Gentlemen-at-Arms: Lord Shepherd.
Lord in Waiting: Lord Hobson.

Certain names, long identified with the Fabian Society, were not specifically noted as members—as, for instance, Lord Gardiner, formerly on the Fabian Executive; or Jennie Lee, widow of Harold Wilson's former chief, Aneurin Bevan. Similarly, Alice Bacon—not starred on the above list—was named in *Fabian News*, September, 1957, as a member of the Leeds local of the Fabian Society. Under the heading, "The General Election," the same issue November-December, 1964 of *Fabian News* (pp. 2-3) also contained the following comments, which can be regarded as official:

Cabinet

The Prime Minister, Harold Wilson, was Chairman of the Society in 1954-55 and for many years a member of the Executive Committee. The Minister of Housing, Dick Crossman, joint editor of *New Fabian Essays*, only retired from the Executive Committee last year after many years service. Lord Gardiner, Patrick Gordon Walker, James Griffiths, Douglas Houghton, Lord Longford and Michael Stewart are all former members of the Executive Committee. Denis Healey was chairman of the International Bureau, Arthur Bottomley sat on the Commonwealth Subcommittee, James Callaghan on the Home Research Committee, and Barbara Castle, the Minister for Overseas Development, has been actively associated with the Society's Commonwealth research.

Other Ministers

Outside the cabinet, Roy Jenkins, the Minister for Aviation, was Chairman of the Society 1957-1958. Anthony Wedgwood Benn, the Postmaster-General, is the Society's new Vice Chairman and is Chairman of the International and Commonwealth Bureau, Anthony Crosland the Economic Secretary to the Treasury, was Chairman in 1961-62. Other active Fabians are George Thomson, Chairman of *Venture* Editorial Board, who has now become Minister of State at the Foreign Office, and Christopher Mayhew, who is an ex-employee.

Junior Appointments

Nearly half the remaining more junior appointments have also gone to members of the Society. Among them, Eirene White, Chairman 1958-59, becomes Parliamentary Secretary at the Colonial Office; H. J. Boyden, one of the hardest working members of the Executive and Vice-Chairman of Local Societies Committee, becomes Joint Parliamentary Secretary of State for Education and Science. Dick Mitchison, who recently went to the House of Lords, becomes Parliamentary Secretary, Ministry of Land and Natural Resources. He was Treasurer of the New Fabian Research Bureau for six years. John Mackie and Lord Walston, who once wrote a Fabian pamphlet on agriculture together, receive appointments in the Ministry of Agriculture and the Foreign Office respectively.

Fabians will have been particularly pleased to hear about the appointments of Bill Rodgers, John Diamond and Arthur Skeffington, who have been so long associated with the work of the Society as General Secretary, Honorary Treasurer, and Chairman of the Local Societies Committee respectively. Bill Rodgers and another Fabian, Maurice Foley, become Joint Parliamentary Under-Secretaries in the Department of Economic Affairs. John Diamond becomes Chief Secretary at the Treasury, and Arthur Skeffington becomes Parliamentary Secretary, Ministry of Land and Natural Resources. Richard Marsh, who joined the Executive Committee last year, becomes a Parliamentary Secretary at the Ministry of Labour.

The following boxed item in the same historic issue of *Fabian News* may also be pertinent:

EXECUTIVE COMMITTEE

The Executive Committee, at its meeting on November 3rd, received with regret the resignations from the Committee of Thomas Balogh and Robert Neild, consequent upon their appointments as Economic Advisers to the Cabinet Office and the Treasury respectively.

Thomas Balogh also resigned his position as Vice-Chairman of the Society. Anthony Wedgwood Benn was appointed Vice-Chairman to succeed him.

THE NEW LABOUR GOVERNMENT

(from *FABIAN NEWS*, Vol. 77, Nos. 4/5 April/May 1966)

Agriculture, Fisheries and Food—Minister: *† Frederick Peart.
　Joint Parliamentary Secretaries—James H. Hoy. † John Mackie.
Aviation—Minister: † Fred Mulley.
　Parliamentary Secretary—Julian Snow.
Colonies—Secretary of State; *† Fred Lee.
　Under-Secretaries of State—† Lord Beswick, †John Stonehouse.
Commonwealth Relations—Secretary of State: *† A. G. Bottomley.
　Minister of State—Judith Hart.
　Under-Secretary of State—† Lord Beswick.
Defence—Secretary of State: *† Denis Healey.
　Minister of Defence for the Army—Gerry Reynolds.
　Minister of Defence for the Royal Navy—† J. P. W. Mallalieu.
　Minister of Defence for the Royal Air Force—Lord Shackleton.
　Under-Secretary of State for Defence for the Royal Navy—† Lord Winterbottom.
　Under-Secretary of State for Defence for the Army—† David Ennals.
　Under-Secretary of State for Defence for the Royal Air Force—† Merlyn Rees.
Duchy of Lancaster—Chancellor: † George Thomson.
Economic Affairs—Minister: *† George Brown.
　Minister of State: † Austen Albu.
　Under-Secretary of State: † W. T. Rodgers.
Education and Science—Secretary of State: *† Anthony Crosland.
　Ministers of State—† Edward Redhead. † Goronwy Roberts.
　Joint Under-Secretaries of State—Denis Howell, Jennie Lee.
Foreign Affairs—Secretary of State: *† Michael Stewart.
　Ministers of State—† Lord Caradon, Lord Chalfont, † Eirene White, W. E. Padley.
　Under-Secretary of State—† Lord Walston.
Health—Minister: † Kenneth Robinson.
　Parliamentary Secretary—Charles Loughlin.
Home Department—Secretary of State—*† Roy Jenkins.
　Minister of State—Alice Bacon.
　Joint Under-Secretaries of State—† Lord Stonham, †Maurice Foley, † Dick Taverne.

Housing and Local Government—Minister: °† R. H. S. Crossman.
  Joint Parliamentary Secretaries—† James MacColl, † R. J. Mellish.
Labour—Minister: °† Ray Gunter.
  Parliamentary Secretary—† Shirley Williams.
Land and Natural Resources—Minister: † Frederick Willey.
  Parliamentary Secretary—† Arthur Skeffington.
Law Officers—Attorney General: † Elwyn Jones.
  Lord Advocate—George Gordon Stott.
  Solicitor-General—Dingle Foot.
  Solicitor-General for Scotland—H. S. Wilson.
Lord Chancellor—° Lord Gardiner.
Lord President of the Council—° Herbert Bowden.
Lord Privy Seal—°† Earl of Longford.
Ministers without Portfolio—°† Douglas Houghton. † Lord Champion.
Overseas Development—Minister: °† Anthony Greenwood.
  Parliamentary Secretary—† A. E. Oram.
Paymaster-General—George Wigg.
Pensions and National Insurance—Minister: † Margaret Herbison.
  Joint Parliamentary Secretaries—† Harold Davies, Norman Pentland.
Post Office—Postmaster-General: † Anthony Wedgwood Benn.
  Assistant Postmaster-General—Joseph Slater.
Power—Minister: °† Richard Marsh.
  Parliamentary Secretary—† Jeremy Bray.
Public Building and Works—Minister: †Reginald Prentice.
  Parliamentary Secretary—† H. J. Boyden.
Scotland—Secretary of State: ° William Ross.
  Minister of State—E. G. Willis.
  Under-Secretaries of State—Lord Hughes, † Bruce Millan, J. Dickson
    Mabon.
Technology—Minister: ° Frank Cousins.
  Joint Parliamentary Secretaries—† Edmund Dell, † Peter Shore.
Trade, Board of—President: °† Douglas Jay.
  Ministers of State—George Darling, † Lord Brown, Roy Mason.
  Parliamentary Secretary—† Lord Rhodes.
Transport—Minister: °† Barbara Castle.
  Joint Parliamentary Secretaries—† Stephen Swingler, John Morris.
Treasury—Prime Minister and First Lord of the Treasury: °† Harold Wilson.
  Chancellor of the Exchequer—°† James Callaghan.
  Chief Secretary—† John Diamond.
  Parliamentary Secretary—Edward Short.
  Financial Secretary—† Niall MacDermot.
  Lords Commissioners—† Alan Fitch, J. Harper, W. Howie, George Law-
    son. William Whitlock.
  Assistant Whips—Edward Bishop, Ronald Brown, H. Gourlay, Walter
    Harrison, Neil McBride, Charles Morris, Brian O'Malley,
Wales—Secretary of State: ° Cledwyn Hughes.
  Minister of State—† George Thomas.
  Under-Secretary of State—† Ifor Davies.

Her Majesty's Household—Treasurer: John Silkin.
  Comptroller: Charles Grey.
  Vice-Chamberlain—John McCann.
  Captain of the Honourable Corps of Gentlemen-at-Arms—† Lord Shepherd.
  Captain of the Yeomen of the Guard—† Lord Bowles.
  Lords in Waiting—Lord Hilton, † Lord Sorensen.
  Baroness in Waiting: Lady Phillips.
          NOTES: * A member of the Cabinet.
                  † A member of the Fabian Society.

APPENDIX II

PARTIAL RECORD OF PAST AND PRESENT "COOPERATORS,"
AS LISTED BY THE [AMERICAN] LEAGUE FOR INDUSTRIAL
DEMOCRACY ON THE OCCASION OF ITS 50TH ANNIVERSARY*
(This list appeared in the Congressional Record of October 12, 1962, origi-
nally prepared by Mina Weisenberg for the 50th Anniversary of the LID)

* further abbreviations added

Some Leaders of College Chapters:

Walter R. Agard, Pres., Amherst ISS, 1914-15; Prof. of Classics, U. of Wisc.;
Pres., American Classical League.

James W. Alexander, former Pres., Princeton ISS; Exec. Com. and Treas.,
ISS, 1920-21; noted mathematician.

Devere Allen, former Pres., Oberlin ISS; Bd. of Dir., LID, 1939-1944; Dir.
and Ed., Worldover Press.

Harold Arnold, Wesleyan ISS; late Director of Research, Bell Telephone
Laboratories (dec.).

Gregory Bardacke, former student leader, Syracuse U. LID; Bd. of Dir.,
LID 1955——; Director, American Trade Union Comm. for Histadrut.

Murray Baron, Member, Brooklyn Law School SLID; Bd. of Dir., LID,
1940——; Public Relations Consultant; Ch., Manhattan Liberal Party.

Thomas S. Behre, Sec., Harvard ISS; New Orleans businessman, active in
liberal movements (dec.).

Daniel Bell, member SLID; Bd. of Dir., LID, 1948——; Labor Ed.,
Fortune Magazine; author; economist.

John K. Benedict, member Union Theological Seminary SLID; formerly
Field Sec., LID.

Walter Bergman, formerly of Michigan ISS; Dir. of Research, Detroit Public
Schools.

Otto S. Beyer, former Pres., U. of Illinois ISS; 1917; labor arbitrator and
consultant; former Ch., National Mediation Bd., (dec.).

Andrew J. Biemiller, former Sec., U. of Pa. and Philadelphia Chaps. LID,
1928-1932; Congressman, 1944-1956; Legislative Comm., AFL.

Carroll Binder, Pres., 1916, Harvard ISS; Editorial Ed. Minneapolis
Tribune.

George H. Bishop, officer U. of Michigan ISS, 1911; faculty, Washington U.
(St. Louis).

Hillman M. Bishop, former Pres., Columbia SLID; Assoc. Prof. of Government, C.C.N.Y.

Julius S. Bixler, former Sec., Amherst ISS; Pres., Colby College.

Bruce Bliven, Pres., Stanford ISS, 1910-1912; Editorial Dir., *New Republio*.

Hyman H. Bookbinder, former student leader, SLID; former N.Y. Exec. Com., LID; political researcher, CIO.

Randolph Bourne, former Columbia ISS; essayist (dec.).

Leroy E. Bowman, Bd. of Dir., LID, 1940——; Field Sec., 1940-41; Assoc. Prof. of Sociology, Brooklyn College.

Robert A. Brady, former U. of California SLID; economist.

Jerome Breslaw, N.Y.U. Chap., SLID; Ch., SLID 1954-55.

Paul F. Brissenden, U. of California ISS; Bd. of Dir., LID, 1923; Prof. of Economics, Columbia U.

Thomas Brooks, Harvard SLID; research staff, T.W.U.A.

Heywood Broun, a founder, Harvard Socialist Club, 1906; Bd. of Dir., LID, 1933-34; columnist; author (dec.).

George Cadbury, U. of Pa. SLID; Bd. of Dir., LID, 1953——; economic consultant.

Maurice S. Calman, organizer of ISS Chap., N.Y. School of Dentistry (1911) and N.Y.U. School of Law; former Socialist Alderman, N.Y.C.; past Pres., Harlem Dental Society.

Wallace J. Campbell, former Pres. U. of Oregon SLID; Bd. of Dir., LID, 1940, 1945-1948; National Council since 1948; Washington Representative, Cooperative League of U.S.A.

Jesse Cavileer, former Pres., Syracuse U. SLID; student Sec., SLID; Bd. of Dir., 1947-1949; National Council LID, 1949——; Unitarian Minister, Cleveland, Ohio.

Alice Cheyney, formerly Pres. Vassar ISS; labor economist.

E. Ralph Cheyney, Pres., U. of Pa. ISS; poet (dec.).

Evans Clark, Pres., Amherst ISS, 1910; Pres. and Vice Pres., ISS and LID, 1918-1923; Dir., Twentieth Century Fund, 1928-1953; editorial writer.

Everett R. Clinchy, member, Wesleyan SLID; Pres., National Council of Christians and Jews.

Ramon P. Coffman, formerly Yale SLID; founder of Uncle Ray Syndicate.

Felix S. Cohen, Pres., C.C.N.Y. LID, 1925-26; former Asst. Solicitor Dept. of Interior, in charge of Indian Affairs; author; teacher; lawyer (dec.). lecturer in Philosophy of Law, Yale, C.C.N.Y.; recipient of LID John Dewey Award, posthumous, 1954.

Cara Cook, Mt. Holyoke SLID; Bd. of Dir., LID, 1950——; Exec. Sec., N.Y. Ethical Culture Society.

Elmer Cope, Ohio Wesleyan SLID; labor economist.

Babette Deutsch, member, Barnard ISS, 1917; poet.

Leonard W. Doob, member, Dartmouth College SLID; Prof. of Psychology, Yale.

Paul H. Douglas, Pres., Columbia ISS, 1915; Exec. Com. ISS, 1915-16; economist; U.S. Senator.

Evelyn Dubrow, formerly N.J. College for Women SLID; Sec., N.Y. ADA.

Tilford Dudley, Wesleyan SLID; Asst. to Pres., PAC-CIO.

Ethan E. Edloff, formerly U. of Michigan ISS and Detroit LID; educator.
George Edwards, formerly Pres., Harvard SLID; former Field Sec., SLID; Judge of Court of Domestic Relations, Detroit.
Gustav Egloff, Pres., Cornell ISS, 1910-1912; leading American chemist.
Samuel A. Eliot, Jr., former Harvard ISS, 1912; Prof. of English, Smith College.
Herbert L. Elvin, Yale SLID; Dir., Dept. of Education, UNESCO.
Boris Emmet, officer, U. of Wisconsin ISS, 1911; labor statistician.
Abraham Epstein, former Pres. U. of Pittsburgh ISS; Bd. of Dir., LID, 1940-41; founder and former Sec., American Assoc. for Social Security; authority on Social Insurance (dec.).
Harold U. Faulkner, Wesleyan ISS, 1913; National Council, LID; Prof. of History, Smith College; authority on Economic History.
William M. Feigenbaum, founder, 1906, of Columbia U. ISS; newspaperman (dec.).
Samuel H. Fine, active in N.Y.U. SLID; former Ch., SLID; Bd. of Dir., 1952-1954; accountant, ILGWU.
Osmond Fraenkel, Pres. Columbia ISS 1910; N.Y. attorney; Counsil, ACLU.
Anna Caples Frank, Vassar SLID; former Membership Sec., LID; public relations counselor.
Isabelle B. Friedman, Hunter College ISS; Bd. of Dir., LID, 1951——; Pres. N.Y. Chapter, 1954-55; representative of LID at N.G.O. of UN.
Samuel H. Friedman, formerly leader C.C.N.Y. ISS Chap.; former Pres., N.Y. Chap., LID; Bd. of Dir., LID 1953——; Pres., Community and Social Agency Employees Union; Socialist leader.
Roland Gibson, formerly with Dartmouth College SLID; formerly, Bd. of Dir., LID; Political Scientist, U. of Illinois.
Louis Gollumb, leader C.C.N.Y. ISS, 1912; writer.
William Gomberg, C.C.N.Y. SLID Chap.; Dir., Management Engineering Dept. ILGWU.
John Temple Graves, officer, Princeton ISS, 1911; author, columnist, lecturer.
William Haber, U. of Wisconsin SLID; Prof. of Economics, U. of Michigan.
Robert Halpern, Pres. C.C.N.Y. Chap., LID; N.Y. attorney.
Elizabeth Healey, formerly Connecticut College; student Sec., SLID, 1947; social worker.
James Henle, Vice Pres., Columbia ISS; Vanguard Press, 1928-1952.
John Herling, formerly Harvard SLID; formerly active in Emergency Com. for Strikers Relief and in LID radio activities; ed., John Herling's Labor Letter.
Sidney Hertzberg, Wisconsin SLID; Bd. of Dir., LID, 1945——; writer; foreign correspondent.
Rene E. Hoguet, former Harvard Chap. ISS; former Pres., N.Y. Chap.; businessman.
Arthur N. Holcombe, Harvard Chap., ISS, 1906; Prof. of Government, Harvard; Pres., American Political Science Assoc., 1936.

Carroll Hollister, Amherst College, SLID; pianist.

Sidney Hook, Pres., C.C.N.Y. Chap., SLID, 1922-23; receiver, LID John Dewey Award, 1953; Ch., Dept. of Philosophy, N.Y.U.; author.

Harold Hutcheson, Yale SLID; Prof. of English, Lake Forest College.

Eugenia Ingerman, Sec., Barnard ISS, 1910; physician.

Morris Iushewitz, Milwaukee State Teachers College SLID; Bd. of Dir., LID, 1951——; Sec.-Treas., N.Y. City CIO Industrial Council.

Nicholas Kelley, charter member, Harvard ISS; Bd. of Dir., LID, 1912-1933; Vice Pres. and General Counsel, Chrysler Corp.

Murray Kempton, member LID Summer School, 1938; Bd. of Dir. and National Council, LID since 1951; columnist.

Freda Kirchwey, Sec. and Pres., Barnard ISS, 1912-1915; former Bd. of Dir., LID; pub., *The Nation.*

William Klare, officer U. of Michigan ISS, 1911; former Vice Pres. Statler Corp.

Maynard Krueger, U. of Pa. and Philadelphia Chap., LID 1928-1932; Prof. of Economics, U. of Chicago.

William Sargent Ladd, Amherst ISS; former Dean, Cornell Medical (dec.).

Harry W. Laidler, Founder, 1905, Wesleyan ISS; Bd. of Dir. of LID since 1905; Exec. Officer ISS-LID since 1910; author, economist, lecturer.

Joseph P. Lash, former Sec. SLID; UN Correspondent, New York *Post.*

John V. P. Lassoe, Jr., Yale SLID; Dir. of Adult Education, A.A.U.N.

William L. Leiserson, Pres. U. of Wisconsin ISS, 1907-08; Economist, former Ch. National Mediation Bd.

Daniel Lerner, formerly N.Y.U. SLID; author; authority on Psychology of Propaganda.

Max Lerner, Brookings Institution SLID at Washington U. (St. Louis); columnist; teacher; writer.

Aaron Levenstein, member, SLID; National Council, LID; Research Institute of America; author.

Grace Mendelsohn Levy, former Brooklyn College SLID and Sec., SLID; Staff, N. Y. C. Housing Authority.

Harold J. Lewack, officer, N.Y.U. LID; National Pres., SLID, 1954; labor educator.

John L. Lewine, Yale SLID; Exec. Com., N.Y. Chap; teacher; Sec., American Institute of France.

John F. Lewis, Jr., formerly U. of Pa. ISS; Philadelphia lawyer and civic reformer.

Marx Lewis, N.Y.U.-SLID; Bd. of Dir., LID, 1945——; Sec.-Treas., United Hat, Cap and Millinery Workers Union.

Walter Lippmann, Pres., Harvard Socialist Club, 1909-10; Exec. Com., ISS, 1911-12; columnist; author.

Karl N. Llewellyn, formerly Yale SLID; Prof. of Law, U. of Chicago; author.

Charlotte Tuttle Lloyd, former Pres., Vassar SLID; former attorney, Dept. of Interior.

Roger S. Loomis, formerly U. of Illinois ISS; Prof. of English Literature, Columbia U.

Jay Lovestone, Pres. C.C.N.Y. ISS; Dir., International Relations, ILGWU.

Isadore Lubin, former Pres., Clark and U. of Missouri ISS; labor statistician; Industrial Commissioner, N.Y. State.

Jerome Lubin, Brooklyn College SLID; former Ch., SLID; City Planner.

Charles Luckman, Sec., Kansas City Junior College SLID; former Pres., Lever Brothers; architect.

Ralph McCallister, member SLID; Dir., Program and Education, Chautauqua.

Arthur McDowell, U. of Pittsburgh; Staff, Upholsterers International Union of N. A.

Kenneth MacGowan, Pres., Harvard ISS, 1910-11; Prof. of Theater Arts, U.C.L.A.; dramatic critic; movie producer.

Charles A. Madison, Pres., U. of Michigan ISS; pub.; author.

Anita Marburg, Vassar ISS; educator.

Otto C. Marckwardt, adviser, U. of Michigan ISS, for many years; English Dept. U. of Michigan.

Will Maslow, active in SLID; Dir., Commission on Law and Social Action, American Jewish Congress.

Daniel Mebane, former Pres. U. of Indiana ISS; former Treas. and Pub., *New Republic.*

Kenneth Meiklejohn, former Swarthmore SLID; specialist in Labor Law.

Inez Milholland, Pres. Vassar ISS; lawyer (dec.).

Spencer Miller, Jr., Amherst ISS; former Sec., Workers Education Bureau and Asst. Sec. of Labor.

Hiram K. Moderwell, Sec. Harvard ISS, 1911; foreign correspondent; dramatic critic (dec.).

Emanuel Muravchik, member, SLID; Bd. of Dir., LID; Field Sec., Jewish Labor Com.

Margaret J. Naumberg, Pres. Barnard ISS, 1910; educator.

Leland Olds, formerly Amherst ISS; receiver of John Dewey Award, LID, 1953; former Ch., Federal Power Commission.

Samuel Orr, N.Y.U. ISS; Exec. Com., N.Y. Chap., 1954——; former Judge; labor lawyer.

Gus Papenek, formerly Cornell SLID; Ch., SLID, 1952; Agricultural Consultant, Pakistan.

Talcott Parsons, Sec., Amherst SLID, 1923-24; Prof. of Sociology, Harvard; author.

Selig Perlman, U. of Wisconsin ISS, 1909-10; Prof. of Economics, U. of Wisconsin; author.

Irving Phillips, formerly Harvard SLID; former Field Sec., SLID; Staff, ILGWU.

Richard Poethig, formerly Wooster SLID; former Sec., SLID; minister.

Justine Wise Polier, formerly Barnard SLID; Justice, Court of Domestic Relations, N.Y.C.

Paul R. Porter, formerly Kansas U. SLID; former Field Sec., LID; former Deputy Administrator, E.C.A., Europe; Pres., Porter International Corp.

Dorothy Psathas, Connecticut College SLID; Sec., SLID, 1951-52; public service.

Carl Raushenbush, Amherst, former Bd. of Dir., LID, National Council; labor consultant.

H. Stephen Raushenbush, Amherst ISS, 1916-17; Sec., LID; Com. on Coal and Power, 1926-1929; author; researcher, Public Affairs Institute.

Paul Raushenbush, former Amherst ISS; economist.

Victor G. Reuther, former Wayne U. SLID; Bd. of Dir., LID, 1950——; Asst. to Pres., CIO.

Walter P. Reuther, Founder and Pres., Wayne U. SLID, 1932; receiver of League's John Dewey Award, 1950; Pres., CIO; Pres., UAW-CIO.

John P. Roche, formerly Cornell SLID; Vice Pres., SLID; Bd. of Dir., 1948; Assoc. of Government, Haverford College.

Will Rogers, Jr., formerly Stanford U. SLID, 1934-35; ed., actor.

Lawrence Rogin, formerly Columbia U. SLID; Educational Dir., T.W.U.A.

Leonore Cohen Rosenfeld, formerly Mt. Holyoke College SLID; housewife.

Henry Rosner, formerly C.C.N.Y. SLID; Dir., Div. of Finance and Statistics, Welfare Dept., N. Y. C.

Harry Rubin, N.Y.U. SLID; Bd. of Dir., 1948-1952.

Morris H. Rubin, Wisconsin U. SLID; Ed., *Progressive* Magazine.

Raymond Rubinow, U. of Pa. SLID; consultant on International Relations.

David J. Saposs, Pres.-Sec., Wisconsin U. ISS, 1910; labor economist; author.

Emil Schlesinger, former Pres. C.C.N.Y. SLID; labor attorney.

Lawrence Seelye, Amherst ISS; former Pres., St. Lawrence U.

Clarence Senior, U. of Kansas SLID; Bd. of Dir., LID; receiver of John Dewey Award, 1953; sociologist; authority on Latin America.

Andre Shifrin, Yale Chap., 1954-55; Exec. Com., SLID.

William Shirer, formerly Sec., Coe College SLID; author; correspondent.

David Sinclair, Wisconsin U. SLID; formerly N.Y. Exec. Com.; physicist.

Albert J. Smallheiser, former Sec. Columbia ISS, 1911-12; Social Science teacher and active spirit in N.Y. Teachers Guild.

Tucker Smith, N.Y.U. ISS; economist.

Boris Stern, U. of Wisconsin ISS; Staff, U.S. Dept. of Labor.

Irving Stone, formerly officer, U. of So. Cal., SLID; novelist.

Monroe Sweetland, formerly Syracuse U. SLID; former Field Sec., SLID; National Council; Ed., Oregon *Democrat*.

Ordway Tead, Pres., Amherst ISS; 1911-12; Research Dir., LID, 1914-15; teacher; pub.; author; former Ch., Bd. of Higher Education, N.Y.C.

Lazar Teper, Johns Hopkins SLID; Research Dir., ILGWU.

Frank Trager, Johns Hopkins U. SLID; Bd. of Dir., LID, 1951——; former Dir., M.S.A., Burma; Prof. of Research, N.Y.U.

Gus Tyler, C.C.N.Y.-SLID; Political Dir., ILGWU.

Jerry Voorhis, formerly Yale SLID; Sec., Cooperative League of U.S.A.

Selman A. Waksman, Sec. Rutgers U. Chap., 1914-15; receiver of John Dewey Award, LID, 1953; co-discoverer of Streptomycin.

James Wechsler, Columbia SLID; Ed., New York *Post*.

Mina Weisenberg, Hunter College ISS; Bd. of Dir., 1954-55; Sec., N.Y. Chap. LID; Treas., N.Y. Teachers Guild, AFL; teacher of Social Studies.

Ray B. Westerfeld, Sec., Yale ISS; economist; banker.

Nathaniel Weyl, Columbia SLID; writer; economist.
Alvin G. Whitney, Pres., Yale ISS, 1910-11; publicist.
Elsie Gibson Whitney, Middlebury College ISS, 1914; publicist.
Simon W. Whitney, formerly Yale SLID; economist.
Paul Willen, founder Oberlin College SLID; writer.
Chester Williams, U.C.L.A.-SLID; writer; lecturer on International Relations.
David Williams, Pres., Marietta College ISS, 1909-10; Unitarian minister.
Frank Winn, formerly U. of Michigan SLID; Ed., *U.A.W.-C.I.O.* Magazine.
Theresa Wolfson, former President Adelphi College ISS; Bd. of Dir., LID, 1944——; receiver of LID John Dewey Award, 1945; Prof. of Economics, Brooklyn College; author.
James Youngdahl, Washington U. SLID; Field Sec., SLID Southwestern Organizer, A.C.-W.A.
Milton Zatinsky, former member SLID; labor economist.
Gertrude Folks Zimand, Pres., Vassar ISS, 1917; Sec., National Child Labor Com.

A Few Past and Present Cooperators:

Leonard D. Abbott, signer of call to ISS; ed., writer (dec.).
Charles Abrams, Bd. of Dir., LID, 1954-55; housing expert; N.Y. State Administrator of Rent Control, 1955.
Luigi Antonini, Bd. of Dir., LID since 1951; First Vice Pres., ILGWU.
Jesse Ashley, Exec. Com., ISS, 1912-13; 1917-18; N.Y. attorney; Prof. of Law; feminist (dec.).
George E. Axtelle, Bd. of Dir., LID, 1954-55; Prof. of Education, N.Y.U.
Fern Babcock, Bd. of Dir., LID, 1946-1955; Program Coordinator, National Council, Y.W.C.A.
George Backer, Bd. of Dir., LID since 1953; businessman; Ed.; former Pres., ORT.
Hope S. Bagger, Exec. Com., N.Y. Chap., LID; author.
Emily G. Balch, Exec. Com., ISS 1919-20; winner of Nobel Peace Prize (1946).
Roger Baldwin, Bd. of Dir., LID, 1920-1923; Dir., ACLU 1917-1952; Ch. of Bd., International League for the Rights of Man.
Angela Bambace, National Council, LID; Staff, Baltimore ILGWU.
Jack Barbash, Bd. of Dir., LID, 1947-1952; National Council since 1952; labor economist; author of "Taft-Hartley Act in Action."
Benjamin W. Barkas, former Ch., Philadelphia Chap., LID; labor educator.
Solomon Barkin, Bd. of Dir., LID since 1953; Dir. of Research, T.W.U.A.
Katrina McCormick Barnes, Bd. of Dir., LID since 1953; Pamphlet Sec. since 1953; Sec. ACLU.
John Bauer, Bd. of Dir., LID, 1938-1942; economist; writer; authority on Public Utilities; author, "America's Struggle for Electric Power."
Charles A. Beard, faculty sponsor ISS; historian.
Helen Marston Beardsley, National Council, LID; housewife; active in peace movements.

Arnold Beichman, Bd. of Dir., LID, 1950-1954; National Council since 1954; Press Representative, International Confederation of Free Trade Unions.

Robert Bendiner, Bd. of Dir., LID, 1948-1952; writer.

Nelson Bengston, Bd. of Dir., LID since 1948; investment counselor.

John C. Bennett, Vice Pres., LID, 1954——; Dean, Union Theological Seminary; author.

Victor L. Berger, guest of honor at League's Carnegie Hall Meeting, 1911; Congressman; Socialist leader (dec.).

Jacob Billikoff, formerly National Council, LID; labor arbitrator (dec.).

Alfred M. Bingham, cooperator, LID; writer; Legislator.

Frederick C. Bird, former Sec., LID Com. on Coal and Power; Dir., Dept. of Municipal Research, Dunn and Bradstreet.

Helen Blankenhorn, Bd. of Dir., LID, 1923-24; writer.

Brand Blanshard, National Council, LID; Prof. of Philosophy, Yale.

Paul Blanshard, Field Sec. and lecturer, LID, 1923-1933; Commissioner of Investigation, N.Y.C., 1933-1937; writer; lecturer.

Harriet Stanton Blatch, former Exec. Com., ISS; suffrage leader.

Anita C. Block, Bd. of Dir., LID, 1923-1933; lecturer, dramatic critic.

Frank Bohn, frequent lecturer for LID; writer; lecturer.

William E. Bohn, formerly active in U. of Michigan ISS; formerly Staff, *Socialist Review*, Ed., *New Leader*.

Karl Borders, former Sec., Chicago Chap., LID; former Chief Administrator, UN International Children's Fund (dec.).

Louis B. Boudin, Exec. Com. ISS, 1917-1921; attorney; authority on Socialism and Labor and Constitutional Problems (dec.).

Bjarne Braatoy, Pres., LID, 1940-1944; Bd. of Dir., LID, 1940-1948; National Council since 1948; author; teacher, technical consultant, German Social Democratic Party.

Phillips Bradley, Bd. of Dir., LID, since 1940; Prof. of Government, Syracuse U.

Rae Brandstein, Exec. Com., N.Y. Chap., LID, since 1954; Exec. Sec., National Com. for Rural Schools.

May Vladeck Bromberg, Bd. of Dir., LID, 1940-1942; social service.

Robert W. Bruere, Exec. Com., ISS, 1908-1910; writer; labor mediator and arbitrator.

Rosemary Bull, Bd. of Dir., LID, since 1954; publicist.

Ralph J. Bunche, receiver of LID Award, 1951; winner of Nobel Peace Prize.

Elizabeth B. Butler, Exec. Com., ISS, 1907-08; writer on labor (dec.).

James B. Carey, National Council, LID; Pres. IUE-CIO; Sec.-Treas. CIO.

Jennie D. Carliph, former Exec. Com., N.Y. Chap,; active in work for Civil Liberties.

J. Henry Carpenter, Bd. of Dir., LID, 1945-1954; former Exec. Sec., Brooklyn Div., Protestant Council (dec.).

Edmund B. Chaffee, former Bd. of Dir., LID; former Dir., Labor Temple, N.Y. (dec.).

Oscar L. Chapman, receiver of LID Award, 1953; former U.S. Sec. of the Interior.

Stuart Chase, Treas., LID in the twenties; lecturer; author of "Waste and the Machine Age."

John L. Childs, Bd. of Dir., LID since 1948; Prof. Emeritus of Philosophy of Education, Teachers College, Columbia; author; former Ch., Liberal Party.

Gordon R. Clapp, Bd. of Dir., LID since 1955; former Ch., TVA; Deputy Administrator, N.Y. C.

Ethel Clyde, Bd. of Dir., LID during thirties; active in many social movements.

William F. Cochran, host of ISS at Summer Conference in 1916; former member National Council (dec.).

Fannia M. Cohn, long member of ISS and LID; former N.Y. Exec. Com., LID; Sec., Education Dept., ILGWU.

M. J. Coldwell, Vice Pres., LID; member Canadian Parliament; leader of C.C.P. of Canada.

McAlister Coleman, LID; lecturer; writer; labor ed.; author (dec.).

George Willis Cooke, Exec. Com., ISS, 1905-1908; minister; writer.

Albert Sprague Coolidge, Bd. of Dir., LID; Dept. of Chemistry, Harvard; active in American Federation of Teachers and other organizations.

Jessica G. Cosgrave, Exec. Com., ISS, 1911-1913; Vice-Pres., 1911-12; former Pres., Finch School (dec.).

George S. Counts, Bd. of Dir., LID since 1954; Prof. of Philosophy of Education, Teachers College, Columbia; former Ch., Liberal Party; author.

Grace L. Coyle, National Council, LID; Prof., School of Applied Social Sciences, Western Reserve University; Pres., National Conference of Social Work 1940.

George F. Cranmore, Bd. of Dir., LID, 1944-1950; Asst. Regional Dir., UAW-CIO (dec.).

Frank R. Crosswaith, frequent League lecturer; Sec., Negro Labor Com.; member, N.Y. C. Housing Authority.

Max Danish, former Bd. of Dir., LID; former Ed., *Justice*.

Clarence Darrow, signer of Call for formation of League; labor and Civil Liberties attorney (dec.).

Maurice P. Davidson, Bd. of Dir., LID, 1946-1954; National Council since 1954; N.Y. attorney; former Commissioner, N.Y. State Power Authority.

Jerome Davis, former Bd. of Dir., LID, 1936-1941; author; lecturer; teacher.

Eugene V. Debs, frequent League lecturer; Socialist leader (dec.).

Jerome De Hunt, former Bd. of Dir., LID; trade union and labor political leader.

Solon De Leon, former Bd. of Dir., LID; economic researcher.

Max Delson, Bd. of Dir., LID since 1950; Ch., Finance Com., since 1952; labor and Civil Liberties attorney.

Albert De Silver, Exec. Com., ISS and Bd. of Dir., LID, 1919-1934; Treas., 1919-20; lawyer; former Dir., ACLU (dec.).

John Dewey, Pres., LID, 1939-40; Honorary Pres., 1940-1953; leading

American educator and philosopher; Prof. of Philosophy, Columbia Univ. (dec.).

Samuel De Witt, Bd. of Dir., LID since 1945; businessman; poet; dramatist; lecturer.

Frank C. Doan, Exec. Com., ISS, 1912-1914; Prof., Meadville Theological Seminary; writer (dec.).

T. C. Douglas, receiver of Award, 1953; Premier of Saskatchewan, Canada.

David Dubinsky, receiver of LID Award, 1949; Pres., ILGWU.

Elizabeth Dutcher, Exec. Com., ISS, 1907-1914; social worker.

Kermit Eby, Bd. of Dir., LID, 1950-1954; National Council since 1954; Assoc. Prof. of Social Sciences, U. of Chicago.

Sherwood Eddy, frequent lecturer for LID; author; writer; religious leader.

John Lovejoy Elliott, former Bd. of Dir., LID; head of Hudson Guild; leader N.Y. Ethical Culture Society (dec.).

Henrietta Epstein, Exec. Com., N.Y. Chap., 1954-55; Social Insurance expert.

Morris Ernst, Bd. of Dir., LID, 1923-24; lawyer; writer; attorney, ACLU.

Samuel B. Eubanks, Bd. of Dir., LID, 1949-1954; National Council since 1954; former Vice-Pres., National Newspaper Guild.

James Farmer, student Field Sec., SLID, since 1950; lecturer; writer.

James T. Farrell, National Council, LID; novelist.

Israel Feinberg, Bd. of Dir., LID, 1950-1954; former Manager, N.Y. Joint Board, Cloakmakers' Union (dec.).

Louis Fischer, Bd. of Dir., LID since 1950; writer; lecturer; author of "Life of Gandhi."

Harry F. Fleischman, Exec. Com., N.Y. Chap., since 1954; Dir., National Labor Service, American Jewish Congress.

Louise Adams Floyd, Exec. Com., ISS and Pres., N.Y. Chap., 1919 to early twenties (dec.).

Walter Frank, frequent host LID meetings; N.Y. attorney; leader in civic and social movements.

Ephraim Frisch, Bd. of Dir., LID, since 1945; Rabbi; former Ch., Commission of Justice and Peace, Central Conference of Jewish Rabbis.

Walter G. Fuller, Bd. of Dir., LID, 1921-22; writer; ed. (dec.).

A. Garrick Fullerton, Exec. Com., N.Y. Chap., since 1954; economic researcher.

Zona Gale, Vice Pres., LID, 1923-1925; novelist (dec.).

Lewis S. Gannett, Bd. of Dir., LID, 1920-1924; Literary Ed., New York *Herald Tribune*.

Benjamin Gebiner, Bd. of Dir., LID, since 1950; Asst. Sec., Workmen's Circle.

Martin Gerber, Bd. of Dir., LID, since 1953; Dir., Region 9, UAW-CIO.

W. J. Ghent, Sec., ISS, 1907-1910; author; Ed.; educator.

Charlotte Perkins Gilman, signer of organization call, ISS; author; feminist.

Elisabeth Gilman, Pres., LID, 1940-41; Sec., Christian Social Justice Fund (dec.).

Arthur Gleason, Exec. Com., ISS and Bd. of Dir., LID, 1918-1923; Pres., ISS, 1920-21; Vice Pres., LID, 1921-1923; writer (dec.).

Louis P. Goldberg, Bd. of Dir., LID, since 1945; National Ch., Social Democratic Federation; N.Y. attorney.

Maurice Goldbloom, formerly N.Y. Exec. Com.; writer on international and inter-cultural affairs.

Clara G. Goldman, National Council, LID; housewife; active in peace movements.

J. King Gordon, Bd. of Dir., LID, 1945-1952; former Managing Ed., *The Nation*; on staff of UN.

Elmer E. Graham, former Ch., Detroit Chap.; Staff, UAW-CIO.

Frances A. Grant, Exec. Com., N.Y. Chap., LID, since 1954; Sec., U.S. Com. of Inter-American Association for Democracy and Freedom.

John H. Gray, National Council, LID; former Pres., American Economic Assoc. (dec.).

Felix Grendon, former Exec. Com., ISS; Shavian authority; teacher.

Murray Gross, Bd. of Dir., LID since 1950; Asst. Manager, N.Y. Joint Board, Dressmakers' Union.

Charles Grossman, Bd. of Dir., LID since 1950; businessman; Ch., Reunion of Old Timers.

Harold M. Groves, National Council, LID, Prof. of Economics, U. of Wisconsin.

Cameron P. Hall, Bd. of Dir., LID, 1947-1949; Exec. Sec., Dept. of Church and Economic Life, National Council of Churches.

Meyer Halushka, Chicago Chap.; educator.

M. V. Halushka, Chicago Chap.; teacher.

Rose Laddon Hanna, former Exec. Sec., ISS; writer; lecturer.

Donald Harrington, National Council, LID; Minister, Community Church, N.Y.C.

A. J. Hayes, Vice Pres., LID since 1954; Pres., International Assoc. of Machinists.

Ellen Hayes, Exec. Com., ISS, 1916-17; author; Prof. of Mathematics, Wellesley College (dec.).

Paul R. Hayes, Bd. of Dir. and National Council, LID since 1951; Prof. of Law, Columbia U.

Timothy Healy, Bd. of Dir., 1925; trade union leader.

Eduard Heimann, National Council, LID; Prof. of Economics, New School; author.

Adolph Held, Bd. of Dir., LID since 1945; Dir., Welfare and Health Benefits, ILGWU; Ch., Jewish Labor Com.

Albert H. Herling, Bd. of Dir., LID, 1952-53; Staff, City of Hope; author.

Mary Fox Herling, Exec. Sec., LID, 1929-1940; National Council since 1940; active in public and cooperative housing.

Hubert C. Herring, Bd. of Dir., LID, 1933-1938; Exec. Dir., Com. on Cultural Relations with Latin America; author.

Thomas Wentworth Higginson, signer of organization call, 1905; author; literary critic.

Morris Hillquit, Treas., ISS, 1908-1915; N.Y. labor attorney; Socialist leader; author (dec.).

Mary W. Hillyer (Blanshard), Bd. of Dir., LID, 1940-1949; Dir., LID Lecture Series in thirties; Staff, Planned Parenthood Assn.

Julius Hochman, Bd. of Dir., LID, 1936-1938; Manager, N.Y. Joint Board, Dressmakers' Union.

John Haynes Holmes, Vice Pres., LID since 1938; Minister Emeritus, N.Y. Community Church.

Darlington Hoopes, LID cooperator; Socialist leader and former Legislator.

Bryn J. Hovde, Vice Pres., LID, 1948-1954; housing authority; former Pres., New School (dec.).

Don Howard, Bd. of Dir., LID, 1941-42; social worker; Dean, School of Social Welfare, U. of California.

Frederick C. Howe, Bd. of Dir., LID, 1923-1925; author; social reformer (dec.).

Quincy Howe, Bd. of Dir., LID, 1939-1941; radio and television commentator; writer; teacher.

Jessie Wallace Hughan, Exec. Com., ISS and Bd. of Dir., LID, 1907-1950; Vice Pres., 1920-21; teacher; author; economist (dec.).

Hubert H. Humphrey, receiver of LID and Reunion of Old Timers 1948 Awards. (Not to be confused with the British Fabian Socialist, Hubert Humphreys.)

Robert Hunter, Exec. Com., ISS, 1905-1911; author; social worker (dec.).

Alex Irvine, former lecturer for ISS; author; minister; lecturer (dec.).

James Weldon Johnson, former Bd. of Dir., LID; author; poet; diplomat; Sec., NAACP (dec.).

Mercer Green Johnston, National Council, LID; minister; social reformer.

John Paul Jones, Bd. of Dir., LID, since 1945; former Pres., N.Y. Chap.; Minister, Union Church, Brooklyn.

Paul Jones, former Bd. of Dir., LID; Bishop, Protestant Episcopal Church (dec.).

Horace M. Kallen, Exec. Com., ISS, 1919-20; educator; philosopher; author.

Leonard S. Kandell, Bd. of Dir., LID, since 1951; Pres., Digby Management Co.

Vladimir Karapetoff, Vice Pres., LID in twenties; Prof. of Engineering, Cornell U.; musician; inventor (dec.).

Florence Kelley, Exec. Com., ISS, 1911-1921; Bd. of Dir., LID, 1921-22; Vice Pres., 1912-1918, 1921-1923; Pres., 1918-1920; Sec., National Consumers League; author; social reformer (dec.).

W. H. Kelley, Exec. Com., ISS, 1907-08; social worker.

Edmond Kelly, Exec. Com., ISS, 1908-1910; lawyer; author; former Counsel for American Embassy, Paris.

Paul Kennaday, Exec. Com., ISS, 1907-1918; Treas., 1907-08; writer; social worker.

A. M. Kidd, National Council, LID; Prof. Emeritus of Economics, U. of California.

William H. Kilpatrick, Bd. of Dir., LID, since 1953; Vice Pres. since 1954; leading American educator.

Clifford Kirkpatrick, National Council, LID; Prof. of Sociology, U. of Indiana.

George R. Kirkpatrick, organizer, ISS, 1908; author; lecturer (dec.).

Cornelius Kruse, National Council, LID; Prof. of Philosophy, Wesleyan U.

Alice Kuebler, Exec. Sec., ISS, 1919-1920 (dec.).

Winthrop D. Lane, Exec. Com., ISS, 1918-1931; writer.

Bruno Lasker, Bd. of Dir., LID, 1921-22; writer; sociologist.

Louis Lasker, Bd. of Dir., LID, since 1948; leader in Public Housing movement.

W. Jett Lauck, former Bd. of Dir., LID, labor economist (dec.).

Algernon Lee, Exec. Com., ISS, 1910-1916; Sec., 1910-11; late Pres., Rand School; author (dec.).

Abraham Lefkowitz, Bd. of Dir., LID, since 1945; Principal, Samuel Tilden High School.

Herbert H. Lehman, receiver of LID Award, 1950; U.S. Senator from N.Y.

William M. Leiserson, Columbia ISS; former Ch., National Mediation Bd.; labor economist.

Alfred Baker Lewis, Bd. of Dir., LID, 1940-1954; Ch. of Bd. 1945; Pres., Union Casualty Co.

Trygve Lie, receiver of LID Award, 1947; former Secretary-General, UN.

Henry R. Linville, formerly Bd. of Dir., LID; teacher; former Pres., New York Teachers Guild (dec.).

Ben E. Lippincott, National Council, LID; Prof. of Economics, U. of Minnesota; author.

Jack London, Pres., ISS, 1905-1907; novelist (dec.).

Cedric Long, Bd. of Dir., LID, 1923-1925; active in Cooperative movement (dec.).

Harry Lopatin, Exec. Com., N.Y. Chap., LID; Managing Ed., *Workmen's Circle Call*; Staff, City of Hope.

Lewis Lorwin, Exec. Com., ISS, 1920-21; author; authority on Labor.

Owen R. Lovejoy, Exec. Com. and Treas., ISS, 1905-06; former Sec., National Child Labor Com.

Robert Morss Lovett, Pres., LID, 1921-1938; Vice Pres., 1938-1949; former Prof. of English Literature, U. of Chicago; former Ed., *New Republic*.

Sara Kaplan Lowe, Sec. to Dr. Laidler since 1925; office manager.

John Lyon, Exec. Com., N.Y. Chap., LID; public relations counselor.

Marcia J. Lyttle, National Council, LID; active in peace movements.

Francis J. McConnell, Vice Pres., LID, 1939-1949; late Bishop, Methodist Church and former Pres., Federal Council of Churches (dec.).

Bertha Mailly, former Bd. of Dir., LID; former Exec. Sec., Rand School.

Julius Manson, Bd. of Dir., LID, 1955; Staff, N.Y. State Board of Mediation.

Edwin Markham, frequent lecturer, ISS; poet.

Jan Masaryk, former Honorary Member, LID; former Foreign Sec. Czechoslovakia (dec.).

James H. Maurer, Vice Pres., LID, 1923-1944; former Pres., Pa. Federation of Labor; former Socialist Legislator (dec.).

George Meany, receiver of LID Award, 1954; Pres., AFL.

Alexander Meiklejohn, Vice Pres., LID, since 1938; former Pres., Amherst; author; lecturer.

Darwin J. Meserole, Exec. Com., ISS, 1918-1921; attorney; Active in Fight Against Unemployment (dec.).

Katherine Maltby Meserole, member 1st Exec. Com, ISS; educator.

Etta Meyer, Vice Pres., N.Y. Chap., LID; social worker.

Edna St. Vincent Millay, former Vassar SLID; poetess (dec.).

Abraham Miller, Bd. of Dir., LID since 1945; Sec., N.Y. Joint Bd., ACWA.

Nathaniel M. Minkoff, Bd. of Dir., LID, since 1952; Ch. of Bd., 1946-1948; Pres. since 1948; Sec. Treas., N.Y. Joint Bd., Dressmakers' Union, ILGWU.

Broadus Mitchell, Johns Hopkins ISS, 1917-18; Bd. of Dir., LID, 1945-1952; Prof. of Economics, Rutgers U.; author.

Hiram K. Moderwell, Sec., Harvard ISS; writer; dramatic critic (dec.).

William P. Montague, Exec. Com., ISS, 1917-18; Bd. of Dir., 1920-1923; Prof. of Philosophy, Columbia (dec.).

Therese H. Moore, Exec. Com., N.Y. Chap., LID; housewife.

Wayne Morse, receiver of LID Award, 1954; U.S. Senator from Oregon.

Amicus Most, Exec. Com., N.Y. Chap., LID, since 1954; former Chief of Industrial Department, E.C.A., Germany; contractor.

Lewis Mumford, former member, N.Y. Chap. Exec. Com., LID; author; city planner.

A. J. Muste, Bd. of Dir., LID, 1921-22; Sec. Emeritus, F.O.R.

Isidore Nagler, Bd. of Dir., LID, 1953——; Manager, N.Y. Joint Bd., Cloakmakers Union, ILGWU.

George Nasmyth, Exec. Com., ISS, 1918-1920; student of International Affairs (dec.).

Benjamin B. Naumoff, Bd. of Dir., LID, 1950——; Pres., N.Y. Chap., 1952-1954; Chief Field Examiner, N.L.R.B., N.Y. Region.

Nellie Seeds Nearing, Bd. of Dir., LID, 1923; author; educator (dec.).

S. L. Newman, Bd. of Dir., LID, 1945-1952; former Vice Pres., International Association of Machinists.

Reinhold Niebuhr, former Pres., N.Y. Chap., LID; former Bd. of Dir. and Treas.; author; Vice Pres., Union Theological Seminary.

Morris S. Novik, Bd. of Dir., LID, 1950——; radio consultant.

Harry A. Overstreet, National Council; author; lecturer; educator.

Mary W. Ovington, Exec. Com., ISS, 1914-15; a founder, NAACP.

Jacob Panken, Bd. of Dir., LID, since 1948; former Justice, Court of Domestic Relations, N.Y.C.

Ernst Papanek, Bd. of Dir., LID, 1955——; Dir., Wiltwyck School.

Herbert W. Payne, Bd. of Dir., LID, 1946-1952; Treas., 1943-1952; late Vice Pres., Textile Workers Union of America (dec.).

Dorothy Pearson, Exec. Com., N.Y. Chap., LID; active in liberal movements.

Orlie Pell, Bd. of Dir., LID; Education and Research Assoc., American Labor Education Services.

Elsie Cole Phillips, Exec. Com., ISS, 1910-1914; Vice Pres., 1910-11.

William Pickens, Bd. of Dir., LID, 1923-1942; author; former Field Sec., NAACP (dec.).

Ernest Poole, Exec. Com., ISS, 1908-1918; Vice Pres., 1912-18; novelist; winner, Pulitzer Prize (dec.).

J. S. Potofsky, Bd. of Dir., LID, 1925-26; Pres., ACWA.

Eliot D. Pratt, Bd. of Dir., LID, 1948-1952; National Council; Ch., Bd. of Trustees, Goddard College.

Sherman D. Pratt, National Council, LID; publicist.

Paul W. Preisler, National Council, LID; teacher; attorney.

Carl Rachlin, Bd. of Dir., LID, since 1950; former Pres., N.Y. Chap.; labor and Civil Liberties attorney.

Walter Rautenstrauch, former Bd. of Dir., LID; Prof. of Industrial Engineering, Columbia (dec.).

Cleveland Rodgers, Bd. of Dir., LID, in forties; formerly Ed., Brooklyn *Eagle* and member, N.Y. City Planning Commission.

George E. Roewer, formerly Boston Chap.; legal consultant; labor lawyer.

Eleanor Roosevelt, recipient of LID Award, 1953; "First Woman of the World."

George Ross, Bd. of Dir., LID, since 1948; businessman; Sec., People's Educational Camp Society.

I. M. Rubinow, Exec. Com., ISS, 1913-1917; authority on Social Insurance.

Charles Edward Russell, frequent lecturer for League; author; writer.

Stanley Ruttenberg, Bd. of Dir., LID, 1950-1952; Dir. of Research and Education, CIO.

Helen Sahler, former Sec., N.Y. Chap.; sculptor; painter (dec.).

Mary R. Sanford, Exec. Com., ISS, 1907-1938; Treas., 1916-1919; Vice Pres., LID, 1938-1948; publicist.

Joseph Schlossberg, Bd. of Dir. LID, 1940——; Treas., 1945—; Sec.-Treas. Emeritus, A.C.W.A.; Member, Board of Higher Education, New York City.

Karl Scholz, National Council, LID; Prof. of Economics, U. of Pa.

Adelaide Schulkind, Vice Pres., N.Y. Chap., 1954——; Sec., League for Mutual Aid.

Leroy Scott, Sec., ISS, 1910-1917; writer; novelist.

Vida D. Scudder, Exec. Com., ISS, 1912-1916; Vice Pres., LID, 1921-1954; Prof. of English Literature, Wellesley (dec.).

H. D. Sedgwick, Exec. Com., ISS, 1912-1917; educator; writer (dec.).

Bert Seidman, former Ch., Washington Chap., LID; Research Dept., AFL.

Toni Sender, frequent League lecturer; Representative of International Confederation of Trade Unions at UN.

Boris Shishkin, Bd. of Dir., LID; economist, AFL.

Upton Sinclair, founder; Vice Pres., ISS, 1905-1917; novelist.

Winifred Smith, National Council, LID; former Prof. of English, Vassar.

George Soule, Bd. of Dir., LID; author; economist; Prof. of Economics, Bennington College.

John Spargo, Exec. Com., ISS, 1916-1919; writer.

Sterling Spero, Bd. of Dir., LID; Prof. of Public Administration, N.Y.U.

Sidney Stark, long LID cooperator; businessman.

Sidney Stark, Jr., National Council, LID; businessman.

Lincoln Steffens, frequent lecturer, LID; writer (dec.).

Charles P. Steinmetz, Vice Pres., LID, 1921-1924; inventor; electric wizard (dec.).

Helen Phelps Stokes, Exec. Com., ISS, 1907-1921; Bd. of Dir., 1921-1940; Vice Pres., 1940 (dec.).

J. G. Phelps Stokes, Exec. Com., ISS, 1905-1918; Pres., 1907-1918; publicist.

Benjamin Stolberg, former Bd. of Dir., LID; writer (dec.).

George Streator, National Council, LID; former Bd. of Dir.; labor editor.
Carol Lloyd Strobell, Exec. Com., ISS, 1913-1921; writer.
Louis Stulberg, Bd. of Dir., LID; Manager, Local 66, ILGWU.
Norman Thomas, Exec. Com., ISS, 1918-1921; Bd. of Dir., LID, since 1921; Exec. Com., 1922-1936; Socialist leader; author; lecturer; Ch. Post War World Council.
John Thurber, former Ch., Washington Chap. LID; labor statistician and historian.
Richard C. Tolman, U. of Illinois ISS; physicist (dec.).
Ashley L. Totten, Bd. of Dir., LID, 1951——; Sec.-Treas., Brotherhood of Sleeping Car Porters.
Thorstein Veblen, National Council, 1925-1929; sociologist (dec.).
Oswald Garrison Villard, Bd. of Dir., LID, 1933-34; former Ed. and Pub. *The Nation* (dec.).
B. Charney Vladeck, Bd. of Dir., LID, in thirties; Business Manager, *Jewish Daily Forward;* former N.Y.C. Councilman (dec.).
Stephen Vladeck, Bd. of Dir., LID, 1955——; labor attorney.
William C. Vladeck, Bd. of Dir., 1953-1955; architect.
Anna Strunsky Walling, active member since 1905.
L. Metcalfe Walling, Bd. of Dir., LID, 1948-1952; former Administrator, Fair Labor Practices; attorney.
William English Walling, Exec. Com., ISS, 1912-1918; author; social scientist (dec.).
Agnes A. Warbasse, Bd. of Dir., 1925-26; leading cooperator (dec.).
Arthur Warner, Bd. of Dir., LID, 1921-1923; writer; ed. (dec.).
Adolph Warshow, formerly Bd. of Dir., LID; businessman (dec.).
Morris Weisz, National Council, LID; labor economist.
Mildred Perlman Westover, Sec., SLID, 1952-53; Bd. of Dir., 1953-1955.
Bertha Poole Weyl, Bd. of Dir., LID, 1922-1945; Vice Pres., since 1945; housewife.
Bouck White, Exec. Com., ISS, 1912-1915; author (dec.).
Samuel S. White, National Council; labor-management relations.
Pearl Willen, Bd. of Dir., LID, since 1952; lecturer; social service.
Norman Williams, Jr., Bd. of Dir., LID; Legal Dept., N.Y.C. Planning Commission.
William Withers, National Council, LID; Prof. of Economics, Queens College.
Herman Wolf, Bd. of Dir., 1953-1955; public relations.
Helen Sumner Woodbury, Exec. Com., ISS and Dir., 1917-1924; labor economist (dec.).
Louis Yagoda, Exec. Com., N.Y. Chap.; N.Y. State Board of Mediation.
Phil Ziegler, National Council, LID; Ed., *Railway Clerk.*
Savel Zimand, Bd. of Dir., LID; 1921-1924; writer; health educator.
Charles Zimmerman, Bd. of Dir., LID; Vice Pres., ILGWU; Manager, Local 22.
Charles Zueblin, Exec. Com., ISS, 1916-1921; author; lecturer (dec.).

APPENDIX III

Grossman, Harold M. Groves, Donald Harrington, Paul R. Hayes, Eduard Heimann, Mary Fox Herling, Mary Hillyer, Sidney Hook, John Paul Jones, Clifford Kirkpatrick, Cornelius Kruse, Aaron Levenstein, Alfred Baker Lewis, Marx Lewis, Harry A. Overstreet, Eliot D. Pratt, Sherman Pratt, Paul W. Preisler, Carl Raushenbush, Asher W. Schwartz, Winifred Smith, George Soule, Monroe Sweetland, Morris Weisz, Samuel S. White, William Withers, Theresa Wolfson.

(Official stationery of LID bears the notation: "Officially Accredited to the United States Mission to the United Nations.")

APPENDIX IV

ORIGINAL OFFICERS AND DIRECTORS OF THE AMERICAN CIVIL LIBERTIES UNION, 1921

Officers

Harry F. Ward, Chairman
Duncan McDonald
Jeannette Rankin, Vice Chairman
*Helen Phelps Stokes, Treasurer
*Albert De Silver
*Roger N. Baldwin

Directors

Walter Nelles, Counsel
Lucille B. Milner, Field Secretary
Louis Budenz, Publicity Director

National Committee

Jane Addams
Herbert S. Bigelow
Sophonisba P. Breckenridge
Robert M. Buck
Joseph D. Cannon
John S. Codman
Lincoln Colcord
James H. Dillard
James A. Duncan
*Crystal Eastman
*John Lovejoy Elliott
Edmund C. Evans
William M. Fincke
John A. Fitch
Elizabeth Gurley Flynn
William Z. Foster
Felix Frankfurter
Ernst Freund
Paul J. Furnas
*Zona Gale
A. B. Gilbert
*Arthur Garfield Hays
*Morris Hillquit
*John Haynes Holmes
*Frederick C. Howe
*James Weldon Johnson
Helen Keller

Agnes Brown Leach
Arthur Le Sueur
*Henry R. Linville
*Robert Morss Lovett
Allen McCurdy
Grenville S. McFarland
Oscar Maddous
Judah L. Magnes
*James H. Maurer
*A. J. Muste
*George W. Nasmyth
*Scott Nearing
Julia O'Connor
*William H. Pickens
William Marion Reedy
John Nevin Sayre
Rose Schneiderman
*Vida D. Scudder
Seymour Stedman
*Norman M. Thomas
Edward D. Tittmann
William S. U'Ren
*Oswald Garrison Villard
*B. Charney Vladeck
George P. West
L. Hollingsworth Wood

* Listed by Mina Weisenberg among "collaborators" of League for Industrial Democracy.

OFFICERS AND DIRECTORS OF THE AMERICAN
CIVIL LIBERTIES UNION, JUNE, 1962

(Names marked * appear on Mina Weisenberg's list of League for Industrial Democracy "collaborators"; names marked † appear on official founders list of Americans for Democratic Action.)

Board of Directors

Ernest Angell=Chairman
Ralph S. Brown, Jr., Sophia Yarnall Jacobs=Vice Chairmen
Edward J. Ennis, *Osmond K. Fraenkel=General Counsel
Dorothy Kenyon=Secretary
B. W. Huebsch=Treasurer
*†Morris L. Ernst, John F. Finerty, *John Holmes, *Norman Thomas=
Directors Emeritus

Robert Bierstedt	Dan Lacy	George Soll
Robert L. Crowell	*Will Maslow	*Stephen C. Vladeck
*Walter Frank	Harry C. Meserve	J. Waties Waring
Lewis Galantiere	Edward O. Miller	Alan Westin
Walter Gellhorn	Walter Millis	Howard Whiteside
Louis M. Hacker	Gerard Piel	Edward Bennett
*August Heckscher	Harriet Pilpel	Williams
Frank S. Horne	Herbert Prashker	
*John Paul Jones	Elmer Rice	

National Executive Staff

John de J. Pemberton, Jr.=Executive Director
Alan Reitman=Associate Director
Melvin L. Wulf=Legal Director
Marie M. Runyon=Membership Director
Lawrence Speiser=Washington Office Director
(1101 Vermont Street, N.W., Washington, D.C.
Telephone: MEtropolitan 8-6602)
Louise C. Floyd, Leanne Golden, Colleen Carmody, Julie Barrows=Executive Assistants
Jeffrey E. Fuller=Staff Associate

National Committee

†Francis Biddle=Chairman
Pearl S. Buck, Howard F. Burns, *Albert Sprague Coolidge, J. Frank Dobie, Lloyd K. Garrison, *Frank P. Graham, †Palmer Hoyt, Karl Menninger, Loren Miller, *Morris Rubin, Lillian E. Smith=Vice Chairmen

Sadie Alexander	*Roger N. Baldwin
J. Garner Anthony	Alan Barth
Thurman Arnold	Dr. Sarah Gibson Blanding
Clarence E. Ayres	*Catherine Drinker Bowen

Prof. Julian P. Boyd
Van Wyck Brooks
John Mason Brown
Dr. Robert K. Carr
Prof. Allan K. Chalmers
*Stuart Chase
Grenville Clark
Dr. Rufus E. Clement
Prof. Henry S. Commager
*Prof. George S. Counts
Prof. Robert E. Cushman
*Melvyn Douglas
Prof. Thomas H. Eliot
Victor Fischer
Walter T. Fisher
James Lawrence Fly
Dr. Erich Fromm
Prof. Ralph F. Fuchs
Prof. Willard E. Goslin
Prof. Mark DeW. Howe
*Quincy Howe
Dr. Robert M. Hutchins
Gerald W. Johnson
Dr. Mordecai W. Johnson
James Kerney
Benjamin H. Kizer
Agnes Brown Leach

*Max Lerner
Prof. Robert S. Lynd
Dr. Millicent C. McIntosh
Patrick Murphy Malin
Prof. Robert Mathews
Prof. Wesley H. Maurer
*Emil Mazey
*Dr. Alexander Meiklejohn
Sylvan Meyer
Donald R. Murphy
Dr. J. Robert Oppenheimer
John B. Orr, Jr.
†Bishop G. Bromley Oxnam
James G. Patton
†A. Philip Randolph
Elmo Roper
†Prof. Arthur Schlesinger, Jr.
Dr. Edward J. Sparling
Prof. George R. Stewart
†Dorothy Tilly
Jose Trias-Monge
William L. White
Thornton Wilder
†Aubrey Williams
Marion A. Wright
Dean Benjamin Youngdahl

OFFICERS OF THE NATIONAL COMMITTEE TO ABOLISH THE HOUSE UN-AMERICAN ACTIVITIES COMMITTEE, AN OFFSHOOT OF THE AMERICAN CIVIL LIBERTIES UNION, 1964

Honorary Chairmen
James Imbrie
Alexander Meiklejohn
Clarence Pickett

Chairman Emeritus
Aubrey W. Williams

Chairman
Harvey O'Connor

Vice Chairmen
Dorothy Marshall
Coordinator

Sylvia E. Crane
Organization Liaison
Charles Jackson
East Coast Region
Harry Barnard
Midwest Region
(to be announced)
Southern Region

Treasurer
Robert W. Kenny

Executive Director-Field Representative
Frank Wilkinson

[Sponsors' List follows. Note interlock with LID, ADA and ACLU.]

SPONSORS
of the
NATIONAL COMMITTEE TO ABOLISH THE HOUSE UN-AMERICAN ACTIVITIES COMMITTEE

(Titles and Institutions Listed for Identification only)

[List as published by above-named Committee in the Bulletin of *Abolition News*, official publication of the National Committee]

EDUCATION

PROF. MAX F. ABELL
Agric. Econ. Emer., U. of N.H.

PROF. JOHN W. ALEXANDER
Assoc. Dean, Columbia College

PROF. ROLAND H. BAINTON
History, Yale University

PROF. STRINGFELLOW BARR
Humanities, Rutgers University

PROF. M. V. L. BENNETT
Neurology, Columbia University

PROF. ERIC BENTLEY
English, Columbia University

PROF. DANIEL M. BERMAN
Government, American University

PROF. ROBERT BIERSTEDT
Sociology-Anthropology, N.Y.U.

PROF. NEAL BILLINGS
U. of Wisconsin-Milwaukee

PROF. HERBERT BLAU
English, San Francisco State

PROF. FRANK J. BOCKHOFF
Chemistry, Fenn College

PROF. DERK BODDE
University of Pennsylvania

PROF. DWIGHT L. BOLINGER
University of Colorado

DEAN WARREN BOWER
English, New York University

PROF. THEODORE BRAMELD
Political Science, Boston Univ.

PROF. EMILY C. BROWN
Vassar College

PROF. R. McAFEE BROWN
Religion, Stanford University

PROF. JUSTUS BUCHLER
Philosophy, Columbia University

PROF. ALLAN M. BUTLER
Pediatrics Emer., Harvard Univ.

PROF. EDMOND CAHN
Law, New York University

PROF. EDWIN S. CAMPBELL
Chemistry, New York University

PROF. THOMAS S. CHECKLEY
Law, University of Pittsburgh

PROF. PAUL F. CLARK
Microbiology Emer., U. of Wis.

PROF. STANLEY COBB
Psychiatry, Harvard University

PROF. WHITFIELD COBB
Statistics, Hollins College

PROF. HUBERT L. COFFEY
Psychology, U. of Calif.-Berkeley

PROF. JULIUS COHEN
Law, Rutgers University

PROF. ROBERT S. COHEN
Physics, Boston University

PROF. CARL W. CONDIT
Northwestern University

PROF. EDWARD U. CONDON
Physics, Washington University

PROF. HOLLIS R. COOLEY
New York University

PROF. ALBERT S. COOLIDGE
Chemistry Emer., Harvard Univ.

PROF. ARTHUR C. DANTO
Philosophy, Columbia University

PROF. WILLIAM C. DAVIDON
Physics, Haverford College

PROF. BERNARD D. DAVIS
Bacteriology, Harvard University

PROF. DAVID B. DAVIS
History, Cornell University

PROF. HORACE B. DAVIS
Social Science, Raleigh, N.C.

PROF. STANTON LING DAVIS
Case Institute of Technology

DR. JAMES P. DIXON
President, Antioch College

PROF. NORMAN DORSEN
Law, New York University

PROF. EDMUND EGAN
Mt. Mercy College

PROF. RUPERT EMERSON
History, Harvard University

PROF. THOMAS I. EMERSON
Law, Yale University

DR. JOHN C. ESTY, JR.
Dean, Amherst College

PROF. ROBERT FINN
Mathematics, Stanford University

PROF. H. BRUCE FRANKLIN
English, Stanford University

PROF. MITCHELL FRANKLIN
Law, Tulane University

PROF. BEN W. FUSON
English, University of Kansas

PROF. JOHN D. GOHEEN
Philosophy, Stanford University

PROF. WILLIAM J. GOODE
Sociology, Columbia University

PROF. GORDON GRIFFITHS
History, University of Washington

PROF. A. D. GUREWITSCH
Columbia-Presbyterian Med. Ctr.

PROF. WALTER E. HAGER
Edu. Emer., Columbia Teach. Col

PROF. BERNARD F. HALEY
Economics Emer., Stanford Univ.

PROF. ALICE HAMILTON
Medicine Emer., Harvard Univ.

PROF. FOWLER HARPER
Law, Yale University

PROF. DOROTHEA HARVEY
Asso. Dean, Columbia University

PROF. ROBERT HAVIGHURST
Education, University of Chicago

PROF. M. HEIDELBERGER
Columbia Univ. P. & S. Emer.;
National Academy of Sciences

PROF. R. L. HEILBRONER
Harvard University

PROF. BURTON HENRY
Education, Los Angeles State Col.

PROF. DAVID HIATT
English, Carroll College

PROF. WILLIAM E. HOCKING
Philosophy Emer., Harvard Univ.

PROF. FRANCIS D. HOLE
Soil Sciences, University of Wis.

PROF. M. DE WOLFE HOWE
Law, Harvard University

PROF. H. STUART HUGHES
History, Harvard University

PROF. HERBERT JEHLE
Physics, George Washington U.

PROF. EARL S. JOHNSON
Univ. of Wisconsin-Milwaukee

PROF. PAUL E. JOHNSON
Boston University

DR. WILMOT R. JONES
Princ. Emer., Frnds. Sch., Wil., Del.

PROF. ERICH KAHLER
Princeton University

PROF. DAVID KETTLER
Political Sci., Ohio State Univ.

PROF. JACK C. KIEFER
Mathematics, Cornell University

DR. JACK E. KITTELL
Headmaster, Dalton School

PROF. LEONARD KITTS
Design, Ohio State University

PROF. PAUL KLEMPERER
Pathology Emer., Mt. Sinai Hosp.

DEAN JOHN W. KNEDLER, JR.
New York University

PROF. I. M. KOLTHOFF
University of Minnesota

PROF. MICHAEL KRAUS
History, Col. of the City of N.Y.

PROF. Y. H. KRIKORIAN
Phil., College of the City of N.Y.

PROF. JOHN C. LAZENBY
Emer., University of Wisconsin

PROF. KAREL DE LEEUW
Mathematics, Stanford University

PROF. HOWARD H. LENTNER
Political Sci., Western Reserve U.

PROF. GEORGE LEPPERT
Mechanical Eng., Stanford Univ.

DEAN LEONARD W. LEVY
Grad. Sch., Brandeis University

DR. FREDERICK J. LIBBY
Washington, D.C.

PROF. LEE LORCH
Mathematics, Univ. of Alberta

PROF. OLIVER S. LOUD
Antioch College

PROF. DAVID RANDALL LUCE
Phil., U. of Wisconsin-Milwaukee

PROF. HELEN M. LYND
Sarah Lawrence College

PROF. C. MAC DOUGALL
Northwestern University

PROF. R. M. MAC IVER
Sociology, Columbia University

PROF. ROLAND P. MACKAY
Neurology, Northwestern Univ.

DR. HANS MAEDER
Director, Stockbridge School

PROF. HUBERT MARSHALL
Political Science, Stanford Univ.

PROF. KIRTLEY F. MATHER
Geology Emer., Harvard Univ.

PROF. WESLEY H. MAURER
Journalism, University of Mich.

PROF. KENNETH O. MAY
Mathematics, Carleton College

PROF. A. MEIKLEJOHN
Phil. Pres. Emer. Amherst Col.
Presidential Medal of Freedom

PROF. KARL MEYER
Biochem., P & S, Columbia Univ.

PROF. CLYDE R. MILLER
Emer., Columbia University

PROF. ARVAL A. MORRIS
Law, University of Washington

PROF. PHILIP MORRISON
Physics, Cornell University

PROF. GLENN R. MORROW
University of Pennsylvania

PROF. LINCOLN E. MOSES
Statistics, Stanford University

PROF. OTTO NATHAN
Economics Emer., New York U.

PROF. HANS NOLL
Biochem., Med. Sch., U. of Ptsbrg.

PROF. PAUL OLYNK
Science, Fenn College

PROF. JAY OREAR
Physics, Cornell University

PROF. ERWIN PANOFSKY
Art Historian, Princeton Univ.

PROF. HOWARD L. PARSONS
Philosophy, Coe College

PROF. LINUS PAULING
Nobel Laureate: Chemistry; Peace

REV. ARTHUR C. PEABODY
Headmaster Emer., Groton School

PROF. ROBERT PREYER
Brandeis University

PROF. JOHN H. RANDALL, JR.
Philosophy, Columbia University

PROF. NORMAN REDLICH
Law, New York University

PROF. ALAN RHODES
Fenn College

PROF. OSCAR K. RICE
Chem., Univ. of North Carolina

PROF. WILLIAM G. RICE
Law, University of Wisconsin

PROF. DONALD H. RIDDLE
Pol. Science, Princeton University

PROF. WALTER B. RIDEOUT
English, Northwestern University

PROF. CLAYTON ROBERTS
History, Ohio State University

PROF. THEODORE ROSEBURY
Washington University

PROF. W. CARSON RYAN
Edu. Emer., U. of North Carolina

PROF. MARIO G. SALVADORI
Indus. Eng., Columbia University

PROF. MEYER SCHAPIRO
Fine Arts, Columbia University

PROF. PAUL A. SCHILPP
Philosophy, Northwestern Univ.

PROF. CARL E. SCHORSKE
History, Univ. of Calif.-Berkeley

PROF. SEYMOUR SCHUSTER
Mathematics, Univ. of Minnesota

PROF. HARLOW SHAPLEY
Astronomy Emer., Harvard Univ.

PROF. THEO. SHEDLOVSKY
Rockefeller Institute

PROF. HENRY NASH SMITH
English, Univ. of Calif.-Berkeley

PROF. ROCKWELL C. SMITH
Northwestern University

PROF. JOHN SOMERVILLE
Phil., City University of N.Y.

PROF. PITIRIM A. SOROKIN
Sociology, Harvard University

PROF. BENJAMIN SPOCK
Ped. & Psychtry. West. Res. Univ.

PROF. KENNETH M. STAMPP
History, Univ. of Calif.-Berkeley

PROF. NORMAN E. STEENROD
Princeton University

PROF. MILTON R. STERN
Asst. Dean, Gen. Education & Ext.,
N.Y.U.

PROF. ERNEST L. TALBERT
University of Cincinnati

DR. HAROLD C. TAYLOR
Former Pres., Sarah Lawrence Col.

PROF. J. HERBERT TAYLOR
Cell Biology, Columbia University

PROF. PAUL TILLITT
Political Science, Rutgers Univ.

PROF. HAROLD C. UREY
Nobel Laureate: Chemistry

DR. MARY VAN KLEECK
Industrial Sociologist

PROF. WILLIAM VICKREY
Economics, Columbia University

PROF. WALTERS S. VINCENT
Med. Sch., Univ. of Pittsburgh

PROF. MAURICE B. VISSCHER
Scientist, Univ. of Minnesota

PROF. WILLIAM VORENBERG
Speech, New York University

PROF. PAUL W. WAGER
University of North Carolina

PROF. LEROY WATERMAN
Emer., University of Michigan

PROF. ROBERT H. WELKER
Case Institute of Technology

PROF. URBAN WHITAKER
Intl. Rel., San Francisco State

DEAN I. G. WHITCHURCH
Kingsfield, Maine

PROF. HAROLD WIDOM
Mathematics, Cornell University

PROF. H. H. WILSON
Politics, Princeton University

PROF. M. WINDMILLER
San Francisco State College

PROF. KURT H. WOLFF
Sociology, Brandeis University

PROF. PAUL R. ZILSEL
Physics, Western Reserve Univ.

RELIGION

RABBI A. N. ABRAMOWITZ
District of Columbia

REV. LYMAN ACHENBACH
Universalist, Columbus, Ohio

REV. GEORGE A. ACKERLY
Meth.; Chrm., World Fel., Inc.

REV. WILLIAM T. BAIRD
Essex Community, Chicago

REV. CHARLES A. BALDWIN
Chaplain, Brown University

DR. JOHN C. BENNETT
Theologian, New York City

DR. ALGERNON D. BLACK
Director, Ethical Culture Society

REV. THEODORE R. BOWEN
Calvary Methodist, D.C.

REV. WALTER R. BOWIE
Theologian, Alexandria, Virginia

DR. EDWIN A. BROWN
Brook Park Methodist, Berea, O.

REV. RAYMOND CALKINS
Congregational, Cambridge, Mass.

DR. J. RAYMOND COPE
Unitarian, Berkeley, California

REV. HENRY HITT CRANE
Cen. Meth. Emer., Detroit, Mich.

REV. JOHN E. EVANS
Unitarian, Plainfield, N.J.

REV. W. W. FINLATOR
Pullen Memorial Baptist,
Raleigh, N.C.

RABBI OSCAR FLEISHAKER
Co-Chrm., Religious Freedom
Committee

REV. S. H. FRITCHMAN
Unitarian, Los Angeles, Calif.

RABBI ROLAND GITTELSOHN
Temple Israel, Boston, Mass.

RABBI JOSEPH B. GLASER
Union of Amer. Hebrew Cong.

RABBI ROBERT E. GOLDBURG
Congregation Mishkan Israel,
New Haven, Conn.

RABBI DAVID GRAUBART
Chicago, Illinois

REV. W. H. HENDERSON
Philadelphia, Pennsylvania

REV. JOHN HAYNES HOLMES
Community Ch. Emer., N.Y.

RABBI PHILIP HOROWITZ
Brith Emeth Cong., Cleveland, O.

REV. STUART J. INNERST
Friends Natl. Com. on Legislation

RABBI LEON A. JICK
Free Synagogue, Mt. Vernon, N.Y.

REV. MARTIN L. KING, JR.
Pres., Southern Christian
Leadership Conference

RABBI EDWARD E. KLEIN
Free Synagogue, New York City

DR. JOHN M. KRUMM
Chaplain, Columbia University

REV. DENNIS G. KUBY
Unitarian Society, Cleveland, O.

REV. JOHN H. LATHROP
Unitarian, Berkeley, California

PROF. PAUL LEHMANN
Theologian, New York City

RABBI EUGENE LIPMAN
Temple Sinai, D.C.

RT. REV. EDGAR A. LOVE
Bishop, Methodist Church,
Baltimore, Md.

DR. JOHN A. MACKAY
Pres. Emer. Princeton Theological
Seminary

RT. REV. WALTER MITCHELL
Episcopal Bishop of Ariz., Ret.

DR. WALTER G. MUELDER
Dean, Boston Theological Sem.

REV. A. J. MUSTE
Secty. Emer., Fellowship for
Reconciliation

DR. REINHOLD NIEBUHR
Theologian, New York City

DR. VICTOR OBENHAUS
Chicago Theological Seminary

REV. ROBERT O'BRIEN
Unitarian, Monterey, California

RT. REV. M. E. PEABODY
Episc. Bish., Central N.Y., Ret.

REV. EDWARD L. PEET
Wesley Meth., Hayward, Calif.

DR. DRYDEN L. PHELPS
Berkeley, California

DR. THEODORE A. RATH
Pres., Bloomfield Col. & Sem.

DR. HARRY B. SCHOLEFIELD
Unitarian, San Francisco, Calif.

DR. HOWARD SCHOMER
Pres., Chicago Theological Sem.

REV. ALBERT L. SEELY
Protestant Chap., U. of Mass.

RABBI BERNARD SEGAL
Dir., United Synagogues of Amer.

DR. D. R. SHARPE
Baptist, Pasadena, California

DR. GUY EMERY SHIPLER
Editor, The Churchman

REV. F. L. SHUTTLESWORTH
Pres., Ala. Christian Movement
Pres., Southern Conf. Edu. Fund

PROF. ARTHUR L. SWIFT, JR.
Theologian

RABBI H. D. TEITELBAUM
Temple Beth Jacob,
Redwood City, Calif.

PROF. BURTON H.
THROCKMORTON, JR.
Bangor Theological Sem., Me.

DR. JAMES D. TYMS
Dean, School of Religion,
Howard University

REV. LUCIUS WALKER
Dir., Northcott Neigh. House,
Milwaukee, Wisconsin

REV. WYATT TEE WALKER
Dir., Southern Christian
Leadership Conference

RABBI JACOB J. WEINSTEIN
KAM Temple, Chicago, Ill.

REV. KENNETH B. WENTZEL
Rockville, Maryland

DR. DAVID RHYS WILLIAMS
Unitarian, Rochester, New York

DR. ROLLAND E. WOLFE
Prof. of Rel., Western Res. Univ.

ARTS AND LETTERS

DONNA ALLEN
Industrial Relations Writer, D.C.

JAMES ARONSON
Editor, National Guardian

MAX AWNER
Editor, Labor News

JAMES BALDWIN
Writer

S. L. M. BARLOW
Writer

HARRY BARNARD
Writer

JOSEPH BARNES
Editor-Writer

PETER BLUME
Painter

KAY BOYLE
Writer

ANNE BRADEN
Editor, Southern Patriot

BENIAMINO BUFANO
Sculptor

ALEXANDER CALDER
Artist

JOHN CIARDI
Poet

GEORGE DANGERFIELD
Historian

BABETTE DEUTSCH
Poet

IRVING DILLIARD
Former Editor—Editorial Page
St. Louis Post Dispatch

LAWRENCE FERLINGHETTI
Poet, Ed./Pub., City Lights Books

SARA BARD FIELD
Poet

WALDO FRANK
Writer

ERICH FROMM
Writer

MAXWELL GEISMAR
Writer

RUSSELL W. GIBBONS
Ed., Writer, Civil Lib. Leader

DR. CARLTON B. GOODLETT
Phys.; Ed./Pub., Sun Times

ROBERT GWATHMEY
Painter

E. Y. HARBURG
Lyricist

STERLING HAYDEN
Actor-Writer

THOMAS B. HESS
Editor, Art News

JOSEPH HIRSCH
Painter

B. W. HUEBSCH
Publisher

JAMES JONES
Writer

MATTHEW JOSEPHSON
Writer

ALBERT E. KAHN
Writer

ROCKWELL KENT
Artist

PHIL KERBY
Editor, Frontier

FREDA KIRCHWEY
Former Editor, The Nation

DR. HELEN LAMB LAMONT
Economic Analyst

JAMES LAWRENCE, JR.
Architect

DENISE LEVERTOV
Poet

BELLA LEWITZKY
Dancer

LENORE MARSHALL
Writer

ALBERT MAYER
Architect

CAREY McWILLIAMS
Editor, The Nation

JESSICA MITFORD
Writer

ASHLEY MONTAGU
Writer-Anthropologist

IRA V. MORRIS
Writer

GEORGE B. MURPHY, JR.
Writer

TRUMAN NELSON
Writer

RUSS NIXON
Manager, National Guardian

HARVEY O'CONNOR
Writer

EMMY LOU PACKARD
Artist

BERNARD B. PERRY
Editor, Indiana Press

BYRON RANDALL
Artist

ROBERT RYAN
Actor

RODERICK SEIDENBERG
Architect

BEN SHAHN
Painter

RAPHAEL SOYER
Painter

I. F. STONE
Writer-Editor

MILTON K. SUSMAN
Writer

MARK VAN DOREN
Writer; Member, Natl. Academy
of Arts & Letters

PIERRE VAN PAASSEN
Writer; Clergyman

DON WEST
Poet

BUSINESS, LABOR AND
THE PROFESSIONS

KURT A. ADLER, M.D., PH.D.
Psychiatrist

ARIS ANAGNOS
Insurance, Beverly Hills

NELSON BENGSTON
Investment Securities, N.Y.C.

DR. WALTER G. BERGMAN
Former Dir., Instruct. Research,
Detroit Public Schools

JESSIE F. BINFORD
Social Worker; Former Dir.,
Hull House

JOHN BRATTIN
Attorney, Lansing, Michigan

JAMES L. BREWER
Attorney, Rochester, New York

HARRY BRIDGES
Pres., Intl. Longshoremen's &
Warehousemen's Union

BENJAMIN J. BUTTENWIESER
New York City, N.Y.

HELEN L. BUTTENWIESER
Attorney, New York City

GRENVILLE CLARK
Attorney-Writer, Dublin, N.H.

JOHN M. COE
Attorney, Pensacola, Florida

JOHN O. CRANE
Found. Trustee, Wds. Hole, Mass.

PERCY M. DAWSON, M.D.
Los Altos, California

JACK G. DAY
Attorney, Cleveland, Ohio

EARL B. DICKERSON
Attorney-Corp. Exec., Chi., Ill.

FRANK J. DONNER
Attorney-Writer, New York City

BENJAMIN DREYFUS
Attorney, San Francisco, Calif.

FYKE FARMER
Attorney, Nashville, Tennessee

OSMOND K. FRAENKEL
Attny.-Civil Lib. Leader, N.Y.C.

A. C. GLASSGOLD
Hotel & Club Employees
Union, AFL-CIO

VIOLA JO GRAHAM
Social Worker, Madison, Wis.

VINCENT HALLINAN
Attorney, San Francisco, Calif.

WILLIAM J. HAYS
Businessman, D.C. & N.Y.C.

FRANCIS HEISLER
Attorney, Carmel, California

HUGH B. HESTER
Brig. General, U.S. Army, Ret.

JAMES IMBRIE
Banker, Ret., Lawrenceville, N.J.

JOHN JURKANIN
Pres. Local 500, Almag.
Meatcutters, AFL-CIO

ROBERT W. KENNY
Attny.; Former Attny. Gen., Cal.

BENJAMIN H. KIZER
Attorney, Spokane, Washington

RAPHAEL KONIGSBERG
Real Estate, Los Angeles, Calif.

WILLIAM M. KUNSTLER
Attny., Civil Lib. Leader, N.Y.C.

MARK LANE
Attny., Former N.Y. Assem.

MORTON LEITSON
Attorney, Flint, Michigan

SIDNEY LENS
Writer; Bus. Mgr. Local #929
AFL-CIO, Chicago, Illinois

CHARLES C. LOCKWOOD
Attorney, Detroit, Michigan

WALTER C. LONGSTRETH
Attorney, Philadelphia, Penn.

BRIAN G. MANION
Attorney, Beverly Hills, Calif.

DAVID A. MARCUS, D.D.S.
Beverly Hills, California

LAFAYETTE MARSH
Attny., Real Est., La Grange, Ill.

C. H. MARSHALL, JR., M.D.
Former Pres., Natl. Medical Asso.

EDWARD A. MARSHALL, M.D.
Cleveland Heights, Ohio

LEO MAYER, M.D.
Orthopedic Surgeon, N.Y.C.

B. F. McLAURIN
Brotherhood of Sleeping Car
Porters, AFL-CIO

JAMES McNAMARA
United Hat, Cap & Millinery
Workers, AFL-CIO

FRANCIS J. McTERNAN
Attorney, San Francisco, Calif.

ROBERT S. MORRIS
Attorney, Los Angeles, California

WALTER M. NELSON
Attorney, Detroit, Michigan

HARRY K. NIER, JR.
Attorney, Denver, Colorado

RICHARD OTTINGER
Attorney, Dist. of Columbia

THOMAS QUINN
Bus. Agent #610, AFL-CIO,
Pittsburgh, Pennsylvania

OSCAR RADEMACHER
Attorney, Medford, Wisconsin

S. ROY REMAR
Attorney, Newton, Massachusetts

DEAN A. ROBB
Attorney-Civil Liberties Leader,
Detroit, Michigan

CATHERINE G. RORABACK
Attorney-Civil Liberties Leader,
New Haven, Connecticut

DR. SUMNER M. ROSEN
Rsch. Asso., Ind. Union Dept.,
AFL-CIO, Boston, Massachusetts

FRANK ROSENBLUM
Secty.-Treas., Amalgamated
Cloth. Wkrs. of Amer., AFL-CIO

HENRY W. SAWYER, III
Attorney-Civil Liberties Leader,
Philadelphia, Pennsylvania

DARBY N. SILVERBERG
Attorney, Torrance, California

BENJAMIN E. SMITH
Attorney-Civil Liberties Leader,
New Orleans, Louisiana

OLIVIA PEARL STOKES, M.D.
Boston, Massachusetts

CARL SUGAR, M.D.
Psychiatrist, Los Angeles, Calif.

JOHN E. THORNE
Attorney, San Jose, Calif.

DONALD E. TWITCHELL
Attorney, Cleveland, Ohio

BRUCE C. WALTZER
Attorney-Civil Liberties Leader,
New Orleans, Louisiana

A. L. WIRIN
Attorney-Civil Liberties Leader,
Los Angeles, California

J. CLARENCE YOUNG
Attorney, Alexandria, Virginia

COMMUNITY

CAROLYN E. ALLEN
YWCA Exec., Ret., Mil., Wisc.

KATHARINE M. ARNETT
Asso. Secty., Women's Intl.
League for Peace & Freedom,
(W.I.L.P.F.) Philadelphia, Pa.

RALPH B. ATKINSON
Monterey, California

WILLIAM V. BANKS
Supreme Grand Master, Intl.
Masons & Eastern Stars

JOSIAH BEEMAN
Pres., Calif. Fed. of Young Dem.

HON. ELMER A. BENSON
Former Gov. of Minnesota

MRS. JOHN C. BERESFORD
Secty., Fairfax County, Virginia
Council on Human Relations

ELIZABETH B. BOYDEN
Cambridge, Massachusetts

CARL BRADEN
Field Organizer, Southern Conf.
Educational Fund, Inc.

DR. THOMAS N. BURBRIDGE
Pres., San Francisco NAACP

ALDEN B. CAMPEN
San Jose, California

MRS. EDWARD C. CARTER
New York City, N.Y.

ELISABETH CHRISTMAN
Washington, D.C.

ETHEL CLYDE
New York City

JOHN COLLIER, SR.
Former U.S. Commissioner of
Indian Affairs

SPENCER COXE

Civil Liberties Leader,
Philadelphia, Pennsylvania

MRS. SYLVIA E. CRANE
Woods Hole, Massachusetts

EDWARD CRAWFORD
Chrm., N.Y. Council to Abolish
IIUAC

MARIAN W. DALGLISH
Chrm., Pittsburgh, Pa. W.I.L.P.F.

DR. JAMES A. DOMBROWSKI
Dir., Southern Conference
Educational Fund, Inc.

JOSEPHINE W. DUVENECK
Los Altos, California

PHYLLIS EDGECUMBE
Civil Liberties Leader,
Los Angeles, California

CARRIE B. EDMONDSON
Milwaukee, Wisconsin

EDWINA E. FERGUSON
Civil Liberties Leader,
Corona del Mar, California

W. H. FERRY
Vice-Pres., Fund for the Republic
Santa Barbara, California

JAMES FORMAN
Dir., Student Non-Violent
Coordinating Committee

HARVEY FURGATCH
Civil Liberties Leader,
La Jolla, California

RUTH GAGE-COLBY
Natl. Bd., W.I.L.P.F.; Stamf., Conn.

MARCUS I. GOLDMAN
Washington, D.C.

JOSEPHINE GOMON
Civil Liberties Leader, Det., Mich.

CHESTER A. GRAHAM
Former Reg. Dir., Friends
Committee on Legislation

ALFRED HASSLER
Ex. Sec. Fellowship of Recon.

ARLENE D. HAYS
Washington, D.C.

BETTY HAYS
Washington, D.C.

DR. EDWIN B. HENDERSON
NAACP Leader, Falls Church, Va.

FRANCES W. HERRING
Women for Peace, Berkeley, Cal.

CHARLES JACKSON
Washington, D.C.

MRS. R. V. INGERSOLL
New York City, N.Y.

MRS. FRED H. IRWIN
Vice-Pres, Cleveland Chapter
United Federalists

KATHLEEN L. JOHNSON
Pasadena, California

CORETTA KING
Atlanta, Georgia

LANGSTON BEACH
Pasadena, California

JOHN LEWIS
Chrm., Student Non-Violent
Coordinating Committee

MRS. CHARLES MADISON
Redding, Connecticut

DOROTHY MARSHALL
Past Pres., Catholic Women's Club
Los Angeles, California

KATHERINE MARSHALL
Former Chrm., Cleveland Voice
of Women, Cleveland, Ohio

FRANCES B. McALLISTER
Pasadena, California

AVA HELEN PAULING
Vice-Pres., National Board,
W.I.L.P.F., Santa Barbara, Calif.

CLARENCE E. PICKETT
Exec. Dir. Emer., Amer. Friends
Serv. Committee, Phila., Pa.

HEDI PIEL
Dist. Ldr., Reform Dem. Club,
New York City

SIDNEY PINES
Chrm. Amer. Zionist Council
of Dallas

HON. JUSTINE WISE POLIER
Judge, New York City

SHAD POLIER
Pres., American Jewish Cong.

MRS. THEODORE ROSEBURY
St. Louis, Missouri

EDWIN A. SANDERS
Exec. Secty., Amer. Friends Serv.
Com., Pac. S. W. Reg. Office

FRANCIS B. SAYRE
Washington, D.C.

MARVIN SCHACTER
Civil Liberties Leader,
West Covina, California

LAURENCE SCOTT
Peace Action Center, Wash., D.C.

DR. BENJAMIN SEGAL
Pres. Phys. Chapt., Amer. Jewish
Cong., New York City, N.Y.

MARGARET T. SIMKIN
Los Angeles Board, W.I.L.P.F.

DR. GEORGE C. SIMKINS
Pres., Greensboro Branch, NAACP

ROBERT H. SOLLEN
Civil Liberties Leader,
Santa Barbara, California

HERBERT S. SOUTHGATE
Alexandria, Virginia

NANCY P. STRAUS
Washington, D.C.

A. BUEL TROWBRIDGE
McLean, Virginia

WILLARD UPHAUS
Dir., World Fellowship, Inc.,
Conway, N.H.

CLARA M. VINCENT
Livonia, Mich. Ldr., W.I.L.P.F.

ROBERT S. VOGEL
Great Neck, N.Y.

EARL L. WALTER
Civil Rights Leader,
Los Angeles, California

HON. J. WATIES WARING
Ret. Judge, New York City, N.Y.

AUBREY W. WILLIAMS
Former Director, National Youth
Administration; Publisher,
The Southern Farmer

MRS. DAGMAR WILSON
Initiator, Women Strike for Peace
BEE R. WOLFE
Tacoma Park, Maryland

APPENDIX V

COMMITTEE OF THE WHOLE, AMERICANS FOR DEMOCRATIC ACTION, AS OF JANUARY 9, 1947

From Hearings before the House Select Committee on Lobbying Activities, 81st Congress, Second Session. *Americans for Democratic Action.* July 11, 12, 1950 (Washington, U.S. Government Printing Office, 1950).

(Names with asterisk appear on the League for Industrial Democracy list.)

Alsop, Joseph, Washington, D.C.; columnist

Alsop, Stewart, Washington, D.C.; columnist

Altman, Jack, New York; executive vice president, United Retail, Wholesale and Department Store Workers of America, CIO

Anderson, Douglas, Chicago; secretary-treasurer, United Railroad Workers of America, CIO

Anderson, Eugenie, Minneapolis; chairman, Democratic-Farm-Labor Party, First District, Minnesota; Ambassador to Denmark

Baldanzi, George, New York; executive vice president, Textile Workers Union of America, CIO

* Bendiner, Robert, New York; associate editor, *Nation*; UDA Board

* Biemiller, Andrew, Milwaukee; Congressman

Bingham, Barry, Louisville; president, Louisville *Courier-Journal*

Blatt, Genevieve, Pittsburgh; chairman, Young Democrats of Pennsylvania

* Bohn, Dr. William, New York; editor, *New Leader*; UDA Board

Bowles, Chester, Essex, Conn.; Governor of Connecticut

Brandt, Evelyn, New York; Friends of Democracy

Brown, Andrew W., Detroit; Michigan Citizens Committee

Brown, Harvey M., New York; president, International Association of Machinists; ECA Labor Chief

* Carey, James B., Washington, D.C.; secretary-treasurer, CIO

Carroll, John A., Denver; Congressman

Carter, Alison E., New York; executive secretary, U.S. Students Assembly, UDA Board

Childs, Marquis, Washington, D.C.; columnist

Clifford, Jerry, Green Bay, Wis.

Crawford, Kenneth, Washington, D.C.; associate editor, *Newsweek*

Cruikshank, Nelson, Washington, D.C.; director, Social Security Activities, AFL, UDA Board

* Danish, Max, New York; editor, *Justice*; ILGWU

Davies, Dr. A. Powell, Washington, D.C.; clergyman, All Souls' Church and American Unitarian Association

Davis, Elmer, Washington, D.C.; radio commentator

Douds, Charles, Englewood, New

521

Jersey; former regional director, NLRB, North Jersey Progressive League

* Dubinsky, David, New York; president, ILGWU-AFL

Edelman, John, Washington, D.C.; legislative representative, Textile Workers Union, CIO, arrangements committee

* Edwards, George, Detroit; president, Detroit Common Council

Edwards, Margaret, Detroit; Michigan Citizens Committee, UDA Board

Ehle, Emily, Philadelphia, Pa.

Epstein, Ethel S., New York; labor arbiter, UDA Board

Ernst, Hugo, Cincinnati; president, Hotel and Restaurant Workers Union, AFL

* Ernst, Morris, New York; counsel, American Civil Liberties Union

Fedder, Herbert L., Baltimore; UDA Baltimore chapter representative

Feder, Michael Ernst, Wellesley; president, U.S. Student Assembly

* Fischer, Louis, New York; author, UDA Board

Fleischman, Bernard, Louisville; UDA Louisville chapter representative

Furstenberg, Dr. Frank, Baltimore; UDA Baltimore chapter representative

Galbraith, J. Kenneth, New York; Harvard professor; former Deputy Director, OPA; *Fortune*

Gamow, Leo, Union City, N.J.; North Jersey Progressive League representative

Gilbert, Richard, Washington, D.C.; former Chief Economist, OPA

Ginsburg, David, Washington, D.C.; former General Counsel, OPA, arrangements committee

Goldblum, A. P., Boston; Harvard Liberal Union, U.S. Student Assembly

Granger, Lester, New York; executive secretary, National Urban League

Green, John, Camden, N.J.; president, Independent Union Marine and Shipbuilding Workers, CIO

Greer, James, New York; Council for Democracy

Grogan, John J., Camden, N.J.; director of organization, Independent Union Marine and Shipbuilding Workers, CIO

Harris, Louis, New York

Harrison, Gilbert, New York; executive vice chairman, now president, American Veterans Committee

* Hayes, A. J., Washington, D.C.; vice president, International Association of Machinists

Hays, Mortimer, New York; UDA Board

Haywood, Allan, Washington, D.C.; vice president and director of organization, CIO

Hedgeman, Anna Arnold, Washington, D.C.

Henderson, Leon, Washington, D.C.

Higgins, Rev. George, Washington, D.C.; National Catholic Welfare Conference

Hildreth, Melvin D., Washington, D.C.; General Counsel, War Relief Control Board

* Hoan, Dan, Milwaukee; former mayor

Hoeber, Johannes U., Philadelphia, Pa.

Hoffman, Sal B., Philadelphia; president, Upholsterers International Union

Holderman, Carl, Newark, N.J.; president, New Jersey State Industrial Union Council, CIO

Holifield, Hon. Chet, Congressman from California

Hollander, Edward, Washington, D.C.; UDA Chapter; arrangements committee

Hook, Frank, Ironwood, Mich.; former Congressman

Hudgens, Robert W., Washington, D.C.; former Deputy Director, Farm Security Administration

Jackson, Gardner, Washington, D.C.; former special assistant to Secretary of Agriculture; arrangements committee

Johnson, Mrs. Clyde, Cincinnati; chairman, Progressive Citizens Committee, UDA Board

Johnson, Morse, Cincinnati; Progressive Citizens Committee

Killen, James S., Washington, D.C.; vice president, International Brotherhood of Pulp, Sulphite and Paper Mill Workers, AFL

Kerr, Chester, New York; Reynal & Hitchcock

Koppelmann, Herman, Hartford, Conn.; former Congressman

Kowal, Leon J., Boston, Mass.; representative, Massachusetts Independent Voters Association

Kyne, Martin, New York; vice president, Retail, Wholesale and Department Store Workers, CIO

*Lash, Joseph P., New York; UDA Director, New York City chapter; arrangements committee

*Lash, Trude Pratt, New York; UDA Board

Lerner, Leo, Chicago; chairman, Independent Voters of Illinois, UDA Board

Levy, Mrs. Newman, New York; representative, New York City chapter, UDA

*Lewis, Alfred Baker, Connecticut; UDA Board

Limbach, Mrs. Sarah, Pittsburgh; Union for Progressive Action

Lindeman, Dr. Edward, New York; president, New York City chapter, UDA

Loeb, James, Jr., Washington, D.C.; national director, UDA: arrangements committee

McCulloch, Frank W., Chicago; vice chairman, Independent Voters of Illinois; director, Labor Education Division, Roosevelt College

*McDowell, A. G., Philadelphia; organization director, Upholsterers International Union, AFL

McLaurin, B. F., New York; International representative, Brotherhood of Sleeping Car Porters, AFL

Messner, Eugene, New York; UDA Board

Montgomery, Don, Washington, D.C.: consumer counsel, United Auto Workers, CIO

Mowrer, Edgar Ansel, Washington, D.C.; columnist

Munger, William L., New York; executive secretary, United Hat, Cap and Millinery Workers, AFL

*Naftalin, Arthur, Minneapolis; secretary to Mayor Hubert Humphrey

*Niebuhr, Dr. Reinhold, New York; chairman, UDA

Oxnam, Bishop G. Bromley, New York; retiring president, Federal Council of Churches

Padover, Saul K., New York; PM

Panek, Nathalie E., Washington, D.C.; UDA national office; arrangements committee

Phillips, Paul L., Albany, N.Y.; first vice president, International Brotherhood of Papermakers, AFL

Pinchot, Cornelia Bryce, Washington, D.C.; UDA Board

*Porter, Paul A., Washington, D.C.; former OPA Director

Poynter, Nelson P., Washington, D.C.; publisher

Prichard, Edward F., Jr., Paris, Ky.; former Deputy Director, OWMR

Rauh, Joseph, Jr., Washington, D.C.; former Deputy Housing Administrator; arrangements committee

Reisenstein, Mrs. Florence, Pittsburgh; Union for Progressive Action

*Reuther, Walter P., Detroit; president, United Auto Workers, CIO

Rieve, Emil, New York; president, Textile Workers Union, CIO

*Roosevelt, Mrs. Franklin D., New York

Roosevelt, Franklin D., Jr. New York

Rosenberg, Marvin, New York; representative, UDA, New York City chapter

Rosenblatt, Will, New York; UDA Board

Rowe, James H., Jr., Washington, D.C.; former Assistant to the President of the United States

Saltzman, Alex E., New York; UDA Board

Scarlett, Rt. Rev. William, St. Louis; Episcopal Bishop of St. Louis

Schachter, Harry, Louisville, Ky.; chairman, Committee for Kentucky

Schlesinger, Arthur M., Jr., Washington, D.C.; arrangements committee; professor, Harvard

Scholle, August, Detroit; president, Michigan State Industrial Union Council, CIO

*Shishkin, Boris, Washington, D.C.; economist, AFL; UDA Board; arrangements committee

Smith, Anthony Wayne, Washington, D.C.; assistant director, Industrial Union Council, CIO; UDA member

Stapleton, Miss Laurence, Bryn Mawr, Pa.

Stokes, Thomas, Washington, D.C.; columnist

Taylor, Barney, Memphis; organization director, National Farm Labor Union, AFL

Tilly, Mrs. M. E., Atlanta; Womens Christian Services Committee, Methodist Church

Townsend, Willard S., Chicago; president, Transport Service Employees; CIO

Tucker, John F. P., Washington, D.C.; UDA national office; arrangements committee

Turner, J. C., Washington, D.C.; business agent, Operating Engineers, AFL; UDA chapter

*Voorhis, H. Jerry, California; former Congressman

Weaver, George L. P., Washington, D.C.; director, Committee to Abolish Discrimination, CIO; UDA Board, arrangements committee

*Wechsler, James, Washington, D.C.; New York *Post*; arrangements committee

Weyler, Edward, Louisville, Ky.; secretary treasurer, Kentucky State Federation of Labor

White, Walter, New York; executive secretary, National Association for the Advancement of Colored People

Wolchok, Samuel, New York; president, Retail, Wholesale and Department Store Employees, CIO

Wyatt, Wilson W., Louisville, Ky.; former Housing Expediter

Young, Hortense, Louisville, Ky.; UDA Louisville chapter

COMMITTEE OF THE WHOLE, AMERICANS FOR DEMOCRATIC ACTION, ADDENDA, JANUARY 22, 1947

Appleby, Paul H., Syracuse, N.Y.; dean, School, Public Administration, Syracuse University

Berger, Clarence, Boston; Independent Voters League

Boettiger, Mr. & Mrs. John, Phoenix, Ariz.; publishers, *Times*

Brandt, Harry, New York; president, Brandt Theaters

Carter, Hodding, Greenville, Miss.; editor, *Democratic Times*

Cluck, Jack R., Seattle; chairman, Progressive Citizens of Washington

Davis, William H., New York; wartime chairman, National War Labor Board

*Douglas, Emily Taft, Chicago; Congresswoman from Illinois

*Douglas, Paul, Chicago; professor, University of Chicago; U.S. Senator

Erickson, Leif, Helena, Mont.; judge, Montana

*Graham, Dr. Frank, Chapel Hill, N.C.; president, University of North Carolina; U.S. Senator

Harrison, Marvin C., Cleveland; attorney; Senatorial candidate

*Heimann, Dr. Edward, New York; dean, Graduate Faculty, New School for Social Research

Howell, Charles R., Trenton, N.J.; businessman; congressional candidate, Congressman

Hoyt, Palmer, Denver; publisher of the Denver *Post*

Kuenzli, Irvin R., Chicago; secretary treasurer, American Federation of Teachers

*Lehman, Herbert H., New York; former Governor of New York; U.S. Senator

*Rogers, Will, Jr., Beverly Hills, Calif.

Smith, Louis P., Boston; treasurer, Massachusetts Independent Voters League

Steinberg, Rabbi Milton, New York; Park Ave. Synagogue

Sweetland, Monroe, Molalla, Oreg.; publisher, Molalla *Pioneer*

Williams, Aubrey, Montgomery, Ala.; editor, *Southern Farmer*

Withers, William, New York; chairman, Division Social Sciences, Queens College

APPENDIX VI

Partial list of ADA members, past or present, in the Kennedy-Johnson Administration between September, 1961 and June, 1962. (Los Angeles *Times, Washington Bureau.*)

Aiken, (Mrs.) Jim G.	Congressional Liaison Officer
Baker, John A.	Department of Agriculture
Belen, Frederic C.	Post Office Department-Operations Section
Bingham, Jonathan B.	U.S. Mission to the United Nations
Bowles, Chester	Department of State-Special Adviser to the President
Cohen, Wilbur J.	Department of Health, Education and Welfare
Conway, Jack T.	Housing and Home Finance Agency
Coombs, Philip	Department of State-Assistant Secretary
Cox, Archibald	Solicitor General
Docking, George	Export-Import Bank
Donahue, Charles	Department of Labor-Solicitor
Elman, Philip	Federal Trade Commission
Finletter, Thomas K.	Department of State-Special Missions
Freeman, Orville	Secretary of Agriculture
Fowler, Henry H.	Under Secretary of the Treasury
Galbraith, John K.	Ambassador to India
Goldberg, Arthur J.	Secretary of Labor
Lewis, Robert G.	Commodity Credit Corporation-Department of Agriculture
Loeb, James Jr.	Ambassador to Peru
Louchheim, Katie	Department of State
McCulloch, Frank W.	Chairman-National Labor Relations Board
Morgan, Howard	Federal Power Commission
Murphy, Charles	Department of Agriculture-Commodity Credit
Peterson, Esther	Assistant Secretary of Labor
Reeves, Frank D.	Commissioner, D.C. (Withdrawn)
Ribicoff, Abraham A.	Secretary of Health, Education and Welfare
Schlesinger, Arthur, Jr.	Assistant to the President
Sorensen, Theodore	Assistant to the President
*Stevenson, Adlai	Special Missions, United Nations (Denied Membership in ADA)
Stoddard, Charles S.	Department of the Interior
Taylor, William L.	Civil Rights Commissions

526

Weaver, George L. P.	International Labor Affairs-Department of Labor
Weaver, Robert C.	Housing and Home Finance Agency
Williams, G. Mennen	Department of State
Wofford, Harrison	Special Assistant to the President
Woolner, Sidney	Housing and Home Finance Agency

*Associated with Independent Voters of Illinois, an ADA affiliate.

SELECTED BIBLIOGRAPHY

BOOKS

AGAR, HERBERT, *Abraham Lincoln*. New York, The Macmillan Company, 1953.

ANGELL, SIR NORMAN, *After All: Autobiography of Sir Norman Angell*. New York, Farrar, Straus and Young, 1951.

ASQUITH, CYNTHIA, *Remember and Be Glad*. New York, Charles Scribner's Sons, 1952.

BAILEY, FOSTER, *Changing Esoteric Values*. London, Lucis Press, Ltd., 1955.

BAKER, RAY STANNARD, *An American Chronicle*. New York, Charles Scribner's Sons, 1945.

————, *What Wilson Did at Paris*. New York, Doubleday, Page and Company, 1919.

————, AND DODD, WILLIAM E., *The Public Papers of Woodrow Wilson*. New York, Harper and Brothers, 1925-1927.

BALDWIN, R. N., AND RANDALL, C. B., *Civil Liberties and Industrial Conflict*. Cambridge, Harvard University Press, 1938.

BARNES, JOSEPH F., *Willkie: The Events He Was Part Of; The Ideas He Fought For*. New York, Simon and Schuster, Inc., 1952.

BARRON, BRYTON, *The Untouchable State Department*. Springfield, Crestwood Books, 1962.

BEER, MAX, *Fifty Years of International Socialism*. London, Allen and Unwin, 1935.

BEER, SAMUEL H., *City of Reason, Harvard Political Studies*. Cambridge, Harvard University Press, 1949.

————, *Treasury Control*. Oxford, Clarendon Press, 1956.

BELLAMY, EDWARD, *Edward Bellamy Speaks Again*. Kansas City, Peerage Press, (Re-print), 1939.

————, *Looking Backward*. Boston, Lee and Shepherd, 1888.

BERLE, ADOLPH A., JR., *The Twentieth Century Capitalist Revolution*. New York, Harcourt, Brace and World, Inc., 1954.

————, AND MEANS, GARDINER C., *The Modern Corporation and Private Property*. New York, The Macmillan Company, 1933.

BERNSTEIN, EDUARD, *My Years of Exile*. New York, Harcourt and Company, 1921.

BEVERIDGE, JANET (Lady), *An Epic of Clare Market*. London, Bell Publishers, 1960.

BEVERIDGE, LORD, *Power and Influence*. New York, The Beechhurst Press, Inc., 1955.

BLACK, EUGENE R., *The Diplomacy of Economic Development*. Cambridge, Harvard University Press, 1060.

BLATCHFORD, ROBERT, *Merrie England*. London, Sonnenschein and Company, 1894.

BLISS, W. D. P. (Rev.), *A Handbook of Socialism*. London, Sonnenschein, 1895.

————, AND BINDER, R. M., *New Encyclopedia of Social Reform*. New York, Funk and Wagnalls Co., Inc., 1908.

BLIVEN, BRUCE, *Previews for Tomorrow*. New York, Alfred A. Knopf, Inc., 1953.

BOHN, WILLIAM E., *I Remember America*. New York, The Macmillan Company, 1962.

BORGEAUD, CHARLES, *Adoption and Amendment of the Constitutions in Europe and America*. New York, The Macmillan Company, 1894.

BOVERI, MARGARET, *Treason in the Twentieth Century*. New York, G. P. Putnam and Company, 1963.

BOWKER, R. R., AND ILES, GEORGE, *Readers Guide in Economic, Social and Political Science*. New York, George Putnam Company, 1891.

BOWMAN, SYLVIA E., *The Year 2000—A Critical Biography of Edward Bellamy*. New York, Bookman Associates, 1958.

BREMNER, ROBERT H., *American Philanthropy*. Chicago, University of Chicago Press, 1960.

BRISSENDEN, PAUL F., *The I.W.W., A Study of American Syndicalism*. New York, Russell and Russell, 1957.

BROCK, CLIFTON, *Americans for Democratic Action*. Washington, Public Affairs Press, 1962.

BROCKWAY, FENNER, *Outside the Right, An Autobiography*. London, Allen and Unwin, 1963.

BRYCE, D. C. L., *The American Commonwealth*. New York, The Macmillan Company, 1894.

BUDENZ, LOUIS F., *This Is My Story*. New York, Whittlesey House-McGraw-Hill, Inc., 1947.

BUNTING, DAVID EDISON, *Liberty and Learning*. Washington, American Council on Public Affairs, 1942.

BURNS, C. DELISLE, *A Short History of the World, 1918-1928*. New York, Payson and Clark, 1928.

BURNS, JAMES MACGREGOR, *The Deadlock of Democracy*. New York, Prentice-Hall, Inc., 1963.

CAINE, SIR SYDNEY, *The History of the London School of Economics*. London, Bell Publishers, 1962.

The Case Against Socialism. A Handbook for Conservative Speakers. With a preface by the Rt. Hon. A. J. Balfour. London, George Allen & Sons, 1909.

CASE, C. M., *Non-Violent Coercion*. New York, D. Appleton-Century Company, 1923.

CATLIN, GEORGE, *The Atlantic Community*. London, Coram, Ltd., 1959.

CHASE, STUART, *American Credos*. New York, Harper and Brothers, 1962.

———, *A New Deal*. New York, The Macmillan Company, 1932.

———, *Rich Land, Poor Land*. New York, Whittlesey House-McGraw-Hill, Inc., 1936.

CHILDS, JOHN L., *Education and Morals*. New York, D. Appleton Company, 1950.

CLAESSENS, AUGUST, *Didn't We Have Fun?* New York, Rand School Press, 1953.

CLARK, KITSON G., *The Making of Victorian England*. London, Methuen and Company, Ltd., 1962.

COLE, G. D. H., *The Post-War Condition of Britain*. New York, Frederick A. Praeger Company.

COLE, MARGARET, *Beatrice Webb*. New York, Harcourt, Brace, 1946.

———, *Growing Up Into Revolution*. London, Longmans, Green and Company, Ltd., 1949.

———, *The Story of Fabian Socialism*. London, Heinemann Educational Books, Ltd., 1961.

The Committee and Its Critics, William F. Buckley, Jr., ed., Chicago, The Henry Regnery Company, 1963.

COURTNEY, PHILIP, *The Economic Munich*. New York, The Philosophical Library, 1949.

COUSINS, NORMAN, *Who Speaks for Man*. New York, The Macmillan Company, 1953.

COWLES, VIRGINIA, *No Cause for Alarm*. New York, Harper and Brothers, 1949.

COWLEY, MALCOLM, *Exile's Return*. New York, The Viking Press, Inc., 1951.

CROSLAND, C. A. R., *The Future of Socialism*. New York, The Macmillan Company, 1957.

———, *The Transition from Capitalism*. London, Turnstile Press, 1952.

DAY, DOROTHY, *The Eleventh Virgin*. New York, A. and C. Boni, 1924.

DAY, HENRY C., *Catholic Democracy*. London, Heath, Cranton and Ousley, 1914.

DEWEY, JOHN, AND DUBINSKY, DAVID, *Pictorial Biography*. New York, Interallied, 1952.

DIES, MARTIN, *The Martin Dies Story*. New York, The Bookmailer, 1963.

DODD, BELLA V., *School of Darkness*. New York, The Devin Adair Company, (Re-issue), 1963.

DOS PASSOS, JOHN, *Mr. Wilson's War*. New York, Doubleday and Company, Inc., 1962.

DOUGLAS, WILLIAM O., *Being An American*. New York, The William Day Company, 1948.

DUGGAN, LAURENCE, *The Americas: The Search for Hemisphere Security*. New York, Henry Holt and Company, 1949.

DUNBAR, JANET, *Mrs. G. B. S. A Biographical Portrait of Charlotte Shaw*. London, Harrap Books, Ltd., 1963.

DURMOND, DWIGHT L., *Roosevelt to Roosevelt*. New York, Henry Holt and Company, 1937.

ECCLES, MARRINER, *Beckoning Frontiers*. New York, Alfred A. Knopf, Inc., 1951.

Economic Classics, W. J. Ashley, ed., New York, The Macmillan Company, 1895.

Economic Essays, Jacob Hollander, ed. (For the American Economic Association). New York, The Macmillan Company, 1927.

ELY, RICHARD T., *Report of the American Economic Association*. Baltimore, J. Murphy Company, 1886.

————, *Socialism and Social Reform*. Boston, T. Y. Crowell and Company, 1894.

ENGELS, FREDERICK, *Socialism, Utopian and Scientific*. London, Sonnenschein and Company, 1892.

ERVINE, ST. JOHN, *Bernard Shaw*. New York, William Morrow and Company, Inc., 1956.

The Essential Lippmann, A Political Philosophy for Liberal Democracy, Clinton Rossiter, and James Lare, eds. New York, Random House, Inc., 1963.

The First International: Minutes of the Hague Congress of 1872, Hans Gerth, ed., Madison, University of Wisconsin Press, 1958.

FLYNN, JOHN T., *The Road Ahead*. New York, The Devin Adair Company, 1949.

FRANK, JEROME, *Courts on Trial*. Princeton, The Press, 1949.

FRANKFURTER, FELIX, *The Case of Sacco-Vanzetti*. New York, Little, Brown and Company, 1922.

GALBRAITH, JOHN K., *The Affluent Society*. Boston, Houghton Mifflin Company, 1958.

————, *American Capitalism*. Cambridge, Harvard University Press, 1952.

————, *American Capitalism: The Concept of Countervailing Power*. Boston, Houghton Mifflin Company, 1956.

————, *The Great Crash, 1929*. Boston, Houghton Mifflin Company, 1955.

GARDINER, A. G., *Pillars of Society*. New York, Dodd, Mead and Company, 1914.

GEORGE, HENRY, *Social Problems*. New York, The National Single Tax League, 1883.

GHENT, WILLIAM J., *Our Benevolent Federalism*. London, The Macmillan Company, 1902.

GIDDINGS, F. H., AND SELIGMAN, E. R. A., *Marginal Utility Testing: The Justice of a Progressive Income Tax*. New York, The Macmillan Company, 1900.

GLENDAY, ROY, *The Economic Consequences of Progress*. London, G. Routledge and Sons, 1934.

GOLDMARK, JOSEPHINE, *Impatient Crusader*. Urbana, University of Illinois Press, 1953.

GOLDSTEIN, DAVID, AND AVERY, MARTHA MOORE, *Socialism: The Nation of Fatherless Children*. Boston, J. Flynn and Company, 1911.

GRONLUND, LAURENCE, *The Co-operative Commonwealth*. Boston, Lee and Shepherd, 1886.

HARRINGTON, MICHAEL, *The Other America: Poverty in the United States*. New York, The Macmillan Company, 1962.

HARRIS, SEYMOUR E. *The Economics of Political Parties*. New York, The Macmillan Company, 1962.

————, *Higher Education: Sources and Finance*. New York, McGraw-Hill, Inc., 1962.

————, *John Maynard Keynes: Economist and Policy Maker*. New York, Charles Scribner's Sons, 1955.

HARRISON, J. F. C., *Learning and Living. A Study in the History of the English Adult Education Movement*. London, Routledge and Kegan Paul, Ltd., 1961.

HARROD, R. F., *The Life of John Maynard Keynes*. New York, The Macmillan Company, 1951.

HEILBRONER, ROBERT L., *The Great Ascent*. New York, Harper and Row, Publishers, 1963.

————, *The Making of Economic Society*. Englewood, Prentice-Hall, Inc., 1962.

————, *The World Philosophers: The Lives, Times and Ideas of the Great Economic Thinkers*. New York, Simon and Schuster, Inc., 1961.

HEILPERIN, MICHAEL, *The Trade of Nations*. New York, Alfred A. Knopf, Inc., 1947.

HENDRICK, BURTON J., *The Life and Letters of Walter Hines Page*. (3 Volumes), New York, Doubleday, Page and Company, 1922-1925.

HILLQUIT, MORRIS, *History of Socialism*. New York, Funk and Wagnalls Co., Inc., 1910.

————, *Loose Leaves from a Busy Life*. New York, The Macmillan Company, 1934.

HOBSON, JOHN A., *Free Thought in the Social Sciences*. London, Allen and Unwin, 1926.

HOBSON, S. G., *Pilgrim to the Left*. London, Longmans, Green and Company, Ltd., 1938.

HOFFMAN, PAUL G., *World Without Want*. New York, Harper and Row, Publishers, 1962.

Holmes-Laski Letters, Mark DeWolf Howe, ed., Cambridge, Harvard University Press, 1953.

(HOUSE, COL. E. M.), *Philip Dru, Administrator*. New York, B. W. Huebsch, 1912.

HOWARD, PETER, *The World Rebuilt*. New York, Duell, Sloan and Pearce, 1951.

HUBBARD, BELA, *Political and Economic Structures*. Caldwell, Caxton Printers, Ltd., 1956.

HUBERMAN, LEO, *The Truth About Socialism*. New York, The Lear Company, 1950.

HUNTER, LESLIE, *The Road to Brighton Pier*. London, Arthur Barker, Ltd., 1959.

HUNTER, ROBERT, *Revolution*. New York, Harper and Brothers, 1940.

HYDE, H. MONTGOMERY, *Room 303*. New York, Dell Publishing Company, (Re-print), 1964.

HYMAN, STANLEY EDGAR, *The Tangled Bank*. New York, Atheneum Publishers, 1962.

HYNDMAN, H. M., *Historical Basis of Socialism in England*. London, Routledge and Kegan Paul, Ltd., 1883.

The Intimate Papers of Colonel House, C. Seymour, ed., Boston, Houghton Mifflin Company, 1926.

JAY, DOUGLAS, M.P., *Socialism in the New Society*. London, Longmans, Green and Company, Ltd., 1963.

JOHNSON, PRESIDENT LYNDON B., *A Time for Action*. (Introduction by Adlai E. Stevenson). New York, Atheneum Publishers, 1964.

JOSEPHSON, MATTHEW, *The Robber Barons*. New York, Harcourt, Brace and Company, 1934.

JOUGHLIN, LOUIS G., AND MORGAN, EDMUND M., *The Legacy of Sacco and Vanzetti*. (Introduction by Arthur M. Schlesinger.) New York, Harcourt, Brace and Company, 1948.

JOUVENAL, BERTRAND DE, *On Power*. New York, The Viking Press, Inc., 1949.

KAUTSKY, KARL, *Social Democracy Versus Communism*. New York, Rand School Press, 1946.

KEEZER, DEXTER M., AND MAY, STACY, *The Public Control of Business: A Study of Anti-Trust Law Enforcement, Public Interest Regulations and Government Participation in Business*. New York, Harper and Brothers, 1930.

KELLY, EDMOND, *Twentieth Century Socialism*. New York, Longmans, Green and Company, Ltd., 1911.

KENNEDY, JOHN F., *Why England Slept*. New York, Doubleday and Company, Inc., 1962.

KENNEDY, ROBERT F., *Just Friends and Brave Enemies*. New York, Harper and Row, 1962.

KERR, CLARK, *The Uses of the University*. Cambridge, Harvard University Press, 1963.

KEYNES, JOHN MAYNARD, *The Economic Consequences of the Peace*. New York, Harcourt, Brace and Company, 1925.

———, *Essays in Biography*. New York, Harcourt, Brace and Company, 1933.

———, *General Theory of Economics*. New York, Harcourt, Brace and Company, 1930.

———, *General Theory of Employment, Interest and Money*. New York, Harcourt, Brace and Company, 1936.

———, *A Short View of Russia*. London, Hogarth Press, 1925.

KINTNER, WILLIAM R., *The Front Is Everywhere*. Norman, University of Oklahoma Press, 1950.

KIPNIS, IRA, *The American Socialist Movement, 1897–1912*. New York, Columbia University Press, 1952.

KLUCKHOHN, FRANK L., *The House that Jack Built, A Candid Look at the Men Around Kennedy.* New York, The Devin Adair Company, 1963.
———, *The Inside on LBJ.* New York, Monarch Books, 1964.
KOLKO, GABRIEL, *Wealth and Power in America.* New York, Frederick A. Praeger, Inc., 1962.
KROPOTKIN, PRINCE, *Mutual Aid: A Factor of Evolution.* New York, Alfred A. Knopf, Inc., 1922.
LANSBURY, GEORGE, *My Life.* London, Constable and Company, 1928.
LASKI, HAROLD, *The Crisis and the Constitution, 1931 and After.* London, Hogarth Press and The Fabian Society, 1932.
———, *Grammar of Politics.* New Haven, Yale University Press, 1928.
LASKY, VICTOR, *John F. Kennedy.* Washington, Free World Press, 1960.
———, *JFK: The Man and the Myth.* New York, The Macmillan Company, 1963.
LAVELEYE, EMILE DE, *Socialism of Today.* London, The Leadenhall Press and Field and Tuer, 1882.
LEONHARD, WOLFGANG, *The Kremlin Since Stalin.* New York, Frederick A. Praeger Company, 1962.
LEWIS, C. S., *The Screwtape Letters.* New York, The Macmillan Company, 1934.
The Liberal Papers, James Roosevelt, ed., New York, Doubleday and Company, Inc., 1962.
LINCOLN, MURRAY D., *Vice President in Charge of Revolution.* New York, McGraw-Hill, Inc., 1960.
LIPPMANN, WALTER, *Preface to Morals.* New York, The Macmillan Company, 1929.
LIPSET, SEYMORE M., *The First New Nation.* New York, Basic Books, Inc., 1963.
LOVETT, ROBERT MORSS, LASKI, HAROLD AND OTHERS, *Recovery Through Revolution.* New York, Covici, Friede, 1933.
LUARD, EVAN, *Nationality and Wealth. A Study in World Government.* London, Oxford University Press, 1964.
LUNN, SIR ARNOLD, *The Science of World Revolution.* New York, Sheed and Ward, 1938.
McCARRAN, MARGARET P., *Fabianism in the Political Life of Britain.* Chicago, Heritage Foundation, 1954.
McWILLIAMS, CAREY, *Witch Hunt: The Revival of Heresy.* Boston, Little, Brown and Company, 1950.
MARTIN, JAMES J., *American Liberalism and World Politics, 1931-1941.* New York, The Devin Adair Company, 1963.
MARTIN, JOHN W., *Dictators and Democracies Today.* Winter Park, The Rollins Press, 1935.
MARTIN, KINGSLEY, *Harold Laski: A Biographical Memoir.* New York, The Viking Press, Inc., 1953.
MARTIN, PRESTONIA MANN, *Is Mankind Advancing?* New York, The Baker and Taylor Company, 1910.
———, *The National Livelihood Plan.* Winter Park, The Rollins Press, 1932.

MARX, KARL, *The Eastern Question*. Eleanor Aveling, ed., London, Sonnenschein and Company, 1899.

MARX, KARL AND ENGELS, FREDERICK, *Selected Correspondence, 1846-1895*. New York, International Publishers, 1942.

MATTHEWS, J. B., *Odyssey of a Fellow Traveler*. New York, Mt. Vernon Publishers, Inc., 1938.

Memorials of Thomas Davidson. The Wandering Scholar, William Knight, ed., Boston and London, Ginn and Company, 1907.

MOLEY, RAYMOND, *The Republican Opportunity*. New York, Duell, Sloan and Pearce, 1962.

MORGAN, ARTHUR E., *Edward Bellamy*. New York, Columbia University Press, 1944.

MORRIS, ROBERT, *No Wonder We Are Losing*. (Eighth Edition). New York, The Bookmailer, 1961.

MUMFORD, LEWIS, *The Conduct of Life*. New York, Harcourt, Brace and Company, 1951.

MYRDAL, GUNNAR, (With the assistance of Richard Sterner and Arnold Rose), *An American Dilemma*. New York, Harper and Brothers, 1944.

NEVINS, ALLEN, *The State Universities and Democracy*. Urbana, University of Illinois Press, 1962.

The New Economics: Keynes Influence on Theory and Public Policy. Seymour E. Harris, ed. A Symposium. New York, Alfred A. Knopf, Inc., 1947.

NIEBUHR, DR. REINHOLD, *Reflexions on the End of an Era*. New York, Charles Scribner's Sons, 1934.

NITTI, FRANCISCO, *Catholic Socialism*. New York, The Macmillan Company, 1895.

NOLAN, ADAM B., *Titoism: The Cominform*. Cambridge, Harvard University Press, 1952.

OVERSTREET, H. A., *A Declaration of Interdependence*. New York, W. W. Norton Company, 1937.

————, *Influencing Human Behavior (Applied Psychology)*. New York, The Peoples Institute Publishing Company, 1925.

OVERSTREET, HARRY AND BONARO, *The War Called Peace (Applied Psychology)*. New York, W. W. Norton Company, 1961.

PAKENHAM, LORD, *Born to Believe*. London, Jonathan Cape, 1953.

PEARSON, HESKETH, *Bernard Shaw*. London, Methuen and Company, Ltd., 1961.

PEASE, EDWARD R., *The History of the Fabian Society*. London, A. C. Fifield, 1916.

————, *History of Socialism*. London, A. & C. Black, 1913.

PERKINS, FRANCES, *The Roosevelt I Knew*. New York, The Viking Press, Inc., 1946.

Politics—1964. Francis M. Carney, and H. Frank Way, eds., Belmont, Wadsworth Publishing Co., 1964.

POSTGATE, RAYMOND, *The Life of George Lansbury*. London, Longmans, Green and Company, Ltd., 1951.

QUINT, HOWARD, *The Forging of American Socialism*. Columbia, University of South Carolina Press, 1953.

REID, D. C., *Effective Industrial Reform*. Stockbridge, D. C. Reid (Privately Published), 1910.

Reinhold Niebuhr: His Religious, Social and Political Thought. Charles W. Kagley and Robert Bretall, eds., New York, The Macmillan Company, 1956.

RIKER, WILLIAM H., *Democracy in the U.S.A.* New York, The Macmillan Company, 1953.

ROBERTS, H. L., *Britain and the United States*. New York, Harper and Brothers, 1953.

ROBERTSON, DENNIS H., *Money*. Chicago, University of Chicago Press, 1959.

ROCKEFELLER, NELSON A., *The Future of Federalism*. Cambridge, Harvard University Press, 1962.

ROSSITER, CLINTON, *Seedtime of the Republic*. New York, Harcourt, Brace and Company, 1953.

ROSTOW, EUGENE V., *Planning for Freedom: The Public Law of American Capitalism*. New Haven, Yale University Press, 1959.

ROSTOW, W. W., *The Dynamics of Soviet Society*. New York, W. W. Norton Company, 1954.

——, *The Stages of Economic Growth*. New York, Harper and Row, 1960.

——, *The United States in the World Arena*. New York, Harper and Row, 1960.

ROSTOW, W. W., AND MILLIKAN, M. F., *A Proposal: Key to an Effective Foreign Policy*. New York, Harper and Brothers, 1957.

RUSSELL, A. E., *Home Life of the Brook Farm Association*. Boston, Little, Brown and Company, 1900.

SANBORN, FRED R., *Design for War*. New York, The Devin Adair Company, 1951.

SCHACHTMAN, MAX, *The Bureaucratic Revolution*. New York, Donald Press, 1962.

SCHLESINGER, ARTHUR M., JR., *The Age of Roosevelt*. Boston, Houghton Mifflin Company, 1957-60.

——, *The Crisis of the Old Order*. Boston, Houghton Mifflin Company, 1957.

——, *The Politics of Hope*. Boston, Houghton Mifflin Company, 1963.

SCHUMAN, FRED L., *The Commonwealth of Man*. New York, Alfred A. Knopf, Inc., 1950.

SCHUMPETER, JOSEPH A., *Capitalism, Socialism and Democracy*. New York, Harper and Row, Publishers, 1950.

SHAW, ALBERT, *Municipal Government in Great Britain*. New York, The Century Company, 1893.

SHAW, GEORGE BERNARD, *Collected Letters*. London, The Bodley Head, 1963.

——, *Complete Plays. With Prefaces*. New York, Dodd, Mead and Company, 1962. Six Volumes.

SHEPHERD, ALBERT, *The Politics of African Nationalism*. New York, Frederick A. Praeger Company, 1962.

SHERWOOD, R. E., *Roosevelt and Hopkins*. New York, Harper and Brothers, 1948, 1950.

SHINWELL, EMANUEL, *Conflict Without Malice, An Autobiography*. London, Odhams Press, Ltd., 1955.

SINCLAIR, UPTON, *A Personal Jesus*. New York, Evans Press, 1952.

————, *The Autobiography of Upton Sinclair*. New York, Harcourt, Brace and World, 1962.

SINNOTT, EDMUND, *Two Roads to Truth*. New York, The Viking Press, Inc., 1950.

SLESSER, HENRY, *Judgment Reserved*. London, Hutchinson & Company, Ltd., 1941.

SMITH, A. D. H., *Mr. House of Texas*. New York, Funk and Wagnalls Co., Inc., 1940.

SMITH, HOWARD K., *Last Train from Berlin*. New York, Alfred A. Knopf, Inc., 1942.

The Social Teachings of the Church. Anne Fremantle, ed., New York, Mentor-Omega, 1963.

Social Unrest, L. P. Powell, ed. (Two volumes). New York, The Review of Reviews Company, 1919.

The Socialism of Our Times. A Symposium. Harry W. Laidler and Norman Thomas, eds. New York, The Vanguard Press-League for Industrial Democracy, 1929.

SOROKIN, P., *Contemporary Sociological Theories (Conflict and Co-operation)*. New York, Harper and Brothers, 1928.

SOULE, GEORGE, *The Coming American Revolution*. New York, The Macmillan Company, 1934.

SOUTHERAN, CHARLES, *Horace Greeley*. New York, Mitchell Kennerly, 1915.

SPARGO, JOHN, *Socialism*. New York, The Macmillan Company, 1913.

SPENDER, STEPHEN, *Forward from Liberalism*. London, V. Gollancz, Ltd., 1937.

SPRAGUE, REV., F. M., *Socialism from Genesis to Revelation*. Boston, Lee and Shepherd, 1892.

SQUIRES, J. D., *British Propaganda in the United States 1914-1917*. Cambridge, Harvard University Press, 1935.

STALEY, EUGENE, *Creating an Industrial Civilization*. New York, Harper and Brothers, 1952.

STEGMAN AND HUGE, *Handbuch der Socialismus*. Zurich, Schabelitz Company, 1894.

STREIT, CLARENCE, *Freedom's Frontier: Atlantic Union Now*. New York, Harper and Brothers, 1962.

————, *Union Now*. New York, Harper and Brothers, 1940.

SWADOS, HARVEY, *A Radical's America*. New York, Little, Brown and Company, 1962.

SWIFT, LINDSAY, *Brook Farm*. New York, The Macmillan Company, 1908.

TAWNEY, R. H., *The Attack*. New York, Harcourt, Brace and Company, 1953.

TAYLOR, OVERTON H., *The Classical Liberalism and the Twentieth Century.* Cambridge, Harvard University Press, 1960.

TELLER, JUDD L., *Scapegoat of Revolution.* New York, Charles Scribner's Sons, 1954.

THEIMER, WALTER, *The Encyclopedia of Modern World Politics.* New York, Rinehart and Company, 1950.

THOMAS, HELEN S., *Felix Frankfurter: Scholar on the Bench.* Baltimore, Johns Hopkins University Press, 1960.

THOMAS, IVOR, *The Socialist Tragedy.* New York, The Macmillan Company, 1953.

THOMPSON, E. P., *The Making of the English Working Class.* London, Pantheon Company, 1964.

TITMUSS, RICHARD M., *Essays on the Welfare State.* New Haven, Yale University Press, 1959.

TOLMAN, W., AND HULL, W. G., *Handbook of Sociological Information.* (With special reference to New York City). New York, City Vigilance League, 1894.

TROWBRIDGE, WILLIAM R. H., *Cagliostro (Savant or Scoundrel?).* New Hyde Park, University Books, 1961.

TRUMAN, HARRY S., *Memoirs.* Garden City, Doubleday and Company, Inc., 1956.

TUTTLE, FLORENCE G., *Women and World Federation.* New York, McBride and Company, 1919.

The Varieties of Economics, Robert Lachman, ed., Cleveland, World Publishing Company, 1962.

VELIE, LESTER, *Labor U.S.A.* New York, Harper and Brothers, 1958.

WAGNER, WARREN W., *H. G. Wells and the World State.* New Haven, Yale University Press, 1961.

WALLACE, HENRY A., *New Frontiers.* New York, Reynal and Hitchcock, 1934.

WALLAS, GRAHAM, *The Great Society* (With Dedication to Walter Lippmann). New York, The Macmillan Company, 1920.

WARNER, AMOS G., *American Charities.* New York, T. Y. Crowell Company, 1893.

WEBB, BEATRICE, *My Apprenticeship.* London, Longmans, Green and Company, Ltd., 1926.

———, *Our Partnership.* London, Longmans, Green and Company, Ltd., 1948.

WEBB, SIDNEY, *Socialism in England.* London, Sonnenschein and Company, 1893.

WEBB, SIDNEY AND BEATRICE, *The Decay of Capitalist Civilisation.* London, The Fabian Society and Allen and Unwin, 1923.

WEINGAST, DAVID E., *Walter Lippmann A Study in Personal Journalism.* New Brunswick, Rutgers Press, 1949.

WEST, HERBERT, *Rebel Thought.* New York, Beacon Press, 1953.

WHITE, THEODORE H., *The Making of the President, 1960.* New York, Atheneum, 1961.

WHITE, THEODORE H., *The Making of the President, 1964*. New York, Atheneum, 1965.

WHITE, WILLIAM S., *Citadel*. New York, Harper and Brothers, 1957.

WIDENER, ALICE, *Behind the U.N. Front*. New York, The Bookmailer, 1962.

WIGGINS, JAMES R., *Freedom or Secrecy*. New York, Oxford Press, 1956.

WILCOX, CLAIR, *Civil Liberties Under Attack*. Philadelphia, University of Pennsylvania Press, 1951.

WILLERT, ARTHUR, *The Road to Safety*. London, Derek Verschoyle, 1952.

WILLEY, MALCOLM, AND RICE, STUART, *Communication Agencies and Social Life*. New York, McGraw-Hill, Inc., 1933.

WILLIAMS, FRANCIS, *Ernest Bevin. Introduction by the Rt. Hon. Clement Attlee, O.M., C.H., M.P.* London, Hutchinson and Company, Ltd., 1952.

WILSON, WOODROW, *The New Freedom*. New York, Doubleday, Page and Company, 1913.

WIRTH, LOUIS, *The Ghetto*. Chicago, The University of Chicago Press, 1929.

WOLFSKILL, GEORGE, *The Revolt of the Conservatives*. Boston, The Macmillan Company, 1962.

WOOLF, LEONARD, *International Government*. New York, Brentano, 1916.

WORMSER, RENE A., *Foundations: Their Power and Influence*. New York, The Devin Adair Company, 1958.

YARDLEY, HERBERT O., *The American Black Chamber*. Indianapolis, The Bobbs-Merrill Company, Inc., 1925.

PUBLICATIONS OF THE LONDON FABIAN SOCIETY

Fabian International Review. Edited by Kenneth Younger, M.P. for the Fabian International Bureau. No. 1, January, 1953 through No. 12, September, 1956. London, Fabian Publications, Ltd.

Fabian Journal. No. 3, March, 1952 through No. 23, November, 1959. London, Fabian Publications, Ltd.

Fabian News. Vol. 8, No. 2, February, 1898 through Vol. 75, No. 11, November–December, 1964. London, The Fabian Society.

Fabian Quarterly. Summer, 1948. London, Fabian Publications, Ltd.

Fabian Research (Pamphlet) Series. London, The Fabian Society.

ARMSTRONG, MICHAEL, AND YOUNG, MICHAEL, *New Look at Comprehensive Schools*. No. 237, January, 1964.

BENENSON, PETER, *A Free Press*. No. 223, June, 1961.

BETTS, T. F., *Bulk Purchase and the Colonies*. Fabian Colonial Bureau, No. 183, November, 1956.

BOYDEN, H. J., M.P., *Councils and Their Public*. No. 221, April, 1961.

BRACK, HARRY, *Building for a New Society*. No. 239, April, 1964.

COOPER, JACK, *Industrial Relations: Sweden Shows the Way*. No. 235, May, 1963.

DONNISON, DAVID AND JAY, PEGGY, AND STEWART, MARY, *The Ingleby Report. Three Critical Essays*. No. 231, December, 1962.

DUMPLETON, C. W., *Colonial Development Corporation*. Fabian Colonial Bureau, No. 186, April, 1957.

ENNALS, DAVID, *A United Nations Police Force?* Fabian International Bureau, No. 210, September, 1959.

ENNALS, DAVID, AND CAMPBELL, IAN, *Middle East Issues.* No. 220, February, 1961.

The General Election and After. Fabian Research Series, No. 102, 1946.

HUGHES, JOHN, *Change in the Trade Unions.* No. 244, August, 1964.

MORRIS, PAULINE, *Prison After-Care: Charity or Public Responsibility.* No. 218, November, 1960.

PAVITT, LAURIE, *The Health of the Nation. The Second Stage of the N. H. S.* No. 236, December, 1963.

ROSS, NORMAN, *The Democratic Firm.* No. 242, July, 1964.

SEGAL, AARON, *Massacre in Rwanda.* No. 240, April, 1964.

SINGLETON, FREDERICK, AND TOPHAM, ANTHONY, *Workers' Control in Jugo-Slavia.* No. 233, February, 1963.

STEWART, MARY, *Consumers' Councils.* Based on Investigations by Local Fabian Societies. Foreword by the Rt. Hon. Hugh Gaitskell, M.P. No. 155, January, 1953.

THORNBERRY, CEDRIC, *Stranger at the Gate.* A study of the Law on Aliens and Commonwealth Citizens. No. 243, August, 1964.

WILLIAMS, SHIRLEY, *Central Africa: The Economics of Inequality.* Fabian Commonwealth Bureau. June, 1960.

Fabian Society Annual Reports. 69th Report, July, 1951–June, 1952 through 81st Report, July, 1963–June, 1964. London: The Fabian Society.

Fabian Tracts. London, The Fabian Society.

ABEL-SMITH, BRIAN, *Freedom in the Welfare State.* No. 353, March, 1964.

BAKER, ASHMORE, *Public vs. Private Electric Supply.* No. 173, 1913.

BALOGH, THOMAS, *Planning for Progress.* A Strategy for Labour. No. 346, July, 1963.

BEAVAN, JOHN, *The Press and the Public.* No. 338, July, 1962.

BROWN, NEVILLE, *Britain in NATO.* No. 357, November, 1964.

COLE, G. D. H., *The Fabian Society Past and Present.* Revised 1952 by Margaret Cole. No. 258.

————, *Labour's Second Term.* London, Fabian Publications, Ltd. and Victor Gollancz, Ltd. No. 273, May, 1949.

CROSSMAN, R. H. S., *Socialism and the New Despotism.* No. 298, February, 1956.

GAITSKELL, HUGH, M.P., *Socialism and Nationalisation.* No. 300, July, 1956.

GOODMAN, GEOFFREY, *Redundancy in the Affluent Society.* No. 340, October, 1962.

HARVEY, AUDREY, *Casualties of the Welfare State.* No. 321, February, 1960.

HEALEY, DENIS, M.P., *A Labour Britain and the World.* No. 352, January, 1964.

HOBSON, S. G., *Public Control of Electric Power and Transit.* No. 119, 1905.

KLEIN, LISL, *The Meaning of Work.* No. 349, October, 1963.

Lynes, Tony, *Pension Rights and Wrongs. A Critique of the Conservative Scheme.* No. 348, September, 1963.

New Patterns for Primary Schools. A Fabian Group. No. 356, September, 1964.

Olivier, Baron Sydney Haldane, *Imperial Trusteeship.* No. 230, 1929.

Pickles, William, *Not With Europe: The Political Case for Staying Out.* Fabian International Bureau. No. 336, April, 1962.

Sargent, J. R., *Out of Stagnation. A Policy for Growth.* No. 343, February, 1963.

Shaw, Bernard, *Report on Fabian Policy.* No. 70, 1896.

——, *Socialism and Superior Brains.* No. 146, 1909.

——, *Vote, Vote, Vote!* No. 43, 1892.

Socialists and Managers. A Fabian Group. No. 351, December, 1963.

Sorensen, Reginald, *Aden, the Protectorates and the Yemen.* Fabian International and Commonwealth Bureau. No. 332, July, 1961.

Stewart, Michael, M.P., *Policy and Weapons in the Nuclear Age.* No. 296, August, 1955.

Stewart, Michael, and Winsbury, Rex, *An Incomes Policy for Labour.* No. 350, October, 1963.

Vaizey, John, *Education in a Class Society. The Queen and Her Horses Reign.* No. 342, November, 1962.

Webb, Sidney, *The War and the Workers.* No. 176, 1914.

What an Education Committee Can Do In Elementary Schools. The Education Group. No. 156, 1911.

Williams, Raymond, *The Existing Alternatives in Communications.* No. 337, June, 1962.

Young, Elizabeth, *Nations and Nuclear Weapons.* No. 347, July, 1963.

Young, Wayland, *Bombs and Votes.* No. 354, May, 1964.

OTHER PUBLICATIONS

The New Fabian Essays, Crossman, R. H. S. ed. With a preface by the Rt. Hon. C. R. Attlee. London, The Turnstile Press, 1952.

Shaw, George Bernard, "Sixty Years of Fabianism," *Fabian Essays.* Jubilee Edition. London, The Fabian Society and Allen and Unwin, 1945.

Social Security. Robson, W. A. ed. London, A Subcommittee of the Fabian Society, 1943.

Starr, Mark, *Labour Politics in the U.S.A.* London, Fabian Publications, Ltd.-Victor Gollancz, Ltd., 1949.

Venture. Vol. 2, No. 2, February, 1949 through Vol. 9, No. 6, November, 1957. Journal of the Fabian Colonial Bureau.

Vol. 15, No. 1, January, 1963 through Vol. 15, No. 2, February, 1963. Journal of the Fabian Commonwealth Bureau.

Vol. 15, No. 3, March, 1963 through Vol. 16, No. 11, October, 1964. Fabian International and Commonwealth Bureau.

London: The Fabian Society.

Woolf, Leonard, and Ward, Barbara, *Hitler's Road to Bagdad,* Fabian

International Research Section, The Fabian Society. London, Allen and Unwin, 1937.

Young Fabian Pamphlets. London, The Fabian Society.

GLENNERSTER, HOWARD, AND PRYKE, RICHARD, *The Public Schools.* No. 7, November, 1964.

The Mechanics of Victory. Prepared by a Study Group. No. 3, February, 1962.

STEELE, DAVID, *More Power to the Regions.* No. 5, March, 1964.

THOMPSON, PAUL, *Architecture: Art or Social Service?* No. 6, March, 1963.

PUBLICATIONS AND BULLETINS OF THE SOCIALIST INTERNATIONAL

Bulletin of the International Council of Social Democratic Women. Vol. III, No. 9, September, 1957 through Vol. X, No. 9, September, 1964, London.

Economic Development and Social Change (Pamphlet). London, The Socialist International. (n.d.—probably 1962 or 1963).

Socialist International Information. Official Bulletin of the Socialist International. Vol. VII, No. 12, March, 1957 through Vol. XIV, No. 24, November, 1964, London.

The World Today . . . The Socialist Perspective. Declaration of the Congress of the Socialist International held in Oslo, Norway in 1962. London, The Socialist International. (n.d.—probably 1962.)

Yearbook of the International Socialist Labour Movement, 1956-1957. Braunthal, Julius, ed. Published under the Auspices of the Socialist International and the Asian Socialist Conference. London, Lincolns-Prager, 1956.

NEWSPAPERS AND PERIODICALS

ABBOTT, LEONARD D., "A Socialist Wedding." *International Socialist Review,* (July, 1901).

ADA World, (November, 1948 through June, 1964). Washington, Americans for Democratic Action.

AFL-CIO Free Trade Union News. Vol. 18, No. 2, February, 1963 through Vol. 19, No. 11, November, 1964. Published monthly by the AFL-CIO Department of International Affairs: Jay Lovestone, Director. Washington and New York.

The American Fabian. Vol. I, No. 1, February, 1895 through Vol. IV, No. 10, October, 1898. Boston and New York.

The American Socialist. Vol. IV, No. 4, April, 1957 through Vol. VI, No. 3, March, 1959. New York.

ANNIS, A. D. AND MEIER, N. C., "The Induction of Opinion Through Suggestion by Means of Planted Content." *The Journal of Social Psychology,* (February, 1934).

BALDWIN, HANSON W., "Slow-Down in the Pentagon." *Foreign Affairs,* (January, 1965).

BELLAMY, EDWARD, "Fourth of July, 1992." *Boston Globe,* (July 4, 1982).
———, "How I Wrote *Looking Backward.*" *Ladies' Home Journal,* Vol. XI, (April, 1894).
———, "Progress of Nationalism in the United States." *North American Review,* (June, 1892).
BOHN, WILLIAM E., "Americans for Democratic Action Celebrates Its Tenth Birthday." *The New Leader,* (April 15, 1957).
BRANDEIS, ELIZABETH, "Memories of a Socialist Snob." *The Progressive,* (August, 1948).
British Information Services Releases, T40, September, 1957 through T43, November, 1962. New York: B.I.S., Rockefeller Plaza.
British Record, No. 7, May 8, 1957 through No. 18, December 4, 1964. New York.
Bulletin of the Atomic Scientists, Vol. XIV, No. 6, June, 1958 through Vol. XX, No. 4, April, 1964. Chicago.
Bulletin of the Rand School of Social Sciences, (1911 through 1935). New York.
The Call, (July, 1917). New York.
Chatanooga News, (March 1, 1935).
Chicago Socialist, (October 30, 1905).
Chicago Sun-Times, (March 30, 1961).
CLARKE, WILLIAM, "The Fabian Society." *The New England Magazine,* Vol. IV, No. 1, (January, 1894). Boston.
The Congregationalist, (June 15, 1901). Boston.
Congressional Record, House of Representatives, (May 3, 1934; May 22, 1950; October 12, 1962).
CONSIDINE, BOB, Interview with General Douglas McArthur. *Hearst Headline Service,* (April 18, 1964).
Current, No. 39, July, 1963 through No. 52, October, 1964. New York.
The Daily Enterprise, (April 18, 1964; June 3, 1964). Riverside, California.
The Daily Worker, (April 20, 1950; December 13, 1961). New York.
The Daily Worker, (May 9, 1936). London.
Department of State Bulletin, (February 3, 1964; February 17, 1964; March 2, 1964; March 16, 1964). Washington.
EFTA Reporter, No. 44, September, 1962 through No. 97, May 15, 1964. Washington: European Free Trade Association Information Office.
FRANKFURTER, FELIX, "The Supreme Court and the Public." *Forum,* (June, 1930).
Freedom, (June, 1919). Stelton, N.J.
Freedom and Union, Vol. VI, No. 9, October, 1951 through Vol. XIX, No. 11, November, 1964. Washington.
German News, Vol. VI, No. 13, November, 1962 through Vol. VII, No. 11, October, 1963. Munich, Published monthly by a nonpartisan group of German parliamentarians.
GLASER, WILLIAM A., "A. M. Simons: American Marxist." *Institute of Social Studies Bulletin,* (1952-53). New York, The Rand School.
HALL, GUS, "The Ultra-Right, Kennedy and the Role of Progressives." *Political Affairs,* (August, 1961).

HARRIS, SEYMOUR E., "Kennedy and the Liberals." *The New Republic,* (June 1, 1963).

Hemispherica, Bulletin of the U.S. Committee of the Inter-American Association for Democracy and Freedom. Vol. I, No. 1, January, 1952 through Vol. XII, No. 10, November, 1963. New York.

HICKEY, D. M., "The Philosophical Argument for World Government." *World Justice, (Justice dans le Monde.)* Vol. VI, No. 2, (December, 1964). Louvain, Belgium, The Louvain University.

Human Events, (January, 1960 through November, 1964). Washington.

The Humanist, (November-December, 1957). Yellow Springs, Ohio.

International Trade Union News, ITN 1, March 1, 1963 through ITN 20, December 15, 1963. Brussels.

KENNEDY, JOHN F., "Inside the Upper House." *The New Leader,* (May 13, 1957).

LENS, SID, "Report on Asian Socialism." *Dissent,* A Quarterly. (Winter, 1955). New York.

Life, (June 30, 1949; January 10, 1964).

LIPPMANN, WALTER, "Notes for a Biography." *The New Republic,* (July 16, 1930).

Lloyd's Bank Review, (January, 1947 through December, 1951). London.

Los Angeles Times, (September 7-12, 1961; February 12, 1962; November 24, 1963; March 22, 1964).

MINOT, PETER, "Inside Schlesinger . . . Slingshot of the New Frontier." *World,* (January 17, 1962). Washington.

MUSTE, A. J., "The Accumulation of Peril." *Liberation,* (December, 1962).

The Nation, Vol. LIX, July, 1894 through Vol. CX, January 1920. New York, The Post Publishing Company; The Nation Press.

Nation and Athenæum, (February 20, 1926). London.

National Review Bulletin, (January 5, 1965). New York.

The New Leader, Vol. XL, No. 18, May 6, 1957 through Vol. XLVII, No. 11, May 25, 1964. Stroudsburg, Pa., The American Labor Conference on International Affairs.

The New Republic, Vol. LXXXIX, No. 11, September, 1958 through Vol. CL, No. 16, April 18, 1964. Washington.

The New Statesman, Vol. LXIV, No. 1654, November 23, 1962 through Vol. LXV, No. 1675, April 19, 1963. London.

The New York Times, (September 21, 1886; December 31, 1933; June 6, 1937; October 11, 1938; April 29, 1941; June 23, 1942; July 5, 11, 1962; September 9, 1963; March 14, 1964).

Press and Radio Service of the International Confederation of Free Trade Unions, Weekly. (PRS/2, January 21, 1963 through PRS/49, December 20, 1963). Brussels.

The Progressive, Vol. XVII, No. 5, May, 1953 through Vol. XXIII, No. 2, February, 1959.

Public Ownership, A monthly journal published by the Public Ownership League of America. Carl D. Thompson, Editor. (December, 1923 through June, 1935). Chicago.

Railway Review, (January 27, 1923). Chicago.
RICH, J. C., "Sixty Years of the *Jewish Daily Forward." The New Leader,* Vol. XL, No. 22, Section 2, (June 3, 1957). (Reprint.)
RYAN, DR. JOHN A., "Men Around Roosevelt." *The Awakener,* (September 1, 1934).
San Francisco Chronicle, (August 19, 1963).
San Francisco Examiner, (August 11, 1963).
SENTNER, DAVID, *Hearst Headline Service,* (September 1, 1963).
SINCLAIR, UPTON, "The Fishpeddler and the Shoemaker." *Institute of Social Studies Bulletin,* (Summer, 1953). New York, The Rand School.
——, "The World As I Want It." *Forum,* (September, 1934).
SMITH, JOHN S., "Organized Labor and Government in the Wilson Era; 1913-1921: Some Conclusions." *Labor History,* Vol. III, No. 3, (Fall, 1962). New York, The Tamiment Institute.
Social Democratic Herald, (May 11, 1912). New York.
Socialist Commentary, (January, 1964 through October, 1964). London.
STARR, MARK, "Cheer Up, Comrade Cole!" *Institute of Social Studies Bulletin,* (Summer, 1953). New York, The Rand School.
——, "Garment Workers: Welfare Unionism." *Current History,* (July, 1954). (Reprint.)
Sudeten Bulletin, A Central European Review. Vol. V, No. 4, April, 1958 through Vol. VI, No. 12, December, 1958. Munich.
The Tablet, (May 4, 1957; September 3, 1960). London.
TARBELL, IDA M., "New Dealers of the Seventies: Henry George and Edward Bellamy." *Forum,* (September, 1934).
The Times, (February 1, 1963). London.
U.S. News and World Report, (May 18, 1964).
VANDERCOOK, JOHN W., "Good News Out of England." *Harper's,* (March, 1947).
The Wanderer, (December 14, 1961). St. Paul, Minnesota.
War/Peace, Vol. II, No. 7, July 1962 through Vol. IV, No. 10, October, 1964.
Washington Evening Star, (November 8, 1931; June 8, 1964).
Washington Post, (January 16, 1947; February 3, 1948; August 30, 1952).
WILLARD, FRANCES E., "An Interview with Edward Bellamy." *Our Day,* Vol. IV, (December 24, 1889). Boston.
WILLIAMS, DAVID C., "Rockefeller in Washington." *The Progressive,* (February, 1959).
W. M. W., "The Communistic Colony of Zoar." *The Southern Cooperator,* (April, 1894). Ocala, Florida.
WRIGHT, DAVID MCCORD, "Mr. Keynes and the 'Day of Judgment'." *Science,* Vol. 128, No. 3334, (November 21, 1958). Published by the American Association for the Advancement of Science. Lancaster, Pa., Lancaster Press.
ZAREMBA, ZIGMUNT, "Socialist-Communist Collaboration." *New Politics,* Journal of Socialist Thought. A Quarterly. Vol. II, No. 1, (Winter, 1964). New York.

REPORTS

American Association of University Professors. *Depression, Recovery and Higher Education*. Malcolm L. Willey, ed. Committee Report. New York and London, McGraw-Hill, Inc., 1937.

———, *Report of Committee on University Teaching*. Washington, 1933.

American Civil Liberties Union 42nd Annual Report. New York, 1962.

American Fund for Public Service Report, 1925-1928. New York.

BALDWIN, R. N., "Freedom to Teach." Proceedings, 1936 Spring Conference, Eastern States Association of Professional Schools for Teachers. New York, Prentice-Hall, Inc., 1936.

British-Polish Friendship Society. *Polish Journey*. Reports from Union Delegates on a Visit to Poland. London, (n.d.).

Committee for Economic Development. *Report of Activities in 1963*. From Thomas B. McCabe, Acting Chairman.

DODD, NORMAN, *The Dodd Report to the Reece Committee on Foundations*. New Canaan, Conn., The Longhouse, Inc., 1954.

International Labor Office. *World Economic Development Report*. Montreal, 1944.

International Ladies Garment Workers Union. *Report of Educational Department*. June 1, 1948 to May 31, 1950. New York.

———, *Report, Education Department*. June, 1951–May, 1953. New York.

———, *Report of the General Executive Board to the 31st Convention, Atlantic City, N.J.* 1962.

———, *Trends and Prospects, Womens Garment Industry, 1947-1950*. Report presented by the General Executive Board to the ILGWU Atlantic City Convention, May, 1950. New York, Educational Department.

LEWIS, FULTON, JR., *The Fund for the Republic*. Washington, Special Reports, Inc., 1955.

Minutes of the American Economic Association. 1885-1889. The American Economic Association, 1905. (No place of publication cited in U.S. Catalogue of Books in Print.)

Papers and Discussion of the Annual Meetings, 12th-17th. Papers Read at 18th Meeting, 1905. Papers Read at 19th Meeting, 1906. American Economic Association, 1906.

Revolutionary Radicalism, Its History, Purpose and Tactics. Report of the Joint Legislative Committee Investigating Seditious Activities, filed April 24, 1920, in the Senate of the State of New York. Albany, J. P. Lyon Company, 1920.

SELIGMAN, E. R. A., *Essays in Colonial Finance*. Report, Special Committee, The American Economic Association. London, E. Sonnenschein Company, 1900.

The Sorge Spy Ring. Section of CIS Periodical Summary No. 23, December 15, 1947. Washington, U.S. Government Printing Office.

Tariffs: The Case Examined. Report, Committee of Economists, Sir William Beveridge, Chairman. London, 1931.

United Nations Bureau of Social Affairs. *Report on the World Social Situation*. New York, United Nations, 1957.

PAMPHLETS, TRACTS, BROCHURES

ALEXANDER, ROBERT J., *World Labor Today*. Highlights of Trade Unions on Six Continents, 1945-1952. New York, League for Industrial Democracy, 1952.

BELLAMY, REV. FRANCIS; GRONLUND, LAURENCE, AND SPRAGUE, REV. P. W., *The Yesterday, Today and Tomorrow of Labor*. Boston, Fabian Educational Company, 1894.

BLISS, REV. W. D. P., *The Social Faith of the Catholic Church*. Boston, Fabian Educational Company, 1894.

———, *Socialism in the Church of England*. Boston, Fabian Educational Company, 1895.

British Labour Party. *British Labor on Reconstruction in War and Peace.* Interim Report of the National Executive Committee of the British Labour Party, approved by the Party Conference under the title, *The Old World and the New Society*. (L.I.D. Pamphlet Series.) New York, League for Industrial Democracy, 1943.

———, *Labour's War Aims*. A British Labour Party Pamphlet. London, The Labour Party, 1917.

———, *Let's Go with Labour for the New Britain*. The Labour Party's Manifesto for the 1964 General Election. London, The Labour Party, 1964.

COLLINS, LEROY; FREEMAN, ORVILLE L.; HUMPHREY, HUBERT H.; MINOW, NEWTON L.; RICKOVER, HYMAN G., AND MARSHALL, THURGOOD, *The Mazes of Modern Government: The States, the Legislature, the Bureaucracy, the Courts*. An Occasional Paper. Santa Barbara, California, Center for the Study of Democratic Institutions, 1963.

Committee for Economic Development. *Union Powers and Union Functions.* A Statement on National Policy by the Research and Policy Committee of the Committee for Economic Development. New York, C.E.D., March, 1964.

Committee on Political Action, AFL-CIO. *How to Win: A Handbook of Political Action*. Washington, AFL-CIO. (n.d.).

Congress of Industrial Organizations. *The C.I.O. and World Affairs*. Policy Statement on Labor's Role in International Affairs. Washington, C.I.O., 1953. (Re-issue).

EDWARDS, ELIZABETH, *The Planners and Bureaucracy*. Liverpool, KRP Publications, (n.d.).

Forty Years of Education. Harry W. Laidler, ed., Symposium by Upton Sinclair and many Others. New York, League for Industrial Democracy, 1945.

Freedom and the Welfare State. Harry W. Laidler, ed., Symposium by Oscar R. Ewing, Herbert H. Lehman, Walter P. Reuther, Margaret Herbison, Clarence Senior and Others. On the Occasion of the 45th Anniversary, L.I.D. New York, League for Industrial Democracy, 1950.

GAITSKELL, HUGH, M.P., AND BROWN, GEORGE, M.P., *Britain and the Common Market*. Texts of speeches made at the 1962 Labour Party

Conference, together with the policy statement accepted by the Conference. London, The Labour Party, 1962.

HALE, REV. EDWARD E.; LIVERMORE, MARY; HIGGINSON, COL. THOMAS W. and Others. *The American Cure for Monopoly and Anarchy.* Pacific National Tract No. 1. Oakland, California. The Nationalist Club, 1904.

How Free Is Free Enterprise? Harry W. Laidler, ed. Symposium by A. J. Hayes, Wayne Morse, Jacob K. Javits, Solomon Barkin, James Farmer, Nathaniel M. Minkoff and Others. Proceedings of 49th Annual Conference L.I.D. New York, League for Industrial Democracy, 1954.

Labor Looks at Labor. Some members of the United Auto Workers undertake a self-examination, Santa Barbara, California, Center for the Study of Democratic Institutions, 1963.

LAIDLER, HARRY W., *Socialism in the United States.* A Brief History. New York, League for Industrial Democracy, 1952.

A Moral Awakening in America. Harry W. Laidler, ed., Symposium by Walter P. Reuther, James B. Carey, Helen Gahagan Douglas, Mark Starr, Jacob K. Javits, Norman Thomas and Others. New York, League for Industrial Democracy, 1952.

The New Britain. The Labour Party's Manifesto for the 1964 General Election. London, The Labour Party, Transport House, 1964.

Political and Economic Planning. *About P.E.P.* London, P.E.P., 1956.

————, Agriculture, the Commonwealth and EEC. London, P.E.P., 1961.

SCHIAVI, PROFESSOR ALESSANDRO, *L'Internazionale Socialista.* Florence, Institute of Socialist Studies, 1964.

SUALL, IRWIN, *The American Ultras: The Extreme Right and the Military-Industrial Complex.* New York, New America Press, 1962.

The Third Freedom: Freedom From Want. Harry W. Laidler, ed., Symposium by Rt. Hon. Arthur Greenwood, R. J. Thomas, Rt. Hon. Margaret Bondfield, Oscar Lange, Nathaniel Minkoff, Mark Starr and Others. New York, League for Industrial Democracy, 1943.

THOMAS, NORMAN, *Democratic Socialism: A New Appraisal.* New York, League for Industrial Democracy, 1953. (Re-issued, with some changes, by the Post War World Council, 1963).

U.S. Department of State. *Freedom from War: The United States Program for General and Complete Disarmament in a Peaceful World.* Department of State Publication 7277, Disarmament Series 5. Washington, Office of Public Services, Bureau of Public Affairs, September, 1961.

Workers' Educational Association. *Workers' Education in Great Britain.* London, W. E. A., 1943.

CONGRESSIONAL HEARINGS

Brewing Investigation. Report and Hearings of the Subcommittee of the Committee on the Judiciary. Senate Document No. 62, 66th Congress. Washington, U.S. Government Printing Office, 1919.

Report and Hearings of Special House of Representatives Committee to Investigate Communist Activities in the United States. Washington, U.S. Government Printing Office, 1931.

Investigation of Un-American Propaganda in the United States. Hearings before a Special Committee, House of Representatives, 75th Congress. Washington, U.S. Government Printing Office, 1938.

Lobbying, Direct and Indirect. Hearings before the Select Committee on Lobbying Activities. House of Representatives, Second Session, 81st Congress. Washington, U.S. Government Printing Office, 1950.

Hearings Regarding Shipments of Atomic Materials to the Soviet Union during World War II. House of Representatives, Committee on Un-American Activities. Washington, U.S. Government Printing Office, 1950.

The Institute of Pacific Relations. Hearings before the Subcommittee to Investigate the Administration of the Internal Security Act and Other Internal Security Laws, of the Senate Committee on the Judiciary. 82nd and 83rd Congress. Washington, U.S. Government Printing Office, 1951, 1952.

Interlocking Subversion in Government Departments. Report and Hearings of the Subcommittee on Internal Security of the Committee on the Judiciary. U.S. Senate, 83rd Congress. Washington, U.S. Government Printing Office, 1953, 1954.

Tax Exempt Foundations. Hearings before the Select Committee to Investigate Tax-Exempt Foundations and Comparable Organizations. House of Representatives, 82nd and 83rd Congress. Washington, U.S. Government Printing Office, 1953, 1954.

Hearings before the Subcommittee to Investigate the Administration of the Internal Security Act and other Internal Security Laws, of the Committee on the Judiciary. U.S. Senate, 87th Congress. Washington, U.S. Government Printing Office, 1962.

Hearings, Joint Economic Committee, First Session, 88th Congress. (January 29, 1963). Washington, U.S. Government Printing Office, 1963.

Tax-Exempt Foundations and Charitable Trusts: Their Impact on Our Economy. Subcommittee Chairman's Reports to Subcommittee No. 1 of the Select Committee on Small Business. House of Representatives, 87th and 88th Congress. Washington, U.S. Government Printing Office, 1962, 1963, 1964.

PAPAL LETTERS

Leo XIII, *Diuturnum, Encyclical Letter on Civil Government.* (June 29, 1881).

————, *Immortale Dei, Encyclical Letter on the Christian Constitution of States.* (November 1, 1885).

————, *Libertas Humana, Encyclical Letter on Human Liberty.* (June 20, 1888).

Pius X, *Motu Proprio On Popular Christian Action.* (December 18, 1903).

Pius XI, *Quadragesimo Anno, Encyclical Letter on Reconstructing the Social Order.* (May 15, 1931).

————, *Divini Redemptoris, Encyclical Letter* (March 14, 1937).

Pius XII, *Summi Pontificatus, Encyclical Letter on the Function of the State in the Modern World.* (October 20, 1939).

UNPUBLISHED MATERIAL

LLOYD, HENRY DEMAREST, *Papers*, University of Illinois, Urbana, Illinois.

Records of the Mixed Claims Commission on German Sabotage in World War I, National Archives, Washington.

ROOSEVELT, FRANKLIN D., *Papers*, Franklin D. Roosevelt Library, Hyde Park, New York.

ROOSEVELT, THEODORE, *Papers*, Manuscript Division, Library of Congress, Washington.

SUNDT, M. EUGENE, *The American Herrenvolk*. (Unpublished manuscript) Albuquerque, New Mexico.

WILSON, WOODROW, *Papers*, Manuscript Division, Library of Congress, Washington.

Index of Persons

General Index